THE SE SUP GROUP DIRECTORY

Twenty-Fourth Edition
2009

A guide to self-help and other support groups in New Jersey with national organizations, model and online groups.

Edited by

Anita M. Broderick
and
Wendy Rodenbaugh

New Jersey Self-Help Group Clearinghouse

Saint Clare's Health System
a member of Catholic Health Initiatives
375 E. McFarlan Street
Dover, NJ 07801-3638

1-800-367-6274 or 973-989-1122
Fax: 973-989-1159
Website: www.selfhelpgroups.org

* In Memoriam *

In loving memory of Mary Ellen Kerin, our former Coordinator of Information and Referral Services who passed away in February of this year. Against the many illnesses and disorders that she faced over the years, she was always a courageous fighter. Mary Ellen, despite her pain, was always upbeat, took joy in life and made every day count. Even after she took medical leave, she continued helping the Clearinghouse as a volunteer working from her home computer, tracking down new state, national and online groups. Mary Ellen will be remembered as a very kind and generous person.

* In Memoriam *

In loving memory of Harry Salle, who was a phone volunteer at the Clearinghouse for many years and very caringly helped thousands of callers. He was an especially kind person who brought laughter and cheer into our office and lives. Harry went on the most extraordinary trips, covering almost every part of the world. But from every port or country, Harry sent us a postcard giving us the opportunity to vicariously travel with him. Even after Harry was stricken with aphasia, he continued to volunteer at the Clearinghouse doing clerical work. Harry will always be remembered as a very caring and kind person.

ISBN 978-1-930683-09-9
Twenty-Fourth Edition
May 2009

ACKNOWLEDGEMENTS

We are grateful to the **Division of Mental Health Services, NJ Department of Human Services** for their initial and continued funding and support that makes the Clearinghouse services possible. We appreciate too, the efforts of the many dedicated **support group representatives** whose volunteer time and energy make this directory possible.

We wish to express our deep appreciation to all of our wonderful and hardworking **volunteers** who have contributed their time and energy in helping callers and extending the services of the Clearinghouse. Our heartfelt thanks go to:

Barbara Blumenfeld	**Pete Lodato**
James Canty	**Baiba Ozols**
Ruth Clark	**Paul Riddleberger**
Pat de la Fuente	**Elaine Romito**
Lois Fallat	**Berit Wenner**
Howard Lerner	

In addition, special thanks to **Kelly Lozito** for her assistance in designing our 2009 Edition cover.

"Everybody can be great...because anybody can serve. You don't have to have a college degree to serve. You don't have to make your subject and verb agree to serve. You only need a heart full of grace. A soul generated by love."-- Martin Luther King, Jr.

TABLE OF CONTENTS

MENTAL HEALTH

MISCELLANEOUS

Need help finding a specific group? Give us a call – we're here to help!
Call 1-800-367-6274

ABOUT THE CLEARINGHOUSE

Our N.J. Self-Help Group Clearinghouse was established in 1981 to promote the awareness, utilization, development and understanding of mutual aid self-help groups. Sponsored by Saint Clare's Health System and funded primarily by state government, the Clearinghouse provides information and referral, consultation services and training primarily to help people find and form self-help groups.

The Clearinghouse maintains a database of information and contacts on over 6,700 groups within the state and over 1,000 national organizations, one-of-a-kind group models and online groups. Easy access to this information is assured through our toll-free phone lines.

An important component of our work is the development of new groups as needs arise. For example, if a caller inquires about a support group for any situation, and our computer search yields nothing in the caller's area, we often invite the caller to consider joining with others to start a group. If they are interested, we can advise them on how they can develop a group, and include them in our database. Subsequent callers would then be referred to this contact person if they were interested in helping them to start that type of a group.

The Clearinghouse also sponsors training conferences and free workshops on starting groups, facilitation skills, publicity, group maintenance and other issues of interest to group leaders.

Other services provided by the Clearinghouse include speaking engagements, a variety of guides and hand-outs on specific and general issues related to group development, research projects, facilitation workshops, speakers' bureau and a website on the Internet. We also work with the media to increase public awareness of self-help groups and their value.

Various volunteer and student opportunities exist at the Clearinghouse. We offer a variety of rewarding volunteer positions, as well as opportunities for internships and applied research that supports self-help groups. Call us for details.

Our Clearinghouse does not permit the marketing of products or services through this directory. No part of this directory may be used for phone solicitation, promotional and/or e-mail mailings, nor other promotional sales in any form without prior written permission from the Clearinghouse.

HOW TO USE THIS DIRECTORY

For an overview of the variety of groups available, review the **Table of Contents**, which is a categorization of self-help groups according to the general problem or concern addressed. To find a mutual aid self-help group for a particular concern, turn to the **Index** at the end of the directory. The index will refer you to pages in the directory where listings of groups dealing with your concern may be found.

Within each category, listings are arranged in a geographical order, with statewide groups shown first, local groups next (in alphabetical order by county), and finally national organizations, model and online groups.

In some categories, there are additional resources at the end of the listing. Note that: **Statewide** listings include New Jersey groups that cover all or a large portion of the state; **Local groups** can either be autonomous groups or chapters of national organizations; **National groups** have chapters in several states and provide assistance to persons interested in starting local chapters; **National Networks** usually don't have face-to-face meetings but link members together for mutual support; **Model** one-of-a-kind groups usually have just one or two local groups but are willing to help others start similar groups in their areas; and **Online groups** and **resources** are included to supplement areas where few face-to-face support groups have been identified.

Each group listing includes the group name, a brief description of the group, meeting and contact information. If there are no dues or fees listed, it means that the group is free of charge, although many groups will "pass the hat" for contributions for refreshments, literature and other group expenses. All of the groups listed are non-profit. If you use a wheelchair, please be sure to call the group first to make sure that the meeting site is wheelchair accessible.

Remember, when calling a group, please show your consideration for others. Many of the phone numbers given are home numbers, so several tries may be necessary, and contact persons may shift periodically from one member to another. With few exceptions, contact numbers are not hotlines (see separate helpline listings beginning on page 657). We request that you not call group contacts too early in the morning or too late at night. In our listings, we have tried to indicate whether the phone numbers are best reached during the day or evening.

If you leave a message on an answering machine, speak very clearly and slowly, and include your area code. Sometimes contact people are unable to return calls because they cannot understand the messages left. Also, please be thoughtful of the type of message you leave for the contact person (either on an answering machine or with another person), especially when it concerns sensitive issues. Leave discreet messages—you never know if the person answering the phone or listening to the messages on the answering machine knows that the contact person is a member of a certain group. These days, you'll probably be checking out the website of the national group that we give you. But if you do write to a national or local group, it's good to enclose a self-addressed stamped envelope to help defer the expenses and make it easier for the group to respond quickly.

When you cannot find an appropriate group, or a group you wanted has disbanded, please call the Clearinghouse to see if there have been any additional groups identified since the directory was printed, or if there are any groups in the process of forming. Also, ask yourself if you or someone you know would be interested in joining with others to form a self-help group. If so, please call us to find out how we can help you.

Don't use this directory after one year has gone by! Much of the information changes in that time. After a year, consider the directory to be out-of-date and ready for the recycling bin. If this directory is replacing an older edition, we request that you take this opportunity now to recycle your older directory. Consider passing the old directory on to a student or colleague to help educate them to the wide variety of groups available. Do tell them they need to call the Clearinghouse for the most current groups and contacts. We are continually updating information on meetings, group contact persons and location changes. We also identify new groups that are added to our database. Please call us for the most up-to-date information on groups.

PLEASE NOTE: The Clearinghouse has made every effort to include as many different support groups as possible. However, the Clearinghouse reserves the right to include or exclude any names, groups or telephone contacts at its absolute discretion. Inclusion of an organization does not signify approval, nor does omission of any organization signify disapproval. A few groups may have escaped our attention. The use of any materials contained herein is entirely the responsibility of the reader. The Clearinghouse further disclaims any and all liability for any use or non-use of the information herein. There are no warranties implied or expressed in any of the information provided. The information provided is based upon that which is supplied by the groups themselves. The Clearinghouse is not responsible for printing, insertion or deletion errors.

Finally, understand that the quality of individual groups will differ, sometimes even among those with the same name. Phone and visit the group to see if it is *for you*. The ultimate evaluation and very survival of any self-help group is determined by those who attend it and decide whether or not to continue as contributing members.

WHAT IS A SELF-HELP GROUP?

Most of the self-help groups listed on the following pages can better be described as mutual aid groups because they derive their energy from members helping one another. Among the various organizations that deal with stressful life situations, we look for those that provide opportunities for mutual help. In addition, three other characteristics constitute a self-help group: the group is composed of peers, i.e. people who share a similar experience or situation; the group is primarily run by and for its members who have a sense of ownership of the group; and the group is voluntary and non-profit in that there are no fees for services, although the group may charge dues or request donations.

While the focus of our Clearinghouse is on the development of self-help groups that are run by members themselves, we include in our listings some support groups that are run by professionals (identified in their listing as "professionally-run"). While professionally-run support groups are not self-help groups, we include them in the directory if the meetings are free or have a nominal charge, the professional does not receive a fee from members for facilitating the group and the purpose of the group is mutual support among peers.

Please understand that there are other types of self-help organizations that do indeed provide mutual aid and support. They include civic, ethnic, fraternal, housing, cultural, political, church and neighborhood groups — some of which spring up naturally without even a name or with little structure beyond mutual help discussions. However, groups in any one of these categories could, by their nature and sheer numbers, warrant a separate directory of their own and are therefore not included here.

"I do not believe that sheer suffering teaches.
If suffering alone taught, all the world would be wise,
since everyone suffers.
To suffering must be added mourning,
understanding, patience, love, openness,
and a willingness to remain vulnerable."
Anne Morrow Lindbergh

HOW SELF-HELP GROUPS HELP

Have you ever noticed that when you have a problem it helps to talk with someone who has had a similar problem? Simply finding others who have "been there" and realizing that "you are not alone" can in itself be a great relief. Providing this opportunity for needed peer support is one way mutual aid self-help groups help.

With time, some self-help groups resemble an extended family, providing a caring community that is often available 24 hours a day without forms, fees or appointments. Yet the groups also emphasize self-reliance, as each member assumes responsibility for helping him or herself.

Within such groups, people who share similar problems and needs gather to help one another cope with the problems they face. The problem may be a disability, a chronic illness, loss of a loved one, an addiction or any one of hundreds of other difficult life situations. Social support can make it easier to cope with a stressful situation. This alleviation of stress can be directly related to the prevention of further illness and distress.

Another important way that self-help groups help is the way in which members not only receive help from their peers but can also provide help to others. Helping someone else deal with a problem you also experience builds self-confidence and reinforces the use of coping strategies that have worked for you and others. Those who have been able to cope with a particular problem can serve as valuable role models for those who are just beginning to reach out for encouragement and practical information.

Self-help groups are not meant to replace needed professional services, although they supplement and sometimes prevent the need for them. Many groups tap professionals as advisors, guest speakers, consultants, trainers and referral resources. When pooling their personal experiences, coping skills and insights, group members will often come to recognize the specific agencies and therapists who best meet their needs. For literature and research study references on additional ways that self-help groups help, please contact the Clearinghouse.

"We make a living by what we get.
We make a life by what we give."
-- Henry Bucher

CHOOSING A SUPPORT GROUP

Whether you are a professional considering groups for your clients, or a person simply looking for a helpful group for yourself, you may wonder if a support group is right for you. Let's examine the choices from those two perspectives.

Professional Considerations

For caring professionals who realize that they cannot be all things to their clients, support groups are welcome community resources that supplement professional assistance. And in so doing, referral to a support group can help prevent professional burnout. Groups also provide support at times when professional offices are closed, whether it is the actual meetings or the phone support often available between meetings. Since the groups provide the unique support of "others who have been there," they can be especially helpful for clients who feel alone and isolated with the stressful situation they face. Groups provide a variety of other benefits: acceptance, positive role models, normalization, coping skills, practical information, education, community, sometimes a "program to work" as in 12-step groups, advocacy and even "helper therapy" - the ability to help others in the group.

In providing a referral, a professional may point out the potential value of a group. It's helpful to suggest to the client that they check out the support group to "see if it is for you." If the client has Internet access and if the local group is part of a national one, suggest they check out the national website to learn more about the group. It's often helpful to have the brochures of particular groups that are most often referred to, since the group's brochure explains what the group offers and takes away the fear of the unknown. Ideally these brochures should be available in the waiting area also.

For the Person Seeking a Group

When looking for a support group, first identify the source of your stress (e.g., the specific illness, addiction, loss, etc.) and any special situation (being a caregiver, parent or friend of the person with the problem). In addition to a group's problem focus, there are many other differences in the types of groups available. Some support groups are member-run, while others have professional facilitators. Some have a very narrow focus while others are very broad. Some are based upon either spiritual or religious beliefs, while many are not. Some are very structured while others have little structure at all. Some focus on emotional support, education or advocacy while others are more social. These differences may be important to you, so the more you learn about a group, the better you will be able to choose the right group for you.

Learn About a Group Before Attending a Meeting The best information about a group comes from the group itself. Most groups have a phone contact person who will answer any questions you have about the group before you attend a meeting. Also, most groups have a national website, brochure and other literature that describes their group's purpose and activities.

Questions You Might Ask In addition to finding out the meeting time and place, there are other questions you may want to ask before attending. You might ask about the people in the group. Do they understand what you are going through because they have had similar experiences? How many usually attend the meeting (more people means more interest and energy, but less time for each member to share concerns)? What is the ratio of men to women, or the age range of the members (if it makes a difference to you)? You might inquire about any meeting formats and any costs associated with joining the group.

The First Meeting You Attend Once you decide to attend a meeting, there are many aspects of the group you can only learn about first hand. One of the first impressions you'll get about the group will be how welcome you feel. Do people welcome you and introduce themselves to you? Do they sit near you, smile at you and in general make you feel like they are glad you're there? How much mutual help occurs within the group? Do people really help each other or is it one or two people giving advice to everyone else? If the group is led by a professional, why is he or she leading the group and what kind of leadership style does he or she exert?

If the members lead the group, how is leadership decided upon? Is it rotated, shared among group members, or limited to just one or two people? What other roles are assumed by group members? How many people help to run the group? Again, a good match between your needs and the group is what you're seeking.

Another observation you can make has to do with general group tone. Does it seem like the group is helpful to its members? Do people seem glad to see each other? Is there positive energy? Humor? Honesty? Do people listen to each other? Do they show concern, respect, understanding and acceptance?

Sometimes you will find a group that is perfect for you on the first try. Other times you may have to try several types of groups or a different meeting of the same group before you've found the best match. The bottom line is whether you feel the group meets your needs. Finally, after you have chosen and benefited from a self-help group, please consider staying for a while to "give back" and help others. Self-help groups depend upon such volunteer efforts. Your volunteer efforts will not only help others, but will most probably benefit you in terms of your own physical and mental well-being.

HOW THE CLEARINGHOUSE HELPS
PEOPLE START GROUPS

If there is no local support in your area addressing your concern, consider joining with others to start a group. This is how most of the thousands of self-help support groups have started throughout New Jersey – from the courage and initial efforts of one person who recognized the value of creating a caring community of people "who truly understand" who share their experiences, strengths and hopes together. Understand how the slogan heard within some self-help groups, "You alone can do it, but you can't do it alone," holds true for developing groups too. We can advise you on ways to start a group, so the effort is not on your shoulders alone, but shared with others. Just phone us for free help, ideas and materials.

Sometimes, we also consult to professionals, who recognize the need for a specific self-help group in the community and want to support people in development of that type of group. In any case, if you are a professional and there's no local group for your client, please consider asking them, "Would you possibly be interested in joining with others to start a local mutual help support group?" If your client is among the few, but very special people, who respond "yes" or even "maybe," let them know of our free services.

Assistance is available to help individuals start self-help groups for any stressful life situations and transitions, medical and emotional problems, parenting and family concerns, addictions or other adversities. There are also varieties of ways in which we can seek to encourage and support your efforts:

Literature: The Clearinghouse offers a wide range of printed materials related to self-help group development and maintenance including:
- General how-to's with suggestions for how to start and run mutual help groups—from finding co-founders to structure a group meeting. For a brief overview of the basics, glance over the "Ideas & Suggestions for Starting a Mutual Aid Self-Help Group" on the following pages 17-20.
- Group development materials from specific groups, detailing how to start that type of group. Our library files and shelves are filled with hundreds of how-to guides for starting many different types of self-help support groups. We can also advise you of any how-to guides online.
- Many other related materials—such as templates for announcing to newspapers you're interested in seeking others willing to help you, how to publicize your group, or ideas for promoting "shared leadership."

Referring Potential Co-founders to You: With your permission, we can list you as a person interested in starting a group on our database. It may be just your first name and a phone number. Then when we receive a call from someone in your area asking for the type of group that doesn't yet exist, but which you want help in starting, we advise the caller: "We're sorry that there is no local group yet available, but would you be interested in helping someone who is trying to get a group going?" This is only one of several ways in which you can find others who are similarly interested in working with you to help create a new group in your area.

Networking You with Other Groups and Resources: To save time and effort and not have to "reinvent the wheel," you can learn from other groups how they started and run their meetings. We can put you in touch with representatives of similar groups. You can call or visit a local group to ask how they got their group started, what they do to find new members, how they plan their meeting activities, and what problems they encounter in their groups and how they solve them. Contact with a national group can often provide the most appropriate group development information, newsletters, pamphlets, brochures, and many other kinds of potential support services. You can contact and learn from others who have started groups. Some national self-help organizations nurture and support a national and/or state network of self-help group leaders by providing them with an online support network of their own - a sort of "self-help group for self-help group representatives."

Phone Help: On-going assistance via the toll-free helpline is always available from your Clearinghouse consultant, who will help you along the way with any concern you have or obstacle you may encounter. Together you can brainstorm ways to resolve any problems and identify potential resources.

Training Workshops: The Clearinghouse offers periodic workshops on issues related to self-help that may be useful to those beginning groups, as well as to leaders of existing groups. The Clearinghouse also periodically co-sponsors special interest conferences with self-help groups and other organizations.

In the interest of maintaining the best climate possible for the development of an independent, member-run mutual aid self-help group, the Clearinghouse primarily provides consultation services—offering advice, suggestions and guidelines on the development of your group, but you are under no obligation to follow through on those suggestions. Like all other self-help groups, your group would be an independent community support group, run by and for its members.

While it's often not easy to start a group, most group founders and co-founders report how very satisfying the effort is to them after they get a group going. So please consider the possibility. The ability of ordinary people to create a mutual support group has been one of the true miracles that self-help groups continue to offer the world, ever since days the great depression when two "drunks" came together to create what became the respected grandfather of so many self-help groups, Alcoholics Anonymous.

IDEAS AND SUGGESTIONS FOR
STARTING A MUTUAL AID SELF-HELP GROUP

Self-help groups offer people who face a common problem the opportunity to meet with others and share their experiences, knowledge, strengths and hopes. Run by and for their members, self-help groups can better be described as "mutual help" groups. Hundreds of these groups are started each week across the nation by ordinary people with a little bit of courage, a fair sense of commitment and a good amount of caring. The following guidelines are based on our experience at the Clearinghouse helping hundreds of individuals to start groups. While there is no one recipe for developing a group (different national groups offer different model approaches), here is an overview of the basic steps and strategies. Call us for additional ideas and specific how-to's.

Don't Re-invent the Wheel: If you are interested in starting a group around a particular concern or problem, find out what groups already exist for it. Call our Clearinghouse to confirm that there are no existing local groups that may address your issue. Check first in this Directory for any national self-help groups that address your concern. Visit their websites. Contact and ask them for what help and "how-to" starter packet information they can provide, and which of their groups might be closest to you. You can also speak to a Clearinghouse group consultant and ask for their help. In addition to free consultation, literature and contacts, the consultant can also list your interest on our computer to network you with any callers interested in helping you. We can provide you with suggestions as to which local organizations and professionals may be able to help.

Think "Mutual-Help" From the Start: Find a few others who share your interest in starting (not simply joining) a self-help group. Starting a group should not be on one person's shoulders alone. So, put out flyers or letters that specifically cite your interest in hearing from those who would be interested in "joining with others to help start" such a group. Include your first name and phone number. Make copies and post them at places you feel most appropriate, e.g., library, community center or post office. Mail copies to key people whom you think would know others like yourself. Post it on any online message boards that deal with the issue or your local community message boards. When, hopefully, you receive calls, discuss with the caller what their interests are, share your vision of what you would like to see the group do, and finally ask if they would be willing to work with you for a specific period of time to try to get the group off the ground. Discuss sharing the workload. Delegate responsibilities, such as: greeting people at the door and introducing new members; bringing refreshments; making coffee; or co-chairing the meeting, etc.

Once a couple of people have said yes, you have a "core group" or "steering committee" - and you won't have to do it alone. It's much easier to start a group if the work is shared. But most importantly, if several people are involved in the

17

initial work at that first meeting (refreshments, publicity, name tags, greeting new people, etc.), you will model for newcomers what your self-help group is all about - not one person doing it all, but the volunteer efforts and the active participation of all the members.

Find a Suitable Meeting Place and Time: Try to obtain free meeting space at a local church, synagogue, library, community center, hospital or social service agency. If you anticipate a small group and feel comfortable with the idea, you could even consider initial meetings in members' homes. Would evening or day meetings be better for members? Many prefer weeknights. It is also easier for people to remember the meeting date if it's a fixed day of the week or month, like the second Thursday of the month, etc.

Publicize and Run Your First Public Meeting: Reaching potential members is never easy. Depending upon the problem area, consider where potential members go. Would they be seen by particular doctors or agencies? Contacting physicians, clergy or other professionals can be one approach to try. Posting flyers in post offices, community centers, hospitals and libraries is another. Free announcements in the community calendar sections of local newspapers can be especially fruitful. Consider simply calling the paper and asking to speak with an editor to suggest an article on the group and the issue. Editors are often grateful for the idea. The first meeting should be arranged so that there will be ample time for you to describe your interest and work, while allowing others the opportunity to share their feelings and concerns. Do those attending agree that such a group is needed? Will they attend another meeting, helping out as needed? What needs do they have in common that the group could address? Based on group consensus, you can make plans for your next meeting.

If your group intends to have guest speakers, another idea for a first meeting is to arrange for a good speaker and topic that can be publicized well in advance. But be sure to build in time for people to discuss the speaker's points in light of their own experiences, i.e., after questions and answers with the speaker, have a discussion group or (if a large turnout) break into smaller discussion groups. Then come together as a full group and present the idea of continuing discussions as an ongoing self-help group.

Identify and Respond to the Felt Needs of Your Members: If your group is new and doesn't follow a set program for helping members help one another, always remember to plan your groups' activities and goals based upon the expressed needs of your members. Share your vision. At the very first meeting, go "round-robin" permitting each member an opportunity to say what they would like to see the group do. Then discuss these needs and come to a consensus as to which needs you will address first. Don't make the mistake of thinking that you know the members' needs without ever asking them.

Remember to regularly ask your new members about their needs, and what they think the group might do to meet those needs. Similarly, be sure to avoid the pitfall of the core group members possibly becoming a clique. The welcoming of new people into the group is a process that continues well beyond welcoming them at the door.

Future Meeting: Considerations for future meetings may be the following:

- *Define the purpose (mission) of the group in no more than two sentences.* Is it clear? You may want to add it to any flyer or brochure that you develop for the group. Some groups also include any guidelines that they have for their meetings right on their flyer or brochure.

- *Membership.* Who can attend meetings and who cannot? Do you want regular membership limited to those with the problem and an associate membership for spouses and family?

- *Meeting format.* What choice or combination of discussion time, education, business meeting, service planning, socializing, etc. best suits your group? What guidelines might you use to assure that discussions be non-judgmental, confidential and informative? Topics can be selected or guest speakers invited. A good discussion group size may be about 7 to 15. As your meeting grows larger, consider breaking down into smaller groups for discussion.

- *Ongoing use of professionals.* Consider using professionals as speakers, advisors, sources of needed space or services, educators, helpful gatekeepers, advocates, possible trainers, researchers, consultants to your group or simply as sources of continued referrals. All you have to do is ask them.

- *Help between meetings.* Many groups encourage the exchange of telephone numbers or a telephone list to provide members with help over the phone when it is needed between meetings. Older groups have a buddy system that pairs newcomers with veteran members.

- *Projects.* Begin with small projects, e.g. developing a flyer, obtaining newspaper coverage by calling editors, beginning a newsletter, etc. Rejoice and pat yourselves on the back when you succeed with these first projects. Then, if the group desires, work your way up to more difficult tasks and projects, e.g. planning a conference, advocating the introduction of specific legislation, developing a visitation program, etc.

- *Sharing responsibilities and nurturing new leaders.* You will want to look for all the different, additional roles that people can play in helping other members and making the group work, e.g., group librarian, arranging for speakers, greeter of new members, group liaison with an agency, etc. In asking for volunteers, it's easier to first ask the group what specific tasks they think would be helpful. If you haven't yet experienced it, you'll come to know the special "helper's high" satisfaction of helping others. Don't be selfish. Remember to let your members feel the fine satisfaction of helping others in the group. By sharing responsibilities you help create opportunities for others to become key members and leaders in the group.

- *Lastly, expect your group to experience regular "ups and downs."* For example, in terms of attendance and enthusiasm. It's natural and to be expected. You may want to consider joining or forming a coalition or state association of leaders from the same or similar types of self-help groups, for your own periodic mutual support and for sharing program ideas and successes.

"One of the most important capabilities of community self-help groups is that ordinary people can develop such groups in their local communities when none exist, and subsequently their group usually serves as an extraordinary resource to many in that area for several years. I still find it amazing that to start a group, a person doesn't need a grant, an agency, or even an office - just the inspiration and a few other people who share their experience and hope. What significantly helps in providing such inspiration is a person's knowledge of an existing national organization or a model group, which can provide them with basic information so they don't have to 're-invent the wheel.' "
- E. Madara, "Mutual Aid Self-Help Group Developments" Community Psychologist, 39 (3), Fall, 2006, p. 21.

A B U S E

CHILD ABUSE (PHYSICAL / EMOTIONAL)
(see also sexual abuse, toll-free helplines)

BERGEN

H.O.P.E.S. (Healing Ourselves Physically, Emotionally and Spiritually) *Professionally-run.* Self-help for adult survivors of any form of child abuse. Meets Thurs. and Fri., 6:30-8pm, St. Mark's Episcopal Church, 118 Chadwick Rd., Teaneck. Call Sara Accordino 201-357-4490, Anne Beemsterboer 201-287-0527 or Parents Anonymous 1-800-843-5437. *Website:* http://www.pa-of-nj.org

BURLINGTON

H.O.P.E.S. (Healing Ourselves Physically, Emotionally and Spiritually) *Professionally-run.* Self-help for adult survivors of any form of child abuse. Meets Tues., 7-9pm, Family Service Center, 770 Woodlane Rd., Suite 23, Mt. Holly. Call Parents Anonymous 1-800-843-5437. *Website:* http://www.pa-of-nj.org

CAMDEN

H.O.P.E.S. (Healing Ourselves Physically, Emotionally and Spiritually) *Professionally-run.* Self-help for adult survivors of any form of child abuse. Meets Mon., 6:30-8:30pm, Global Substance Abuse, 1419 Baird Blvd., Camden. Call Margaret Rogers Darian 856-963-2800. *Website:* http://www.pa-of-nj.org

MORRIS

H.O.P.E.S. (Healing Ourselves Physically, Emotionally and Spiritually) *Professionally-run.* Self-help for adult survivors of any form of child abuse. Meets Wed., 7:30-9:30pm, First Presbyterian Church, 35 Church St., Rockaway. Before attending call Janice Taitel 973-586-8979 or Parents Anonymous 1-800-843-5437. *Website:* http://www.pa-of-nj.org

NATIONAL

Adult Survivors of Child Abuse *International. 11 affiliated groups. Founded 1991.* Mutual support for adult survivors of physical, sexual and/or emotional child abuse or neglect. Encourages victims to become survivors, then thrivers.

Online support group meetings, phone meetings, monthly newsletter, group starter manual and general information. Offers assistance in starting groups. Write: Survivors, P.O. Box 14477, San Francisco, CA 94114-0038. Call 415-928-4576. *Website:* http://www.ascasupport.org *E-mail:* ascaoutreach@yahoo.com

Shaken Baby Alliance *National. Founded 1998.* Promotes public awareness, education, victim and family support. Offers networking, victim advocacy and literature. Provides assistance in starting groups. Provides case consultation services to professionals involved in diagnosing, investigating and prosecuting physical child abuse. Online listserv. Write: Shaken Baby Alliance, 4516 Boat Club Rd., Suite 114, Fort Worth, TX 76135. Call 817-882-8686; Fax: 817-882-8687. *Website:* http://www.shakenbaby.com *E-mail:* info@shakenbaby.com

ONLINE

Abused Survivors *Online. 510 members. Founded 1998.* Support group that offers an outstretched hand to adult survivors of abuse (physical, verbal, emotional or sexual). Open only to survivors. *Website:* http://health.groups.yahoo.com/group/abusedsurvivors

SEXUAL ABUSE / INCEST / RAPE
(see also child abuse, toll-free helplines)

STATEWIDE

SNAP (Survivors Network of those Abused by Priests) Support for men and women who were sexually abused by any clergy person (priest, brother, nun, deacon, teacher, etc.) Extensive phone network, newsletter, advocacy, conferences, information and referrals. Call 201-715-6510 or 732-632-7687. *E-mail:* pat.serrano1@gmail.com or mecrawf@comcast.net

Survivors of Incest Anonymous 12-Step. Program for men and women 18 yrs. or older who have been victims of child sexual abuse and want to be survivors. Write: SIANYC, Murray Hill Station, P.O. Box 1603, New York, NY 10156. Call SIA regional office 212-501-4325 (leave message and call will be returned). For possible New Jersey support, visit the website and complete the inquiry form. *Website*: http://www.sianyc.org

"When we feel love and kindness toward others, it not only makes others feel loved and cared for, but it helps us also to develop inner happiness and peace." -- Dalai Lama

BERGEN

H.O.P.E.S. (Healing Ourselves Physically, Emotionally and Spiritually) *Professionally-run.* Self-help for adult survivors of any form of child abuse. Meets Thurs. and Fri., 6:30-8pm, St. Mark's Episcopal Church, 118 Chadwick Rd., Teaneck. Call Sara Accordino 201-357-4490 (day), Anne Beemsterboer 201-287-0527 or Parents Anonymous 1-800-843-5437. *Website:* http://www.pa-of-nj.org

Men's Survivor Group *Professionally-run.* Mutual support for male survivors of child sexual abuse. Group runs for 10 sessions, 2-3 times/yr. Meetings vary, YWCA of Bergen County, Rape Crisis Center, Hackensack. Leave name and phone number with answering service. Your call will be returned. Call 201-487-2227 (24 hr. hotline); TDD: 201-487-9609. *Website:* http://www.bergencountyrapecrisis.org *E-mail:* bcrcc@aol.com

Survivors of Rape *Professionally-run.* Support for adult female survivors of sexual assault. Meets Thurs., YWCA, Oak St., Ridgewood. Before attending call 201-487-2227 (24 hr.); TTY: 201-487-0916. *Website:* http://www.bergencountyrapecrisis.org *E-mail:* bcrcc@aol.com

BURLINGTON

H.O.P.E.S. (Healing Ourselves Physically, Emotionally and Spiritually) *Professionally-run.* Self-help for adult survivors of any form of child abuse. Meets Tues., 7-9pm, Family Service Center, 770 Woodlane Rd., Suite 23, Mt. Holly. Call Parents Anonymous 1-800-843-5437. *Website:* http://www.pa-of-nj.org

CAMDEN

H.O.P.E.S. (Healing Ourselves Physically, Emotionally and Spiritually) *Professionally-run.* Self-help for adult survivors of any form of child abuse. Meets Mon., 6:30-8:30pm, Global Substance Abuse, 1419 Baird Blvd., Camden. Call Margaret Rogers Darian 856-963-2800. *Website:* http://www.pa-of-nj.org

Survivors of Incest Anonymous 12-Step. Program for men and women, 18 yrs. or older, who have been victims of child sexual abuse, are not abusing any child and want to be survivors. Literature and newsletter. Building is handicapped accessible. Meets Sat., 9:30-11am, The Starting Point, 215 Highland Ave., Suite C, Westmont. Call Annie 856-858-5630 (eve.) or Helen 856-768-1925 (day).

ESSEX

Victims and Survivors of Sexual Violence *Professionally-run.* Support for adult women who are victims and/or survivors of sexual violence. Literature. Meetings vary, Essex County Rape Care Center, 204 Claremont Ave., Montclair. Registration required. Before attending call Christine Ferro, LSW 973-746-0800 ext. 22 (day). *E-mail:* cferro@familyserviceleague.org

HUNTERDON

SAFE in Hunterdon *Professionally-run.* Support for victims of domestic violence and sexual assault. Also provides shelters and other services. Building is handicapped accessible. Meetings vary, SAFE in Hunterdon, 47 E. Main St., Flemington. Call 908-788-7666 (day) or hotline 1-888-988-4033 (24 hr.); TTY: 1-866-954-0100. *Website:* http://www.safeinhunterdon.org *E-mail:* agencyinfo@womenscrisisservices.org

MERCER

SASS (Sexual Abuse Survivor Support) *Professionally-run.* Mutual support, education and coping skills for female rape survivors ages 13-26. Rap sessions. Building is handicapped accessible. Meets Thurs., 7:30-9pm, HiTOPS, 21 Wiggins St., Princeton. Before attending call Elizabeth Walters 609-683-0179 ext. 218 (day). *E-mail:* elizabeth@hitops.org

MIDDLESEX

Adult Survivors of Sexual Assault *Professionally-run.* Provides a safe, confidential environment for female survivors to share and receive support. Rap sessions. Group runs for 19 weeks, 2 times/yr., Edison. Pre-registration required. Call 1-877-665-7273 ext. 321 (day).

Male Survivors of Sexual Abuse/Assault *Professionally-run.* Provides a safe, confidential environment for male survivors of sexual abuse or assault to learn to cope with the effects of the abuse. Rap sessions. Runs for 19 weeks, 2 times/yr., Edison. Call 1-877-665-7273 ext. 321 (day).

MONMOUTH

Women Survivors of Sexual Abuse / Incest *Professionally-run.* Support for the empowerment of women who have been sexually victimized. Helps deal with the isolation, shame and powerlessness that can result. Members encouraged to be in therapy and must not be actively abusing substances. Dues

$5. Building is handicapped accessible. Meets Wed., 6:30-8:30pm, Freehold Township Municipal Building, 1 Municipal Plaza, Freehold. Pre-registration required. Before attending call Anitra or Danielle 732-409-6260 (Mon. or Wed. after 3:30pm).

MORRIS

Adult Survivors Group *(BILINGUAL) (WOMEN ONLY) Professionally-run.* Mutual support for female survivors of sexual abuse. Helps survivors process their feelings and understand the pain. Education, guest speakers and rap sessions. Groups meet for 12 consecutive weeks in Denville. Call Sonia Reyes 973-216-6432.

H.O.P.E.S. (Healing Ourselves Physically, Emotionally and Spiritually) *Professionally-run.* Self-help for adult survivors of any form of child abuse. Meets Wed., 7:30-9:30pm, First Presbyterian Church, 35 Church St., Rockaway. Before attending call Janice Taitel 973-586-8979 or Parents Anonymous 1-800-843-5437. *Website:* http://www.pa-of-nj.org

SNAP (Survivors Network of those Abused by Priests) North NJ Support for men and women who were sexually abused by any clergy person (priest, brother, nun, deacon, teacher, etc.). Survivors and immediate family only. Meets 1st Tues., 7-9pm, Grace Lutheran Church, 65 East Main St., Mendham. Call Kevin 908-630-9235. *E-mail:* kevinkingree@yahoo.com

OCEAN

Jersey Shore Survivors of Incest Anonymous 12-Step. Support for men and women who want to recover from having been sexually abused. Literature. Meets Thurs., 7-8:30pm, United Church of Christ, 1681 Ridgeway Rd. (Route 571), Toms River. Call Cathy 732-363-3839 (eve.). *E-mail:* jerseyshoresia@verizon.net

PASSAIC

12 Steps To Healing With a Christian Emphasis 12-Step. Mutual support for adult and youth survivors of sexual assault. The group meets for 12 weeks. Each week a different step is reviewed. Meeting location varies throughout Passaic and Sussex counties. For information call Erin 973-398-2862. *E-mail:* thadnerin@optonline.net

Passaic County Women's Center *(BILINGUAL) Professionally-run.* Support groups for survivors of domestic violence and/or sexual assault. Discussions include coping skills, legal issues and parenting skills. Groups meet weekly in Paterson. Call Tracy Francese 973-881-0725 (day) or 973-881-1450 (24 hr. hotline).

SALEM

Survivors of Childhood Sexual Abuse *Professionally-run.* Support, education and information for survivors of childhood sexual abuse and their families. Opportunity to share with other survivors. Groups offered periodically based on needs and run for 6-8 weeks. For information call 856-935-6655 (24 hr.); TTY: 856-935-7118.

SOMERSET

Survivors of Sexual Violence *Professionally-run.* Supportive and confidential group for adult female survivors of sexual assault and abuse. Provides a therapeutic environment to aid in the healing of sexual trauma. Rap sessions and literature. Building is handicapped accessible. Meets for 8 week sessions several times a year, Women's Health and Counseling Center, Somerville. Pre-registration required. Before attending call Caitlin 908-526-2335 ext. 132 (day). *Website:* http://www.womenandhealth.org *E-mail:* sass@womenandhealth.org

SUSSEX

12 Steps To Healing With a Christian Emphasis 12-Step. Mutual support for adult and youth survivors of sexual assault. The group meets for 12 weeks. Each week a different step is reviewed. Meeting location varies throughout Sussex and Passaic counties. For information call Erin 973-398-2862. *E-mail:* thadnerin@optonline.net

WARREN

Women's Domestic Violence Support Group *Professionally-run.* Supportive and confidential environment to help women victims of domestic violence work towards healing. Need prior screening to attend. Educational series. Building is handicapped accessible. Meets Tues., 11:30am-1pm, Hackettstown. For information on meeting call 908-453-4181 ext. 303; TTY: 908-453-2553. *Website:* http://www.darccwc.org

NATIONAL

Adult Survivors of Child Abuse *International. 11 affiliated groups. Founded 1991.* Mutual support for adult survivors of physical, sexual and/or emotional child abuse or neglect. Encourages victims to become survivors, then thrivers. Online support group meetings, phone meetings, monthly newsletter, group starter manuals and general information. Offers assistance in starting groups. Write: Adult Survivors, P.O. Box 14477, San Francisco, CA 94114-0038. Call 415-928-4576. *Website:* http://www.ascasupport.org *E-mail:* ascaoutreach@yahoo.com

Incest Resources, Inc. *Resource. Support groups in the Boston, MA area. Founded 1980.* Provides educational and resource materials for female and male survivors of childhood sexual abuse, and the professionals who work with them. International listing of survivor self-help groups, manual for starting survivor self-help groups and many other resources. For complete information send self-addressed envelope with two 1st class stamps. Write: Incest Resources, Inc., 46 Pleasant St., Cambridge, MA 02139. (NO CALLS PLEASE) *Website:* http://www.incestresourcesinc.org

Incest Survivors Anonymous (I.S.A.) *International. Founded 1980.* Uses 12-step/12-traditions, principles and tools of recovery. Fellowship of men, women and teens who meet to share their experience, strength and hope so that they may recover from their incest experiences and break free to freedom and a new peace of mind. Offers several packets of information, pen pals, I.S.A. E-mail Family Letter, CDs and cassettes. Not open to initiators, pedophiles, child molesters or satanists. Provides assistance in starting I.S.A. groups. When writing send a self-addressed stamped envelope (2 stamps). Write: I.S.A., P.O. Box 17245, Long Beach, CA 90807-7245. Call 562-428-5599. *Website:* http://www.lafn.org/medical/isa *E-mail:* isa@lafn.org

Male Survivor: National Organization Against Male Sexual Victimization *National. Founded 1995.* Information and referrals for male survivors of sexual assault and the professionals working with them. Conference every two years, referrals to local resources, newsletter, periodic regional retreats offered, online bulletin board and chatroom. Write: Male Survivor, PMB 103, 5505 Connecticut Ave. NW, Washington, DC 20015-2601. Call 1-800-738-4181. *Website:* http://www.malesurvivor.org

Molesters Anonymous *Model. Founded 1985.* Provides support with anonymity and confidentiality for men who molest children. Use of "thought stoppage" technique and buddy system. Groups are initiated by a professional but become member-run. Group development manual $9.95. Write: Jerry

Goffman, 1040 S. Mt. Vernon Ave., G-306, Colton, CA 92324. Call Jerry Goffman 951-312-1041. *E-mail:* jerrygoffman@hotmail.com

SNAP (Survivors Network of those Abused by Priests) *International. 50+ affiliated groups. Founded 1989.* Support for men and women who were sexually abused by any clergy person (priest, brother, nun, deacon, teacher, etc.) Extensive phone network, newsletter, advocacy, conferences, information and referrals. Information on finding support groups. Dues $25 (optional). Write: SNAP, P.O. Box 6416, Chicago, IL 60680. Call 312-409-2720. *Website:* http://www.snapnetwork.org *E-mail:* snapblaine@hotmail.com

Survivors of Incest Anonymous *International. 300 groups. Founded 1982.* 12-Step. Program for men and women, 18 yrs. or older, who have been victims of child sexual abuse, are not abusing any child and want to be survivors. Newsletter $15/yr., literature $30/13 pieces. Offers assistance in starting groups, volunteer information, referral line and speakers' bureau. Send self-addressed stamped envelope when writing (include a donation if possible). Write: SIA, P.O. Box 190, Benson, MD 21018-9998. Call 410-893-3322. *Website:* http://www.siawso.org *E-mail:* feedback@siawso.org

ONLINE

Abused Survivors *Online. 510 members. Founded 1998.* Support group that offers an outstretched hand to adult survivors of abuse (physical, verbal, emotional or sexual). Open only to survivors. *Website:* http://health.groups.yahoo.com/group/abusedsurvivors

Pandora's Aquarium, Inc. *Online. Founded 1999.* Provides support, education and resources to sexual violence survivors and their supporters. Operates an online support group, message board and chatroom for rape and sexual abuse survivors. Offers a Sexual Assault Lending Library, which lends materials on sexual violence and recovery, free of charge. Newsletter, literature and national conference. *Website:* http://www.pandorasaquarium.org

"Take the first step in faith. You don't have to see the whole staircase, just take the first step." --Martin Luther King Jr.

Positive Partners of Survivors *Online.* Support for anyone who has a loved one who was sexually abused. Offers mutual support and understanding. Provides chatroom, e-group and message board. *Website:* http://health.groups.yahoo.com/group/positivepartnersofsurvivors *E-mail:* hrtfelt32@aol.com or simonshek@idirect.com

Stigma, Inc. *Online.* Support for individuals conceived by rape or incest. Also, support to women who have been pregnant by assault or are raising rape or incest conceived children. In addition, there is a community forum for supportive visitors to discuss issues. E-mail support lists, chatroom, optional contacts to obtain general support and information. *Website:* http://www.stigmatized.org

SPOUSAL ABUSE / DOMESTIC VIOLENCE
(see also toll-free helplines)

BURLINGTON

Providence House *Professionally-run.* Support, education, counseling and shelter for victims who are, or have been, in abusive situations. Meets in Delran. Children's counseling services. Call 1-877-871-7551.

CAMDEN

Women's Domestic Violence Support Group *(BILINGUAL) Professionally-run.* Mutual support for female victims/survivors of domestic violence. Educational series and advocacy. Call 856-963-5668 (day). *Website:* http://www.ccwomenscenter.org
    Camden Meets Thurs., noon-2pm.
    Collingswood Meets Tues., 6-8pm.

CAPE MAY

CARA Buddy System *Professionally-run.* Confidential support for battered women to discuss problems and share resources. Rap sessions, guest speakers, phone help and literature. Building is handicapped accessible. Meets Wed., 7:30pm, CARA, Cape May Court House. Before attending call Juanita Battle 609-522-6489 (day) or CARA 1-877-294-2272; TTY: 609-463-0818. *E-mail:* carasafe1@verizon.net

M.E.N.D. (Men Exploring New Directions) *Professionally-run.* Support for men to learn other ways of coping with anger and stop violence in families. Rap sessions, phone help and literature. Meets Thurs., 7-9pm, Cape Regional Medical Center, Cape May Court House. Pre-registration required. Before attending call 609-522-6489 (day) or 1-877-294-2272; TTY: 609-463-0818.

CUMBERLAND

ACT (Abuse Ceases Today) *Professionally-run.* Mutual support for men to help deal with their anger. Educational series, rap sessions and literature. Building is handicapped accessible. Meets Tues., 6-8pm, Vineland. For meeting information call 856-691-3713 (day); TTY: 856-691-6024.

ESSEX

Babyland Family Violence Program *Professionally-run.* Support for women who have been in abusive relationships. Aim is to educate, liberate and empower domestic violence victims and survivors. Shelter and hotline. Pre-requisite requirements. Also offers a men's PEACE group ($2 fee). Meets at various locations in Essex County. Call 973-484-4446 (24 hr.). *Website:* http://www.babylandfamilyservices.org

GLOUCESTER

SERV (Services Empowering Rights of Victims) Support and education for women survivors of domestic violence. Meets Mon., 6:30pm, Glassboro. Call 856-881-3335.

HUDSON

Women's Project Groups *Professionally-run.* Support, education, workshops and groups to help women on subjects such as self-esteem, separation/divorce, domestic violence, employment and stress management. Meetings vary, Christ Hospital, 176 Palisade Ave., Jersey City. Before attending call Michele Bernstein 201-795-8375 ext. 8416 (day).

HUNTERDON

SAFE in Hunterdon *Professionally-run.* Support group and services for victims of domestic violence and sexual assault. Also serves children who are witnesses of domestic violence. Offers a men's compassion therapy program for a fee. Building is handicapped accessible. Meetings vary, SAFE in Hunterdon, 47 E. Main St., Flemington. Call 908-788-7666 (day) or 1-888-988-4033 (24 hr.

hotline); TTY: 1-866-954-0100. *Website:* http://www.safeinhunterdon.org *E-mail:* agency@safeinhunterdon.org

MIDDLESEX

Manavi *(SOUTH ASIAN) Professionally-run.* Provides emotional support for any South Asian woman (Indian, Pakistan, Bangladishi, Nepali, Sri Lankan) as they work through the effects of abuse. A safe space for women to share personal experiences. Provides a comfortable atmosphere to develop relationships which are trusting and caring. Meetings vary, 3-4:30pm, Manavi, New Brunswick. Childcare available. For meeting information call 732-435-1414. *Website:* http://www.manavi.org *E-mail:* manavi@manavi.org

Next Step, The *Professionally-run.* Emotional support for current and former victims of domestic violence (regardless of marital status or sexual orientation). Group explores options and tools to get control back into their lives. Various meeting locations throughout Middlesex County. For information call 732-725-1689 (all calls are confidential.)

Women Aware, Inc. *(BILINGUAL) Professionally-run.* Support groups, education and advocacy for battered women. Information on emergency shelter and other services. Call 732-249-4504 (voice/TTY) (24 hr.); legal advocacy 732-937-9525 (day). *Website:* http://www.womenaware.net *E-mail:* womenaware@aol.com

MORRIS

Jersey Battered Women's Service, Inc. *(BILINGUAL) Professionally-run.* Provides support groups and a safe home for victims or survivors of domestic violence and/or abusive relationships. Spanish-speaking groups available. Children's program services available. Legal advocacy. Call 973-267-4763 (helpline); TTY: 973-285-9095 (24 hr.). Also Jersey Center for Non-Violence offers services to assist batterers in stopping abuse and in developing alternative behaviors. Call 973-539-7801. *Website:* http://www.jbws.org *E-mail:* info@jbws.org

PASSAIC

Domestic Violence/Parenting Support Group *Professionally-run.* Provides emotional support and networking for women who are, or who have been, in domestic violent situations. Educational series, social group, advocacy and guest speakers. Also offers parenting classes. Meets Thurs., 6-8pm, Senior Citizen Center, 330A Passaic St., Passaic. Call Miriam Torres 973-365-5740 (day) or

Tom Fischetti 973-365-5741 (day). *Website:* http://www.passaicalliance.org *E-mail:* prevention@passaicalliance.org

Passaic County Women's Center *(BILINGUAL) Professionally-run.* Support groups for survivors of domestic violence and/or sexual assault. Discussions include coping skills, legal issues and parenting skills. Various groups meet weekly in Paterson. Call Tracy Francese 973-881-0725 (day) or Hotline 973-881-1450 (24 hr.).

SALEM

Female Victims and Survivors of Family Violence *Professionally-run.* Support, education and information for women to share with other victims. Building is handicapped accessible. Meets bi-weekly in a confidential location in Salem. Men's batterers program also. Call 856-935-6655 (24 hr.); TTY/TDD: 856-935-7118.

SUSSEX

Domestic Abuse Services, Inc. Mutual support for survivors of domestic violence and abuse. Meets in Newton. Call 973-579-2386 or 973-875-1211 (24 hr. hotline); TTY: 973-875-6369 (24 hr). *Website:* http://www.dasi.org *E-mail:* info@dasi.org

UNION

Project Protect *Professionally-run.* Provides support to victims of domestic violence. Meetings vary in Cranford. Call 908-355-4357 (24 hr.).

WARREN

Women's Domestic Violence Support Group *Professionally-run.* Supportive and confidential environment to help women victims of domestic violence work towards healing. Need prior screening to attend. Educational series. Building is handicapped accessible. Meets Tues., 11:30am-1pm, Hackettstown. For information on meeting call 908-453-4181 ext. 303; TTY: 908-453-2553. *Website:* http://www.darccwc.org

NATIONAL

Batterers Anonymous *National. Founded 1980.* Self-help program for men who wish to control their anger and eliminate their abusive behavior toward women. Buddy system. Group development manual ($9.95). Write: Batterers

Anonymous, c/o Dr. Jerry Goffman, 1040 S. Mt. Vernon Ave., G-306, Colton, CA 92324. Call Dr. Jerry Goffman 951-312-1041 (leave message and return address). *E-mail:* jerrygoffman@hotmail.com

Pathways To Peace, Inc. *International. 11 groups. Founded 1998.* Self-help program for anger management. In addition, offers education and assistance with starting groups. Write: Pathways To Peace, Inc., P.O. Box 259, Cassadaga, NY 14718. Call 1-800-775-4212; Fax: 716-595-3886. *Website:* http://www.pathwaystopeaceinc.com *E-mail:* transfrm@netsync.net

ONLINE

Abused Guys *Online.* Provides support for male victims of domestic violence. Offers online chatroom and message forum. Must join the group to post. *Website:* http://health.groups.yahoo.com/group/abusedguys *E-mail:* abusedguy@yahoo.com

Battered Husbands Support *Online. Founded 1998.* Support for men who have been or who are currently being battered by his female or male partner. Offers message boards, chatroom and useful links. *Website:* http://health.groups.yahoo.com/group/batteredhusbandssupport

Woman's Emotional Abuse Support *Online. Founded 1999.* Offers mutual support and understanding for victims of verbal abuse. Provides message boards, chatroom, links and e-mail group. *Website:* http://health.groups.yahoo.com/group/womansemotionalabusesupport

"Sometimes when you think you are done, it is just the edge of beginning. Probably that's why we decide we're done. It's getting too scary. We are touching down onto something real. It is beyond the point when you think you are done that often something strong comes out."--Natalie Goldberg

SUPPORT

Come and lean on me a bit;
I know just how you feel.
I've felt your fear and loneliness;
I know your pain is real.

For I have been where you are now,
Walking that long, dark road.
Then someone came to comfort me
And share my heavy load.

They helped me find new courage
And hope when I had none.
They let me lean on them awhile,
'Til my battle was won.

So come and lean on me a bit,
'Til your ordeal is through,
Then find someone who needs your help.
And let them lean on you.

--Martha J. Morrison

ADDICTIONS / DEPENDENCIES

ALCOHOL ABUSE
(see also toll-free helplines)

STATEWIDE

Al-Anon Family Groups 12-Step. Fellowship of families and friends of alcoholics. Offers comfort, hope and friendship through shared experiences. Includes groups for parents, children and adult children, gays, men and women. Several groups offer babysitting. Weekly meetings throughout New Jersey.
   North Jersey Information Service *(MULTILINGUAL)* (Covers Bergen, Essex, Hudson, Hunterdon, Middlesex, Monmouth, Morris, Passaic, Somerset, Sussex, Union and Warren counties) Call Al-Anon Information Service 973-744-8686 (day); Spanish-speaking 973-268-1260. Write: Al-Anon Family Groups, 73 S. Fullerton Ave., Montclair, NJ 07042. *Website:* http://www.northjerseyal-anon.org
   South Jersey Intergroup (Covers Atlantic, Burlington, Camden, Cape May, Cumberland, Gloucester, Mercer, Ocean and Salem counties) Write: Al-Anon Family Groups, South Jersey Information Service, 116 White Horse Pike, Haddon Heights, NJ 08035. Call Al-Anon Information Service 856-547-0855 (10am-3pm); Spanish-speaking 973-268-1260; Fax: 856-547-7111. *Website:* http://www.nj-al-anon.org

Al-Anon's Adult Children 12-Step. Fellowship offering comfort, hope and friendship through shared experiences for adult children of alcoholics. Weekly meetings available throughout New Jersey. Write: Al-Anon's Adult Children, 73 S. Fullerton Ave., 2nd Floor, Montclair, NJ 07042. For local meeting information call Al-Anon Information Service North New Jersey 973-744-8686 (day) or South New Jersey 856-547-0855 (day). *Website:* http://www.northjerseyal-anon.org

Alcoholics Anonymous 12-Step. Fellowship of men and women who share their experience, strength and hope to help each other recover from alcoholism. Groups meet weekly throughout New Jersey.
   Cape Atlantic Intergroup (Covers Atlantic and Cape May counties) Write: A.A., 32 Blackhorse Pike, P.O. Box 905, Pleasantville, NJ 08232. Call 1-800-604-4357 (not available with all cell phones) or 609-641-8855. *Website:* http://www.capeatlanticintergroup.org

Central Jersey Intergroup *(BILINGUAL)* (Covers Mercer County and parts of Ocean, Monmouth, Middlesex, Somerset and Hunterdon counties) Write: A.A. Central Jersey Intergroup, P.O. Box 4096, Trenton, NJ 08610. Call 609-656-8900 (24 hr.); Spanish-speaking 973-824-0555. *Website:* http://www.centraljerseyintergroup.org

North Jersey Intergroup *(BILINGUAL)* (Covers Bergen, Essex, Hudson, Hunterdon, Middlesex, Monmouth, Morris, Ocean, Passaic, Somerset, Sussex, Union and Warren counties) Write: A.A., 2400 Morris Ave., Union, NJ 07083. Call 1-800-245-1377 or 908-687-8566 (24 hr.). Spanish speaking 973-824-0555. *Website:* http://www.nnjaa.org

South Jersey Intergroup *(BILINGUAL)* (Covers Burlington, Camden, Cumberland, Gloucester and Salem counties) Write: A.A., P.O. Box 2514, Cherry Hill, NJ 08034. Call 1-866-920-1212 or 856-486-4444 (24 hr.); Spanish-speaking 973-824-0555. *Website:* http://www.aasj.org

Families Anonymous 12-Step. Program for relatives and friends concerned about the use of drugs, alcohol or related behavioral problems. Meetings throughout NJ. Call 1-800-736-9805. *Website:* http://www.familiesanonymous.org

Lawyers Concerned for Lawyers Statewide network of independent, self-help groups that support attorneys, judges and law students in recovery from alcoholism and drug dependence. Based on the 12-steps but not affiliated with A.A., and is not meant to be a substitute for participation in A.A. or other fellowships. The NJ Lawyers Assistance Program performs an "intergroup function" for Lawyers Concerned for Lawyers. All services are free and confidential. Write: NJLAP, NJ Law Center, One Constitution Square, New Brunswick, NJ 08901-1520. Call 1-800-246-5527 or 732-937-7549 (day). For information about women's group, call Denise 732-937-7541. *Website:* http://www.njlap.org *E-mail:* njlap@aol.com

Nurse Recovery Group *Professionally-run.* Mutual support and information for nurses who are recovering from addictions. Sharing of professional concerns and encouragement. Meets in Bergen, Burlington, Camden, Cape May, Cumberland, Essex, Hunterdon, Mercer, Middlesex, Monmouth, Morris, Ocean, Passaic and Sussex counties. Write: Peer Assistance Project, 1479 Pennington Rd., Trenton, NJ 08618. Call 1-800-662-0108 (day). *Website:* http://www.njsna.org (click on RAMP; next click on Peer Assistance)

Signs of Sobriety, Inc. (SOS) *Professionally-run.* Provides alcoholism and drug addiction services to persons who are deaf or hard-of-hearing. Makes referrals to deaf and sign interpreted 12-step groups throughout NJ (alcohol or drug addiction, gambling, families of alcoholics, etc). Offers prevention awareness, education classes, Sober Camp annual summer retreat and Sober/Deaf activities for deaf or hard-of-hearing individuals in recovery. Newsletter. Write: Signs Of Sobriety, Inc., 100 Scotch Rd., 2nd Floor, Ewing, NJ 08628. Call TTY/VP: 609-882-7177; Voice: 609-882-7677 or 1-800-332-7677 (day); Fax: 609-882-6808. *Website:* http://www.signsofsobriety.org *E-mail:* info@signsofsobriety.org

ATLANTIC

Al-Anon Family Groups 12-Step. Fellowship of families and friends of alcoholics. Offers comfort, hope and friendship through shared experiences. Includes groups for children and adult children. Call Al-Anon Information Services 856-547-0855 (10am-3pm) or 973-744-8686 (day); Spanish-speaking 973-268-1260. *Website:* http://www.nj-al-anon.org

Alcoholics Anonymous *(BILINGUAL)* 12-Step. Fellowship of men and women who share their experience, strength and hope with each other that they may solve their common problem and help others to recover from alcoholism. Young people's groups also available. Call 1-800-604-4357 (not available with all cell phones) or 609-641-8855. *Website:* http://www.capeatlanticintergroup.org

Dual Recovery Anonymous *Professionally-run.* 12-Step. Mutual support for people who suffer from a mental illness and struggle with substance abuse issues. Families welcome. Guest speakers. Meets Tues., 3-4pm, CSP of NJ, 1147 North New Rd., Absecon. Call Cathy Flanagan 609-383-1190 ext. 309 (day). *E-mail:* cflanagan@cspnj.org

Dual Recovery Anonymous 12-Step. Fellowship for persons diagnosed with both a mental illness and an addiction. Building is handicapped accessible. Rap sessions. Meets Wed., 6pm, Atlantic City Rescue Mission, Bacharach Blvd., Atlantic City. Call 609-272-1700 ext. 303 (day).

Family Support Group Mutual support for parents and families of persons diagnosed with both a mental illness and alcohol or chemical addiction. Sharing of emotional and practical coping skills. Guest speakers. Meets 2nd Thurs., 10:30am and 4th Thurs., 5:30pm, Mental Health Association, 1127 North New Rd., Absecon. Call Christine Gromadzyn, MSW 609-272-1700 (day).

Need help finding a specific group? Give us a call – we're here to help!
*Call **1-800-367-6274**.*

Lawyers Concerned for Lawyers Self-help group that supports recovery from alcoholism and drug dependence for attorneys, judges, law students and others in the legal system. Based on the 12-step program adapted from A.A. All inquiries are confidential. Meets Wed., 5:30pm, 1555 Zion Rd., Suite 201, Northfield. Before attending call John 609-641-2266 (day) or NJ Lawyers Assistance Program 1-800-246-5527. *Website:* http://www.njlap.org *E-mail:* njlap@aol.com

BERGEN

A Jewish Approach to Recovery Incorporates Jewish teachings related to recovery plus the 12-steps of Alcoholics Anonymous. Mutual support for all Jews in recovery and their family members. Guest speakers and literature. Building is handicapped accessible. Meets Wed., 7:30pm, The Living Room at Jewish Family Service, 1485 Teaneck Rd., Teaneck. Before attending call 201-837-9090 (day), Marty 201-281-0498, Dan 201-244-1244 (day) or 201-394-8802 (eve). *E-mail:* thelivingroom@jfsbergen.org

Al-Anon Family Groups 12-Step. Fellowship of families and friends of alcoholics. Offers comfort, hope and friendship through shared experiences. Includes groups for children and adult children. Call Al-Anon Information Services 973-744-8686 (day); Spanish-speaking 973-268-1260. *Website:* http://www.northjerseyal-anon.org

Al-Anon's Adult Children 12-Step. Fellowship offering comfort, hope and friendship through shared experiences for adult children of alcoholics. Meets Sat., 10:30am, First Reformed Church, 2420 Lemoine Ave., Fort Lee. Call Al-Anon Information Services 973-744-8686 (day). *Website:* http://www.northjerseyal-anon.org

Alateen 12-Step. Fellowship of young persons (ages 10-18) whose lives have been affected by someone else's drinking. An active adult member of Al-Anon serves as a sponsor. Call Al-Anon Information Services 973-744-8686 (day). *Website:* http://www.northjerseyal-anon.org
>   **Hillsdale** Meets Sun., 7:30pm, Pascack Bible Church, 181 Piermont Ave. Use back door entrance.
>   **Teaneck** Meets Tues., 7:30pm, St. Mark's Episcopal Church, 118 Chadwick Rd.

Alcoholics Anonymous *(BILINGUAL)* 12-Step. Fellowship of men and women who share their experience, strength and hope with each other that they may solve their common problem and help others to recover from alcoholism. Young people's groups also available. Call 1-800-245-1377 or 908-687-8566 (24 hr.); Spanish-speaking 973-824-0555. *Website:* http://www.nnjaa.org

CARE (Christians, Addictions, Recovery and Education) 12-Step. Support ministry for substance abusers and their families to help find sobriety, solace and a way to a comfortable non-judgmental Christian walk. Meets Mon., 7:30pm, Church of the Nazarene, 285 E. Midland Ave., Paramus. Call 201-262-3323 (Mon., Wed., Thurs.; 9:30am-4pm). *Website:* http://www.maranathanj.org

Double Trouble in Recovery 12-Step. Support and encouragement for those who are chemically addicted and are also in recovery from a psychiatric illness. Meets Wed., 7pm, On Our Own Self-Help Center, 179 Main St., 2nd Floor, Hackensack. Call On Our Own Self-Help Center 201-489-8402.

Families Anonymous 12-Step. Mutual support for relatives and friends concerned about the use of drugs or related behavioral problems. *Website:* http://www.familiesanonymous.org

    Englewood Meets Fri., 7:30pm, Englewood Hospital, 350 Engle St., Medical Learning Center, Main Floor. Call Geri 201-585-8091.

    Mahwah Meets Wed., 7:30-8:30pm, Church of the Immaculate Conception, 900 Darlington Ave. Call Richard or Barbara 201-327-0748. *E-mail:* famahwah@verizon.net

    Tenafly Meets Tues., 7:30pm, Trinity Lutheran Church, Basement, 430 Knickerbocker Rd. Call Judy or Gene 201-262-7758 (day).

Lawyers Concerned for Lawyers Self-help group that supports recovery from alcoholism and drug dependence for attorneys, judges, law students and others in the legal system. Based on the 12-step program adapted from A.A. All inquiries are confidential. Meets Wed., 6:30pm, Church of the Good Shepard, 1576 Palisades Ave., Chapel, Fort Lee. Before attending call NJ Lawyers Assistance Program 1-800-246-5527. *Website:* http://www.njlap.org *E-mail:* njlap@aol.com

Nurse Recovery Group *Professionally-run.* Mutual support and information for nurses who are recovering from addictions. Sharing of professional concerns and encouragement. Meets in Teaneck and Paramus. Call 1-800-662-0108 (day). *Website:* http://www.njsna.org (click on RAMP; next click Peer Assistance)

Parent Support Group - New Jersey, Inc. *Professionally-run.* Confidential support group for parents of children (ages 13-40+) who are chemically dependent. Meets Mon., 6:30pm, Behavioral Health Center, Bergen Pines Hospital, Room E218, Paramus. Call Karol Sullivan or Adrienne Mellana

1-800-561-4299   or   973-736-3344   (day).   *Website:*
http://www.psgnjhomestead.com

Psychiatrically Recovering Alcoholics Mutual support for psychiatrically recovering alcoholics who suffer from emotional and mental disorders to share experience, strength and hope while recovering from alcoholism and psychiatric disorders. Meets Tues., 7-8pm, Bethany Presbyterian Church, Palisade Ave. and William St., Englewood. Call Ed 201-541-8452.

Seniors Count *Professionally-run.* 12-Step. Support for persons (ages 60+) who are recovering from substance abuse or co-dependency. Meets Fri., 1:30-3pm, Vantage Building, 93 West Palisades Ave., Englewood. Call Anne Wennhold 201-569-6667 ext. 3298. *Website:* http://www.vanostinstitute.org *E-mail:* awennhold@vanostinstitute.org

Women For Sobriety Self-help group designed specifically to help women with addictions achieve sobriety. Helps develop self-esteem and coping skills. Donation $2. Meets Thurs., 7-8:30pm (new members 6:45pm), YWCA, 112 Oak St., Ridgewood. Call Nina Wegener 201-612-0511 (day) or Jennifer Rosa 201-881-1721 (day).

BURLINGTON

12 Steps God's Way Christian-focused recovery group for anyone suffering from any type of addiction, dependency or compulsive disorder. Meets Thurs., 7pm, Fellowship Alliance Chapel, 199 Church Rd., Medford. Call 609-953-7333 (day).

Addictions Victorious of South Jersey, Inc. 12-Step. Christ-centered support group for men and women who, in their struggle with substance abuse and emotional problems, come together that they may solve their problems and help others as well. Guest speakers, rap sessions, phone help, literature and newsletter. Optional donation. Meets Tues., 7pm, Lighthouse Tabernacle, 716 Main St., Lumberton. Call Ronnie and Harry 609-267-2657 or Mike 609-267-5499. *Website:* http://www.addvicinc.org

Al-Anon Family Groups 12-Step. Fellowship of families and friends of alcoholics. Offers comfort, hope and friendship through shared experiences. Includes groups for children and adult children. Call Al-Anon Information Services 856-547-0855 (10am-3pm) or 973-744-8686 (day); Spanish-speaking 973-268-1260. *Website:* http://www.nj-al-anon.org

Alcoholics Anonymous *(BILINGUAL)* 12-Step. Fellowship of men and women who share their experience, strength and hope with each other that they may solve their common problem and help others to recover from alcoholism. Young people's groups also available. Call 1-866-920-1212 or 856-486-4444 (24 hr.); Spanish-speaking 973-824-0555. *Website:* http://www.aasj.org

Double Trouble in Recovery Mutual support for persons with a substance abuse problem who are also taking medication for psychiatric problems. Meets Sun., Mon. and Wed., 8:30pm, Hampton Hospital, 650 Rancocas Rd., Cafeteria, Westampton. Call Greg Pryor 609-267-7000 ext. 2148 (day).

Families Anonymous 12-Step. Support for parents, families and friends of persons with drug, alcohol or related behavioral problems. Meets Wed., 7:30pm, Marlton United Methodist Church, Plymouth Ave. and Marlboro Ave., Marlton. Call 856-461-7076 (eve). *Website:* http://www.familiesanonymous.org

Lawyers Concerned for Lawyers Self-help group that supports recovery from alcoholism and drug dependence for attorneys, judges, law students and others in the legal system. Based on the 12-step program adapted from A.A. All inquiries are confidential. Meets 1st and 3rd Wed., 5:30pm, The Daily Grind, 48 High St., Mount Holly. Before attending call NJ Lawyers Assistance Program 1-800-246-5527. *Website:* http://www.njlap.org *E-mail:* njlap@aol.com

Nurse Recovery Group *Professionally-run.* Mutual support and information for nurses who are recovering from addictions. Sharing of professional concerns and encouragement. Meets in Moorestown. Call 1-800-662-0108 (day). *Website:* http://www.njsna.org (click on RAMP; next click Peer Assistance)

Rap Room Parent-to-Parent Coalition *Professionally-run.* Support and education for parents of teens and adult children dealing with substance/alcohol addictions. Mutual sharing, advocacy, guest speakers, crisis intervention and referral. Meets 1st Tues., 7-9pm, Greentree Executive Campus, 1003A Lincoln Drive West, Marlton. Call Louise 856-983-3328. *Website:* http://www.raproom.org

CAMDEN

ACOA (Adult Children Of Alcoholics) 12-Step. Support for adult children of alcoholics. Meets Tues., 6:30pm, Starting Point, 215 Highland Ave., Suite C, Westmont. Call 856-854-3155 ext. 0.

Addictions Victorious of South Jersey, Inc. 12-Step. Christ-centered support group for men and women who, in their struggle with substance abuse and emotional problems, come together that they may solve their problems and help others as well. Guest speakers, rap sessions, phone help, literature and newsletter. Optional donation. *Website:* http://www.addvicinc.org

> **Barrington** Meets Mon., 7pm, Grace Bible Church, 887 Clements Bridge Rd. Call Ginny 856-232-0207 or Bob 856-869-3077.
>
> **Blackwood** Meets Thurs., 7pm, Community Wesleyan Church, 508 Woodbury-Turnersville Rd. Call Norman 856-243-2205.
>
> **Camden** Meets Tues., noon, Fellowship House, 1722 S. Broadway. Call Lucy 856-964-4545.
>
> **Camden** Meets Thurs., 7:30pm, New Hope Temple, 488 Jackson St. Call Deborah or Anita 856-966-0343.
>
> **Camden** Meets 1st and 3rd Fri., 8pm, Assembly of God, 518 Market St. Call Kevin or Eugene 856-966-8141.
>
> **Camden** Meets 2nd and 4th Thurs., 6pm, Evangelism Today, 1658 Mt. Ephraim Ave., 2nd Floor. Call Elaine 856-541-7977.
>
> **Collingswood** Meets Wed., 7pm, First United Methodist Church, 201 Dayton Ave. Call Richard 856-240-1667.
>
> **Lindenwold** Meets Mon., 7pm, Garden Lake Bible Church, 63 First Ave. Call Pastor Dave 856-357-4194 or Harry 609-502-0773.
>
> **Lindenwold** Meets Thurs., 7:30pm, Christ Community Church, 325 Linden Ave. Call David 856-346-2220.
>
> **Pennsauken** Meets Sun., 5pm, Calvary Assembly of God, 4921 Camden Ave. and Browning Rd. Call Will or Lucy 856-964-4545.
>
> **Pine Hill** Meets Tues., 7:30pm, Hope Chapel C.M.A., New Hope Ministries, 28 East Branch Ave. Call Skip 856-566-4134.
>
> **Somerdale** Meets Thurs., 7pm, Park Avenue Community Church, 431 Hilltop Ave. Call Jeannine 856-435-0309.

Al-Anon Family Groups 12-Step. Fellowship of families and friends of alcoholics. Offers comfort, hope and friendship through shared experiences. Includes groups for children and adult children. Call Al-Anon Information Services 856-547-0855 (10am-3pm) or 973-744-8686 (day); Spanish-speaking 973-268-1260. *Website:* http://www.nj-al-anon.org

Alateen 12-Step. Fellowship of young persons whose lives have been affected by someone else's drinking. An active adult member of Al-Anon serves as a sponsor. Call Al-Anon Information Services 856-547-0855 (10am-3pm). *Website:* http://www.nj-al-anon.org

> **Cherry Hill** Meets Wed., 8-9pm, JFK Hospital, Chapel Ave. and Cooper Landing Rd., 5th Floor, Conference Room C.

Cherry Hill Meets Sun., 8:15pm, St. Peter Celestine School, 402 Kings Highway North.

Alcoholics Anonymous *(BILINGUAL)* 12-Step. Fellowship of men and women who share their experience, strength and hope with each other that they may solve their common problem and help others to recover from alcoholism. Young people's groups also available. Call 1-866-920-1212 or 856-486-4444 (24 hr.); Spanish-speaking call 973-824-0555. *Website:* http://www.aasj.org

Calix Society Mutual support to promote the spiritual development of Catholic alcoholics. Members of other faiths welcome. Group followed by mass. Meets 1st Sat., 4pm, St. Bartholomew Church, Kaighn Blvd., Camden. Call Joe 856-384-9791.

Camden County Parent-to-Parent Mutual support for parents of children of any age who have alcohol or drug-related problems. Guest speakers, literature and phone help. Building is handicapped accessible. Meets 2nd and 4th Tues., 6:30-8:30pm, Bellmawr Library, 35 E. Browning Rd., Bellmawr. Call 856-225-5071 (day).

Dual Recovery Anonymous 12-Step. Mutual support for alcoholics/addicts who are taking medication for psychiatric problems.
    Cherry Hill Meetings vary, 3:30-4:30pm, MICA Club, 498 Marlboro Ave., Before attending call 856-662-0955 (voice/TDD; day).
    Westmont Meets Mon., 8pm, Starting Point, 215 Highland Ave. Call Tom 856-495-2676.

Nurse Recovery Group *Professionally-run.* Mutual support and information for nurses who are recovering from addictions. Sharing of professional concerns and encouragement. Meets in Haddonfield. Call 1-800-662-0108 (day). *Website:* http://www.njsna.org (click on RAMP; next click Peer Assistance)

CAPE MAY

Al-Anon Family Groups 12-Step. Fellowship of families and friends of alcoholics. Offers comfort, hope and friendship through shared experiences. Includes groups for children and adult children. Call Al-Anon Information Service 856-547-0855 (10am-3pm) or 973-744-8686 (day); Spanish-speaking 973-268-1260. *Website:* http://www.nj-al-anon.org

Consider passing this Directory on to a student or staff member - browsing through the Directory pages can often provide helpful education as to the wide variety of groups available.

Alateen 12-Step. Fellowship of young persons whose lives have been affected by someone else's drinking. An active adult member of Al-Anon serves as a sponsor. Call Al-Anon Information Services 856-547-0855 (10am-3pm).
   Cape May Courthouse Meets Thurs., 8:30am, Cape Educational Compact, 204 Moore Rd.
   Marmora Meets Thurs., 8pm, Church of the Resurrection, 200 W. Tuckahoe Rd.

Alcoholics Anonymous 12-Step. Fellowship of men and women who share their experience, strength and hope with each other that they may solve their common problem and help others to recover from alcoholism. Young people's groups also available. Call 1-800-604-4357 (not available with all cell phones) or 609-641-8855. *Website:* http://www.capeatlanticinterrgroup.org

Celebrate Recovery Christian 12-Step. Fellowship sharing experiences, strengths and hopes with others who are going through recovery. Rap sessions, guest speakers and literature. Meets Fri., 7-9pm, Seashore Church of the Nazarene, 446 Seashore Rd., Erma. Call Michael Austin 609-886-6196 (day). *E-mail:* celebrate_at_seashore@msn.com

Nurse Recovery Group *Professionally-run.* Mutual support and information for nurses who are recovering from addictions. Sharing of professional concerns and encouragement. Meets in Marmora. Call 1-800-662-0108 (day). *Website:* http://www.njsna.org (click on RAMP; next click Peer Assistance)

CUMBERLAND

Al-Anon Family Groups 12-Step. Fellowship of families and friends of alcoholics. Offers comfort, hope and friendship through shared experiences. Includes groups for children and adult children. Call Al-Anon Information Services 856-547-0855 (10am-3pm) or 973-744-8686 (day); Spanish-speaking 973-268-1260. *Website:* http://www.nj-al-anon.org

Alateen 12-Step. Fellowship of young persons whose lives have been affected by someone else's drinking. An active adult member of Al-Anon serves as a sponsor. Meets Thurs., 8pm, First Presbyterian Church, 119 North 2nd St., Millville. Call Al-Anon Information Services 856-547-0855 (10am-3pm).

Alcoholics Anonymous *(BILINGUAL)* 12-Step. Fellowship of men and women who share their experience, strength and hope with each other that they may solve their common problem and help others to recover from alcoholism. Young people's groups also available. Call 1-866-920-1212 or 856-486-4444 (24 hr.); Spanish-speaking 973-824-0555. *Website:* http://www.aasj.org

Dual Recovery Anonymous 12-Step. Assists consumers who suffer a severe and persistent mental illness to work on their recovery from addiction to substances. Meets Tues., 1-3pm, Special Needs Adult Partial Care Program, Cumberland County Guidance Center, 2038 Carmel Rd., Millville. Call 856-825-6810 ext. 269.

Nurse Recovery Group *Professionally-run.* Mutual support and information for nurses who are recovering from addictions. Sharing of professional concerns and encouragement. Meets in Seabrook. Call 1-800-662-0108 (day). *Website:* http://www.njsna.org (click on RAMP; next click Peer Assistance)

Overcomer's Outreach Christian 12-Step. Fellowship to overcome any type of addiction or compulsive behavior, anxiety, depression or loneliness using God's word as a basis of recovery. Bible study, discussion, prayer and phone help. Meets Thurs., 7-8pm, Shiloh Seventh Day Baptist Church, East Ave., Shiloh. Call Frank B. Mulford 856-451-8698 (day) or Rev. Chroniger 856-455-0488 (day). *E-mail:* ahfarm@hotmail.com

ESSEX

Al-Anon Family Groups 12-Step. Fellowship of families and friends of alcoholics. Offers comfort, hope and friendship through shared experiences. Includes groups for children and adult children. Call Al-Anon Information Services 973-744-8686 (day); Spanish-speaking 973-268-1260. *Website:* http://www.northjerseyal-anon.org

Al-Anon's Adult Children 12-Step. Fellowship offering comfort, hope and friendship through shared experiences for adult children of alcoholics. Meets Tues., 8pm, First Presbyterian Church, 10 Fairview Ave., Verona. Call Al-Anon Information Services 973-744-8686. *Website:* http://www.northjerseyal-anon.org

Alcoholics Anonymous *(BILINGUAL)* 12-Step. Fellowship of men and women who share their experience, strength and hope with each other that they may solve their common problem and help others to recover from alcoholism. Young people's groups also available. Call 1-800-245-1377 or 908-687-8566 (24 hr.); Spanish-speaking 973-824-0555. *Website:* http://www.nnjaa.org

BASA (Brothers And Sisters of Addicts) *Professionally-run.* Confidential support group for siblings with a chemically dependent sibling. Meets Mon., 7pm, St. Cloud Presbyterian Church, Old Indian Rd. and Ridgeway Ave., West Orange. Call Karol Sullivan or Adrienne Mellana 973-736-3344 (day) or 1-800-561-3299. *Website:* http://www.psgnjhomestead.com *E-mail:* psgnj1@aol.com

Double Trouble in Recovery Support for persons in dual recovery from a mental illness and a substance or alcohol addiction. Meets Mon., 5-6pm, Where Peaceful Waters Flow, 47 Cleveland St., Orange. Call Richard 973-677-7700 (day) or 973-651-7382.

Families Anonymous 12-Step. Support for families and friends concerned about the use of drugs or related behavioral problems. Sharing of experiences, strengths and hopes. Dues $1. Meets Wed., 7:30pm, First Episcopal Church of the Holy Spirit, 36 Gould St., Verona. Call Cathy 201-991-5711 or Roxy 973-667-1067. *Website:* http://www.familiesanonymous.org

Lawyers Concerned for Lawyers Self-help group that supports recovery from alcoholism and drug dependence for attorneys, judges, law students and others in the legal system. Based on the 12-step program adapted from A.A. All inquiries are confidential. Meets Tues., 7:30pm, United Way Building, 60 S. Fullerton Ave., Room 211A, Montclair. Before attending call Kenneth 973-429-5588 (day), 973-509-6062 (eve.) or NJ Lawyers Assistance Program 1-800-246-5527. *Website:* http://www.njlap.org *E-mail:* njlap@aol.com

MICA Support Group 12-Step. Support to help those who have dual disorders of recovery from an alcohol/drug addiction and also in recovery from a psychiatric illness. Meets Wed., 5:30-6:30pm, Pleasant Moments Self-Help Center, 465 Broadway, Conference Room, Newark. Call Scott 973-751-5922.

Nurse Recovery Group *Professionally-run.* Mutual support and information for nurses who are recovering from addictions. Sharing of professional concerns and encouragement. Meets in Montclair. Call 1-800-662-0108 (day). *Website:* http://www.njsna.org (click on RAMP; next click Peer Assistance)

Parents Support Group - New Jersey Inc. *Professionally-run.* Confidential support group for parents of children (ages 13-40+) who are chemically dependent. Meets Wed., 6pm and Thurs., 6:30pm, St. Cloud Presbyterian Church, Old Indian Rd. and Ridgeway Ave., West Orange. Call Karol Sullivan 973-736-3344 (9am-3pm) or 1-800-561-4299 (24 hr. hotline).

"Adapt yourself to the things among which your lot has been cast and love sincerely the fellow creatures with whom destiny has ordained that you shall live." —Marcus Aurelius

GLOUCESTER

Addiction Support Group - Families and Friends *Professionally-run.* Support for families of persons with addiction issues. Offers encouragement, information and guidance with a Jewish perspective. Group is open to people of any faith. Meetings vary, 6 week sessions, 2-3 times/yr., 7-8:30pm, Jewish Family and Child Services, 702 Birchfield Rd., Mount Laurel. Pre-registration required. Before attending call Meira Itzkowitz 856-778-7775.

Addictions Victorious of South Jersey, Inc. 12-Step. Christ-centered support group for men and women who in their struggle with substance abuse and emotional problems come together that they may solve their problems and help others as well. Guest speakers, rap sessions, phone help, literature and newsletter. Optional donation. *Website:* http://www.addvicinc.org

> **Glassboro** Meets Tues., 7pm, Olivet Wesleyan Church, 711 Heston Rd. Call Chip 609-706-6597.
> **Pitman** Meets Mon. and Thurs., 7:30pm, The Rock Church, 205 Esplanade Ave. Call Laura 856-582-2277.
> **Williamstown** Meets Thurs., 6pm, Community Bible Fellowship Church, Broadlane Rd. Call Fabian 609-605-1671.
> **Woodbury** Meets Tues., 7:30pm, Gateway Christian Church, 751 Delaware St. Call David 856-761-2356 or Dan 856-848-5252.

Al-Anon Family Groups 12-Step. Fellowship of families and friends of alcoholics. Offers comfort, hope and friendship through shared experiences. Includes groups for children and adult children. Call Al-Anon Information Services 856-547-0855 (10am-3pm) or 973-744-8686 (day); Spanish-speaking 973-268-1260. *Website:* http://www.nj-al-anon.org

Alcoholics Anonymous *(BILINGUAL)* 12-Step. Fellowship of men and women who share their experience, strength and hope with each other that they may solve their common problem and help others to recover from alcoholism. Young people's groups also available. Call 1-866-920-1212 or 856-486-4444 (24 hr.); Spanish-speaking 973-824-0555. *Website:* http://www.aasj.org

Gloucester County Parent To Parent Coalition *Professionally-run.* Confidential meetings and focus on providing parents with support, information, resources and referrals for dealing with substance abuse and related problems. Guest speakers, educational series and literature. Building is handicapped accessible. Meets 2nd and 4th Mon., 7:30-9:30pm, Washington Township Municipal Building, 523 Egg Harbor Rd., Meeting Room C, Washington Township. Call 856-589-6446 (day).

Teens Recovery Group *Professionally-run.* Support group for teenagers (ages 13-20) in recovery from drugs and/or alcohol. Meets Thurs., 7-8:30pm, Washington Township Municipal Building, 523 Egg Harbor Rd., Meeting Room C, Sewell. Call Donna Rullo 856-589-6446 (day). *E-mail:* wtfcs@twp.washington.nj.us

HUDSON

Al-Anon Family Groups 12-Step. Fellowship of families and friends of alcoholics. Offers comfort, hope and friendship through shared experiences. Includes groups for children and adult children. Call Al-Anon Information Services 973-744-8686 (day); Spanish-speaking 973-268-1260. Spanish-speaking 973-268-1260. *Website:* http://www.northjerseyal-anon.org

Alcoholics Anonymous *(BILINGUAL)* 12-Step. Fellowship of men and women who share their experience, strength and hope with each other that they may solve their common problem and help others to recover from alcoholism. Young people's groups also available. Call 1-800-245-1377 or 908-687-8566 (24 hr.); Spanish-speaking 973-824-0555. *Website:* http://www.nnjaa.org

Double Trouble in Recovery 12-Step. Support and encouragement for those who are chemically addicted and are also in recovery from a psychiatric illness. Meets Tues., 10:30am, Hudson County Self-Help Center, 880 Bergen Ave., Suite 605, Jersey City. Call Wayne Vivian 201-420-8013.

HUNTERDON

Al-Anon Family Groups 12-Step. Fellowship of families and friends of alcoholics. Offers comfort, hope and friendship through shared experiences. Includes groups for children and adult children. Call Al-Anon Information Services 973-744-8686 (day); Spanish-speaking 973-268-1260. *Website:* http://www.northjerseyal-anon.org

Alcoholics Anonymous *(BILINGUAL)* 12-Step. Fellowship of men and women who share their experience, strength and hope with each other that they may solve their common problem and help others to recover from alcoholism. Young people's groups also available. Call 1-800-245-1377 or 908-687-8566 (24 hr.); Spanish-speaking 973-824-0555. *Website:* http://www.nnjaa.org

Nurse Recovery Group *Professionally-run.* Mutual support and information for nurses who are recovering from addictions. Sharing of professional concerns and encouragement. Meets in Flemington. Call 1-800-662-0108 (day). *Website:* http://www.njsna.org (click on RAMP; next click on Peer Assistance)

MERCER

Al-Anon Family Groups 12-Step. Fellowship of families and friends of alcoholics. Offers comfort, hope and friendship through shared experiences. Includes groups for children and adult children. Call Al-Anon Information Services 856-547-0855 (10am-3pm) or 973-744-8686 (day); Spanish-speaking 973-268-1260. *Website:* http://www.nj-al-anon.org

Alateen 12-Step. Fellowship of young persons whose lives have been affected by someone else's drinking. An active adult member of Al-Anon serves as a sponsor. Meets Wed., 8pm, St. Anthony's Church, Route 33 and Maxwell Ave., Hightstown. Call Al-Anon Information Services 856-547-0855 (10am-3pm). *Website:* http://www.nj-al-anon.org

Alcoholics Anonymous *(BILINGUAL)* 12-Step. Fellowship of men and women who share their experience, strength and hope with each other that they may solve their common problem and help others to recover from alcoholism. Young people's groups also available. Call 609-656-8900 (24 hr.); Spanish-speaking 973-824-0555. *Website:* http://www.centraljerseyintergroup.org

Families Anonymous 12-Step. Program for families, especially parents of those with substance abuse or other disruptive behavioral problems. Building is handicapped accessible. Meets Mon., 7:30pm, St. Lawrence Rehab Center, 2381 Lawrenceville Rd. (Route 206 South), Lawrenceville. Call Joan 609-883-1403. *Website:* http://www.familiesanonymous.org *E-mail:* joan@brra.com

Nurse Recovery Group *Professionally-run.* Mutual support and information for nurses who are recovering from addictions. Sharing of professional concerns and encouragement. Meets in Trenton. Call 1-800-662-0108 (day). *Website:* http://www.njsna.org (click on RAMP; next click Peer Assistance)

Princeton ACA (Adult Children of Alcoholics/Dysfunctional Families) 12-Step. Fellowship for adult children from alcoholic or dysfunctional families. Optional meeting donation $1. Meets Thurs., 7:30-9pm, Unitarian Church of Princeton, 50 Cherry Hill Rd., Princeton. Call Audrey 609-716-8063.

MIDDLESEX

Al-Anon Family Groups 12-Step. Fellowship of families and friends of alcoholics. Offers comfort, hope and friendship through shared experiences. Includes groups for children and adult children. Call Al-Anon Information Services 973-744-8686 (day); Spanish-speaking 973-268-1260. *Website:* http://www.northjerseyal-anon.org

Alateen 12-Step. Fellowship of young persons (ages 12-19) whose lives have been affected by someone else's drinking. An active adult member of Al-Anon serves as a sponsor. Meets Fri., 8pm, St. Joseph's Parish Center, 80 High St., Carteret. Call Al-Anon Information Services 973-744-8686. *Website:* http://www.northjerseyal-anon.org

Alcoholics Anonymous *(BILINGUAL)* 12-Step. Fellowship of men and women who share their experience, strength and hope with each other that they may solve their common problem and help others to recover from alcoholism. Young people's groups also available. Call 1-800-245-1377 or 908-687-8566 (24 hr.); Spanish-speaking 973-824-0555. *Website:* http://www.nnjaa.org

Double Trouble in Recovery 12-Step. Support and encouragement for those who are chemically addicted and are also in recovery from a psychiatric illness. Meets Wed., 7:30-9:30pm, Moving Forward Self-Help Center, 35 Elizabeth St., 2nd Floor, Suite 2B, New Brunswick. Call Donna Wittmann 609-275-5454 or 732-213-3224. *E-mail:* dwittmann@servbhs.org

Lawyers Concerned for Lawyers *(WOMEN ONLY)* Self-help group that supports recovery from alcoholism and drug dependence for attorneys, judges, law students and others in the legal system. Based on the 12-step program adapted from A.A. All inquiries are confidential. Meets 2nd Sat., One Constitution Square, New Brunswick. Pre-registration required. Before attending call Denise at NJ Lawyers Assistance Program 732-937-7541 or 1-800-246-5527 (day). *Website:* http://www.njlap.org *E-mail:* njlap@aol.com

Nurse Recovery Group *Professionally-run.* Mutual support and information for nurses who are recovering from addictions. Sharing of professional concerns and encouragement. Meets in Woodbridge. Call 1-800-662-0108 (day). *Website:* http://www.njsna.org (click on RAMP; next click Peer Assistance)

Parent Support Group - New Jersey, Inc. Confidential support group for parents of children (ages 13-40+) who are chemically dependent. Meets Thurs., 7pm, St. Peter's Episcopal Church, 505 Main St., Spotswood. Call Karol Sullivan or Adrienne Mellana 1-800-561-4299 or 973-736-3344 (day). *Website:* http://www.psgnjhomestead.com

"Be kind, for everyone you meet is fighting a hard battle." —Plato

Overcomer's Outreach Christian 12-Step. Fellowship to overcome any type of addiction or compulsive behavior, anxiety, depression or loneliness using God's word as a basis of recovery. Bible study, discussion, prayer and phone help. Meets Tues., 6:30-7:30pm, Metuchen Assembly of God, 130 Whitman St., Metuchen. Call Janet 732-388-2856 (eve.).

SMART Recovery (Self-Management And Recovery Training) *Professionally-run.* Self-help group for individuals wanting to gain their independence from addictive behaviors (drugs, alcohol, nicotine and other compulsive behaviors including gambling and eating disorders). SMART is a abstinence program based on cognitive-behavioral education and principles, especially those of rational-emotive behavior therapy. Building is handicapped accessible. Meets Thurs., 6-7:30pm, Rutgers University, 152 Frelinghuysen Rd., Busch Campus, Psychology Building, Room A340, 2nd Floor, Piscataway. Call Ayelet Kattan 732-445-6111 ext. 871 (day).

MONMOUTH

Al-Anon Adult Children 12- Step. Fellowship offering comfort, hope and friendship through shared experiences for adult children of alcoholics. Meets Sun., 7:30pm, First Baptist Church, 86 Maple Ave., Red Bank. Call Al-Anon Information Services 973-744-8686 (day); Spanish-speaking 973-268-1260. *Website:* http://www.northjerseyal-anon.org

Al-Anon Family Groups 12-Step. Fellowship of families and friends of alcoholics. Offers comfort, hope and friendship through shared experiences. Includes groups for children and adult children. Call Al-Anon Information Services 973-744-8686 (day); Spanish-speaking 973-268-1260. *Website:* http://www.northjerseyal-anon.org

Alateen 12-Step. Fellowship of young persons (ages 12-18) whose lives have been affected by someone else's drinking. An active adult member of Al-Anon serves as a sponsor. Call Al-Anon Information Services 973-744-8686 (day). *Website:* http://www.northjerseyal-anon.org
    Red Bank Meets Mon., 8pm, Trinity Episcopal Church, 65 W. Front St.
    Red Bank Meets Wed., Holy Trinity Lutheran Church, 150 River Rd.

"One head doesn't carry the roof." Malawian proverb

Alcoholics Anonymous *(BILINGUAL)* 12-Step. Fellowship of men and women who share their experience, strength and hope with each other that they may solve their common problem and help others to recover from alcoholism. Young people's groups also available. Call 1-800-245-1377, 908-687-8566 or 609-656-8900 (24 hr.); Spanish-speaking 973-824-0555. *Website:* http://www.centraljerseyintergroup.org

Celebrate Recovery Christian 12-Step. Fellowship sharing experiences, strengths and hopes with others who are going through recovery. Rap sessions, guest speakers and literature. Meets Thurs., 7-9pm, Abundant Life Church of God, 632 Colts Neck Rd. (Route 537 East), Freehold. Call Joanne 732-409-2923 (day). *Website:* http://www.alcog.org/celebrate_recovery.html

Double Trouble Dual Recovery 12-Step. Support for those who have an emotional/psychiatric illness and are alcohol/chemically addicted. Meets Mon. and Thurs., 10:15-11am, Park Place Program, 1011 Bond St., Asbury Park. Call Mark 732-869-2781 (day) or Mike Rafter 732-869-2765 (day). *E-mail:* msullivan@meridianhealth.com

Dual Recovery Support Group Mutual support for alcoholics or drug abusers who are taking medication for psychiatric problems. Call George 732-431-6000 ext. 5848 or Michelle 732-431-6000 ext. 4614.
> **Freehold** Meets Tues., 7pm, Freehold Self-Help Center, 17 Bannard St. Transportation available.
> **Red Bank** Meets Fri., 7pm, Riverview Hospital, One Riverview Plaza.

Families Anonymous 12-Step. Mutual support for relatives and friends concerned about the use of drugs, alcohol or related behavioral problems. *Website:* http://www.familiesanonymous.org Call 908-770-1659 (day). *E-mail:* higley@optonline.net
> **Colts Neck** Meets Wed., 7:30pm, St. Mary's Church, Phalanx Rd. and Route 34.
> **Leonardo** Meets Mon., 7:30pm, Middletown Township Complex, 900 Leonardville Rd., Croydon Hall. Call 732-383-8852.
> **Red Bank** Meets Thurs., 7:30-9pm, United Methodist Church, 247 Broad St., Basement.

Nurse Recovery Group *Professionally-run.* Mutual support and information for nurses who are recovering from addictions. Sharing of professional concerns and encouragement. Meets in Freehold and Neptune. Call 1-800-662-0108 (day). *Website:* http://www.sjsna.org (click on RAMP; next click Peer Assistance)

Parent Support Group - New Jersey, Inc. Confidential support group for parents of children (ages 13-40+) who are chemically dependent. Meets Tues., 7pm, Church of the Nativity, 180 Ridge Rd., Fair Haven. Call Karol Sullivan or Adrienne Mellana 1-800-561-4299 or 973-736-3344 (day). *Website:* http://www.psgnjhomestead.com *E-mail:* psgnj1@aol.com

MORRIS

Al-Anon Family Groups 12-Step. Fellowship of families and friends of alcoholics. Offers comfort, hope and friendship through shared experiences. Includes groups for children and adult children. Call Al-Anon Information Services 973-744-8686 (day); Spanish-speaking 973-268-1260. *Website:* http://www.northjerseyal-anon.org

Al-Anon's Adult Children 12-Step. Fellowship offering comfort, hope and friendship through shared experiences for adult children of alcoholics. Call Al-Anon Information Services 973-744-8686. *Website:* http://www.al-anon.org
> **Dover** Meets Tues., 7pm, First Memorial Presbyterian Church, 51 W. Blackwell St.
> **Parsippany** Meets Sat., 7:30pm, St. Gregory Episcopal Church, 480 South Beverwyck Rd.
> **Stirling** Meets Fri., 8:15pm, First Presbyterian Church, 158 Central Ave.

Alateen 12-Step. Fellowship of young persons (ages 11-18) whose lives have been affected by someone else's drinking. An active adult member of Al-Anon serves as a sponsor. Meets Thurs., 7:30pm, Presbyterian Church of Chatham Township, 240 Southern Blvd. (back entrance - downstairs), Chatham. Call Al-Anon Information Services 973-744-8686 (day). *Website:* http://www.northjerseyal-anon.org

Alcoholics Anonymous *(BILINGUAL)* 12-Step. Fellowship of men and women who share their experience, strength and hope with each other that they may solve their common problem and help others to recover from alcoholism. Young people's groups also available. Call 1-800-245-1377 or 908-687-8566 (24 hr.); Spanish-speaking 973-824-0555. *Website:* http://www.nnjaa.org

Calix Society Mutual support to promote the spiritual development of Catholic alcoholics. Members of other faiths welcome. Mass followed by group discussion. Meets last Sat., 10am, Chester. Call Thomas 908-876-4343 or Bob 908-684-8399.

Families Anonymous 12-Step. Mutual support for parents, relatives and friends of persons with drug or alcohol problems. Peer-counseling. Meets Tues., 7:30-9pm, First Presbyterian Church, 35 Church St., Rockaway. Call 973-586-2440 (eve.). *Website:* http://www.familiesanonymous.org

Family Support Group *Professionally-run.* Support and education for families of individuals with substance abuse and/or mental health issues. Literature. Meets Thurs., 6pm, Morristown Memorial Hospital, Atlantic Rehabilitation Institute, 95 Mt. Kemble Ave., 6th Floor, Morristown. Call Diana Krafcik 973-971-4742 (day).

Lawyers Concerned for Lawyers Self-help group that supports recovery from alcoholism and drug dependence for attorneys, judges, law students and others in the legal system. Based on the 12-step program adapted from A.A. All inquiries are confidential. Meets Wed., 7:30pm, Center for Behavioral Health, 95 Mt. Kemble Ave., Morristown. Before attending call NJ Lawyers Assistance Program 1-800-246-5527. *Website:* http://www.njlap.org *E-mail:* njlap@aol.com

Mental Health and Alcohol/Drug Family Education Group *Professionally-run.* Support and education for families facing a mental health and/or substance abuse disorder in a family member. Building is handicapped accessible. Meets Thurs., 6-7pm, Atlantic Rehabilitation Institute, 95 Kemble Ave., Morristown. Pre-registration required. Before attending call 973-971-4700.

Nurse Recovery Group *Professionally-run.* Mutual support and information for nurses who are recovering from addictions. Sharing of professional concerns and encouragement. Meets in Boonton. Call 1-800-662-0108 (day). *Website:* http://www.njsna.org (click on RAMP; next click Peer Assistance)

Psychiatrically Recovering 12-Step. Mutual support for psychiatrically recovering people who wish to refrain from using alcohol or drugs, abusing food or any other compulsive behavior. Building is handicapped accessible. Call Richie S. 973-865-4851.

> **Cedar Knolls** Meets Mon. and Thurs., 10am, Saint Clare's Behavioral Health Center, 100 East Hanover Ave., 1st Floor.
> **Denville** Meets Mon., 1pm, Saint Clare's Behavioral Health Center, 50 Morris Ave., Room B-1.
> **Pompton Plains** Meets Fri., 11am, New Bridge, 640 Newark-Pompton Turnpike.

SMART Recovery (Self-Management And Recovery Training) Self-help group for individuals wanting to gain their independence from addictive behaviors (alcohol, drugs, nicotine and other compulsive behaviors including gambling and eating disorders). SMART is a abstinence program based on cognitive-behavioral education and principles, especially those of rational-emotive behavior therapy. Meets Thurs., 7-8:30pm, Family Services, 62 Elm St., Morristown. Call Rich 973-983-8755 or Glenn 973-255-7296. *Website:* http://www.smartrecovery.org

OCEAN

Adult Children of Alcoholics Self-help group for adult children of alcoholics or dysfunctional families. Follows the 12-step program adapted from A.A. Meets Tues. and Fri., 7:45-9pm, Toms River Church of Christ, 1126 Hooper Ave., Toms River. Call Stephanie 732-573-1535 (answering machine). *Website:* http://www.adultchildren.org *E-mail:* trtuesaca@aol.com

Al-Anon Family Groups 12-Step. Fellowship of families and friends of alcoholics. Offers comfort, hope and friendship through shared experiences. Includes groups for children and adult children. Call Al-Anon Information Services 856-547-0855 (10am-3pm); Spanish-speaking 973-268-1260. *Website:* http://www.nj-al-anon.org

Al-Anon's Adult Children 12-Step. Fellowship offering comfort, hope and friendship through shared experiences for adult children of alcoholics. Meets Sun., 7pm, Ocean Medical Center, Jack Martin Blvd., Second Floor, Conference Room, Brick. Call Al-Anon Information Services 856-547-0855 (Mon.-Fri., 10am-3pm). *Website:* http://www.nj-al-anon.org

Addictions Victorious of South Jersey, Inc. 12-Step. Christ-centered support group for men and women who, in their struggle with substance abuse and emotional problems, come together that they may solve their problems and help others as well. Guest speakers, rap sessions, phone help, literature and newsletter. Optional donation. Meets Fri., 7pm, Redeemer Orthodox Presbyterian Church, 1600 Central Ave., Seaside Heights. Call Geoff 732-458-1119. *Website:* http://www.addvicinc.org

We can also refer callers to over 100 individuals who are seeking others to help start new support groups throughout NJ. Give us a call for more information. ***1-800-367-6274***

Alateen 12-Step. Fellowship of young persons whose lives have been affected by someone else's drinking. An active adult member of Al-Anon serves as a sponsor. Call Al-Anon Information Services 856-547-0855 (10am-3pm). *Website:* http://www.nj-al-anon.org

> **Brick** Meets Sat., 11am, Ocean Medical Center, 425 Jack Martin Blvd., Basement Conference Room.
> **Manahawkin** Meets Tues., Southern Ocean County Hospital, 1140 Route 72 West.

Alcoholics Anonymous *(BILINGUAL)* 12-Step. Fellowship of men and women who share their experience, strength and hope with each other that they may solve their common problem and help others to recover from alcoholism. Young people's groups also available. Call 1-800-245-1377, 908-687-8566 or 609-656-8900 (24 hr.). For Long Beach Island/Southern Ocean City call 609-494-5130; Spanish-speaking 973-824-0555. *Website:* http://www.aasj.org

Double Trouble in Recovery 12-Step. Fellowship offering mutual support for persons with a substance abuse problem who are also taking medication for psychiatric problems.

> **Barnegat** Meets Tues. and Thurs., 7pm, Journey to Wellness Self-Help Center, 575 N. Main St. Call 609-698-8889.
> **Bayville** Meets Mon., 6-7pm, Ocean Mental Health Services, 160 Route 9. Call 732-905-1132 (day).
> **Jackson** Meets Wed., 7:30-8:30pm, Brighter Days Self-Help Center, 268 Bennetts Mills Rd. Call 732-534-9960 (day).
> **Toms River** Meets Fri., 7:30-8:30pm, St. Barnabas Hospital, 1691 Route 9. Call 732-905-1132 (day).
> **Waretown** Meets Sun., 5pm, St. Stephen's Episcopal Church, 367 Route 9. Call 609-698-8889.

Families Anonymous 12-Step. Mutual support for relatives and friends concerned about the use of drugs or related behavioral problems. Meets Tues., 7:30pm, St. Andrews United Methodist Church, 1528 Church Rd., Toms River. Call 732-864-0548. *Website:* http://www.familiesanonymous.org *E-mail:* famanontr@comcast.net

Lawyers Concerned for Lawyers Self-help group that supports recovery from alcoholism and drug dependence for attorneys, judges, law students and others in the legal system. Based on the 12-step program adapted from A.A. All inquiries are confidential. Meets Tues., 7:15pm, St. Mary's By The Sea, 804 Bay Ave., Meeting Room, Point Pleasant. Before attending call NJ Lawyers Assistance Program 1-800-246-5527. *Website:* http://www.njlap.org *E-mail:* njlap@aol.com

Nurse Recovery Group *Professionally-run.* Mutual support and information for nurses who are recovering from addictions. Sharing of professional concerns and encouragement. Meets in Manahawkin and Toms River. Call 1-800-662-0108 (day). *Website:* http://www.njsna.org (click on RAMP; next click Peer Assistance)

Overcomers In Christ Recovery program that deals with every aspect of addiction and dysfunction (spiritual, physical, mental, emotional and social). Uses Overcomers goals which are Christ-centered. Resources, literature, information and referrals. Meets Mon., 7-8:30pm, America's Keswick, 601 Route 530, Whiting. Separate groups for men and women. For women's group call Diane Hunt 732-350-1187 ext. 47. For men's group call Chaplain Jim Freed 732-350-1187 ext. 43. *Website:* http://www.americaskeswick.org

Parent Support Group - New Jersey, Inc. Confidential support group for parents of children (ages 13-40+) who are chemically dependent. Meets Mon., 7pm, Presbyterian Church of Toms River, 1070 Hooper Ave., Toms River. Call Karol Sullivan or Adrienne Mellana 1-800-561-4299 or 973-736-3344 (day). *Website:* http://www.psgnjhomestead.com *E-mail:* psgnj1@aol.com

Thursday Night Recovery Support to help overcome dependencies and addictions through accountability, encouragement and spiritual development. Meets Thurs., 7-8:30pm, Shore Vineyard Church, 320 Compass Ave., Beachwood. Call 732-244-3888 (day).

Women For Sobriety Self-help group designed specifically to help women with addictions achieve sobriety. Helps develop self-esteem and coping skills. Meets Mon., 7-8:30pm, Center for Healthy Living (house is next to Kimball Medical Center, off of parking lot), 198 Prospect St., Lakewood. Call Women For Sobriety 215-536-8026 (national).

PASSAIC

Al-Anon Family Groups 12-Step. Fellowship of families and friends of alcoholics. Offers comfort, hope and friendship through shared experiences. Includes groups for children and adult children. Call Al-Anon Information Services 973-744-8686 (day); Spanish-speaking 973-268-1260. *Website:* http://www.northjerseyal-anon.org

Al-Anon's Adult Children 12-Step. Fellowship offering comfort, hope and friendship through shared experiences for adult children of alcoholics. Meets Tues., 8pm (beginners 7pm), Preakness Reformed Church, 131 Church Lane,

Wayne. Call Al-Anon Information Services 973-744-8686 (day). *Website:* http://www.northjerseyal-anon.org

Alateen 12-Step. Fellowship of young persons (ages 13-19) whose lives have been affected by someone else's drinking. An active adult member of Al-Anon serves as a sponsor. Meets Tues., 8pm, Preakness Reformed Church, 131 Church Lane, Wayne. Call Al-Anon Information Services 973-744-8686 (day). *Website:* http://www.northjerseyal-anon.org

Alcoholics Anonymous *(BILINGUAL)* 12-Step. Fellowship of men and women who share their experience, strength and hope with each other that they may solve their common problem and help others to recover from alcoholism. Young people's groups also available. For meeting information call 1-800-245-1377 or 908-687-8566 (24 hr.); Spanish-speaking call 973-824-0555. *Website:* http://www.nnjaa.org

Double Trouble in Recovery 12-Step. Support and encouragement for those who are chemically addicted and are also in recovery from a psychiatric illness. Meets Mon., 5-6pm, Mental Health Association in Passaic County, 404 Clifton Ave., 1st Floor, Clifton. Call Amanda 973-478-4444 ext. 62 (day).

MICA Support Group *Professionally-run.* Mutual support for persons diagnosed with substance abuse and a mental illness. Meets 2nd and 4th Tues., 4-5pm, Our House Self-Help Center, 750 Broadway, Paterson. Call 973-553-1101 (day).

Nurse Recovery Group *Professionally-run.* Mutual support and information for nurses who are recovering from addictions. Sharing of professional concerns and encouragement. Meets in Passaic. Call 1-800-662-0108 (day). *Website:* http://www.njsna.org (click on RAMP; next click Peer Assistance)

Parent Support Group - New Jersey, Inc. *Professionally-run.* Confidential support group for parents of children (ages 13-40+) who are chemically dependent. Meets Mon., 6:30pm, St. Joseph's Hospital, 224 Hamburg Turnpike, 6th Floor, Room 6B, Wayne. Call Karol Sullivan or Adrienne Mellana 1-800-561-4299 or 973-736-3344 (day). *Website:* http://www.psgnjhomestead.com *E-mail:* psgnj1@aol.com

Psychiatrically Recovering 12-Step. Mutual support for psychiatrically recovering people who wish to refrain from using alcohol or drugs, abusing food or any compulsive behavior. Building is handicapped accessible. Meets Fri., 9:45am, New Bridge: Visions, 22 Riverview Dr., Wayne. Call Richie S. 973-865-4851.

SALEM

Al-Anon Family Groups 12-Step. Fellowship of families and friends of alcoholics. Offers comfort, hope and friendship through shared experiences. Includes groups for children and adult children. Call Al-Anon Information Services 856-547-0855 (10am-3pm); Spanish-speaking 973-268-1260. *Website:* http://www.nj-al-anon.org

Alcoholics Anonymous *(BILINGUAL)* 12-Step. Fellowship of men and women who share their experience, strength and hope with each other that they may solve their common problem and help others to recover from alcoholism. Young people's groups also available. Call 1-866-920-1212 or 856-486-4444 (24 hr.); Spanish-speaking 973-824-0555. *Website:* http://www.aasj.org

SOMERSET

Al-Anon Family Groups 12-Step. Fellowship of families and friends of alcoholics. Offers comfort, hope and friendship through shared experiences. Includes groups for children and adult children. Call Al-Anon Information Services 973-744-8686 (day); Spanish-speaking 973-268-1260. *Website:* http://www.northjerseyal-anon.org

Alateen 12-Step. Fellowship of young persons (ages 11-17) whose lives have been affected by someone else's drinking. An active adult member of Al-Anon serves as a sponsor. Meets Sun., 8pm, St. Elizabeth's School, 141 Seney Dr., Bernardsville. Call Al-Anon Information Services 973-744-8686 (day). *Website:* http://www.northjerseyal-anon.org

Alcoholics Anonymous *(BILINGUAL)* 12-Step. Fellowship of men and women who share their experience, strength and hope with each other that they may solve their common problem and help others to recover from alcoholism. Young people's groups also available. Call 1-800-245-1377 or 908-687-8566 (24 hr.); Spanish-speaking 973-824-0555. *Website:* http://www.nnjaa.org

Bright Futures for Kids *Professionally-run.* Provides support, education and counseling for children (ages 4-12) who are affected by a family member's alcohol and/or drug addiction. Children learn how to express their feelings, develop coping skills, a sense of responsibility and the ability to resist peer pressure. Meets Sun., 11am-1pm, Carrier Clinic, Atkinson Amphitheater, 252 Route 601, Classroom 3, Belle Mead. Call Community Relations Dept. 908-281-1513.

Lawyers Concerned for Lawyers Self-help group that supports recovery from alcoholism and drug dependence for attorneys, judges, law students and others in the legal system. Based on the 12-step program adapted from A.A. All inquires are confidential. Meets Tues., 6pm, 70 Grove St., Somerville. Before attending call NJ Lawyers Assistance Program 1-800-246-5527. *Website:* http://www.njlap.org *E-mail:* njlap@aol.com

Parent Support Group - New Jersey, Inc. Confidential support group for parents of children (ages 13-40+) who are chemically dependent. Meets Mon., 7pm, Carrier Foundation, Admissions Building, Chapel, Belle Mead. Call Karol Sullivan or Adrienne Mellana 1-800-561-4299 or 973-736-3344 (day). *Website:* http://www.psgnjhomestead.com *E-mail:* psgnj1@aol.com

Psychiatrically Recovering 12-Step. Mutual support for psychiatrically recovering people who wish to refrain from using alcohol or drugs, abusing food or any other compulsive behavior. Building is handicapped accessible. Meets Thurs., 7:30pm, Richard Hall Community Mental Health Center, 500 N. Bridge St., Room 121, Bridgewater. Call Richie S. 973-865-4851.

SUSSEX

Al-Anon Family Groups 12-Step. Fellowship of families and friends of alcoholics. Offers comfort, hope and friendship through shared experiences. Includes groups for children and adult children. Call Al-Anon Information Services 973-744-8686 (day); Spanish-speaking 973-268-1260. *Website:* http://www.northjerseyal-anon.org

Alateen 12 Step. Fellowship of young persons (ages 13-19) whose lives have been affected by someone else's drinking. An active adult member of Al-Anon serves as a sponsor. Meets Mon., 7:30pm, West Side United Methodist Church, 16 Maxim Dr., Hopatcong. Call Al-Anon Information Services 973-744-8686 (day). *Website:* http://www.northjerseyal-anon.org

Alcoholics Anonymous *(BILINGUAL)* 12-Step. Fellowship of men and women who share their experience, strength and hope with each other that they may solve their common problem and help others to recover from alcoholism. Young people's groups also available. Call 1-800-245-1377 or 908-687-8566 (24 hr.); Spanish-speaking 973-824-0555. *Website:* http://www.nnjaa.org

Nurse Recovery Group *Professionally-run.* Mutual support and information for nurses who are recovering from addictions. Sharing of professional concerns and encouragement. Meets in Newton. Call 1-800-662-0108 (day). *Website:* http://www.sjsna.org (click on RAMP; next click Peer Assistance)

UNION

Al-Anon Family Groups 12-Step. Fellowship of families and friends of alcoholics. Offers comfort, hope and friendship through shared experiences. Includes groups for children and adult children. Call Al-Anon Information Services 973-744-8686 (day); Spanish-speaking 973-268-1260. *Website:* http://www.northjerseyal-anon.org

Alcohol and Drug Family Education *Professionally-run.* Support for families facing the chemical dependency of a family member. Deals with co-dependency issues. Building is handicapped accessible. Meets Tues., 6:30-8pm, Overlook Hospital, Behavioral Health Dept., 46-48 Beauvoir Ave., Summit. Call 908-522-4800 (day).

Alcoholics Anonymous *(BILINGUAL)* 12-Step. Fellowship of men and women who share their experience, strength and hope with each other that they may solve their common problem and help others to recover from alcoholism. Young people's groups also available. Call 1-800-245-1377 or 908-687-8566 (24 hr.); Spanish-speaking 973-824-0555. *Website:* http://www.nnjaa.org

Double Trouble in Recovery 12-Step. Support and encouragement for those who are chemically addicted and are also in recovery from a psychiatric illness. Rap sessions and guest speakers. Meets Wed., 4:30-5pm, Park Avenue Self-Help Center, 333 Park Ave., Plainfield. Call Andre Lawson 908-757-1350 (day).

Families Anonymous 12-Step. Support for parents, families and friends concerned about the use of drugs, alcohol or related behavioral problems. Meets Thurs., 7:30pm, Central Presbyterian Church, Maple St. and Morris Ave., Summit. Before attending call Barbara 973-267-2475 (day). *Website:* http://www.familiesanonymous.org

Families of Addiction *Professionally-run.* Mutual support for families of persons with an alcohol or drug addiction. Building is handicapped accessible. Meets Tues., 6:30-8pm, Overlook Hospital, Behavioral Health Dept., 46-48 Beauvoir Ave., Summit. Before attending call Rosemary Walsh 908-522-4878.

Parent Support Group - New Jersey, Inc. *Professionally-run.* Confidential support group for parents of children (ages 13-40+) who are chemically dependent. Meets Tues., 6:30pm, Central Presbyterian Church, 70 Maple Ave., Library Room, Summit. Call Karol Sullivan or Adrienne Mellana 1-800-561-4299 or 973-736-3344 (day). *Website:* http://wwwpsgnjhomestead.com *E-mail:* psgn1@aol.com

Psychiatrically Recovering 12-Step. Mutual support for psychiatrically recovering people who wish to refrain from using alcohol or drugs, abusing food or any other compulsive behavior. Building is handicapped accessible. Meets Tues., 9:30am, Occupational Center of Union County, New Building, 291 Cox St., Activity Room, Roselle. Call Richie S. 973-865-4851.

WARREN

Al-Anon Family Groups 12-Step. Fellowship of families and friends of alcoholics. Offers comfort, hope and friendship through shared experiences. Includes groups for children and adult children. Call Al-Anon Information Services 973-744-8686 (day); Spanish-speaking 973-268-1260. *Website:* http://www.northjerseyal-anon.org

Alcoholics Anonymous *(BILINGUAL)* 12-Step. Fellowship of men and women who share their experience, strength and hope with each other that they may solve their common problem and help others to recover from alcoholism. Young people's groups also available. Call 1-800-245-1377 or 908-687-8566 (24 hr.); Spanish-speaking 973-824-0555. *Website:* http://www.nnjaa.org

Double Trouble in Recovery Mutual support for alcoholics or drug addicts who are taking medication for psychiatric problems. Meets Wed., 7-8pm, Better Future Self-Help Center, 21 West Washington Ave., Washington. Call Elena 908-835-1180.

NATIONAL

Adult Children of Alcoholics World Services Organization *International. 1500+ meetings. Founded 1977.* 12-Step. Program of recovery for individuals who were raised in an alcoholic or otherwise dysfunctional household. Group development guidelines, newsletter and literature. Send a self-addressed stamped envelope when writing. Write: ACAWSO, P.O. Box 3216, Torrance, CA 90510. Call 310-534-1815 (directs you to website or postal address for request). *Website:* http://adultchildren.org *E-mail:* info@adultchildren.org

Al-Anon Family Groups, Inc. World Services Headquarters *(MULTILINGUAL) International. 24,000 groups. Founded 1951.* 12-Step. Fellowship of men, women, adult children and children whose lives have been affected by the drinking of a family member or friend. Opportunity for personal recovery and growth. Guidelines for starting groups. Literature is available in over 34 languages. Write: Al-Anon Family Group Headquarters, Inc., 1600 Corporate Landing Parkway, Virginia Beach, VA 23454-5617. Call 757-563-1600; for meeting information call 1-888-425-2666 (Mon.-Fri., 8am-6pm EST)

(English/French/Spanish); Fax: 757-563-1655. *Website:* http://www.al-anon.alateen.org *E-mail:* wso@al-anon.org

Alateen *(MULTILINGUAL) International. 1770 groups. Founded 1957.* 12-Step. Fellowship of young persons whose lives have been affected by someone else's drinking. An active adult member of Al-Anon who is certified as eligible to serve as a sponsor for each group. Group development guidelines and newsletter. Literature is available in over 30 languages. Write: Alateen, c/o Al-Anon Family Group Headquarters Inc., 1600 Corporate Landing Parkway, Virginia Beach, VA 23454-5617. Call 757-563-1600; for meeting information call 1-888-425-2666 (Mon.-Fri., 8am-6pm EST; English/French/Spanish); Fax: 757-563-1655. *Website:* http://www.al-anon.alateen.org *E-mail:* wso@al-anon.org

Alcoholics Anonymous World Services, Inc. *(MULTILINGUAL) International. 106,000 groups worldwide. Founded 1935.* 12-Step. Fellowship of women and men who are seeking a solution to their drinking problem. The only requirement for membership is a desire to stop drinking. Supported by voluntary contributions of its members and groups. A.A. neither seeks nor accepts outside funding. Members observe personal anonymity at the public level, thus emphasizing A.A. principles rather than personalities. For more information check your local phone directory. Write: General Service Office, P.O. Box 459, Grand Central Station, New York, NY 10163. Call 212-870-3400; Fax: 212-870-3003. *Website:* http://www.aa.org

Alcoholics Victorious *International. 150 affiliated groups. Founded 1948.* 12-Step. Christian-oriented group for those recovering from alcohol or chemical dependency. Information and referrals, literature, phone support, conferences, support group meetings and newsletter. Assistance in starting groups. How-to materials. Write: Alcoholics Victorious, c/o FootPrints, Inc., 4501 Troost St., Kansas City, MO 64110. Call 816-561-0567; Fax: 816-561-0572. *Website:* http://www.alcoholicsvictorious.org *E-mail:* info@alcoholicsvictorious.org

Anesthetists in Recovery *National network. Founded 1984. 150 members.* Network of recovering nurse anesthetists. Provides phone support, information and referrals to groups and treatment. Write: AIR, c/o Art, 8233 Brookside Rd., Elkins Park, PA 19027. Call 215-635-0183 or 215-872-6821. *Website:* http://health.groups.yahoo.com/group/airforsobriety *E-mail:* a.to.z@comcast.net

Calix Society *International. 20 chapters. Founded 1947.* Fellowship of Catholic alcoholics maintaining their sobriety through Alcoholics Anonymous. Concerned with total abstinence, spiritual development and sanctification of the whole personality of each member. Bimonthly newsletter. Assistance in chapter development. Write: Calix Society, 3881 Highland Ave., Suite 201, White Bear Lake, MN 55110. Call 651-773-3117 or 1-800-398-0524. *Website:* http://www.calixsociety.org *E-mail:* calix@usfamily.net

Chemically Dependent Anonymous *National. 65 affiliated groups. Founded 1980.* Purpose is to carry the message of recovery to the chemically dependent person. For those with a desire to abstain from drugs or alcohol. Information, referrals, phone support and conferences. Group development guidelines. Write: Chemically Dependent Anonymous, P.O. Box 813, Annapolis, MD 21401. Call 1-888-232-4673. *Website:* http://www.cdaweb.org

Double Trouble in Recovery, Inc. *National. 250+ affiliated groups. Founded 1989.* Fellowship of men and women who share their experience, strength and hope with each other so that they may solve their common problems and help others to recover from their particular addiction(s) and mental disorders. For persons dually-diagnosed with an addiction as well as a mental disorder. Literature, information, referrals and conferences. Double Trouble in Recovery Basic Guide Book also available. Assistance in starting new groups. Write: Double Trouble in Recovery, Inc., P.O. Box 245055, Brooklyn, NY 11224. Call 718-373-2684. *Website:* http://www.doubletroubleinrecovery.org *E-mail:* HV613@aol.com

Dual Recovery Anonymous *International. Chapters worldwide. Founded 1989.* A self-help program for individuals who experience a dual disorder of chemical dependency and a psychiatric or emotional illness. Based on the principles of the 12-steps and the personal experiences of individuals in dual recovery. Literature, newsletter and assistance in starting local groups. Write: Dual Recovery Anonymous, P.O. Box 8107, Prairie Village, KS 66208. Call 913-991-2703. *Website:* http://www.draonline.org (Note: listings of groups on this website may be out-of-date call the contact number listed for the group before attending) *E-mail:* draws@draonline.org

Families Anonymous *International. 500+ groups. Founded 1971.* 12-Step. Fellowship for relatives and friends of persons with drug, alcohol or behavioral problems. Members learn to achieve their own serenity in spite of the turmoil which surrounds them. Besides many booklets, pamphlets and bookmarks, publications include daily thought book, "Today A Better Way" and a bi-monthly newsletter "The Twelve-Step Rag." Offers group development guidelines. Write: Families Anonymous, P.O. Box 3475, Culver City, CA 90231-3475. Call 1-800-736-9805 (Mon., Wed., Fri., 10:30am-4:30pm PST); Fax: 310-815-9682. *Website:* http://www.familiesanonymous.org *E-mail:* famanon@familiesanonymous.org

Free N One Recovery *National. 55 affiliated groups. Founded 1985.* Group teaches people to be free mentally and spiritually, as well as free of drugs and alcohol. Family support groups available. Information and referrals, phone support, literature and conferences. Assistance in starting local chapters. Write: Free N One Recovery, 5838 S. Overhill Dr., Los Angeles, CA 90043. Call 323-295-0009; Fax: 310-764-5439. *Website:* http://www.freenone.net *E-mail:* freenone@msn.com

Intercongregational Addictions Program (ICAP) *International. Founded 1979.* Network of recovering alcoholic women in religious orders. Helps Roman Catholic women who are, or have been, members of religious orders and are alcoholic or chemically dependent, compulsive eaters, compulsive gamblers, etc. Information, referrals, assistance in meeting other members, phone support, conferences and e-mail support. Write: ICAP, 7777 Lake St., Suite 115, River Forest, IL 60305-1734. Call 708-488-9770; Fax: 708-488-9774. *E-mail:* icapsrs@sbcglobal.net

International Doctors in Alcoholics Anonymous *International network. 6000 members. 175 affiliated groups. Founded 1949.* Opportunity for doctoral level health care professionals to discuss common problems and find common solutions to drug and alcohol problems. Annual meetings (1st week Aug.), phone support, newsletter, information and referrals. Mutual help meetings at conferences of other organizations. Also, Al-Anon program of helping families and friends of alcoholics recover from the effects of living with the problem drinking of a relative or friend. In addition, website provides links to several listgroups (ongoing recovery-related meetings conducted by e-mail). Write: IDAA, c/o Dale Syfert, 2616 N.W. 25th Place, Gainsville, FL 32605-2826. Call 352-375-0240. *Website:* http://www.idaa.org

International Lawyers in Alcoholics Anonymous *International. 40+ affiliated groups. Founded 1975.* Serves as a clearinghouse for support groups for lawyers who are recovering alcoholics or have other chemical dependencies. Newsletter, annual conventions and group development guidelines. Write: ILAA, c/o Eli Gauna, 14123 Victory Blvd., Van Nuys, CA 91401. Call 818-785-6541 (day); Fax: 818-785-3887. *Website:* http://www.ilaa.org

"Community is no longer something that we are born into. It is now something that we must choose."-- Dr. Robert Wuthnow, in his book, Sharing the Journey: Support Groups and America's New Quest for Community, 1994

International Ministers and Pastors in Recovery *International. Founded 1988.* Provides mutual support for pastors and ministers recovering from addictions and actively participating in a 12-step recovery program. Provides phone network, meetings at an international 12-step conference, information and referrals. Assistance in starting local/regional groups. Write: International Ministers and Pastors in Recovery, P.O. Box 219, Augusta, MO 63332. Call 314-808-5470. *E-mail:* fresh12st@aol.com

JACS (Jewish Alcoholics, Chemically Dependent Persons and Significant Others) *International. Founded 1980.* For alcoholic and chemically dependent Jews, families, friends, associates and the community. Networking, community outreach, retreats, newsletter, literature, spiritual events and speakers bureau. Write: JACS, 120 W. 57th St., New York, NY 10019. Call 212-397-4197 (day); Fax: 212-399-3525. *Website:* http://www.jacsweb.org *E-mail:* jacs@jacsweb.org

LifeRing Secular Recovery *International. Founded 1999.* Secular community of persons who are building lives free of dependency on alcohol and other drugs. Group activities are not associated with religion or spirituality. Members practice complete abstinence from alcohol and other addicting drugs. Peer support, literature, information, referrals and advocacy activities. Guidelines available for starting similar groups. Large online e-mail support group and several smaller special interest groups (women, weight loss, stop smoking, etc). Online chats and forum. Publishes sobriety literature. Write: LifeRing Secular Recovery, 1440 Broadway, Suite 312, Oakland, CA 94612-2023. Call 1-800-811-4142 or 510-763-0779. *Website:* http://www.unhooked.com *E-mail:* service@lifering.org

Men for Sobriety *International. 5 affiliated groups. Founded 1976.* Purpose is to help all men recover from chemical addiction through the discovery of self, gained by sharing experiences, hopes and encouragement with other men in similar circumstances. Recognizes men's complex role in today's society. Write: Men for Sobriety, P.O. Box 618, Quakertown, PA 18951-0618. Call 215-536-8026; Fax: 215-538-9026. *E-mail:* NewLife@nni.com

Moderation Management *International. 25 groups. Founded 1993.* Behavioral change program and support network for people concerned about their drinking and who desire to make positive lifestyle changes. Empowers individuals to accept personal responsibility for choosing and maintaining their own path, whether moderation or abstinence. Promotes early self-recognition of risky drinking behavior when moderation is a more easily achievable goal. Online meetings, chatroom topic meetings, listservs and moderation-friendly therapist listings. Write: Moderation Management Network, Inc., 22 West 27th St., New

York, NY 10001. Call 212-871-0974. *Website:* http://moderation.org *E-mail:* mm@moderation.org

Overcomers In Christ *International. Founded 1987.* Recovery program that deals with every aspect of addiction and dysfunction (spiritual, physical, mental, emotional and social). Uses Overcomers goals which are Christ-centered. Resources, literature, information and referrals. Assistance in starting new groups. Write: Overcomers In Christ, P.O. Box 34460, Omaha, NE 68134-04604. Call 1-866-573-0966 or 402-573-0966. *Website:* http://www.overcomersinchrist.org *E-mail:* oic@overcomersinchrist.org

Overcomers Outreach, Inc. *International. 700 affiliated groups. Founded 1985.* 12-Step. Christ-centered support group for anyone affected by addictions, as well as their families and friends. Uses 12-steps of A.A. and applies them to the Scriptures. Uses Jesus Christ as "higher power." Supplements involvement in other 12-step groups. Newsletter, group development guidelines and conferences. Write: Overcomers Outreach, Inc., P.O. Box 922950, Sylmar, CA 91392-2950. Call 1-800-310-3001. *Website:* http://www.overcomersoutreach.org *E-mail:* info@overcomersoutreach.org

Psychologists Helping Psychologists *National network. Founded 1980.* For doctoral-level psychologists or students who have had a personal experience with alcohol or drugs. Aim is to support each other in recovery. Regional/national get-togethers and newsletter. Write: Psychologists Helping Psychologists, 3484 S. Utah St., Arlington, VA 22206-1921. Call Ann 703-243-4470; Fax: 703-243-7125. *E-mail:* AnnS@Erols.com

Recoveries Anonymous *International. 50 chapters.* Spiritual recovery group for anyone seeking solution for any kind of addiction, problem or behavior. Families and friends welcome. "How To Begin..." guides and "Start A Group" kit can be downloaded for free from the website. Write: Recoveries Anonymous Universal Services, P.O. Box 1212, East Northport, NY 11731. *Website:* http://www.r-a.org *E-mail:* raus@r-a.org

Secular Organizations for Sobriety (Save Ourselves) *International. Founded 1986.* Mutual help for alcoholics and addicts who want to acknowledge their addiction and maintain sobriety as a separate issue from religion or spirituality. Newsletter. Guidelines and assistance available for starting groups. Real-time online chats and e-groups available. Write: Secular Organizations for Sobriety, 4773 Hollywood Blvd., Hollywood, CA 90027. Call 323-666-4295; Fax: 323-666-4271. *Website:* http://www.cfiwest.org/sos *E-mail:* sos@cfiwest.org

SMART Recovery (r) (Self-Management And Recovery Training) *National. 225+ affiliated groups. Founded 1994.* Network of self-help groups for individuals wanting to gain their independence from addictive and compulsive behaviors. SMART Recovery is a abstinence program based on cognitive-behavioral principles, especially those of rational-emotive behavior therapy. Newsletter, information, referrals, literature and assistance in starting local groups. Write: SMART Recovery, 7537 Mentor Ave., Suite 306, Mentor, OH 44060. Call 1-866-951-5357 or 440-951-5357; Fax: 440-951-5358. *Website:* http://www.smartrecovery.org *E-mail:* info@smartrecovery.org

Social Workers Helping Social Workers *National network. Founded 1981.* Supports recovery from alcohol or other chemical dependence, either their own or that of a significant other, among social workers (BSW/MSW) or BSW/MSW students. Social workers with other addictions are welcome to attend meetings. Newsletter, annual conferences, some regional retreats/meetings, continuing education, daily e-mail digest and group development guidelines. Write: Social Workers Helping Social Workers, c/o Betty Check, 5228 S. Kenwood Ave., Chicago, IL 60615-4006. Call Betty 773-493-6940 (confidential voice mail). *Website:* http://www.socialworkershelping.org *E-mail:* swhswil@aol.com

Veterinarians in Recovery *National network. Founded 1990.* Support network for veterinarians in recovery from alcoholism and addiction. Provides information and referrals, phone support and newsletter. Online e-mail listserv. Maintains database of members for support. Al-Anon members and recovering veterinarian staff welcome at meetings. Many VIR members also are members of International Doctors in A.A., and meet during their annual conference. Write: Veterinarians in Recovery, c/o Jeff H., 180 County Rd. 741, Clanton, AL 35046. Call 205-335-4222.

Women For Sobriety *International. 150 groups. Founded 1976.* Program designed specifically to help chemically addicted women achieve sobriety. Addresses need to overcome depressed feelings and guilt. Monthly newsletter, information and referrals, phone support, group meetings, conferences and group development guidelines. Write: Women for Sobriety, P.O. Box 618, Quakertown, PA 18951-0618. Call 215-536-8026; Fax: 215-538-9026. *Website:* http://www.womenforsobriety.org *E-mail:* NewLife@nni.com

ONLINE

Conduct Disorders Parent Message Board *Online. 7080 members. Founded 1995.* Support for parents living with a child with one of the many behavior disorders including: attention deficit hyperactivity disorder, oppositional defiance disorder, conduct disorder, depression and substance abuse. Parents with children of all ages welcome. *Website:* http://www.conductdisorders.com

HAMS: Harm Reduction for Alcohol and Other Substances *Online. 225 members. Founded 2007.* Support and information for people who choose to practice safe intoxication, as well as those choosing moderate drinking or quitting as a goal. Members offer simple and pragmatic strategies for reducing the risks of recreational intoxication to self and others. *Website:* http://health.groups.yahoo.com/group/hamshrn

CO-DEPENDENCY / DYSFUNCTIONAL FAMILIES

BERGEN

Co-DA (Co-Dependents Anonymous) 12-Step. Fellowship of men and women whose common purpose is to develop healthy relationships. For those who have a desire for healthy, fulfilling relationships with others and themselves. Donation $1-2. Meets Thurs., 8pm, Paramus Congregational Church, 205 Spring Valley Rd., Paramus. Call John 973-751-0919.

Seniors Count 12-Step. Support for persons (ages 60+) who are recovering from substance abuse or co-dependency. Meets Fri., 1:30-3pm, Vantage Building, 93 West Palisades Ave., Englewood. Call Anne Wennhold 201-569-6667 ext. 3298. *Website:* http://www.vanostinstitute.org *E-mail:* awennhold@vanostinstitute.org

CAMDEN

Co-DA (Co-Dependents Anonymous) 12-Step. Fellowship for men and women whose common purpose is to develop healthy relationships. For those who want to learn to develop healthy, fulfilling relationships with others and themselves. Meets Fri., 7:30pm and Sun., 7pm, The Starting Point, 215 Highland Ave., Suite C, Westmont. Call 856-854-3155 (day). *Website:* http://www.startingpoint.org *E-mail:* info@startingpoint.org

MERCER

Princeton ACA (Adult Children of Alcoholics/Dysfunctional Families) 12-Step. Fellowship for adult children from alcoholic and dysfunctional families. Optional meeting donation $1/wk. Meets Thurs., 7:30-9pm, Unitarian Church of Princeton, 50 Cherry Hill Rd., Princeton. Call Audrey 609-716-8063.

MORRIS

Co-DA (Co-Dependents Anonymous) 12-Step. Fellowship of men and women whose common purpose is to develop healthy relationships. For those who have a desire for healthy, fulfilling relationships with others and themselves. Meets Mon., 6:30pm, The Church of the Savior, 155 Morris Ave., Denville. Call Kristy 973-713-4438.

OCEAN

Adult Children of Alcoholics 12-Step. Self-help group for adult children of alcoholics or dysfunctional families. Meets Tues. and Fri., 7:45-9pm, Toms River Church of Christ, 1126 Hooper Ave., Toms River. Call Stephanie 732-573-1535 (answering machine). *Website:* http://www.adultchildren.org *E-mail:* trtuesaca@aol.com

Overcomers In Christ Recovery program that deals with every aspect of addiction and dysfunction (spiritual, physical, mental, emotional and social). Uses Overcomers goals which are Christ-centered. Resources, literature, information and referrals. Meets Mon., 7-8:30pm, America's Keswick, 601 Route 530, Whiting. Separate groups for men and women. Women's group call Diane Hunt 732-350-1187 ext. 47. Men's group call Chaplain Jim Freed 732-350-1187 ext. 43. *Website:* http://www.americaskeswick.org

SOMERSET

Co-DA (Co-Dependents Anonymous) 12-Step. Fellowship of men and women whose common purpose is to develop healthy relationships. For those with a desire for healthy, fulfilling relationships with others and themselves. Building is handicapped accessible. Meets Sat., 9-10:30am; Sun., 4pm; Mon., 7-8:15pm and Fri., 7:30pm, United Methodist Church, 9 Church St., Kingston. Call Carmella 609-291-0461 or church 609-921-6812 (day).

UNION

Co-DA (Co-Dependents Anonymous) 12-Step. Fellowship of men and women whose common purpose is to develop healthy relationships. For those who have a desire to build and maintain fulfilling relationships with others and themselves. Meets Tues., 7:30-9pm, All Saints Episcopal Church, 559 Park Ave., Scotch Plains. Call Joe F. 908-272-1926 (before 10pm).

NATIONAL

Co-Dependents Anonymous *International. Founded 1986.* 12-Step. Self-help program of recovery from co-dependence. Members share experience, strength and hope in an effort to find freedom and peace in relationships with themselves and others. Library of literature and audio tapes. Guidelines on starting a similar group available. Newsletter and listing of local support groups online. Write: CoDA, P.O. Box 33577, Phoenix, AZ 85067-3577. For local support groups call 602-277-7991. *Website:* http://www.coda.org *E-mail:* outreach@coda.org

Overcomers In Christ *International. Founded 1987.* Recovery program that deals with every aspect of addiction and dysfunction (spiritual, physical, mental, emotional and social). Uses Overcomers goals which are Christ-centered. Resources, literature, information and referrals. Assistance in starting new groups. Write: Overcomers In Christ, P.O. Box 34460, Omaha, NE 68134-0460. Call 1-866-573-0966 or 402-573-0966. *Website:* http://www.overcomersinchrist.org *E-mail:* oic@overcomersinchrist.org

DEBT / OVERSPENDING
(see also toll-free helplines)

BERGEN

Debtor's Anonymous 12-Step. Program for those who wish to stop incurring debt. Call 1-877-717-3328. *Website:* http://www.njpada.org
> **Teaneck** Meets Fri., 7:30-9pm, St. Paul's Lutheran Church, Church St. and Longfellow Rd.
> **Teaneck** Meets Sun., 4pm, St. Mark's Episcopal Church, 118 Chadwick Rd.

BURLINGTON

12 Steps God's Way Christian-focused recovery group for anyone suffering from any type of addiction, dependency or compulsive disorder. Meets Thurs., 7pm, Fellowship Alliance Chapel, 199 Church Rd., Medford. Call 609-953-7333 (day).

"None of us is as smart as all of us." -- Ziggy

CAMDEN

Debtor's Anonymous 12-Step. Program for those who wish to stop incurring debt. Meets Thurs., 7:30-8:30pm, Starting Point, 215 Highland Ave., Suite C, Room 14, Westmont. Call Judy P. 856-482-6892 or 1-877-717-3328. *Website:* http://www.njpada.org

CUMBERLAND

Overcomer's Outreach Christian 12-Step. Fellowship to overcome any type of addiction or compulsive behavior, anxiety, depression or loneliness using God's word as a basis of recovery. Bible study, discussion, prayer and phone help. Meets Thurs., 7-8pm, Shiloh Seventh Day Baptist Church, East Ave., Shiloh. Call Frank B. Mulford 856-451-8698 (day) or Rev. Chroniger 856-455-0488. *E-mail:* ahfarm@hotmail.com

ESSEX

Debtors Anonymous 12-Step. Program for those who wish to stop incurring debt. Call 1-877-717-3328. *Website:* http://www.njpada.org
> **Bloomfield** Meets Mon., 8pm (beginners 7:30pm), Watchung Presbyterian Church, 375 Watchung Ave., (GSP exit 151). Call Jane 973-667-2404 (day).
> **South Orange** Meets Tues., 6:30pm, Our Lady of Sorrows Church, 217 Prospect St. (enter on 4th St. side), Kateri Room.

MERCER

Debtors Anonymous 12-Step. Program for those who wish to stop incurring debt. Meets Thurs., 7:45pm, Slackwood Presbyterian Church, 2020 Brunswick Ave., Route 1, Lawrenceville. Call Karen B. 609-577-3346 (day) or 1-877-717-3328. *Website:* http://www.njpada.org

MIDDLESEX

Debtors Anonymous 12-Step. Support for people to share experiences and common problem of incurring debt. Goal is to stay solvent and help other compulsive debtors achieve solvency. Call 1-877-717-3328. *Website:* http://www.njpada.org
> **Highland Park** Meets Mon., 7:30-8:30pm, Reformed Church of Highland Park, 19-21 South 2nd Ave.
> **Metuchen** Meets Sun., 7pm (beginners 6:30pm), St. Luke's Episcopal Church, Oak St. and Route 27 North. Call Josephine 732-448-0021.

Overcomer's Outreach Christian 12-Step. Fellowship to overcome any type of addiction or compulsive behavior, anxiety, depression loneliness using God's word as a basis of recovery. Bible study, discussion, prayer and phone help. Meets Tues., 6:30-7:30pm, Metuchen Assembly of God, 130 Whitman St., Metuchen. Call Janet 732-388-2856 (eve.).

MORRIS

Debtors Anonymous 12-Step. Program for those who wish to stop incurring debt. Meets Wed., 8pm, Saint Clare's Hospital, 130 Powerville Rd., Boonton. Call 1-877-717-3328. *Website:* http://www.njpada.org

SMART Recovery (Self-Management And Recovery Training) Self-help group for individuals wanting to gain their independence from addictive behaviors (alcohol, drugs, nicotine and other compulsive behaviors including gambling and eating disorders). SMART is an abstinence program based on cognitive-behavioral education and principles, especially those of rational-emotive behavior therapy. Meets Thurs., 7-8:30pm, Family Services, 62 Elm St., Morristown. Call Rich 973-983-8755 or Glenn 973-255-7296. *Website:* http://www.smartrecovery.org

OCEAN

Overcomers In Christ Recovery program that deals with every aspect of addiction and dysfunction (spiritual, physical, mental, emotional and social). Uses Overcomers goals which are Christ-centered. Resources, literature, information and referrals. Meets Mon., 7-8:30pm, America's Keswick, 601 Route 530, Whiting. Separate groups for men and women. Women's group call Diane Hunt 732-350-1187 ext. 47. Men's group call Chaplain Jim Freed 732-350-1187 ext. 43. *Website:* http://www.americaskeswick.org

SOMERSET

Debtors Anonymous 12-Step. Program for those who wish to stop incurring debt. Meets Tues., 7:30-8:30pm (beginners 7pm), Presbyterian Church of Basking Ridge, 1 East Oak St., Basking Ridge. Call Diana D. 908-647-7659 (eve.), Debi P. 862-684-5108 or 1-877-717-3328. *Website:* http://www.njpada.org

"One person can make a difference, and every person must try."-- John F. Kennedy

SUSSEX

Debtors Anonymous 12-Step. Program for those who wish to stop incurring debt. Meets Fri., 5:30-6:30pm, Tri-Co Federal Credit Union, Tri-Co Plaza, 47 Route 206 (use rear entrance to Community Room), Augusta. Call 1-877-717-3328. *Website:* http://www.njpada.org

NATIONAL

Debtors Anonymous *International. 520 groups. Founded 1976.* 12-Step. Fellowship that provides mutual help in recovering from compulsive indebtedness. Primary purpose of members is to stay solvent and help other compulsive debtors achieve solvency. Newsletter and phone support network. Offers online support and listings of local meetings. Write: Debtors Anonymous, P.O. Box 920888, Needham, MA 02492-0009. Call 781-453-2743; Fax: 781-453-2745. *Website:* http://www.debtorsanonymous.org *E-mail:* new@debtorsanonymous.org

Intercongregational Addictions Program (ICAP) *International. Founded 1979.* Network of recovering alcoholic women in religious orders. Helps Roman Catholic women who are, or have been, members of religious orders and are alcoholic or chemically dependent, compulsive eaters, compulsive gamblers, etc. Information, referrals, assistance in meeting other members, phone support, conferences and e-mail support. Write: ICAP, 7777 Lake St., Suite 115, River Forest, IL 60305-1734. Call 708-488-9770; Fax: 708-488-9774. *E-mail:* icapsrs@sbcglobal.netn

Overcomers In Christ *International. Founded 1987.* Recovery program that deals with every aspect of addiction and dysfunction (spiritual, physical, mental, emotional and social). Uses Overcomers goals which are Christ-centered. Resources, literature, information and referrals. Assistance in starting new groups. Write: Overcomers In Christ, P.O. Box 34460, Omaha, NE 68134-0460. Call 1-866-573-0966 or 402-573-0966. *Website:* http://www.overcomersinchrist.org *E-mail:* oic@overcomersinchrist.org

"The glory of friendship is not the outstretched hand, nor the kindly smile, nor the joy of companionship; it is the spiritual inspiration that comes to one when you discover that someone else believes in you and is willing to trust you with a friendship."
—*Ralph Waldo Emerson, Adapted*

Overcomers Outreach, Inc. *International. 700 affiliated groups. Founded 1985.* 12-Step. Christ-centered support group for anyone affected by addictions, as well as their families and friends. Uses 12-steps of A.A. and applies them to the Scriptures. Uses Jesus Christ as "higher power." Supplements involvement in other 12-step groups. Newsletter, group development guidelines and conferences. Write: Overcomers Outreach, Inc., P.O. Box 922950, Sylmar, CA 91392-2950. Call 1-800-310-3001. *Website:* http://www.overcomersoutreach.org *E-mail:* info@overcomersoutreach.org

Spenders Anonymous *National.* Support for those who have problems spending compulsively using the 12-step approach. Script for running a meeting is on website. Call 651-649-4573 (meeting information). *Website:* http://www.spenders.org

ONLINE

Shopping Addicts Support *Online.* For people who are, or think they may be, addicted to shopping to help and support each other. For anyone who has a problem and is trying to overcome it. *Website:* http://health.groups.yahoo.com/group/shopping_addicts

DRUG ABUSE
(see also toll-free helplines)

STATEWIDE

Cocaine Anonymous 12-Step. Fellowship of men and women who share their experiences, strengths and hopes that they may solve their common problem and help others to recover from addiction. Call Dominick 732-620-5829 (day) or 212-262-2463 northern NJ (recording); 1-866-777-0983 southern NJ.

Families Anonymous 12-Step. Program for relatives and friends concerned about the use of drugs, alcohol or related behavioral problems. Meetings throughout NJ. Call 1-800-736-9805. *Website:* http://www.familiesanonymous.org

Lawyers Concerned for Lawyers Statewide network of independent, self-help groups that support attorneys, judges, law students others in the legal system in recovery from alcoholism and drug dependence. Based on the 12-steps but not affiliated with A.A. Not meant to be a substitute for participation in A.A. or other fellowships. The NJ Lawyers Assistance Program performs an "intergroup function" for Lawyers Concerned for Lawyers. All services are free and confidential. Write: NJLAP, NJ Law Center, One Constitution Square, New Brunswick, NJ 08901-1520. Call 1-800-246-5527 or 732-937-7549 (day). *Website:* http://www.LawyersAssistance.org *E-mail:* njlap@aol.com

Nar-Anon Family Group/Narateen Provides help for family members and friends of drug abusers by offering comfort, hope and friendship through shared experiences. Meeting locations throughout New Jersey. For information call Nar-Anon Answering Service 1-800-238-2333, 1-877-424-4491 or 609-587-7215. *Website:* http://www.naranonofnj.org

Narcotics Anonymous *(BILINGUAL)* 12-Step. Fellowship of men and women seeking recovery from drug addiction. The only requirement for membership is the desire to stop using drugs. Meeting locations statewide, including several bilingual groups. Write: Central South Jersey Regional Service Conference, P.O. Box 4257, Trenton, NJ 08610; North New Jersey Regional Service Conference, P.O. Box 8224, Newark, NJ 07103. Call 1-800-992-0401 or 732-933-0462. *Website:* http://www.nanj.org

Nurse Recovery Group *Professionally-run.* Mutual support and information for nurses who are recovering from addictions. Sharing of professional concerns and encouragement. Meets in Bergen, Burlington, Camden, Cape May, Cumberland, Essex, Hunterdon, Mercer, Middlesex, Monmouth, Morris, Ocean, Passaic and Sussex counties. Write: Peer Assistance Project, 1479 Pennington Rd., Trenton, NJ 08618. Call 1-800-662-0108 (day). *Website:* http://www.njsna.org (click on RAMP; next click Peer Assistance)

Signs of Sobriety, Inc. (SOS) *Professionally-run.* Provides alcoholism and drug addiction services to persons who are deaf or hard-of-hearing. Makes referrals to deaf and sign interpreted 12-step groups throughout NJ (alcohol or drug addiction, gambling, families of alcoholics, etc). Offers prevention awareness, education classes, SoberCamp-annual summer retreat and Sober/Deaf activities for deaf or hard-of-hearing individuals in recovery. Newsletter. Write: Signs Of Sobriety, Inc. 100 Scotch Rd., 2nd Floor, Ewing, NJ 08628. Call TTY/VP: 609-882-7177; Voice: 609-882-7677 or 1-800-332-7677 (day); Fax: 609-882-6808. *Website:* http://www.signsofsobriety.org *E-mail:* info@signsofsobriety.org

ATLANTIC

Dual Recovery Anonymous *Professionally-run.* 12-Step. Mutual support for people who suffer from a mental illness and struggle with substance abuse issues. Families welcome. Guest speakers. Meets Tues., 3-4pm, CSP of NJ, 1147 North New Rd., Absecon. Call Cathy Flanagan 609-383-1190 ext. 301 (day). *E-mail:* cflanagan@cspnj.org

Dual Recovery Anonymous 12-Step. Fellowship for persons diagnosed with both a mental illness and an addiction. Building is handicapped accessible. Rap sessions. Meets Wed., 6pm, Atlantic City Rescue Mission, Bacharach Blvd., Atlantic City. Call 609-272-1700 ext. 303 (day).

Family Support Group Mutual support for parents and families of persons diagnosed with both a mental illness and alcohol or chemical addiction. Sharing of emotional and practical coping skills. Guest speakers. Meets 2nd Thurs., 10:30am and 4th Thurs., 5:30pm, Mental Health Association, 1127 North New Rd., Absecon. Call Christine Gromadzyn, MSW 609-272-1700 (day).

Lawyers Concerned for Lawyers Self-help group that supports recovery from alcoholism and drug dependence for attorneys, judges, law students and others in the legal system. Based on the 12-step program adapted from A.A. All inquiries are confidential. Meets Wed., 5:30pm, 1555 Zion Rd., Suite 201, Northfield. Before attending call John 609-641-2266 (day) or NJ Lawyers Assistance Program 1-800-246-5527. *Website:* http://www.njlap.org *E-mail:* njlap@aol.com

Nar-Anon Family Group Provides help for family members and friends of drug abusers by offering comfort, hope and friendship through shared experiences. Meeting locations throughout New Jersey. For information call Nar-Anon Answering Service 1-800-238-2333, 1-877-424-4491 or 609-587-7215. *Website:* http://www.naranonofnj.org

Narcotics Anonymous 12-Step. Fellowship of men and women seeking recovery from drug addiction. The only requirement for membership is the desire to stop using drugs. Call 1-800-992-0401 or 732-933-0462. *Website:* http://www.nanj.org

BERGEN

A Jewish Approach to Recovery Incorporates Jewish teachings related to recovery plus the 12-steps of Alcoholic Anonymous. Mutual support for all Jews in recovery and their family members. Guest speakers and literature. Meets Wed., 7:30pm, The Living Room at Jewish Family Service, 1485 Teaneck Rd., Teaneck. Before attending call 201-837-9090 (day), Marty 201-281-0498, Dan 201-244-1244 (day) or 201-394-8802 (eve.). *E-mail:* thelivingroom@jfsbergen.org

CARE (Christians, Addictions, Recovery and Education) 12-Step. Support ministry for substance abusers and their families to help our brothers sisters find sobriety, solace and a way to a comfortable non-judgmental Christian walk.

Meets Mon., 7:30pm, Church of the Nazarene, 285 East Midland Ave., Paramus. Call 201-262-3323 (Mon., Wed., Thurs.; 9:30am-4pm). *Website:* http://www.maranathanj.org

Cocaine Anonymous 12-Step. Fellowship of men and women who share their experiences, strengths and hopes that they may solve their common problem help others to recover from addiction. Call 212-262-2463 for taped meeting information and confirm meeting. *Website:* http://www.ca-ny.org/newjersey.htm

> **Ridgewood** Meets Sun., 8pm, Westside Community Church, 6 South Monroe St.
>
> **Teaneck** Meets Thurs., 8pm, Church of St. Anastasia, 1095 Teaneck Rd. Building is handicapped accessible.

Double Jeopardy Peer Support Group *Professionally-run.* Emotional support and information for men and women who have HIV/HCV and substance abuse issues. Building is handicapped accessible. Meets Thurs., 6-8pm, Buddies of New Jersey, 149 Hudson St., Hackensack. Call Susan 201-489-2900 (10am-6pm). *Website:* http://www.njbuddies.org

Double Trouble in Recovery 12-Step. Support and encouragement for those who are chemically addicted and are also in recovery from a psychiatric illness. Meets Wed., 7pm, On Our Own Self-Help Center, 179 Main St., 2nd Floor, Hackensack. Call On Our Own Self-Help Center 201-489-8402.

Families Anonymous 12-Step. Mutual support for relatives and friends concerned about the use of drugs or related behavioral problems. *Website:* http://www.familiesanonymous.org

> **Englewood** Meets Fri., 7:30pm, Englewood Hospital, 350 Engle St., Medical Learning Center, Main Floor. Call Geri 201-585-8091.
>
> **Mahwah** Meets Wed., 7:30-8:30pm, Church of the Immaculate Conception, 900 Darlington Ave. Call Richard or Barbara 201-327-0748. Building is handicapped accessible. *E-mail:* famahwah@verizon.net
>
> **Tenafly** Meets Tues., 7:30pm, Trinity Lutheran Church, 430 Knickerbocker Rd. Call Judy or Gene 201-262-7758 (day).

Lawyers Concerned for Lawyers Self-help group that supports recovery from alcoholism and drug dependence for attorneys, judges, law students and others in the legal system. Based on the 12-step program adapted from A.A. All inquiries are confidential. Meets Wed., 6:30pm, Church of the Good Shepard, 1576 Palisades Ave., Chapel, Fort Lee. Before attending call NJ Lawyers Assistance Program 1-800-246-5527. *Website:* http://www.njlap.org *E-mail:* njlap@aol.com

Marijuana Anonymous Fellowship of men and women who share their experiences, strengths and hopes with each other so they may solve their common problem and help others to recover from marijuana addiction. Meets Sun., 7pm, Bergen Regional Hospital, 230 Ridgewood Ave., Behavioral Health Pavilion, Room E003, Paramus. Call 201-873-2109. *Website:* http://www.marijuana-anonymous.org

Nar-Anon Family Group 12-Step. Provides help for family members and friends of drug abusers by offering comfort, hope and friendship through shared experiences. Call Nar-Anon Answering Service 1-800-238-2333, 1-877-424-4491 or 609-587-7215. *Website:* http://www.naranonofnj.org

Narcotics Anonymous 12-Step. Fellowship of men and women seeking recovery from drug addiction. The only requirement for membership is the desire to stop using drugs. Call 1-800-992-0401 or 732-933-0462. *Website:* http://www.nanj.org

Nurse Recovery Group *Professionally-run.* Mutual support and information for nurses who are recovering from addictions. Sharing of professional concerns and encouragement. Meets in Teaneck and Paramus. Call 1-800-662-0108 (day). *Website:* http://www.njsna.org (click on RAMP; next click Peer Assistance)

Parent Support Group - New Jersey, Inc. *Professionally-run.* Confidential support group for parents of children (ages 13-40+) who are chemically dependent. Meets Mon., 6:30pm, Behavioral Health Center, Bergen Pines Hospital, Room E218, Paramus. Call Karol Sullivan or Adrienne Mellana 1-800-561-4299 or 973-736-3344 (day). *Website:* http://www.psgnjhomestead.com

Seniors Count *Professionally-run.* 12-Step. Support for persons (ages 60+) recovering from substance abuse or co-dependency. Meets Fri., 1:30-3pm, Vantage Building, 93 West Palisades Ave., Englewood. Call Anne Wennhold 201-569-6667 ext. 3298. *Website:* http://www.vanostinstitute.org *E-mail:* awennhold@vanostinstitute.org

Women For Sobriety Self-help group designed specifically to help women with addictions achieve sobriety. Helps develop self-esteem and coping skills. Donation $2. Meets Thurs., 7-8:30pm (new members 6:45pm), YWCA, 112 Oak St., Ridgewood. Call Nina Wegener 201-612-0511 (day) or Jennifer Rosa 201-881-1721 (day).

BURLINGTON

12 Steps God's Way Christian-focused recovery group for anyone suffering from any type of addiction, dependency or compulsive disorder. Meets Thurs., 7pm, Fellowship Alliance Chapel, 199 Church Rd., Medford. Call 609-953-7333 (day).

Addictions Victorious of South Jersey, Inc. 12-Step. Christ-centered support group for men and women who in their struggle with substance abuse and emotional problems come together that they may solve their problems and help others as well. Guest speakers, rap sessions, phone help, literature and newsletter. Optional donation. Meets Tues., 7pm, Lighthouse Tabernacle, 716 Main St., Lumberton. Call Ronnie and Harry 609-267-2657 or Mike 609-267-5499. *Website:* http://www.addvicinc.org

Double Trouble in Recovery Mutual support for persons with a substance abuse problem who are also taking medication for psychiatric problems. Meets Sun., Mon. and Wed., 8:30pm, Hampton Hospital, 650 Rancocas Rd., Cafeteria, Westampton. Call Greg Pryor 609-267-7000 ext. 2148 (day).

Families Anonymous 12-Step. Support for parents, families and friends of persons with drug, alcohol or related behavioral problems. Meets Wed., 7:30pm, Marlton United Methodist Church, Plymouth Ave. and Marlboro Ave., Marlton. Call 856-461-7076 (eve). *Website:* http://www.familiesanonymous.org

Lawyers Concerned for Lawyers Self-help group that supports recovery from alcoholism and drug dependence for attorneys, judges, law students and others in the legal system. Based on the 12-step program adapted from A.A. All inquiries are confidential. Meets 1st and 3rd Wed., 5:30pm, The Daily Grind, 48 High St., Mount Holly. Before attending call NJ Lawyers Assistance Program 1-800-246-5527. *Website:* http://www.njlap.org *E-mail:* njlap@aol.com

Nar-Anon Family Group 12-Step. Provides help for families and friends of drug abusers by offering comfort, hope and friendship through shared experiences. For meeting information call Nar-Anon Answering Service 1-800-238-2333, 1-877-424-4491 or 609-587-7215. *Website:* http://www.naranonofnj.org

Narcotics Anonymous 12-Step. Fellowship of men and women seeking recovery from drug addiction. The only requirement for membership is the desire to stop using drugs. Several meeting locations throughout the county. For meeting information call 1-800-992-0401 or 732-933-0462. *Website:* http://www.nanj.org

Nurse Recovery Group *Professionally-run.* Mutual support and information for nurses who are recovering from addictions. Sharing of professional concerns and encouragement. Meets in Moorestown. Call 1-800-662-0108 (day). *Website:* http://www.njsna.org (click on RAMP; next click Peer Assistance)

Rap Room Parent-to-Parent Coalition *Professionally-run.* Support and education for parents of teens and adult children dealing with substance/alcohol addictions. Mutual sharing, advocacy, guest speakers, crisis intervention and referrals. Meets 1st Tues., 7-9pm, Greentree Executive Campus, 1003A Lincoln Drive West, Marlton. Call Louise 856-983-3328. *Website:* http://www.raproom.org

CAMDEN

Addictions Victorious of South Jersey, Inc. 12-Step. Christ-centered support group for men and women who in their struggle with substance abuse and emotional problems come together that they may solve their problems and help others as well. Guest speakers, rap sessions, phone help, literature and newsletter. Optional donation. *Website:* http://www.addvicinc.org

Barrington Meets Mon., 7pm, Grace Bible Church, 887 Clements Bridge Rd. Call Ginny 856-232-0207 or Bob 856-869-3077.

Blackwood Meets Thurs., 7pm, Community Wesleyan Church, 508 Woodbury-Turnersville Rd. Call Norman 856-243-2205.

Camden Meets Tues., noon, Fellowship House, 1722 S. Broadway. Call Lucy 856-964-4545.

Camden Meets 1st and 3rd Fri., 8pm, Assembly of God, 518 Market St. Call Kevin or Eugene 856-966-8141.

Camden Meets 2nd and 4th Thurs., 6pm, Evangelism Today, 1658 Mt. Ephraim Ave., 2nd Floor. Call Elaine 856-541-7977

Camden Meets Thurs., 7:30pm, New Hope Temple, 488 Jackson St. Call Deborah or Anita 856-966-0343.

Collingswood Meets Wed., 7pm, First United Methodist Church, 201 Dayton Ave. Call Richard 856-240-1667.

Lindenwold Meets Mon., 7pm, Garden Lake Bible Church, 63 First Ave. Call Pastor Dave 856-357-4194 or Harry 609-502-0773.

Lindenwold Meets Thurs., 7:30pm, Christ Community Church, 325 Linden Ave. Call David 856-346-2220.

Pennsauken Meets Sun., 5pm, Calvary Assembly of God, 4921 Camden Ave. and Browning Rd. Call Will or Lucy 856-964-4545.

Pine Hill Meets Tues., 7:30pm, Hope Chapel C.M.A., New Hope Ministries, 28 East Branch Ave. Call Skip 856-566-4134.

Somerdale Meets Thurs., 7pm, Park Avenue Community Church, 431 Hilltop Ave. Call Jeannine 856-435-0309.

Camden County Parent-to-Parent Mutual support for parents of children of any age who have alcohol or drug related problems. Guest speakers, literature and phone help. Building is handicapped accessible. Meets 2nd and 4th Tues., 6:30-8:30pm, Bellmawr Library, 35 E. Browning Rd., Bellmawr. Call 856-225-5071 (day).

Dual Recovery Anonymous (DRA) 12-Step. Mutual support for alcoholics/addicts who are taking medication for psychiatric problems.
> **Cherry Hill** Meetings vary, 3:30-4:30pm, MICA Club, 498 Marlboro Ave. Before attending call 856-662-0955 (voice/TDD; day).
> **Westmont** Meets Mon., 8pm, Starting Point, 215 Highland Ave. Call Tom 856-495-2676.

Nar-Anon Family Group 12-Step. Provides help for family members and friends of drug abusers by offering comfort, hope and friendship through shared experiences. Call Nar-Anon Answering Service 1-800-238-2333, 1-877-424-4491 or 609-587-7215. *Website:* http://www.naranonofnj.org

Narcotics Anonymous 12-Step. Fellowship of men and women seeking recovery from drug addiction. The only requirement for membership is the desire to stop using drugs. Call 1-800-992-0401 or 732-933-0462. *Website:* http://www.nanj.org

Nurse Recovery Group *Professionally-run.* Mutual support and information for nurses who are recovering from addictions. Sharing of professional concerns and encouragement. Meets in Haddonfield. Call 1-800-662-0108 (day). *Website:* http://www.njsna.org (click on RAMP; next click Peer Assistance)

CAPE MAY

Celebrate Recovery Christian 12-Step. Fellowship sharing experiences, strengths and hopes with others who are going through recovery. Rap sessions, guest speakers and literature. Meets Fri., 7-9pm, Seashore Church of the Nazarene, 446 Seashore Rd., Erma. Call Michael Austin 609-886-6196 (day). *E-mail:* celebrate_at_seashore@msn.com

Nar-Anon Family Group 12-Step. Provides help for family members and friends of drug abusers by offering comfort, hope and friendship through shared experiences. Call Nar-Anon Answering Service 1-800-238-2333, 1-877-424-4491 or 609-587-7215. *Website:* http://www.naranonofnj.org

Narcotics Anonymous 12-Step. Fellowship of men and women seeking recovery from drug addiction. The only requirement for membership is the desire to stop using drugs. Call 1-800-992-0401 or 732-933-0462. *Website:* http://www.nanj.org

Nurse Recovery Group *Professionally-run.* Mutual support and information for nurses who are recovering from addictions. Sharing of professional concerns and encouragement. Meets in Marmora. Call 1-800-662-0108 (day). *Website:* http://www.njsna.org (click on RAMP; next click Peer Assistance)

CUMBERLAND

Dual Recovery Anonymous 12-Step. Assists consumers who suffer a severe and persistent mental illness to work on their recovery from addiction to substances. Meets Tues., 1-3pm, Special Needs Adult Partial Care Program, Cumberland County Guidance Center, 2038 Carmel Rd., Millville. Call 856-825-6810 ext. 269.

Nar-Anon Family Group 12-Step. Provides help for family members and friends of drug abusers by offering comfort, hope and friendship through shared experiences. Call Nar-Anon Answering Service 1-800-238-2333, 1-877-424-4491 or 609-587-7215. *Website:* http://www.naranonofnj.org

Narcotics Anonymous 12-Step. Fellowship of men and women seeking recovery from drug addiction. The only requirement for membership is the desire to stop using drugs. Call 1-800-992-0401 or 732-933-0462. *Website:* http://www.nanj.org

Nurse Recovery Group *Professionally-run.* Mutual support and information for nurses who are recovering from addictions. Sharing of professional concerns and encouragement. Meets in Seabrook. Call 1-800-662-0108 (day). *Website:* http://www.njsna.org (click on RAMP; next click Peer Assistance)

Overcomer's Outreach Christian 12-Step. Fellowship to overcome any type of addiction or compulsive behavior, anxiety, depression or loneliness using God's word as a basis of recovery. Bible study, discussion, prayer and phone help. Meets Thurs., 7-8pm, Shiloh Seventh Day Baptist Church, East Ave., Shiloh. Call Frank B. Mulford 856-451-8698 (day) or Rev. Chroniger 856-455-0488 (day). *E-mail:* ahfarm@hotmail.com

ESSEX

BASA (Brothers And Sisters of Addicts) *Professionally-run.* Confidential support group for siblings with a chemically dependent sibling. Meets Mon., 7pm, St. Cloud Presbyterian Church, Old Indian Rd. and Ridgeway Ave., West

Orange. Call Karol Sullivan or Adrienne Mellana 973-736-3344 (day) or 1-800-561-3299. *Website:* http://www.psgnjhomestead.com *E-mail:* psgnj1@aol.com

Double Trouble in Recovery Support for persons in dual recovery from a mental illness and a substance or alcohol addiction. Meets Mon., 5-6pm, Where Peaceful Waters Flow, 47 Cleveland St., Orange. Call Richard 973-677-7700 (day) or 973-651-7382.

Double Trouble in Recovery *Professionally-run.* Support for HIV+ persons who are also substance abusers. Meets Wed., noon-2pm, North Jersey Community Research Initiative, 393 Central Ave., 2nd Floor, Newark. Call 973-483-3444 ext. 122.

Families Anonymous 12-Step. Support for families and friends concerned about the use of drugs or related behavioral problems. Sharing of experiences, strengths and hopes. Meets Wed., 7:30pm, First Episcopal Church of the Holy Spirit, 36 Gould St., Verona. Call Cathy 201-991-5711 or Roxy 973-667-1067. *Website:* http://www.familiesanonymous.org

Lawyers Concerned for Lawyers (LCL) Self-help group that supports recovery from alcoholism and drug dependence for attorneys, judges, law students and others in the legal system. Based on the 12-step program adapted from A.A. All inquiries are confidential. Meets Tues., 7:30pm, United Way Building, 60 S. Fullerton Ave., Room 211A, Montclair. Before attending call Kenneth 973-429-5588 (day) or 973-509-6062 (eve.) or NJ Lawyers Assistance Program 1-800-246-5527. *Website:* http://www.njlap.org *E-mail:* njlap@aol.com

MICA Support Group 12-Step. Support to help those who have dual disorders of recovery from an alcohol/drug addiction and also in recovery from a psychiatric illness. Meets Wed., 5:30-6:30pm, Pleasant Moments Self-Help Center, 465 Broadway, Conference Room, Newark. Call Scott 973-751-5922.

Nar-Anon Family Group 12-Step. Provides help for family members and friends of drug abusers by offering comfort, hope and friendship through shared experiences. Call Nar-Anon Answering Service 1-800-238-2333, 1-877-424-4491 or 609-587-7215. *Website:* http://www.naranonofnj.org

Narcotics Anonymous 12-Step. Fellowship of men and women seeking recovery from drug addiction. The only requirement for membership is the desire to stop using drugs. Call 1-800-992-0401 or 732-933-0462. *Website:* http://www.nanj.org

Nurse Recovery Group *Professionally-run.* Mutual support and information for nurses who are recovering from addictions. Sharing of professional concerns and encouragement. Meets in Montclair. Call 1-800-662-0108 (day). *Website:* http://www.njsna.org (click on RAMP; next click Peer Assistance)

Parents Support Group - New Jersey Inc. *Professionally-run.* Confidential support group for parents of children (ages 13-40+) who are chemically dependent. Meets Wed., 6pm and Thurs., 6:30pm, St. Cloud Presbyterian Church, Old Indian Rd. and Ridgeway Ave., West Orange. Call Karol Sullivan 973-736-3344 (9am-3pm) or 1-800-561-4299 (24 hr. hotline).

GLOUCESTER

Addiction Support Group - Families and Friends *Professionally-run.* Support for families of persons with addiction issues. Offers encouragement, information and guidance with a Jewish perspective. Group is open to people of any faith. Meetings vary, 6 week sessions, 2-3 times/yr., 7-8:30pm, Jewish Family and Child Services, 702 Birchfield Rd., Mount Laurel. Pre-registration required. Call Lisa Weissbach 856-778-7775.

Addictions Victorious of South Jersey, Inc. 12-Step. Christ-centered support group for men and women who in their struggle with substance abuse and emotional problems come together that they may solve their problems and help others as well. Guest speakers, rap sessions, phone help, literature and newsletter. Optional donation. *Website:* http://www.addvicinc.org

> **Glassboro** Meets Tues., 7pm, Olivet Wesleyan Church, 711 Heston Rd. Call Chip 609-706-6597.
> **Pitman** Meets Mon. and Thurs., 7:30pm, The Rock Church, 205 Esplanade Ave. Call Laura 856-582-2277.
> **Williamstown** Meets Thurs., 6pm, Community Bible Fellowship Church, Broadlane Rd. Call Fabian 609-605-1671.

Gloucester County Parent To Parent Coalition *Professionally-run.* Confidential meetings and focus on providing parents with support, information, resources and referrals for dealing with substance abuse and related problems. Guest speakers, educational series and literature. Building is handicapped accessible. Meets 2nd and 4th Mon., 7:30-9:30pm, Washington Township Municipal Building, 523 Egg Harbor Rd., Meeting Room C, Washington Township. Call 856-589-6446 (day).

Nar-Anon Family Group 12-Step. Provides help for family members and friends of drug abusers by offering comfort, hope and friendship through shared experiences. Call Nar-Anon Answering Service 1-800-238-2333, 1-877-424-4491 or 609-587-7215. *Website:* http://www.naranonofnj.org

Narcotics Anonymous 12-Step. Fellowship of men and women seeking recovery from drug addiction. The only requirement for membership is the desire to stop using drugs. Call 1-800-992-0401 or 732-933-0462. *Website:* http://www.nanj.org

Teens Recovery Group *Professionally-run.* Support group for teenagers (ages 13-20) in recovery from drugs and/or alcohol. Meets Thurs., 7-8:30pm, Washington Township Municipal Building, 523 Egg Harbor Rd., Meeting Room C, Sewell. Call Donna Rullo 856-589-6446 (day). *E-mail:* wtfcs@twp.washington.nj.us

HUDSON

Double Trouble in Recovery 12-Step. Support and encouragement for those who are chemically addicted and are also in recovery from a psychiatric illness. Meets Tues., 10:30am, Hudson County Self-Help Center, 880 Bergen Ave., Suite 605, Jersey City. Call Wayne Vivian 201-420-8013.

Nar-Anon Family Group 12-Step. Provides help for family members and friends of drug abusers by offering comfort, hope and friendship through shared experiences. Call Nar-Anon Answering Service 1-800-238-2333, 1-877-424-4491 or 609-587-7215. *Website:* http://www.naranonofnj.org

Narcotics Anonymous 12-Step. Fellowship of men and women seeking recovery from drug addiction. The only requirement for membership is the desire to stop using drugs. Call 1-800-992-0401 or 732-933-0462. *Website:* http://www.nanj.org

HUNTERDON

Nar-Anon Family Group 12-Step. Provides help for family members and friends of drug abusers by offering comfort, hope and friendship through shared experiences. Call Nar-Anon Answering Service 1-800-238-2333, 1-877-424-4491 or 609-587-7215. *Website:* http://www.naranonofnj.org

Narcotics Anonymous 12-Step. Fellowship of men and women seeking recovery from drug addiction. The only requirement for membership is the desire to stop using drugs. Call 732-933-0462. *Website:* http://www.nanj.org

Nurse Recovery Group *Professionally-run.* Mutual support and information for nurses who are recovering from addictions. Sharing of professional concerns and encouragement. Meets in Flemington. Call 1-800-662-0108 (day). *Website:* http://www.njsna.org (click on RAMP; next click Peer Assistance)

MERCER

Cocaine Anonymous 12-Step. Fellowship of men and women who share their experiences, strengths and hopes that they may solve their common problem and help others to recover from addiction. Meets Tues., 8-9:30pm, Last Chance Recovery, 917 S. Broad St., Trenton. Call Steve 609-638-7176. *Website:* http://www.caphilly.org

Families Anonymous 12-Step. Program for families, especially parents of those with substance abuse or other disruptive behavioral problems. Meets Mon., 7:30pm, St. Lawrence Rehabilitation Center, 2381 Lawrenceville Rd. (Route 206 South), Lawrenceville. Call Joan 609-883-1403 (eve.). *Website:* http://www.familiesanonymous.org *E-mail:* joan@brra.com

Nar-Anon Family Group 12-Step. Provides help for family members and friends of drug abusers by offering comfort, hope and friendship through shared experiences. Call Nar-Anon Answering Service 1-800-238-2333, 1-877-424-4491 or 609-587-7215. *Website:* http://www.naranonofnj.org

Narcotics Anonymous 12-Step. Fellowship of men and women seeking recovery from drug addiction. The only requirement for membership is the desire to stop using drugs. Call 1-800-992-0401 or 732-933-0462. *Website:* http://www.nanj.org

Nurse Recovery Group *Professionally-run.* Mutual support and information for nurses who are recovering from addictions. Sharing of professional concerns and encouragement. Meets in Trenton. Call 1-800-662-0108 (day). *Website:* http://www.njsna.org (click on RAMP; next click Peer Assistance)

MIDDLESEX

Cocaine Anonymous 12-Step. Fellowship of men and women who share their experiences, strengths and hopes that they may solve their common problem and help others to recover from addiction. Meets Mon., 7:30-8:45pm, Christ Church, 257 Fourth St., South Amboy. Call 212-262-2463 for taped meeting information and confirm meeting. *Website:* http:www.ca-ny.org/newjersey.htm

Double Trouble in Recovery 12-Step. Support and encouragement for those who are chemically addicted and are also in recovery from a psychiatric illness. Meets Wed., 7:30-9:30pm, Moving Forward Self-Help Center, 35 Elizabeth St., 2nd Floor, Suite 2B, New Brunswick. Call Donna Wittmann 609-275-5454 or 732-213-3224. *E-mail:* dwittmann@servbhs.org

Lawyers Concerned for Lawyers (LCL) Self-help group that supports recovery from alcoholism and drug dependence for attorneys, judges, law students and others in the legal system. Based on the 12-step program adapted from A.A. All inquiries are confidential. Meets 2nd Sat., One Constitution Square, New Brunswick. Pre-registration required. Before attending call Denise at NJ Lawyers Assistance Program 732-937-7541 or 1-800-246-5527 (day). *Website:* http://www.njlap.org *E-mail:* njlap@aol.com

Nar-Anon Family Group 12-Step. Provides help for family members and friends of drug abusers by offering comfort, hope and friendship through shared experiences. Call Nar-Anon Answering Service 1-800-238-2333, 1-877-424-4491 or 609-587-7215. *Website:* http://www.naranonofnj.org

Narcotics Anonymous 12-Step. Fellowship of men and women seeking recovery from drug addiction. The only requirement for membership is the desire to stop using drugs. Call 1-800-992-0401 or 732-933-0462. *Website:* http://www.nanj.org

Nurse Recovery Group *Professionally-run.* Mutual support and information for nurses who are recovering from addictions. Sharing of professional concerns and encouragement. Meets in Woodbridge. Call 1-800-662-0108 (day). *Website:* http://www.njsna.org (click on RAMP; next click Peer Assistance)

Overcomer's Outreach Christian 12-Step. Fellowship to overcome any type of addiction or compulsive behavior, anxiety, depression or loneliness using God's word as a basis of recovery. Bible study, discussion, prayer and phone help. Meets Tues., 6:30-7:30pm, Metuchen Assembly of God, 130 Whitman St., Metuchen. Call Janet 732-388-2856 (eve.).

Parent Support Group - New Jersey, Inc. Confidential support group for parents of children (ages 13-40+) who are chemically dependent. Meets Thurs., 7pm, St. Peter's Episcopal Church, 505 Main St., Spotswood. Call Linda Leck, Karol Sullivan, or Adrienne Mellana 1-800-561-4299 or 973-736-3344 (day). *Website:* http://www.psgnjhomestead.com

SMART Recovery (Self-Management And Recovery Training) *Professionally-run.* Self-help group for individuals wanting to gain their independence from addictive behaviors (drugs, alcohol, nicotine and other compulsive behaviors including gambling and eating disorders). SMART is a abstinence program based on cognitive-behavioral education and principles, especially those of rational-emotive behavior therapy. Building is handicapped accessible. Meets Thurs., 6-7:30pm, Rutgers University, 152 Frelinghuysen Rd., Busch Campus, Psychology Building, Room A340, 2nd Floor, Piscataway. Call Ayelet Kattan 732-445-6111 ext. 871 (day).

MONMOUTH

Celebrate Recovery Christian 12-Step. Fellowship sharing experiences, strengths and hopes with others who are going through recovery. Rap sessions, guest speakers and literature. Meets Thurs., 7-9pm, Abundant Life Church of God, 632 Colts Neck Rd. (Route 537 East), Freehold. Call Joanne 732-409-2923 (day). *Website:* http://www.alcog.org/celebrate_recovery.html

Cocaine Anonymous 12-Step. Fellowship of men and women who share their experiences, strengths and hopes that they may solve their common problem and help others to recover from addiction. Building is handicapped accessible. Call 212-262-2463 for taped meeting information and confirm before attending. *Website:* http://www.ca-ny.org/newjersey.htm

> **Atlantic Highlands** Meets Sun., 7pm, United Methodist Church, 95 3rd Ave.
> **Freehold** Meets Fri., 8:30-9:30pm, New Attitudes Clubhouse, 42 Throckmorton St. Call Phil W. 732-580-1588 (day).
> **Keyport** Meets Thurs., 8-9:15pm, Calvary Methodist Church, 3rd and Osborn St.

Double Trouble Dual Recovery 12-Step. Support for those who have an emotional/psychiatric illness and are alcohol/chemically addicted. Meets Mon. and Thurs., 10:15-11am, Park Place Program, 1011 Bond St., Asbury Park. Call Mark 732-869-2781 (day) or Mike Rafter 732-869-2765 (day). *E-mail:* msullivan@meridianhealth.com

Dual Recovery Support Group Mutual support for alcoholics or drug abusers who are taking medication for psychiatric problems. Call George 732-431-6000 or Michelle 732-431-6000 ext. 4614 (day).

> **Freehold** Meets Tues., 7pm, Freehold Self-Help Center, 17 Bannard St. Transportation available.
> **Red Bank** Meets Fri., 7pm, Riverview Hospital, One Riverview Plaza.

Families Anonymous 12-Step. Mutual support for relatives and friends concerned about the use of drugs, alcohol or related behavioral problems. Call 908-770-1659 (day). *Website:* http://www.familiesanonymous.org

> **Colts Neck** Meets Wed., 7:30pm, St. Mary's Church, Phalanx Rd. and Route 34.
> **Leonardo** Meets Mon., 7:30pm, Middletown Township Complex, 900 Leonardville Rd., Croydon Hall. Call 732-383-8852.
> **Red Bank** Meets Thurs., 7:30-9pm, United Methodist Church, 247 Broad St., Basement. *E-mail:* higley@optonline.net

Nar-Anon Family Group Provides help for family members and friends of drug abusers by offering comfort, hope and friendship through shared experiences. Meeting locations throughout New Jersey. For information call Nar-Anon Answering Service 1-800-238-2333, 1-877-424-4491 or 609-587-7215. *Website:* http://www.naranonofnj.org

Narcotics Anonymous 12-Step. Fellowship of men and women seeking recovery from drug addiction. The only requirement for membership is the desire to stop using drugs. Call 1-800-992-0401 or 732-933-0462. *Website:* http://www.nanj.org

Nurse Recovery Group *Professionally-run.* Mutual support and information for nurses who are recovering from addictions. Sharing of professional concerns and encouragement. Meets in Freehold and Neptune. Call 1-800-662-0108 (day). *Website:* http://www.njsna.org (click on RAMP; next click on Peer Assistance)

Parent Support Group - New Jersey, Inc. Confidential support group for parents of children (ages 13-40+) who are chemically dependent. Meets Tues., 7pm, Church of the Nativity, Hance Ridge Rd., Fair Haven. Call Karol Sullivan or Adrienne Mellana 1-800-561-4299 or 973-736-3344 (day). *Website:* http://www.psgnjhomestead.com *E-mail:* psgnj1@aol.com

MORRIS

Families Anonymous 12-Step. Mutual support for parents, relatives and friends of persons with drug or alcohol problems. Peer-counseling. Meets Tues., 7:30-9pm, First Presbyterian Church, 35 Church St., Rockaway. Call 973-586-2440 (eve.). *Website:* http://www.familiesanonymous.org

Family Support Group *Professionally-run.* Support and education for families of individuals with substance abuse and/or mental health issues. Literature. Meets Thurs., 6pm, Morristown Memorial Hospital, Atlantic Rehabilitation

Institute, 95 Mt. Kemble Ave., 6th Floor, Morristown. Call Diana Krafcik 973-971-4742 (day).

Lawyers Concerned for Lawyers (LCL) Self-help group that supports recovery from alcoholism and drug dependence for attorneys, judges, law students and others in the legal system. Based on the 12-step program adapted from A.A. All inquiries are confidential. Meets Wed., 7:30pm, Center for Behavioral Health, 95 Mt. Kemble Ave., Morristown. Before attending call NJ Lawyers Assistance Program 1-800-246-5527. *Website:* http://www.njlap.org *E-mail:* njlap@aol.com

Mental Health and Alcohol/Drug Family Education Group *Professionally-run..* Support and education for families facing a mental health and/or substance abuse disorder in a family member. Building is handicapped accessible. Meets Thurs., 6-7pm, Atlantic Rehabilitation Institute, 95 Kemble Ave., Morristown. Pre-registration required. Before attending call 973-971-4700.

Nar-Anon Family Group 12-Step. Provides help for family members and friends of drug abusers by offering comfort, hope and friendship through shared experiences. Call Nar-Anon Answering Service 1-800-238-2333, 1-877-424-4491 or 609-587-7215. *Website:* http://www.naranonofnj.org

Narcotics Anonymous 12-Step. Fellowship of men and women seeking recovery from drug addiction. The only requirement for membership is the desire to stop using drugs. Call 1-800-992-0401 or 732-933-0462. *Website:* http://www.nanj.org

Narcotics Anonymous for MICA Patients Fellowship of men and women seeking recovery from drug addiction who also have a mental illness. Meets Thurs., 7:30pm, New Views, Greystone Park Hospital, 59 Koch Ave., Morris Plains. Call Marcia Brands 973-898-4940 (day). *E-mail:* newviews@nac.net

Nurse Recovery Group *Professionally-run.* Mutual support and information for nurses who are recovering from addictions. Sharing of professional concerns and encouragement. Meets in Boonton. Call 1-800-662-0108 (day). *Website:* http://www.njsna.org (click on RAMP; next click Peer Assistance)

Psychiatrically Recovering 12-Step. Mutual support for psychiatrically recovering people who wish to refrain from using alcohol or drugs, abusing food or any other compulsive behavior. Building is handicapped accessible. Call Richie S. 973-865-4851.

>**Cedar Knolls** Meets Mon. and Thurs., 10am, Saint Clare's Behavioral Health Center, 100 East Hanover Ave., Group Room, 1st Floor.

Denville Meets Mon., 1pm, Saint Clare's Behavioral Health Center, 50 Morris Ave., Room B-1.

Pompton Plains Meets Fri., 11am, New Bridge, 640 Newark-Pompton Turnpike.

SMART Recovery (Self-Management And Recovery Training) Self-help group for individuals wanting to gain their independence from addictive behaviors (alcohol, drugs, nicotine and other compulsive behaviors including gambling and eating disorders). SMART is a abstinence program based on cognitive-behavioral education and principles, especially those of rational-emotive behavior therapy. Meets Wed., 7-8:30pm, Daily Planit, 150-152 Speedwell Ave., Morristown. Call Rich 973-983-8755 or Glenn 973-255-7296. *Website:* http://www.smartrecovery.org

OCEAN

Addictions Victorious of South Jersey, Inc. 12-Step. Christ-centered support group for men and women who, in their struggle with substance abuse and emotional problems, come together that they may solve their problems and help others as well. Guest speakers, rap sessions, phone help, literature and newsletter. Optional donation. Meets Fri., 7pm, Redeemer Orthodox Presbyterian Church, 1600 Central Ave., Seaside Heights. Call Geoff 732-458-1119. *Website:* http://www.addvicinc.org

Double Trouble in Recovery 12-Step. Fellowship offering mutual support for persons with a substance abuse problem who are also taking medication for psychiatric problems.

Barnegat Meets Tues. and Thurs., 7pm, Journey to Wellness Self-Help Center, 575 N. Main St. Call 609-698-8889.

Bayville Meets Mon., 6-7pm, Ocean Mental Health Services, 160 Route 9. Call 732-905-1132 (day).

Jackson Meets Wed., 7:30-8:30pm, Brighter Days Self-Help Center, 268 Bennetts Mills Rd. Call 732-534-9960 (day). Building is handicapped accessible.

Toms River Meets Fri., 7:30-8:30pm, St. Barnabas Hospital, 1691 Route 9. Call 732-905-1132 (day).

Waretown Meets Sun., 5pm, St. Stephen's Episcopal Church, 367 Route 9. Call 609-698-8889.

Families Anonymous 12-Step. Mutual support for relatives and friends concerned about the use of drugs or related behavioral problems. Meets Tues., 7:30pm, St. Andrews United Methodist Church, 1528 Church Rd., Toms River.

Call 732-864-0548. *Website:* http://www.familiesanonymous.org *E-mail:* famanontr@comcast.net

Lawyers Concerned for Lawyers (LCL) Self-help group that supports recovery from alcoholism and drug dependence for attorneys, judges, law students and others in the legal system. Based on the 12-step program adapted from A.A. All inquiries are confidential. Meets Tues., 7:15pm, St. Mary's By The Sea, 804 Bay Ave., Meeting Room, Point Pleasant. Before attending call NJ Lawyers Assistance Program 1-800-246-5527. *Website:* http://www.njlap.org *E-mail:* njlap@aol.com

Nar-Anon Family Group 12-Step. Provides help for family members and friends of drug abusers by offering comfort, hope and friendship through shared experiences. Call Nar-Anon Answering Service 1-800-238-2333, 1-877-424-4491 or 609-587-7215. *Website:* http://www.naranonofnj.org

Narcotics Anonymous 12-Step. Fellowship of men and women seeking recovery from drug addiction. The only requirement for membership is the desire to stop using drugs. Call 1-800-992-0401 or 732-933-0462. *Website:* http://www.nanj.org

Nurse Recovery Group *Professionally-run.* Mutual support and information for nurses who are recovering from addictions. Sharing of professional concerns and encouragement. Meets in Manahawkin and Toms River. Call 1-800-662-0108 (day). *Website:* http://www.njsna.org (click on RAMP; next click Peer Assistance)

Overcomers In Christ Recovery program that deals with every aspect of addiction and dysfunction (spiritual, physical, mental, emotional and social). Uses Overcomers goals which are Christ-centered. Resources, literature, information and referrals. Meets Mon., 7-8:30pm, America's Keswick, 601 Route 530, Whiting. Separate groups for men and women. For women's group call Diane Hunt 732-350-1187 ext. 47. For men's group call Chaplain Jim Freed 732-350-1187 ext. 43. *Website:* http://www.americaskeswick.org

Parent Support Group - New Jersey, Inc. Confidential support group for parents of children (ages 13-40+) who are chemically dependent. Meets Mon., 7pm, Presbyterian Church of Toms River, 1070 Hooper Ave., Toms River. Call Karol Sullivan or Adrienne Mellana 1-800-561-4299 or 973-736-3344 (day). *Website:* http://www.psgnjhomestead.com *E-mail:* psgnj1@aol.com

Thursday Night Recovery Support to help overcome dependencies and addictions through accountability, encouragement and spiritual development. Meets Thurs., 7-8:30pm, Shore Vineyard Church, 320 Compass Ave., Beachwood. Call 732-244-3888 (day).

Women For Sobriety Self-help group designed specifically to help women with addictions achieve sobriety. Helps develop self-esteem and coping skills. Meets Mon., 7-8:30pm, Center for Healthy Living (house is next to Kimball Medical Center, off of parking lot), 198 Prospect St., Lakewood. Call Women For Sobriety 215-536-8026 (national).

PASSAIC

Double Trouble in Recovery 12-Step. Support and encouragement for those who are chemically addicted and are also in recovery from a psychiatric illness. Meets Mon., 5-6pm, Mental Health Association in Passaic County, 404 Clifton Ave., 1st Floor, Clifton. Call Amanda 973-478-4444 ext. 62 (day).

MICA Support Group *Professionally-run.* Mutual support for persons diagnosed with substance abuse and a mental illness. Meets 2nd and 4th Tues., 4-5pm, Our House Self-Help Center, 750 Broadway, Paterson. Call 973-553-1101 (day).

Nar-Anon Family Group 12-Step. Provides help for family members and friends of drug abusers by offering comfort, hope and friendship through shared experiences. Call Nar-Anon Answering Service 1-800-238-2333, 1-877-424-4491 or 609-587-7215. *Website:* http://www.naranonofnj.org

Narcotics Anonymous 12-Step. Fellowship of men and women seeking recovery from drug addiction. The only requirement for membership is the desire to stop using drugs. Call 1-800-992-0401 or 732-933-0462. *Website:* http://www.nanj.org

Nurse Recovery Group *Professionally-run.* Mutual support and information for nurses who are recovering from addictions. Sharing of professional concerns and encouragement. Meets in Passaic. Call 1-800-662-0108 (day). *Website:* http://www.njsna.org (click on RAMP; next click Peer Assistance)

Parent Support Group - New Jersey, Inc. Confidential support group for parents of children (ages 13-40+) who are chemically dependent. Meets Mon., 6:30pm, St. Joseph's Hospital, 224 Hamburg Turnpike, 6th Floor, Room 6B, Wayne. Call Karol Sullivan or Adrienne Mellana 1-800-561-4299 or 973-736-3344 (day). *Website:* http://www.psgnjhomestead.com *E-mail:* psgnj1@aol.com

Psychiatrically Recovering 12-Step. Mutual support for psychiatrically recovering people who wish to refrain from using alcohol or drugs, abusing food or any other compulsive behavior. Building is handicapped accessible. Meets Fri., 9:45am, New Bridge: Visions, 22 Riverview Dr., Wayne. Call Richie S. 973-865-4851.

SALEM

Narcotics Anonymous 12-Step. Fellowship of men and women seeking recovery from drug addiction. The only requirement for membership is the desire to stop using drugs. Call 1-800-992-0401 or 732-933-0462. *Website:* http://www.nanj.org

SOMERSET

Bright Futures for Kids *Professionally-run.* Provides support, education and counseling for children (ages 4-12) who are affected by a family members alcohol and/or drug addiction in learning how to express their feelings, coping skills, a sense of responsibility and the ability to resist peer pressure. Meets Sun., 11am-1pm, Carrier Clinic, Atkinson Amphitheater, 252 Route 601, Classroom 3, Belle Mead. Call Community Relations 908-281-1513.

Lawyers Concerned for Lawyers (LCL) Self-help group that supports recovery from alcoholism and drug dependence for attorneys, judges, law students and others in the legal system. Based on the 12-step program adapted from A.A. All inquires are confidential. Meets Tues., 6pm, 70 Grove St., Somerville. Before attending call NJ Lawyers Assistance Program 1-800-246-5527. *Website:* http://www.njlap.org *E-mail:* njlap@aol.com

Nar-Anon Family Group 12-Step. Provides help for family members and friends of drug abusers by offering comfort, hope and friendship through shared experiences. Call Nar-Anon Answering Service 1-800-238-2333, 1-877-424-4491 or 609-587-7215. *Website:* http://www.naranonofnj.org

Narcotics Anonymous 12-Step. Fellowship of men and women seeking recovery from drug addiction. The only requirement for membership is the desire to stop using drugs. Call 1-800-992-0401 or 732-933-0462. *Website:* http://www.nanj.org

"We cannot hold a torch to light another's path without brightening our own."
-- Ben Sweetland

Parent Support Group - New Jersey, Inc. *Professionally-run.* Confidential support for parents of children (ages 13-40+) who are chemically dependent. Meets Mon., 7pm, Carrier Foundation, Admissions Building, Belle Mead. Call Karol Sullivan or Adrienne Mellana 1-800-561-4299 or 973-736-3344 (day). *Website:* http://www.psgnjhomestead.com *E-mail:* psgnj1@aol.com

Psychiatrically Recovering 12-Step. Mutual support for psychiatrically recovering people who wish to refrain from using alcohol or drugs, abusing food or any other compulsive behavior. Building is handicapped accessible. Meets Thurs., 7:30pm, Richard Hall Community Mental Health Center, 500 North Bridge St., Room 121, Bridgewater. Call Richie S. 973-865-4851.

SUSSEX

Nar-Anon Family Group 12-Step. Provides help for family members and friends of drug abusers by offering comfort, hope and friendship through shared experiences. Call Nar-Anon Answering Service 1-800-238-2333, 1-877-424-4491 or 609-587-7215. *Website:* http://www.naranonofnj.org

Narcotics Anonymous 12-Step. Fellowship of men and women seeking recovery from drug addiction. The only requirement for membership is the desire to stop using drugs. Several meeting locations throughout the county. For meeting information call 1-800-992-0401 or 732-933-0462. *Website:* http://www.nanj.org

Nurse Recovery Group *Professionally-run.* Mutual support and information for nurses who are recovering from addictions. Sharing of professional concerns and encouragement. Meets in Newton. Call 1-800-662-0108 (day). *Website:* http://www.njsna.org (click on RAMP; next click on Peer Assistance)

UNION

Alcohol and Drug Family Education *Professionally-run.* Support for families facing the chemical dependency of a family member. Deals with co-dependency issues. Building is handicapped accessible. Meets Tues., 6:30-8pm, Overlook Hospital, Behavioral Health Dept., 46-48 Beauvoir Ave., Summit. Call 908-522-4800 (day).

Double Trouble in Recovery 12-Step. Support and encouragement for those who are chemically addicted and are also in recovery from a psychiatric illness. Rap sessions and guest speakers. Meets Wed., 4:30-5pm, Park Avenue Self-Help Center, 333 Park Ave., Plainfield. Call Andre Lawson 908-757-1350 (day).

Families Anonymous 12-Step. Support for parents, families and friends concerned about the use of drugs, alcohol or related behavioral problems. Meets Thurs., 7:30pm, Central Presbyterian Church, Maple St. and Morris Ave., Summit. Before attending call Barbara 973-267-2475 (day). *Website:* http://www.familiesanonymous.org

Families of Addiction *Professionally-run.* Mutual support for families of persons with an alcohol or drug addiction. Building is handicapped accessible. Meets Wed., 6:30-8pm, Overlook Hospital, Behavioral Health Dept., 46-48 Beauvoir Ave., Summit. Before attending call Rosemary Walsh 908-522-4800.

Nar-Anon Family Group 12-Step. Provides help for family members and friends of drug abusers by offering comfort, hope and friendship through shared experiences. Call Nar-Anon Answering Service 1-800-238-2333, 1-877-424-4491 or 609-587-7215. *Website:* http://www.naranonofnj.org

Narcotics Anonymous 12-Step. Fellowship of men and women seeking recovery from drug addiction. The only requirement for membership is the desire to stop using drugs. Call 1-800-992-0401 or 732-933-0462. *Website:* http://www.nanj.org

Parent Support Group - New Jersey, Inc. Confidential support group for parents of children (ages 13-40+) who are chemically dependent. Meets Tues., 6:30pm, Central Presbyterian Church, 70 Maple Ave., Library Room, Summit. Call Karol Sullivan or Adrienne Mellana 1-800-561-4299 or 973-736-3344 (day). *Website:* http://www.psgnjhomestead.com *E-mail:* psgnj1@aol.com

Psychiatrically Recovering 12-Step. Mutual support for psychiatrically recovering people who wish to refrain from using alcohol or drugs, abusing food or any other compulsive behavior. Building is handicapped accessible. Meets Tues., 9:30am, Occupational Center of Union County, New Building, 291 Cox St., Activity Room, Roselle. Call Richie S. 973-865-4851.

WARREN

Double Trouble in Recovery Mutual support for alcoholics or drug addicts who are taking medication for psychiatric problems. Meets Wed., 7-8pm, Better Future Self-Help Center, 21 West Washington Ave., Washington. Call Elena 908-835-1180.

Nar-Anon Family Group 12-Step. Provides help for family members and friends of drug abusers by offering comfort, hope and friendship through shared experiences. Call Nar-Anon Answering Service 1-800-238-2333, 1-877-424-4491 or 609-587-7215. *Website:* http://www.naranonofnj.org

Narcotics Anonymous 12-Step. Fellowship of men and women seeking recovery from drug addiction. The only requirement for membership is the desire to stop using drugs. Call 1-800-992-0401 or 732-933-0462. *Website:* http://www.nanj.org

NATIONAL

Alcoholics Victorious *International. 150 affiliated groups. Founded 1948.* 12-Step. Christian-oriented group for those recovering from alcohol or chemical dependency. Information and referrals, literature, phone support, conferences, support group meetings and newsletter. Assistance in starting groups. How-to materials. Write: Alcoholics Victorious, c/o Footprints, Inc., 4501 Troost St., Kansas City, MO 64110. Call 816-561-0567; Fax: 816-561-0572. *Website:* http://alcoholicsvictorious.org *E-mail:* info@alcoholicsvictorious.org

Anesthetists in Recovery *National network. 150+ members. Founded 1984.* Network of recovering nurse anesthetists. Provides phone support, information and referrals to groups and treatment. Write: AIR, c/o Art, 8233 Brookside Rd., Elkins Park, PA 19027. Call 215-635-0183 or 215-872-6821; Fax: 215-829-8757. *Website:* http://health.groups.yahooo.com/group/airforsobriety/ *E-mail:* a.to.z@comcast.net

Chemically Dependent Anonymous *National. 65 affiliated groups. Founded 1980.* Purpose is to carry the message of recovery to the chemically dependent person. For those with a desire to abstain from drugs/alcohol. Information and referrals, phone support, conferences and group development guidelines. Write: Chemically Dependent Anonymous, P.O. Box 813, Annapolis, MD 21401. Call 1-888-232-4673. *Website:* http://www.cdaweb.org

Co-Anon Family Groups *International. 28 groups. Founded 1985.* 12-Step. Program for families and friends of cocaine, crack and other drug addicts, whether they are actively using or not. Online e-mail and face-to-face meetings. Provides assistance in starting new groups. Write: Co-Anon Family Groups, P.O. Box 12722, Tucson, AZ 85732-2722. Call 1-800-898-9985 or 520-513-5028. *Website:* http://www.co-anon.org *E-mail:* info@co-anon.org

Cocaine Anonymous, Inc. *International. 2500 chapters. Founded 1982.* 12-Step. Fellowship of men and women who share their experience, strength and hope that they may solve their common problem and help others to recover from addiction. Quarterly newsletter. Group starter kit available. Write: Cocaine Anonymous, 3740 Overland Ave., Suite C, Los Angeles, CA 90034-6337. For local chapters call 1-800-347-8998 (24 hr.) or 310-559-5833 (business office); Fax: 310-559-2554. *Website:* http://ca.org *E-mail:* cawso@ca.org

Crystal Meth Anonymous *National.* 12-Step. Fellowship for those in recovery from addiction to crystal meth. Open to families and friends. Information on starting a group available. Meetings list available on website. Write: Crystal Meth Anonymous, 8205 Santa Monica Blvd., PMB 1-114, West Hollywood, CA 90046-5977. Call 213-488-4455. *Website:* http://www.crystalmeth.org

Double Trouble in Recovery, Inc. *National. 800+ affiliated groups. Founded 1989.* Fellowship of men and women who share their experience, strength and hope with each other so that they may solve their common problems and help others to recover from their particular addiction(s) and mental disorders. For persons dually-diagnosed with an addiction as well as a mental disorder. Literature, conferences, information and referrals. Double Trouble in Recovery Basic Guide Book also available. Assistance in starting new groups. Write: Double Trouble in Recovery, Inc., P.O. Box 245055, Brooklyn, NY 11224. Call 718-373-2684. *Website:* http://www.doubletroubleinrecovery.org *E-mail:* HV613@aol.com

Dual Recovery Anonymous *International. Chapters worldwide. Founded 1989.* A self-help program for individuals who experience a dual disorder of chemical dependency and a psychiatric or emotional illness. Based on the principles of the 12-steps and the personal experiences of individuals in dual recovery. Literature, newsletter and assistance in starting local groups. Write: Dual Recovery Anonymous, P.O. Box 8107, Prairie Village, KS 66208. Call 913-991-2703. *Website:* http://www.draonline.org (Note: listings of groups on this website may be out-of-date - be sure to call the contact number listed for the group before attending) *E-mail:* draws@draonline.org

"Feelings of worth can flourish only in an atmosphere where individual differences are appreciated, mistakes are tolerated, communication is open and rules are flexible – the kind of atmosphere that is found in a nurturing family." -- Virginia Satir

Families Anonymous *International. 500+ groups. Founded 1971.* 12-Step. Fellowship for relatives and friends of persons with drug, alcohol or behavioral problems. Members learn to achieve their own serenity in spite of the turmoil which surrounds them. Besides many booklets, pamphlets and bookmarks, publications include daily thought book, "Today A Better Way" and a bimonthly newsletter "The Twelve-Step Rag." Offers group development guidelines. Write: Families Anonymous, P.O. Box 3475, Culver City, CA 90231-3475. Call 1-800-736-9805 (Mon., Wed., Fri., 10:30am-4:30pm PST); Fax: 310-815-9682. *Website:* http://www.familiesanonymous.org *E-mail:* famanon@familiesanonymous.org

Free N One Recovery *National. 55 affiliated groups. Founded 1985.* Group teaches people to be free mentally and spiritually, as well as free of drugs and alcohol. Family support groups available. Information and referrals, phone support, literature and conferences. Assistance in starting local chapters. Write: Free N One Recovery, 5838 S. Overhill Dr., Los Angeles, CA 90043. Call 323-395-0009; Fax: 310-764-5439. *Website:* http://www.freenone.net *E-mail:* freenone@msn.com

Intercongregational Addictions Program (ICAP) *International. Founded 1979.* Network of recovering alcoholic women in religious orders. Helps Roman Catholic women who are or have been members of religious orders and are alcoholic or chemically dependent, compulsive eaters, compulsive gamblers, etc. Information, referrals, assistance in meeting other members, phone support, conferences and e-mail support. Write: ICAP, 7777 Lake St., Suite 115, River Forest, IL 60305-1734. Call 708-488-9770; Fax: 708-488-9774. *E-mail:* icapsrs@sbcglobal.net

International Doctors in Alcoholics Anonymous *International network. 6000 members. 175 affiliated groups. Founded 1949.* Opportunity for doctoral level health care professionals to discuss common problems and find common solutions to drug and alcohol problems. Annual meetings (1st week Aug.), phone support, newsletter, information and referrals. Mutual help meetings at conferences of other organizations. Also, Al-Anon program of helping families and friends of alcoholics recover from the effects of living with the problem drinking of a relative or friend. In addition, website provides links to several listgroups (ongoing recovery-related meetings conducted by e-mail). Write: International Doctors in Alcoholics Anonymous, c/o Dale Syfert, 2616 N.W. 25th Place, Gainsville, FL 32605-2826. Call 352-375-0240. *Website:* http://www.idaa.org

International Lawyers in Alcoholics Anonymous *International. 40+ affiliated groups. Founded 1975.* Serves as a clearinghouse for support groups for lawyers who are recovering alcoholics or have other chemical dependencies. Newsletter, annual conventions and group development guidelines. Write: International Lawyers in A.A., c/o Eli Gauna, 14123 Victory Blvd., Van Nuys, CA 91401. Call 818-785-6541; Fax: 818-785-3887. *Website:* http://www.ilaa.org

International Ministers and Pastors in Recovery *International. Founded 1988.* Provides mutual support for pastors and ministers recovering from addictions and actively participating in a 12-step recovery program. Provides phone network, meetings at an international 12-step conference, information and referrals. Assistance in starting local/regional groups. Write: International Ministers and Pastors in Recovery, P.O. Box 219, Augusta, MO 63332. Call 314-808-5470. *E-mail:* fresh12st@aol.com

JACS (Jewish Alcoholics, Chemically Dependent Persons and Significant Others) *International. Founded 1980.* For alcoholic and chemically dependent Jews, families, friends, associates and the community. Networking, community outreach, retreats, newsletter, literature, spiritual events and speakers bureau. Write: JACS, 120 W. 57th St., New York, NY 10019. Call 212-397-4197 (day); Fax: 212-399-3525. *Website:* http://www.jacsweb.org *E-mail:* jacs@jacsweb.org

LifeRing Secular Recovery *International. Founded 1999.* Secular community of persons who are building lives free of dependency on alcohol and other drugs. Group activities are not associated with religion or spirituality. Members practice complete abstinence from alcohol and other addicting drugs. Peer support, literature, information, referrals and advocacy activities. Guidelines available for starting similar groups. Large online e-mail support group and several smaller special interest groups (women, weight loss, stop smoking, etc). Online chats and forum. Publishes sobriety literature. Write: LifeRing Secular Recovery, 1440 Broadway, Suite 312, Oakland, CA 94612-2023. Call 1-800-811-4142 or 510-763-0779. *Website:* http://www.unhooked.com *E-mail:* service@lifering.org

Marijuana Anonymous World Services *International. 50+ groups. Founded 1989.* 12-Step. Fellowship of men and women who desire to stay clean of marijuana. Literature and starter packets. Various online meetings. Write: M.A., P.O. Box 2912, Van Nuys, CA 91404. Call 1-800-766-6779 (recorded message). *Website:* http://www.marijuana-anonymous.org *E-mail:* office@marijuana-anonymous.org

Methadone Anonymous Support Inter*national. 400+ affiliated groups. Founded 1991.* Self-help group for, and led by, current and former methadone maintenance treatment patients. Open to anyone interested in recovery from chemical dependency. Literature, conferences, support group meetings and online chatrooms (methadone users, detox, chronic pain, buprenorphine/suboxone treatment, caregivers, methadone pregnancy information, etc). Online meetings daily. Assistance in starting local groups. *Website:* http://www.methadonesupport.org *E-mail:* carol@methadonesupport.org

Nar-Anon Family Group Headquarters, Inc. *International. 1600 groups. Founded 1967.* 12-Step. Group offering self-help recovery to families and friends of addicts. Members share their experience, hope and strength with each other. Packet of information for starting new groups. Nar-Ateen and Nar-Atot programs available. Write: Nar-Anon Family World Group Headquarters, Inc., 22527 Crenshaw Blvd., Suite 200B, Torrance, CA 90505. Call 1-800-477-6291 or 310-534-8188; Fax: 310-534-8688. *Website:* http://www.nar-anon.org *E-mail:* naranonwso@hotmail.com

Narcotics Anonymous *(MULTILINGUAL) International. 44,000+ meetings per week in 127 countries. Founded 1953.* 12-Step. Worldwide multicultural organization whose primary purpose is to help any individual stop using drugs. No dues, fees or registration. The only requirement for membership is the desire to stop using drugs. Information is available in several languages, on audio tape, CD and in Braille. Write: NAWS, P.O. Box 9999, Van Nuys, CA 91409. Call 818-773-9999; Fax: 818-700-0700. *Website:* http://www.na.org *E-mail:* fsmail@na.org

National Family Partnership (formerly Parents for Drug-Free Youth) *National. 58 affiliates. Founded 1980.* Support, drug prevention education, information and networking for parents to address drug prevention. Legislative advocacy on federal level and information resource for state and local efforts. Annual Red Ribbon Campaign, resource center, drug prevention and anti-tobacco resource. Write: National Family Partnership, 2490 Coral Way, Suite 501, Miami, FL 33145. Call 1-800-705-8997 (Mon.-Fri., 8:30am-5pm EST); Fax: 305-856-4815. *Website:* http://www.nfp.org *E-mail:* ireyes@informedfamilies.org

Overcomers In Christ *International. Founded 1987.* Recovery program that deals with every aspect of addiction and dysfunction (spiritual, physical, mental, emotional and social). Uses Overcomers goals which are Christ-centered. Resources, literature, information and referrals. Assistance in starting new groups. Write: Overcomers In Christ, P.O. Box 34460, Omaha, NE 68134-0460.

Call 1-866-573-0966 or 402-573-0966. *Website:* http://www.overcomersinchrist.org *E-mail:* oic@overcomersinchrist.org

Overcomers Outreach, Inc. *International. 700 affiliated groups. Founded 1985.* 12-Step. Christ-centered support group for anyone affected by addictions, as well as their families and friends. Uses 12-steps of A.A. and applies them to the Scriptures. Uses Jesus Christ as "higher power." Supplements involvement in other 12-step groups. Newsletter, group development guidelines and conferences. Write: Overcomers Outreach, Inc., P.O. Box 922950, Sylmar, CA 91392-2950. Call 1-800-310-3001. *Website:* http://www.overcomersoutreach.org *E-mail:* info@overcomersoutreach.org

Pills Anonymous *Model. 1 group in New York City.* Self-help, self-supporting, anonymous 12-step program, based on the principles of A.A., for those who want to help themselves and others recover from chemical addiction. Call 212-874-0700. *Website:* http://www.pillsanonymous.org *E-mail:* panonjh@yahoo.com

Psychologists Helping Psychologists *National network. Founded 1980.* For doctoral-level psychologists or students who have had a personal experience with alcohol or drugs. Aim is to support each other in recovery. Aims to educate psychology community. Regional/national get-togethers and newsletter. Write: Psychologists Helping Psychologists, 3484 S. Utah St., Arlington, VA 22206-1921. Call Ann 703-243-4470; Fax: 703-243-7125. *E-mail:* anns@erols.com

Recoveries Anonymous *International. 50 chapters.* Spiritual recovery group for anyone seeking a solution for any kind of addiction. Family and friends welcome. "How To Begin..." guides and "Start A Group" kit can be downloaded free from the website. Write: R.A. Universal Services, P.O. Box 1212, East Northport, NY 11731. *Website:* http://www.r-a.org *E-mail:* raus@r-a.org

Secular Organizations for Sobriety (Save Ourselves) *International. Founded 1986.* Mutual help for alcoholics and addicts who want to acknowledge their addiction and maintain sobriety as a separate issue from religion or spirituality. Newsletter. Guidelines and assistance available for starting groups. Real-time online chats and e-groups available. Write: Secular Organizations for Sobriety, 4773 Hollywood Blvd., Hollywood, CA 90027. Call 323-666-4295; Fax: 323-666-4271. *Website:* http://www.cfiwest.org/sos/ *E-mail:* sos@cfiwest.org

SMART Recovery (r) (Self-Management And Recovery Training) *National. 225+ affiliated groups. Founded 1994.* Network of self-help groups for individuals wanting to gain their independence from addictive and compulsive behaviors. SMART Recovery is a abstinence program based on cognitive-behavioral principles, especially those of rational-emotive behavior therapy. Newsletter, information, referrals, literature and assistance in starting local groups. Write: SMART Recovery, 7537 Mentor Ave., Suite 306, Mentor, OH 44060. Call 1-866-951-5357 or 440-951-5357; Fax: 440-951-5358. *Website:* http://www.smartrecovery.org *E-mail:* info@smartrecovery.org

Social Workers Helping Social Workers *National network. Founded 1981.* Supports recovery from alcohol or other chemical dependence, either their own or that of a significant other, among social workers (BSW/MSW) or BSW/MSW students. Social workers with other addictions are welcome to attend meetings. Newsletter, annual conferences, some regional retreats/meetings, continuing education, daily e-mail digest and group development guidelines. Write: Social Workers Helping Social Workers, c/o Betty Check, 5228 S. Kenwood Ave., Chicago, IL 60615-4006. Call Betty 773-493-6940 (confidential voice mail). *Website:* http://www.socialworkershelping.org *E-mail:* swhswil@aol.com

Veterinarians in Recovery *National network. Founded 1990.* Support network for veterinarians in recovery from alcoholism and addiction. Provides information and referrals, phone support and newsletter. Online e-mail listserv. Maintains database of members for support. Al-Anon members and recovering veterinarian staff welcome at meetings. Many VIR members also are members of International Doctors in A.A., and meet during their annual conference. Write: Veterinarians in Recovery, c/o Jeff H., 180 County Rd. 741, Clanton, AL 35046. Call 205-335-4222.

ONLINE

Benzo *Online. Founded 1999.* Benzodiazepine withdrawal support network for those who want to end benzodiazepine dependency/addiction and recover from the withdrawal syndrome. *Website:* http://health.groups.yahoo.com/group/benzo/

Benzoprotracted *Online. 489 members. Founded 2001.* Supportive environment to those who suffer from withdrawal symptoms after months, or years, of being free from benzodiazepine drugs. *Website:* http://groups.yahoo.com/group/benzoprotracted

Conduct Disorders Parent Message Board *Online. 7080 members. Founded 1995.* Support for parents living with a child with one of the many behavior disorders including: attention deficit hyperactivity disorder, oppositional defiance disorder, conduct disorder, depression and substance abuse. Parents with children of all ages welcome. *Website:* http://www.conductdisorders.com

HAMS: Harm Reduction for Alcohol and Other Substances *Online. 225 members. Founded 2007.* Support and information for people who choose to practice safe intoxication, as well as those choosing moderate drinking or quitting as a goal. Members offer simple and pragmatic strategies for reducing the risks of recreational intoxication to self and others. *Website:* http://health.groups.yahoo.com/group/hamshrn

GAMBLING
(see also toll-free helplines)

STATEWIDE

Gam-Anon 12-Step. Fellowship of family members and friends of compulsive gamblers. Follows the 12-step program adapted from A.A. Various meeting locations throughout New Jersey. Write: Gam-Anon, P.O. Box 177, Lodi, NJ 07644. Call 973-815-0988. *Website:* http://www.njgamanon.org

Gamblers Anonymous - New Jersey Intergroup 12-Step. Fellowship of men and women who share their experiences, strengths and hopes with each other in order to recover from their common problem of compulsive gambling. Various meeting locations throughout New Jersey. Write: G.A., P.O. Box 283, Kearny, NJ 07032. Call 1-888-424-3577 (24 hr). *Website:* http://www.ga4nj.com

Signs of Sobriety, Inc. (SOS) *Professionally-run.* Provides alcoholism and drug addiction services to persons who are deaf or hard-of-hearing. Makes referrals to deaf and sign interpreted 12-step groups throughout NJ (alcohol or drug addiction, gambling, families of alcoholics and general 12-step meetings). Provides prevention and education classes. Offers SoberCamp-annual summer retreat and Sober/Deaf activities for deaf and hard-of-hearing individuals in recovery. Newsletter. Write: Signs Of Sobriety, Inc., 100 Scotch Rd., 2nd Floor, Ewing, NJ 08628. Call TTY/VP: 609-882-7177; Voice: 609-882-7677 or 1-800-332-7677 (day); Fax: 609-882-6808. *Website:* http://www.signsofsobriety.org *E-mail:* info@signsofsobriety.org

ATLANTIC

Gam-Anon 12-Step. Fellowship of family members and friends of compulsive gamblers. Meets Thurs., 8-10pm, Our Lady of Sorrow Church, Wabash and Popular Ave., Linwood. Call Gam-Anon Hotline 973-815-0988. *Website:* http://www.njgamanon.org

Gamblers Anonymous 12-Step. Fellowship of men and women who share experiences, strengths and hopes with each other to recover from compulsive gambling. Follows 12-step program. Call 1-888-424-3577 (24 hr.). *Website:* http://www.ga4nj.com

> **Brigantine** Meets Sat., 10am-noon, Community Presbyterian Church, 1501 Brigantine Ave. and 15th St.
> **Linwood** Meets Thurs., 8-10pm, Our Lady of Sorrow Church, Wabash Ave. and Poplar Ave.
> **Margate** Meets Sun., 10:30am-noon, Margate Library, 8100 Atlantic Ave.

BERGEN

Gam-Anon 12-Step. Fellowship of family members and friends of compulsive gamblers. Building is handicapped accessible. Call Gam-Anon Hotline 973-815-0988. *Website:* http://www.njgamanon.org

> **Fair Lawn** Meets Fri., 8pm, Episcopal Church of Atonement, 1-36 30th St. and Rosalie Ave. Building is handicapped accessible.
> **Paramus** Meets Tues., 7pm, Care Plus NJ, Inc., 610 Valley Health Plaza.
> **Paramus** Meets Tues., 8-9pm, Bergen Pines Hospital, 230 East Ridgewood Ave.

Gamblers Anonymous 12-Step. Fellowship of men and women who share experiences, strengths and hopes with each other to recover from compulsive gambling. Call 1-888-424-3577 (24 hr.). *Website:* http://www.ga4nj.com

> **Carlstadt** *(STEP MEETING ONLY)* Meets Mon., 6:30-7:30pm and Wed., 7:30-9:45pm, First Presbyterian Church, 457 Division Ave. Building is handicapped accessible.
> **Fair Lawn** Meets Tues., 7-8:30pm, Wed. and Fri., 8-10pm, Episcopal Church of Atonement, 1-36 30th St. Building is handicapped accessible.
> **Hasbrouck Heights** Meets Sat., 10am-noon, St. John the Divine Episcopal Church, Terrace Ave. and Jefferson Ave.
> **Paramus** Meets Tues., 7-8:30pm, Care Plus NJ, 610 Valley Health Plaza, Industrial Ave.
> **Westwood** Meets Sun., 7:30-9:30pm, United Methodist Church, 105 Fairview Ave.

"Come to the edge," He said. They said, "We are afraid." "Come to the edge," He said.
They came. He pushed them ... and they flew. – G. Apollinaire

BURLINGTON

12 Steps God's Way Christian-focused recovery group for anyone suffering from any type of addiction, dependency or compulsive disorder. Rap sessions, guest speakers and literature. Meets Thurs., 7pm, Fellowship Alliance Chapel, 199 Church Rd., Medford. Call 609-953-7333 (day).

Gam-Anon 12-Step. Fellowship of family members and friends of compulsive gamblers. Call Gam-Anon Hotline 973-815-0988. *Website:* http://www.njgamanon.org
> **Marlton** Meets Thurs., 7-9pm, Virtua West Jersey Hospital, 90 Brick Rd.
> **Rancocas** Meets Sun., 5:30-6pm, Hampton Hospital, 650 Rancocas Rd., 2nd Floor, Recovery Room.

Gamblers Anonymous 12-Step. Fellowship of men and women who share experiences, strengths and hopes with each other to recover from compulsive gambling. Call 1-888-424-3577 (24 hr.). *Website:* http://www.ga4nj.com
> **Marlton** Meets Thurs., 7-9pm; Fri., 8:30-10pm and Sat., 9-10:30am, Virtua West Jersey Hospital, 90 Brick Rd.
> **Moorestown** Meets Mon., 8-9:30pm, Trinity Church, Main St.
> **Rancocas** Meets Wed., 7:30-9pm and Sun., 5:30-6:30pm, Hampton Hospital, 650 Rancocas Rd.

CAPE MAY

Gamblers Anonymous 12-Step. Fellowship of men and women who share experiences, strengths and hopes with each other to recover from compulsive gambling. Meets Sun., 7-8pm, Holy Trinity Episcopal Church, 2998 Bay Ave., Ocean City. Call 1-888-424-3577 (24 hr.). *Website:* http://www.ga4nj.com

CUMBERLAND

Overcomer's Outreach Christian 12-Step. Fellowship to overcome any type of addiction or compulsive behavior, anxiety, depression or loneliness using God's word as a basis of recovery. Bible study, discussion, prayer and phone help. Meets Thurs., 7-8pm, Shiloh Seventh Day Baptist Church, East Ave., Shiloh. Call Frank B. Mulford 856-451-8698 (day) or Rev. Chroniger 856-455-0488 (day). *E-mail:* ahfarm@hotmail.com

ESSEX

Gam-Anon 12-Step. Fellowship of family members and friends of compulsive gamblers. Call Gam-Anon Hotline 973-815-0988. *Website:* http://www.njgamanon.org

> **Bloomfield** Meets Tues., 8:30-10:30pm, Bethany United Presbyterian Church, 293 West Passaic St.
>
> **Nutley** Meets Mon., 8pm and Fri., 8:30pm, St. Paul's Congregational Church, 10 St. Paul's Place.

Gamblers Anonymous 12-Step. Fellowship of men and women who share experiences, strengths and hopes with each other to recover from compulsive gambling. Call 1-888-424-3577 (24 hr.). *Website:* http://www.ga4nj.com

> **Bloomfield** Meets Tues. and Thurs., 8:30-10:30pm, Bethany United Presbyterian Church, 293 W. Passaic Ave., Lower Level.
>
> **Nutley** Meets Mon., 8-10pm, St. Paul's Congregational Church, 10 St. Paul's Place, 1st Floor (side entrance).
>
> **South Orange** Meets Wed., 1-2pm and Thurs., 8-9:30pm, St. Andrew and Holy Communion, 160 West South Orange Ave. (front entrance closest to Church St.), 2nd Floor.
>
> **West Orange** Meets Tues., 8-9pm, St. Cloud Presbyterian Church, 5 Ridgeway Ave., Lower Level, Rear Entrance.

GLOUCESTER

Gamblers Anonymous 12-Step. Fellowship of men and women who share experiences, strengths and hopes with each other to recover from compulsive gambling. Call 1-888-424-3577 (24 hr.). *Website:* http://www.ga4nj.com

> **Blackwood** Meets Fri., 8-10pm, Blackwood Methodist Church, 35 East Church St.
>
> **Egg Harbor City** Meets Wed., 7-9pm, Holy Trinity Greek Orthodox Church, 7004 Ridge Ave.
>
> **Mantua** Meets Tues., 10am, Cedar Grove Park, 1 A Whipporwill Way, Club House.
>
> **Sewell** Meets Wed., 7:30-9pm, Church of the Holy Family, 226 Hurfville Rd.
>
> **Woodbury** Meets Tues., 7-8:30pm, St. Stephen's Lutheran Church, 230 North Evergreen Ave.

HUDSON

Gamblers Anonymous 12-Step. Fellowship of men and women who share their experiences, strengths and hopes with each other to recover from compulsive gambling. Building is handicapped accessible. Call 1-888-424-3577 (24 hr.). *Website:* http://www.ga4nj.com

> **Bayonne** Meets Tues., 8-9pm, Bayonne Senior Center, 16 West 4th St.
> **Jersey City** *(BILINGUAL)* Meets Wed., 8-9:30pm, Old Bergen Church, Highland Ave. and Bergen Ave., Rear Entrance. Two separate groups one in English and one in Spanish.

MERCER

Gamblers Anonymous 12-Step. Fellowship of men and women who share experiences, strengths and hopes with each other to recover from compulsive gambling. Meets Tues., 8-10pm, University Office Plaza, 3635 Quakerbridge Rd., Suite 7, Hamilton. Call 1-888-424-3577 (24 hr.). *Website:* http://www.ga4nj.com

MIDDLESEX

Gam-Anon 12-Step. Fellowship of family members and friends of compulsive gamblers. Building is handicapped accessible. Call Gam-Anon Hotline 973-815-0988. *Website:* http://www.njgamanon.org

> **Metuchen** Meets Tues., 7pm, St. Luke's Episcopal Church, 17 Oak St.
> **Old Bridge** Meets Wed., 8pm, Sayre Woods Bible Church, 2290 Highway 9, Room 201 and 202.
> **Parlin** Meets Thurs., 8pm, Messiah Lutheran Church, 3091 Bordentown Ave.

Gamblers Anonymous 12-Step. Fellowship of men and women who share experiences, strengths and hopes with each other to recover from compulsive gambling. Building is handicapped accessible. Call 1-888-424-3577 (24 hr.). *Website:* http://www.ga4nj.com

> **Edison** Meets Sat., 10-11:30am, Oak Tree Presbyterian Church, 455 Plainfield Rd.
> **Metuchen** *(Young Gamblers)* Meets Tues., 7-9pm, St. Luke's Episcopal Church, 17 Oak St., Room #2.
> **Old Bridge** *(Young Gamblers)* Meets Wed., 8-9:30pm, Sayre Woods Bible Church, 2290 Highway Route 9 South, Room 201 and 202.
> **Parlin** *(Young Gamblers)* Meets Thurs., 8-9:30pm, Messiah Lutheran Church, 3091 Bordentown Ave., Main Entrance, 1st Floor.

"You give but little when you give of your possessions. It is when you give of yourself that you truly give." -- Kahlil Gibran

Overcomer's Outreach Christian 12-Step. Fellowship to overcome any type of addiction or compulsive behavior, anxiety, depression or loneliness using God's word as a basis of recovery. Bible study, discussion, prayer and phone help. Meets Tues., 6:30-7:30pm, Metuchen Assembly of God, 130 Whitman St., Metuchen. Call Janet 732-388-2856 (eve.).

SMART Recovery (Self-Management Recovery Training) *Professionally-run.* Self-help group for individuals wanting to gain their independence from addictive behaviors (drugs, alcohol, nicotine and other compulsive behaviors including gambling and eating disorders). SMART is a abstinence program based on cognitive-behavioral education and principles, especially those of rational-emotive behavior therapy. Building is handicapped accessible. Meets Thurs., 6-7:30pm, Rutgers University, 152 Frelinghuysen Rd, Busch Campus, Psychology Building, Room A340, 2nd Floor, Piscataway. Call Ayelet Kattan 732-445-6111 ext. 871 (day).

MONMOUTH

Gam-Anon 12-Step. *(STEP MEETING ONLY)* Fellowship of family members and friends of compulsive gamblers. Building is handicapped accessible. Meets Sun., 6:30pm, St. Mary's Church, Route 34 and Phalanx Rd., Colts Neck. Call Gam-Anon Hotline 973-815-0988. *Website:* http://www.njgamanon.org

Gamblers Anonymous 12-Step. Fellowship of men and women who share experiences, strengths and hopes with each other to recover from compulsive gambling. Building is handicapped accessible. Call 1-888-424-3577 (24 hr.). *Website:* http://www.ga4nj.com

> **Colts Neck** *(STEP MEETING ONY),* Meets Tues., 8-9:30pm and Sun. 6:30-8pm St. Mary's Church, Spiritual Center Building, Route 34 and Phalanx Rd.
> **Freehold** Meets Fri., 8-9:30pm, Hope Lutheran Church, 211 Elton-Adelphia Rd., Route 524.
> **Manasquan** Meets Wed., 7:30-9:30pm, Holy Trinity Lutheran Church, 6 Osborn Ave., Grahn Room (downstairs).
> **Ocean Township** Meets Mon., 7:30-9:30pm, Church of St. Anselm, 1028 Wayside Rd.

MORRIS

Gam-Anon 12-Step. Fellowship of family members and friends of compulsive gamblers. Building is handicapped accessible. Meets Tues., 8-10pm, Saint Clare's Behavioral Health Center, Powerville Rd., Boonton. Call Gam-Anon Hotline 973-815-0988. *Website:* http://www.njgamanon.org

Gamblers Anonymous 12-Step. Fellowship of men and women who share experiences, strengths and hopes with each other to recover from compulsive gambling. Building is handicapped accessible. Meets Tues., 8-10pm, Saint Clare's Behavioral Health Center, Powerville Rd., Boonton. Call 1-888-424-3577 (24 hr.). *Website:* http://www.ga4nj.com

SMART Recovery (Self-Management And Recovery Training) Self-help group for individuals wanting to gain their independence from addictive behaviors (alcohol, drugs, nicotine and other compulsive behaviors including gambling and eating disorders). SMART is a abstinence program based on cognitive-behavioral education and principles, especially those of rational-emotive behavior therapy. Meets Thurs., 7-8:30pm, Family Services, 62 Elm St., Morristown. Call Rich 973-983-8755 or Glenn 973-255-7296. *Website:* http://www.smartrecovery.org

OCEAN

Gam-Anon 12-Step. Fellowship of family members and friends of compulsive gamblers. Call Gam-Anon Hotline 973-815-0988. *Website:* http://www.njgamanon.org
> **Toms River** Meets Thurs., 8-9pm and Sat., 9:30-11:30am, The Presbyterian Church of Toms River, 1070 Hooper Ave. Building is handicapped accessible.
> **Toms River** Meets Fri., 7:30-9pm, Holy Cross Lutheran Church, 1500 Hooper Ave.

Gamblers Anonymous 12-Step. Fellowship of men and women who share experiences, strengths and hopes with each other to recover from compulsive gambling. Call 1-888-424-3577 (24 hr.). *Website:* http://www.ga4nj.com
> **Toms River** Meets Thurs., 7-9pm and Sat. 9:30-11:30am, Presbyterian Church of Toms River, 1070 Hooper Ave. Building is handicapped accessible.
> **Toms River** Meets Fri., 7:30-9pm, Holy Cross Lutheran Church, 1500 Hooper Ave.

Overcomers In Christ Recovery program that deals with every aspect of addiction and dysfunction (spiritual, physical, mental, emotional and social). Uses Overcomers goals which are Christ-centered. Resources, literature, information and referrals. Meets Mon., 7-8:30pm, America's Keswick, 601 Route 530, Whiting. Separate groups for men and women. Women's group call Diane Hunt 732-350-1187 ext. 47. Men's group call Chaplain Jim Freed 732-350-1187 ext. 43. *Website:* http://www.americaskeswick.org

Thursday Night Recovery Support to help overcome dependencies and addictions through accountability, encouragement and spiritual development. Meets Thurs., 7-8:30pm, Shore Vineyard Church, 320 Compass Ave., Beachwood. Call 732-244-3888 (day).

SOMERSET

Gam-Anon 12-Step. Fellowship of family members and friends of compulsive gamblers. Building is handicapped accessible. Meets Thurs., 7-8:30pm, Lyons Veterans Administration Medical Center, Building 143, 1st Floor, Multipurpose Room, Lyons. Call Gam-Anon Hotline 973-815-0988. *Website:* http://www.njgamanon.org

Gamblers Anonymous 12-Step. Fellowship of men and women who share their experiences, strengths and hopes with each other in order to recover from their common problem of compulsive gambling. Building is handicapped accessible. Call 1-888-424-3577 (24 hr.). *Website:* http://www.ga4nj.com
> **Basking Ridge** Meets Sat., 10-11:30am, St. James Church, Parish Community Center, 184 South Finley Ave., Room 4.
> **Lyons** Meets Thurs., 7-8:30pm, Lyons Veterans Administration Medical Center, Building 143, Multi-Purpose Room, 151 Knollcroft Rd.

UNION

Gam-Anon 12-Step. Fellowship of family members and friends of compulsive gamblers. Call Gam-Anon Hotline 973-815-0988. *Website:* http://www.njgamanon.org
> **Clark** Meets Mon., 7:45-10pm, Temple Beth Or, 111 Valley Rd., 1st Floor.
> **Summit** Meets Mon., 7:45-10pm, Beth Hatikva, 36 Chatham Rd.

Gamblers Anonymous 12-Step. Fellowship of men and women who share experiences, strengths and hopes with each other to recover from compulsive gambling. Call 1-888-424-3577 (24 hr.). *Website:* http://www.ga4nj.com
> **Clark** Meets Mon., 7:45-10pm, Temple Beth Or/Beth Torah, 111 Valley Rd., 1st Floor, Room 7.
> **Summit** Meets Mon., 7:45-10pm, Congregation Beth Hatikvah, 36 Chatham Rd.
> **Union** Meets Sun., 7-9pm, Union Methodist Church, Berwyn St. and Overlook Terrace (rear entrance), Lower Level.

NATIONAL

Bettors Anonymous *Model. 5 groups in Massachusetts. Founded 1990.* 12-Step. Fellowship who share their experience, hope and strength with each other in order to help themselves and others recover from compulsive gambling. The only requirement for membership is a desire to stop gambling. Literature, phone help, information and referrals. Meetings in Massachusetts. Provides assistance in starting local groups. Write: Bettors Anonymous, P.O. Box 304, Wilmington, MA 01887. Call 978-988-1777 or 781-662-5199. *Website:* http://www.bettorsanonymous.org

Gam-Anon Family Groups *International. 325 groups. Founded 1960.* 12-Step. Fellowship for men and women who are husbands, wives, relatives or friends of compulsive gamblers, who have been affected by the gambling problem. Purpose is to learn acceptance and understanding of the gambling illness, to use the program to rebuild lives and give assistance to those who suffer. A few groups have Gam-a-teen groups for children of gamblers. Write: Gam-Anon, P.O. Box 157, Whitestone, NY 11357. Call 718-352-1671 (Tues. and Thurs., 9am-5pm EST); Fax: 718-746-2571. *Website:* http://www.gam-anon.org

Gamblers Anonymous *International. Approximately 2400 chapters. Founded 1957.* 12-Step. Fellowship of men and women who share experiences, strengths and hopes with each other to recover from compulsive gambling. Monthly bulletin for members. Offers assistance in starting new groups. Write: G.A., P.O. Box 17173, Los Angeles, CA 90017. Call 213-386-8789; Fax: 213-386-0030. *Website:* http://www.gamblersanonymous.org *E-mail:* isomain@gamblersanonymous.org

Intercongregational Addictions Program (ICAP) *International. Founded 1979.* Network of recovering alcoholic women in religious orders. Helps Roman Catholic women who are, or have been, members of religious orders and are alcoholic or chemically dependent, compulsive eaters, compulsive gamblers, etc. Information, referrals, assistance in meeting other members, phone support, conferences and e-mail support. Write: ICAP, 7777 Lake Street, Suite 115, River Forest, IL 60305-1734. Call 708-488-9770; Fax: 708-488-9774. *E-mail:* icapsrs@sbcglobal.net

Need help finding a specific group? Give us a call – we're here to help!
Call 1-800-367-6274.

Overcomers In Christ *International. Founded 1987.* Recovery program that deals with every aspect of addiction and dysfunction (spiritual, physical, mental, emotional and social). Uses Overcomers goals which are Christ-centered. Resources, literature, information and referrals. Assistance in starting new groups. Write: Overcomers In Christ, P.O. Box 34460, Omaha, NE 68134-0460. Call 1-866-573-0966 or 402-573-0966. *Website:* http://www.overcomersinchrist.org *E-mail:* oic@overcomersinchrist.org

Overcomers Outreach, Inc. *International. 700 affiliated groups. Founded 1985.* 12-Step. Christ-centered support group for anyone affected by addictions, as well as their families and friends. Uses 12-steps of A.A. and applies them to the Scriptures. Uses Jesus Christ as "higher power." Supplements involvement in other 12-step groups. Newsletter, group development guidelines and conferences. Write: Overcomers Outreach, Inc., P.O. Box 922950, Sylmar, CA 91392-2950. Call 1-800-310-3001. *Website:* http://www.overcomersoutreach.org *E-mail:* info@overcomersoutreach.org

Recoveries Anonymous *International. 50 chapters.* Spiritual recovery group for anyone seeking a solution for any kind of addiction, problem or behavior. Family and friends welcome. "How To Begin..." guides and "Start A Group" kit can be downloaded free from the website. Write: R.A. Universal Services, P.O. Box 1212, East Northport, NY 11731. *Website:* http://www.r-a.org *E-mail:* raus@r-a.org

GAMERS

ONLINE

On-Line Gamers Anonymous *Online.* 12-Step. Fellowship of people sharing their experience, strengths and hope to help each other recover and heal from the problems caused by excessive and/or obsessive game playing (computer/video/console/on-line games). Support for family and friends of gamers also available. *Website:* http://www.olganonboard.org/

Gamer Widow *Online.* Message boards for partners, family and friends of people who play computer games compulsively. Several forums for specific types of games, such as multiplayer online role play, fantasy and action/fighting games. *Website:* http://www.gamerwidow.com/

OVEREATING / OVERWEIGHT
(see also eating disorders, toll-free helplines)

STATEWIDE

Overeaters Anonymous 12-Step. Fellowship of men, women and children who meet to help one another understand and overcome their common problem of compulsive overeating. Follows the O.A. 12-step program. Meetings throughout New Jersey.

> **Central Jersey Intergroup** Covers Hunterdon, Mercer, Middlesex, Monmouth, Somerset and Union counties. Write: Overeaters Anonymous, P.O. Box 284, Woodbridge, NJ 07095. Call 908-253-3464 or Margaret 732-326-1934. *Website:* http://www.oa-centraljersey.org

> **Jersey Shore Intergroup** Covers Atlantic, Cape May and Ocean counties. Write: Overeaters Anonymous, P.O. Box 571, Manahawkin, NJ 08050. Call Jersey Shore Intergroup 609-698-0244. *Website:* http://www.oa.org

> **North Jersey Intergroup** Covers Bergen, Essex, Hudson, Morris, Passaic, Sussex, Union and Warren counties. Write: Overeaters Anonymous, P.O. Box 827, Fairlawn, NJ 07410-0827. Call 973-746-8787. *Website:* http://www.njioa.org

> **South Jersey Intergroup** Covers Burlington, Camden, Cumberland, Gloucester and Salem counties. Write: Overeaters Anonymous, South Jersey Intergroup, P.O. Box 766, Voorhees, NJ 08044. Call South Jersey Intergroup 609-239-0022. *Website:* http://www.southjerseyoa.org

TOPS (Take Off Pounds Sensibly) *45+ groups.* Helps overweight persons lose weight through medical supervision, competition and group process. Open to children 7 years and older. Phone network, buddy system, peer-counseling and newsletter. Dues $26/yr. Meetings throughout NJ. For information call Sue Anne Cress 856-797-8601 (leave message). Check website for local meetings. *Website:* http://www.tops.org

ATLANTIC

Overeaters Anonymous 12-Step. Fellowship who meet to help one another understand and overcome their common problem of compulsive overeating. For information on local meetings call Jersey Shore Intergroup 609-698-0244.

BERGEN

Food Addicts in Recovery Anonymous 12-Step. Fellowship of those recovering from the disease of food addiction, obesity, anorexia and bulimia. *Website:* http://www.foodaddicts.org
> **Maywood** Meets Mon. and Tues., 10:30am-noon, St. Martin's Episcopal Church, 29 Parkway. Call Deb 201-843-1667.
> **Paramus** Meets Thurs., 6:30-8pm, Kraft Center, 15 Essex Rd. Call Joe S. 973-243-8807.

Gastric Bypass Support Group *Professionally-run.* Mutual support and education for persons who have had bariatric surgery (gastric stapling) within the last year or are considering the procedure. Guest speakers and phone help. Meets 3rd Wed., 5:30-7pm, Englewood Hospital, 350 Engle St., Englewood. Before attending call 201-227-5534 (day).

Lap Band Support Group *Professionally-run.* Mutual support and education for persons who have had lap band surgery or are considering the procedure. Meets 3rd Tues., 5:30pm, Englewood Hospital, 350 Engle St., Englewood. Before attending call 201-227-5534 (day).

Laparoscopic Gastric Band or Laparoscopic Gastric Bypass *Professionally-run.* Support and education for persons who have had laparoscopic gastric band or laparoscopic gastric bypass surgery. Meets 4th Thurs., 6pm (except July and Dec.), Holy Name Hospital, 718 Teaneck Rd., Teaneck. Pre-registration required. Before attending call 973-437-8020 (day). Website: http://www.myprogramforlife.com

Overeaters Anonymous 12-Step. Fellowship who meet to help one another understand and overcome their common problem of compulsive overeating. For local meeting information by day of week call 973-746-8787.

TOPS (Take Off Pounds Sensibly) Helps overweight persons lose weight through medical supervision, competition and group process. Open to children 7 years and older. Phone network, buddy system, peer-counseling and newsletter. Membership $26/yr. For meeting information call Sue Anne Cress 856-797-8601 (leave message). Check website for local meetings. *Website:* http://www.tops.org

BURLINGTON

12 Steps God's Way Christian-focused recovery group for anyone suffering from any type of addiction, dependency or compulsive disorder. Meets Thurs.,

7pm, Fellowship Alliance Chapel, 199 Church Rd., Medford. Call 609-953-7333 (day).

Overeaters Anonymous 12-Step. Fellowship who meet to help one another understand and overcome their common problem of compulsive overeating. For local meetings call the Overeaters Anonymous South Jersey Intergroup 609-239-0022.

TOPS (Take Off Pounds Sensibly) Helps overweight persons lose weight through medical supervision, competition and group process. Open to children 7 years and older. Phone network, buddy system, peer-counseling and newsletter. Membership $26/yr. For meeting information call Sue Anne Cress 856-797-8601 (leave message). Check website for local meetings. *Website:* http://www.tops.org

CAMDEN

Overeaters Anonymous 12-Step. Fellowship who meet to help one another understand and overcome their common problem of compulsive overeating. For local meetings call the Overeaters Anonymous South Jersey Intergroup 609-239-0022.

TOPS (Take Off Pounds Sensibly) Helps overweight persons lose weight through medical supervision, competition and group process. Open to children 7 years and older. Phone network, buddy system, peer-counseling and newsletter. Membership $26/yr. For meeting information call Sue Anne Cress 856-797-8601 (leave message). Check website for local meetings. *Website:* http://www.tops.org

CAPE MAY

Bariatric Bodies *Professionally-run.* Support and education to promote healthy lifestyles for post-bariatric patients. Topics include nutrition and exercise. Rap sessions, guest speakers, literature and buddy system. Building is handicapped accessible. Meetings vary, 6:30-7:30pm, Cape May County Library, Bayshore Rd., Lower Division, Villas. Before attending call Susan Shropshire, RN 856-641-8398 (day) or Deena Snyder 609-889-6607 (day).

Overeaters Anonymous 12-Step. Fellowship who meet to help one another understand and overcome their common problem of compulsive overeating. For local meetings call the Overeaters Anonymous Jersey Shore Intergroup at 609-698-0244.

TOPS (Take Off Pounds Sensibly) Helps overweight persons lose weight through medical supervision, competition and group process. Open to children 7 years and older. Phone network, buddy system, peer-counseling and newsletter. Membership $26/yr. For meeting information call Sue Anne Cress 856-797-8601 (leave message). Check website for local meetings. *Website:* http://www.tops.org

CUMBERLAND

Gastric Bypass Support Group *Professionally-run.* Mutual support for those who have or are planning to have gastric bypass surgery. Under 18 welcome. Rap sessions. Meets 4th Wed., 7pm, South Jersey Healthcare, Fitness Connection, 1430 W. Sherman Ave., Vineland. Call Susan 856-641-8398 (day).

Overeaters Anonymous 12-Step. Fellowship who meet to help one another understand and overcome their common problem of compulsive overeating. For local meetings call the Overeaters Anonymous South Jersey Intergroup 609-239-0022.

South Jersey Healthcare "Graduate" Support Group *Professionally-run.* Support and education for patients 12-60+ months post-op bariatric (weight loss) surgery. Topics include staying on or getting back on track, weight management, coping skills and lifestyle adjustments. Guest speakers and phone help. Building is handicapped accessible. Meets 2nd Wed., 7-8pm, Fitness Connection, Orchard Rd. and Sherman Ave., 2nd Floor, Conference Room, Vineland. Call Susan Shropshire, RN, CBN 856-641-8398 (day). *E-mail:* shropshires@sjhs.com

South Jersey Healthcare Information Support Group *Professionally-run.* Support and education for pre-op patients and those seeking information about bariatric (weight loss) surgery. Guest speakers and phone help. Building is handicapped accessible. Meets 4th Wed., 7-8pm, Fitness Connection, Orchard Rd. and Sherman Ave., 2nd Floor, Conference Room, Vineland. Call Susan Shropshire, RN, CBN 856-641-8398 (day). *E-mail:* shropshires@sjhs.com

South Jersey Healthcare "New Beginnings" Support Group *Professionally-run.* Support and education for patients up to 12 months post-op bariatric (weight loss) surgery. Topics include healthy eating, changing habits, emotional issues and exercise. Guest speakers, literature and phone help. Building is handicapped accessible. Meets 1st Wed., 7-8pm, Fitness Connection, Orchard Rd. and Sherman Ave., 2nd Floor, Conference Room, Vineland. Call Susan Shropshire, RN, CBN 856-641-8398 (day). *E-mail:* shropshires@sjhs.com

TOPS (Take Off Pounds Sensibly) Helps overweight persons lose weight through medical supervision, competition and group process. Open to children 7 years and older. Phone network, buddy system, peer-counseling and newsletter. Membership $26/yr. For meeting information call Sue Anne Cress 856-797-8601 (leave message). Check website for local meetings. *Website:* http://www.tops.org

ESSEX

Food Addicts Anonymous 12-Step. Fellowship to recover from food addiction. Primary purpose is to maintain abstinence from sugar, flour and wheat. Meets Sun., 7:30-8:30pm, St. Peter's Episcopal Church, 94 East Mount Pleasant Ave., Livingston. Call Roger 908-403-6535 or Lisa 973-403-0333 (day).

Overeaters Anonymous 12-Step. Fellowship who meet to help one another understand and overcome their common problem of compulsive overeating. For local meeting information by day of week call 973-746-8787.

TOPS (Take Off Pounds Sensibly) Helps overweight persons lose weight through medical supervision, competition and group process. Open to children 7 years and older. Phone network, buddy system, peer-counseling and newsletter. Membership $26/yr. For meeting information call Sue Anne Cress 856-797-8601 (leave message). Check website for local meetings. *Website:* http://www.tops.org

GLOUCESTER

Overeaters Anonymous 12-Step. Fellowship who meet to help one another understand and overcome their common problem of compulsive overeating. For information on local meetings call the Overeaters Anonymous South Jersey Intergroup 609-239-0022.

South Jersey Bariatric Support System Support for persons who have had gastric bypass or are considering the procedure. Families welcome. Rap sessions, online support and literature. Building is handicapped accessible. Meets every other Wed., 7pm, Gloucester County Office of Education, 1492 Tanyard Rd., Sewell. For meeting information call Chrissie 856-256-9066 (day). *E-mail:* sjbss@verizon.net

TOPS (Take Off Pounds Sensibly) Helps overweight persons lose weight through medical supervision, competition and group process. Open to children 7 years and older. Phone network, buddy system, peer-counseling and newsletter. Membership $26/yr. For meeting information call Sue Anne Cress 856-797-

8601 (leave message). Check website for local meetings. *Website:* http://www.tops.org

HUDSON

Laparoscopic Gastric Band or Laparoscopic Gastric Bypass *Professionally-run.* Support and education for persons who have had laparoscopic gastric band or laparoscopic gastric bypass surgery. Meets 3rd Wed., 6pm (except Aug. and Dec.), Knights of Columbus, 669 Ave. C and 30th St., Bayonne. Pre-registration required. Before attending call 973-437-8020 (day). Website: http://www.myprogramforlife.com

Overeaters Anonymous 12-Step. Fellowship who meet to help one another understand and overcome their common problem of compulsive overeating. For local meeting information by day of week call 973-746-8787.

HUNTERDON

Overeaters Anonymous 12-Step. Fellowship who meet to help one another understand and overcome their common problem of compulsive overeating. For local meeting information call the Overeaters Anonymous Central Intergroup 908-253-3464 or 732-634-6695.

TOPS (Take Off Pounds Sensibly) Helps overweight persons lose weight through medical supervision, competition and group process. Open to children 7 years and older. Phone network, buddy system, peer-counseling and newsletter. Membership $26/yr. For meeting information call Sue Anne Cress 856-797-8601 (leave message). Check website for local meetings. *Website:* http://www.tops.org

MERCER

Bariatric Surgery Weight Loss Support Group *Professionally-run.* Support and education for persons who have had bariatric surgery (gastric bypass or lap band) or are considering the procedure. Building is handicapped accessible. Meets 3rd Thurs., 6-8pm, Robert Wood Johnson Center for Health and Wellness, 3100 Quakerbridge Rd., Hamilton. Pre-registration required. Before attending call 609-584-5900 (day).

Overeaters Anonymous 12-Step. Fellowship who meet to help one another understand and overcome their common problem of compulsive overeating. For local meetings call the Overeaters Anonymous Central Intergroup 732-634-6695.

TOPS (Take Off Pounds Sensibly) Helps overweight persons lose weight through medical supervision, competition and group process. Open to children 7 years and older. Phone network, buddy system, peer-counseling and newsletter. Membership $26/yr. For meeting information call Sue Anne Cress 856-797-8601 (leave message). Check website for local meetings. *Website:* http://www.tops.org

MIDDLESEX

Laparoscopic Gastric Band or Laparoscopic Gastric Bypass *Professionally-run.* Support and education for persons who have had laparoscopic gastric band or laparoscopic gastric bypass surgery. Meets 2nd Thurs., 6pm, St. Peter's University Hospital, 254 Easton Ave., New Brunswick. Pre-registration required. Before attending call 973-437-8020 (day). Website: http://www.myprogramforlife.com

NJ Bariatrics Lap Band Support Group *Professionally-run.* Mutual support and education for persons who have had lap band surgery or are considering the procedure. Guest speakers, literature and phone help. Meets 1st Wed., 7pm, NJ Bariatrics, 666 Plainsboro Rd., Building 600, Suite 640, Plainsboro. Pre-registration required. Before attending call Donna 609-785-5870 (day).

NJ Bariatrics Support Group *Professionally-run.* Mutual support and education for persons who have had gastric bypass surgery or are considering the procedure. Guest speakers, literature and phone help. Meets 1st Mon., 7pm, Old Bridge. Pre-registration required. Before attending call Donna 609-785-5870 (day).

Overeaters Anonymous 12-Step. Fellowship who meet to help one another understand and overcome their common problem of compulsive overeating. For local meeting information call the Overeaters Anonymous Central Intergroup 908-253-3464 or 732-634-6695.

SMART Recovery (Self-Management Recovery Training) *Professionally-run.* Self-help group for individuals wanting to gain their independence from addictive behaviors (drugs, alcohol, nicotine and other compulsive behaviors including gambling and eating disorders). SMART is a abstinence program based on cognitive-behavioral education and principles, especially those of rational-emotive behavior therapy. Building is handicapped accessible. Meets Thurs., 6-7:30pm, Rutgers University, 152 Frelinghuysen Rd., Busch Campus, Psychology Building, Room A340, 2nd Floor, Piscataway. Call Ayelet Kattan 732-445-6111 ext. 871 (day).

TOPS (Take Off Pounds Sensibly) Helps overweight persons lose weight through medical supervision, competition and group process. Open to children 7 years and older. Phone network, buddy system, peer-counseling and newsletter. Membership $26/yr. For meeting information call Sue Anne Cress 856-797-8601 (leave message). Check website for local meetings. *Website:* http://www.tops.org

MONMOUTH

Bariatric Angels *Professionally-run.* Mutual support for bariatric surgery patients using a 12-step program. Education, advocacy, rap sessions, buddy system, socials, newsletter and phone help. Pre-surgery individuals are welcome 1st meeting of each month. Meets Fri., 8pm; Sat., 10am (surgery less than 4 months) and 11am (surgery more than 4 months) Angels Cove Retreat, 164 West Front St., Keyport. Pre-registration required. Before attending call Kate Fenimore 732-203-2322 (eve.).

Bariatric Surgery Support Group *Professionally-run.* Support for individuals who have undergone gastric bypass surgery or to those considering surgery. Meets 4th Thurs., 7-9pm (3rd Thurs., Nov. and Dec.), Monmouth Medical Center, 300 Second Ave., Long Branch. Registration is required. Before attending call 1-888-724-7123 (day).

Overeaters Anonymous 12-Step. Fellowship who meet to help one another understand and overcome their common problem of compulsive overeating. For local meeting information call Overeaters Anonymous Central Jersey Intergroup 908-253-3464 or 732-634-6695.

TOPS (Take Off Pounds Sensibly) Helps overweight persons lose weight through medical supervision, competition and group process. Open to children 7 years and older. Phone network, buddy system, peer-counseling and newsletter. Membership $26/yr. For meeting information call Sue Anne Cress 856-797-8601 (leave message). Check website for local meetings. *Website:* http://www.tops.org

MORRIS

Band Support Group *Professionally-run.* Mutual support for those who have had or are planning to have adjustable gastric band surgery. Families welcome. Rap sessions, advocacy and guest speakers. Meets last Wed., 7-8pm, 147 Columbia Turnpike, Suite 301, Florham Park. Call Jennifer Levine 973-410-0452.

Food Addicts in Recovery Anonymous 12-Step. Fellowship of those recovering from the disease of food addiction, obesity, anorexia and bulimia. Building is handicapped accessible. Meets Sat., 9-10:30am, Saint Clare's Hospital, 400 West Blackwell St., Conference Room C, Dover. Call Joe 201-704-0931 (day). *Website:* http://www.foodaddicts.org

Gastric Band Support Group *Professionally-run.* Support for those who have undergone, or are considering gastric band surgery. Literature and phone help. Meets 4th Wed., 7:15-8:15pm, St. Clares Hospital Dover, Sister Catherine Health Center, 400 West Blackwell St., Dover. Call Cheryl Iannicelli 973-989-3805 (day) or Pat Kanya 973-989-3644 (day).

Gastric Bypass Support Group *Professionally-run.* Support for those who have undergone, or are considering gastric bypass surgery. Literature and phone help. Meets 4th Wed., 6-7pm, St. Clare's Hospital Dover, Sister Catherine Health Center, 400 West Blackwell St., Dover. Call Cheryl Iannicelli 973-989-3805 (day) or Pat Kanya 973-989-3644 (day).

Overeaters Anonymous 12-Step. Fellowship who meet to help one another understand and overcome their common problem of compulsive overeating. For local meeting information by day of week call 973-746-8787.

SMART Recovery (Self-Management And Recovery Training) Self-help group for individuals wanting to gain their independence from addictive behaviors (alcohol, drugs, nicotine and other compulsive behaviors including gambling and eating disorders). SMART is a abstinence program based on cognitive-behavioral education and principles, especially those of rational-emotive behavior therapy. Meets Thurs., 7-8:30pm, Family Services, 62 Elm St., Morristown. Call Rich 973-983-8755 or Glenn 973-255-7296. *Website:* http://www.smartrecovery.org

TOPS (Take Off Pounds Sensibly) Helps overweight persons lose weight through medical supervision, competition and group process. Open to children 7 years and older. Phone network, buddy system, peer-counseling and newsletter. Membership $26/yr. For meeting information call Sue Anne Cress 856-797-8601 (leave message). Check website for local meetings. *Website:* http://www.tops.org

"Confront your fears, list them, get to know them, and only then will you be able to put them aside and move ahead." --Jerry Gillies

OCEAN

Food Addicts Anonymous 12-Step. Fellowship to recover from food addiction. Primary purpose is to maintain abstinence from sugar, flour and wheat. Call Phyllis 732-244-4324 (Mon. group) or Barbara 732-864-9611 (Thurs. group).

> **Brick** Meets Mon., 11am and Thurs., 7:30pm, First Baptist Church of Laurelton, 1824 Route 88 East.
>
> **Toms River** Meets Thurs., 11am, Presbyterian Church of Toms River, Hooper Ave. and Chestnut St. (use back entrance).

Overcomers In Christ Recovery program that deals with every aspect of addiction and dysfunction (spiritual, physical, mental, emotional and social). Uses Overcomers goals which are Christ-centered. Resources, literature, information and referrals. Meets Mon., 7-8:30pm, America's Keswick, 601 Route 530, Whiting. Separate groups for men and women. Women's group call Diane Hunt 732-350-1187 ext. 47. Men's group call Chaplain Jim Freed 732-350-1187 ext. 43. *Website:* http://www.americaskeswick.org

Overeaters Anonymous 12-Step. Fellowship who meet to help one another understand and overcome their common problem of compulsive overeating. For information on local meetings call Jersey Shore Intergroup 609-698-0244.

Thursday Night Recovery Support to help overcome dependencies and addictions through accountability, encouragement and spiritual development. Meets Thurs., 7-8:30pm, Shore Vineyard Church, 320 Compass Ave., Beachwood. Call 732-244-3888 (day).

TOPS (Take Off Pounds Sensibly) Helps overweight persons lose weight through medical supervision, competition and group process. Open to children 7 years and older. Phone network, buddy system, peer-counseling and newsletter. Membership $26/yr. For meeting information call Sue Anne Cress 856-797-8601 (leave message). Check website for local meetings. *Website:* http://www.tops.org

PASSAIC

Food Addicts in Recovery Anonymous 12-Step. Fellowship of those recovering from the disease of food addiction, obesity, anorexia and bulimia. Meets Sun., 8-9:30am, Eva's Village, 393 Main St., Paterson. Call Naomi 201-265-6917. *Website:* http://www.foodaddicts.org

Overeaters Anonymous 12-Step. Fellowship who meet to help one another understand and overcome their common problem of compulsive overeating. For local meeting information by day of week call 973-746-8787.

TOPS (Take Off Pounds Sensibly) Helps overweight persons lose weight through medical supervision, competition and group process. Open to children 7 years and older. Phone network, buddy system, peer-counseling and newsletter. Membership $26/yr. For meeting information call Sue Anne Cress 856-797-8601 (leave message). Check website for local meetings. *Website:* http://www.tops.org

SALEM

Overeaters Anonymous 12-Step. Fellowship who meet to help one another understand and overcome their common problem of compulsive overeating. For information on local meetings call the Overeaters Anonymous South Jersey Intergroup 609-239-0022.

TOPS (Take Off Pounds Sensibly) Helps overweight persons lose weight through medical supervision, competition and group process. Open to children 7 years and older. Phone network, buddy system, peer-counseling and newsletter. Membership $26/yr. For meeting information call Sue Anne Cress 856-797-8601 (leave message). Check website for local meetings. *Website:* http://www.tops.org

SOMERSET

Bariatric Angels *Professionally-run.* Mutual support for bariatric surgery patients using a 12-step program. Education, advocacy, rap sessions, buddy system, socials, newsletter and phone help. Pre-surgery individuals are welcome 1st meeting of each month. Meets Tues., 7pm (surgery less than 4 months) and 8pm (surgery more than 4 months), Presbyterian Church of Bound Brook, 950 Mountain Ave. and Route 28 (Union Ave.), Bound Brook. Pre-registration required. Before attending call Kate Fenimore 732-203-2322 (eve.).

Overeaters Anonymous 12-Step. Fellowship who meet to help one another understand and overcome their common problem of compulsive overeating. For local meeting information call Overeaters Anonymous Central Intergroup 908-253-3464 or 732-634-6695.

SUSSEX

Overeaters Anonymous 12-Step. Fellowship who meet to help one another understand and overcome their common problem of compulsive overeating. For local meeting information by day of week call 973-746-8787.

TOPS (Take Off Pounds Sensibly) Helps overweight persons lose weight through medical supervision, competition and group process. Open to children 7 years and older. Phone network, buddy system, peer-counseling and newsletter. Membership $26/yr. For meeting information call Sue Anne Cress 856-797-8601 (leave message). Check website for local meetings. *Website:* http://www.tops.org

UNION

Food Addicts Anonymous 12-Step. Fellowship to recover from food addiction. Primary purpose is to maintain abstinence from sugar, flour and wheat. Meets Mon., 8pm, Clark Public Library, 303 Westfield Ave., Board Room, 2nd Floor, Clark. Call Phyllis 732-244-4324. *Website:* http://www.foodaddictsanonymous.org

Overeaters Anonymous 12-Step. Fellowship who meet to help one another understand and overcome their common problem of compulsive overeating. For local meeting information by day of week call 908-253-3464.

WARREN

Overeaters Anonymous 12-Step. Fellowship who meet to help one another understand and overcome their common problem of compulsive overeating. For local meeting information by day of week call 973-746-8787.

TOPS (Take Off Pounds Sensibly) Helps overweight persons lose weight through medical supervision, competition and group process. Open to children 7 years and older. Phone network, buddy system, peer-counseling and newsletter. Membership $26/yr. For meeting information call Sue Anne Cress 856-797-8601 (leave message). Check website for local meetings. *Website:* http://www.tops.org

NATIONAL

Compulsive Eaters Anonymous - H.O.W. *International. 500 affiliated groups. Founded 1985.* 12-Step. Fellowship to share experience, strength and hope in order to help themselves and others who suffer from the self-destruction of compulsive eating. H.O.W. (Honesty, Open-mindedness and Willingness) groups use a food plan which includes an abstinence of sugar and flour. Plan allows only three weighed and measured meals per day. Write: Compulsive Eaters Anonymous - H.O.W., 5500 E. Atherton St., Suite 227 B, Long Beach, CA 90815-4017. Call 562-342-9344 (Mon.-Fri., 9am-1pm PST). *Website:* http://www.ceahow.org *E-mail:* gso@ceahow.org

Eating Addictions Anonymous -SANE Fellowship *National. 6 affiliated chapters.* 12-Step. Recovery program for men and women recovering from all forms of eating and body image addictions. Includes anorexia, bulimia, binge eating, overeating, exercise bulimics, etc. Focuses on internal growth and reclaiming bodies rather than weight or appearance. Write: Eating Addictions Anonymous, P.O. Box 8151, Silver Spring, MD 20907-8151. Call 202-882-6528. *Website:* http://www.eatingaddictionsanonymous.org *E-mail:* 12n12@tidalwave.net

Eating Disorders Anonymous *International. Founded 2000.* Fellowship of men and women who share their experience, strength and hope with each other that they may solve their common problems and help others to recover from their eating disorders. Focuses on the solution; not the problem. Endorses sound nutrition. Pen pals, phone support, literature, information and referrals. Assistance in starting groups. Offers local support group referrals online. Write: General Service Board of Eating Disorders Anonymous, P.O. Box 55876, Phoenix, AZ 85078-5876. *Website:* http://www.eatingdisordersanonymous.org

Food Addicts Anonymous *International. 146 affiliated groups worldwide. Founded 1987.* 12-Step. Fellowship of men and women who are willing to recover from the disease of food addiction. Primary purpose is to maintain abstinence from sugar, flour and wheat. Pen pals, online chatroom, e-mail loop, phone meetings, conferences, information and referral. Assistance in starting groups. Online listing of local support groups. Write: Food Addicts Anonymous, 4623 Forest Hill Blvd., Suite 109-4, W. Palm Beach, FL 33415. Call 561-967-3871; Fax: 561-967-9815. *Website:* http://www.foodaddictsanonymous.org *E-mail:* info@foodaddictsanonymous.org

Food Addicts In Recovery Anonymous *International. Founded 1998.* A 12-step fellowship addressing all forms of food addiction, e.g. undereating, overeating and bulimia through purging and/or exercise. FA members are all ages and walks of life. Literature, phone support, assistance in starting new groups and on-line listing of meetings. Write: Food Addicts Anonymous, 400 West Cummings Park, Suite 1700, Woburn, MA 01801. Call 781-932-6300; Fax: 781-932-6322. *Website:* http://www.foodaddicts.org *E-mail:* fa@foodaddicts.org

Intercongregational Addictions Program (ICAP) *International. Founded 1979.* Network of recovering alcoholic women in religious orders. Helps Roman Catholic women who are or have been members of religious orders and are alcoholic or chemically dependent, compulsive eaters, compulsive gamblers, etc. Information, referrals, assistance in meeting other members, phone support, conferences and e-mail support. Write: ICAP, 7777 Lake St., Suite 115, River Forest, IL 60305-1734. Call 708-488-9770; Fax: 708-488-9774. *E-mail:* icapsrs@sbcglobal.net

National Association to Advance Fat Acceptance (NAAFA) *National. 50 chapters. Founded 1969.* Fights size discrimination and provides fat people with the tools for self-empowerment. Public education regarding obesity. Provides a forum for peer support and activism. Dues $35 (includes newsletter), educational materials, group development guidelines and annual convention. Special interest groups include: youth, families, gays, diabetics, men, women, sleep apnea, military, mental health professionals and couples. Write: National Association to Advance Fat Acceptance, P.O. Box 22510, Oakland, CA 94609. Call 916-558-6880. *Website:* http://www.naafa.org

Overcomers In Christ *International. Founded 1987.* Recovery program that deals with every aspect of addiction and dysfunction (spiritual, physical, mental, emotional and social). Uses Overcomers goals which are Christ-centered. Resources, literature, information and referrals. Assistance in starting new groups. Write: Overcomers In Christ, P.O. Box 34460, Omaha, NE 68134-0460. Call 1-866-573-0966 or 402-573-0966. *Website:* http://www.overcomersinchrist.org *E-mail:* oic@overcomersinchrist.org

Overcomers Outreach, Inc. *International. 700 affiliated groups. Founded 1985.* 12-Step. Christ-centered support group for anyone affected by addictions, as well as their families and friends. Uses 12-steps of A.A. and applies them to the Scriptures. Uses Jesus Christ as "higher power." Supplements involvement in other 12-step groups. Newsletter, group development guidelines and conferences. Write: Overcomers Outreach, Inc., P.O. Box 2204, Oakhurst, CA 93644. Call 1-800-310-3001. *Website:* http://www.overcomersoutreach.org *E-mail:* info@overcomersoutreach.org

Overeaters Anonymous *International. 6500 groups. Founded 1960.* A 12-step fellowship of men and women who meet to help one another understand and overcome compulsive eating. Also groups and literature for young persons and teens. Monthly magazine, literature and group development guidelines. Write: Overeaters Anonymous, P.O. Box 44020, Rio Rancho, New Mexico 87174-4020. Call 505-891-2664 or look in white pages for local number; Fax: 505-891-4320. *Website:* http://www.oa.org *E-mail:* info@oa.org

Recoveries Anonymous *International. 50 chapters.* Spiritual recovery group for anyone seeking a solution for any kind of addiction, problem or behavior. Family and friends welcome. "How To Begin..." guides and "Start A Group" kit can be downloaded free from the website. Write: R.A. Universal Services, P.O. Box 1212, East Northport, NY 11731. *Website:* http://www.r-a.org *E-mail:* raus@r-a.org

T.O.P.S. (Take Off Pounds Sensibly) *International. 10,000 chapters. Founded 1948.* Members use professionally prepared materials on menu planning, food exchanges, motivation and exercise. Promotes a sensible approach to managing weight as a life choice. Weekly meetings emphasize recognition and support. Newsletter, tools for weight management and chapter development. New chapters may be started by a minimum of four people. Support group locations available online. Dues $24/USA; $30/Canada. Write: TOPS, 4575 South 5th St., Milwaukee, WI 53207. Call 1-800-932-8677. *Website:* http://www.tops.org

SEX / LOVE ADDICTION

STATEWIDE

New Jersey/Delaware Valley Sexaholics Anonymous Intergroup Mutual support for those who want to stop their sexually self-destructive thinking and behavior to become sexually sober. Several meeting locations throughout NJ. Call 1-888-258-6104. *Website:* http://www.sa.org

BERGEN

S-Anon 12-Step. Offers support for family members and the loved ones of those who are sexually addicted. Literature, phone help and newsletter. Donation $2. Meets Tues., 7:30-8:30pm, First Presbyterian Church, 64 Passaic St., Hackensack. Call Phil 973-773-0291.

Sexaholics Anonymous Mutual support for those who want to stop their sexually self-destructive thinking and behavior to become sexually sober. For information call NJ Intergroup 1-888-258-6104. *Website:* http://www.njessay.org

> **Teaneck** Meets Tues., Wed. and Fri., 7am, Church of St. Anastasia, 1095 Teaneck Rd.
> **Wyckoff** Meets Tues., 7pm, Bethany Church, 568 Wellington Dr., Cornerstone Room.

BURLINGTON

S-Anon 12-Step. Offers support for family members and the loved ones of those who are sexually addicted. Literature. Building is handicapped accessible. Meets Mon., 7:30-8:30pm, Prince of Peace Lutheran Church, 61 Route 70 East, Marlton. Call 856-751-3545 (day).

S-Anon Couples Group 12-Step. Offers support for couples dealing with a sexual addiction. Building is handicapped accessible. Meets 3rd Sat., 7:30pm, Prince of Peace Lutheran Church, 61 Route 70 East, Marlton. Call 856-751-3545 (day).

CAMDEN

Sexaholics Anonymous Mutual support for those who want to stop their sexually self-destructive thinking and behavior to become sexually sober. For information call NJ Intergroup 1-888-258-6104. *Website:* http://www.njessay.org
> **Cherry Hill** Meets Thurs., 7pm, Kennedy Memorial Hospital, 2201 Chapel Ave. West.
> **Westmont** Meets Sat., 8am, Starting Point Inc., 215 Highland Ave.

S.L.A.A. (Sex and Love Addicts Anonymous) 12-Step. Fellowship for those who desire to stop living out a pattern of sex and love addiction, compulsive sexual behavior or emotional attachment.
> **Cherry Hill** Meets Sun., 7pm; Tues., 7:30pm and Sat., 7pm, Kennedy Memorial Hospital, 2201 Chapel Ave. West. Call Ken 856-235-1018 (Sun. and Tues. mtg.) or Melissa 856-745-4844 (Sat. mtg.).
> **Gibbsboro** Meets Mon., 7:30pm, St. Andrew the Apostle Church, Gibbsboro-Kresson Rd. Call Michael 856-534-8453.

ESSEX

Sexaholics Anonymous Mutual support for those who want to stop their sexually self-destructive thinking and behavior to become sexually sober. Meets Thurs., 8pm, Unitarian Church, 67 Church St., Montclair. For information call NJ Intergroup 1-888-258-6104. *Website:* http://www.njessay.org

S.L.A.A. (Sex and Love Addicts Anonymous) 12-Step. Fellowship for those who desire to stop living out a pattern of sex and love addiction, compulsive sexual behavior or emotional attachment. Meets Mon., Wed. and Fri., 7:30pm (beginners) and 8:30pm (regular), First Lutheran Church, Clark St., Montclair. Call George 973-481-5267.

HUDSON

Hoboken S.A.A. (Serenity Acceptance Affirmation) 12-Step. Support group for anyone concerned about their own addictive or compulsive sexual behavior. Meets Sun., 7-8:30pm, St. Matthew Trinity Lutheran Parish Center, 8th St. and Washington St., Hoboken. Call Dave 201-459-8858. *Website:* http://www.saa-recovery.org

Sexaholics Anonymous Mutual support for those who want to stop their sexually self-destructive thinking and behavior to become sexually sober. Meets Tues., 7:30pm, Mt. Carmel Guild Catholic Services, 249 Virginia Ave., Jersey City. For information call NJ Intergroup 1-888-258-6104. *Website:* http://www.njessay.org

MIDDLESEX

Sexaholics Anonymous Mutual support for those who want to stop their sexually self-destructive thinking and behavior to become sexually sober. Meets Sun., 5pm and Wed., 7:30pm, St. Luke's Episcopal Church, Oak Ave., Metuchen. For information call NJ Intergroup 1-888-258-6104. *Website:* http://www.njessay.org

MONMOUTH

S-Anon Offers support for family members and the loved ones of those who are sexually addicted. Meets Mon., 7:30pm and Thurs., 11:30am, United Methodist Church, Broad St., Red Bank. Before attending call Lisa 732-610-6400.

"All of us are, to some extent, victims of what we are. We are not limited by our imaginations, but by our ability to do what we imagine. We are not too often limited by our abilities as much as by circumstances. And we are not as often limited by our circumstances as much as by the lack of the will to respond."--Dee Bowman

Sexaholics Anonymous Mutual support for those who want to stop their sexually self-destructive thinking and behavior to become sexually sober. For information call NJ Intergroup 1-888-258-6104. *Website:* http://www.orgsites.com/nj/sa

> **Kingston** Meets Wed. and Sat., 7am, United Methodist Church, 9 Church St., Anderson House (end of path behind church).
> **Lincroft** Meets Mon., 7pm, St. Leo's Church, Hurley's Lane.
> **Neptune** Meets Fri., 7:30pm, Jersey Shore Medical Center, Route 33 West.
> **Red Bank** Meets Sun., 8am, Riverview Medical Center, Blazedale Bldg., 5th Floor Auditorium, Riverview Plaza.
> **Red Bank** Meets Wed., 12:30pm, First Baptist Church, 84 Maple Ave.
> **West Long Branch** Meets Tues., 7:30pm, West Long Branch Community Center, 116 Locust Ave.

MORRIS

S-Anon Support for family members and loved ones of those who are sexually addicted. Donation $2/mtg. Meets Mon., 8-9pm, St. John's Episcopal Church, 11 South Bergen St., Dover. Call Barbara 973-659-0901.

Sexaholics Anonymous Mutual support for those who want to stop their sexually self-destructive thinking and behavior to become sexually sober. For information call NJ Intergroup 1-888-258-6104. *Website:* http://www.njessay.org

> **Dover** Meets Mon., 8pm, St. John's Episcopal Church, 11 South Bergen St.
> **Morris Plains** Meets Tues., Thurs. and Fri., noon, St. Paul's Episcopal Church, Hillview Ave. and Mountain Way.

S.L.A.A. (Sex and Love Addictions Anonymous) 12-Step. Fellowship for those who desire to stop living out a pattern of sex and love addiction, compulsive sexual behavior or emotional attachment. Meets Tues., Thurs. and Sat., 7:30-8:45pm, Morristown Memorial Hospital, 100 Madison Ave., Franklin Wing, Room F571, Morristown. Call Lee 908-876-4081.

OCEAN

Overcomers In Christ Recovery program that deals with every aspect of addiction and dysfunction (spiritual, physical, mental, emotional and social). Uses Overcomers goals which are Christ-centered. Resources, literature, information and referrals. Meets Mon., 7-8:30pm, America's Keswick, 601 Route 530, Whiting. Separate groups for men and women. Women's group call

Diane Hunt 732-350-1187 ext. 47. Men's group call Chaplain Jim Freed 732-350-1187 ext. 43. *Website:* http://www.americaskeswick.org

Sexaholics Anonymous Mutual support for those who want to stop their sexually self-destructive thinking and behavior to become sexually sober. For information call NJ Intergroup 1-888-258-6104. *Website:* http://www.njessay.org

> **Beachwood** Meets Tues., 8pm, St. Paul Lutheran Church, 130 Cable Ave.
>
> **Toms River** Meets Sat., 9:30am, Presbyterian Church of Toms River, 1070 Hooper Ave.

PASSAIC

Sexaholics Anonymous Mutual support for those who want to stop their sexually self-destructive thinking and behavior to become sexually sober. Meets Mon., 7:30pm and Sat., 7:30am, United Methodist Church, 139 Main St., Little Falls. For information call NJ Intergroup 1-888-258-6104. *Website:* http://www.njessay.org

SOMERSET

Freedom Group 12-Step. Christ-based support group for men wanting freedom from being sexually driven. Confidential. Rap sessions, phone help, literature and guest speakers. Meetings vary, Millington Baptist Church, 520 King George Rd., Basking Ridge. Before attending call Millington Baptist Church 908-647-0594 ext. 27.

S.L.A.A. (Sex and Love Addicts Anonymous) 12-Step. Fellowship for those who desire to stop living out a pattern of sex and love addiction, compulsive sexual behavior or emotional attachment. Meets Sun., 8pm, Bound Brook Presbyterian Church, 409 Mountain Ave. and E. Union Ave., Bound Brook. Call Steve 908-413-2470.

"How can we communicate love? I think three things are involved. We must reach out to a person, make contact. We must listen with the heart, be sensitive to the other's needs. We must respond in a language that the person can understand. Many of us do all the talking. We must learn to listen and to keep on listening."--Princess Pale Moon

UNION

Sexaholics Anonymous Mutual support for those who want to stop their sexually self-destructive thinking and behavior to become sexually sober. For information call NJ Intergroup 1-888-258-6104. *Website:* http://www.njessay.org

> **Cranford** Meets Mon. and Wed., 7:15am; Mon., Tues., Thurs. and Fri., noon; Fri., 8pm; Sat., 7:30pm and Sun., 1:30pm, Cranford United Methodist Church, 201 Lincoln Ave.
>
> **Elizabeth** Meets Sat., noon, St. Mary's of the Assumption Church, 155 Washington Ave.

NATIONAL

COSA (Codependents Of Sex Addicts) *International. 50+ affiliated groups. Founded 1980.* Self-help program of recovery using the 12 steps adapted from A.A. Al-Anon, for those involved in relationships with people who have compulsive sexual behavior. Assistance in starting new groups. Newsletter ($24). Write: COSA, Inc., P.O. Box 14537, Minneapolis, MN 55414. Call 763-537-6904 (answering service - leave message). *Website:* http://www.cosa-recovery.org *E-mail:* info@cosa-recovery.org

Overcomers In Christ *International. Founded 1987.* Recovery program that deals with every aspect of addiction and dysfunction (spiritual, physical, mental, emotional and social). Uses Overcomers goals which are Christ-centered. Resources, literature, information and referrals. Assistance in starting new groups. Write: Overcomers In Christ, P.O. Box 34460, Omaha, NE 68134-0460. Call 1-866-573-0966 or 402-573-0966. *Website:* http://www.overcomersinchrist.org *E-mail:* oic@overcomersinchrist.org

Overcomers Outreach, Inc. *International. 700 affiliated groups. Founded 1985.* 12-Step. Christ-centered support group for anyone affected by addictions, as well as their families and friends. Uses 12-steps of A.A. and applies them to the Scriptures. Uses Jesus Christ as "higher power." Supplements involvement in other 12-step groups. Newsletter, group development guidelines and conferences. Write: Overcomers Outreach, Inc., P.O. Box 922950, Sylmar, CA 91392-2950. Call 1-800-310-3001. *Website:* http://www.overcomersoutreach.org *E-mail:* info@overcomersoutreach.org

Recoveries Anonymous *International. 50 chapters.* Spiritual recovery group for anyone seeking a solution for any kind of addition, problem or behavior. Family and friends welcome. "How To Begin..." guides and "Start A Group" kit can be downloaded free from the website. Write: R.A. Universal Services, P.O. Box

1212, East Northport, NY 11731. *Website:* http://www.r-a.org *E-mail:* raus@r-a.org

S-Anon International. *280 affiliated groups. Founded 1984.* 12-Step. Support group for persons who have a friend or family member with a sexual addiction. Assistance available for starting groups. Conferences and quarterly newsletter ($14). Write: S-Anon, P.O. Box 111242, Nashville, TN 37222. Call 1-800-210-8141. *Website:* http://www.sanon.org *E-mail:* sanon@sanon.org

Sex Addicts Anonymous *International. 736 groups. Founded 1977.* 12-Step. Fellowship of men and women who share their experience, strength and hope with each other so they may overcome their sexual addiction or dependency. Open to all who share a desire to stop compulsive sexual dependency. Bimonthly newsletter. Write: International Service Organization of SAA, P.O. Box 70949, Houston, TX 77270. Call 713-869-4902 or 1-800-477-8191 (Mon.-Fri., 10am-6pm CST). *Website:* http://www.saa-recovery.org *E-mail:* info@saa-recovery.org

Sexaholics Anonymous *International. 700 chapters. Founded 1979.* Program of recovery for those who want to stop their sexually self-destructive thinking and behavior. Mutual support to achieve and maintain sexual sobriety. Phone network, quarterly newsletter, literature and books. Guidelines to help start a similar group. Write: S.A., P.O. Box 3565, Brentwood, TN 37024-3565. Call 615-370-6062 or 1-866-424-8777; Fax: 615-370-0882. *Website:* http://www.sa.org *E-mail:* saico@sa.org

Sexual Compulsives Anonymous *(BILINGUAL) International. 118+ groups. Founded 1982.* 12-Step. Fellowship of men and women who share their experience, strength and hope that they may solve their common problem and help others to recover from sexual compulsion. Based on the 12-step model of recovery. Newsletter, information and referrals, phone support and conferences. Guidelines for starting similar groups. Write: Sexual Compulsives Anonymous, P.O. Box 1585, Old Chelsea Station, New York, NY 10011. Call 1-800-977-4325. *Website:* http://www.sca-recovery.org *E-mail:* info@sca-recovery.org

Sexual Recovery Anonymous *International. 32 affiliated groups. Founded 1990.* 12-Step. Fellowship of men and women who share their experience, strength and hope with each other that they may solve their common problem and help others to recover. For those with a desire to stop compulsive sexual behavior. Online referrals, literature and support also available. Write: Sexual Recovery Anonymous, P.O. Box 1296, Redondo Beach, CA 90278. Call 212-340-4650 (leave message for call back); 323-850-8565 (Los Angeles area) or 604-290-9382 (BC, Canada). *Website:* http://www.sexualrecovery.org

SMOKING / NICOTINE
(see also toll-free helplines)

STATEWIDE

Nicotine Anonymous 12-Step. Self-help program of recovery for people who want to help themselves and others recover from nicotine addiction and live free of nicotine in all forms. For meeting information call Bill 201-947-3305. *Website:* http://www.nicotine-anonymous.org

ATLANTIC

Nicotine Anonymous 12-Step. Mutual support for persons wishing to stop smoking and their use of nicotine.
> **Galloway** Meets Tues., 7:45pm, St. Mark's All Saints Episcopal Church, 429 S. Pitney Rd. Call Lori 609-404-4644.
> **Somers Point** Meets Mon., 7pm, Shore Memorial Hospital, Shore Rd., Conference Center. Call Alice 609-748-0747.

BERGEN

Nicotine Anonymous 12-Step. Mutual support for persons wishing to stop smoking and their use of nicotine.
> **Paramus** Meets Wed., 7pm, Valley Hospital, 15 Essex Rd. Call Bill 201-947-3305.
> **Teaneck** Meets Sat., 7pm, St. Mark's Episcopal Church, 118 Chadwick Rd. Call Bill 201-947-3305.

CAMDEN

Nicotine Anonymous 12-Step. Fellowship of men and women who want to achieve and maintain a nicotine-free life. Meets Mon., 7pm, Kennedy Hospital, Chapel Ave., 5th Floor, Cherry Hill. Call Ellie 856-354-0887.

CAPE MAY

Nicotine Anonymous 12-Step. Fellowship of men and women who want to achieve and maintain a nicotine-free life. Meets Sat., 3:30-4:30pm, The Hut, 113 West Oak Ave., Wildwood. Call Joseph 609-729-9145.

CUMBERLAND

Overcomer's Outreach Christian 12-Step. Fellowship to overcome any type of addiction or compulsive behavior, anxiety, depression or loneliness using God's word as a basis of recovery. Bible study, discussion, prayer and phone help. Meets Thurs., 7-8pm, Shiloh Seventh Day Baptist Church, East Ave., Shiloh. Call Frank B. Mulford 856-451-8698 (day) or Rev. Chroniger 856-455-0488 (day). *E-mail:* ahfarm@hotmail.com

MERCER

Nicotine Anonymous 12-Step. Fellowship of men and women who want to achieve and maintain a nicotine-free life.
> **Hamilton** Meets Fri., 7pm, Hamilton Hospital, Library (near Gift Shop), Whitehorse-Hamilton Square Rd. Call Josephine 609-890-9176.
> **Lawrenceville** Meets Fri., 7pm, Lawrence Neighborhood Center, 295 Eggerts Crossing Rd., 2nd Floor. Call Jim 609-771-8157.

MIDDLESEX

Nicotine Anonymous 12-Step. Fellowship of men and women who want to achieve and maintain a nicotine-free life.
> **East Brunswick** Meets Wed., 7pm, Trinity Presbyterian Church, 367 Cranbury Rd. Call Fuzzy 732-742-3836.
> **Metuchen** Meets Mon., 7:30-8:30pm, Centenary United Methodist Church, 200 Hillside Ave., Room 20. Call Frank 732-485-7874.

Overcomer's Outreach Christian 12-Step. Fellowship to overcome any type of addiction or compulsive behavior, anxiety, depression or loneliness using God's word as a basis of recovery. Bible study, discussion, prayer and phone help. Meets Tues., 6:30-7:30pm, Metuchen Assembly of God, 130 Whitman St., Metuchen. Call Janet 732-388-2856 (eve.).

SMART Recovery (Self-Management Recovery Training) *Professionally-run.* Self-help group for individuals wanting to gain their independence from addictive behaviors (drugs, alcohol, nicotine and other compulsive behaviors including gambling and eating disorders). SMART is a abstinence program based on cognitive-behavioral education and principles, especially those of rational-emotive behavior therapy. Building is handicapped accessible. Meets Thurs., 6-7:30pm, Rutgers University, 152 Frelinghuysen Rd., Busch Campus, Psychology Building, Room A340, 2nd Floor, Piscataway. Call Ayelet Kattan 732-445-6111 ext. 871 (day).

MONMOUTH

Smoke Free Support Group *Professionally-run.* Offers support and education for those who are thinking about quitting, recently quit or are struggling to quit smoking. Building is handicapped accessible. Meets 4th Tues., 7-9pm (except June, July, Aug.), Monmouth Medical Center, Community Health Education, 300 Second Ave., Long Branch. Pre-registration required. Before attending call 732-923-6990 (day).

MORRIS

SMART Recovery (Self-Management And Recovery Training) Self-help group for individuals wanting to gain their independence from addictive behaviors (alcohol, drugs, nicotine and other compulsive behaviors including gambling and eating disorders). SMART is a abstinence program based on cognitive-behavioral education and principles, especially those of rational-emotive behavior therapy. Meets Wed., 7-8:30pm, Daily Planit, 150-152 Speedwell Ave., Morristown. Call Rich 973-983-8755 or Glenn 973-255-7296. *Website:* http://www.smartrecovery.org

NATIONAL

Nicotine Anonymous World Services *International. 500+ groups. Founded 1985.* 12-Step. Program for people who want to recover from nicotine addiction and live free of nicotine in all forms. Welcomes all, including persons using cessation programs and nicotine withdrawal aids. Write: Nicotine Anonymous World Services, 419 Main St. PMB #370, Huntington Beach, CA 92648. Call 1-877-879-6422 or 415-750-0328. *Website:* http://www.nicotine-anonymous.org

Recoveries Anonymous *International. 50 chapters.* Spiritual recovery group for anyone seeking a solution for any kind of addiction, problem or behavior. Family and friends welcome. "How To Begin..." guides and "Start A Group" kit can be downloaded free from the website. Write: R.A. Universal Services, P.O. Box 1212, East Northport, NY 11731. *Website:* http://www.r-a.org *E-mail:* raus@r-a.org

ONLINE

New Jersey Quitnet *Online.* Provides access to peer support groups where one can learn from others who are quitting and get advice from those who have successfully quit. Once registered, members get a Quitting Guide to help them develop their individually tailored plan for quitting. *Website:* http://www.nj.quitnet.com

BEREAVEMENT

BEREAVEMENT (GENERAL)
(see also death of a child, widows and widowers, survivors of suicide)

STATEWIDE

Concerns Of Police Survivors, Inc. **(COPS)** *(Garden State Chapter)* Peer support for families and co-workers of police officers who have died in the line of duty. Mutual sharing, phone help, rap sessions and social events. Call 1-866-576-2677. *Website:* http://www.gardenstatecops.com *E-mail:* info@gardenstatecops.com

Iraq/Afghanistan War Family Bereavement Groups *Professionally-run.* Veteran centers in New Jersey have support groups and related services for families of military killed in the war. Building is handicapped accessible. Meetings vary. Write: Ann Talmage, Newark Vet Center, 2 Broad St., Suite 703, Bloomfield, NJ 07003. For information contact the nearest center: Newark (Essex) 973-748-0980; Jersey City (Hudson) 201-748-4467; Trenton (Mercer) 609-882-5744; Ventnor (Atlantic) 609-487-8387. *Website:* http://www.va.gov/rcs *E-mail:* ann.talmage@va.gov

Rainbows, Inc. *Professionally-run.* Time-limited support groups for children and teens (ages 4-17) who are grieving a loss due to death, divorce, abandonment or other life-altering experience. Groups meet for a specific number of sessions and are held periodically. Some programs have concurrent groups for the parents. Helps implement programs throughout the state in schools, churches and social service agencies. *Website:* http://www.rainbowsnj.org

    Central New Jersey (Covers Burlington, Mercer, Monmouth and Ocean counties). Write: Marilyn Schipp, Trenton Diocese Family Life Office, P.O. Box 5147, Trenton, NJ 08638-0147. For any upcoming group sessions planned call Marilyn Schipp 609-406-7400 ext. 5557 (day).

    Northern New Jersey (Covers Bergen, Essex, Hudson, Hunterdon, Middlesex, Morris, Passaic, Somerset, Sussex, Union and Warren counties). Write: Rainbows, Inc., NJ State Chapter, 73 South Fullerton Ave., 2nd Floor, Montclair, NJ 07042. For any upcoming group sessions planned call Alice Forsyth 973-744-7676 (day).

    Southern New Jersey (Covers Atlantic, Camden, Cape May, Cumberland, Gloucester and Salem counties). Write: Sister Pat

McGrenra, Gesu School, 1700 West Thompson St., Philadelphia, PA 19121. For any upcoming group sessions planned call Sister Pat McGrenra 215-763-3660 ext. 204 (day).

ATLANTIC

Atlantic City Grief Support Group *Professionally-run.* Mutual support for anyone who has lost a loved one due to natural causes, suicide, homicide or sudden death. Meets 2nd Wed., 6:30-8:30pm, AtlantiCare Healthplex, 1401 Atlantic Ave., Atlantic City. Pre-registration is required. Before attending call AtlantiCare Hospice 609-272-2424 or AtlantiCare Access 1-888-569-1000 (day).

Coping With Loss *Professionally-run.* Mutual support and education for persons grieving the death of a loved one. Group runs for 6 week sessions, 4 times per/year, Egg Harbor Township. Call 609-272-2424 (day).

Living with Loss *Professionally-run.* Support for anyone who has lost a loved one to cancer. Building is handicapped accessible. Meets Thurs., 6-8pm, Gilda's Club South Jersey, 555 Bay Ave., Somers Point. Before attending call Barbara Ferrera 609-926-2699 (day). *Website:* http://www.gildasclubsouthjersey.org *E-mail:* info@gildasclubsouthjersey.org

BERGEN

Bereavement Support Group *Professionally-run.* Mutual support and education for persons experiencing the grief and loss of a loved one. Groups run for approximately 6 sessions, and are offered periodically throughout the year. Building is handicapped accessible. Meets at Englewood Hospital Medical Center, Home Health and Hospice Services, 350 Engle St., Englewood. Pre-registration required. Before attending call Jessica Pressler, LCSW 201-541-2676 (day).

Bereavement Support Group *Professionally-run.* Support for those who have lost a loved one or friend to cancer. Rap sessions. Building is handicapped accessible. Meets Thurs., 6:30-8pm, Gilda's Club Northern NJ, 575 Main St., Hackensack. Call Carley Anne Tsaglos 201-457-1670 ext. 123 (day). *Website:* http://www.gildasclubnnj.org

Bereavement Support Group *Professionally-run.* Mutual support for persons who have suffered the loss of a loved one. Meets 4th Mon., 6:30-8pm, Hillsdale Library, 509 Hillsdale Ave., Hillsdale. Call Dawn Thomas 201-358-2900 ext. 2673 (day).

Bereavement Support Group *Professionally-run.* Offers support to help persons grieve for a loved one. Groups run for approximately 7 weeks, 2 times/yr. Building is handicapped accessible. Meets at Holy Name Hospital, 718 Teaneck Rd., Teaneck. Call 201-833-3740 ext. 2709 (day).

Bereavement Support Group *Professionally-run.* Support and comfort for those grieving the loss of a loved one. Building is handicapped accessible (has chair lift - must be able to transfer). Meets for 8 week sessions, several times a year, Wallington Presbyterian Church, Paterson St. and Bond St., Wallington. For meeting information call Rev. Peter Carey 973-779-2640.

Journeys Bereavement Group for Children Support and education for children (ages 3-17) who have experienced the death of a loved one and/or life-threatening illness of a family member. Meeting day and time varies, 10 week sessions, 3 times/yr., Paramus. Before attending call Henry Fersco-Weiss 201-291-6243.

Pet Bereavement Support Group *Professionally-run.* Support for individuals to honor the lives of departed animal companions and promote healing from the loss. Rap sessions. Meets Mon., 7-8:15pm, Oradell Animal Hospital, 580 Winters Ave., Paramus. Call Lisa Davis 201-262-0100 (day) or Susan Stone 201-567-5596 (day).

Rainbows Peer Support Group *Professionally-run.* Peer support for children, (ages 4 - teens), who have experienced a family loss because of death, separation, divorce or abandonment. Goals are to provide peer support, furnish an understanding of the grief experience, assist in building a stronger sense of self-esteem and teach appropriate coping mechanisms. Parents' group meets concurrently. Meets Tues., 7-8pm (Sept.-Dec.), and Wed., 7-8pm (Jan.-Apr.), Ridgewood YMCA, 112 Oak St., Ridgewood. Registration required. Call Kathi Meding 201-444-5600 ext. 332 (day). For any other new group sessions planned, call the regional representative, Alice Forsyth 973-744-7676 (day). *E-mail:* kmeding@ridgewoodym.org

Safe Space Support for bereaved high school teens who have lost a loved one through death. Education, mutual sharing and literature. Meets for 8 week sessions, Creative Living Center, 37E Allendale Ave., Allendale. Call Dan Bottorff 201-327-2424 ext. 253 or Penny Gadzini 201-327-2424 ext 254. *Website:* http://www.creativelivingresource.org

Need help finding a specific group? Give us a call – we're here to help!
Call 1-800-367-6274.

Separated, Divorced and Bereaved Catholics Referrals to groups for emotional/spiritual support and social activities for separated, divorced or bereaved men and women. Groups are sponsored by various parishes throughout the counties and are open to people of any faith. Call Family Life Ministries, Catholic Diocese of Newark 973-497-4327.

BURLINGTON

Bereavement Support Group Mutual support for those suffering the loss of a loved one. Various meeting locations and times. Call Office of Family Life, Trenton Diocese 609-406-7400 ext. 5557 (day). See group listings and contacts online at: http://www.dioceseoftrenton.org/church/consolation.asp (scroll down to "Support Groups for Bereavement").

Bereavement Support Group for Friends and Family *Professionally-run.* Support for friends and family grieving the death of a loved one to help cope with the loss. Building is handicapped accessible. Meets 3rd Wed., 7-8:30pm (except July/Aug.), Dougherty's Funeral Home, 2200 Trenton Rd., Levittown, PA. Call Deborah Gawthrop 215-624-8190 (day). *E-mail:* dgawthropcnlt@verizon.net

Big Hurts, Little Tears *Professionally-run.* Support group for 3-5 year-olds who have been affected by a loss. Meetings vary, Samaritan Hospice, Marlton. Pre-registration required. Before attending call The Samaritan Center for Grief Support 1-800-596-8550.

Daughters Without Mothers *Professionally-run.* Support group for women who are grieving the loss of a mother. Education, discussions and an opportunity to share stories. Meetings vary, Samaritan Hospice, Marlton. Pre-registration required. Before attending call The Samaritan Center for Grief Support 1-800-596-8550.

Helping Hand Grief Support Group Christian-based support for anyone bereaving the loss of a loved one (including death of a child, loss to homicide or suicide) through education, encouragement, counseling and understanding. Families welcome. Meets 1st and 3rd Mon., 7-9pm, Fellowship Alliance Chapel (Log house in back of church), 199 Church Rd., Medford. Call Wanda and George Stein 609-953-7333 ext. 309.

Just the Guys *Professionally-run.* Mutual support for adult men grieving the loss of a family member or friend. Meetings vary, Samaritan Hospice, Marlton. Pre-registration required. Before attending call The Samaritan Center for Grief Support 856-596-8550.

SIGH (Sharing In Grief and Hope) *Professionally-run.* Mutual support for anyone who has experienced the death of a loved one. Meets in Marlton. Pre-registration required. Before attending call The Samaritan Center for Grief Support 1-800-596-8550.

Standing on the Promises Mutual support, encouragement and understanding for anyone who has lost a loved one. Rap sessions. Building is handicapped accessible. Meets 4th Sat., 4pm, Bethel AME Church, 8216 Park Ave., Pennsauken. Call Shirley Braver 856-983-6444.

VITAS Hospice - Living With Loss *Professionally-run.* Forum for sharing one's grief experience, giving and receiving support, learning about the grief process and promoting healing. Meets for 6 weeks, 4 times/yr., Kennedy Hospital, 18 E. Laurel Rd., Stratford. Call James K. Chrysler 856-346-7325 (day).

CAMDEN

Bereavement Support Group *Professionally-run.* Support for newly bereaved adults grieving the loss of a loved one within the past year. Families welcome. Phone help and literature. Meets for 6 week sessions (Spring and Fall), Underwood Memorial Hospital, Woodbury. Call Bereavement Coordinator 856-414-1155 (day).

Breath of Life Bereavement Support Group *Professionally-run.* Mutual support for anyone grieving the loss of a loved one. Education, rap sessions, guest speakers and phone help. Meets 2nd and 4th Tues., 7:30-8:30pm, Bethany Baptist Church, 10 Foster Ave., Gibbsboro. Pre-registration required. Before attending call Cynthia Faison 856-784-2220 ext. 114 (day) or Rev. Niki Brown 856-782-6749 (day). *Website:* http://www.abundantharvest.com *E-mail:* revnbrown@verizon.net

Counseling Network for Loss and Transition Grief Groups *Professionally-run.* Provides emotional and educational support for persons grieving the loss of a loved one. Offers various groups, both time-limited and on-going, for general bereavement, loss of spouse and a group for young widows. Meeting time and location varies in NE Philadelphia (Bucks and Montgomery counties), PA. For information call Debbie Gawthrop 215-624-8190 (day). *E-mail:* dgawthropcnlt@verizon.net

Grief Management of St. Rose of Lima Mutual support for anyone grieving the loss of a significant person in their life due to death, separation or divorce. Families welcome. Meets Thurs., 7:30-9:30pm (for 12 week sessions), St. Rose of Lima Church, 300 Kings Highway, Parish Lounge, Haddon Heights. Before attending call Trish 856-310-1770. *Website:* http://www.strosenj.com

St. Agnes Grief Support Ministry Mutual support for anyone who is grieving the loss of a loved one. Literature and phone help. Building is handicapped accessible. Meets for 8 weeks, 3 times per/yr., St. Agnes Church, 701 Little Gloucester Rd., Conference Room Rectory, Blackwood. Before attending call Pat Reilly 856-228-7906 (eve.).

VITAS Hospice - Living With Loss *Professionally-run.* Forum for sharing one's grief experience, giving and receiving support, learning about the grief process and promoting healing. Building is handicapped accessible. Meets for 6 weeks/3 times/yr., Kennedy Hospital - Stratford, 18 E. Laurel Rd., 3rd Floor Conference Room, Stratford. Call James K. Chrysler 856-778-0222 (day) or 856-914-2837. *E-mail:* james.chrysler@vitas.com

CUMBERLAND

Adults Living With a Loss *Professionally-run.* Support for bereaved adults who have lost a loved one. Literature. Registration fee $25 (can be waived). Meets Tues., 7-9pm (8 week sessions, 5 times/yr.), Fitness Connection, Sherman Ave. and Orchard Rd., Vineland. Before attending call Fred Goos 856-575-4277 (day).

ESSEX

Adult Bereavement Group *Professionally-run.* Mutual support for adults bereaving the death of a loved one. Newly bereaved group meets twice a month for eight weeks. Also offers an ongoing group for persons who have already attended a professionally-run bereavement group or had professional counseling. Meets 1st and 3rd Mon., 6-7pm, Hospice of NJ, 400 Broadacres Dr., 1st Floor, Bloomfield. Call Michael Teague 973-893-0818 ext. 213. *E-mail:* michael.teague@americanhospice.com

Daughter's Bereavement Mutual support for adult women who have experienced the loss of their mother. Meets for 6 week sessions, St. Barnabas Hospice and Palliative Care Center, 95 Old Short Hills Rd., West Orange. For meeting information call Judith Zucker, LCSW 973-322-4817 (day).

Growing Through Loss Bereavement Group *Professionally-run.* Offers a caring and supportive environment for adults grieving the loss of a loved one. Loss must be between 3 and 13 months prior to attending group. Building is handicapped accessible. Meets for 8 week sessions, 6-7 times/yr., St. Barnabas

Medical Center, Old Short Hills Rd., Livingston. Pre-registration required. Call Pastoral Care 973-322-5015 (day).

Our Lady of The Lake Bethany Support Group *Professionally-run.* Provides mutual support for persons affected by the loss of a loved one. Offers mutual sharing, education, literature and guest speakers. Meets twice a month, 7:30-9pm, Our Lady of the Lake Church, 32 Lakeside Ave., Rectory, Verona. Call JoAnn 973-585-7278 (eve.).

Rainbows, Inc. *Professionally-run.* Peer support for children (kindergarten - sixth grade) who are grieving a loss due to death, divorce, abandonment or other life altering situation. For any other new group sessions planned call the regional representative Alice Forsyth 973-744-7676 (day).

> **Livingston** Meets Mon., 5:30-6:30pm, Linda and Rudy Slucker NCJW Center for Women, 513 West Mt. Pleasant Ave. Call 973-994-4994 (day). *Website:* http://www.centerforwomennj.org *E-mail:* centerforwomen@ncjwessex.org
>
> **Verona** Meets Mon., 7 week sessions (Spring/Fall), First Presbyterian Church, 10 Fairview Ave. Before attending call 973-239-3561 (day).

Separated, Divorced and Bereaved Catholics Referrals to groups for emotional/spiritual support and social activities for separated, divorced or bereaved men and women. Groups are sponsored by various churches throughout the county and are open to people of any faith. For information call Family Life Ministry, Catholic Diocese of Newark 973-497-4327.

Survivors of Murdered Children *Professionally-run.* Mutual support and understanding for families and friends who have lost a loved one to murder. Guest speakers, advocacy, speakers' bureau, social and buddy system. Meets 2nd Fri., 6:30pm, ECHOES, The Grief Center, 116 Main St., Orange. Call Beverly Henderson 973-675-1199.

GLOUCESTER

Center for People in Transition *Professionally-run.* Assists displaced homemakers whose major source of financial support has been lost due to separation/divorce, death or disability of a spouse. Helps individuals to become emotionally and economically self-sufficient through life skills training, career decision making, education or vocational training and supportive services. Evening divorce and bereavement support groups for men and women. Call 856-415-2222 (day). *E-mail:* peopleintransition@gccnj.edu

HUDSON

Bereavement Support *Professionally-run.* Support for anyone grieving the loss of a loved one. Building is handicapped accessible. Meets Thurs., 6:30pm, Christ Hospital, Palisades Ave., Chapel, Jersey City. Before attending call Pastoral Care Dept. 201-795-8397.

Hudson Hospice Bereavement Group *Professionally-run.* Provides a supportive environment for those grieving the recent death of someone close. The overall goal of the group is to help people move toward the reconciliation of grief. Meets 1st and 3rd Wed., 6:30pm, Bayonne. For meeting information call Hospice 201-433-6225 (day). *E-mail:* ols9395@comcast.net

Hudson Hospice Children's Bereavement Support Group *Professionally-run.* Program to help grieving families. Children (ages 4-17) attend a weekly art therapy group while the parents participate in a companion parent group. Group meets for 10 week sessions, 3 times per/yr., in Bayonne. Call Sharon or Sister Alice McCoy 201-433-6225 (day). *E-mail:* ols9395@comcast.net

Pet Loss and Bereavement Support Group *Professionally-run.* Support for anyone coping with the loss or impending loss of their companion animal. Meets 1st Sun., 2pm, Liberty Humane Society, 235 Jersey City Blvd., Jersey City. Call Allison 201-547-4147 ext. 500 (day).

Separated, Divorced and Bereaved Catholics Referrals to groups for emotional/spiritual support and social activities for separated, divorced or bereaved men and women. Groups are sponsored by various churches throughout the county and are open to people of any faith. For information call Family Life Ministry, Catholic Diocese of Newark 973-497-4327.

HUNTERDON

Grieving and Growing Through Loss *Professionally-run.* Mutual support for persons going through the grief process. Building is handicapped accessible. Meets 2nd and 4th Thurs., 7-8:30pm, Hunterdon Hospice Office, Hunterdon Regional Community Health Care, 5 Bartles Corner Rd., Flemington. Call 908-788-6600 (day).

MERCER

Bereavement Support Group *Professionally-run.* Mutual support for individuals whose loss has occurred at least 2 or more months ago. Building is handicapped accessible. Meets 2nd and 4th Thurs., 5-6:30pm, Cancer Institute of NJ at Hamilton, 2575 Klockner Rd., Hamilton. Before attending call Chaplain Ted Taylor 609-631-6980 (day).

Bereavement Support Group Mutual support for those suffering the loss of a loved one. Various meeting locations and times. Call Office of Family Life, Trenton 609-406-7400 ext. 5557. See group listings at: http://www.dioceseoftrenton.org/church/consolation.asp (scroll down to "Support Groups for Bereavement").

Caring and Sharing *Professionally-run.* Mutual support for anyone suffering the loss of a loved one. Meets 1st Wed., 7-8:30pm, Saul Colonial Home, 3795 Nottingham Way, Hamilton Square. Call Mary Lou Pizzullo 609-587-7072 (day). *Website:* http://www.saulfuneralhomes.com *E-mail:* mlpizzullo@saulfuneralhomes.com

Coping with Bereavement *Professionally-run.* Support for those who have lost a family member or friend. Building is handicapped accessible. Meets 3rd Mon., 1-2:30pm, Princeton Senior Resource Center, Suzanne Patterson Building (behind Borough Hall), 45 Stockton St., Princeton. Call Joann Laveman, LCSW or Ann Schoonover 609-497-4900 (day). *Website:* http://www.princetonsenior.org

MIDDLESEX

Bereavement Support Group *Professionally-run.* Provides a safe environment where individuals can identify and communicate about their losses in order to facilitate the healing process. Rap sessions, literature, newsletter, phone help and buddy system. Building is handicapped accessible. Meets Wed., 10:30am-noon and 7-8:30pm, Costello-Runyon Funeral Home, 568 Middlesex Ave., Metuchen. Call Carol H. Burner 732-562-8565. *E-mail:* carolhburner@aol.com

Bereavement Support Group *Professionally-run.* Provides a safe environment where individuals can identify and communicate about their losses in order to facilitate the healing process. Rap sessions, literature, newsletter, phone help and buddy system. Meets 3rd Mon. and 3rd Tues., 7-8:30pm, Middlesex Funeral Home, 528 Bound Brook Rd., Middlesex. Call Carol H. Burner 732-562-8565. *E-mail:* carolhburner@aol.com

Bereavement Support Group *Professionally-run.* Mutual support for anyone suffering the loss of a loved one. Meets 1st and 3rd Thurs., 7-8:30pm, St. Peter's University Hospital, 254 Easton Ave., New Brunswick. Call Barbara 908-418-7241 (day) or Eve 908-403-7174 (day).

Bereavement Support Group *Professionally-run.* Provides a safe environment where individuals can identify and communicate about their losses in order to facilitate the healing process. Rap sessions, literature, newsletter, phone help and buddy system. Meets 1st Mon. and 1st Tues., 7-8:30pm, South Plainfield Funeral Home, 2456 Plainfield Ave., South Plainfield. Call Carol H. Burner 732-562-8565. *E-mail:* carolhburner@aol.com

MONMOUTH

Adult Bereavement Support Group *Professionally-run.* Support for adults who have experienced the death of a loved one. Building is handicapped accessible. Meetings vary, 8 sessions, 2-3 times/yr., Visiting Nurse Association, 176 Riverside Ave., Red Bank. Before attending call Rosemarie Reilly 732-493-2220 ext. 4641 (day). *E-mail:* rreilly@vnacj.org

Adults Grieving Parents *Professionally-run.* Support for adults who are grieving the loss of a parent. Building is handicapped accessible. Meets Sat., 9:30-11am, Visiting Nurse Association, 176 Riverside Ave., Red Bank. Call Rosemarie Reilly 732-493-2220 ext. 4641 (day). *E-mail:* rreilly@vnacj.org

Art Therapy for Bereaved Children *Professionally-run.* Bereavement program for children (ages 6-9) who have experienced the death of a loved one. Uses art therapy to help children express their feelings. Separate group for parents. Building is handicapped accessible. Meets 3 times/yr., 3:30pm, Visiting Nurse Association, 1100 Wayside Rd., Tinton Falls. Pre-registration required. Before attending call Rosemarie Reilly 732-493-2220 ext. 4641 (day). *E-mail:* rreilly@vnacj.org

Art Therapy for Bereaved Children *Professionally-run.* Bereavement program for children who have lost a loved one. Uses art therapy to help children (ages 4 1/2 - 13 yrs.) address their feelings. Building is handicapped accessible. Meets periodically for 7 week sessions, Riverview Medical Center, 1 Riverview Plaza, Red Bank. Call Jane Weinheimer 732-530-2382 ext. 3035.

Bereavement Support Group *Professionally-run.* Mutual support for adults dealing with the death of a loved one. Building is handicapped accessible. Meets 2nd and 4th Tues., 7:30pm, Bayshore Community Hospital, 727 N. Beers St., TCU Activity Room (main lobby to 2 East Floor), Holmdel. Call Chaplain Anna Esposito 732-739-5888 (day).

Bereavement Support Group *Professionally-run.* Mutual support for the loss of a spouse and adult children bereaving the death of a parent. Meets for 6 weeks, several times per year, Riverview Medical Center, Cancer Center, 1 Riverview Plaza, Red Bank. Call Terry Suruda 732-530-2382 ext. 3036.

Bereavement Support Group Mutual support for those suffering the loss of a loved one. Various meeting locations and times. Call Office of Family Life, Trenton Diocese 609-406-7400 ext. 5557 (day). See group listings at: http://www.dioceseoftrenton.org/church/consolation.asp (scroll down to "Support Groups for Bereavement").

Living With Loss *Professionally-run.* Mutual support for persons who have experienced the loss of a loved one. Building is handicapped accessible. Meets Mon., 11:30am-1pm, Centra State Medical Center, Route 537, Freehold. Call Bunny Salomon 732-617-2221.

Saint Rose Bereavement Support Group *Professionally-run.* Support for those who are experiencing grief due to the death of a loved one. Offers support to members while working through the changes in their lives by sharing their stories in a faith community. Guest speakers, phone help, literature, prayer and music. Building is handicapped accessible. Meets 1st and 3rd Thurs., 7:30-8:30pm (June/July meets 1st Thurs.; Aug. meets 3rd Thurs.), St. Rose Rectory, 603 7th Ave., Belmar. Call Deacon Normand 732-681-0512 ext. 423 or Rosemarie Reilly 732-681-3901.

MORRIS

Adult Bereavement Support Group *Professionally-run.* Support for bereaved adults who have lost a loved one due to cancer or other long-term illness. Building is handicapped accessible. Runs for 8-week sessions, St. Clare's Hospital, Pocono Rd., Denville. For information call Brandy Johnson, MSW 973-625-6176 (day). *E-mail:* bjohnson@saintclares.org

Children's Bereavement Group *Professionally-run.* Provides support to children (ages 6-13) who have experienced a recent loss due to cancer. Building is handicapped accessible. Runs for 8 week sessions, St. Clares Hospital, 25 Pocono Rd., Denville. For information call Brandy Johnson, MSW 973-625-6176 (day). *E-mail:* bjohnson@saintclares.org

Healing Hands *Professionally-run.* Art workshop for children (ages 4-12) who have lost a parent due to death. Parent or caregiver must attend the group with child. Building is handicapped accessible. Meetings vary, 6:30pm, Family Services, 62 Elm St., Morristown. Pre-registration required. Before attending call Tammy Rosenthal 973-538-5260. *Website:* http://www.fsmc.org *E-mail:* trosenthal@fsmc.org

My Rainbows Place Peer support for children and adolescents (kindergarten - eighth grade) who are grieving a loss due to death, divorce or abandonment. Group runs for 14 weeks in the winter and 7 weeks in the summer. Building is handicapped accessible. Meets Tues., 7-7:45pm, St. Francis Residential Community, 122 Diamond Spring Rd., Denville. Separate group for parents. Before attending call Diane 973-627-2134 or Wendy 973-625-3352. For any other new group sessions planned, call the regional representative, Alice Forsyth 973-744-7676 (day).

Path to Happiness Emotional and spiritual support for men and women in all stages of separation, divorce, bereavement, emotional healing and purpose in life. Phone help, pen pals and buddy system. Meets Thurs., 6:30pm, St. Rose of Lima Church, 312 Ridgedale Ave., East Hanover. Call Laura 973-581-1636. *E-mail:* pathtohappiness@aol.com

Pet Loss Support Group *Professionally-run.* Helps individuals cope with the loss or impending loss of their companion animal to work through feelings of grief and mourning. Under 18 welcome. Building is handicapped accessible. Meets 1st and 3rd Tues., 7:30pm, St. Hubert's Giralda, Woodland Ave., Madison. For information call 973-377-7094 (day).

Rainbows and Prism *Professionally-run.* Peer support for children and adolescents (kindergarten - eighth grade) who are grieving the loss of a parent due to death or divorce. Parent group meets concurrently. Building is handicapped accessible. Meets Tues., 7:15-8pm (Sept.-Jan.), Our Lady of Magnificat, 2 Miller Rd., Kinnelon. Call Claudette Meehan 973-492-9406 (eve.) or Peggy Tana 973-838-7265.

OCEAN

Bereavement for Adults Mutual support for adults bereaving the loss of a loved one. Educational series, rap sessions and guest speakers. Meets 1st and 3rd Wed., 6:30-8pm, Hospice of NJ-Toms River, 40 Bey Lea Rd., Toms River. Call 732-818-3460 (day).

Bereavement Support Group *Professionally-run.* Support for anyone bereaving the loss of a loved one. Meets Mon., 1pm, Congregation B'nai Israel, 1488 Old Freehold Rd., Toms River. Call Rita Sason, LCSW 732-363-8010 (Mon.-Thurs.).

Bereavement Support Group Mutual support for those suffering the loss a loved one. Various meeting locations and times. Call Office of Family Life, Trenton Diocese 609-406-7400 ext. 5557 (day). See group listings at: http://www.dioceseoftrenton.org/church/consolation.asp (scroll down to "Support Groups for Bereavement").

Better Bereavement Support for anyone bereaving the loss of a loved one. Meets 1st and 3rd Tues., 7:30-9pm (schedule varies June/Aug.), Ocean Medical Center, 425 Jack Martin Blvd., Dining Room, Brick. Pre-registration required. Before attending call 1-800-560-9990 (day).

Grief Share Support, education and sharing for persons grieving the loss of someone close to them. Families welcome. Meets Mon., 7pm, Shore Vineyard Church, 320 Compass Ave., Beachwood. Call Jackie 732-244-3888 (day). *E-mail:* jackiekerry64@yahoo.com

Journey Through Grief *Professionally-run.* Support for men and women of all ages to work through the normal stages of grief with education and group support. Focuses on situations which frequently occur after the loss of a loved one. Building is handicapped accessible. Meetings vary, St. Francis Center, 4700 Long Beach Blvd., Brant Beach. Before attending call 609-494-1554 (day).

Kids Bereavement Support Group *Professionally-run.* Support for children (ages 7-14) who are bereaving the loss of a parent, grandparent, sibling or friend. Rap sessions. Building is handicapped accessible. Meets 1st Thurs., 5:30-6:30pm, Center for Kids and Family, 591 Lakehurst Rd., Toms River. Call 732-505-5437 (day).

PASSAIC

Adult Bereavement Group *Professionally-run.* Mutual support for adults bereaving the death of a loved one. Meetings vary, 6-7:15pm, Preakness Reformed Church, 131 Church Lane, Wayne. Before attending call Michael Teague 973-893-0818 ext. 213 (day). *E-mail:* michael.teague@americanhospice.com

Lighted Path, The *Professionally-run.* Mutual support for persons who have suffered the loss of a loved one. Meets for 6 week sessions (Spring and Fall), Pathways Counseling Center, 16 Pompton Ave., Pompton Lakes. Call Peg Buczek 973-835-6337 (day).

Passaic Valley Hospice Bereavement Support Group *Professionally-run.* Offers mutual support and education for anyone who has experienced the death of a loved one. Sharing of feelings and experiences in a safe supportive environment. Literature and guest speakers. Building is handicapped accessible. Meets for 6 week sessions, 4 times/yr., Passaic Valley Hospice, 783 Riverview Dr., Totowa. Call Al Jousset, Hospice Chaplain 973-785-7406 (day).

SALEM

Bereavement Support Group *Professionally-run.* Mutual support to help facilitate an individual's grief process within a safe and confidential environment. Under 18 welcome. Building is handicapped accessible. Meets for 8 week sessions, Mon., 7-8:30pm, Memorial Hospital of Salem County, 310 Salem-Woodstown Rd., Salem. Before attending call Rev. Walt Kellen 856-678-8500 ext. 302 (day).

SOMERSET

Bereavement Support Group *Professionally-run.* Support for individuals who have experienced the death of a loved one from cancer. Share thoughts, feelings and information. Meetings vary, The Wellness Community of Central New Jersey, 3 Crossroads Dr., Bedminster. Pre-registration required. Before attending call Ellen Levine, LCSW 908-658-5400 (day). *Website:* http://www.thewellnesscommunity.org/cnj *E-mail:* elevine@thewellnesscommunity.org

Bereavement Support Group *Professionally-run.* Provides a safe environment where individuals can identify and communicate about their losses in order to facilitate the healing process. Rap sessions, literature, newsletter, phone help and buddy system. Meets Tues., 10-11:30am, Branchburg Funeral Home, 910 Route 202 South, Branchburg. Call Carol H. Burner 732-562-8565. *E-mail:* carolhburner@aol.com

Friends of Nikki Support for individuals to cope with the loss or impending loss of their companion animal. Meets 3rd Sun., 1-2:30pm, Somerset. Call Donna 732-246-2124 (day).

JANUS Bereavement Group *Professionally-run.* Support and education for anyone who has experienced a loss through death, separation/divorce, retirement, loss of a job, health or relocation. Helps individuals accept and adjust to the loss. Building is handicapped accessible. Meets 2nd Tues., 7:30-9pm, Bridgewater and Raritan. Call Barbara Ronca, LCSW, PhD 908-218-9062 (Mon.-Fri., 9am-3pm).

Kids Connect / Parents Connect Bereavement Groups *Professionally-run.* Support for children and surviving spouses who have experienced the death of a parent/spouse from cancer. Share thoughts, feelings and information. Rap sessions. Meetings vary, The Wellness Community of Central New Jersey, 3 Crossroads Dr., Bedminster. Call Ellen Levine, LCSW 908-658-5400 ext. 2. *Website:* http://www.thewellnesscommunity.org /cnj

Visiting Nurse Association of Somerset Hills *Professionally-run.* Mutual support for family and friends bereaving the loss of a loved one. Building is handicapped accessible. Meets 2nd and 4th Wed., 10:30am-noon, VNA Somerset Hills, 200 Mt. Airy Rd., Basking Ridge. Call Mary Lou Daley, LCSW 908-766-0180 ext. 242 (day). *E-mail:* mldaley@visitingnurse.org

SUSSEX

Bereavement Support Group Support for anyone who has suffered a loss. Rap sessions, phone help and literature. Building is handicapped accessible. Meets 2nd and 4th Wed., 7-8:30pm, Office of Dr. Dennis Fielding, 17 Route 23 North, Hamburg. Call Linda Marion 973-827-8518 (eve.). *E-mail:* ljpatete@yahoo.com

Coping with Loss *Professionally-run.* Support for those grieving the loss of a loved one through death. Building is handicapped accessible. Meets 4th Tues., 10-11:30am, United Methodist Church, West Ann St., Milford, PA. Call Lorri Opitz or Diana Sebzda 973-383-0115 (day). *Website:* http://www.karenannquinlanhospice.org *E-mail:* bereavement@karenannquinlanhospice.org

Coping with Loss Support Group *Professionally-run.* Support for those grieving the loss of a loved one through death. Building is handicapped accessible. Meets 1st Wed., 12:30-2pm and 2nd Mon., 7-8:30pm, Karen Ann Quinlan Hospice, 99 Sparta Ave., Newton. Call Diana Sebzda 973-383-0115 or 1-800-882-1117 (day). *Website:* http://www.karenannquinlanhospice.org *E-mail:* Bereavement@karenannquinlanhospice.org

"Deep listening is miraculous for both listener and speaker. When someone receives us with open-hearted, non-judging, intensely interested listening, our spirits expand." --Sue Patton Thoele

Pet Loss Support Group *Professionally-run.* Support for individuals coping with the loss of their companion animal to work through feelings of grief and mourning. Dues $5/mtg. Building is handicapped accessible. Meets 3rd Mon., 11am-12:30pm, Karen Ann Quinlan Hospice, 99 Sparta Ave., Newton. Pre-registration required. Call Diana Sebzda 973-383-0115 or 1-800-882-1117 (day). *Website:* http://www.karenannquinlanhospice.org *E-mail:* bereavement@karenannquinlanhospice.org

Project Self-Sufficiency *Professionally-run.* Support for single parents, teen parents, displaced homemakers and low-income families. Offers peer support groups for single parents and teen parents, loss recovery groups for children, parenting skills training and support, family activities, home visitation, family stabilization, physical and emotional health educational seminars, comprehensive job training and educational services designed to promote self-sufficiency. Meetings vary. Call Deborah Berry-Toon 973-383-5129 (day). *E-mail:* pss@garden.net

UNION

Bereavement Support Group *Professionally-run.* Mutual support for persons grieving the loss of a loved one. Meets for 5 week sessions, 3 times/yr. Separate groups for spouses and other family members. Meetings vary, United Methodist Church, 1441 Springfield Ave., New Providence. Call Bereavement Coordinator 973-379-8440 (day).

Center For Hope Hospice Bereavement Support Group *Professionally-run.* Separate support groups for adults, teens and children (ages 5+) who have experienced the death of a loved one. Donations accepted. Meetings vary, Center for Hope Hospice, Acadia House, 175 Glenside Ave., Scotch Plains. Before attending call Center for Hope Hospice 908-654-3711 (day). *Website:* http://www.centerforhope.com

Good Grief *Professionally-run.* Support for children (ages 3-17) and young adults (ages 18-30) who have lost a parent, sibling or other important person in their life due to death. Groups are in different age categories. Concurrent parent group is offered. Building is handicapped accessible. Meetings vary, 6:30-8pm, Good Grief, 561 Springfield Ave., Summit. Pre-registration is required. Before attending call Joe Primo 908-522-1999 (day). *E-mail:* info@good-grief.org

Homicide Survivors *Professionally-run.* Provides support to family members and friends of homicide victims. Rap sessions and guest speakers. Building is handicapped accessible. Meets 3rd Mon., 7:15-9pm (except July/Aug.), Robert Wood Johnson Hospital, Rahway. Call Elaine O'Neal 908-527-4596 (day).

Separated, Divorced and Bereaved Catholics Referrals to groups for emotional/spiritual support, and social activities for separated, divorced or bereaved men and women. Groups are sponsored by various churches throughout the county and are open to people of any faith. Call Family Life Ministry, Catholic Diocese of Newark 973-497-4327.

WARREN

Coping with Loss Support Group *Professionally-run.* Support for those grieving the loss of a loved one through death. Meets 3rd Tues., 10-11:30am, Joseph T. Quinlan Bereavement Center, 214 Washington St., Hackettstown. Call Diana Sebzda 973-383-0115 (day). *Website:* http://www.karenannquinlanhospice.org *E-mail:* bereavement@karenannquinlanhospice.org

Grief Recovery Program *Professionally-run.* Provides comfort, support and healing to persons (ages 18+) who have suffered the loss of a loved one. Building is handicapped accessible. Groups run for 4 weeks, 7-9pm (April and October), Hackettstown Regional Medical Center, 651 Willow Grove St., Hackettstown. Call Carl Bannister 908-850-7757 (day).

Grief Support Group *Professionally-run.* Provides support for those coping with the loss of a partner, child, parent or friend. Dues $20 (literature, refreshments, handouts, etc.) per 6 week session. Building is handicapped accessible. Meets 4 times/yr., Warren Hospital, Chapel, 185 Roseberry St., Phillipsburg. Call 908-859-6700 ext. 2048 (day).

Pet Loss Support Group *Professionally-run.* Support for individuals coping with the loss of their companion animal to work through feelings of grief and mourning. Dues $5/mtg. Meets 3rd Tues., 12:30-2pm (Jan., Mar., May, July, Sept., Nov.), Joseph T. Quinlan Bereavement Center, 214 Washington St., Hackettstown. Call Diana Sebzda 973-383-0115 (day). *Website:* karenannquinlanhospice.org *E-mail:* bereavement@karenannquinlanhospice.org

NATIONAL

ACCESS (AirCraft Casualty Emotional Support Services) *National network. Founded 1996.* Matches persons who have lost a loved one in an aircraft-related tragedy to volunteers who previously experienced a similar loss. Goal is to help fill the void that occurs when the emergency and disaster relief organizations disband, the initial shock subsides and the natural grieving process intensifies. Offers guidelines to help start a similar group. Persons communicate through e-mail or by phone. Online newsletter. Write: ACCESS, 1202 Lexington Ave.,

Suite 335, New York, NY 10028. Call 1-877-227-6435. *Website:* http://www.accesshelp.org *E-mail:* info@accesshelp.org

Concerns Of Police Survivors, Inc. (COPS) *National. 50 chapters. Founded 1984.* Provides resources for the surviving families of law enforcement officers killed in the line of duty according to Federal criteria. Also offers law enforcement training. Quarterly newsletter, departmental guidelines and peer support. Provides annual National Police Survivors' Conference each May during National Police Week. Special hands-on programs for survivors. Summer camp for children (ages 6-14) and their parent/guardian, parents' retreats and spouses get-aways. Outward Bound experiences for young adults (ages 15-20), siblings retreat, adult children and in-laws retreat. Write: COPS, P.O. Box 3199, 3096 South State Highway 5, Camdenton, MO 65020. Call 573-346-4911; Fax: 573-346-1414. *Website:* http://www.nationalcops.org *E-mail:* cops@nationalcops.org

GriefShare *Resource.* Biblically based 13-week support group for churches to offer to those grieving the death of a loved one. Group members view a video each session, followed by discussion and complete weekly exercises. Workbooks are required for each member. Basic kit $340.00 for 5 workbooks; Ministry Kit $440.00 for 15 workbooks; Total Ministry kit $540.00 for 25 workbooks (plus postage). GriefShare meeting locations may found listed on the website. Write: GriefShare, Church Initiatives Inc., P.O. Box 1739, Wake Forest, NC 27588. Call 1-800-395-5755 or 919-562-2112. *Website:* http://www.griefshare.org *E-mail:* info@griefshare.org

National Donor Family Council *National. Founded 1992.* Bereavement support and educational resources for families of deceased organ and tissue donors. Provides free literature, educational programs and numerous ways to honor a loved one. National Donor Family Quilt, quarterly newsletter, pen pals and advocacy efforts. Write: National Donor Family Council, National Kidney Foundation, 30 E. 33rd St., New York, NY 10016. Call 212-889-2210 or 1-800-622-9010; Fax: 212-689-9261. *Website:* http://www.donorfamily.org *E-mail:* donorfamily@kidney.org

National Fallen Firefighters Foundation. Survivors Support Network *National network. Founded 1992.* Provides emotional support to spouses, families and friends of firefighters who have died in the line of duty. Members are matched with survivors of similar experiences to help them cope during the difficult months following the death. Write: National Fallen Firefighters Foundation, P.O. Drawer 498, Emmitsburg, MD 21727. Call 301-447-1365. *Website:* http://www.firehero.org *E-mail:* firehero@firehero.org

National Students of Ailing Mothers and Fathers Support Network *International.* Network of university students helping each other cope with the serious illness or death of a parent or loved one. Campus-based mutual support groups, online newsletter, online chats and service projects. Website provides information, group development guidelines and a listing of universities currently interested in group development. Write: National Students of AMF, 514 Daniels St., Suite 356, Raleigh, NC 27605. *Website:* http://www.studentsofamf.org

Parents Of Murdered Children, Inc. (POMC) *National. Over 230 chapters in US, Canada and Costa Rica. Founded 1978.* Self-help support organization for the family and friends of those who have died by violence. Newsletter published 3 times a year. Court accompaniment also provided by many chapters. Parole Block Program and Second Opinion Service also available. Offers assistance in starting local chapters. Write: Parents of Murdered Children, 100 E. Eighth St., Suite 202, Cincinnati, OH 45202. Call 1-888-818-7662 or 513-721-5683 (office) (Mon.-Fri., 8am-5pm EST); Fax: 513-345-4489. *Website:* http://www.pomc.org *E-mail:* natlpomc@aol.com

RAINBOWS *International. 8600 affiliated groups. Founded 1983.* Establishes peer support groups in churches, schools or social agencies for children and adults who are grieving a death, divorce or other painful transition in their family. Groups are led by trained adults. Online newsletter, information and referrals. Write: RAINBOWS, 2100 Golf Rd., Suite 370, Rolling Meadows, IL 60008-4231. Call 1-800-266-3206 or 847-952-1770; Fax: 847-952-1774. *Website:* http://www.rainbows.org *E-mail:* info@rainbows.org

Tragedy Assistance Program for Survivors (TAPS) *National network.* Provides support for persons who have lost a loved one while serving in the armed forces (Army, Air Force, Navy, Marine Corps, National Guard, Reserves, Service Academies, Coast Guard and contractors serving beside the military). Offers networking, crisis information, problem solving assistance and liaison with military agencies. Also TAPS youth programs. Annual seminar. Write: TAPS, 910 17th Street NW, Suite 800, Washington, DC 20006. Call 1-800-959-8277 or 202-588-8277; Fax: 202-457-8278. *Website:* http://www.taps.org *E-mail:* info@taps.org

Twinless Twin Support Group *International network. 12 regional directors. Founded 1986.* Mutual support for twins and other multiples who have lost their twin or multiple(s). Phone support, chatroom, information, local meetings and annual conference. Parents of infant/child age survivor twins welcome. Publishes "Twinless Times." Dues $50/yr. Write: Twinless Twin Support Group, P.O. Box 980481, Ypsilanti, MI 48198. Call 1-888-205-8962. *Website:* http://www.twinlesstwins.org *E-mail:* contact@twinlesstwins.org

Wings of Light, Inc. *National. 3 support networks. Founded 1995.* Support and information network for individuals whose lives have been touched by aviation accidents. Separate networks for airplane accident survivors, families and friends of persons killed in airplane accidents and persons involved in rescue, recovery and investigation of crashes. Information, referrals and phone support. Write: Wings of Light, Inc., P.O. Box 1097, Sun City, AZ 85372. Call 623-516-1115. *Website:* http://www.wingsoflight.org

ONLINE

Adult Sibling Grief *Online.* Support for those who have suffered the devastating loss of an adult sibling. Chatrooms, message board and resources. *Website:* http://www.adultsiblinggrief.com

Autoerotic Asphyxiation Support *Online. Founded 1999.* Supportive message board for family and friends of those who have died by autoerotic asphyxiation. *Website:* http://groups.yahoo.com/group/autoeroticasphyxiationsupport

Delta Society *Online.* Maintains a list of pet bereavement support groups, pet loss resource persons, counselors and hotlines. Call 425-679-5500; Fax: 425-679-5539. *Website:* http://www.deltasociety.org *E-mail:* info@deltasociety.org

Drowning Support Network *Online. Founded 2002.* Offers support for people who have lost loved ones due to drowning or other water accidents, especially those in which no remains were found or in which the recovery process has been lengthy or difficult. *Website:* http://health.groups.yahoo.com/group/drowningsupportnetwork

Grief Recovery Online - Widows and Widowers (GROWW) *Online.* Support groups for persons bereaving the loss of a loved one. Offers a large variety of chatrooms, run by volunteers, dealing with specific issues (loss of a child, sibling, significant other or parent; loss due to drugs, long-term illness, sudden death or violence). Monthly newsletter. *Website:* http://www.groww.org

Pet Loss Grief Support *(MULTILINGUAL) Online.* Moderated board that offers support and understanding for persons grieving the loss of their pet or who have a pet that is ill. Provides personal support and thoughtful advice. Also offers "Monday Pet Loss Candle Ceremony," a chatroom, tribute pages and other resources. *Website:* http://www.petloss.com

DEATH OF A CHILD / FETAL LOSS
(see also bereavement, suicide, crime)

ATLANTIC

Compassionate Friends Support for parents, grandparents and siblings bereaving the death of a child. Meets 2nd Wed., 7:30-9pm, Grace Lutheran Church, Shore Rd. and Dawes Ave., Somers Point. Call Gail Katten 609-653-8451 or Compassionate Friends 1-877-969-0010. *Website:* http://www.compassionatefriends.org *E-mail:* tcfnj@comcast.net

BERGEN

Compassionate Friends Support for parents grieving the death of a child. Grandparents and siblings are welcomed. Speakers' bureau. Building is handicapped accessible. Meets 4th Tues., 7:30-9:30pm (beginners 7:15pm), Christian Healthcare Center, Mountain Ave., Wyckoff. Call Compassionate Friends 201-567-0089. *Website:* http://www.compassionatefriends.org

Parents Who Have Lost A Child Support Group Mutual support, education and spirituality for parents who have lost a child. Meets 3rd Mon., 7:30pm, St. Peter the Apostle Church, 445 Fifth Ave., Rectory Basement, River Edge. Call Mary Davis 201-261-5400 (day) or 201-265-3688 (eve.).

Perinatal Bereavement Support Group *Professionally-run.* Support for parents and significant others who have experienced the loss of a pregnancy or infant death. Building is handicapped accessible. Meets 3rd Wed., 7:30pm, Englewood Hospital, Englewood. Call Sue Dziemian 201-384-8258.

Perinatal Bereavement - Healing Hearts *Professionally-run.* Provides support for parents who have experienced a miscarriage, ectopic pregnancy, stillbirth or infant death to help with the grieving process. Building is handicapped accessible. Meets 3rd Thurs., 7:30-9pm, Valley Hospital, 233 N. Van Dien Ave., Conference Center, Room #2, Ridgewood. Before attending call Trudy Heerema, LCSW 201-447-8539 (day).

Pregnancy and Newborn Loss Support Group *Professionally-run.* An opportunity for parents who have experienced the loss of an infant, miscarriage or stillbirth to share their experiences with other parents. Provides information and resources for parents, families and friends on perinatal grief. Guest speakers. Meets 1st Tues., 7:30-9pm, Holy Name Hospital, 718 Teaneck Rd., Teaneck. Call Perinatal Bereavement Hotline 201-833-3058 (day).

SIDS/Infant Loss Support Group *(BILINGUAL) Professionally-run.* Support for parents who have lost a child to a sudden infant death. Families welcome. Building is handicapped accessible. Meets 2nd Thurs., 7-8:30pm, Hackensack University Medical Center, Hackensack. Before attending call 1-800-545-7437.

Turning Point - A Women's Resource Center *Professionally-run.* Confidential post-abortion support group using God's word as a basis for inner healing. Building is handicapped accessible. Group meets for 8-12 weeks as needed in Bergenfield. Call Turning Point 201-501-8876.

BURLINGTON

Bereaved Parents *Professionally-run.* Support for parents bereaving the loss of a child. Meetings vary, Samaritan Hospice, Marlton. Pre-registration required. Before attending call The Samaritan Center for Grief Support 1-800-596-8550. *Website:* http://www.samaritanhospice.org

Compassionate Friends Support for parents grieving the death of a child. Meets 2nd Fri., 7:30pm, Family Services Building, 770 Woodlane Rd., Suite 23, Mount Holly. Call Jack 856-983-2242. *Website:* http://www.compassionatefriends.org

Grief Recovery After Substance Passing (GRASP) Support for parents who have suffered the death of a child due to substance abuse. Provides opportunity for parents to share their grief and experiences without shame or recrimination. Meets 3rd Tues., 6pm, 1003 Lincoln Dr. West (off Route 73), Rap Room, Suite A, Marlton. Call 856-983-3328 (day).

Helping Hand Grief Support Group Christian-based support for anyone bereaving the loss of a loved one (including death of a child, loss to homicide or suicide) through education, encouragement, counseling and understanding. Families welcome. Meets 1st and 3rd Mon., 7-9pm, Fellowship Alliance Chapel (log house in back of church), 199 Church Rd., Medford. Call Wanda and George Stein 609-953-7333 ext. 309.

SIDS/Infant Loss Support Group *(BILINGUAL) Professionally-run.* Support for parents who have lost a child to sudden infant death. Families welcome. Building is handicapped accessible. Meets 1st Thurs., 7-8:30pm, West Jersey Hospital, Marlton. Before attending call 1-800-545-7437.

UNITE Grief Support *Professionally-run.* Mutual support for parents who have experienced the loss of a child, either during pregnancy, at birth or up to the first year of life. Discussion of experiences and feelings in an atmosphere of support and respect. Meets 2nd Mon., 7:30-9pm, Virtua Memorial, 175 Madison Ave., Conference Center, Mt. Holly. Before attending call 1-888-847-8823 (day).

CAMDEN

Compassionate Friends Support for parents bereaving the death of a child. Grandparents and relatives welcome. Rap sessions and newsletter. Meets 3rd Fri., 8-9:30pm, Audubon Senior Center, Oak Ave. and Oakland Ave., Audubon. Call Compassionate Friends 1-877-969-0010. *Website:* http://www.compassionatefriends.org

UNITE Grief Support *Professionally-run.* Mutual support for parents who have experienced the loss of a child, either during pregnancy, at birth or up to the first year of life. Discussion of experiences and feelings in an atmosphere of support and respect. Meets 1st and 3rd Mon., 7-9pm, Virtua Health's Barry Brown Health Education Center, 106 Carnie Blvd., Voorhees. Before attending call 1-888-847-8823.

CUMBERLAND

Helping Hands *Professionally-run.* Provides emotional support for parents who have lost a child to miscarriage, stillbirth or infant death. Open to grandparents. Meets 2nd Mon., 7pm, South Jersey Health Care, Vineland. Before attending call Judy Ford, RN BSN 856-507-2768 (day).

Parents Living with a Loss *Professionally-run.* Support for parents grieving the loss of a child. Meets 4th Thurs., 7-9pm, South Jersey Healthcare Hospice Care, Vineland Health Center, South State St., Room 240, Vineland. Pre-registration required. Before attending call 856-575-4277 (day).

ESSEX

Compassionate Friends Offers friendship and understanding for parents bereaving the death of a child. Meets 3rd Mon., Nutley area. For meeting information call Rose Rappaport 973-239-1711 or Pat Gerges 973-535-9022 (eve.). *Website:* http://www.compassionatefriends.org

Fathers Whose Children Have Died *Professionally-run.* Support for fathers bereaving the death of a child. Phone help. Meets 4 times/yr., Mar., June, Sept. and Dec., Notre Dame Roman Catholic Church, 358 Central Ave., Parish Center, North Caldwell. Before attending call Family Life Office 973-497-4327.

HOPE (Helping Other Parents Endure) Mutual support, education and spirituality for parents who have lost a child. Meets 1st Wed., 7:30-9:30pm (July and August meets 7pm), St. Thomas the Apostle Church, 60 Byrd Ave., Parish Center, Bloomfield. Call Mary Margaret or Bob Corriston 201-288-6886 or Ann and Jack Muller 201-358-8752. *E-mail:* bmmc917@optonline.net or mulleraj@optonline.net

Mothers of Murdered Sons and Daughters Support and advocacy for mothers and families of murdered children. Rap sessions and guest speakers. Meets 3rd Sun., 5pm (except Nov./Dec.), East Orange General Hospital, 300 Central Ave., East Orange. Before attending call Christine Johnson 973-399-5029.

Perinatal Bereavement Group *Professionally-run.* Mutual support for parents who have experienced a miscarriage, infant death or stillbirth. Building is handicapped accessible. Meets 1st Wed., 7:30pm, Saint Barnabas Medical Center, 94 Old Short Hills Rd., Livingston. Call Dorothy Kurzweil, LCSW 973-322-5745 (day) or Social Services 973-322-5855 (day).

Survivors of Murdered Children *Professionally-run.* Mutual support, education and understanding for families and friends who have lost a loved one to murder. Guest speakers, advocacy, speakers' bureau, social and buddy system. Meets 2nd Fri., 6:30-8pm, ECHOES, The Grief Center, 116 Main St., Orange. Call Beverly Henderson 973-675-1199.

GLOUCESTER

Grief Group for Parents Support for parents grieving the loss of a child to drugs. Rap sessions and buddy system. Building is handicapped accessible. Meets 1st and 3rd Wed., 7:30-8:30pm, Washington Township Municipal Building, 523 Egg Harbor Rd., Meeting Room C, Sewell. Call Donna Rullo 856-589-6446 (day). *E-mail:* wtfcs@twp.washington.nj.us

HOPING (Helping Other Parents In Normal Grief) *Professionally-run.* Support for parents who have experienced miscarriage, stillbirth, ectopic pregnancy or newborn death. Building is handicapped accessible. Meets 4 times/yr. Underwood Memorial Hospital, 509 N. Broad St., Woodbury. Before attending call 856-845-0100 ext. 2749 (day); TTY: 856-845-0100.

HUNTERDON

Compassionate Friends Support for parents bereaving the death of a child. Group discussions, lectures, literature and phone help available. Meets last Sat., 7-9pm, High Bridge. For meeting information call James and Roselee Persinko

908-638-8717 (eve./weekends) or Compassionate Friends 1-877-969-0010. *Website:* http://www.compassionatefriends.org

MERCER

Compassionate Friends Mutual support for parents, grandparents or adult siblings bereaving the death of a child. Guest speakers, phone help and newsletter. Building is handicapped accessible. Meets 1st Mon., 7:30pm, Capital Health System, 1445 Whitehorse-Mercerville Rd., Hamilton Campus, Hamilton. Call 609-516-8047. *Website:* http://www.tcfmercer.org *E-mail:* tcfmercer@optonline.net

MIDDLESEX

Compassionate Friends - *Central Jersey Chapter* Mutual support for parents, grandparents or siblings grieving the death of a child. Phone help, guest speakers, rap sessions, literature and newsletter. Meets 2nd Sun., 2-4pm, St. Peter's Episcopal Church, 505 Main St., Parish Hall, Spotswood. Call Susan 732-690-6673 or Compassionate Friends 1-877-969-0010. *Website:* http://www.compassionatefriends.org

Perinatal and Neonatal Support Group *Professionally-run.* Support for parents who have suffered the loss of a baby during any stage of pregnancy or shortly after birth. Networking with caring, supportive, bereaved parents with similar losses. Offers an opportunity to share experiences, emotions and information in a confidential, non-judgmental manner. Meets 1st Mon., 6-8pm, Bristol Myers Squibb Children's Hospital, Robert Wood Johnson University Hospital, 1 Robert Wood Johnson Place, First Floor Conference Room, New Brunswick. Pre-registration required. Call 732-828-3000 ext. 4475.

Share Pregnancy and Infant Loss Support, Inc. *Professionally-run.* Provides support for parents, their families and friends who have experienced miscarriage, stillbirth or neonatal death. Offers phone help and literature. Meets 2nd Thurs., 7-9pm, St. Peter's University Hospital, 254 Easton Ave., New Brunswick. Call Dawn Brady 732-745-8600 ext. 5214 (day).

"One of the hardest things in life is having words in your heart that you can't utter."
-- James Earl Jones

MONMOUTH

C.H.I.L.D. (Caring Help In Lost Dreams) *Professionally-run.* Bereavement group for parents and surviving siblings who have lost a child of any age. Offers emotional support to help cope with the unnatural loss of a deeply loved child. Building is handicapped accessible. Meets 1st Thurs., 7:30-9pm, CentraState Medical Center, Route 537, Freehold. Call Bunny Salomon 732-617-2221.

Compassionate Friends Support for parents, grandparents and siblings bereaving the death of a child. Building is handicapped accessible. Literature, newsletter and phone help. Meets 3rd Tues., 7:30-9:30pm, Good Shepherd Lutheran Church, 112 Middletown Rd., Holmdel. Call Terri Dassing 908-358-2268 (day) or 732-787-3866 (eve.). *Website:* http://www.monmouthcountycf.org *E-mail:* tdassing@optonline.net

SHARE *Professionally-run.* Support group for parents, grandparents and other adults close to the parents who have experienced a loss due to miscarriage, stillbirth or neonatal death. Also provides information on how to help children cope with the loss of a sibling. Meets 4th Tues., 7:30pm, Monmouth Medical Center, 300 Second Ave., Stanley Wing, Room 206, Long Branch. Registration is required. Before attending call Jennifer Pawlak, APN, 732-923-7344 (day).

Share Pregnancy and Infant Loss Support, Inc. *Professionally-run.* Provides support for parents grieving the loss of an infant through miscarriage, ectopic pregnancy, stillbirth or death of a newborn. Newsletter, phone help, guest speakers and literature. Meets 2nd Tues., 7:30-9:30pm, Riverview Medical Center, 1 River Plaza, Booker Conference Room, Red Bank. Call Pam Rossano 732-530-2315 (day) or 1-800-560-9990 (day).

MORRIS

Compassionate Friends Mutual support for parents, grandparents and siblings bereaving the death of a child. Phone help and newsletter. Call 973-270-7908. *Website:* http://www.compassionatefriendsnj.org *E-mail:* tcf_nj@yahoo.com
> **Chatham** Meets 3rd Sun., 7-9:30pm (2nd Sun., June and Dec.), Chatham Township Presbyterian Church, 240 Southern Blvd.
> **Parsippany** Meets 2nd Thurs., 7:30-10pm, St. Christopher's Church, 1050 Littleton Rd., Room 101.

M.I.D.S. (Miscarriage, Infant Death, Stillbirth) Mutual support and information for bereaved parents who have experienced stillbirth, miscarriage, infant death or ectopic pregnancy. Meets 2nd Wed., 8pm, Parsippany. Call Janet

Tischler 973-884-1016. *Website:* http://www.midsinc.org *E-mail:* mids1982@yahoo.com

PELA (Parents Enduring Loss from Addiction) Mutual support and understanding in a non-judgmental environment for parents who have lost a child of any age to a drug or alcohol overdose. Building is handicapped accessible. Meets 3rd Thurs., 5:30-7pm, The Willow Tree Center, 415 Speedwell Ave., Morris Plains. Before attending call 973-682-8733. *Website:* http://www.willowtree.org *E-mail:* charlie@willowtree.org

RTS Perinatal Bereavement Services *Professionally-run.* Support for families who have experienced the loss of a baby through miscarriage, ectopic pregnancy, stillbirth or newborn death. Meets 3rd Wed., 7:30-9pm, Morristown Memorial Hospital, 100 Madison Ave., Morristown. Before attending call Labor and Delivery 973-971-5748.

Share Pregnancy and Infant Loss Support Group *Professionally-run.* Provides support for parents who have lost a baby through neonatal death, miscarriage, ectopic pregnancy or stillbirth. Pen pals, monthly meetings, guest speakers, lending library and phone help available. Meets 3rd Tues., 7:30-9pm, 28 Drake Rd., Mendham. To confirm meeting date call Lucy 973-543-2495 (day). *Website:* http://www.shareatlanta.org *E-mail:* sharenonj@msn.com

OCEAN

Compassionate Friends Mutual support for parents and siblings grieving the death of a child. Includes parents of stillbirth or fetal death. Monthly newsletter, occasional speakers and library. Meets 1st Tues., 7:30pm, Building at Children's Memorial Garden, Winding River Park, Toms River. Call Compassionate Friends 732-730-1726. *Website:* http://www.oceantcf.com *E-mail:* oceantcf@yahoo.com

SOMERSET

Compassionate Friends Provides mutual support for parents bereaving the death of a child. Rap sessions, guest speakers and newsletter. Building is handicapped accessible. Meets 4th Sun., 7:30pm, Temple Sholom, Bridgewater. Call Dossie Weissbein 908-725-7736, Marilyn and Fred Mountjoy 908-722-6199 or Compassionate Friends 1-877-969-0010. *Website:* http://www.freewebs.com/cfbridgewater

UNION

F.A.T.E. (Feelings After Termination Experience) *Professionally-run.* Support for couples or individuals who have terminated a pregnancy due to fetal abnormalities. Building is handicapped accessible. Meetings vary, Overlook Hospital, 99 Beauvoir Ave., Summit. Call Gisela Rodriguez 973-972-3302 (day). *E-mail:* rodriggi@umdnj.edu

NATIONAL

AGAST *International. Founded 1989.* Dedicated to supporting grandparents when a grandchild dies. Offers personal support, literature packet (information to help own child, siblings, etc.), provides online message board and newsletter. Telephone support and subject matter support available (one twin died, grandchild murdered, etc.). Helps with the development of new groups. Write: AGAST-MISS, P.O. Box 5333, Peoria, AZ 85385-5333. Call 1-888-774-7437 or 1-800-455-6477; Fax: 623-979-1001. *Website:* http://www.agast.org or http://www.missfoundation.org *E-mail:* reachout@agast.org or info@missfoundation.org

Alive Alone, Inc. *National network. Founded 1988.* Self-help network of parents who have lost an only child or all of their children. Provides education and publications to promote communication and healing, to assist in resolving grief and to develop means to reinvest lives for a positive future. Bimonthly newsletter. Write: Alive Alone, c/o Kay Bevington, 1112 Champaign Dr., Van Wert, OH 45891. *Website:* http://www.alivealone.org *E-mail:* alivalon@bright.net

AMEND (Aiding Mothers and Fathers Experiencing Neonatal Death) *National network. Founded 1974.* Offers support and encouragement to parents having a normal grief reaction to the loss of their baby. Provides one-to-one peer counseling with trained volunteers. Write: AMEND, 4324 Berrywick Terrace, St. Louis, MO 63128. Call 314-487-7582. *Website:* http://www.amendgroup.com *E-mail:* martha@amendgroup.com or amendgroup@charter.net

Bereaved Parents of the USA *(BILINGUAL) National. 80+ affiliated groups. Founded 1995.* Designed to aid and support bereaved parents and their families who are struggling to survive their grief after the death of a child. Information and referrals, newsletter, phone support, conferences and support group meetings. Assistance and guidelines in starting groups. Write: Bereaved Parents of the USA, P.O. Box 95, Park Forest, IL 60466. Call 708-748-7866 (voice/fax). *Website:* http://www.bereavedparentsusa.org

CLIMB, Inc. (Center for Loss In Multiple Birth) *International network.* *Founded 1987.* Support by and for parents who have experienced the death of one or more of their twins or higher multiples during pregnancy, birth, infancy or childhood. Newsletter, information on specialized topics, pen pals and phone support. Write: CLIMB, P.O. Box 91377, Anchorage, AK 99509. Call 907-222-5321. *Website:* http://www.climb-support.org *E-mail:* climb@pobox.alaska.net

Compassionate Friends, The *National. Approximately 600 chapters. Founded 1969.* Offers mutual support, friendship and understanding to families grieving the death of a child of any age, from any cause. Provides information on the grieving process, referrals to local chapter meetings and publishes quarterly magazine ($20/yr). Also has a sibling network. Write: The Compassionate Friends, P.O. Box 3696, Oak Brook, IL 60522-3696. Call 1-877-969-0010; Fax: 630-990-0246. *Website:* http://www.compassionatefriends.org *E-mail:* nationaloffice@compassionatefriends.org

First Candle/SIDS Alliance *(BILINGUAL) National. 50 chapters. Founded 1987.* Provides education, advocacy, research, support for families of babies who have died from SIDS (sudden infant death syndrome), stillbirth and miscarriages. Bilingual grief counselors available 24 hrs. Newsletter, conferences and chapter development guidelines. Write: First Candle/SIDS Alliance, 1314 Bedford Ave., Suite 210, Baltimore, MD 21208. Call 1-800-221-7437 or 410-653-8226; Fax: 410-653-8709. *Website:* http://www.firstcandle.org *E-mail:* info@firstcandle.org

GRASP (Grief Recovery After Substance Passing) *National. 6 affiliated groups. Founded 2002.* Support and advocacy group for parents who have suffered the death of a child due to substance abuse. Provides opportunity for parents to share their grief and experiences without shame or recrimination. Provides information and suggestions for those wanting to start new chapters. Write: GRASP, c/o Patricia Wittberger, 62 Holly Ribbons Circle, Bluffton, SC 29909. Call 843-705-2217. *Website:* http://www.grasphelp.com *E-mail:* mom@jennysjourney.org

M.I.S.S. Foundation, The *International. 20 affiliated groups. Founded 1995.* Offers emergency and on-going support for families suffering from the loss a child. Provides information, referrals, phone support, newsletter, pen pals, literature, advocacy and online chatroom support. Information on local group development. Local support group listings online. Write: M.I.S.S., P.O. Box 5333, Peoria, AZ 85385-5333. Call 623-979-1000; Fax: 623-979-1001. *Website:* http://www.missfoundation.org *E-mail:* joanne@missfoundation.org

Parents of Murdered Children, Inc. (POMC) *National. Over 230 chapters in the U.S., Canada and Costa Rica. Founded 1978.* Self-help support organization for families and friends of those who have died by violence. Newsletter 3 times a year. Court accompaniment also provided by many chapters. Parole Block Program and Second Opinion Service also available. Offers assistance in starting local chapters. Write: Parents of Murdered Children, Inc., 100 E. Eighth St., Suite 202, Cincinnati, OH 45202. Call 1-888-818-7662 or 513-721-5683 (office) (Mon.-Fri., 8am-5pm EST); Fax: 513-345-4489. *Website:* http://www.pomc.org *E-mail:* natlpomc@aol.com

Share Pregnancy and Infant Loss Support, Inc. *National. 100 chapters. Founded 1977.* Mutual support for bereaved parents and families whose lives have been touched by the tragic death of a baby through early pregnancy loss, stillbirth or in the first few months of life. Provides support toward positive resolution of grief experienced at the time of, or following, the death of a baby. Information, education and resources on the needs and rights of bereaved parents, grandparents and siblings. Online newsletter, calendar of upcoming events, helpful hints for caregivers, chapter development opportunities and guidelines available on website. Online message board and chatrooms. Write: National Share Office, St. Joseph Health Center, 402 Jackson St., St. Charles, MO 63301. Call 1-800-821-6819 or 636-947-6164; Fax: 636-947-7486. *Website:* http://www.nationalshare.com *E-mail:* share@nationalshare.com

UNITE, Inc. *National. 12 groups. Founded 1975.* Support for parents grieving a miscarriage, stillbirth or infant death. Also provides support for parents through subsequent pregnancies. Group meetings, phone help, newsletter, lending libraries and annual conference. Offers guidelines for starting and facilitating a group. Grief counselor training programs. Professionals in advisory roles. Online referrals to local support group meetings and times. Write: UNITE, Inc., P.O. Box 65, Drexel Hill, PA 19026. Call 1-888-488-6483 (tape). *Website:* http://www.unitegriefsupport.org *E-mail:* administrator@unitegriefsupport.org

ONLINE

A Heartbreaking Choice *Online.* Resource for parents who have had to terminate a wanted pregnancy due to prenatal news such as birth defects or risk to the well-being of the mother. Listserv e-mail list, discussion forum and grandparents forum. *Website:* http://www.aheartbreakingchoice.com

Angels of Addiction *Online. 136 members. Founded 2005.* Mutual support for bereaved parents who have lost a child of any age to the use of drugs or drug overdose. *Website:* http://health.groups.yahoo.com/group/angelsofaddiction/

MyMolarPregnancy.com *Online. Founded 2001.* Information, links, references and a number of interactive web features for women who have had a molar pregnancy. Support group, message board and chatroom. *Website:* http://www.mymolarpregnancy.com

Parent Soup Message Boards *Online.* Offers a large variety of message boards which deal with parenting issues including infertility, pregnancy, parenting challenges, parents of disabled, pregnancy loss, newborn babies, toddlers, adoption, family issues, etc. *Website:* http://www.parentsoup.com/messageboards

Triplet Connection, The *Online. Founded 1983.* Online support forum of parents who have lost one or more children in multiple births. Write: The Triplet Connection, P.O. Box 429, Spring City, UT 84662. Call 435-851-1105. *Website:* http://www.tripletconnection.org/triplet_forum/dcboard.php *E-mail:* tc@tripletconnection.org

SUICIDE SURVIVORS
(see also bereavement, death of a child, widows)

ATLANTIC

Atlantic City Grief Support Group *Professionally-run.* Mutual support for anyone who has lost a loved one due to natural causes, suicide, homicide or sudden death. Meets 2nd Wed., 6:30-8:30pm, AtlantiCare Healthplex, 1401 Atlantic Ave., Atlantic City. Pre-registration is required. Before attending call AtlantiCare Hospice 609-272-2424 or AtlantiCare Access 1-888-569-1000 (day).

Heartbreak to Healing Mutual support and understanding for persons who have lost a loved one to suicide. Group meets last Tues., 7:30pm, Grace Lutheran Church, Somers Point. For information call Dolores Thomas 609-345-3230.

BERGEN

Survivors After Suicide *Professionally-run.* Provides support for family members and friends of people who died by suicide. Open to all. Meets 1st and 3rd Wed., 7:15-8:45pm, Vantage Health System, 2 Park Ave., Dumont. Call Michelle Weinberg 201-818-7133 or Vantage Health System 201-385-4400 ext. 0 (day).

BURLINGTON

Helping Hand Grief Support Group Christian-based support for anyone bereaving the loss of a loved one (including death of a child, loss to homicide or suicide) through education, encouragement, counseling and understanding. Families welcome. Meets 1st and 3rd Mon., 7-9pm, Fellowship Alliance Chapel (Log house in back of church), 199 Church Rd., Medford. Call Wanda and George Stein 609-953-7333 ext. 309.

Living Through Suicide *Professionally-run.* Christian-based support for those who have lost a loved one to suicide. Meets 4th Mon., 7-9pm, Fellowship Alliance Chapel (small chapel in back parking lot), 199 Church Rd., Medford. Call Wanda Stein 609-953-7333 ext. 309.

Sharing Suicide's Sorrows *Professionally-run.* Support for family and friends grieving a death from suicide. Meetings vary, The Center for Grief Support, 5 Eves Dr., Suite 180, Marlton. Call 1-800-596-8550.

CAMDEN

Friends and Families of Suicide Support for those who have lost a loved one to suicide. Meets 2nd Tues., 7:45pm, Barrington Borough Municipal Building, 229 Trenton Ave., Barrington. Call Barbara 856-307-0331 or Gail 856-858-7044. *E-mail:* survivingsuicidenj@yahoo.com

ESSEX

Surviving After Suicide *Professionally-run.* Support for those who have lost a loved one to suicide. Guest speakers, literature and phone help. Childcare available. Building is handicapped accessible. Meetings vary, Brandt Life Therapy Center, 15 Bloomfield Ave., Suite 2, Verona. Before attending call 973-239-0954. *E-mail:* dougbrandt@comcast.net

MERCER

Surviving After Suicide *Professionally-run.* Support for those who have lost a loved one to suicide. Quarterly newsletter. Meets 3rd Wed., 7:30pm, Trinity United Methodist Church, 1985 Pennington Rd., Ewing. Call Daniel Casselberry 609-434-0061. *E-mail:* dbcassel@comcast.net

Need help finding a specific group? Give us a call – we're here to help!
*Call **1-800-367-6274**.*

MIDDLESEX

Surviving After Suicide *Professionally-run.* Group for survivors after the suicide of a family member or friend. Meets 3rd Mon., 7:30-9:30pm, University of Medicine and Dentistry of NJ, University Behavioral Health Care, 671 Hoes Lane, Piscataway. Call Peggy Farrell 732-462-5267. *E-mail:* farrmarg@aol.com

MONMOUTH

Surviving After Suicide *Professionally-run.* Group for survivors after the suicide of a family member or friend. Building is handicapped accessible. Meets 2nd Tues., 7:30-9:30pm, Bayshore Memorial Hospital, Conference Room A, 717 N. Beers St., Holmdel. Call Peggy Farrell 732-462-5267. *E-mail:* farrmarg@aol.com

MORRIS

Survivors of Suicide Mutual support and discussion for people who have had someone close to them commit suicide. Meets 2nd and 4th Wed., 7:30-9pm, Grace Episcopal Church, 4 Madison Ave., Madison. Call Jane Cole 973-786-5178.

OCEAN

Survivors After Suicide Support for those who have lost a loved one to suicide. Meets 2nd Thurs., 7:30pm, St. Francis Center, Long Beach Blvd., Brant Beach. Call Jo and Roger 609-361-7608.

Survivors of Suicide Grief support and understanding for those who have lost a loved one to suicide. Meets 2nd Wed., 7:30-9:30pm, Ocean Medical Center, 425 Jack Martin Blvd., Brick. Before attending call Dave Thelen 732-899-8483 (eve.).

Survivors of Suicide Mutual support for those who have lost a loved one to suicide. Meets 3rd Tues., 7-9pm, Kimball Medical Center, Center for Healthy Living, 198 Prospect St., Lakewood. Call Jim Romer 732-886-4475 (day). *E-mail:* jromer@sbhcs.com

NATIONAL

American Association of Suicidology *National. 350 affiliated groups.* Referrals to local support groups for survivors of suicide nationwide. Directory of groups ($15). Newsletter, pamphlets and brochures available for a fee. Book available on starting self-help groups ($30). Write: American Association of Suicidology, 5221 Wisconsin Ave. NW, 2nd Floor, Washington, DC 20015. Call 202-237-2280; Fax: 202-237-2282. *Website:* http://www.suicidology.org *E-mail:* info@suicidology.org

American Foundation for Suicide Prevention *Resource. Founded 1987.* Provides state-by-state directory of survivor support groups for families and friends who have lost someone to suicide. Training programs available to start similar groups. Write: American Foundation For Suicide Prevention, 120 Wall St., 22nd Floor, New York, NY 10005. Call 1-888-333-2377 or 212-363-3500 ext. 10; Fax: 212-363-6237. *Website:* http://www.afsp.org

Heartbeat *International. 35 chapters. Founded 1980.* Mutual support for those who have lost a loved one through suicide. Information, referrals, phone support and chapter development guidelines on-line. Speakers on suicide bereavement. Write: Heartbeat, 2015 Devon St., Colorado Springs, CO 80909. Call 719-596-2575. *Website:* http://heartbeatsurvivorsaftersuicide.org

ONLINE

Friends And Family Of Suicide *Online. Founded 1998.* Provides online support to survivors of suicide. Offers moderated e-mail mailing list, chatroom, retreats and various memorial projects. *Website:* http://www.pos-ffos.com Direct sign up address: http://health.groups.yahoo.com/group/ffofsuicides *E-mail:* arlynsmom@bellsouth.net

Parents of Suicide *Online. Founded 1998.* Support for parents whose sons and daughters have died by suicide. Annual retreat. Offers private chatroom, e-mail discussion group and listserv. *Website:* http://www.pos-ffos.com Direct sign up address: http://health.groups.yahoo.com/group/parentsofsuicides *E-mail:* arlynsmom@bellsouth.net

SOLES (Survivors Of Law Enforcement Suicide) *Online. Founded 1995.* Provides emotional support to families of police officers who died by suicide. Information and referrals on national and local resources including support groups, conferences and grief workshops. E-mail discussion list and weekly online chat. *Website:* http://www.tearsofacop.com/police/soles

"If we all tried to make other people's paths easy, our own feet would have a smooth even place to walk on." – Myrtle Reed (A Weaver of Dreams)

WIDOWS / WIDOWERS
(see also bereavement, suicide, crime)

STATEWIDE

Catholic Divorce Ministry (The Ministry of the North American Conference of Separated and Divorced Catholics) Ministry serving individuals experiencing separation, divorce or death of a spouse. Offers leadership training conferences, resources materials and social activities. Referrals to self-help groups statewide. Call Charlie Rauh 201-986-9676. *Website:* http://www.nacsdc.org (click into Region 3) *E-mail:* sam4sdw@gmail.com

ATLANTIC

H.O.P.E. (Helping Other People Evolve, Inc.) Helps the recently widowed to cope with their loss and to move forward to become self-reliant persons. Group runs for 10 week sessions, 4 times per year. Registration fee $25 for 10 sessions. Meets Wed., 11am-12:30pm, Smithville. Call Anthony 609-748-2532, Joan 609-296-1966 or H.O.P.E. 1-888-920-2201 (Mon.-Fri., 10am-1pm). *E-mail:* hopesnj@juno.com

BERGEN

Partners Bereavement Support Group *Professionally-run.* Support for spouses/partners bereaving the loss of a loved one to cancer in the past year. Group meets for 8 week sessions, 4 times/yr., Cancer Care, 141 Dayton St., Ridgewood. For information call 201-444-6630 ext. 0 (day). *Website:* http://www.cancercare.org *E-mail:* njinfo@cancercare.org

Separated, Divorced and Bereaved Catholics Referrals to groups for emotional/spiritual support, and social activities for separated, divorced or bereaved men and women. Groups are sponsored by various churches throughout the county and are open to people of any faith. For information call Family Life Ministry, Catholic Diocese of Newark 973-497-4327.

Widows and Widowers Support Group *Professionally-run.* Mutual support and education for spouses. Groups run for approximately 6 sessions periodically throughout the year. Building is handicapped accessible. Meetings vary, Englewood Hospital and Medical Center, Home Health and Hospice Services, 75 Demarest Ave., Englewood. Pre-registration required. Before attending call Jessica Pressler, LCSW 201-541-2676 (day).

BURLINGTON

Early Endings *Professionally-run.* Support for young widows and widowers who have lost a spouse or companion early in their lives. Meetings vary, Samaritan Hospice, Marlton. Pre-registration required. Before attending call The Samaritan Center for Grief Support 1-800-596-8550 (Mon.-Fri., 8:30am-4:30pm). *Website:* http://www.samaritanhospice.org

Grieving the Love of Your Life *Professionally-run.* Support for anyone, age 50 and over, grieving the loss of a spouse or a partner. Building is handicapped accessible. Meeting days and locations vary. Pre-registration required. Before attending call The Samaritan Center for Grief Support 1-800-596-8550. *Website:* http://www.samaritanhospice.org

H.O.P.E. (Helping Other People Evolve, Inc.) Support and information for recently (up to 2 yrs.) widowed men and women of all ages. Group runs for 10 week sessions, 4 times per year. Registration fee $25 for 10 sessions. Meets in various locations. Call H.O.P.E. 1-888-920-2201 (Mon.-Fri., 10am-1pm).

Widows and Widowers Support Group *Professionally-run.* Provides mutual support for widows and widowers grieving the loss of their spouse. Building is handicapped accessible. Meets 2nd and 4th Wed., 1:30-2:45pm (except July/Aug.), Dougherty's Funeral Home, 2200 Trenton Rd., Levittown, PA. Call Deborah Gawthrop 215-624-8190 (day). *E-mail:* dgawthropcnlt@verizon.net

Widows and Widowers Support Group Mutual support for anyone feeling the loss of their spouse. Building is handicapped accessible. Meets 1st Sat., 7pm, Lourdes Medical Center of Burlington County Hospital, 218A Sunset Rd., Willingboro. Before attending call Helen Pellerin 609-871-0783.

CAMDEN

Counseling Network for Loss and Transition Grief Groups *Professionally-run.* Provides emotional and educational support for persons grieving the loss of a loved one. Offer various groups, both time-limited and on-going, for general bereavement, loss of spouse and a group for young widows. Meeting time and location varies in Philadelphia (Bucks and Montgomery counties), PA area. For information call Debbie Gawthrop 215-624-8190 (day). *E-mail:* dgawthropcnlt@verizon.net

H.O.P.E. (Helping Other People Evolve, Inc.) Helps the recently widowed to cope with their loss and move forward to become self-reliant persons. Group runs for 10 week sessions, 4 times per year. Registration fee $25 for 10 sessions.

Meets in various locations. Call H.O.P.E. 1-888-920-2201 (Mon.-Fri., 10am-1pm). *E-mail:* hopesnj@juno.com

To Live Again Support and encouragement for widows and widowers (ages 45+). Newly widowed meets Tues., 7pm, Queen of Heaven Church, Cherry Hill. General group meets 2nd Mon., 7:30pm, St. Peter's Celestine School, Cafeteria, Cherry Hill. Dues $15/yr. Call Rita 856-779-9438 (day) or Stanley 856-662-6754 (eve.).

CAPE MAY

H.O.P.E. (Helping Other People Evolve, Inc.) Support and information for recently (up to 2 yrs.) widowed men and women of all ages. Group runs for 10 week sessions, 4 times per year. Registration fee $25 for 10 sessions. Meets in various locations. Call H.O.P.E. 1-888-920-2201 (Mon.-Fri., 10am-1pm). *E-mail:* hopesnj@juno.com

ESSEX

Separated, Divorced and Bereaved Catholics Referrals to groups for emotional and spiritual support for separated, divorced or bereaved men and women. Groups are sponsored by various churches throughout the county and are open to people of any faith. For information call Family Life Ministry, Catholic Diocese of Newark 973-497-4327.

Widows Moving On Support for widows that have dealt with the bereavement phase and now want to meet other widows to talk about getting on with their lives. Groups start periodically and run for 6 weeks. Registration fee $45. Building is handicapped accessible. Meets at Linda and Rudy Slucker NCJW Center for Women, 513 West Mt. Pleasant Ave., Livingston. Call Center for Women 973-994-4994 (day). *Website:* http://www.centerforwomennj.org *E-mail:* centerforwomen@ncjwessex.org

Widows Support Groups Mutual support for widows of all ages. Groups start periodically and run for 6 weeks. Registration fee $45. Building is handicapped accessible. Meets at Linda and Rudy Slucker NCJW Center for Women, 513 West Mt. Pleasant Ave., Livingston. Call 973-994-4994. *Website:* http://www.centerforwomennj.org *E-mail:* centerforwomen@ncjwessex.org

Widows and Widowers Support Group *Professionally-run.* Support for those who have lost their spouses. Meets for 6 weeks, St. Barnabas Hospice and Pallative Care Center, 95 Old Short Hills Rd., West Orange. Before attending call Judith Zucker, LCSW 973-322-4817 (day).

Young Widows Moving On Support for young widows that have dealt with the bereavement phase and now want to meet other young widows to talk about getting on with their lives. Groups start periodically and run for 6 weeks. Registration fee $45. Building is handicapped accessible. Meets at Linda and Rudy Slucker NCJW Center for Women, 513 West Mt. Pleasant Ave., Livingston. Call Center for Women 973-994-4994 (day). *Website:* http://www.centerforwomennj.org *E-mail:* centerforwomen@ncjwessex.org

Young Widows Support Group Mutual support for widows in their 40's and younger. Groups start periodically and run for 6 weeks. Registration fee $45. Building is handicapped accessible. Meets at Linda and Rudy Slucker NCJW Center for Women, 513 West Mt. Pleasant Ave., Livingston. Call 973-994-4994. *Website:* http://www.centerforwomennj.org *E-mail:* centerforwomen@ncjwessex.org

GLOUCESTER

H.O.P.E. (Helping Other People Evolve, Inc.) Helps the recently widowed to cope with their loss, move forward and become self-reliant. Group runs for 10 week sessions, 4 times per year. Registration fee $25 for 10 sessions. Meets in Mantua. Call H.O.P.E. 1-888-920-2201 (Mon.-Fri., 10am-1pm). *E-mail:* hopesnj@juno.com

HUDSON

Separated, Divorced and Bereaved Catholics Referrals to groups for emotional/spiritual support for separated, divorced or bereaved men and women. Groups are sponsored by various churches throughout the county and are open to people of any faith. Call Family Life Ministry, Catholic Diocese of Newark 973-497-4327.

HUNTERDON

Catholic Widows and Widowers Mutual support for widowed persons of any faith. Groups for the recently bereaved as well as for those further along. Various meeting locations and times. Call Family Life Office 732-562-1990 ext. 1624 (day).

Consider passing this Directory on to a student or staff member - browsing through the Directory pages can often provide helpful education as to the wide variety of groups available.

MERCER

H.O.P.E. (Helping Other People Evolve, Inc.) Support and information for recently (up to 2 yrs.) widowed men and women of all ages. Group runs for 10 week sessions, 4 times per year. Registration fee $25 for 10 sessions. Meets in various locations. Call H.O.P.E. 1-888-920-2201 (Mon.-Fri., 10am-1pm).

Starting Over *Professionally-run.* Support for widows and widowers under the age of 50 or those with dependent children. Meets 1st and 3rd Tues., 7-8:30pm, Saul Colonial Home, 3795 Nottingham Way, Hamilton Square. Before attending call Mary Lou Pizzullo or Deborah Myslinski 609-587-7072 (day). *Website:* http://www.saulfuneralhomes.com *E-mail:* mlpizzullo@saulfuneralhomes.com

MIDDLESEX

Catholic Widows and Widowers Mutual support for widowed persons of any faith. Groups for the recently bereaved as well as for those further along. Various meeting locations and times. For information call the Family Life Office, Metuchen Diocese 732-562-1990 ext. 1624 (day).

Spousal Bereavement Group *Professionally-run.* Helps persons who have lost their spouse within the last two years to understand the grieving process and share feelings, while adjusting to new roles. Building is handicapped accessible. Young widows/widowers (under age 55), 2nd Tues., 7-8:15pm and widows/widowers (age 55 and over), 3rd Tues., 7-8:15pm, JFK Medical Center, 65 James St., Edison. Pre-registration required. Before attending call 732-321-7769 (day).

St. Thomas WOW'S (Widows Or Widowers) Mutual support for widows and widowers. Open to persons of any faith. Rap sessions, education, prayer, scripture, social and guest speakers. Building is handicapped accessible. Annual dues $8 per year, $1 per meeting. Meets 1st Tues., 7pm (except July/Aug.), St. Thomas the Apostle Church, One St. Thomas Plaza, Pastoral Center, Old Bridge. Call Deacon John J. Fitzsimmons 732-251-4000 (day) or Irene Sutton 732-251-1458 (eve.).

MONMOUTH

Bereavement Support Group *Professionally-run.* Mutual support for the loss of a spouse and adult children bereaving the death of a parent. Meets for 6 weeks, several times per year, Riverview Medical Center, Cancer Center, 1 Riverview Plaza, Red Bank. Call Terry Suruda 732-530-2382 ext. 3036.

Growing Through Loss *Professionally-run.* Mutual bereavement support for younger widows and widowers (ages 30-60, plus or minus). Non-sectarian. Opportunity to share thoughts. Meets 1st and 3rd Mon., 7:30-9pm (once a month in Jan., Feb., Mar.), Temple Shaari Emeth, 400 Craig Rd., Manalapan. For meeting information call Temple Shaari Emeth 732-462-7744 or Bunny Salomon 732-617-2221.

Separated / Divorced / Widows and Widowers Support Group Support for persons who have lost their spouse due to separation, divorce or death (past the bereavement stage) to help members get on with their lives. Not for crisis situations. Not intended as a social group. Meets Tues., 7:30pm, St. Veronica's Rectory Cellar, Route 9 North, Howell. Call Ree 732-431-0446. *Website:* http://www.divorceheadquarters.com *E-mail:* Reegroup@aol.com

Spouse Bereavement Group *Professionally-run.* Mutual support for persons bereaving the death of a spouse. Building is handicapped accessible. Meets for 6 weeks, several times per year, Riverview Medical Center, 1 Riverview Plaza, Red Bank. Before attending call 732-530-2382.

Women's Support Group Helps women who are displaced homemakers facing the loss of their primary source of income due to separation, divorce, disability or death of spouse. Issues addressed include self-sufficiency, career development, assertiveness, self-esteem, divorce, separation, widowhood and other related topics. Meets Fri., 10am-noon, Brookdale Community College, Lincroft. Pre-registration required. Before attending call Robin Vogel 732-495-4496 ext. 4007 (day) or Mary Ann O'Brien 732-229-8675.

MORRIS

Widow/Widower Support Group *Professionally-run.* Opportunity for widows and widowers to share experiences and feelings with other newly bereaved who are living through similar circumstances. Rap sessions. Meets 4th Tues., 1-2:30pm, Chilton Health Network Building, 242 West Parkway, 2nd Floor, Pompton Plains. Before attending call Joan Beloff 973-831-5167 (day).

Widows and Widowers Support Group *Professionally-run.* Provides support, education and mutual sharing for widows and widowers. Literature. Building is handicapped accessible. Meets 4 times year, for 8 week sessions, Morristown Memorial Hospital, 100 Madison Ave., Morristown. Before attending call Zsuzsa 973-971-5402 (day).

OCEAN

Community Medical Center Bereavement Support Group *Professionally-run.* Support for adults who have experienced the recent loss of a spouse. Building is handicapped accessible. Meets Mon., 10-11:30am, Community Medical Center, Hooper Ave., Toms River. Pre-registration required. Before attending call Bereavement Coordinator 732-818-6826 (day).

PASSAIC

Widow/Widower Support Group *Professionally-run.* Support and sharing of experiences for newly widowed persons. Meets for 6 week sessions, 2-3 times/yr., Pathways Counseling Center, 16 Pompton Avenue, Pompton Lakes. Registration required. Call Peg Buczek 973-835-6337 (day).

Widows/Widowers Support Group Mutual support for all widowed persons. Provides guest speakers, group discussions, phone help, peer-counseling, visitation and refreshments. Building is handicapped accessible. Meets 2nd and 4th Wed., 7:30pm (only newly bereaved persons); 2nd and 4th Mon., 7:30pm (past the newly bereaved stage), St. Philip the Apostle Church, Valley Rd., Clifton. Call John Cerullo 973-472-4494.

SOMERSET

Catholic Widows and Widowers Mutual support for widowed persons of any faith. Groups for the recently bereaved as well as for those further along. Various meeting locations and times. Call Family Life Office, Metuchen Diocese 732-562-1990 ext. 1624 (day).

JANUS Bereavement Group *Professionally-run.* Support and education for anyone who has experienced a loss through death, separation, divorce, retirement, loss of a job, health or relocation. Helps individuals accept and adjust to the loss. Building is handicapped accessible. Meets 2nd Tues., 7:30-9pm, Bridgewater and Raritan. Call Barbara Ronca, LCSW, PhD 908-218-9062 (Mon.-Fri., 9am-3pm).

"Kindness is a language which the deaf can hear and the blind can see." --Mark Twain

Single Senior Women Support for women (ages 60+) who are divorced, separated or widowed. Meets 2nd and 4th Thurs., 10am-noon, Office on Aging, 27 Warren St., Somerville. Call Erin 908-704-6339 (day).

UNION

Hospice Bereavement Support Group *Professionally-run.* Mutual support for persons bereaving the death of a spouse. Rap sessions, literature and guest speakers. Group runs for 8 weeks (Spring/Fall). Building is handicapped accessible. Meets Wed., Robert Wood Johnson University Hospital at Rahway, 865 Stone St., Rahway. Before attending call Shannon Wiese 732-499-6169 (day). *E-mail:* swiese@rwjuhr.com

Separated, Divorced and Bereaved Catholics Referrals to groups for emotional and spiritual support for separated, divorced or bereaved men and women. Groups are sponsored by various churches throughout the county and are open to people of any faith. Call Family Life Ministry, Catholic Diocese of Newark 973-497-4327.

WARREN

Catholic Widows and Widowers Mutual support for widowed persons of any faith. Groups for the recently bereaved as well as for those further along. Various meeting locations and times. Call the Family Life Office, Metuchen 732-562-1990 ext. 1624 (day).

NATIONAL

Beginning Experience, The *International. 112 teams. Founded 1974.* Support programs for divorced, widowed and separated adults (and their children) enabling them to work through the grief of a lost marriage. Write: The Beginning Experience, c/o International Ministry Center, 1657 Commerce Dr., South Bend, IN 46628. Call 574-283-0279 or 1-866-610-8877; Fax: 574-283-0287. *Website:* http://www.beginningexperience.org *E-mail:* jan@beginningexperience.org

Concerns Of Police Survivors, Inc. (COPS) *National. 48 chapters. Founded 1984.* Provides resources for the surviving families of law enforcement officers killed in the line of duty according to Federal criteria. Also offers law enforcement training. Quarterly newsletter, departmental guidelines and peer support. Provides annual National Police Survivors' Conference each May during National Police Week. Special hands-on programs for survivors. Summer camp for children (ages 6-14) and their parent/guardian. Parents' retreats, spouse get-away, Outward Bound experiences for young adults (ages 15-20), siblings retreat, adult children and in-laws retreats. Write: COPS, P.O. Box 3199, 3096 South State Highway 5, Camdenton, MO 65020. Call 573-346-4911; Fax: 573-346-1414. *Website:* http://www.nationalcops.org *E-mail:* cops@nationalcops.org

North American Conference of Separated and Divorced Catholics *International. 3000+ groups. Founded 1974.* Religious, educational and emotional aspects of separation, divorce, remarriage and widowhood are addressed through self-help groups, conferences and training programs. Families of all faiths are welcome. Group development guidelines. Newsletter. Membership dues start at $35/yr. (includes newsletter, discounts and resources). Write: North American Conference of Separated and Divorced Catholics, P.O. Box 10, Hancock, MI 49930. Call 906-482-0494; Fax: 906-482-7470. *Website:* http://www.nacsdc.org *E-mail:* office@nacsdc.org

Society of Military Widows *National. 24 chapters. Founded 1968.* Support and assistance for widows of members of all U.S. uniformed services. Helps people in coping with adjustment to life on their own. Promotes public awareness. Bimonthly magazine/journal. Dues $12/yr. Chapter development guidelines. Online listing of local chapters. Write: Society of Military Widows, 5535 Hempstead Way, Springfield, VA 22151. Call 1-800-842-3451 ext. 1005 or 253-750-1342. *Website:* http://www.militarywidows.org *E-mail:* president@militarywidows.org or patschecter@earthlink.net

ONLINE

Grief Recovery Online - Widows and Widowers (GROWW) *Online.* Support for widowed and other persons grieving the loss of a loved one. Offers a large variety of chatrooms, run by volunteers, dealing with specific issues (loss of a child, sibling, significant other or parent; loss due to drugs, long-term illness, sudden death or violence). Monthly newsletter. *Website:* http://www.groww.org

Young Widow - Chapter Two *Online.* Mutual support group for young widows and widowers, who share experiences, and strengths through its message board. Also provides a listing of local face-to-face groups, links to other related online e-mail discussion groups and websites for the young widowed persons. *Website:* http://www.youngwidow.org

Can't find an appropriate group in your area? The Clearinghouse helps people start groups. Give us a call at 1-800-367-6274.

"Oh, the comfort, the inexpressible comfort of feeling safe with a person; having neither to weigh thoughts nor measure words, but to pour them all out, just as they are, chaff and grain together, knowing that a faithful hand will take and sift them, keep what is worth keeping, and then, with the breath of kindness, blow the rest away."
—George Eliot

DISABILITIES

AMPUTATION / LIMB DIFFERENCES
(see also general disabilities and *specific disorder)*

BERGEN

Kessler Leg Amputee Support Group *Professionally-run.* Provides mutual support for both trans-tibial (below knee) and trans-femoral (above knee) amputees. Families welcome. Rap sessions, guest speakers, literature and buddy system. Building is handicapped accessible. Meets 3rd Thurs., 6-7:30pm, Kessler Institute, 300 Market St., Saddle Brook. Call Cynthia Macaluso 201-368-6087 (day).

BURLINGTON

Amputee Support Group Offers mutual support for physical, emotional and social issues for patients and their families dealing with an amputation. Rap sessions and guest speakers. Building is handicapped accessible. Meets 3rd Wed., 7-8:30pm, Marlton Rehab Hospital, 92 Brick Rd., Marlton. Call Andrea Varone 856-988-8778 ext. 2030.

ESSEX

S.H.A.G. (Self-Help Amputee Group) Mutual support for amputees and their families. Phone support. Meets 1st Sat., 10am, Kessler Institute, West Orange. Call Ann Silvestrini 973-748-8785.

MONMOUTH

Amputees on the Move Provides mutual support, education and social events for amputees and their families. Guest speakers, rap sessions and phone help. Meets 1st Mon., 1:30-3pm, Healthsouth, 2 Centre Plaza, Tinton Falls. Call Sharon Collins 732-760-5378 (day) or Pete Dacchille 732-602-0188 (day). *E-mail:* sharon.collins@healthsouth.com

Can't find an appropriate group in your area? The Clearinghouse helps people start groups. Give us a call at 1-800-367-6274.

OCEAN

James F. Gorman Amputee Support Group of NJ Mutual support, encouragement and education for amputees, families, friends, caregivers or anyone who has involvement with an amputee. Rap sessions, guest speakers, literature, social activities, phone help and buddy system. Dues $5. Meets 1st Wed., noon-2pm, Health South Rehabilitation Hospital of Toms River, 14 Hospital Dr., Toms River. Call Scott 609-971-0006 or Jim 732-938-4805.

NATIONAL

American Amputee Foundation, Inc. *National. Founded 1975.* Self-help and educational information, referrals and peer support for amputees. Hospital visitation and counseling. Group development guidelines, national resource directory for patients, families and caregivers. Write: American Amputee Foundation, P.O. Box 94227, North Little Rock, AR 72190. Call 501-835-9290; Fax: 501-835-9292. *Website:* http://www.americanamputee.org *E-mail:* info@americanamputee.org

Amputee Coalition of America *National. 240 affiliated groups.* Mission is to reach out to people with limb loss and to empower them through education, support and advocacy. Maintains the National Limb Loss Information Center which is a comprehensive source of information for people living with limb differences. Offers referrals to ACA certified peer visitors. Publishes information packet on starting a support group and two magazines, "inMotion" and "First Step: A Guide for Adapting to Limb Loss." Write: Amputee Coalition of America, 900 East Hill Ave., Suite 205, Knoxville, TN 37915. Call 1-888-267-5669 (Mon.-Fri., 8am-5pm EST); Fax: 865-525-7917. *Website:* http://www.amputee-coalition.org *E-mail:* acainfo@amputee-coalition.org

National Amputation Foundation, Inc. *National. Founded 1919.* Offers support, referrals and information to all amputees. "Amp to Amp" program links individuals with others with similar amputations. Newsletter, information and referrals. Dues $25/yr. Donated medical equipment given to any person in need. Items must be picked up at the office. Scholarship program open to full-time college students who have a major limb amputation. Write: National Amputation Foundation, 40 Church St., Malverne, NY 11565. Call 516-887-3600; Fax: 516-887-3667. *Website:* http://www.nationalamputation.org *E-mail:* amps76@aol.com

ONLINE

AMP-L Amputee List *Online. Founded 1995.* Moderated forum for adult amputees and interested others to exchange ideas and to discuss matters of mutual interest. Provides support and a platform to discuss the amputee experience from many different perspectives. *Website:* http://www.amp-info.net/amp-l.htm

I-CAN (International Child Amputee Network) *Online. 350 members. Founded 1995.* Mailing list for parents of children with either acquired or congenital limb loss. Opportunity to share experiences with other parents and mentors who grew up as amputees. *Website:* http://www.child-amputee.net *Listserv:* i-can@listserv.icors.org *E-mail:* jbaughn@child-amputee.net

LimbDifferences.org *Online. Founded 1981.* A comprehensive resource for families and friends of children with limb differences. Establishes contact with other families of children with limb differences through its forum. *Website:* http://www.limbdifferences.org

AUTISM / ASPERGER SYNDROME
(see also parents of the disabled)

STATEWIDE

ASPEN (Asperger Syndrome Education Network) Information and support for parents of children with Asperger syndrome, pervasive developmental disorders and high functioning autism. Discussion groups, guest speakers and statewide workshops. Dues: $35/yr. (parents); $55/yr. (professionals). Write: ASPEN, 9 Aspen Circle, Edison, NJ 08820. Call Lori Shery 732-321-0880 (9am-2pm). *Website:* http://www.aspennj.org

Autism New Jersey (formerly COSAC) *(BILINGUAL) Professionally-run.* Helps families, individuals, teachers and agencies concerned about the welfare and treatment of children and adults with autism. Pen pals for siblings, guest speakers, information, referral, advocacy assistance and workshops. Support groups statewide. Newsletter. Write: Autism New Jersey, 1450 Parkside Ave., Suite 22, Ewing, NJ 08638. Call 1-800-428-8476 (day) or 609-883-8100 ext. 28. *Website:* http://www.njcosac.org *E-mail:* information@njcosac.org

ONLINE

Autism_Parents_and_Pros_NJ *Online. 129 members. Founded 2004.* New Jersey support group for family members and professionals in the world of autism to connect and share support and information about experiences. *Website:* http://health.groups.yahoo.com/group/autism_parents_and_pros_nj

ATLANTIC

FACES (Families for Autistic Children, Education and Support) Group Discusses topics important to families touched by autism. Guest speakers, literature, workshops, play groups and social opportunities. *Website:* http://www.faces-autismsupport.org *Online chatroom:* http://health.groups.yahoo.com/group/facesautism *E-mail:* facesgroup@comcast.net

> **Egg Harbor Township** Meets 4th Thurs., 6-7:30pm, South Jersey Children's Museum, Shore Mall. Call Mary Ann 609-641-1877.
> **Hammonton** Meets 1st Wed., 6:30-8:30pm, Hammonton Early Childhood Education Center, 601C North 4th St. Call Colleen 609-270-7438. *E-mail:* faceshammonton@yahoo.com

BERGEN

ASPEN (Asperger Syndrome Parents Education Network) Provides resource information, education, caring, sharing and understanding to parents of children with Asperger syndrome. Phone help, literature and newsletter. Dues $35/yr. Meets 2nd Mon., 7:30pm, Good Shepherd Lutheran Church, 233 South Highwood Ave., Glen Rock. Call 201-391-0758. *Website:* http://www.aspennj.org *E-mail:* aspenbergencounty@yahoo.com

Autism New Jersey (formerly COSAC) *Professionally-run.* Mutual support for parents of children with autism. Families welcome. Guest speakers, literature and phone help. *Website:* http://www.njcosac.org

> **Paramus** Meets 3rd Fri., 7-9pm, Bergen Community College, 400 Paramus Rd. Call Kathy Kientz 963-655-8066 (Mon.-Fri., 6:30pm-10pm; Sat. and Sun., day).
> **Ridgewood** Meets 1st Fri., 7-9pm, Mt. Carmel Church, Passaic St. Call Gary 201-503-9476.

BURLINGTON

ASPEN (Asperger Syndrome Education Network) Support and information for parents of children with Asperger syndrome, pervasive developmental disorder-NOS, high functioning autism and nonverbal learning disabilities. Dues $35/yr. Meets 3rd Wed., 6:45-8:45pm, Mount Laurel Library, 100 Walt Whitman Ave., Mount Laurel. Call Debbie 856-616-0877 (day). *E-mail:* dschmidt6verizon.net or jackieppr@comcast.net

Autism New Jersey (formerly COSAC) *Professionally-run.* Mutual support for parents of children with autism. Families welcome. Guest speakers, literature and phone help. Meetings vary, 7-9pm, Olde York Country Club, 228 Old York Rd., Chesterfield. Call 609-883-8100 ext. 45 (day). *Website:* http://www.njcosac.org

P.A.C.T (Chapter of Autism Society of America) Support and sharing of information by parents of autistic children. Outside activities with siblings and families. Newsletter. Building is handicapped accessible. Meets 2nd Tues., 7pm (Sept.-June), Durand Academy, 111 Gaithers Dr., Suite 101, Mt. Laurel. Call 856-722-8518 (day). *Website:* http://www.solvingthepuzzle.com

CAMDEN

Autism New Jersey (formerly COSAC) *Professionally-run.* Mutual support for parents of children with autism. Families welcome. Guest speakers, literature and phone help. Meetings vary, 7-9pm, YCS Sawtelle South, 550 Magill Ave., West Collingswood. Call 609-883-8100 ext. 45 (day). *Website:* http://www.njcosac.org

GRASP (Global and Regional Asperger Syndrome Partnership) Support network for adults diagnosed with high functioning autism or Asperger syndrome. Building is handicapped accessible. Meets 2nd Sat., 2-4pm, Easttown Library, 720 First Ave., Berwyn, PA. Call Robert 610-993-8096. *Website:* http://health.groups.yahoo.com/group/grasp_Philadelphia_pa

CAPE MAY

FACES (Families for Autistic Children, Education and Support) Group Discusses topics important to families touched by autism. Guest speakers, workshops, play groups and social opportunities. Free childcare provided (call first). Meets 1st Mon., 6:30pm, Ocean Academy School, 148 Crest Haven Ave., Cape May Court House. Call Linda Kelly 609-465-0086 or FACES 609-412-3750. *Website:* http://www.faces-autismsupport.org *Online chatroom:* http://health.groups.yahoo.com/group/facesautism *E-mail:* facesgroup@comcast.net

ESSEX

ADD Action Group Information about alternative solutions for attention deficit disorder, learning disabilities, hyperactivity, dyslexia and autism. Educational series, guest speakers, literature and phone help. Meets 3rd Thurs., 7-8:45pm, Millburn Public Library, 200 Glen Ave., Millburn. Pre-registration required. Before attending call Lynne 973-731-2189. *E-mail:* ltberke@aol.com

ASPEN (Asperger Syndrome Parents Education Network) Support and information for parents and families of children whose lives are affected by Asperger syndrome/PDD-NOS and high functioning autism. Guest speakers and literature. Dues $35/yr. Meets 3rd Mon., 7:30-9:30pm, JCC of Metrowest, 760 Northfield Ave., West Orange. Call Anita 973-669-5757 (day). *Website:* http://www.aspennj.org *E-mail:* ednee@aol.com

Autism New Jersey (formerly COSAC) *Professionally-run.* Mutual support for parents of children with autism. Families welcome. Guest speakers, literature and phone help. *Website:* http://www.njcosac.org
> **Montclair** *(parents of adult children)* Meets 3rd Tues., 7-9pm, Montclair Kimberley Academy, 201 Valley Rd. Building is handicapped accessible. Call Alice 973-324-2131 or 609-883-8100 ext. 45 (day).
> **Verona** Meets 1st Mon., 7-9pm (except Aug.), Congregation Beth Ahm, 56 Grove Ave. Call Dr. Michele Havens 201-486-5607 or 609-883-8100 ext. 45 (day). *E-mail:* mhavens523@aol.com

Autista Soy Amame Pacientemente (I am autistic – love me with passion) *(SPANISH)* Mutual support for parents of children with autism. Families welcome. Meets 1st Tues., in Newark. For meeting information call Luis 973-484-0863 (eve.) or Dina 201-997-0656 (eve.).

HUDSON

Autism New Jersey (formerly COSAC) *Professionally-run.* Mutual support for parents of children with autism. Families welcome. Guest speakers, literature and phone help. *Website:* http://www.njcosac.org
> **Bayonne** Meets 1st Wed., 7pm, Jewish Community Center, 1050 Kennedy Blvd. Call 609-883-8100 ext. 45 (day).
> **Union City** Meets 1st Thurs., 7-9pm, Iglesia San Augustin, 3900 New York Ave. Call Susana 201-864-7262.

HUNTERDON

ASPEN (Asperger Syndrome Education Network) *(Hunterdon County Adult Issues)* Young adult group for persons (ages 18 and up) who have Asperger syndrome, high functioning autism or PDD. Discussion, social activities and guest speakers. Meets 3rd Sun., 3-5pm (except Nov./Dec.), Health Quest, 310 Highway 31 North, Flemington. Call Matt and Carolyn 908-236-6153 (day). *Website:* http://www.aspergerfriends.com

Autism New Jersey (formerly COSAC) *Professionally-run.* Mutual support for parents of children with autism. Families welcome. Meets 2nd Mon., 7:30pm, JW Tumbles, 186 Center St., Clinton. Call Marybeth Ruchlin 908-730-7002 (day) or 908-387-1383 (eve.). *Website:* http://www.njcosac.org

Sharing and Caring of Bucks County Information and support for parents of children with autism, Asperger syndrome, mental retardation and related disorders. Discussion groups, guest speakers, Sib-Shop sibling support group, social and recreational activities. Meets 2nd Thurs., 7-9pm (except June, July, Aug.), St. Vincent DePaul Church, Hatboro Rd., Education Building, Richboro, PA. Call Holly 215-321-3202 (Mon.-Fri., 10am-6pm).

MERCER

Autism New Jersey (formerly COSAC) *Professionally-run.* Mutual support for parents of children with autism. Families welcome. Meets 3rd Fri., 7-9pm, Hamilton YMCA, 1315 Whitehorse-Mercerville Rd., Hamilton. Call Kelly 609-584-8825 (eve.). *Website:* http://www.njcosac.org

MIDDLESEX

ASPEN (Asperger Syndrome Parents Education Network) Support and information for parents of children with Asperger syndrome, PDD-NOS and high functioning autism. Discussion groups and guest speakers. Dues families: $35/yr.; professionals: $55/yr. Building is handicapped accessible. Meetings vary, 7:30-9:30pm, Jewish Community Center, 1775 Oak Tree Rd., Edison. Call Lori Shery 732-321-0880 (day). *Website:* http://www.aspennj.org *E-mail:* info@aspennj.org

Autism New Jersey (formerly COSAC) *Professionally-run.* Mutual support for parents of children with autism. Families welcome. Meets 1st Thurs., 7-9pm, Raritan Valley Academy, Stelton Rd., Piscataway. Call Laura 732-980-9008 (eve.). *Website:* http://www.njcosac.org

MONMOUTH

ASPEN (Asperger Syndrome Education Network) Support and information for parents of children with Asperger syndrome/PDD-NOS and high functioning autism. Discussion groups and guest speakers. Building is handicapped accessible. Meets 3rd Wed., 7-9pm, Monmouth County Library, Headquarters, 125 Symmes Rd., Manalapan. Call Ann Hiller 732-446-7610 (day). *Website:* http://www.aspennj.org *E-mail:* ann0912@aol.com

Atlantic Highlands Autism Meetup Support for parents of children with autism. Rap sessions, sharing of strategies and treatments. Building is handicapped accessible. Meets Fri., 7-9pm, Panera Bread, 776 Highway 35, Middletown. Call Jodi 732-291-1662. *Website:* http://autism.meetup.com/434 *E-mail:* lieutenant2nd@verizon.net

Autism New Jersey (formerly COSAC) *Professionally-run.* Mutual support for parents of children with autism. Families welcome. Meets 4th Thurs., 6:30-8:35pm, Monmouth County Library, 125 Symmes Rd., Manalapan. Call 609-883-8100 ext. 45 (day). *Website:* http://www.njcosac.org

MORRIS

ASPEN (Asperger Syndrome Parents Education Network) Support and information for parents and families of children with Asperger syndrome, high functioning autism and other pervasive developmental disorders. Provides support, education, advocacy, sharing of resources, guest speakers and literature. Dues $25/yr. Building is handicapped accessible. Meets last Wed., 7:30-9:30pm, Saint Clare's Hospital, 400 West Blackwell St., Conference Room D, Dover. Call Janice 973-541-0178. *Website:* http://www.aspennj.org *E-mail:* janmlem1@hotmail.com

OCEAN

Autism New Jersey (formerly COSAC) *Professionally-run.* Mutual support for parents of children with autism. Families welcome. Guest speakers, literature and phone help. Building is handicapped accessible. Meetings vary, 7:30-9pm, Children's Specialized Hospital, 94 Stevens Rd., Toms River. Call Maria and Brandon Chornobroff 732-363-6228. *Website:* http://www.njcosac.org

"Shared pain decreases; shared joy increases." -- *Author Unknown*

SALEM

Salem County Autism Support Group Mutual support and education for anyone with children or adults with autism. Families and friends welcome. Guest speakers, literature and newsletter. Meets 2nd Wed., 7-9pm, Concorde Professional Building, 390 North Broadway, Suite 1200, Pennsville. Call 856-678-9400 (day).

SOMERSET

Autism New Jersey (formerly COSAC) *Professionally-run.* Mutual support for parents of children with autism. Families welcome. Meets 1st Mon., 7-9pm, Clarence Dillon Public Library, 2336 Lamington Rd., Bedminster. Call 609-883-8100 ext. 45. *Website:* http://www.njcosac.org *E-mail:* barbara.wells@njcosac.org

UNION

Autism New Jersey (formerly COSAC) *Professionally-run.* Mutual support for parents of children with autism. Building is handicapped accessible. Meets 4th Tues., 7:30-9:30pm (except July and Dec.), Children's Specialized Hospital, New Providence Rd., Mountainside. Before attending call Deb 908-233-8510 (1-5pm only). *Website:* http://www.njcosac.org

Group S.P.I.R.I.T. (Spectrum Parents Inspired with Resources, Information and Teamwork!) Mutual support for parents with children on the autistic spectrum. Families welcome. Rap sessions, guest speakers and literature. Childcare available. Meets 1st Thurs., 7-8:30pm, Scotch Plains Library, 1927 Bartle Ave., Lower Level, Scotch Plains. Call Christine Gee 908-889-8173 (day). *E-mail:* groupspirit@aol.com

WARREN

Autism New Jersey (formerly COSAC) *Professionally-run.* Mutual support for parents of children with autism. Families welcome. Guest speakers, literature and phone help. Building is handicapped accessible. Meets 4th Wed., 7:30-9pm, Hackettstown Hospital, Willow Grove St., Hackettstown. Call Jodi 973-663-2505 (day). *Website:* http://www.njcosac.org

Need help finding a specific group? Give us a call – we're here to help!
*Call **1-800-367-6274**.*

NATIONAL

Autism Network International *International. Founded 1992.* Organization run by and for autistic people. Provides peer support and tips for coping and problem-solving. Online listserv, advocacy, education, retreats/conferences, information and referrals. Write: Autism Network International, P.O. Box 35448, Syracuse, NY 13235-5448. Call 315-476-2462 (long-distance calls will be returned collect). *Website:* http://www.ani.ac *E-mail:* jisincla@mailbox.syr.edu

Autism Society of America *National. 200+ chapters. Founded 1965.* Organization of parents, professionals and citizens working together via education, advocacy, research for children and adults on the autism spectrum. Magazine, searchable database and annual conference. Write: Autism Society of America, 7910 Woodmont Ave., Suite 300, Bethesda, MD 20814. Call 301-657-0881; 1-800-328-8476 (information and referral only; Mon.-Fri., 9am-5pm EST); Fax: 301-657-0869. *Website:* http://www.autismsocietyofamerica.org *E-mail:* info@autism-society.org

GRASP (Global and Regional Asperger Syndrome Partnership) *National. 15 chapters. Founded 2003.* Support network for adults with a diagnosis on the autism spectrum with high functioning autism, Asperger syndrome or pervasive developmental disorder. Newsletter, literature, advocacy, information and referrals. Assistance in starting local chapters. Also has an Orthodox Jewish Network for the Tri-State area in New York, along with a teen group. Write: GRASP, 666 Broadway, Suite 830, New York, NY 10012. Call 646-242-4003; Fax: 212-529-9996. *Website:* http://www.grasp.org *E-mail:* info@grasp.org

ONLINE

Families of Adults Afflicted with Asperger's Syndrome *Online.* Offers support to the family members of adult individuals with Asperger's syndrome. Membership dues $29.95. Bulletin board, e-mail list and resources. *Website:* http://www.faaas.org

Online Asperger Syndrome Information and Support (OASIS) *Online.* Interactive webpage providing information and support for Asperger syndrome and related disorders. Includes local, national and international support groups, research papers and descriptions. Message boards, chatrooms, family contributions, research projects, links to evaluators and other Asperger syndrome online resources. Forums for families affected by Asperger syndrome and the professionals working with them. *Website:* http://www.aspergersyndrome.org

BLIND / VISUALLY IMPAIRED
(see also specific disorder, toll-free helplines)

STATEWIDE

Adjustment to Vision Loss Groups Resource that provides information on support groups for those with vision loss in the following northern and central NJ area. Counties served are: Bergen, Essex, Hudson, Hunterdon, Mercer, Middlesex, Monmouth, Morris, Ocean, Passaic, Sussex, Union and Warren. Free group development assistance also available. Call Susan Vanino 201-996-9100 ext. 26.

DOROT/University Without Walls Telephone Support Teleconference support groups for persons with limited mobility who are coping with vision loss, anxiety, aging issues, etc. There is a $10 registration fee and $15 tuition per support group. Scholarships are available. Write: DOROT, 171 W. 85th St., New York, NY 10024. For more information call 1-877-819-9147 or Fran Rod 973-763-1511. *Website:* http://www.dorotusa.org

National Federation of the Blind of New Jersey Support, advocacy, self-help and education for blind persons, their families and friends. Under 18 welcome. Visitation, phone help, guest speakers, annual state conference and quarterly newsletter "Sounding Board" available in print and cassette. Dues $5/yr. Write: NFBNJ, 254 Spruce St., Bloomfield, NJ 07003. Call Joe Ruffalo 973-743-0075 (9am-5pm). *Website:* http://www.nfb.org *E-mail:* nfbnj@yahoo.com

New Jersey Association of the Deaf-Blind, Inc. *Professionally-run.* Purpose of group is to meet the needs of the deaf-blind, deaf, blind or communication impaired and their families in NJ. Provides advocacy, case management, education, information and referrals. Residential, community support, employment, family support and training services available. Write: NJADB, Inc., 24 K Worlds Fair Dr., Somerset, NJ 08873. Call 732-805-1912 (voice/TTY).

New Jersey Council of the Blind, Inc. *5 chapters.* Goal is to increase the independence of people with visual impairments through networking, mentoring and education. Membership is primarily made up of legally blind people age 18 and older. Interested sighted members are also welcome. Meetings are held in January, April and July. Annual convention is held in October. Members receive 4 quarterly issues of the New Jersey Council of the Blind, Inc. Chronicle and about 10 issues of the American Council of the Blind Braille Forum. Write: New Jersey Council of the Blind, Inc., 520 Ewingville Rd., Ewing, NJ 08638. Call

Ottilie Lucas 609-882-2446. *Website:* http://www.njcounciloftheblind.org *E-mail:* njcounciloftheblind@verizon.net

Parents of Blind Children - NJ Support, information, training and advocacy for parents of blind and visually impaired children. Technology demonstration site, newsletter and seminars. Dues $10/yr. Write: POBC, 23 Alexander Ave., Madison, NJ 07940. Call Carol Castellano 973-377-0976 (day). *Website:* http://www.blindchildren.org *E-mail:* blindchildren@verizon.net

ATLANTIC

VIP Flyers Mutual support for individuals who are blind or visually impaired. Families welcome. Rap sessions, guest speakers, literature, phone help, buddy system and speakers' bureau. Meets 4th Tues., 11am-1pm, John D. Young Blind Center, 100 Crestview Ave., Absecon. Call Ann Burns 609-677-1199 (Tues., Wed., Thurs., 9:30am-4:30pm).

BERGEN

Adjustment to Vision Loss Support Mutual support for persons dealing with vision loss to exchange helpful information, offer and obtain emotional support while learning practical solutions for dealing with vision loss. For information on groups in Cresskill, Englewood, Fort Lee, Park Ridge and Washington Township call Susan Vanino 201-996-9100 ext. 26 (day).

Focus on Eyes Support Group for the Visually-Impaired Mutual support for blind and visually impaired persons. Building is handicapped accessible. Meets 1st Tues., 10am-noon (except July/Aug.), Fair Lawn Municipal Building, Fair Lawn Ave., Fair Lawn. Call Marion 201-797-6937 or Helen Markowitz 201-797-8839. *E-mail:* marionslacke@gmail.com

BURLINGTON

Choices Support Group Mutual support for blind and visually impaired persons, their families and friends. Rap sessions, phone help, guest speakers, literature, buddy system and speakers' bureau. Building is handicapped accessible. Meets 4th Tues., 10am-noon, Resources for Independent Living, Inc., 351 High St., Burlington. Call Joe Zesski 609-747-7745; TTY: 609-747-1875. *Website:* http://www.rilnj.org *E-mail:* jzesski@rilnj.org

CAMDEN

National Federation of the Blind of New Jersey Mutual support, information and advocacy for blind persons, their families and friends. Under 18 welcome. Visitation, phone help and guest speakers. Dues $1.50 a month. Meets 3rd Sat., 10am-noon (except July), Kennedy Memorial Hospital, 5th Floor, Conference Room A, Cherry Hill. Call Linda Deberardinis 856-764-7014 or Edward Godfrey 856-906-4516 (day).

PILOTS (People Interested in Lending Others Their Support) Offers mutual support, education and social group for blind or visually-impaired persons (ages 35-65). Meets 2nd Fri., 1-3pm (except Nov.; meets 3rd Fri.), Magnolia Diner, 510 Whitehorse Pike South, Magnolia. Call Linda 856-764-7014.

ESSEX

Adjustment to Vision Loss Support Mutual support for persons dealing with vision loss to exchange helpful information, offer and obtain emotional support while learning practical solutions for dealing with vision loss. For information on groups in Irvington, Newark and West Caldwell call Susan Vanino 201-996-9100 ext. 26 (day).

E.C.H.O. (Eyes Closed Hearts Open) Provides support and recreational opportunities for persons who are visually impaired or blind. Guest speakers and rap sessions. Building is handicapped accessible. Meets 3rd Wed., noon-2:30pm, Eagle Rock Diner, 410 Eagle Ave., West Orange. Call Jane 973-736-5785.

S.C.I.L.S. (Senior Community Independent Living Services) *Professionally-run.* Support for seniors (age 55+) who are visually impaired or blind. Family and friends are welcome. Offers rap sessions, social group, literature, educational materials, mutual sharing and guest speakers. Transportation provided. Meets 3rd Wed., 1:30-2:45pm (except June, July, Aug.), Bloomfield Civic Center, 84 Broad St., Bloomfield. Call Lauri Matera 201-656-6001 ext. 152.

Sight Beyond Sight Support group for persons with visual impairments. Opportunity to exchange resource information. Guest speakers, social events and group discussions. Meets 1st Thurs., 1-4pm, Orange Public Library, Main St., Orange. Call Marcus 973-280-6290. *E-mail:* marcusscenario@gmail.com

GLOUCESTER

SHADES, Inc. Mutual support for blind and visually impaired persons. Sharing of experiences, guest speakers and information. Building is handicapped accessible. Dues $3/mtg. Meets 4th Thurs., 11am-2pm, Gloucester County Library, Route 45, Mullica Hill. Before attending call Kathryn 856-589-5438.

HUDSON

Adjustment to Vision Loss Support Mutual support for persons dealing with vision loss to exchange helpful information, offer and obtain emotional support while learning practical solutions for dealing with vision loss. For information on groups in Jersey City and Secaucus call Susan Vanino 201-996-9100 ext. 26 (day).

S.C.I.L.S. (Senior Community Independent Living Services) *(BILINGUAL) Professionally-run.* Support for interpersonal sharing and personal growth for blind and visually impaired persons (age 55+). Several small informal groups meet in various locations. Spanish-speaking group available. Call 201-656-6001 (Mon.-Fri., 8:30am-4:30pm).

HUNTERDON

Hunterdon Eye Openers Support for persons dealing with vision loss to exchange helpful information, offer and obtain emotional support while learning practical solutions for dealing with vision loss. Meets 1st Thurs., 11:30am, Senior Services, Building #3, Gauntt Pl., Flemington. Call Hank 908-751-1697.

MERCER

Adjustment to Vision Loss Support Mutual support for persons dealing with vision loss to exchange helpful information, offer and obtain emotional support while learning practical solutions for dealing with vision loss. Dues $10/yr. Meets 3rd Thurs., 7:30-9:30pm, 1985 Pennington Rd., Ewing. Call Ottilie Lucas 609-882-2446. *E-mail:* ottilie@verizon.net

National Federation of the Blind Support and advocacy for the blind community. Family and friends are welcome to attend. Dues $10/yr. Meets 3rd Sat., 10am-noon, Lawrence Library, 2751 Brunswick Pike, Lawrenceville. Call Mary Jo 609-888-5459 (eve.).

MIDDLESEX

Adjustment to Vision Loss Support Mutual support for persons dealing with vision loss to exchange helpful information, offer and obtain emotional support while learning practical solutions for dealing with vision loss.

> **Edison, Metuchen and Milltown** Meetings vary. Call Susan Vanino 201-996-9100 ext. 26 (day).
>
> **Metuchen** Meets 4th Thurs., 7-9pm (except Jan., Feb., July, Aug.), Metuchen Public Library, 480 Middlesex Ave. (rear entrance). Building is handicapped accessible. Call Phyllis Boeddinghaus 732-548-1391.
>
> **Monroe Township** Meets 3rd Thurs., 10:30am-noon, Monroe Township Senior Center, 1 Municipal Plaza. Building is handicapped accessible. Call Laura Petix or Judy Kalman 732-521-6111.
>
> **Monroe Township** Meetings vary, Monroe Village. Building is handicapped accessible. Call Ted Alter 732-521-6418. *E-mail:* talter@phsnet.org
>
> **Perth Amboy** Meets 2nd Wed., 7:30-9pm, Grace Lutheran Church, 600 New Brunswick Ave. Dues $10/yr. Building handicapped accessible. Call Kellyanne 732-388-1322.

Beyond the Eyes Multicultural resource and support group for men and women who are visually impaired. Rap sessions and education. Membership $25/yr. Building is handicapped accessible. Meets last Fri., 1-4pm, Heritage at Clara Barton, 1015 Amboy Ave., Edison. Call Diane Robinson 973-733-9565 or James 973-763-6308.

Eye Openers Of Central New Jersey Mutual aid self-help for blind and visually impaired persons. Emotional support, sharing of experience and information. Meets 1st Thurs., 7:15-9:15pm, at local restaurants. Call Bernard Zuckerman 732-494-0753.

MONMOUTH

Adjustment to Vision Loss Support Mutual support for persons dealing with vision loss to exchange helpful information, offer and obtain emotional support while learning practical solutions for dealing with vision loss. For information on groups in Tinton Falls and Wall Township call Susan Vanino 201-996-9100 ext. 26 (day).

Middletown Area Visually Challenged Group Support for persons dealing with vision loss to exchange helpful information, offer and obtain emotional support while learning practical solutions for dealing with vision loss. Meetings vary, 11am-noon, New Jersey Blind Citizens Association, Inc., Camp

Happiness, 18 Burlington Ave., Leonardo. Before attending call Charles Blood 732-671-9371.

MORRIS

Adjustment to Vision Loss Support Mutual support for persons dealing with vision loss to exchange helpful information, offer and obtain emotional support while learning practical solutions for dealing with vision loss. For information on groups in Denville and Pompton Plains call Susan Vanino 201-996-9100 ext. 26 (day).

North Jersey Retinitis Pigmentosa Support Group Mutual support for persons with retinitis pigmentosa, macular degeneration, Usher's syndrome or related disorders and their families. Provides education, referrals, phone help, rap sessions and guest speakers. Meetings vary, 1:30-4pm, Morristown. Before attending call Jean and Don Perlman 973-584-6471, Susan Strechay 973-267-2419 (eve.) or Glorie Isakower 609-409-7985 (Usher's syndrome).

V.I.P. (Visually Impaired Persons) Mutual aid self-help for blind and visually impaired persons. Emotional support, sharing of experiences and information. Meets 2nd Wed., 11am-1:30pm (except July and Aug.), Diamond Spring Lodge, 230 Diamond Spring Rd., Denville. Call Mary Ann Speenburgh 973-884-0039.

OCEAN

Adjustment to Vision Loss Support Mutual support for persons dealing with vision loss to exchange helpful information, offer and obtain emotional support while learning practical solutions for dealing with vision loss.
> **Lakewood** Meets 2nd Tues., 11am-noon, Leisure Village East, 1015 B Aberdeen Dr. Call Betty 732-920-1522.
> **Mayetta, Toms River and Whiting** For information on groups call Susan Vanino 201-996-9100 ext. 26 (day).

Eye Openers Of Point Pleasant/Brick Mutual aid self-help for blind and visually impaired persons. Emotional support, sharing of experiences and information. Building is handicapped accessible.
> **Point Pleasant Beach** Meets 2nd and 4th Tues., 10am-noon, Pt. Pleasant Presbyterian Church, Bay Ave. and Forman Ave. Call George 732-892-5117.
> **Toms River** Meets 3rd Tues., 12:30-2:30pm, Toms River Library, Washington St. Call Jim Fox 732-244-7057 (day). *E-mail:* Jim2447057@comcast.net

Low Vision Support Group Support for persons afflicted with low vision, their families and friends. Guest speakers, mutual sharing and educational programs. Meets 1st Wed., 1pm (except July and Aug.), Ocean Club, 700 Route 9 South, Stafford Township. Call Judi 609-978-3559 (Tues-Fri.; 9am-4:30pm).

National Federation of the Blind of New Jersey Mutual support, information and advocacy for blind persons, their families and friends. Dues $5/yr. Meets 2nd Sat., 10am-noon, Denny's Restaurant, Brick Blvd., Bricktown. Call Mary 732-349-2456.

PASSAIC

Adjustment to Vision Loss Support Mutual support for persons dealing with vision loss to exchange helpful information, offer and obtain emotional support while learning practical solutions for dealing with vision loss. For information on groups in Clifton, Paterson and Wayne call Susan Vanino 201-996-9100 ext. 26 (day).

SUSSEX

Adjustment to Vision Loss Support Mutual support for persons dealing with vision loss to exchange helpful information, offer and obtain emotional support while learning practical solutions for dealing with vision loss. For information on groups in Sparta call Susan Vanino 201-996-9100 ext. 26 (day).

UNION

Adjustment to Vision Loss Support Mutual support for persons dealing with vision loss to exchange helpful information, offer and obtain emotional support while learning practical solutions for dealing with vision loss. For information on groups in Cranford and Roselle call Susan Vanino 201-996-9100 ext. 26 (day).

Macular Degeneration Support Group Support, coping skills, visual aids and research for persons with macular degeneration. Meets 2nd Sat., 11am-12:30pm, Overlook Hospital, 99 Beauvoir Ave., Conference Room 2, Summit. Call Janet Rowley-Cebula 973-972-2097 (day).

Self-Help Group for the Visually-Impaired Provides mutual support and education for those who are blind or visually-impaired. Meets 1st Thurs., noon-2pm (except July/Aug.), Senior Citizen Center, Bonnel Court, Union. Call Agnes 908-790-9336 (eve.).

NATIONAL

American Council of the Blind *National. 70 affiliates. Founded 1961.* Aims to improve the well-being of all blind or visually impaired people and their families through education, support and advocacy. National conference, information and referrals, phone support, state and special interest affiliates (e.g. guide dog users, blind lawyers, teachers and students) and magazine published ten times per year (available in Braille, half speed cassette, large print, CD-ROM, online or via e-mail). Scholarships. Online job bank. Chapter development guidelines. Write: American Council of the Blind, 1155 15th St. NW, Suite 1004, Washington, DC 20005. Call 1-800-424-8666 or 202-467-5081; Fax: 202-467-5085. *Website:* http://www.acb.org *E-mail:* info@acb.org

Aniridia Foundation International *International. Founded 2002.* Offers support, data studies, research and education to the public, medical community and members. Provides information, referrals, literature, newsletter, phone support, pen pals and conferences. Online e-mail support and chatrooms. Also supports those with low vision or blindness who experience the same associated conditions such as glaucoma, corneal disease and cataracts. OPTIC program helps those with Stevens-Johnson syndrome, chemical and thermal burns to the eyes and other corneal dystrophy patients. Write: Aniridia Foundation International, c/o Hamilton Eye Institute, 930 Madison Ave., Suite 314, Memphis, TN 38163. Call 901-448-2380; Fax: 901-448-2382. *Website:* http://www.aniridia.net *E-mail:* info@aniridia.net

Association for Macular Diseases, Inc. *National. Founded 1978.* Support for persons suffering from macular diseases and their families. Distributes information on vision equipment. Supports national eye bank donor projects devoted solely to macular disease research. Quarterly newsletter, phone support network, participates in seminars and group development guidelines. Dues $20/year. Write: Association for Macular Diseases, 210 E. 64th St., New York, NY 10021. Call 212-605-3719 (eve.); Fax: 212-605-3795. *Website:* http://www.macula.org

Blinded Veterans Association *National. 53 regional groups. Founded 1945.* Support, information and outreach to blinded veterans including those who were blinded in combat and those suffering from age-related macular degeneration and other eye diseases. Help in obtaining prosthetic devices and accessing the latest technological advances to assist the blind. Information on benefits and rehabilitation programs. Quarterly newsletter. Regional meetings. Write: BVA, 477 H St., NW, Washington, DC 20001. Call 202-371-8880 or 1-800-669-7079; Fax: 202-371-8258. *Website:* http://www.bva.org *E-mail:* bva@bva.org

Council of Citizens with Low Vision International *International. Founded 1979.* Encourages low vision people to make full use of vision through use of equipment, technology and services. Education, advocacy, quarterly magazine, group development guidelines, scholarships, conferences, information and referrals. Write: Council of Citizens with Low Vision International, 2200 Wilson Blvd., Arlington, VA 22201. Call 1-800-733-2258 (Mon.-Fri, 9am-4pm PST). *Website:* http://www.cclvi.org

Foundation Fighting Blindness, Inc., The *National. Founded 1971.* Offers information and referral services for affected individuals and their families, as well as doctors and eye care professionals. Provides comprehensive information kits on retinitis pigmentosa, macular degeneration and Usher syndrome. Newsletter presents articles on coping, research updates and Foundation news. Supports research into the causes, treatments, preventive methods and cures for the entire spectrum of retinal degenerative diseases. Newsletter "InFocus" published 3 times/yr. E-newsletter "InSight" published 5 times/yr. National conference held every year. Write: Foundation Fighting Blindness, Inc., 11435 Cronhill Dr., Owings Mill, MD 21117-2220. Call 1-800-683-5555 (Mon.-Fri., 9am-4pm EST); 1-800-683-5551 (TDD). *Website:* http://www.fightblindness.org *E-mail:* info@fightblindness.org

Jewish Guild for the Blind, The *National. Founded 1914.* Support for persons of all ages who are visually impaired, blind and those with additional disabilities. Telephone support network brings together parents from around the country whose children have the same condition (retinopathy of prematurity, retinitis pigmentosa, cortical visual impairment, Leber's congenital amaurosis and Stargardt disease) to speak with parents in the same situation. Newsletter, literature and how-to materials for starting a support group available on the website or in hard copy. Write: The Jewish Guild for the Blind, 15 West 65th Street, New York, NY 10023. Call 1-800-284-4422 or 212-769-7800. *Website:* http://www.jgb.org *E-mail:* info@jgb.org

Lighthouse International *Resource.* Mission is to overcome vision impairment for people of all ages through rehabilitation services, education, research and advocacy. Free literature on eye diseases (macular degeneration, glaucoma, cataracts, diabetes and more) and various resource lists (reading options, adaptive computer technology, financial aid, etc.) Provides contact information for support groups, low vision services, rehabilitation agencies, state agencies and advocacy groups. Write: Lighthouse International, 111 East 59th St., New York, NY 10022. Call 1-800-829-0500 or 212-821-9200 (Mon.-Fri., 9am-5pm EST); Fax: 212-821-9707; TDD: 212-821-9713. *Website:* http://www.lighthouse.org *E-mail:* info@lighthouse.org

MAB Community Services *National. 34 groups. Founded 1903.* Support network for persons coping with sight loss. Sponsors support groups for elders and mixed ages. Outreach services, community volunteers, recording studio, cassettes and newsletter. Write: MAB Community Services, 313 Pleasant St., Watertown, MA 02472. Call 617-926-4232 or 1-800-852-3029 (MA only) (Mon.-Fri., 9am-5pm EST); Fax: 617-926-1412. *Website:* http://www.mabcommunity.org *E-mail:* fweisse@mabcommunity.org or jbreda@mabcommunity.org

National Association for Parents of Children with Visual Impairments *(BILINGUAL) National. 21 groups. Founded 1980.* Outreach and support for parents of children with visual impairments. Promotes formation of local parent support groups. Increases public awareness. Quarterly newsletter. Dues $25/family. Group development guidelines. Write: NAPVI, Inc., P.O. Box 317, Watertown, MA 02471-0317. Call 1-800-562-6265; Fax: 617-972-7444. *Website:* http://www.napvi.org *E-mail:* napvi@perkins.org

National Association for Visually Handicapped *(MULTILINGUAL) National. Founded 1954.* Support for visually impaired adults and seniors. Newsletter, phone support, information and referrals. Bimonthly support group for visually impaired seniors. Guide to starting groups for elders losing sight. Free large print loan library by mail and optical library. Large print informational materials available in English, some in Russian, Spanish and Chinese. Write: National Association for Visually Handicapped, c/o C. Gomez, 22 West 21st St., 6th Floor, New York, NY 10010. Call 212-889-3141 or 1-888-205-5951; Fax: 212-727-2931. *Website:* http://www.navh.org *E-mail:* navh@navh.org

National Federation of the Blind *National. 52 affiliates. Founded 1940.* Serves as both an advocacy and a public information vehicle. Contacts newly blind persons to help with adjustment. Provides information on services and applicable laws. Student scholarships. Assists blind persons who are victims of discrimination. Literature, monthly meetings and magazine. Assistance in starting new groups. Write: National Federation of the Blind, 1800 Johnson St., Baltimore, MD 21230-4998. Call 410-659-9314; Fax: 410-685-5653. *Website:* http://www.nfb.org *E-mail:* nfb@nfb.org

National Keratoconus Foundation *National network. Founded 1986.* Provides information and support to persons with keratoconus, an eye condition where the cornea progressively thins causing a cone-like bulge. Newsletter, phone support, information and referrals. Online support group. Encourages research into cause and treatment. Write: National Keratoconus Foundation, 8733 Beverly Blvd., Suite 201, Los Angeles, CA 90048. Call 1-800-521-2524; Fax: 310-623-1837. *Website:* http://www.nkcf.org *E-mail:* info@nkcf.org

National Organization of Parents of Blind Children *National. 25 chapters. Founded 1983.* Serves as both an advocacy and public information vehicle. Provides information on services available. Offers positive philosophy and insights into blindness and practical guidance in raising a blind child. "Future Reflections" magazine, parent seminars, free parents' information packet, meetings and conventions. Dues $8. Write: National Organization of Parents of Blind Children, c/o Barbara Cheadle, National Federation of the Blind, 1800 Johnson St., Baltimore, MD 21230. Call 410-659-9314 ext. 2360; Fax: 410-685-5653. *Website:* http://www.nfb.org/nopbc *E-mail:* bcheadle@nfb.org

Vision Northwest *Model. 42 groups (support groups in WA and OR). Founded 1983.* Mission is to promote independent living for people affected by vision loss through individual and group support, low vision aids, information and education. Helps people with vision loss to become more independent through a network of peer support groups and individual peer counseling. Information and referral, newsletters, low vision accessory store and loan-lending optical aids network. Write: Vision Northwest, 9225 SW Hall Blvd., Suite G, Tigard, OR 97223. Call 503-684-8389; Fax: 503-684-9359. *Website:* http://www.visionnw.com *E-mail:* info@visionnw.com

ONLINE

Duane's Retraction Syndrome *Online. 1150 members. Founded 1999.* A place for those affected by Duane's retraction syndrome (an eye mobility disorder) to share experiences and information with others. *Website:* http://health.groups.yahoo.com/group/duanes

EyesApart *Online. 581 members. Founded 2006.* Support forum for adults, teens and parents of children with strabismus (also known as: squint, crossed eyes, lazy eye, wall eyes, double vision, turned, floating, wandering, wayward, drifting eyes) to discuss knowledge, experiences, problems and ideas related to strabismus. *Website:* http://health.groups.yahoo.com/group/eyesapart

LazyEye *Online. 927 members. Founded 1999.* Provides emotional support and direction to resources for parents of children with amblyopia, strabismus or other conditions associated with "lazy eye." Adult amblyopes are welcome as well. *Website:* http://health.groups.yahoo.com/group/lazyeye

Leber's Congenital Amaurosis eGroup *Online. 568 members. Founded 1999.* Provides a listserv for persons who are interested in sharing, support and information relating to the genetic disorder. *Website:* http://groups.yahoo.com/group/lca

VitreousFloaters *Online. 2703 members. Founded 2000.* Support for those with eye floaters or vitreous detachment. Opportunity to share experiences, ideas for treatment and strategies for living with floaters. *Website:* http://health.groups.yahoo.com/group/vitreousfloaters

BRAIN INJURY / COMA
(see also general disabilities, specific disorder, toll-free helplines)

STATEWIDE

Brain Injury Association of New Jersey Provides information, education, outreach, prevention, advocacy and support services to all persons affected by brain injury. Write: Brain Injury Association of New Jersey, 825 Georges Rd., 2nd Floor, North Brunswick, NJ 08902. Call 732-745-0200 (day) or 1-800-669-4323 (day); Fax: 732-745-0211. *Website:* http://www.bianj.org *E-mail:* info@bianj.org

ATLANTIC

Brain Injury Association of New Jersey *Professionally-run.* Emotional support and education for persons with brain injuries, their families and friends. Meets 2nd Thurs., 7pm, Bacharach Institute for Rehabilitation, 61 W. Jimmie Leeds Rd., Pomona. Call Nutan Ravani 856-589-5797 (day) or helpline 1-800-669-4323. *Website:* http://www.bianj.org *E-mail:* info@bianj.org

BERGEN

Brain Injury Support Group Emotional support and education for persons with brain injuries, their families and friends. Building is handicapped accessible. Meets 3rd Mon., 6:30pm, Englewood Hospital, Engle St., Englewood. Call Joe Concato 201-666-2015 (day).

Voices That Count *Professionally-run.* Support group for brain injury survivors. Families, friends and caregivers group meets concurrently. Guest speakers and literature. Building is handicapped accessible. Meets 2nd Wed., 6:30-8pm, Rehabilitation Specialists, 18-01 Pollitt Dr., Suite 1A, Fair Lawn. Call Carly Schoener 201-478-4200 ext. 26 (survivors); Dawn King, ME 201-478-4200 ext. 19 or Jennifer Victoria-Proano, MA 201-478-4200 ext. 31 (families, friends and caregivers). *E-mail:* (survivors) cschoener@rehab-specialists.com; (families, friends and caregivers) dscala@rehab-specialists.com or jvictoria @rehab-specialists.com

BURLINGTON

Brain Injury Association of New Jersey *Professionally-run.* Support group for survivors of mild/moderate brain injuries and their families. Guest speakers and literature. Meets 2nd and 4th Wed., 7pm, Marlton Rehabilitation Hospital, 92 Brick Rd., Marlton. Call Nutan Ravani 856-988-4118 (day) or helpline 1-800-669-4323.

CAMDEN

Burlington/Camden County Support Group *Professionally-run.* Support for persons with brain injuries, their families and caregivers. Guest speakers. Meets 3rd Mon., 7-9pm, Lebensfeld Bancrof, 201 South Kings Highway, Camden. Call Katie Kelly 609-799-8400 (day) or Kristin Lukianovich 856-616-6433 (day). *E-mail:* kkelly@bnh.org

ESSEX

Brain Injury Association of New Jersey *Professionally-run.* Emotional support and education for persons with brain injuries, their families and friends. Meets 2nd and last Tues., 6:30pm, Kessler Institute for Rehabilitation, 1199 Pleasant Valley Way, West Orange. Call Betty Collins 973-414-4743 (day).

GLOUCESTER

Brain Injury Support Group Mutual support, friendship, networking and social activities for individuals who have sustained a brain injury.

> **Turnersville** Meets Wed., 7-9:30pm, Apostles Lutheran Church, 4401 Black Horse Pike. Call Teresa May 856-629-8487 or the church 856-629-4228.
>
> **Woodbury** Meets 4th Mon., 6:30pm, Moss Rehab, Drucker Brain Injury Center, 135 South Broad St. Building is handicapped accessible. Call Dayna Scott 856-853-9900 ext. 102.

*We can also refer callers to over 100 individuals who are seeking others to help start new support groups throughout NJ. For more information call **1-800-367-6274.***

HUNTERDON

Brain Injury Association of New Jersey *Professionally-run.* Emotional support and education for persons with brain injuries and their families. Building is handicapped accessible. Meets 2nd Thurs., 7pm (except July/Aug.), Hunterdon Medical Center, 2100 Wescott Dr., Meeting Room C, Flemington. Call Gwen Bartlett-Palmer 908-391-5503.

MERCER

Brain Injury Association of New Jersey *Professionally-run.* Emotional support and education for persons with brain injuries, their families and friends. Building is handicapped accessible. Meets 1st Wed., 6:30pm, St. Lawrence Rehab Hospital, 2381 Lawrenceville Rd., Room 117, Lawrenceville. Call David Searles 609-896-9500 ext. 2244 or helpline 1-800-669-4323.

MIDDLESEX

Brain Injury Association of New Jersey *Professionally-run.* Emotional support and education for persons with head injuries and their families. Building is handicapped accessible. Meets 2nd Tues., 6pm, JFK Center for Head Injuries, 2048 Oak Tree Rd., Edison. Call Sabrina Wisniewski 732-906-2640 ext. 42656 (day).

COPSA Spouse Support Group *Professionally-run.* Mutual support and understanding for spouses of persons with any type of memory loss including Alzheimer's, Parkinson's, vascular disease, stroke, head injury and dementia. Meets 1st and 3rd Mon., 9:30-11am, University Behavioral Healthcare Center, 671 Hoes Lane, Piscataway. Call Mary Catherine Lundquist 732-235-2858 (day). *E-mail:* lundqumc@umdnj.edu

MONMOUTH

Brain Injury Association of New Jersey *Professionally-run.* Emotional support and education for persons with head injuries and their families. Meets 1st Tues., 7pm, Dorbrook Park Recreation Area, Route 537, Colts Neck. Call 732-745-0200.

OCEAN

Brain Injury Association of New Jersey *Professionally-run.* Emotional support and education for persons with head injuries, their families and friends. Meets 3rd Tues., 6pm, Community Medical Center, 99 Highway 37 West, Toms

River. Call Vicki Hardy 732-557-8000 ext. 10226 or Pam Lightfoot 732-557-8000 ext. 11547.

SUSSEX

Brain Injury Association of New Jersey *Professionally-run.* Emotional support and education for persons with brain injuries, their families and friends. Meets 2nd Wed., 8pm (except Jan., Feb., Dec.), Redeemer Lutheran Church, 37 Newton-Sparta Rd., Newton. Call Vince Dorio 732-627-9890 ext. 220 (day) or helpline 1-800-669-4323.

NATIONAL

Brain Injury Association, Inc. *National. 42 state associations. 600 affiliated groups. Founded 1980.* Advocacy organization providing services to persons with brain injuries, their families and professionals. Increases public awareness through state associations, support groups, information and resource network, seminars, conferences, literature and prevention programs. Guidelines for starting similar groups. Write: Brain Injury Association, 1608 Spring Hill Road, Suite 110, Vienna, VA 22182. Call 1-800-444-6443 (National Brain Injury Information Center) or 703-761-0750; Fax: 703-761-0755. *Website:* http://www.biausa.org *E-mail:* braininjuryinfo@biausa.org

Coma/Traumatic Brain Injury Recovery Association *National network. Founded 1980.* Support and advocacy for families of coma and traumatic brain injury survivors. Provides information, referrals and support group for family members and survivors. Quarterly newsletter and yearly conferences for families, brain injury professionals and survivors. Write: Coma/Traumatic Brain Injury Recovery Association, 8300 Republic Airport, Suite 106, Farmingdale, NY 11735. Call 631-756-1826; Fax: 631-756-1827. *Website:* http://www.comarecovery.org *E-mail:* inquiry@comarecovery.org

BURN SURVIVORS
(see also facial disfigurement)

ESSEX

Burn Peer Support Group Support and education for burn patients and their families. Visitations and phone help. Building is handicapped accessible. Meets monthly, St. Barnabas Medical Center, Old Short Hills Rd., Livingston. Call Susan Fischer 973-322-5276 (day).

NATIONAL

Burns United Support Group *National. 1 affiliated group. Founded 1986.* Mutual support for children and adults who have survived being burned, no matter how major or minor the burn. Also for the family and friends of the survivor. Outreach visitation, newsletter, pen pals, phone support and assistance in starting groups. Write: Burns United Support Group, c/o Donna Schneck, P.O. Box 36416, Detroit, MI 48236. Call 313-881-5577.

Phoenix Society for Burn Survivors, Inc., The *International. Founded 1977.* Mission is to uplift and inspire anyone affected by burns through peer support, collaboration, education and advocacy. Includes support services, referrals and quarterly newsletter "Burn Support News." SOAR Peer Support Program, annual World Burn Congress, family services, toll-free information and referral line, online chat sessions, advocacy and educational programs. Write: The Phoenix Society, 1835 RW Berends Dr. SW, Grand Rapids, MI 49519. Call 1-800-888-2876 or 616-458-2773; Fax: 616-458-2831. *Website:* http://www.phoenix-society.org *E-mail:* info@phoenix-society.org

ONLINE

Burn Survivors Online *Online.* Information and support for burn survivors and their families throughout the world. Burn survivor profiles, burn statistics, peer support scheduled chats, outreach to newly burned patients and families. Newsletter, list of books, articles, question and answer forum. *Website:* http://www.burnsurvivorsonline.com

CEREBRAL PALSY
(see also general disabilities, parents of disabled)

STATEWIDE

Advancing Opportunities (Formerly Cerebral Palsy of New Jersey) Provides services statewide to advance the independence of children and adults with all types of disabilities. Programs include advocacy, employment services, family support, respite, assistive technology, substance abuse prevention, information and referral, personal assistance services and a technology lending center. Write: Cerebral Palsy of New Jersey, 1005 Whitehead Rd., Suite 1-A, Ewing, NJ 08638. Call 1-888-322-1918 or 609-882-0620; TTY: 609-882-0620. *Website:* http://www.cpofnj.org *E-mail:* info@cpofnj.org

NATIONAL

United Cerebral Palsy Association, Inc. *National. 140 affiliates. Founded 1949.* Supports local affiliates that run programs for individuals with cerebral palsy and other disabilities. Local programs include support groups for parents and adults with cerebral palsy. Advocacy, research reports, referrals and information packets. Write: United Cerebral Palsy Association, Inc., 1660 L St., NW, Suite 700, Washington, DC 20036-5603. Call 1-800-872-5827; Fax: 202-776-0414. *Website:* http://www.ucp.org

ONLINE

Cerebral Palsy Network *Online. 1289 members. Founded 2000.* Aim is to make a difference in the lives of individuals with cerebral palsy and their loved ones. *Website:* http://groups.yahoo.com/group/cerebralpalsynetwork

DEAF / HEARING IMPAIRED / TINNITIS
(see also vestibular, toll-free helplines)

STATEWIDE

ALDA (Association of Late-Deafened Adults) - Garden State Support, education and advocacy on behalf of all people with hearing loss, especially the post-lingually deafened. Accessible education workshops, guest speakers, advocacy and social events. Yearly dues: $15/individual; $20/family. Free newsletter on request. All education meetings provide sign language interpreters and CART captioning. Call Elinore Bullock 908-832-5083 (CapTel). *Website:* http://www.alda-gs.org *E-mail:* elinorebullock7@embarqmail.com

New Jersey Association of the Deaf-Blind, Inc. *Professionally-run.* Purpose of group is to meet the needs of the deaf-blind, deaf, blind or communication impaired and their families in NJ. Provides advocacy, case management, education, information and referrals. Residential, community, family, employment support and training services. Write: NJ Association of Deaf-Blind, Inc., 24 K Worlds Fair Drive, Somerset, NJ 08873. Call 732-805-1912 (voice/TTY).

Signs of Sobriety, Inc. (SOS) Provides alcoholism and drug addiction services to persons who are deaf or hard-of-hearing. Makes referrals to deaf and sign interpreted 12-step programs. Provides prevention and education classes. Offers S.T.E.P.S. Program, a weekly peer support group for recovering individuals. Sponsors sober/deaf activities. Newsletter. Write: Signs Of Sobriety, Inc., 100 Scotch Rd., 2nd Floor, Ewing, NJ 08628-2507. Call TTY/VP: 609-882-7177; Voice: 609-882-7677 or 1-800-332-7677 (day); Fax: 609-882-6808. *Website:* http://www.signsofsobriety.org *E-mail:* info@signsofsobriety.org

BERGEN

Hearing Loss Association of America (HLA) *(Bergen County Chapter)* Mutual support and information for people who are hard-of-hearing. Guest speakers. Dues $10/yr. Meetings vary, 1-3pm (Apr., June, Sept.), Puffin Cultural Forum, 1 Puffin Way, Teaneck. Call Arlene 201-995-9594 (voice/TTY). *E-mail:* aromoff@aol.com

CAMDEN

South Jersey Tinnitus Support Group *Professionally-run.* Support and information for tinnitus sufferers and family members. Building is handicapped accessible. Meets 1st Thurs., 7:30pm (except July/Aug.), Virtua Hospital, Barry Brown Education Building, Voorhees. Call Linda Beach 856-346-0200 or Mary Ann Halladay 609-429-5055 ext. 25; TDD: 856-346-0623 (day). *Website:* http://www.pro-oto.com *E-mail:* linda.beach@gmail.com

MERCER

Tinnitus Association of New Jersey *Professionally-run.* Mutual support for persons afflicted with tinnitus, their families and friends. Rap sessions, guest speakers, coping skills, literature and newsletter. Meets 1st Sat., 10-11:30am, First Presbyterian Church, Ewing. Call Dhyan Cassie 856-983-8981 (day).

MIDDLESEX

Hearing Loss Association of America (HLA) *(Middlesex County Chapter)* Mutual support and information for people who are hard-of-hearing. Rap sessions and guest speakers. Dues $10/yr. includes monthly newsletter. Building is handicapped accessible. Meets 3rd Tues., 7:30-9pm (except July/Aug.), First Baptist Church of South Plainfield, 201 Hamilton Blvd., South Plainfield. Call Marie Nordling 732-721-4183. *E-mail:* mcnord@yahoo.com

New Jersey CODA (Children Of Deaf Adults) Provides mutual support for hearing adult children (ages 18+) of deaf parents. Also open to deaf parents with children under age 18. Promotes family awareness and individual growth in hearing children of deaf parents. Speakers' bureau, discussion sessions and phone assistance. Call Mariann Linfante Jacobson 732-548-2571. *E-mail:* jac2003@prodigy.net

MONMOUTH

Hearing Loss Association of America (HLA) *(Monmouth/Ocean Chapter)* Mutual support and information for people who cannot hear well. Guest speakers, rap sessions and literature. Families welcome. Donation $10/yr. Building is handicapped accessible. Meets 1st Sun., 1:30-4pm, Lakewood. Call Lois Walker 732-222-5546 (CapTel). *E-mail:* oceanmonmouthhla@yahoo.com

PASSAIC

DIAL, Inc. - Center for Independent Living Provides referral, peer counseling, advocacy and independent living skills program for people with disabilities. Deaf and hard-of-hearing outreach services. Dues $15/yr./individual, $25/yr./family. Building is handicapped accessible. Meets last Tues., 6:30-9:30pm, Clifton Center for Seniors and Citizens with Disabilities, Clifton. Call 1-866-277-1733 or 973-470-8090 (day); TTY: 973-470-2521. *Website:* http://www.dial-cil.org *E-mail:* info@dial-cil.org

NATIONAL

Alexander Graham Bell Association for Deaf and Hard of Hearing *Founded 1958.* Network of parents whose members promote advocating independence through listening and talking. Concerned with early diagnosis and auditory, language and speech training for children who are deaf or hard-of-hearing. Works to preserve parent and children's rights by advocating auditory-oral and auditory-verbal education. Serves as clearinghouse to dispense information and exchange ideas. Write: Alexander Graham Bell Association 3417 Volta Pl. NW, Suite 310, Washington, DC 20007. Call 202-337-5220; TTY: 202-337-5221; Fax: 202-337-8314. *Website:* http://www.agbell.org *E-mail:* info@agbell.org

American Society for Deaf Children *National. 120 affiliates. Founded 1967.* Information and support for parents and families with children who are deaf or hard-of-hearing. Quarterly magazine, biennial conventions, information and referral. Guidelines for starting similar groups. Dues $40/yr. Write: American Society for Deaf Children, 3820 Hartzdale Dr., Camp Hill, PA 17011. Call hotline: 1-800-942-2732, 1-866-895-4206 or 717-909-5577 (voice/TTY); Fax: 717-909-5599. *Website:* http://www.deafchildren.org *E-mail:* asdc1@aol.com

American Tinnitus Association *National. 50 groups. Founded 1971.* Provides support, information, education and advocacy for persons affected by tinnitus. Funds research. Dues $35/yr includes "Tinnitus Today" magazine. Write: American Tinnitus Association, P.O. Box 5, Portland, OR 97207. Call 1-800-634-8978 or 503-248-9985. *Website:* http://www.ata.org *E-mail:* tinnitus@ata.org

Children Of Deaf Adults *International. 12 affiliated groups. Founded 1983.* Provides mutual support for hearing children (over the age of 18) of deaf parents. Promotes family awareness and individual growth through self-help groups, educational programs, advocacy and resource development. Newsletter, assistance in starting groups, information and referrals. Dues $25/yr. Write: Children of Deaf Adults, Box 30715, Santa Barbara, CA 93130. Call 805-682-0997 (voice/TTY) (9am-9pm PST). *Website:* http://www.coda-international.org

Hearing Loss Association of America *International. 200 chapters and groups. Founded 1979.* Aim is to open the world of communication to people with hearing loss by providing support, information, education, referrals and advocacy. Bimonthly journal, online local group and chapter listings. Assistance in starting groups. Write: Hearing Loss Association of America, 7910 Woodmont Ave., Suite 1200, Bethesda, MD 20814. Call 301-657-2248 (voice) or 301-657-2249 (TTY); Fax: 301-913-9413. *Website:* http://www.hearingloss.org *E-mail:* info@hearingloss.org

National Association of the Deaf *National. 51 affiliated groups. Founded 1880.* Federation of state associations, organizational and business affiliates that fights for the civil rights of deaf and hard-of-hearing Americans. Offers grassroots and youth leadership development and legal expertise across a broad spectrum of areas including, but not limited to, accessibility, education, employment, healthcare, mental health, rehabilitation, technology, telecommunications and transportation. Provides advocacy information and resources. Write: National Association of the Deaf, 8630 Fenton St., Suite 820, Silver Spring, MD 20910-3819. Call 301-587-1789 (TTY); 301-587-1788 (voice); Fax: 301-587-1791. *Website:* http://www.nad.org

Rainbow Alliance of the Deaf *National. 23 affiliated chapters. Founded 1977.* Promotes the educational, economical and social welfare of deaf and hard-of-hearing gay, lesbian, bisexual, transgendered persons and their friends. Discussion of practical problems and solutions. Advocacy, conferences, newsletter, assistance in starting groups. Online information on contacting a local chapter. Write: Rainbow Alliance of the Deaf, c/o Steven Schumacher, 9804 Walker House Rd., Suite 4, Montgomery Village, MD 20886. *Website:* http://www.rad.org *E-mail:* president@rad.org

DEVELOPMENTAL DISABILITIES / DOWN SYNDROME
(see also parents of disabled, specific syndrome, toll-free helplines)

STATEWIDE

Arc of NJ, The *Professionally-run.* Services and advocacy for children and adults with intellectual and developmental disabilities and their families. Parent support groups available at the chapter offices in each county. Membership dues vary for each chapter. Write: The Arc of NJ, 985 Livingston Ave., North Brunswick, NJ 08902. Call 732-246-2525 (day). *Website:* http://www.arcnj.org *E-mail:* info@arcnj.org

New Jersey Self-Advocacy Project and Statewide Self-Advocacy Provides information on groups statewide forming the Statewide Self-Advocacy Network of individual self-advocacy groups and five regional councils. Works cooperatively to foster change and increase community awareness about issues related to people with intellectual and developmental disabilities, helps individuals with disabilities set up their own self-help groups and assists in the maintenance of those groups. Members learn skills such as assertiveness, decision making, goal setting and effective communication skills. Write: New Jersey Self-Advocacy Project, 985 Livingston Ave., North Brunswick, NJ 08902. Call Randy Goodwin 732-246-2525 ext. 30 (day). *Website:* http://www.njselfadvocacyproject.org

ATLANTIC

21 Down - Down Syndrome Awareness Group Inc. Support for families of a loved one with a developmental disability. Guest speakers. Meets 4 times/yr., local restaurants in Galloway and Tuckahoe. Call Pam 609-390-5645 (day). *Website:* http://www.21down.org

ESSEX

North Jersey Parent Support Group *Professionally-run.* Support, education and resources to parents of children with developmental disabilities. Provides information of specific services and programs available. Guest speakers, rap sessions and literature. Childcare available if requested. Building is handicapped accessible. Meetings vary, 7:30-9pm, Trinity Covenant Church, 343 East Cedar

213

St., Fellowship Hall, Livingston. Before attending call Donna Ruberto 973-992-9830 (day) or Judy Bellina 973-535-1181 ext. 1223 (day). *E-mail:* jbellina@arcessex.org

HUDSON

Family Support Group *(BILINGUAL)* Support for families and friends of people with developmental disabilities. Mutual sharing, socialization, education, lectures and advocacy for parents and others concerned about people with developmental disabilities. Building is handicapped accessible. Meets 2nd Fri., 6-8pm, 405-09 36th St., Union City. Call Nadia Cabana 201-319-9229 (day). *Website:* http://www.archudson.org *E-mail:* ncabana.arc@verizon.net

HUNTERDON

Sharing and Caring of Bucks County Information and support for parents of children with autism, Asperger syndrome, mental retardation and related disorders. Discussion groups, guest speakers, Sib-Shop sibling support group, social and recreational activities. Meets 2nd Thurs., 7-9pm (except June, July, Aug.), St. Vincent DePaul Church, Hatboro Rd., Education Building, Richboro, PA. Call Holly 215-321-3202 (Mon.-Fri., 10am-6pm).

MERCER

Down Syndrome Association of Central NJ Mutual support for parents and family members of children with Down syndrome. Guest speakers, literature, newsletter, phone help and visitation. Meetings vary, The Arc of Mercer County, 180 Ewingville Rd., Ewing. Call 1-866-369-6796 (answering machine), Carron 609-333-1077 or Kathy 609-799-0187. *Website:* http://www.dsacnj.org

MIDDLESEX

Network 21: Supporting Families with Down Syndrome *Professionally-run.* Support group for parents of children with Down syndrome. Meets monthly in Metuchen and East Brunswick. Quarterly family fun days. Call Amy 732-390-0108 (day). *Website:* http://www.dsnetwork21.org *E-mail:* geoffroyamy@gmail.com

"It is one of those beautiful compensations of this life that no one can sincerely try to help another without helping himself." -- Ralph Waldo Emerson

MONMOUTH

Down Syndrome Parent Support Group *Professionally-run.* Mutual support for parents of children with Down syndrome. Meets quarterly, 8-11pm, in members' homes. Call Susan Levine 732-747-5310 (day). *Website:* http://www.frainc.org

MORRIS

Down Syndrome Support Group *Professionally-run.* Support for parents of children with Down Syndrome from birth to 5 years. Meets Wed., 7-9pm, P.G. Chambers School, 15 Halko Dr., Cedar Knolls. Pre-registration required. Before attending call Sarah Ehinger 973-829-8484 (day).

SUSSEX

Self-Advocacy Group *Professionally-run.* Fosters independence and responsibility in developmentally disabled adults. Education on advocating for one's own rights. Meetings vary, 112 Phil Hardin Rd., Fredon. Call 973-383-8574.

UNION

Central NJ Down Syndrome Parent Advocacy Group Provides support for parents of children with Down Syndrome. Guest speakers, social and recreational outings, lending library, literature in English and Spanish. Meets last Tues., 7pm, Children's Specialized Hospital, 150 New Providence Rd., Mountainside. Call Sandy 908-756-6774. *Website:* http://dsparentgroup.com

WARREN

Go-Getters *Professionally-run.* Self-advocacy group for persons with developmental disabilities. Peer counseling and guest speakers. Meets 1st Wed., 3:30-5:30pm, The Arc, 319 West Washington Ave., Washington. Before attending call Bonnie Hill 908-689-7525 (day). *Website:* http://www.arcwarren.org

NATIONAL

Arc, The *National. 1100 chapters. Founded 1950.* Provides support for people with mental retardation and their families. Advocacy groups and direct services. Quarterly newspaper. Chapter development guidelines. Local group information on website. Write: The Arc, 1010 Wayne Ave., Suite 650, Silver Spring, MD

20910. Call 301-565-3842 (day); Fax: 301-565-3843. *Website:* http://www.thearc.org *E-mail:* info@thearc.org

National Down Syndrome Congress *National. 150+ parent group networks. Founded 1974.* Support, information and advocacy for families affected by Down syndrome. Promotes research and public awareness. Serves as clearinghouse and network for parent groups. Newsletter ($25/yr). Annual convention, phone support and chapter development guidelines. Write: National Down Syndrome Congress, 1370 Center Dr., Suite 102, Atlanta, GA 30338. Call 1-800-232-6372 or 770-604-9500 (Mon.-Fri., 9am-5:30pm EST); Fax: 770-604-9898. *Website:* http://www.ndsccenter.org *E-mail:* info@ndsccenter.org

People First *Model. 33 groups in Washington. 7 high school clubs. Founded 1977.* Self-help advocacy organization created by and for people with developmental disabilities. Provides help in starting new chapters. Quarterly newsletter. Write: People First, P.O. Box 648, Clarkston, WA 99403. Call 509-758-1123; Fax: 509-758-1289. *E-mail:* pfow@clarkston.com

Speaking For Ourselves *Model. 13 groups. Founded 1982.* Self-help advocacy for people with developmental disabilities. Monthly chapter meetings. Members help each other resolve problems, gain self-confidence and learn leadership skills. Chapter development guidelines and newsletter. Write: Speaking For Ourselves, 100 W. Main St., Suite 510, Lansdale, PA 19446. Call 1-800-867-3330 or 215-361-3100; Fax: 215-361-3101. *Website:* http://www.speaking.org *E-mail:* info@speaking.org

Voice of the Retarded *National. 160 affiliated groups. Founded 1983.* Works to empower families of persons with mental retardation through information and advocacy. Weekly e-mail updates and quarterly newsletter for members. Networking, information and referrals, advocacy, phone support and conferences. Annual dues $25. Write: Voice of the Retarded, 836 S. Arlington Heights Rd., #351, Arlington Heights, IL 60007. Call 1-877-399-4867; Fax: 847-253-0675. *Website:* http://www.vor.net *E-mail:* tamie327@hotmail.com

We can also refer callers to over 100 individuals who are seeking others to help start new support groups throughout NJ. Give us a call for more information.
1-800-367-6274

DISABILITIES (GENERAL) /
SPINAL CORD INJURY
(see also parents of the disabled, specific disability, toll-free helplines)

STATEWIDE

Advancing Opportunities (Formerly Cerebral Palsy of New Jersey) Provides services statewide to advance the independence of children and adults with all types of disabilities. Programs include: advocacy, employment services, family support, respite, assistive technology, substance abuse prevention, information and referral, personal assistance services and a technology lending center. Write: Cerebral Palsy of New Jersey, 1005 Whitehead Rd., Suite 1-A, Ewing, NJ 08638. Call 1-888-322-1918 or 609-882-4182; TTY: 609-882-0620. *Website:* http://www.cpofnj.org *E-mail:* info@cpofnj.org

Monday Morning Project, The Grassroots movement of people with disabilities, their families, friends and neighbors. Made up of advocacy networks in each county, it brings together ordinary citizens to work with local, state and federal officials on public policy issues important to people with disabilities. Some of the groups will help a new member with a personal advocacy issue. Meetings are held monthly in Bergen, Burlington, Camden, Cumberland, Essex, Gloucester, Hudson, Hunterdon, Mercer, Middlesex, Monmouth, Morris, Ocean, Passaic, Salem, Somerset, Union and Warren counties. For information on your local county network call 1-800-792-8858 or 609-292-3745 (day); TTD: 609-777-3228. *Website:* http://njddc.org

BERGEN

Heightened Independence and Progress (hip) Support groups, information, referrals, advocacy, peer counseling, recreational and other services for people with all types of disabilities who have equipment and assistive devices. Meets various times, Heightened Independence and Progress, 131 Main St., Suite 120, Hackensack. Call Paula Walsh 201-996-9100; TTY: 201-996-9424. *Website:* http://www.hipcil.org

Post Stroke and Disabled Adult Program *Professionally-run. (BERGEN COUNTY RESIDENTS ONLY)* Mutual support for post-stroke patients and disabled adults. Program functions include group discussions, various activities that promote physical fitness, arts and crafts, games, exercises and occasional recreational events. Meets various times and days, East Rutherford, Englewood, Paramus and Maywood. Call Anika Davis 201-336-6502 (day); TTY/TDD: 201-336-6505.

Women With Disabilities Support Group Discussion and education for disabled women. Meets 1st and 3rd Mon., 11am-1pm, Heightened Independence and Progress, 131 Main St., Suite 120, Hackensack. Call Paula Walsh 201-996-9100 (day); TTY: 201-996-9424 *Website:* http://www.hipcil.org

ESSEX

Monday Morning Network of Essex County Advocacy support group organized by and for people with disabilities. Purpose is to provide support and improve the quality of life for persons with disabilities by having a voice in government policy making and legislation. Helps members with individual advocacy issues. Family and friends welcome. Newsletter. Meets 2nd Thurs., 6:30-8:30pm, Camptown Garden, 624 Nye Ave., Community Room, Irvington. Call Frances Grant 973-470-8090 or Opportunity Project 973-921-1000 (day).

NJ Coalition on Women and Disabilities *(Essex County Chapter)* Support to empower, educate and motivate women with disabilities. Advocacy and guest speakers. Dues $12/yr. Meets 3rd Mon., 6:30-8:30pm, Pope John Paul Pavillion, 135 South Center St., Orange. Call Cynthia DeSouza 862-215-6869. *E-mail:* njcwd_essexchapter@verizon.net

Spinal Cord Injury Support Group Peer support group where individuals with spinal cord injuries share their experiences. Literature and buddy system. Meets 4th Thurs., 6-7pm, Kessler Institute for Rehabilitation, New Building, 1199 Pleasant Valley Way, SCI Day Room, 2nd Floor, West Orange. Pre-registration required. Before attending call Sandy or Ron 973-243-6927 (day).

MERCER

Disability Support Group *Professionally-run.* Support for persons with any disability to share feelings, thoughts and resources. Under 18 welcome. Phone help and newsletter. Meets monthly, Progressive Center for Independent Living, 1262 Whitehorse-Hamilton Square Rd., Suite 102, Hamilton. Before attending call Susan Jacobsen 609-581-4500 (day); TDD: 609-581-4550. *Website:* http://www.pcil.org *E-mail:* info@pcil.org

MIDDLESEX

Alliance for Disabled in Action, Inc. Support for persons with any disability. Family members are welcome. Information, advocacy, education, referrals for housing, employment, transportation and assistive technology. Promotes barrier-free environments. Meets 3rd Thurs., 7pm, Brunswick Municipal Complex, 710

Hermann Rd., North Brunswick. Call Kathleen Orsetti 732-738-4388; TDD: 732-738-9644. *Website:* http://www.adacil.org *E-mail:* korsetti@adacil.org

Parents and Grandparents Support Group Support, education, information and resource sharing for parents and grandparents who have disabilities. Rap sessions and buddy system. Meets 3rd Thurs., 6:30-8:30pm, Alliance for Disabled in Action, 629 Amboy Ave., Edison. Call Kathleen 732-738-4388 (day), Paul 908-561-5464 (eve.) or Janet 732-743-1579 (eve.); TDD: 732-738-9644.

MONMOUTH

Disability Support Group Support for men and women with any type of physical disability including Multiple Sclerosis. Guest speakers and phone help. Meets Wed., 11am-2pm, St. Anselm's Church, 1028 Wayside Rd., Wayside. Call Rhoda 732-462-0401 (day).

PASSAIC

DIAL, Inc. - Center for Independent Living Provides information and referral, peer counseling, advocacy and independent living skills program for people with disabilities. Deaf and hard-of-hearing outreach services. Dues $15/yr./individual; $25/yr./family. Building is handicapped accessible. Meets last Tues., 6:30-9:30pm, Clifton Center for Seniors and Citizens with Disabilities, Clifton. Call 1-866-277-1733 or 973-470-8090 (day); TTY: 973-470-2521. *Website:* http://www.dial-cil.org *E-mail:* info@dial-cil.org

Monday Morning Project Support and advocacy for persons with a disability. Meets monthly, 10am-noon, Wayne Public Library, 461 Valley Rd., Wayne. Call 973-694-4272.

SOMERSET

Raritan Valley Post-Polio Support Group Support and information sharing for post-polio survivors. Anyone with a physical disability is also welcome to attend. Networking with professionals and other groups. Phone help, speakers and monthly newsletter. Dues $10/yr. Meets 1st Sat. (Mar., Apr., Oct., Nov., Dec.), Manville Library, Manville. Call Arthur Siegfried 908-722-7212 (eve.). *Website:* http://www.njpolio.org/rvppsg

UNION

Alliance For Disabled in Action, Inc. Support for persons with any disability. Family members are welcome. Information, advocacy, education, referrals for housing, employment, transportation and assistive technology. Promotes barrier-free environments. Call Kathleen Orsetti 732-738-4388; TDD: 732-738-9644. *Website:* http://www.adacil.org *E-mail:* korsetti@adacil.org

> **Berkeley Heights** Meets last Thurs., 1pm, Runnells Specialized Hospital, 40 Watchung Way.
> **Rahway** Meets 3rd Mon., 1pm, Rahway Public Library.

FOCAS Peer Support Group Mutual support for those with disabilities to enhance their daily living. Rap sessions and guest speakers. Meets 2nd Mon., 7-8:30pm, 35 Sumner Ave., Union. Call 908-355-3299 (day). *E-mail:* susysnowflake2002@yahoo.com

WARREN

Totally Kids Network *Professionally-run.* Support for siblings (ages 5-10) that have a sibling with a disability. Children are given the opportunity to share feelings in a relaxing, recreational atmosphere. Meets monthly on Sat., Phillipsburg and Columbia. For meeting information call 908-689-7525 ext. 209. *Website:* http://www.arcwarren.org

NATIONAL

Barn Builders Peer Support Network *National network. Founded 1979.* Provides peer support through networking for farmers and ranchers with disabilities. Connects recently injured individuals with persons with similar disability. Support through talking, correspondence and visitation. Write: Breaking New Ground, ABE Building, 225 South University St., West Lafayette, IN 47907-2093. Call 765-494-5088 (Voice/TTY) or 1-800-825-4264; Fax: 765-496-1356. *Website:* http://www.barnbuilders.info *E-mail:* bng@ecn.purdue.edu

National Spinal Cord Injury Association *National. 35 chapters and support groups. Founded 1948.* Provides information and referrals on many topics to persons with spinal cord injuries and diseases, their families and interested professionals. Group development guidelines, monthly newsletter, support groups and peer counseling. Online listing of local chapters. Write: National Spinal Cord Injury Association, 6701 Democracy Blvd., Suite 300-9, Bethesda, MD 20817. Call 1-800-962-9629 (Mon.-Fri., 8:30am-5pm EST); Fax: 301-990-0445. *Website:* http://www.spinalcord.org *E-mail:* info@spinalcord.org

Paralyzed Veterans of America *National. 34 chapters and 58 field service offices.* Aim is to ensure that spinal cord injured or diseased veterans achieve the highest quality of life possible. Membership is available solely to individuals who are American citizens with spinal cord dysfunction as a result of trauma or disease. Must have served on active duty and had an other than dishonorable discharge. Support groups, publications, VA benefits counseling, magazine, information and referrals. Write: Paralyzed Veterans of America, 801 18th St. NW, Washington, DC 20006. Call 1-800-424-8200 or 202-872-1300 (Mon.-Fri., 8:30am-5pm EST). *Website:* http://www.pva.org *E-mail:* info@pva.org

Project DOCC (Delivery Of Chronic Care) *International. 28 chapters. Founded 1994.* Provides education regarding the impact of chronic illness and/or disability on a family. Information, referrals, phone support, e-mail correspondence and "how-to" guides on developing a local group. Write: Project DOCC, 18 Dunster Rd., Great Neck, NY 11771. Call 516-829-0786; Fax: 516-498-1899. *Website:* http://projectdocc.org *E-mail:* projdocc@aol.com

Sibling Support Project *National. 200 affiliated groups. Founded 1990.* Organization dedicated to the life long concerns of brothers and sisters of children with special health, developmental and mental health concerns. Provides training and technical assistance regarding Sibshops and workshops for school-age siblings. Write: Sibling Support Project, c/o Donald Meyer, 6512 23rd Ave. NW, Suite 213, Seattle, WA 98117. Call 206-297-6368; Fax: 509-752-6789. *Website:* http://www.siblingsupport.org *E-mail:* donmeyer@siblingsupport.org

United Spinal Association *National. Founded 1946.* Aim is to provide support and improve the quality of life for all Americans with spinal cord injuries and disorders. Write: United Spinal Association, 75-20 Astoria Blvd., Jackson Heights, NY 11370-1177. Call 718-803-3782 ext. 1203.

ONLINE

Ability Online Support Network *Online. Founded 1992.* A family friendly monitored electronic message system that enables children and adolescents with disabilities or chronic illness (also parents/caregivers/siblings) to share experiences, information, encouragement, support and hope through messages. Registration is free. Call 1-866-650-6207. *Website:* http://www.abilityonline.org *E-mail:* information@ablelink.org

Family Village *Online.* A global community that integrates information, resources and communication opportunities for persons with cognitive and other disabilities, their families and professionals. Broad range of discussion boards. *Website:* http://www.familyvillage.wisc.edu *E-mail:* familyvillage@waisman.wisc.edu

Quad-List *Online.* Provides a forum for quadriplegics (tetraplegics) to support and communicate with others who share the same condition. Not strictly a SCI (spinal cord injury) forum. Forum is for anyone who suffers a partial or full loss of function of all 4 extremities of the body, i.e. a quad due to any reason not just from a spinal cord injury. *Website:* http://www.makoa.org/quadlist.htm

SibNet *Online. 1157 members. Founded 1998.* Listserv for and about adult brothers and sisters of people with special health, developmental and emotional needs. Opportunity for young adults and adult brothers and sisters to share information and discuss issues of common interest. Subscribers can connect with their peers, seek information about local services, create connections for their siblings and discuss the proper policies agencies should have toward brothers and sisters. *Website:* http://groups.yahoo.com/group/sibnet

LEARNING DISABILITY / ATTENTION DEFICIT DISORDER
(see also toll-free helplines)

STATEWIDE / NATIONAL

ADDA (Attention Deficit Disorder Association) *National network. Founded 1989.* Mission is to provide information, resources and networking to adults with attention deficit hyperactivity disorder and to the professionals working with them. Aims to generate hope, awareness, empowerment and connections worldwide in the field of ADHD through bringing together science and the human experience. The information and resources provided to individual and families affected with ADHD focus on diagnosis, treatment, strategies and techniques for helping adults with ADHD lead better lives. Membership $45/yr. individual; $150/yr. professional. Write: ADDA, 15000 Commerce Parkway, Suite C, Mount Laurel, NJ 08054. Call 856-439-9099; Fax: 856-439-0525. *Website:* http://www.add.org

*Can't find an appropriate group in your area? The Clearinghouse helps people start groups. Give us a call at **1-800-367-6274**.*

BERGEN

CHADD Support and education for adults and parents of children with attention deficit disorder. Membership $45/yr. Building is handicapped accessible. Meets 3rd Wed., 7:30-8:30pm (Oct.-June), Valley Hospital, 223 Van Dien Ave., First Floor, Terrace Room, Ridgewood. Call CHADD 201-664-1313. *Website:* http://www.chaddbc.org

CAMDEN

ADDventure for Adults Lends an attentive ear and helping hand to all who have adult ADD or a connection with someone who has adult ADD. Rap sessions, guest speakers, literature and speakers bureau. Dues $5/mtg. Meets 2nd Thurs., 7:30-9pm, Barry D. Brown Health Education Center, Virtua West Jersey Hospital, 106 Carnie Blvd., Voorhees. Call 856-596-5520. *Website:* http://www.addventureforadults.org

CHADD of Southern NJ *Professionally-run.* Support for adults and parents of children with attention deficit hyperactivity disorder. Membership dues $45/yr. Building is handicapped accessible. Meetings vary, 7-8:30pm (except June, July, Aug., Dec.), Barry D. Brown Health Education Center, Virtua West Jersey Hospital, 106 Carnie Blvd., Voorhees. Call Mary Fagnani or Linda Karanzalis 856-482-0756 (day). *Website:* http://www.chadd.org

ESSEX

ADD Action Group Information about alternative solutions for attention deficit disorder, learning disabilities, hyperactivity, dyslexia and autism. Educational series, guest speakers, literature and phone help. Meets 3rd Thurs., 7-8:45pm, Millburn Public Library, 200 Glen Ave., Millburn. Pre-registration required. Before attending call Lynne 973-731-2189. *E-mail:* ltberke@aol.com

CHADD Support and education for adults and parents of children with attention deficit disorder/hyperactivity disorder. Membership dues $45/yr. *Website:* http://www.chadd.net/976

> **Montclair** Meets 3rd Mon., 7pm, Montclair Public Library, 50 South Fullerton Ave., Rose Cafe, First Floor. Call Julia 973-773-7745 (day) or Cindy 973-661-2997 (day).
> **Nutley** Meets 2nd Mon., 7pm, Grace Church, 200 Highfield Lane, Church Office. Call Julia 973-773-7745 (day).

MERCER

CHADD Princeton-Mercer County Support and education for adults and parents of children with attention deficit disorder. Membership dues $45/yr. Meetings vary, 7-9pm (except July and Aug.), Riverside Elementary School, 58 Riverside Dr., Princeton. Call Jane Milrod 609-683-8787 (day). *Website:* http://www.chadd.org *E-mail:* janemilrod@aol.com

MONMOUTH

Adult ADD Self-Help Support Group *Professionally-run.* Support for adults who have attention deficit disorder or those who suspect that they may. Significant others welcome. Building is handicapped accessible. Meets 4th Thurs., 7:30-9:30pm (except June, July, Aug.; 3rd Thurs. in Nov. and Dec.), Monmouth Medical Center, 300 2nd Ave., Long Branch. Pre-registration required. Before attending call Dr. Robert LoPresti 732-842-4553 (day). *Website:* http://www.drlopresti.com

MORRIS

Learning Disabilities Association of New Jersey Support and information for families of children with learning disabilities. Conferences, newsletters, literature, resources and referrals. Dues $30/yr. Meets at various locations and times. Call Terry Cavanaugh 973-265-4303 (voice mail). *Website:* http://www.ldaamerica.org *E-mail:* ldanj@optonline.net

SOMERSET

Adults with Attention Deficit Disorder *Professionally-run.* Provides support for adults who have attention deficit disorder. Meets 1st and 3rd Wed., 7:30-9:30pm, Somerset Medical Center, 110 Rehill Ave., Library, Community Health, South Fuld Bldg., Somerville. Call 908-685-2814 (day).

SUSSEX

New Jersey Special Education Parent Association Mutual support, education and advocacy for parents of children with specific learning disabilities which often overlap with auditory processing, reading, writing and listening skills. Rap sessions and phone help. Building is handicapped accessible. Meetings vary, 7pm (except June, July, Aug.), First Presbyterian Church, Pearson Hall, Sparta. For meeting information call Brenda 973-726-3029.

UNION

Adult ADHD Support Group *Professionally-run.* Provides support and education for adults who have attention deficit disorder or hyperactivity disorder. Family members welcome. Guest speakers, literature, phone help and buddy system. Meets Tues. and Thurs., 7pm, Stepping Forward Counseling Center, 18 Bank St., Summit. Before attending call Christine Robertello 973-533-6990 (day).

NATIONAL

CHADD (Children and Adults with Attention-Deficit/Hyperactivity Disorder) *(BILINGUAL) International. 200 chapters. Founded 1987.* Support network for individuals, parents and caregivers of children with attention deficit/hyperactivity disorder. Provides information for parents, adults, teachers and professionals. Bimonthly magazine and annual conference. Guidelines and assistance on starting self-help groups. Dues $45; student $35; healthcare professionals $110. Online listing of local support groups. Write: CHADD, 8181 Professional Pl., Suite 150, Landover, MD 20785. Call 1-800-233-4050 or 301-306-7070 (day); Fax: 301-306-7090. *Website:* http://www.chadd.org

Feingold Association of the U.S. *National. Founded 1976.* Help for families of children with learning or behavior problems, including attention deficit disorder. Supports members in implementing the Feingold program. Generates public awareness re: food and synthetic additives. Newsletter and phone support network. Write: Feingold Association of the US, 554 East Main St., Suite 301, Riverhead, NY 11901. Call 1-800-321-3287 (US only) or 631-369-9340. *Website:* http://www.feingold.org *E-mail:* help@feingold.org

GT/LD Network *National network. Founded 1984.* Mutual support and information for parents of gifted children who are also learning disabled. Membership is predominantly parents, but it is also open to students and educators. Referrals, advocacy, parent collaboration and support, literature, conferences, online discussion support group and local meetings in Maryland. Dues $45. Write: GT/LD Network, c/o Topping, 9601 Windcroft Way, Potomac, MD 20854. *Website:* http://www.gtldnetwork.org *E-mail:* webmaster@gtldnetwork.org

ONLINE

ADD Forums *Online.* Wide variety of specific online message boards including those for men, women and teens with ADD/ADHD. Also, boards for those with co-existing conditions such as ADD/ADHD and substance abuse, bipolar disorder, depression, eating disorders, and autism/Asperger's syndrome. Blogs and chatrooms available. *Website:* http://www.addforums.com/forums/index.php

Conduct Disorders Parent Message Board *Online. 7080 members. Founded 1995.* Support for parents living with a child with one of the many behavior disorders such as attention deficit hyperactivity disorder, oppositional defiance disorder, conduct disorder, depression and substance abuse. Parents with children of all ages welcome. *Website:* http://www.conductdisorders.com

Dyslexia Support 2 *Online. 341 members. Founded 2003.* Support list for parents of children who are dyslexic. Resource for parents to share ideas and exchange ways of helping. *Website:* http://health.groups.yahoo.com/group/dyslexiasupport2

Dyslexia Talk *Online.* Support for anyone affected by dyslexia. Offers message board, open discussions and separate support group for parents. *Website:* http://www.dyslexiatalk.com

NLD-In-Common *Online.* Opportunity for loved ones of people with non-verbal learning disabilities (NLD), adults with NLD and certain professionals to come together to communicate. Provides listserv support and information. Membership subject to approval. *Website:* http://www.groups.yahoo.com/group/nld-in-common

Premature Baby - Premature Child *Online. Founded 1997.* Offers support for parents of premature babies that are age 4+ years old for any of their special needs, e.g. mental, physical, emotional or learning disability. Provides support, discussion listserv, prematurity forums, advocacy and educational links. Special children's show-and-tell section. *Website:* http://www.prematurity.org

"Respect your fellow human beings, treat them fairly, disagree with them honestly, enjoy their friendship, explore your thoughts about one another candidly, work together for a common goal and help one another achieve it. No destructive lies. No ridiculous fears. No debilitating anger." -- Bill Bradley

FAMILY / PARENTING

ADOPTION
(see also parenting, toll-free helplines)

STATEWIDE

Foster and Adoptive Family Services Provides support services, comprehensive information, education and training to foster and adoptive parents. Advocates on behalf of foster and adoptive parents and their children for improved foster care and adoption services. Information for persons wishing to become foster parents. Call 1-800-222-0047. *Website:* http://www.fafsonline.org

NJ Adoption Resource Clearing House (NJ ARCH) Provides adoption advocacy, support, education, information and referral services to birth parents, adoptive and pre-adoptive families throughout New Jersey, as well as to families interested in adopting children and to professionals, family and community members interested in adoption issues. Literature, resource directory, library, newsletter, speakers' bureau and workshops. Write: NJ Adoption Resource Clearing House, 76 South Orange Ave., Suite 209, South Orange. Call 1-877-427-2465. *Website:* http://www.njarch.org *E-mail:* warmline@njarch.org

NJ Families For Russian Ukrainian Adoptions Support Group Support for people who have adopted or plan to adopt from Eastern Europe. Guest speakers, phone help, literature and newsletter. Dues $35/yr. Call Mirna Rucci 908-431-0318. *Website:* http://www.frua.org *E-mail:* mirucci@earthlink.net

BERGEN

Adoptive Parents Committee, Inc. Support and education for adoptive parents and those interested in adoption. Advocacy, social group, guest speakers, phone help, newsletter and annual conference. Dues $65/1st yr., $35/thereafter. Meetings vary in Paramus. Call 201-689-0995. *Website:* http://www.adoptiveparents.org *E-mail:* apcconf2003@msn.com

Foster and Adoptive Family Services Mutual support for foster parents, adoptive parents and relative care providers. Guest speakers, literature, social events and newsletter. Meetings vary, Tues., Division of Youth and Family Services, 125 State St., Hackensack. Before attending call Rosanne Doyle 201-965-6513 (day).

FULL CIRCLE Triad Post-Adoption Group of North Jersey Mutual support and education for adoptees, adoptive and birth parents. Building is handicapped accessible. Meets 2nd Wed., 7:30pm, Panera Bread (Kohl's shopping center), Route 4 West, Community Room, Paramus. Before attending call Cindi Addesso 973-427-4521. Check website to confirm meeting date. *Website:* http://www.fullcircletriadnj.com *E-mail:* cindilouwho@mindspring.com

BURLINGTON

Foster and Adoptive Family Services Mutual support for foster parents, adoptive parents and relative care providers. Guest speakers, literature, social events and newsletter. Childcare available. Meets 2nd Mon., 6-8pm, First Methodist Church, 25 Brainerd St., Mt. Holly. Call Joyce 609-267-3712.

CAMDEN

Foster and Adoptive Family Services Mutual support for foster parents and adoptive parents. Guest speakers, social events and newsletter. Meets 2nd Tues., 7pm, Division of Youth and Family Services, 201 Laurel Rd., Voorhees. Call Delores 856-863-8641 (day).

CAPE MAY

Foster and Adoptive Family Services Mutual support for foster parents, adoptive parents and relative care providers. Guest speakers, literature, social events and newsletter. Meets 3rd Wed., Martin Luther King Center, 207 West Main St., Whitesboro. Before attending call Stacy 609-231-1025 (day).

ESSEX

Foster and Adoptive Family Services Mutual support for foster parents, adoptive parents and relative care providers. Guest speakers, literature, social events and newsletter. Meets 4th Tues., 7pm, Community Hills Day Care Center, 85 Irvine Turner Blvd., 2nd Floor, Newark. Call Mike Johnstone 1-800-334-6930 (day).

GLOUCESTER

Foster and Adoptive Family Services Mutual support for foster parents, adoptive parents and relative care providers. Guest speakers, literature, social events and newsletter. Meets last Mon., 7pm, Mantua Methodist Church, 201 Mantua Blvd., Mantua. Call Cynthia 856-241-1612 (day).

HUNTERDON

Adoptive Families Group NJ/PA Support, child and adult socialization, education on various adoption issues for all adoptive families, including those considering adoption. Also open to adult adoptees, birthmothers who have made adoption plans for their children and any others who share an adoption connection. Monthly meetings in Hunterdon and Warren counties. Rap sessions, guest speakers, literature, phone help and buddy system. Call Patricia Blum 908-475-8944 (day).

MERCER

Adoptive Parents Organization of Central New Jersey Mutual support to inform, discuss and learn about all aspects of adoption including families waiting as well as families thinking about adoption. Membership $30/yr. Childcare available. Guest speaker, advocacy, book discussions and social activities. Meets 3rd Wed., 7-9pm (except June, July, Aug.), St. Gregory the Great Parish Center, 4680 Nottingham Way, Hamilton Square. Call Lisa Valenti 609-575-2082. *Website:* http://apocnj.tripod.com *E-mail:* apocentralnj@gmail.com

MIDDLESEX

Foster and Adoptive Family Services Mutual support for foster parents and adoptive parents. Guest speakers, social events and newsletter. Childcare available upon request. Meets 2nd Thurs., 7:30pm, Division of Youth and Family Services, 53 Knightsbridge Rd., Piscataway. Call Debi 732-317-2105 (day).

MONMOUTH

Foster and Adoptive Family Services Mutual support for foster parents, adoptive parents and relative care providers. Guest speakers, literature, social events and newsletter. Meetings vary, Middletown Library, 55 Monmouth Rd., Middletown. Before attending call Lisa 732-229-3207 or Lori 732-739-6780.

Monmouth/Ocean County Adoptive Parents Support Group Provides support, education and a network for all members of the adoption triad (pre- and post-adoption), especially those adopting transracially. Literature, guest speakers, phone help and buddy system. Dues $25/yr. Building is handicapped accessible. Meets 3rd Fri., 7:30-9:30pm, St. Mary's Church, Spiritual Center, Phalanx Rd. and Route 34 North, Colts Neck. Call Danielle 732-845-0791 or

Liz 732-473-9113. *Website:* http://www.freewebs.com/mocafsg *E-mail:* webbymisha@hotmail.com

MORRIS

Concerned Persons for Adoption Organization working to support those who wish to adopt. Also provides educational and networking resources to those who have adopted. Educational programs, social events and annual conference "Let's Talk Adoption." Membership dues $25/1st yr., $20/thereafter. Meetings are free. Meetings vary, 7:45pm, First Presbyterian Church, 494 Route 10 West, Whippany. Call Joan Walsh 973-625-8440 or Grace Boehm 908-221-0537. *Website:* http://www.cpfanj.org

Morris County Foster Parents Association Provides social and emotional support to foster parents and their children. Dues $20/yr. Building is handicapped accessible. Meets 3rd Wed., 7pm (except July/Aug.), Division of Youth and Family Services of Morris County, 855 Route 10 East, Randolph. Call Michele Cannaveno 908-850-8303 (day). *Website:* http://www.morrisfpa.org *E-mail:* webmaster@morrisfpa.org

NJ Coalition for Adoption Reform and Education *(Formerly known as NJ Coalition for Openness in Adoption)* Organization that supports honesty in adoption through educational outreach and legislative advocacy. Workshops. Links to statewide search and support groups. Building is handicapped accessible. Meets Mon., 7pm, Presbyterian Church, Parish House, 65 South St., Morristown. Call Jane Nast 973-267-8698, Judy Foster 973-455-1268 or Pam Hasegawa 973-292-2440. *Website:* http://www.nj-care.org *E-mail:* janenast@compuserve.com

Post-Adoption Support Group Support and education for adoptees, adoptive parents, birth parents and professionals. Under 18 welcome. Donation $3. Guest speakers, advocacy, speakers' bureau and search assistance. Building is handicapped accessible. Meets 1st Sat., 1pm, Presbyterian Church Parish House, 65 South St., Morristown. Call Jane Nast 973-267-8698 or Judy Foster 973-455-1268. *Website:* http://www.nj-care.org *E-mail:* janenast@compuserve.com

OCEAN

Foster and Adoptive Parent Group Mutual support for anyone who is a foster parent or adoptive parent. Opportunity for parents to share experiences and adjustment issues. Education, literature and phone help. Childcare available. Call in advance to arrange childcare. Building is handicapped accessible. Meets

3rd Wed., 7-9pm, Ocean County Family Support Organization, 44 Washington St., Room 2A, Toms River. Call Annie Hercules 732-281-5770 ext. 16 (day).

Parents Of Adoptive Children with Fetal Alcohol Syndrome Mutual support and information for parents who have adopted a child with fetal alcohol syndrome. Group meets various days and times. For meeting information call Shannon 732-600-7657.

PASSAIC

Foster and Adoptive Family Services Mutual support for foster parents, adoptive parents and relative care providers. Guest speakers, literature, social events and newsletter. Meets 2nd Thurs., 7pm, St. Joseph's Hospital, 224 Hamburg Turnpike, 1st Floor, Meyer Conference Room, Wayne. Call Marion 973-742-1436.

SUSSEX

Foster and Adoptive Family Services Mutual support for foster parents, adoptive parents and relative care providers. Guest speakers, literature, social events and newsletter. Meets 4th Mon., 7pm, Division of Youth and Family Service, 20 Clinton St., Newton. Call Cheryl 973-875-7549.

WARREN

Adoptive Families Group NJ/PA Support, education, child and adult socialization on various adoption issues for all adoptive families, including those considering adoption. Also open to adult adoptees, birthmothers who have made adoption plans for their children and any others who share an adoption connection. Monthly meetings in Hunterdon and Warren counties. Rap sessions, guest speakers, literature, phone help and buddy system. Call Patricia Blum 908-475-8944 (day) or Barbara Hurte 908-213-0184 (day). *E-mail:* pblum@netcarrier.com

Foster and Adoptive Family Services Mutual support for foster parents, adoptive parents and relative care providers. Guest speakers, literature, social events and newsletter. Meets 3rd Mon., Harmony Presbyterian Church, 2727 Belvidere Rd., Harmony. Call Tammi 908-454-7574 (day). *Website:* http://www.wcfafs.org

NATIONAL

Adoption Crossroads *International. 475 affiliated groups. Founded 1990.* Mutual support for persons separated by adoption. Referrals to adoption search and support groups. Newsletter, phone support and conferences. Provides information and referrals to support group meetings. Assistance in starting groups. Write: Adoption Crossroads, c/o Joe Soll, 74 Lakewood Dr., Congers, NY 10920. Call 845-268-0283; Fax: 845-267-2736. *Website:* http://www.adoptioncrossroads.org *E-mail:* info@adoptioncrossroads.org

ALMA Society (Adoptees' Liberty Movement Association) *International network. Founded 1971.* Provides moral support and guidance for adopted children in finding their birth parents and/or siblings. Also helps parents find the children they gave up for adoption. Open to foster children (ages 18+). International reunion registry. One-time tax deductible contribution $50. Write: ALMA Society, 3476 Manor Grove Circle, Glen Allen, VA 23059. Call 804-264-0164. *Website:* http://www.almasociety.org *E-mail:* manderson@almasociety.org

Concerned United Birthparents, Inc. *National. 11 branches. Founded 1976.* Support for adoption-affected people in coping with adoption. Prevention of unnecessary separations. Dues $40/yr. Online chatroom, quarterly newsletter, pen pals and phone network. Provides assistance starting local groups. Write: CUB, P.O. Box 503475, San Diego, CA 92150-3475. Call 1-800-822-2777; Fax: 858-712-3317. *Website:* http://www.cubirthparents.org *E-mail:* info@cubirthparents.org

Korean American Adoptee Adoptive Family Network *International.* Mission is to support networking and build understanding among adoptees, adoptive families, Koreans and Korean Americans. Annual conference and weekly newsletter. Write: KAAN, P.O. Box 5585, El Dorado Hills, CA 95762. Call 916-933-1447. *Website:* http://www.kaanet.com *E-mail:* kaanet@aol.com

North American Council on Adoptable Children *International (US/Canada). Founded 1974.* Focuses on special needs adoption. Provides referrals and maintains current listing of adoptive parent support groups which conduct a wide range of activities. Helps new groups get started, and sponsors an annual adoption conference which features workshops for adoptive parents, prospective parents, foster parents, child welfare professionals and other child advocates. Newsletter. Membership $45/US and $50/Canada. Parent group manual free online. Write: North American Council on Adoptable Children, 970 Raymond Ave., Suite 106, St. Paul, MN 55114-1149. Call 651-644-3036 (day); Fax: 651-644-9848. *Website:* http://www.nacac.org *E-mail:* info@nacac.org

Stars of David, Inc. *International. 32+ chapters.* Support and advocacy group for Jewish or interfaith adoptive families, extended families, interested clergy, social service agencies and adoption professionals. Socials, phone help, literature, education, online listserv and newsletter. Online directory of local groups. Dues $50/family; $125/professional. Write: Stars of David, 3175 Commercial Ave., Suite 100, Norbrook, IL 60062-1915. Call 1-800-782-7349 or 847-274-1527. *Website:* http://www.starsofdavid.org

ONLINE

Parent Soup Message Boards *Online.* Offers a large variety of message boards which deal with parenting issues including infertility, pregnancy, parenting challenges, parents of disabled, pregnancy loss, newborn babies, toddlers, adoption, family issues, etc. *Website:* http://www.parentsoup.com/messageboards

CESAREAN BIRTH
(see also childbirth, premature/high risk infants)

NATIONAL

ICAN, Inc. (International Cesarean Awareness Network) *Online.* Support for women healing from Cesarean birth. Encouragement and information for those wanting vaginal birth after previous Cesarean. Aims to lower the high Cesarean rate through prevention and education. Newsletter. Chapter development guidebook. *Website:* http://www.ican-online.org *E-mail:* info@ican-online.org

CHILDBIRTH / BREASTFEEDING / PREGNANCY
(see also parenting, toll-free helplines)

BERGEN

La Leche League of Teaneck Support and education for pregnant and breastfeeding women. Discussion group, mutual sharing, phone help and literature. Dues $40/yr. Meetings and locations vary, Teaneck. Call Carmen Clark 201-837-7646, Susan Esserman 201-385-2377 (day) or Julie Rosen 201-837-5910. *Website:* http://www.lalecheleaguenj.org

New Mother Skills and Socialization Group *Professionally-run.* Support, education, information and socialization for pregnant and new mothers adjusting to emotional changes. Rap sessions. Meets Wed., 7-8:15pm, Blue Skye Consulting, 560 Sylvan Ave., Englewood Cliffs. Pre-registration is required. Before attending call Susan Stone 201-567-5596 (day). *E-mail:* susanstonelcsw@aol.com

BURLINGTON

Breastfeeding Support Group *Professionally-run.* Support and education for nursing mothers regardless of the age of the child. Meets Wed., 11am-12:30pm, Virtua Health, 175 Madison Ave., Conference Center, Mt. Holly. Before attending call 1-888-847-8823 (day).

CAMDEN

Breastfeeding Support Group *Professionally-run.* Support and education for nursing mothers regardless of the age of the child. Meets Wed., 1:30-3pm, Virtua Health's Barry D. Brown Health Education Center, 106 Carnie Blvd., Voorhees. Before attending call 1-888-847-8823 (day).

HUNTERDON

Breastfeeding Support Group *Professionally-run.* Mutual support and education for women who are breastfeeding their infants. Moms are welcome to bring lunch. Babies welcome. Building is handicapped accessible. Meets 1st Thurs., noon-1pm, Hunterdon Medical Center, 2100 Westcott Dr., Flemington. Before attending call Jean Jamele, RN 908-788-6634 (day). *Website:* http://hunterdonhealthcare.org *E-mail:* jamele.jean@hunterdonhealthcare.org

MERCER

Breastfeeding Support Group *Professionally-run.* Support and education for new mothers. Learn breastfeeding techniques and parenting issues. Babies welcome. Building is handicapped accessible. Meets Tues., 1:30pm, Robert Wood Johnson Center for Health and Wellness, 3100 Quakerbridge Rd., Classroom 2 and 3, Hamilton. Call Heather or Debbie 609-584-5904 (day).

Pregnancy and Postpartum Support Group *Professionally-run.* Support for pregnant and new mothers adjusting to emotional issues such as blues, depression, obsessive compulsive disorder and anxiety. Children and significant others welcome. Meets 3rd Sat., 10:30am-noon, Mary Jacobs County Library, Route 518, Rocky Hill. Pre-registration required. Before attending call Joyce

609-921-3555, Terry 908-752-3797, Leah 732-255-6896 (eve.) or Gail 732-248-4921 (eve.).

MIDDLESEX

Pregnant Again *Professionally-run.* Mutual support for anyone who has lost a child by miscarriage, stillbirth or infant death and are pregnant again. Literature and phone help. Meets 2nd Mon., 6-8pm, St. Peter's University Hospital, 254 Easton Ave., Conference Room 5, New Brunswick. Pre-registration required. Before attending call Dawn Brady 732-745-8600 ext. 5214 (day).

MONMOUTH

Breastfeeding Support Group *Professionally-run.* Mutual support and education for women who are breastfeeding their infants. Meets Wed., 11am-12:30pm, Monmouth Medical Center, Goldsmith Wellness Center, 300 Second Ave., 4th Floor, Long Branch. Registration is required. Before attending call 732-923-6857 (day).

Mother to Mother Support Group *Professionally-run.* Provides support and education for new mothers to help with topics such as feeding, sleeping, crying, recovery from childbirth and postpartum depression. Newborns to 6 months welcome. Building is handicapped accessible. Meets Mon., 11am-noon, Monmouth Medical Center, 300 Second Ave., Ronald McDonald Family Conference Room, Borden Wing, 2nd Floor, Long Branch. Pre-registration required. Before attending call 732-923-6990 (day).

SOMERSET

YoungLives Support Group *Professionally-run.* Support and education for teenagers (under age 20) who are pregnant or recently gave birth. Childcare available. Rap sessions, guest speakers, literature, newsletter, phone help and buddy system. Building is handicapped accessible. Meets 1st Fri., 7pm (except June, July, Aug.), St. Luke's Church, 300 Clinton Ave., North Plainfield. Call Lucy Droege 908-791-4455 (day).

UNION

Latino YoungLives Support Group *(SPANISH) Professionally-run.* Support and education for teenagers (under age 20) who are pregnant or recently gave birth. Childcare available. Rap sessions, guest speakers, literature, newsletter, phone help and buddy system. Meets 3rd Fri., 7pm, First Christian Assembly, 718 Central Ave., Plainfield. Call Lucy Droege 908-791-4455 (day).

Prevention Through Parenting *Professionally-run.* Support and education for teenagers who are pregnant or parents of young children. Fathers are welcome also. Literature and phone help. Meets Thurs., 3:30-5pm, United Family and Children's Society, 305 West 7th St., Plainfield. Call Karen Flanagan, CSW 908-755-4848. *E-mail:* kflanagan@unitedfamily.org

NATIONAL

La Leche League *International. 3500 groups. Founded 1956.* Support and education for breastfeeding mothers. Group discussions, personal help, classes and conferences. Publishes literature on breastfeeding and parenting. Bi-monthly newsletter, quarterly abstracts and phone support network. Assistance with starting new groups. Write: La Leche League International, 957 N. Plum Grove Rd., Schaumburg, IL 60168-4079. Call 1-800-525-3243 (day) or 847-519-7730; Fax: 847-969-0460; TTY/TDD: 847-592-7570 *Website:* http://www.lalecheleague.org *E-mail:* llli@llli.org

Lamaze International *International. Founded 1960.* Dedicated to promoting normal, natural, healthy and fulfilling childbearing, breastfeeding and early parenting experiences through education, advocacy and reform. Newsletter and publications. Write: Lamaze International, 2025 M St., NW, Suite 800, Washington, DC 20036-3309. Call 1-800-368-4404 (Mon-Fri, 9am-5pm EST); Fax: 202-367-2128. *Website:* http://www.lamaze.org *E-mail:* info@lamaze.org

National Association of Mothers' Centers *National. 40 sites. Founded 1975.* Warm, welcoming environment of support. Discussion groups and other activities regarding parenting, pregnancy, childbirth and childrearing. National and some local newsletters, conference and advocacy. Has up-to-date information on contacting local Mothers' Center programs, starting a center and how employers in NY/NJ/CT can offer a program for working parents. Write: National Association of Mothers' Centers, 1740 Old Jericho Turnpike, Jericho, NY 11753. Call 1-877-939-6667 or 516-939-6667; Fax: 516-750-5365. *Website:* http://www.motherscenter.org *E-mail:* info@motherscenter.org

Sidelines High Risk Pregnancy Support *National network. Founded 1991.* Trained former high risk pregnancy moms provide support to current high risk patients and their families. Provides educational resources, advocacy and emotional support via phone and e-mail. Write: Sidelines National Support Network, P.O. Box 1808, Laguna Beach, CA 92652. Call 1-888-447-4754; Fax: 949-497-5598. *Website:* http://www.sidelines.org *E-mail:* sidelines@sidelines.org

ONLINE

Diabetic Mommies *Online. Founded 2001.* Support for all women with diabetes (type 1, type 1.5, type 2, gestational and pre-diabetes) at all stages of life whether already a mom, during pregnancy or trying to conceive. Articles, forum, chatroom, surveys, networking and newsletters. *Website:* http://www.diabeticmommy.com *E-mail:* editor@diabeticmommy.com

Expecting Parents Meetup Groups *Online.* Meet other new or expecting parents to exchange advice, support and laughs. Message boards. *Website:* http://newparents.meetup.com

Parent Soup Message Boards *Online.* Offers a large variety of message boards which deal with parenting issues including infertility, pregnancy, parenting challenges, parents of disabled, pregnancy loss, newborn babies, toddlers, adoption, family issues, etc. *Website:* http://www.parentsoup.com/messageboards

Postpartum Hemorrhage Survivors *Online.* E-mail list for women who are supporting each other after a postpartum hemorrhage and hysterectomy. *Website:* http://health.groups.yahoo.com/group/pph-survivors

Preeclampsia Foundation *Online.* Organization dedicated to providing support, funding research, raising public awareness and education for those whose lives have been touched by preeclampsia and other hypertensive disorders while pregnant. Forums. *Website:* http://www.preeclampsia.org

Pregnant Teen Support *Online.* E-mail list support group for teens (ages 12-20) facing an unplanned, unexpected or unwanted pregnancy. *Website:* http://health.groups.yahoo.com/group/pregnant_teen_support

Consider passing this Directory on to a student or staff member - browsing through the Directory pages can often provide helpful education as to the wide variety of groups available.

FOSTER FAMILIES
(see also toll-free helplines)

STATEWIDE

Foster and Adoptive Family Services Provides support services, comprehensive information, education and training to foster and adoptive parents. Advocates on behalf of foster and adoptive parents and their children for improved foster care and adoption services. Information for persons wishing to become foster parents. Call 1-800-222-0047. *Website:* http://www.fafsonline.org

BERGEN

Foster and Adoptive Family Services Mutual support for foster parents, adoptive parents and relative care providers. Guest speakers, literature, social events and newsletter. Meetings vary, Tues., Division of Youth and Family Services, 125 State St., Hackensack. Before attending call Rosanne Doyle 201-965-6513 (day).

BURLINGTON

Foster and Adoptive Family Services Mutual support for foster parents, adoptive parents and relative care providers. Guest speakers, literature, social events and newsletter. Childcare available. Meets 2nd Mon., 6-8pm, First Methodist Church, 25 Brainerd St., Mt. Holly. Call Joyce 609-267-3712.

CAMDEN

Foster and Adoptive Family Services Mutual support for foster parents and adoptive parents. Guest speakers, social events and newsletter. Meets 2nd Tues., 7pm, Division of Youth and Family Services, 201 Laurel Rd., Voorhees. Call Delores 856-863-8641 (day).

CAPE MAY

Foster and Adoptive Family Services Mutual support for foster parents, adoptive parents and relative care providers. Guest speakers, literature, social events and newsletter. Meets 3rd Wed., Martin Luther King Center, 207 West Main St., Whitesboro. Before attending call Stacy 609-231-1025 (day).

ESSEX

Foster and Adoptive Family Services Mutual support for foster parents, adoptive parents and relative care providers. Guest speakers, literature, social events and newsletter. Meets 4th Tues., 7pm, Community Hills Day Care Center, 85 Irvine Turner Blvd., 2nd Floor, Newark. Call Mike Johnstone 1-800-334-6930 (day).

Grandma K.A.R.E.S., Inc. (Kinship, Advocacy, Resources, Education and Support) *Professionally-run.* Educational, inspirational and motivational support group for "Kinship-Caregivers" and foster parents. Building is handicapped accessible. Guest speakers, literature, newsletter, phone help and buddy system. Meets 3rd Fri., 1-3pm, South Orange Library, 65 Scotland Rd., South Orange. Call Louise Eagle 973-327-4114. *E-mail:* grandmakares@optonline.net

GLOUCESTER

Foster and Adoptive Family Services Mutual support for foster parents, adoptive parents and relative care providers. Guest speakers, literature, social events and newsletter. Meets last Mon., 7pm, Mantua Methodist Church, 201 Mantua Blvd., Mantua. Call Cynthia 856-241-1612 (day).

MIDDLESEX

Foster and Adoptive Family Services Mutual support for foster parents and adoptive parents. Guest speakers, social events and newsletter. Childcare available on request. Meets 2nd Thurs., 7:30pm, Division of Youth and Family Services, 53 Knightsbridge Rd., Piscataway. Call Debi 732-317-2105 (day).

MONMOUTH

Foster and Adoptive Family Services Mutual support for foster parents, adoptive parents and relative care providers. Guest speakers, literature, social events and newsletter. Meetings vary, Middletown Library, 55 Monmouth Rd., Middletown. Before attending call Lisa Van Dam 732-229-3207.

"The best way out is always through." – Robert Frost

MORRIS

Morris County Foster Parents Association Provides social and emotional support to foster parents and their children. Dues $20/yr. Building is handicapped accessible. Meets 3rd Wed., 7pm (except July/Aug.), Division of Youth Family Services of Morris County, 855 Route 10 East, Randolph. Call Michele Cannaveno 908-850-8303 (day). *Website:* http://www.morrisfpa.org *E-mail:* webmaster@morrisfpa.org

OCEAN

Foster and Adoptive Parent Group Mutual support for anyone who is a foster parent or adoptive parent. Opportunity for parents to share experiences and adjustment issues. Education, literature and phone help. Childcare available. Call in advance to arrange childcare. Building is handicapped accessible. Meets 3rd Wed., 7-9pm, Ocean County Family Support Organization, 44 Washington St., Room 2A, Toms River. Call Annie Hercules 732-281-5770 ext. 16 (day).

PASSAIC

Foster and Adoptive Family Services Mutual support for foster parents, adoptive parents and relative care providers. Guest speakers, literature, social events and newsletter. Meets 2nd Thurs., 7pm, St. Joseph's Hospital, 224 Hamburg Turnpike, 1st Floor, Meyer Conference Room, Wayne. Call Marion 973-742-1436.

SUSSEX

Foster and Adoptive Family Services Mutual support for foster parents, adoptive parents and relative care providers. Guest speakers, literature, social events and newsletter. Meets 4th Mon., 7pm, Division of Youth and Family Service, 20 Clinton St., Newton. Call Cheryl 973-875-7549.

WARREN

Foster and Adoptive Family Services Mutual support for foster parents, adoptive parents and relative care providers. Guest speakers, literature, social events and newsletter. Meets 3rd Mon., Harmony Presbyterian Church, 2727 Belvidere Rd., Harmony. Call Tammi 908-454-7574 (day). *Website:* http://www.wcfafs.org

NATIONAL

Fostered Adult Children Together (FACT) *Model. 1 group in MI. Founded 1999.* Provides mutual support for former foster children. Literature. Provides assistance in starting similar groups. Write: FACT, c/o Carol Lucas, 226 S. Burkhart Rd., Howell, MI 48843. Call 517-546-7818 (voice/fax). *Website:* http://www.factsupportgroup.com *E-mail:* carolannlucas@hotmail.com

National Foster Parent Association, Inc. *National. 50 affiliated groups. Founded 1972.* Support, education and advocacy for foster parents and their children. Resource center for foster care information. Quarterly newsletter, annual national conference and workshops. Chapter development guidelines. Write: National Foster Parent Association, 7512 Stanich Lane, Suite 6, Gig Harbor, WA 98335. Call 1-800-557-5238 or 253-853-4000 (Mon.-Fri., 7:30am-3:30pm PST); Fax: 253-853-4001. *Website:* http://www.nfpainc.org *E-mail:* info@nfpainc.org

GRANDPARENTING

ATLANTIC

AtlantiCare Grandparents and Kin Support Group *(BILINGUAL) Professionally-run.* Provides information, advocacy and economic assistance to grandparents and kin raising other family members' children. Families welcome. Rap sessions, guest speakers, literature, educational series and phone help. Building is handicapped accessible. Meets 2nd Tues., 6-8pm, Uptown School Complex, 323 Madison Ave., Atlantic City. Call 609-441-0102 (day). *E-mail:* rnorrellnance@atlanticare.org

BERGEN

Grandparents Raising Grandchildren Support Group Mutual support, information and encouragement for grandparents raising grandchildren. Rap sessions and guest speakers. Meets 3rd Thurs., 10-11:30am, Russell Major Liberty School, 12 Tenafly Rd., Englewood. Pre-registration required. Before attending call 201-796-6209.

"There is no power greater than right action in the present moment." -- *Yaga Vasistha*

BURLINGTON

BCCAP Headstart Grandparent Support Group Support for grandparents, great-grandparents, great-aunts/uncles, etc. who are raising grandchildren. Building is handicapped accessible. Meets monthly, 7-9pm (except July/Aug.), Human Services Building, 795 Woodlane Rd., Mt. Holly. Call Sue Dietz 609-261-2323 (day).

CAMDEN

Grandparents Raising Grandchildren Support and education for women and men who are caring for their grandchildren struggling with emotional, behavioral and mental challenges. Guest speakers, literature, social, advocacy and buddy system. Meets 4th Mon., 6:30-8:30pm, Holy Trinity Lutheran Church, 325 South Whitehorse Pike, Audubon. Call Marge Varneke 856-547-1620 (eve.) or Susan A. Doherty-Funke 856-662-2600 (day). *Website:* http://www.camdenfso.org *E-mail:* sdoherty-funke@camdenfso.org

CAPE MAY

Grandparents Raising Grandchildren *Professionally-run.* Support and educational workshops for grandparents raising their grandchildren. Members share ideas, challenges and learn new skills. Newsletter. Meets monthly, Rutgers Cooperative Research and Extension, 355 Court House/South Dennis Rd., Cape May Court House. For specific date and times call Marian 609-465-5115 ext. 609.

ESSEX

GrandFamilies Support Groups *Professionally-run.* Educational and emotional support for grandparents raising grandchildren. Meets 2nd Wed., 11am-noon, Salvation Army West Side Community Center, 699 Springfield Ave., Newark and 1st Thurs., 10:30-11:30am, Salvation Army Community Center, 430 Martin Luther King Jr. Blvd., East Orange. Before attending call Erica Lewis 973-623-5959 ext. 207.

Grandma K.A.R.E.S., Inc. (Kinship, Advocacy, Resources, Education and Support) *Professionally-run.* Educational, inspirational and motivational support group for "Kinship-Caregivers" and foster parents. Building is handicapped accessible. Guest speakers, literature, newsletter, phone help and buddy system. Meets 3rd Fri., 1-3pm, South Orange Library, 65 Scotland Rd., South Orange. Call Louise Eagle 973-327-4114. *E-mail:* grandmakares@optonline.net

Grandparents United Group *Professionally-run.* Provides support, encouragement and information to grandparents raising grandchildren. Meets 3rd Wed., 11am-1pm, Family Support Organization of Essex County, 60 Evergreen Place, Suite 410, East Orange. Call Nicole 973-395-1441 (day). *Website:* http://www.fsoec.org

MERCER

Grand-Parent Support Group *(MERCER COUNTY RESIDENTS ONLY) Professionally-run.* Provides support and education for grandparents who provide full-time or part-time care for grandchildren. On-going and short term groups. Building is handicapped accessible. For meeting day, time and location call Barbara Stender 609-396-6788 ext. 241 (day). *E-mail:* bstender@gtbhc.org

Grandparents Need More Than A Hug Emotional support for grandparents raising their grandchildren. Meets 3rd Thurs., 6pm, Trenton. Before attending call Harriet Jones 609-695-4260 (5-9pm). *E-mail:* grandparentsneedhugs@mac.com

MIDDLESEX

Middlesex County Grandparents Raising Grandchildren Coalition, Inc. Support and advocacy organization committed to providing kinship caregivers the tools necessary to provide a stable, nurturing and secure environment for each child in their care. Dues $10/per mtg./family. Children welcome. Childcare provided. Building is handicapped accessible. Meets 2nd Mon., 7-9pm, Edison Senior Center, 2963 Woodbridge Ave., Edison. Call Jill Williams 732-248-8255. *E-mail:* dmwjas@aol.com.

OCEAN

Grandparents Support Group *Professionally-run.* Support for grandparents, especially grandparents raising grandchildren, a chance to share knowledge, hopes and strengths. Provides a safe environment for guidance and validation. Topics will include: estrangement issues, divorce of children, raising grandchildren, long-distance grandparenting, step-grandparenting, family tensions, etc. Guest speakers, rap sessions and social activities. Meets 1st and 3rd Tues., 10-11:30am, Holy Spirit Episcopal Church, 220 E. Main St., Library, Tuckerton. Pre-registration required. Before attending call 609-296-8300 option #4.

UNION

Grandparents Raising Grandchildren *(SPANISH)* *Professionally-run.* Support for grandparents raising grandchildren. Members share ideas, challenges, new skills and crafts. Meets Tues., 4:30-5:45pm, Josephine's Place, 622 Elizabeth Ave., Elizabeth. Call Sister Judy 908-436-0099 or 908-789-7625.

NATIONAL

GAP (Grandparents As Parents) *Model. 9 groups throughout LA county. Founded 1987.* Support network, sharing of experiences and feelings between grandparents and other relative caregivers who are raising their grandchildren for various reasons. Phone support, networking, advocacy, social activities, group member listings, emergency assistance, information and referrals. Assistance in starting similar groups. Write: GAP, 22048 Sherman Way, #217, Canoga Park, CA 91303. Call 818-264-0880; Fax: 818-264-0882. *E-mail:* madelyn@grandparentsasparents.com

MARRIAGE / FAMILY

BERGEN

S.O.U.R.C.E., The *Professionally-run.* Support, information, networking and referrals for all family concerns. Phone help, drop-in center, guest speakers, groups for parents and kids. Building is handicapped accessible. Meets various times, The Source Building, 1 West Plaza, Glen Rock. Call Jean Baker Wunder 201-670-4673 or 201-652-8332 (day).

BURLINGTON

Third Option *Professionally-run.* Christian-focused group for persons with marital problems or couples who want to strengthen their marriages. Rap sessions, literature, lecture and education. Building is handicapped accessible. Meets 1st and 3rd Thurs., 7-9pm, Fellowship Alliance Chapel, 199 Church Rd., Medford. Call Rev. Ed Stiegel 609-953-7333 ext. 129.

NATIONAL

ACME (Association for Couples in Marriage Enrichment) *National network. Founded 1973.* Network of couples who want to enhance their own relationship, as well as help strengthen marriages of other couples. Local chapters sponsor support groups, retreats and workshops. Bi-monthly newsletter, leadership training and conferences. Write: ACME, P.O. Box 21374, Winston-Salem, NC 27120. Call 1-800-634-8325 or 336-724-1526; Fax: 336-721-4746. *Website:* http://www.bettermarriages.org *E-mail:* acme@bettermarriages.org

No Kidding! *International. 50 chapters in five countries. Founded 1984.* Mutual support and social activities for married and single people who either have decided not to have children, are postponing parenthood, are undecided or are unable to have children. Chapter development guidelines. Write: No Kidding!, Box 2802, Vancouver, BC, Canada V6B 3X2. Call 604-538-7736 (24 hr.). *Website:* http://www.nokidding.net *E-mail:* info@nokidding.net

Recovering Couples Anonymous *National. 130 groups. Founded 1988.* 12-Step. Goal is to assist couples find freedom from dysfunctional patterns in their relationships. RCA is made up of couples committed to restoring healthy communication and developing a caring and functional relationship. Offers local support group information. Write: RCA, P.O. Box 11029, Oakland, CA 94611. Call 510-663-2312. *Website:* http://www.recovering-couples.org

ONLINE

After the Affair *Online.* Discussion forum to help persons recover after an extra-marital affair. *Website:* http://members3.boardhost.com/affair

PARENTING (GENERAL)
(see also parents of adolescents, childbirth, toll-free helplines)

STATEWIDE

Mocha Moms Support for stay-at-home mothers of color. Sponsors support group meetings, monthly moms-only events and community projects. There are presently 7 local groups in Bergen, Burlington, Essex, Mercer, Monmouth, Somerset and Union counties. Visit their national website for contact information and details on status of NJ groups. *Website:* http://www.mochamoms.org

MOMS Club Support for stay-at-home moms. There are several groups that meet in NJ. Check website for local groups. *Website:* http://www.momsclub.org (scroll to bottom, then click on to chapter links).

MOPS (Mothers Of Preschoolers) Provides non-denominational Christian support for mothers of preschoolers. There are about 131 MOPS groups that meet in NJ. For information about a local chapter call 1-800-929-1287. *Website:* http://www.mops.org

Mothers and More Support groups for women who have altered their career paths to care for their children at home. 7 chapters in NJ. Check website for listing of these chapters. Call 630-941-3553 (national office in Illinois). *Website:* http://www.mothersandmore.org

Mothers of Only Children of Northern NJ Provides support and social activities to families that have an only child (ages 2-12) whether by choice or not. For information contact Joanne via e-mail. *E-mail:* jkowalski_makeovers@yahoo.com

NJ Kinship Legal Guardianship Clearinghouse (KinKonnect) Information and referral service for any caregiver raising a family member. Resource directory, lending library, handbooks, advocacy, publications and newsletter. Call 1-877-554-5463. *Website:* http://www.kinkonnect.org

Parents Anonymous *(BILINGUAL) Professionally-run.* Self-help for parents who are under stress and who want to improve their relationships with their children. Groups meet weekly and are facilitated by a volunteer professional. Many groups provide childcare. Groups meet in most counties throughout the state with some bilingual groups available. Online parent support group available. Write: Parents Anonymous, 127 Route 206, Suite 10, Hamilton, NJ 08610. Call 1-800-843-5437 (stressline) or 609-585-7666 (office). *Website:* www.pa-of-nj.org *E-mail:* panjstress@aol.com

Unschoolers Network Information and encouragement for families who educate their children at home. Guest speakers, literature and phone help. For local group information call Nancy Plent 732-938-2473. *Website:* http://www.unschoolersnetwork.bravehost.com *E-mail:* unnet@aol.com

ATLANTIC

MOPS (Mothers Of Pre-Schoolers) Support and encouragement for mothers of pre-schoolers. Program includes fellowship, lectures on Christian womanhood, discussion groups and crafts. Suggested $5/mtg. Meets 1st and 3rd Mon., 9:30-11:30am, Shore Fellowship Church, 1049 Ocean Heights Ave., Egg Harbor Township. Call Jennifer Christiansen 609-909-9702 or church 609-646-4693 (day).

Parents Anonymous *Professionally-run.* Self-help for parents who are under stress and who want to improve their relationships with their children. Before attending call Parents Anonymous 1-800-843-5437.

> **Atlantic City** Meets Tues., 5-7pm, Interstate Reality Management, 925 Caspean Ave.
>
> **Northfield** Meets Tues., 10-11:30am, Family Support Organization, 1601 Tilton Rd., Unit 1. Before attending call Andrea Burleigh 609-485-0575.

BERGEN

Holistic Moms Network Mutual support for moms with an interest in natural health, alternative therapies and mindful parenting. Families welcome. Rap sessions and guest speakers. Dues $35/yr. Meets in Hillside. For monthly meeting information call 1-877-465-6667. *Website:* http://www.holisticmoms.org

Mocha Moms Support for stay-at-home mothers of color. Sponsors support group meetings, monthly moms-only events and community projects. *Website:* http://www.bergencountymochamoms.org

Parents Anonymous *Professionally-run.* Self-help for parents who are under stress and who want to improve their relationships with their children. Meets Wed., 7-8pm, Family Support Organization, 0-108 29th St., Fairlawn. Before attending call Parents Anonymous 1-800-843-5437 or Lynne Bolson 201-796-6209 ext. 102.

BURLINGTON

Mocha Moms Support for stay-at-home mothers of color. Sponsors support group meetings, monthly moms-only events and community projects. *Website:* http://www.njmochamoms.org

*Can't find an appropriate group in your area? The Clearinghouse helps people start groups. Give us a call at **1-800-367-6274**.*

Parents Anonymous *Professionally-run.* Self-help for parents who are under stress and who want to improve their relationships with their children. Before attending all Parents Anonymous 1-800-843-5437.

> **Lumberton** Meets Tues., 7-9pm, Family Support Organization, 774 Eayrestown Rd. Before attending call Maggie Kaupp 609-265-8838.
>
> **Westampton** Meets Thurs., 7-9pm, Family Service Center, 770 Woodlane Rd., Suite 23. Childcare available. Before attending call Charles Robinson 609-526-4117.
>
> **Willingboro** Meets Tues., 7:30-9pm, New Life Deliverance, Salem Rd. and Levitt Parkway. Childcare available. Before attending call Pastor Rose Sparrow Melton 609-871-8798.

CAMDEN

Parents Anonymous *Professionally-run.* Self-help for parents who are under stress and who want to improve their relationships with their children. Before attending call Parents Anonymous 1-800-843-5437.

> **Camden** Meets Wed., 6-8:30pm, Camden Village Wrap, Inc., 112 N. 7th St.
>
> **Merchantville** Meets Thurs., 6:30-8:30pm, Family Support Organization, 23 West Park Ave., Suite 103-104. Before attending call Susan Doherty-Funke 856-662-2600.

CAPE MAY

Parents Anonymous *Professionally-run.* Mutual support for any parent or caregiver of a child. Opportunity to discuss troubling issues and exchange information on raising healthy, confident and loving children. Rap sessions. Childcare available. Meets Wed., 6:30-8pm, Cape Counseling Service, 128 Crest Haven Rd., Bldg. D, Cape May Court House. Call Patricia Rocanella, BSW 609-465-4100 ext. 244 (day).

CUMBERLAND

Parents Anonymous *Professionally-run.* Self-help for parents who are under stress and who want to improve their relationships with their children. Before attending call Parents Anonymous 1-800-843-5437.

> **Bridgeton** Meets Wed., 6-8pm, Gateway Family Enrichment Center, 155 Spruce St.
>
> **Elmer** Meets Tues., 6-8pm, Family Support Organization CGS, 1226 E. Landis Ave. Childcare available. Before attending call Lisa Gates 856-507-9400.

Millville Meets Tues., 6:30-8pm, Holly City Help Center, 221 E. Broad St. Before attending call Amy Richter 856-765-0205.

ESSEX

Holistic Moms Network Mutual support for moms with an interest in natural health, alternative therapies and mindful parenting. Families welcome. Rap sessions and guest speakers. Dues $35/yr. Meets in Montclair. For monthly meeting information call 1-877-465-6667. *Website:* http://www.holisticmoms.org

Mocha Moms Support for stay-at-home mothers of color. Sponsors support group meetings, monthly moms-only events and community projects. *Website:* http://mochamomsofessexco.clubspaces.com

MOPS (Mothers Of Preschoolers) Provides non-denominational Christian support for mothers with children under school age. Education, group discussions, socials, guest speakers and crafts. For women with the desire to be the best mother they can be. Donation $6 (can be waived). Meets 4th Thurs., 9:30am-noon (except July/Aug.), Montclair Community Church, 143 Watchung Ave., Upper Montclair. Before attending call 973-746-0042. *Website:* http://www.mops.org

New Moms' Circle *Professionally-run.* Support group for new mothers to openly discuss the ups and downs of adjusting to motherhood. Topics to be covered include: myths of motherhood, shifting identity, postpartum depression, attempting to balance it all, marriage and the transition to parenthood. Meets Tues., 10-11:30am, Saint Barnabas Ambulatory Care Center, 200 South Orange Ave. (across from the Livingston Mall), Livingston. For information call Saint Barnabas Women's Health Education 973-322-5360 or Dr. Lauren Meisels, PhD 973-762-4147. Infants in strollers or car seats are welcome to attend and free childcare is available, if needed, by calling 973-322-7309 at least 24 hours in advance.

"I am only one, but I still am one. I cannot do everything, but I still can do something. And because I cannot do everything, I will not refuse to do the something that I can do."
-- Helen Keller

Parents Anonymous *Professionally-run.* Self-help for parents who are under stress and who want to improve their relationships with their children. Before attending call Parents Anonymous 1-800-843-5437.

> **East Orange** *(GRANDPARENTS)* Meets Thurs., noon-2pm, East Orange Child Development Center, 42 Chestnut St. Before attending call Ms. Rutledge 973-676-1110.
>
> **Irvington** Meets Wed., 9-11am, Grove Street Elementary School, 602 Grove St. Stop at the security desk and ask for parent group meeting room. Before attending call Donna Alston 973-399-6949.
>
> **Orange** Meets Wed., 4:30-6pm, Norjenes Day Care Center, 95 South Essex Ave. Before attending call Audrey Garres and Sherri Featherstone 973-677-4299.

GLOUCESTER

Bring-Along-Baby Morning *Professionally-run.* An informal support group for moms and their babies under 2 years of age. Fee $3/mtg. Building is handicapped accessible. Meets Fri., 9:30-11am (except July/Aug.), Central Baptist Church, West Centre St. and South Jackson St., Woodbury. Pre-registration required. Before attending call 856-845-0100 ext. 2456 (day).

Holistic Moms Network *(Tri-County Chapter)* Mutual support for moms with an interest in natural health, alternative therapies and mindful parenting. Families welcome. Rap sessions and guest speakers. Dues $35/yr. Meets in Pitman. For monthly meeting information call 1-877-465-6667. *Website:* http://www.holisticmoms.org

Parents Anonymous *Professionally-run.* Self-help for parents who are under stress and who want to improve their relationships with their children. Meets Thurs., 6:30-8:30pm, Woodbury Child Development Center, 36 Carpenter St., Woodbury. Before attending call Parents Anonymous 1-800-843-5437 or Donna Backus 609-458-7901.

Tag-Along-Toddler Morning *Professionally-run.* An informal support group for moms and their toddlers under 3 years of age. Fee $3/mtg. Building is handicapped accessible. Meets Wed., 9:30-11am (except July/Aug.), Central Baptist Church, West Centre St. and South Jackson St., Woodbury. Pre-registration is required. Before attending call 856-845-0100 ext. 2456 (day).

"It is in giving oneself, that one receives." – Francis of Assisi

HUDSON

D.I.G. (Dads Involved Group) *Professionally-run.* Opportunity for fathers to provide support and encouragement to each other. Meets 2nd Mon., 6-8pm, Family Support Organization of Hudson County, 705 Bergen Ave., Jersey City. Call 201-915-5143.

Parents Anonymous *Professionally-run.* Self-help for parents who are under stress and who want to improve their relationships with their children. Before attending call Parents Anonymous 1-800-843-5437.

> **Jersey City** Meets Sat., noon-2pm, Family Support Organization of Hudson County, 705 Bergen Ave. Before attending call Roslyn Gibbs-Muse 201-915-5140.

> **Jersey City** *(Teenage Parents Group)* Meets Mon., 6-8pm, Hudson County Child Abuse Prevention Center, 880 Bergen Ave., Room 302. Before attending call Tamir Reyes 201-798-5588.

HUNTERDON

Holistic Moms Network Mutual support for moms with an interest in natural health, alternative therapies and mindful parenting. Families welcome. Rap sessions and guest speakers. Dues $35/yr. For monthly meeting information call 1-877-465-6667. *Website:* http://www.holisticmoms.org

MERCER

Hispanic Parenting Support Group *(SPANISH) Professionally-run.* Provides mutual support and education for parents. Rap sessions, guest speakers and literature. Life skills and parenting workshops. Also offers bilingual and multicultural parenting skills. Lunch provided. Meets Fri., 10:30am-1pm, Latinas Unidas, YWCA of Trenton, 140 E. Hanover St., Trenton. Call Cecy Weeast 609-396-3040 (day).

Holistic Moms Network Mutual support for moms with an interest in natural health, alternative therapies and mindful parenting. Families welcome. Rap sessions and guest speakers. Dues $35/yr. Meets in Lawrenceville. For monthly meeting information call 1-877-465-6667. *Website:* http://www.holisticmoms.org

Mercer County Mocha Moms Mutual support for full or part-time stay-at-home mothers of color. Encourages community activism among the membership. Advocacy, social, newsletter, guest speakers and online message board. Dues $34/yr. Meets 1st Sat., 9-10am, Panera Bread, Nassau Park

Shopping Center, 510 Nassau Park Blvd., West Windsor. Check website to confirm meeting day. *Website:* http://mercer.nj.mochamoms.tripod.com

New Moms Group Support designed for moms and their babies from birth to nine months. Offers mutual support discussing the ups and downs of a new baby on the family. Registration fee $36. Meets for 6-8 week sessions, 2-3 times/yr., Princeton area. Pre-registration required. Before attending call Debra Levenstein 609-987-8100 (day). *Website:* http://www.jfcsonline.org *E-mail:* debral@jfcsonline.org

Parents Anonymous *Professionally-run.* Self-help for parents and caregivers who wish to improve family relationships. Building is handicapped accessible. Before attending call Parents Anonymous 1-800-843-5437.

> **Hamilton** Meets Wed., 10am-noon, Ibis Plaza, 3535 Quakerbridge Rd., Suite 400. Call Paulette Mader 609-586-1200 ext. 225 or Laurie Townsend 609-586-1200 ext. 322 (day).

> **Hamilton** *(Parents of Teenagers)* Self-help for parents of teenagers who are under stress and who want to improve their relationships with their children. Meets Wed., 6-8pm, Parents Anonymous Office, 127 Route 206 South, Suite 10. Before attending call Orysia Kaufman 609-585-7666.

MIDDLESEX

Holistic Moms Network Mutual support for moms with an interest in natural health, alternative therapies and mindful parenting. Families welcome. Rap sessions and guest speakers. Dues $35/yr. Meets in Metuchen. For monthly meeting information call 1-877-465-6667. *Website:* http://www.holisticmoms.org

New Moms - New Babies *Professionally-run.* Support and discussion group for new moms. Babies welcome. Topics to be discussed include: postpartum, sleep deprivation, breast feeding, childcare issues and more. Building is handicapped accessible. Meets 2nd and 4th Thurs., 12:30-2pm, Robert Wood Johnson University Hospital, One Robert Wood Johnson Place, BMSCH 1st Floor Conference Room, New Brunswick. Call 732-253-3871.

MONMOUTH

Holistic Moms Network Mutual support for moms with an interest in natural health, alternative therapies and mindful parenting. Families welcome. Rap sessions and guest speakers. Dues $35/yr. Meets in Shrewsbury. For monthly meeting information call 1-877-465-6667. *Website:* http://www.holisticmoms.org

Mocha Moms Support for stay-at-home mothers of color. Sponsors support group meetings, monthly moms-only events and community projects. *Website:* http://www.monmouthmochas.org

MOPS (Mothers Of Pre-Schoolers) Support and encouragement to mothers of preschoolers. Program includes fellowship, lectures on Christian womanhood, discussion groups and crafts. Suggested $4/mtg. Meetings vary, 9-11am (Sept.-May), First Presbyterian Church at Red Bank, 255 Harding Rd., Red Bank. Call Carol Andrews 732-671-0553 (day) or 732-747-1348 (day).

Mother to Mother Support Group *Professionally-run.* Provides support and education for new mothers to help with topics such as feeding, sleeping, crying, recovery from childbirth and postpartum depression. Newborns to 6 months welcome. Building is handicapped accessible. Meets Mon., 11am-noon, Monmouth Medical Center, 300 Second Ave., Ronald McDonald Family Conference Room, Borden Wing, 2 Floor, Long Branch. Pre-registration required. Before attending call 732-923-6990 (day).

New Moms Network at Jersey Shore University Medical Center *Professionally-run.* Support and information for mothers of infants (ages birth to 12 months). Rap sessions, guest speakers and phone help. Building is handicapped accessible. Meets Thurs., 1-3pm, Jersey Shore University Medical Center, 1945 Route 33, Lance B 104, Neptune. Call Linda Carroll 732-776-4281 (day). *E-mail:* lcarroll@meridianhealth.com

Parent Linking Program Opportunity for parents to discuss parenting skills, child development and parent-child interaction. Some groups welcome young fathers and grandparents. Various meeting locations. For information call Jill Brown 732-246-8060 (day). *Website:* http://www.preventchildabusenj.org

Parents Anonymous *Professionally-run.* Self-help for parents who are under stress and who want to improve their relationships with their children. Before attending call Parents Anonymous 1-800-843-5437.
> **Freehold** Meets Tues., 10am-noon, Monmouth County Human Services Building, 3000 Kozloski Rd., First Floor. Call before attending group if childcare is needed. Before attending call Mary Ellen Hemenway 732-845-2073.
> **Keansburg** *(KEANSBURG RESIDENTS ONLY)* Meets Wed., 9:30-11:30am, Bolger Middle School, 100 Palmer Pl. Before attending call Jeff Johnson 732-787-2007 ext. 2554.

MORRIS

Holistic Moms Network Mutual support for moms with an interest in natural health, alternative therapies and mindful parenting. Families welcome. Rap sessions and guest speakers. Dues $35/yr. Meets in Morris Plains and Long Valley. For monthly meeting information call 1-877-465-6667. *Website:* http://www.holisticmoms.org

PASSAIC

Holistic Moms Network Mutual support for moms with an interest in natural health, alternative therapies and mindful parenting. Families welcome. Rap sessions and guest speakers. Dues $35/yr. Meets in Wayne. For monthly meeting information call 1-877-465-6667. *Website:* http://www.holisticmoms.org

SALEM

Parents Anonymous *Professionally-run.* Self-help for parents who are under stress and who want to improve their relationships with their children. Meets Wed., 6-8pm, Inter-Agency Council, 98 Market St., Salem. Childcare available. Before attending call Parents Anonymous 1-800-843-5437 or Cora Santiago 856-935-7510 ext. 8319.

SOMERSET

Holistic Moms Network Mutual support for moms with an interest in natural health, alternative therapies and mindful parenting. Families welcome. Rap sessions and guest speakers. Dues $35/yr. Meets in Bridgewater. For monthly meeting information call 1-877-465-6667. *Website:* http://www.holisticmoms.org

Mocha Moms Support for stay-at-home mothers of color. Sponsors support group meetings, monthly moms-only events and community projects. *Website:* http://www.somersetunionmochas.com

YoungLives Support Group *Professionally-run.* Support and education for teenagers (under age 20) who are pregnant or recently gave birth. Childcare available. Rap sessions, guest speakers, literature, newsletter, phone help and buddy system. Building is handicapped accessible. Meets 1st Fri., 7pm (except June, July, Aug.), St. Luke's Church, 300 Clinton Ave., North Plainfield. Call Lucy Droege 908-791-4455 (day).

SUSSEX

Holistic Moms Network Mutual support for moms with an interest in natural health, alternative therapies and mindful parenting. Families welcome. Rap sessions and guest speakers. Dues $35/yr. Meets in Lafayette. For monthly meeting information call 1-877-465-6667. *Website:* http://www.holisticmoms.org

Project Self-Sufficiency *Professionally-run.* Support for single parents, teen parents, displaced homemakers and low-income families. Offers peer support groups for single parents and teen parents, loss recovery groups for children, parenting skills training and support. Also family activities, physical and emotional health educational seminars, home visitation, family stabilization, comprehensive job training and educational services designed to promote self-sufficiency. Meetings vary. Call Deborah Berry-Toon 973-383-5129 (day). *E-mail:* pss@garden.net

UNION

Holistic Moms Network Mutual support for moms with an interest in natural health, alternative therapies and mindful parenting. Families welcome. Rap sessions and guest speakers. Dues $35/yr. Meets in Cranford. For monthly meeting information call 1-877-465-6667. *Website:* http://www.holisticmoms.org

Latino YoungLives Support Group *(SPANISH) Professionally-run.* Support and education for teenagers (under age 20) who are pregnant or recently gave birth. Childcare available. Rap sessions, guest speakers, literature, newsletter, phone help and buddy system. Meets 3rd Fri., 7pm, First Christian Assembly, 718 Central Ave., Plainfield. Call Lucy Droege 908-791-4455 (day).

Mocha Moms Support for stay-at-home mothers of color. Sponsors support group meetings, monthly moms-only events and community projects. *Website:* http://www.somersetunionmochas.com

"No man or woman of the humblest sort can really be strong, gentle and good, without the world being better for it, without somebody being helped and comforted by the very existence of that goodness." -- Alan Alda

Parents Anonymous *Professionally-run.* Self-help for parents who are under stress and who want to improve their relationships with their children. Group is primarily for parents of children with behavioral and emotional disorders. Before attending call Parents Anonymous 1-800-843-5437.

> **Plainfield** Meets 2nd and 4th Wed., 6:30-8pm, Center for Stronger Families, Plainfield High School (enter old building), 925 Arlington Ave. Childcare available. Before attending call Agness McLean 908-731-4360 ext. 5381.
> **Roselle** Meets Thurs., 6:30-8:30pm, Chestnut Street Community Church, 303 Chestnut St. Childcare available. Before attending call Jackie Mitchell 908-620-1775.
> **Westfield** Meets 2nd and 4th Wed., 6:30-8:30pm, Family Support Organization, 143 Elmer St. Before attending call Rosalie Kennedy 908-789-7625.

Prevention Through Parenting *Professionally-run.* Support and education for teenagers who are pregnant or parents of young children. Fathers are welcome also. Literature and phone help. Meets Thurs., 3:30-5pm, United Family and Children's Society, 305 West 7th St., Plainfield. Call Karen Flanagan, CSW 908-755-4848. *E-mail:* kflanagan@unitedfamily.org

WARREN

Holistic Moms Network Mutual support for moms with an interest in natural health, alternative therapies and mindful parenting. Families welcome. Rap sessions and guest speakers. Dues $35/yr. Meets in Blairstown. For monthly meeting information call 1-877-465-6667. *Website:* http://www.holisticmoms.org

NATIONAL

Attachment Parenting International *International. Founded 1994.* Promotes parenting practices to create strong, healthy emotional bonds between parents and their child. Dues $35/yr. Offers support group referrals, newsletter, advocacy, literature, information and referrals. Write: Attachment Parenting International, P.O. Box 4615, Alpharetta, GA 30022. Call 1-800-850-8320. *Website:* http://www.attachmentparenting.org *E-mail:* info@attachmentparenting.org

Family Equality Council *National. 160+ local groups. Founded 1979.* Support, education and advocacy for gay, lesbian or transgendered parents and prospective parents. Families welcome. Information and referrals, phone support, family events, literature and newsletter. Assistance in starting groups.

Write: Family Equality Council, P.O. Box 206, Boston, MA 02133. Call 617-502-8700; Fax: 617-502-8701. *Website:* http://www.familyequality.org *E-mail:* info@familyequality.org

Holistic Moms Network *International. Chapters across the US and Canada. Founded 2002.* Purpose is to provide support, awareness and education for holistic parenting. Provides a nurturing, open-minded and respectful community for parents to share these ideals. Encourages moms and dads to parent naturally and educate themselves about alternative health, mindful parenting and natural healing. Assists persons in starting new chapters. Write: Holistic Moms Network, P.O. Box 408, Caldwell, NJ 07006. Call 1-877-465-6667. *Website:* http://www.holisticmoms.org *E-mail:* info@holisticmoms.org

MAD DADS, Inc. (Men Against Destruction Defending Against Drugs and Social-disorder) *National. 60 affiliated groups in 17 states. Founded 1989.* Grassroots organization of fathers aimed at fighting gang and drug-related violence. Provides family and community activities and leadership, community education and mobilization, speaking engagements regarding goals and objectives and chapter formation. They present themselves as "surrogate fathers" who listen to and care about street teens. National signature program: Neighborhood Street Mentoring Patrols. Members provide assistance in starting chapters in hard-to-reach neighborhoods. Also, groups for kids, mothers and grandparents. Write: MAD DADS, Inc., 5732 Normandy Blvd., Suite 8, Jacksonville, FL 32205. Call 904-781-0905. *Website:* http://www.maddads.com *E-mail:* national@maddads.com

Mocha Moms, Inc. *National. 100+ affiliated groups. Founded 1997.* Provides support for at-home mothers of color. Sponsors weekly support group meetings, monthly moms-only events, on-going community service and volunteer opportunities. Dues $20/year. Bulletins, information, assistance with starting local chapters and referrals to existing groups. Write: Mocha Moms, Inc., P.O. Box 1995, Upper Marlboro, MD 20773. Fax: 301-805-8147. *Website:* http://www.mochamoms.org *E-mail:* nationaloffice@mochamoms.org

MOMS Club *International. 2000+ affiliated groups. Founded 1983.* Mutual support for mothers-at-home. Groups provide at-home mothers of children of all ages emotional and moral support, as well as a wide variety of activities. Provides assistance in starting and maintaining or locating chapters through local coordinators (enclose $2 to cover postage). Write: MOMS Club, 1464 Madera Rd., #N 191, Simi Valley, CA 93065. *Website:* http://www.momsclub.org *E-mail:* momsclub@aol.com

MOPS, International (Mothers Of Pre-Schoolers) *International. 3600 affiliated groups. Founded 1973.* Offers a non-denominational Christian support group for mothers with children from infancy to 6 years old. MOPS groups meet in churches throughout the U.S., Canada and 15 other countries. Provides assistance in starting local groups. Write: MOPS, International, 2370 South Trenton Way, Denver, CO 80231. Call 1-800-929-1287 or 303-733-5353 (group referrals); 1-888-910-6677 (to start a MOPS group); Fax: 303-733-5770. *Website:* http://www.mops.org *E-mail:* info@mops.org

Mothers and More *National. 180 chapters. Founded 1987.* Support and advocacy for women who have altered their career paths to care for their children at home. It is not about opposing mothers who work outside the home; rather it is about respecting, supporting and advocating for choice in how one combines working and parenting. Provides ongoing support for a woman's personal needs and interests with regard to active parenting. Also advocates for public and employment policies that accommodate stay-at-home mothers. Newsletter and chapter development guidelines. Write: Mothers and More, P.O. Box 31, Elmhurst, IL 60126. Call 630-941-3553; Fax: 630-941-3551. *Website:* http://www.mothersandmore.org *E-mail:* nationaloffice@mothersandmore.org

NATHHAN (National Challenged Homeschoolers) *National network. Founded 1990.* Christian, non-profit organization encouraging families with special needs, particularly those who home educate. Bi-annual magazine, lending library, family phone book, phone support, program for parents of special need pre-borns, information and referrals. Dues $25/yr. Write: NATHHAN, P.O. Box 310, Moyie Springs, ID 83845. Call 208-267-6246. *Website:* http://www.nathhan.com *E-mail:* nathanews@aol.com

National Association of Mothers' Centers *National. 40 sites. Founded 1975.* Warm, welcoming environment of support. Discussion groups and other activities regarding parenting, pregnancy, childbirth and childrearing. National and some local newsletters, conference and advocacy. Has up-to-date information on contacting local Mothers' Center programs, starting a center and how employers in NY/NJ/CT can offer a program for working parents. Write: National Association of Mothers' Centers, 1740 Old Jericho Turnpike, Jericho, NY 11753. Call 1-877-939-6667 or 516-939-6667; Fax: 516-750-5365. *Website:* http://www.motherscenter.org *E-mail:* info@motherscenter.org

Parents Anonymous, Inc. *National. Founded 1969.* Country's oldest child abuse prevention organization. Opportunity for parents to learn new skills, transform their attitudes and behaviors and create lasting changes in their lives. Group meetings offer structured children's programs. Helps to develop new community groups by providing training, technical assistance, materials and networking. Write: Parents Anonymous, Inc., 675 W. Foothill Blvd., Suite 220, Claremont, CA 91711-3475. Call 909-621-6184; Fax: 909-625-6304. *Website:* http://www.parentsanonymous.org *E-mail:* parentsanonymous@parentsanonymous.org

PEP (Postpartum Education for Parents) *Model. 1 group in California. Founded 1977.* Volunteer-run group that provides emotional peer support for parents. Helps parents adjust to the changes in their lives that a baby brings. Education on basic infant care and parent adjustment. Phone help. Group development guidelines. Write: PEP, P.O. Box 6154, Santa Barbara, CA 93130. Call 805-564-3888 (8am-8pm PST). *Website:* http://www.sbpep.org *E-mail:* pepboard@gmail.com

ONLINE

At Home Dad Network, The *Online. Founded 1997.* Support and resources for stay-at-home fathers. Discussion forum, chatroom, information and events. *Website:* http://www.athomedad.com

CentralJerseyMoms.com *Online.* A place for women to connect and support each other. Information, ideas and input on questions or offer advice in a safe, reliable online environment. Current news, forums, events and activities. *Website:* http://www.centraljerseymoms.com

Conduct Disorders Parent Message Board *Online. 7080 members. Founded 1995.* Support for parents living with a child with one of the many behavior disorders including: attention deficit hyperactivity disorder, oppositional defiance disorder, conduct disorder, depression and substance abuse. Parents with children of all ages welcome. *Website:* http://www.conductdisorders.com

Expecting Parents Meetup Groups *Online.* Meet other new or expecting parents to exchange advice, support and laughs. Message boards. *Website:* http://newparents.meetup.com

Jersey Dads *Online.* Support for stay-at-home dads to discuss parenting and household skills. *Website:* http://www.jerseydads.com *E-mail:* njdads@hotmail.com

Mothers of Freshmen *Online.* Support group for mothers of college freshmen where they share their various concerns unique to sending a child off to college, from how to support their child to coping with "Empty Nest Syndrome." Has a variety of topical message boards and evening chat sessions. *Website:* http://www.mofchat.com

Parent Empowerment Network *Online. Founded 1996.* E-mail group for parents with disabilities. *Website:* http://www.disabledparents.net *E-mail:* trish@disabledparents.net

Parent Soup Message Boards *Online.* Offers a large variety of message boards which deal with parenting issues including infertility, pregnancy, parenting challenges, parents of disabled, pregnancy loss, newborn babies, toddlers, adoption, family issues, etc. *Website:* http://www.parentsoup.com/messageboards

Stay At Home Moms University (SAHMU) *Online. 745 members. Founded 1999.* Support, encouragement and discussions regarding the unique challenges faced by stay-at-home moms. Discussion topics include parenting, teenagers, infants, marriages, homeschooling, home business and budget. Pregnant SAHMs-to-be are welcome. *Website:* http://groups.yahoo.com/group/sahmu

PARENTS OF CHILDREN WITH BEHAVIORAL PROBLEMS
(see also drugs, alcohol, parenting, toll-free helplines)

STATEWIDE

New Jersey Parents' Caucus *(BILINGUAL)* Statewide coalition of families of children with special emotional and behavioral needs. Works to ensure that the needs of children are met through parent support groups, parent empowerment training, advocacy efforts and direct services at local offices. Helps parents to start local groups. Training and materials also in Spanish. Write: New Jersey Parents' Caucus, 236 South Salem St., Randolph, NJ 07869. Call 1-866-560-6572 or 973-989-8866; Fax: 973-989-8867. *Website:* http://www.newjerseyparentscaucus.org *E-mail:* info@njparentcaucus.org

ATLANTIC

Family Support Organization *(Parents Supporting Parents)* Provides support, education and advocacy for parents and caregivers of children with emotional, mental and behavioral challenges. Guest speakers, buddy system, literature, speakers' bureau, newsletter and phone help. Building is handicapped accessible. Meets 1st and 3rd Wed., 6:30-8:30pm, Atlantic Cape Family Support Organization, 1601 Tilton Rd., Unit #1, Northfield. Call Laura Marcy 609-485-0575 (day). *Website:* http://www.acfamsupport.org *E-mail:* lmarcy@acfamsupport.org

BERGEN

Family Support Organization *Professionally-run.* Provides support, education and advocacy to families and caregivers of children with complex emotional and behavioral challenges. Meets Wed., 7-8:30pm, Family Support Organization of Bergen County, 0-108 29th St., Fair Lawn. Childcare available. Before attending call 201-796-6209 (day). *Website:* http://www.fsobergen.org

BURLINGTON

B.I.L.Y. (Because I Love You) Mutual support to help parents with children (of any age) who have behavioral challenges. Guest speakers. Meets 1st and 3rd Thurs., 6:30-8:30pm, Sisterhood, Inc., 132-136 E. Broad St., Burlington. Call 609-265-8838 (day). *E-mail:* familyvoices@fsoburlco.org

Family Support Organization of Burlington/Mercer Counties *Professionally-run.* Provides support and advocacy to families and caregivers of children with complex emotional and behavioral challenges. Educational lectures offered. Meets Tues., 7-9pm, Family Support Organization of Burlington and Mercer county, 774 Eayrestown Rd., Lumberton. Call Russ or Terry 609-265-8838 (day).

CAMDEN

Grandparents Raising Grandchildren Support and education for women and men who are caring for their grandchildren struggling with emotional, behavioral and mental challenges. Guest speakers, literature, social, advocacy and buddy system. Meets 4th Mon., 6:30-8:30pm, Holy Trinity Lutheran Church, 325 South Whitehorse Pike, Audubon. Call Marge Varneke 856-547-1620 (eve.) or Susan A. Doherty-Funke 856-662-2600 (day). *Website:* http://www.camdenfso.org *E-mail:* sdoherty-funke@camdenfso.org

NJ Parents' Caucus Support Group *(BILINGUAL)* Mutual support and help provided for and by parents or caregivers of children with special emotional/behavioral needs. Guest speakers, phone help and speakers' bureau. Before attending call 1-866-560-6572 or 856-964-5155.

> **Camden** Meets 2nd Wed., noon-2pm, Ferry Avenue Branch Library, 852 Ferry Ave.
> **Camden** Meetings vary, 6-8pm, New Jersey Parents' Caucus of Camden County, 1419 Baird Blvd.

Parents Empowering Parents Provides support and advocacy for parents and caregivers of children with complex emotional and behavioral challenges. Rap sessions, guest speakers, literature and phone help. Childcare provided. Meets Tues. and Thurs., 6:30-8:30pm, Family Support Organization of Camden County, 23 West Park Ave., Suite 103-104, Merchantville. Call 856-662-2600. *Website:* http://www.camdenfso.org

CAPE MAY

Family Support Organization *(Parents Supporting Parents)* Support, education and advocacy for parents and caregivers of children with emotional and behavioral challenges. Rap sessions, guest speakers, buddy system, newsletter and phone support. Meets 4th Wed., 6:30-8:30pm, The Court House Church of Christ, 102 East Pacific Ave., Cape May Court House. Call Chris Haas 609-729-2034 (day). *Website:* http://www.acfamsupport.org *E-mail:* chaas@acfamsupport.org

ESSEX

Parents Self-Help Group Mutual support for parents disturbed by their children's unacceptable behavior. Helps parents take a firm stand with their kids. Building is handicapped accessible. Meets Tues., 7:45pm, Senior Community Center, Livingston. Call Debbie 973-533-1319, Helene and Jerry 973-994-4034 or Paul and Nancy 908-464-1590.

GLOUCESTER

Gloucester County Parent To Parent Coalition *Professionally-run.* Confidential meetings and focus on providing parents with support, information, resources and referrals for dealing with substance abuse and related problems. Guest speakers, educational series and literature. Building is handicapped accessible. Meets 2nd and 4th Mon., 7:30-9:30pm, Washington Township Municipal Building, 523 Egg Harbor Rd., Meeting Room C, Washington Township. Call 856-589-6446 (day).

HUDSON

F.S.O. - "I Need You, You Need Me" Parent Group *Professionally-run.* Support for parents raising a child with emotional and/or behavioral challenges. Educational series, advocacy, guest speakers, phone help, literature and buddy system. Building is handicapped accessible. Meets 2nd Sat., 10am-noon, Family Support Organization of Hudson County, 705 Bergen Ave., Jersey City. Call

Roslyn Gibbs-Muse 201-915-5140 (day). *Website:* http://www.fsohc.org *E-mail:* rgibbs-muse@fsohc.org

HUNTERDON

Family Support Organization *Professionally-run.* Support for parents and caregivers raising a child with emotional and behavioral challenges. Building is handicapped accessible. Meeting days and times vary, Family Support Organization, 4 Minneakoning Rd., Flemington. Call Stanley Croughter 908-788-8585 (day). *Website:* http://www.fsohsw.org

MERCER

Parent Support Group *Professionally-run.* Support for parents whose children are experiencing emotional and behavioral problems. Meets last Sat., 3:30-5pm, Lawrence Commons, 3371 Brunswick Pike, Suite 124, Lawrenceville. Use entrance in back of building. Call Joanna Harrison-Smith 609-799-8994 (day).

Parent Support Group *Professionally-run.* Support and information for parents of adolescents. Opportunity to share ideas, concerns, strategies, learn helpful parenting skills and techniques. Meets Mon., 6-7pm, Anchor House, 482 Centre St., Trenton. Call 609-396-8329.

MIDDLESEX

B.I.L.Y. (Because I Love You) Mutual support to help parents with children (of any age) who have behavioral challenges. Meets Wed., 6-8pm, Family Support Organization of Middlesex County, 1 Ethel Rd., Suite 108A, Edison. Pre-registration required. Before attending call 732-287-8701 (day).

P.A.C.E.S. (Parent and Caregivers Emotional Support) *Professionally-run.* Mutual support to help parents and caregivers with children of any age, who have behavioral, emotional or mental health challenges. Educational series, advocacy and coping skills. Meets Mon., 6:30-8:30pm, Family Support Organization of Middlesex County, 1 Ethel Rd., Suite 108A, Edison. Before attending call Bryn Schain 732-287-8701 (day). *E-mail:* brynschain1325@msn.com

We can also refer callers to over 100 individuals who are seeking others to help start new support groups throughout NJ.
Give us a call for more information. ***1-800-367-6274***

MONMOUTH

Parent Support Group Mutual support for parents with children experiencing emotional and behavioral problems. Rap sessions, guest speakers, literature, phone help and newsletter. Childcare and limited transportation. Before attending call 732-571-3272 (day).

> **Keansburg** Meets Mon., 6:30pm, First United Methodist Church, 21 Church St. Building is handicapped accessible. Pre-registration required.
> **Long Branch** Meets Thurs., 7-9pm, Family Based Services Association, 279 Broadway, Suite 400.
> **Long Branch** *(SPANISH)* Meets Wed., 7-9pm, Family Based Services Association, 279 Broadway, Suite 400. Call Luz Velasquez 732-546-1996 (day).

MORRIS

Family Support Organization *Professionally-run.* Provides support and advocacy to families and caregivers of children with complex emotional and behavioral challenges. Educational lectures offered. Building is handicapped accessible. Meets 2nd Wed., 10:30am-noon and 1st Mon., 7-8:30pm, Family Support Organization, 200 Valley Rd., Suite 405, Mt. Arlington. Childcare and refreshments provided. Call Norma 973-770-2700 (day). *Website:* http://www.fso-ms.org

OCEAN

Parents Empowering Parents Support, education and advocacy for parents and caregivers of children with emotional and behavioral challenges. Rap sessions and guest speakers. Meets 2nd and 4th Tues., 7-9pm, Ocean County Family Support Organization, 44 Washington St., Suite 2A, Toms River. Call Annie Hercules 732-281-5770 ext. 16 (day). *Website:* http://www.ocfso.org *E-mail:* annie.hercules@ocfso.org

PASSAIC

Behavioral Support Group *Professionally-run.* Support for parents raising a child with behavioral challenges. Literature and phone help. Meets last Tues., 7pm, Hillcrest Community Center, 1810 Macopin Rd., Room 25, West Milford. Before attending call Julie Rikon 973-728-0999 (day).

Family Support Organization of Passaic County Support for parents and caregivers raising a child with emotional and behavioral challenges. Building is handicapped accessible. Pre-registration required. Before attending call 973-427-0100. *Website:* http://www.fso-pc.org

> **North Haledon** Meets Wed., 7-8:30pm, Family Support Organization of Passaic County, 810 Belmont Ave., 2nd Floor.
>
> **North Haledon** *(SPANISH)* Meets Tues., 7-8:30pm, Family Support Organization of Passaic County, 810 Belmont Ave., 2nd Floor.

SOMERSET

Fathering Support Group *Professionally-run.* Support group for fathers of children (ages 5-18) with mental health and behavioral issues in the Hunterdon, Somerset or Warren county area only. Meets twice a month in Branchburg. Fathers must initially speak with Dr. Richard Horowitz prior to group enrollment. Call 908-526-3900 ext. 114. *E-mail:* rhorowitz@tricountycmo.org

SUSSEX

Family Support Organization *Professionally-run.* Provides support and advocacy to families and caregivers of children with complex emotional and behavioral challenges. Educational lectures offered. Childcare and refreshments provided. Meets 1st and 3rd Thurs., 6:30-8pm, Family Support Organization, 67A Spring St., Newton. Call Bessy 973-940-3194 (day).

UNION

NJ Parents' Caucus Support Group *(BILINGUAL)* Mutual support and help provided for and by parents or caregivers of children with special emotional/behavioral needs. Guest speakers, phone help and speakers' bureau. Childcare provided. Building is handicapped accessible. Meets 2nd Mon., 7-9pm, Trinitas Hospital, 655 East Jersey St., Grassman Hall (basement), Elizabeth. Call Linda Mc Conneyhead or Jainette Tiru 908-994-7471.

NATIONAL

B.I.L.Y. (Because I Love You: The Parent Support Group) *National. 47 affiliated groups. Founded 1982.* Self-help groups for parents who have children of all ages with behavioral problems such as truancy, substance abuse or other forms of defiance of authority. Focus is on parents getting back their self-esteem and control of their home. Write: B.I.L.Y., P.O. Box 2062, Winnetka, CA 91396-2062. Call 818-884-8242; Fax: 805-493-2714. *Website:* http://www.becauseiloveyou.org *E-mail:* bily1982@aol.com

ONLINE

Conduct Disorders Parent Message Board *Online. 7080 members. Founded 1995.* Support for parents living with a child with one of the many behavior disorders including: attention deficit hyperactivity disorder, oppositional defiance disorder, conduct disorder, depression and substance abuse. Parents with children of all ages welcome. *Website:* http://www.conductdisorders.com

PARENTS OF CHILDREN WITH DISABILITIES / ILL CHILDREN
(see also specific disability, toll-free helplines)

STATEWIDE

S.P.A.N. (Statewide Parent Advocacy Network) *(BILINGUAL) Professionally-run.* Training, information, technical assistance, leadership development and support for parents concerning education and healthcare issues for children from birth to age 21. Special focus on children at risk due to disabilities, special healthcare or emotional needs, poverty, language or race. Workshops on laws, effective education practices and advocacy strategies. Assists parents of children with special health needs in medical insurance and advocacy. Newsletter, phone help and bilingual materials. Parent-to-Parent program (call 1-800-372-6510) matches families of children on a one-to-one basis with similar disabilities or other special health needs. The START Project helps parents of children who have special needs and are in public schools to find and/or start their own parent support groups. Call 1-800-654-7726 (within NJ; voice/TDD) or 973-642-8100 (day). *Website:* http://www.spannj.org *E-mail:* span@spannj.org

BERGEN

Supporting Parents of Exceptional Children Provides support, education and resources to help families of children with special needs. For meeting information call Lori Ruschman 201-280-2924 (day) or Joanna 201-519-0340 (eve.).

CAMDEN

STEPS (Special Teachers Exceptional Parents and Students) Support, education and advocacy group for parents, teachers and school administrators who are involved with and concerned about children with special learning needs.

Guest speakers, literature, newsletter and phone help. Meets 1st Mon., 7:30-9:30pm (Oct.-June), Glenview Avenue School, 1700 Sycamore St., Library, Haddon Heights. Call Deborah 856-672-0124 or Colleen 856-547-4164 (eve.). *Website:* http://www.hhsteps.com *E-mail:* contact@hhsteps.com

MERCER

Special Education Support Group Support and education for parents and caregivers whose children have or need special education services. Building is handicapped accessible. Childcare available. Meets 1st Wed., 6-8pm, Ibis Plaza 3535 Quakerbridge Rd., Suite 400, Hamilton. Call Laurie Townsend or Luvia Vian 609-586-1200 (day).

MONMOUTH

Parents Of Children With Multiple Impairments *Professionally-run.* Support for parents of children with multiple impairments. Meets monthly, 7:30-9pm, Family Resource Associates, 35 Haddon Ave., Shrewsbury. Call Susan Levine 732-747-5310 (day).

MORRIS

Hearts and Hands Mutual support for moms with special needs children. Guest speakers, literature and phone help. Building is handicapped accessible. Meets Thurs., 9:30-11am (except June/July/Aug.), Bethlehem Church, 758 Route 10, 3rd Floor, Randolph. Call Dorie 973-455-0159 or church 973-366-3434 (day). *E-mail:* tiel@optonline.net

Mount Olive Special Kids Group Opportunity for parents of special needs children to share experiences, joys, frustrations and failures as well as to offer information and resources to other parents of children with disabilities or other special needs. Guest speakers. Meets last Thurs., 6:45pm (except July/Aug.), Mount Olive Public Library, Wolfe Rd., Budd Lake. Call Awilda 973-252-9424. *E-mail:* mtospecialkids@optonline.net

"Strange is our situation here upon earth. Each of us comes for a short visit, not knowing why, yet sometimes seeming to divine a purpose. From the standpoint of daily life, however, there is one thing we do know: That man is here for the sake of other men."--Unknown

PASSAIC

Parents Place/Club de Padres Catholic Family and Community Services *(BILINGUAL)* Support for parents and families of children with disabilities. Information and referrals, translation and interpretation services available, educational issues, technical assistance, immigration assistance, advocacy, recreation, training, employment and respite care. Childcare and local transportation available. Meets 3rd Sat., 1:30-3:30pm, 26 DeGrasse St., Paterson. Call 973-523-8404 ext. 45 (day). *E-mail:* parentsplace26@aol.com

Supporting Special Families *Professionally-run.* Support for parents of children (ages birth - 21) with any type of disability. Buddy system, newsletter and phone help. Meets 3rd Wed., 7:30pm, Hillcrest Community Center, 1810 Macopin Rd., Room 25, West Milford. Pre-registration required. Before attending call 973-728-8744 (day).

SOMERSET

Care-to-Share Support Network Provides families, educators and advocates opportunities to meet and share resources on a variety of topics in support of children with special needs. Guest speakers, literature, phone help and buddy system. Meets 2nd Tues., 7-9:30pm, The ARC of Somerset, 141 Main St., Manville. Call Tina Rear 908-450-5691 (day). *Website:* http://www.caretosharenj.org

WARREN

North Warren Special Education Advocacy Group Support and advocacy for parents and guardians of children with special needs. Rap sessions, guest speakers and phone help. Dues $10/yr. Meetings vary, Catherine Dickson Hofman Library, 4 Lambert Rd., Blairstown. Before attending call Margaret Scocozza 908-362-9066.

NATIONAL

Birth Defect Research for Children *National network. Founded 1982.* Links parents of children with similar birth defects for mutual sharing and support. Provides information about birth defects, as well as services and resources that may be helpful to families. Sponsors the National Birth Defect Registry. Maintains database on medical/scientific literature and research. Monthly electronic newsletter. Write: Birth Defect Research for Children, 800 Celebration Ave., Suite 225, Celebration, FL 34747. Call 407-566-8304; Fax:

407-566-8341. *Website:* http://www.birthdefects.org *E-mail:* staff@birthdefects.org

Family Voices *(BILINGUAL) National. 50 affiliated groups. Founded 1995.* Grassroots organization that speaks on behalf of children with special healthcare needs at the national, state and local levels. Encourages and supports families who want to play a role in their child's healthcare. Advocacy. Literature (Spanish and English). Write: Family Voices, 2340 Alamo SE, Suite 102, Albuquerque, NM 87106. Call 1-888-835-5669 or 505-872-4774 (Mon.-Fri., 8am-5pm MST); Fax: 505-872-4780. *Website:* http://www.familyvoices.org *E-mail:* kidshealth@familyvoices.org

MUMS National Parent-to-Parent Network *National. 36 affiliated groups. Founded 1979.* Mutual support and networking for parents or care providers of children with any disability, rare disorder, chromosomal abnormality or health condition using a database of over 23,000 families from 54 countries, covering 3500 disorders, very rare syndromes or undiagnosed conditions. Provides referrals to support groups and assistance in starting groups. Newsletter ($15/parents; $25/ professionals). Matching services $5. Hyperbaric Oxygen Therapy as a Treatment for Brain Damage packet, $25 USA/$35 other countries. Various literature available. Write: MUMS National Parent-to-Parent Network, 150 Custer Court, Green Bay, WI 54301-1243. Call 1-877-336-5333 (parents only) or 920-336-5333 (day); Fax: 920-339-0995. *Website:* http://www.netnet.net/mums *E-mail:* mums@netnet.net

NATHHAN (National Challenged Homeschoolers) *National network. Founded 1990.* Christian, non-profit organization encouraging families with special needs, particularly those who home educate. Bi-annual magazine, lending library, family phone book, phone support, program for parents of special need pre-borns, information and referrals. Dues $25/yr. Write: NATHHAN, P.O. Box 310, Moyie Springs, ID 83845. Call 208-267-6246. *Website:* http://www.nathhan.com *E-mail:* nathanews@aol.com

Parents Helping Parents *(MULTILINGUAL) Model. 22 groups. Founded 1976.* Parent-directed family resource center serving children with special needs (due to illness, accident, conditions of birth, learning differences or family stress), their families and the professionals who serve them. Information and referral, specialty programs, family support groups, peer counseling, training and library. Newsletter, group development guidelines and national resource directory online. Outreach in Spanish, Japanese and Vietnamese. Write: PHP, 1400 Parkmoor Ave., Suite 100, San Jose, CA 95126. Call 408-727-5775; Fax: 408-286-1116. *Website:* http://www.php.com *E-mail:* info@php.com

Sibling Support Project *National. 200 affiliated groups. Founded 1990.* Organization dedicated to the life-long concerns of brothers and sisters of people with special health, developmental and mental health concerns. Provides training and technical assistance regarding Sibshops and workshops for school-age siblings. Write: Sibling Support Project, c/o Donald Meyer, 6512 23rd Ave. NW, Suite 213, Seattle, WA 98117. Call 206-297-6368; Fax: 509-752-6789. *Website:* http://www.siblingsupport.org *E-mail:* donmeyer@siblingsupport.org

Washington PAVE *Model. 1 group in Washington. Founded 1979.* Parent-directed organization to increase independence, empowerment and opportunities for special needs children and their families through training, information, referrals and support. Newsletter, lending library of resources, networking between parents through internet, workshops on many issues, phone support and conferences on special education issues. Has special program that focuses on military family concerns. Write: Washington PAVE, 6316 S. 12th, Tacoma, WA 98465. Call 1-800-572-7368 (voice/TTY) or 253-565-2266 (voice/TTY); Fax: 253-566-8052. *Website:* http://www.washingtonpave.org *E-mail:* wapave9@washingtonpave.com

Washington State Fathers Network *Model. 15 groups in Washington. Founded 1986.* Provides mutual support and resources for fathers and families raising children with special needs and developmental disabilities. Print newsletters, e-newsletter, web page with extensive links, photo album of men and children, articles by dads and materials for providers regarding family-centered, culturally competent care. Videos and monographs available. Statewide and regional conferences. Write: WSFN, 16120 N.E. Eighth St., Bellevue, WA 98008. Call Greg Schell 425-747-4004; Fax: 425-474-1069. *Website:* http://www.fathersnetwork.org *E-mail:* greg.schell@kindering.org

ONLINE

Mothers From Hell 2 *Online. National network. Founded 1992.* Support and advocacy for families of children with any type of disability. Mission is to improve the quality of the lives and education of persons with developmental and other disabilities. Seeks to promote understanding and acceptance of people with disabilities. Dues $13/yr. Newsletter, referral network and training packets. Assistance in starting local groups. *Website:* http://www.mothersfromhell2.org *E-mail:* mfh2_kim@sbcglobal.net

Parent Soup Message Boards *Online.* Offers a large variety of message boards which deal with parenting issues including infertility, pregnancy, parenting challenges, parents of disabled, pregnancy loss, newborn babies, toddlers, adoption, family issues, etc. *Website:* http://www.parentsoup.com/messageboards

Premature Baby - Premature Child *Online. Founded 1997.* Offers support for parents of premature babies that are age 4+ years old for any of their special needs, e.g. mental, physical, emotional or learning disability. Provides support, discussion listserv, prematurity forums, advocacy and educational links. Special children's show-and-tell section. *Website:* http://www.prematurity.org

SibNet *Online. 1157 members. Founded 1998.* Listserv for and about adult brothers and sisters of people with special health, developmental and emotional needs. Opportunity for young adults and adult brothers and sisters to share information and discuss issues of common interest. Subscribers can connect with their peers, seek information about local services, create connections for their siblings and discuss the proper policies agencies should have toward brothers and sisters. *Website:* http://groups.yahoo.com/group/sibnet

PARENTS OF PREMATURE / HIGH RISK INFANTS
(see also parents of twins and triplets, specific disabilities, toll-free helplines)

NATIONAL

Sidelines High Risk Pregnancy Support *National network. Founded 1991.* Trained former high risk pregnancy moms provide support to current high risk patients and their families. Provides educational resources, advocacy and emotional support via phone and e-mail. Write: Sidelines National Support Network, P.O. Box 1808, Laguna Beach, CA 92652. Call 1-888-447-4754; Fax: 949-497-5598. *Website:* http://www.sidelines.org *E-mail:* sidelines@sidelines.org

ONLINE

Preemie-List *Online.* Mutual discussion forum of support for parents with children born six weeks or more before due date. Families and friends are welcome to join discussions. *Website:* http://groups.yahoo.com/group/preemie-list

Need help finding a specific group? Give us a call – we're here to help!
*Call **1-800-367-6274**.*

Premature Baby - Premature Child *Online. Founded 1997.* Offers support for parents of premature babies that are age 4+ years old, for any of their special needs, e.g. mental, physical, emotional or learning disability. Provides support, discussion listserv, prematurity forums, advocacy and educational links. Special children's show-and-tell section. *Website:* http://www.prematurity.org

PARENTS OF TWINS / TRIPLETS / MULTIPLES

BERGEN

Twins Mothers Club of Bergen County Provides support, advice and camaraderie for mothers of multiples. Rap sessions, guest speakers, literature and buddy system. Dues $35/yr. Meets 4th Wed., 7:15-9:30pm (except June, July, Aug., Dec.), Unitarian Society of Ridgewood, 113 College Place, Ridgewood. Call Pixie 201-669-8251.

CAMDEN

South Jersey Mothers of Multiples Moral support for mothers of multiple births. Hospital visits, clothing sales, children activities, speakers and newsletters. Dues $30/yr. Meets 1st Wed., 7:30pm, Lions Lake Park Building, Route 73, Voorhees. Call Lisa 856-797-9863 (day).

MERCER

Central Jersey Mothers of Multiples Support for mothers and legal guardians of multiples (twins, triplets or more). Education, events and friendship. Guest speakers, literature, newsletter, buddy system, online message board, social and pen pals. Also offers support to women who are currently pregnant with multiples. Membership $30/yr. Building is handicapped accessible. Meets 1st Wed., 7-9pm (Sept.-May), Reynolds Middle School, 2145 Yardville-Hamilton Square Rd., Hamilton. Contact Jennifer Hogan through e-mail address. *Website:* http://www.cjmom.org *E-mail:* membership@cjmom.org

MONMOUTH

Mid-Jersey Mothers of Multiples Mothers of multiples share information and advice on dealing with their unique problems and joys. Guest speakers and activities for adults and children. Dues $35/yr. Meets 4th Tues., 8pm, Jackson Street Firehouse, Matawan. Call Lisa 732-238-7682 or Cheryl 732-787-8642 (day). *E-mail:* seeleys@comcast.net

MORRIS

Twins and Triplets Mothers of Morris County Mothers of multiples share information and advice on dealing with their unique problems and joys. Newsletter. Dues $30/yr. Meeting dates and locations vary. Call Alison 973-601-3043. *E-mail:* harrington_john@yahoo.com

SOMERSET

Raritan Valley M.O.M.S. Support for moms of multiples. Friendship, guest speakers and newsletter. Dues $25/yr. Meets 4th Mon., 7:30pm (except July, Aug., Dec.) , Fellowship Church, 109 New Amwell Rd., Hillsborough. Call Liz Pollard 908-575-9385 (day). *Website:* http://www.rvmom.net

NATIONAL

Mothers Of Super Twins (MOST) *International. Founded 1987.* Support network of families who are expecting, or are already the parents of twins, triplets or more. Provides information, support, resources, empathy during pregnancy, infancy, toddlerhood and school age. Magazine, catalogue, networking, phone and online support. Specific resource persons for individual challenges. Help in starting groups. Write: MOST, P.O. Box 306, East Islip, NY 11730-0306. Call Maureen 631-859-1110; Fax: 631-859-3580. *Website:* http://www.mostonline.org *E-mail:* info@mostonline.org

National Organization of Mothers of Twins Clubs *National. 475 clubs. Founded 1960.* Opportunity for parents of multiple birth children (twins, triplets, quads) to share information, concerns and advice on dealing with their unique challenges. Literature, quarterly newspaper ($15/yr), group development guidelines, educational materials, pen pal program, special needs and bereavement support. Membership through local chapters or as individual affiliate members. Write: National Organization of Mothers of Twins Clubs, P.O. Box 700860, Plymouth, MI 48170-0955. Call 1-877-540-2200 (referrals) or 248-231-4480. *Website:* http://www.nomotc.org *E-mail:* nomotc@aol.com

Triplet Connection *International network. Founded 1983.* Network of caring and sharing for families with multiples. Emphasis is on providing quality information regarding pregnancy management and preterm birth prevention for high risk multiple pregnancies. Expectant parent's packet, new parent's packet, quarterly newsletter, phone support and area resources. Write: Triplet Connection, P.O. Box 429, Spring City, UT 84662. Call 435-851-1105; Fax: 435-462-7466. *Website:* http://www.tripletconnection.org *E-mail:* tc@tripletconnection.org

SEPARATION / DIVORCE
(see also men, women, single parenting and toll-free helplines)

STATEWIDE

Catholic Divorce Ministry (The Ministry of the North American Conference of Separated and Divorced Catholics) Ministry serving individuals experiencing separation, divorce or death of a spouse. Offers leadership training conferences, resources, materials and social activities. Referrals to self-help groups statewide. Call Charlie Rauh 201-986-9676. *Website:* http://www.nacsdc.org (click into Region 3) *E-mail:* sam4sdw@gmail.com

F.A.C.E. (Father's And Children's Equality) Support group for non-custodial parents, their families and others involved with Family Court. Helps members effectively represent themselves in court, and/or effectively direct their lawyers. Areas of interest include: divorce, child custody, parental alienation, false allegations of child or domestic abuse and male victims of domestic violence. Write: F.A.C.E., P.O. Box 2471, Cinnaminson, NJ 08077. Call 856-786-3223 (hotline). *Website:* http://www.facenj.org *E-mail:* faceinfo@facenj.org

Rainbows, Inc. *Professionally-run.* Time-limited support groups for children and teens (ages 4-17) who are grieving a loss due to death, divorce, abandonment or other life-altering experiences. Groups meet for a specific number of sessions and are held periodically. Some programs have concurrent groups for the parents. Helps implement programs throughout the state in schools, churches and social service agencies. *Website:* http://www.rainbowsnj.org

> **Central New Jersey** (Covers Burlington, Mercer, Monmouth and Ocean counties). Write: Marilyn Schipp, Trenton Diocese Family Life Office, P.O. Box 5147, Trenton, NJ 08638-0147. For any upcoming group sessions planned call Marilyn Schipp 609-406-7400 ext. 5557 (day).
>
> **Northern New Jersey** (Covers Bergen, Essex, Hudson, Hunterdon, Middlesex, Morris, Passaic, Somerset, Sussex, Union and Warren counties). Write: Rainbows, Inc., NJ State Chapter, 73 South Fullerton Ave., 2nd Floor, Montclair, NJ 07042. For any upcoming group sessions planned call Alice Forsyth 973-744-7676 (day).
>
> **Southern New Jersey** (Covers Atlantic, Camden, Cape May, Cumberland, Gloucester and Salem counties). Write: Sister Pat McGrenra, Gesu School, 1700 West Thompson St., Philadelphia, PA 19121. For any upcoming group sessions planned call Sister Pat McGrenra 215-763-3660 ext. 204 (day).

BERGEN

New Beginnings *Professionally-run.* Support group for separated or divorced persons. Building is handicapped accessible. Meets Tues., 7:30pm, Montvale Evangelical Free Church, 141 West Grand Ave., Montvale. Call Dr. Brian Cistola 845-353-1433 or 201-391-6233 (day).

Rainbows Peer Support Group *Professionally-run.* Peer support for children (ages 4-teens) who experienced a family loss because of separation, divorce, death or abandonment. Goals are to provide peer support, furnish an understanding of the grief experience, assist in building a stronger sense of self-esteem and teach appropriate coping mechanisms. Parents' group meets concurrently. Meets Tues., 7-8pm (Sept.-Dec.) and Wed., 7-8pm (Jan.-Apr.), Ridgewood YMCA, 112 Oak St., Ridgewood. Registration required. Call Kathi Meding 201-444-5600 ext. 332 (day). For any other new group sessions planned, call regional representative, Alice Forsyth 973-744-7676 (day). *E-mail:* kmeding@ridgewoodym.org

Separated, Divorced and Bereaved Catholics Referrals to groups for emotional, spiritual support and social activities for separated, divorced or bereaved men and women. Groups are sponsored by various churches throughout the county and are open to people of any faith. For information call Family Life Ministry, Catholic Diocese of Newark 973-497-4327.

St. Peter's Support Group Offers peer-to-peer support for anyone coping with a divorce, loss of a spouse or who have never been married. Guest speakers, rap sessions and social activities. Donation $1. Meets Thurs., 7:30-9:30pm, St. Peter the Apostle Church, 431 5th Ave., Parish Center, River Edge. Call Mary Sabino 201-261-8159 (eve.) or Bob Setzer 201-712-9272 (eve.). *Website:* http://www.support-group-nj.com

BURLINGTON

Initial Care/Divorce Recovery Support Group *Professionally-run.* Christian-based psychoeducation and support group for persons going through divorce. Open to people of any faith. Facilitators have gone through divorce. Rap sessions. Building is handicapped accessible. Meets Wed., 7:30-9pm, Fellowship Alliance Chapel, 199 Church Rd., Room C-9, Medford. Call Rev. Ed Stiegel 609-953-7333 (day).

Separated and Divorced Catholics Mutual support for separated or divorced men and women. Open to people of any faith. Various meeting locations and times. Call Office of Family Life, Catholic Diocese of Trenton 609-406-7400

ext. 5557 (day). See group listings and contacts online at: http://www.dioceseoftrenton.org/church/consolation.asp (scroll down to "Support Groups for Separated and Divorced")

CAMDEN

F.A.C.E. (Fathers' and Children's Equality) Support for non-custodial parents, their families and others involved with Family Court. Building is handicapped accessible. Meets 2nd Tues., 7-9pm, Kennedy Hospital, 2201 West Chapel Ave., Cherry Hill. Call 856-786-3223 (hotline). *Website:* http://www.facenj.org *E-mail:* info@facenj.org

Grief Management of St. Rose of Lima Mutual support for anyone grieving the loss of a significant person in their life due to death, separation or divorce. Families welcome. Meets Thurs., 7:30-9:30pm (for 12 week sessions), St. Rose of Lima Church, 300 Kings Highway, Parish Lounge, Haddon Heights. Before attending call Trish 856-310-1770. *Website:* http://www.strosenj.com

CUMBERLAND

DivorceCare Christian-based support group that helps in recovery from separation and divorce. Sharing of experiences, video showings, education, guest speakers and phone help. Building is handicapped accessible. Childcare available. Meets Thurs., 6:30-7:45pm, Vineland Nazarene Church, North Delsea Dr. and Forest Grove Rd., Vineland. Call Sandy or Fred Bohren 856-697-4945. *Website:* http://www.vinelandnaz.com

ESSEX

Divorced Women Moving On Support for women who are already divorced, have dealt with that issue and now want to meet other women to talk about getting on with their lives. Groups start periodically and run for 6 weeks. Registration fee $45. Building is handicapped accessible. Meets at Linda and Rudy Slucker NCJW Center for Women, 513 West Mt. Pleasant Ave., Livingston. Call 973-994-4994 (day). *Website:* http://www.centerforwomennj.org *E-mail:* centerforwomen@ncjwessex.org

"The best way to cheer yourself up is to try to cheer somebody else up."-- Mark Twain

Rainbows, Inc. *Professionally-run.* Peer support for children (kindergarten - sixth grade) who are grieving a loss due to death, divorce, abandonment or other life altering situation. For any other new group sessions planned call the regional representative, Alice Forsyth 973-744-7676 (day).

> **Livingston** Meets Mon., 5:30-6:30pm, Linda and Rudy Slucker NCJW Center for Women, 513 West Mt. Pleasant Ave. Call 973-994-4994 (day). *Website:* http://www.centerforwomennj.org *E-mail:* centerforwomen@ncjwessex.org
>
> **Verona** Meets Mon., 7 week sessions (Spring/Fall), First Presbyterian Church, 10 Fairview Ave. Before attending call 973-239-3561 (day).

Separated, Divorced and Bereaved Catholics *Professionally-run.* Emotional and spiritual support for separated, divorced or bereaved men and women. Groups are held at various churches throughout the diocese and are open to people of any faith. For information call Family Life Ministry, Catholic Diocese of Newark 973-497-4327.

Women Coping with Separation and Divorce Support for women coping with separation and divorce. Groups start periodically and run for 6 weeks. Registration fee $45. Building is handicapped accessible. Meetings vary, Linda and Rudy Slucker NCJW Center for Women, 513 West Mt. Pleasant Ave., Livingston. Call 973-994-4994 (day). *Website:* http://www.centerforwomennj.org *E-mail:* centerforwomen@ncjwessex.org

GLOUCESTER

Center for People in Transition *Professionally-run.* Assists displaced homemakers whose major source of financial support has been lost due to separation/divorce, death or disability of a spouse. Helps individuals to become emotionally and economically self-sufficient through life skills training, career decision making, education or vocational training and supportive services. Evening divorce and bereavement support groups open to men and women. For information call 856-415-2222 (Mon.-Fri.). *E-mail:* peopleintransition@gccnj.edu

HUDSON

Separated, Divorced and Bereaved Catholics *Professionally-run.* Emotional and spiritual support for separated, divorced or bereaved men and women. Groups are sponsored by various churches throughout the county and are open to people of any faith. For information call Family Life Ministry, Catholic Diocese of Newark 973-497-4327.

Women's Project Groups *Professionally-run.* Support, education, workshops and groups to help women on subjects such as self-esteem, separation/divorce, domestic violence, employment and stress management. Meets various days and times, Christ Hospital, 176 Palisade Ave., Jersey City. Before attending call Michele Bernstein 201-795-8375 ext. 8416 (day).

HUNTERDON

Separated and Divorced Catholics Mutual support and social events for separated or divorced men and women. Open to people of any faith. Various meeting times and locations. For information call the Office of Family Life, Catholic Diocese of Metuchen 732-562-1990 ext. 1624 (day).

MERCER

Divorce Recovery Program *Professionally-run.* Support and education seminar for separated or divorced persons. Building is handicapped accessible. Support group meets 1st and 4th Fri., 7:30pm; seminar meets 2nd Fri., 7:30pm, Princeton Church of Christ, 33 River Rd., Princeton. Call Phyllis Rich 609-581-3889 (eve.). *Website:* http://www.princetonchurchofchrist.com/divorcerecovery.shtml *E-mail:* divorcerecovery@softhome.net

Separated and Divorced Catholics Mutual support for separated or divorced men and women. Open to people of any faith. Various meeting locations and times. Call Office of Family Life, Catholic Diocese of Trenton 609-406-7400 ext. 5557 (day). See group listings and contacts online at: http://www.dioceseoftrenton.org/church/consolation.asp (scroll down to "Support Groups for Separated and Divorced")

Separated and Divorced Support Group Helps people through the pain and trauma of separation and divorce to grow into well-adjusted, self-sufficient, whole single people. Encourages sharing and support among members with an end towards friendship. Not for singles seeking dates. Meets Wed., 8pm, Hopewell Presbyterian Church, 80 W. Broad St., Hopewell. Call Jill 609-213-9509 or 609-466-0758 (day).

St. James Separated and Divorced Support Group *Professionally-run.* Mutual support for men and women in all stages of separation and divorce. Guest speakers, literature and buddy system. Meets 2nd and 4th Mon., 7-9pm, St. James Church, 115 E. Delaware Ave., Pennington. Call 609-737-0122 (day).

MIDDLESEX

CONCORDS Mutual support for divorced or separated people. Meets 2nd Wed., 8pm (except July/Aug.), Our Lady of Fatima, 50 Van Winkle Pl., Piscataway. Call Mel 732-926-1963 or Lucy 732-968-4093 (6-7pm).

Passages Support for separated or divorced persons to help them regain self-esteem, confidence and the ability to go on with their lives. Donation $3 per mtg. Rap session and social group. Building is handicapped accessible. Meets Tues., 7:30-9:30pm, St. Peter's Episcopal Church, 505 Main St., Spotswood. Call Robin 732-238-7822 (eve.) or Alan 732-828-5880. *Website:* http:/www.freewebs.com/passagesnj *E-mail:* passages@excite.com

Separated and Divorced Catholics Mutual support for recently separated or divorced men and women. Open to people of any faith. Various meeting times and locations. For information call the Family Life Office, Catholic Diocese of Metuchen 732-562-1990 ext. 1624 (day).

MONMOUTH

Separated / Divorced / Widows and Widowers Support Group Support for persons who have lost their spouse due to separation, divorce or death (past the bereavement stage) to help members get on with their lives. Not for crisis situations. Not intended as a social group. Meets Tues., 7:30pm, St. Veronica's Rectory Cellar, Route 9 North, Howell. Call Ree 732-431-0446. *Website:* http://www.divorceheadquarters.com *E-mail:* reegroup@aol.com

Separated and Divorced Catholics Mutual support for separated or divorced men and women. Open to people of any faith. Various meeting locations and times. Call Office of Family Life, Catholic Diocese of Trenton 609-406-7400 ext. 5557 (day). See group listings and contacts online at: http://www.dioceseoftrenton.org/church/consolation.asp (scroll down to "Support Groups for Separated and Divorced")

Transitions Support for persons in all stages of separation and divorce to provide comfort, support and recovery. Rap sessions. Building is handicapped accessible. Meets Tues., 7:30-8:45pm, Monmouth County Library, 125 Symmes Dr., Manalapan. Call David Nasoff 732-888-4440.

Women's Support Group Helps women who are displaced homemakers (facing the loss of their primary source of income due to separation, divorce, disability or death of spouse). Issues addressed include self-sufficiency, career development, assertiveness, self-esteem, divorce, separation, widowhood and other related topics. Meets Fri., 10am-noon, Brookdale Community College, Lincroft. Pre-registration required. Before attending call Robin Vogel 732-495-4496 ext. 4007 (day) or Mary Ann O'Brien 732-229-8675.

MORRIS

Divorced and Separated Support Group Support for separated and divorced persons. Open to anyone who has experienced the pain of a broken marriage. Meets Sun., 7-8:30pm, St. Peter the Apostle Church, 189 Baldwin Rd., Annex, Parsippany. Call Tim 908-418-1745.

My Rainbows Place Peer support for children and adolescents (kindergarten - eighth grade) who are grieving a loss due to death, divorce or abandonment. Group runs for 14 weeks in the winter and 7 weeks in the summer. Building is handicapped accessible. Meets Tues., 7-7:45pm, St. Francis Residential Community, 122 Diamond Spring Rd., Denville. Separate group for parents. Before attending call Diane 973-627-2134 or Wendy 973-625-3352. For any other new group sessions planned, call the regional representative, Alice Forsyth 973-744-7676 (day).

Path to Happiness Emotional and spiritual support for men and women in all stages of separation, divorce, bereavement, emotional healing and purpose in life. Phone help, pen pals and buddy system. Meets Thurs., 6:30pm, St. Rose of Lima Church, 312 Ridgedale Ave., East Hanover. Call Laura 973-581-1636. *E-mail:* pathtohappiness@aol.com

Rainbows and Prism Peer support for children and adolescents (kindergarten - eighth grade) who are grieving the loss of a parent due to death or divorce. Parent group meets concurrently. Building is handicapped accessible. Meets Tues., 7:15-8pm (Sept.-Jan.), Our Lady of Magnificat, 2 Miller Rd., Kinnelon. Call Claudette Meehan 973-492-9406 (eve.) or Peggy Tana 973-838-7265.

"The isolated individual is not a real person. A real person is one who lives in and for others. And the more personal relationships we form with others, the more we truly realize ourselves as persons. It has even been said that there can be no true person unless there are two, entering into communication with one another."--Kallistos Ware

OCEAN

Kids and Divorce Support Group *Professionally-run.* Support for children (ages 7-12) who have experienced a separation or divorce in their family. Rap sessions. Building is handicapped accessible. Meets 2nd Sat., 9:30-10:30am, Center for Kids and Family, 591 Lakehurst Rd., Toms River. Call 732-505-5437 (day).

Separated and Divorced Catholics Mutual support for separated or divorced men and women. Open to people of any faith. Various meeting locations and times. Call Office of Family Life, Catholic Diocese of Trenton 609-406-7400 ext. 5557 (day). See group listings and contacts online at: http://www.dioceseoftrenton.org/church/consolation.asp (scroll down to "Support Groups for Separated and Divorced")

PASSAIC

Circle of Friendship Mutual support for those who are separated and divorced. Phone help, social and guest speakers. Meets Thurs., 7:30pm, St. Mary's School, 17 Pompton Ave., Pompton Lakes. Call Christine Scott 973-335-9880, Donna White 973-831-8825 or church 973-835-0374.

Separation and Divorce Support Group Mutual support and education to help women through the emotional, legal, financial and family issues which arise during the divorce process. Building is handicapped accessible. Meetings vary, Women In Transition, 1022 Hamburg Turnpike, Wayne. Before attending call Kate McAteer 973-694-9215 (day).

SOMERSET

JANUS Bereavement Group *Professionally-run.* Support and education for anyone who has experienced a loss such as a separation/divorce, death, retirement, loss of a job, health or relocation. Helps individuals accept and adjust to the loss. Building is handicapped accessible. Meets 2nd Tues., 7:30-9pm, Bridgewater and Raritan. Call Barbara Ronca, LCSW, PhD 908-218-9062 (Mon.-Fri., 9am-3pm).

MASH (Mutual Aid Self-Help) Group for Separated or Divorced Men and Women, The Support, education and discussion. Social activities between meetings. Donation $3/mtg. Meets Mon., 7:30-9pm, St. Luke's Roman Catholic Church, 300 Clinton Ave., North Plainfield. Call 908-889-7243 or 732-548-6580. *E-mail:* debviolin4@aol.com

Separated and Divorced Catholics Mutual support and social events for separated or divorced men and women. Open to people of any faith. Various meeting times and locations. For information call the Office of Family Life, Catholic Diocese of Metuchen 732-562-1990 ext. 1624 (day).

Single Senior Women Support for women (ages 60+) who are divorced, separated, widowed, never married or who have a spouse who is ill. Recreational activities. Meets 2nd and 4th Thurs., 10am-noon, Office on Aging, 27 Warren St., Somerville. Call Erin 908-704-6339 (day).

SUSSEX

Separated and Divorced Support Group *Professionally-run.* Support, discussion and encouragement for separated and divorced people. Donation $5. Meets Wed., 7:30-9:30pm, Partnership for Social Services, 48 Wyker Rd., Franklin. Pre-registration required. Before attending call 973-827-4702. *Website:* http://www.partnershipforsocialservice.org *E-mail:* psocserv@catholicharities.org

UNION

DivorceCare *Professionally-run.* Christian-based support group for persons recovering from a separation or divorce. Offers video program and mutual sharing. Workbook provided for $12. Meets Tues., 7:30-9pm (8-12 sessions, several times a year), New Providence, Basking Ridge and Liberty Corner. Pre-registration required. Before attending call Maury 908-665-2994. *E-mail:* fletcher@pcnp.org

Holy Spirit Church Divorce Support Group Mutual support for separated and divorced persons. Open to people of any faith. Meets Thurs., 7:30pm, Holy Spirit Roman Catholic Church, 984 Suburban Rd., Drexler Hall, Union. Call John 908-964-1683 or Marie 908-931-9073.

Separated, Divorced and Bereaved Catholics *Professionally-run.* Emotional and spiritual support for separated, divorced or bereaved men and women. Groups are sponsored by various churches throughout the county and are open to people of any faith. For information call Family Life Ministry, Catholic Diocese of Newark 973-497-4327.

WARREN

Separated and Divorced Catholics Mutual support and social events for separated or divorced men and women. Open to people of any faith. Various meeting times and locations. For information call the Office of Family Life, Catholic Diocese of Metuchen 732-562-1990 ext. 1624 (day).

NATIONAL

Association for Children for Enforcement of Support (ACES) *National. 400 affiliated groups. Founded 1984.* Support and information for parents who have custody of their children and have difficulty collecting child support payments. Location service on non-payers. Assistance in starting local support groups. Newsletter, information and referrals. Write: Association for Children for Enforcement of Support, P.O. Box 7842, Fredericksburg, VA 22404. Call 1-800-738-2237; Fax: 540-582-3386. *Website:* http://www.childsupport-aces.org *E-mail:* aces@childsupport-aces.org

Beginning Experience, The *International. 112 teams. Founded 1974.* Support programs for divorced, widowed, separated adults and their children enabling them to work through the grief of a lost marriage. Write: The Beginning Experience, c/o International Ministry Center, 1657 Commerce Dr., South Bend, IN 46628. Call 1-866-610-8877 or 574-283-0279; Fax: 574-283-0287. *Website:* http://www.beginningexperience.org *E-mail:* jan@beginningexperience.org

Children's Rights Council *International. 53 chapters in 37 states, 8 countries. Founded 1985.* Concerned parents provide education and advocacy for reform of the legal system regarding child custody. Offers help with visitation, mediation, custody and support groups. Newsletter, information and referrals, directory of parenting organizations, neutral drop-off and pick-up centers for children and supervised access in various states, catalog of resources, conferences and group development guidelines. Write: CRC, c/o David L. Levy, CEO, 8181 Professional Pl., Suite 240, Landover, MD 20785. Call 1-800-787-5437 or 301-459-1220; Fax: 301-459-1227. *Website:* http://www.crckids.org *E-mail:* info@crckids.org

DivorceCare *Resource.* Biblically based 13-week support program for churches that want to help those going through separation or divorce. Members view a video at each session, followed by discussion, and complete weekly exercises. Workbooks are required for each member. Basic kit $340.00/5 workbooks; ministry kit $440.00/15 workbooks; total ministry kit $540.00/25 workbooks (plus postage). Website contains listing of groups. Write: DivorceCare, Church Initiatives Inc., P.O. Box 1739, Wake Forest, NC 27588. Call 1-800-395-5755 or 919-562-2112. *Website:* http://www.divorcecare.org *E-mail:* info@divorcecare.org

EX-POSE (Ex-Partners Of Servicemembers for Equality) *National membership. Founded 1980.* Primary information resource for spouses facing separation and divorce from a service member, active duty or retired. Lawyer referral service. Quarterly newsletter. Publishes a New Member Information Letter. Membership dues $25. Write: EX-POSE, P.O. Box 11191, Alexandria, VA 22312. Call 703-941-5844 (Tues.-Thurs., 11am-3pm EST). *Website:* http://www.ex-pose.org *E-mail:* ex-pose@juno.com

Grandparents Rights Organization *National. Founded 1984.* Advocates and educates on behalf of grandparent-grandchild relationships, primarily with respect to grandparent visits. Assists in the formation of local support groups dealing with the denial of grandparent visitation by custodial parent or guardian. Newsletter, conferences, information and referrals. Donations $40/yr. Write: Grandparents Rights Organization, 100 W. Long Lake Rd., Suite 250, Bloomfield Hills, MI 48304. Call 248-646-7191 (day); Fax: 248-646-9722. *Website:* http://www.grandparentsrights.org *E-mail:* rsvlaw@aol.com

North American Conference of Separated and Divorced Catholics *International. 3000+ groups. Founded 1974.* Religious, educational and emotional aspects of separation, divorce, remarriage and widowhood are addressed through self-help groups, conferences and training programs. Families of all faiths are welcome. Group development guidelines. Newsletter. Membership dues starting at $35/yr. (includes newsletter, discounts and resources). Write: North American Conference of Separated and Divorced Catholics, P.O. Box 10, Hancock, MI 49930. Call 906-482-0494; Fax: 906-482-7470. *Website:* http://www.nacsdc.org *E-mail:* office@nacsdc.org

RAINBOWS *International. 8300 affiliated groups. Founded 1983.* Establishes peer support groups in churches, schools or social agencies for children and adults who are grieving a death, divorce or other painful transition in their family. Groups are led by trained adults. Online newsletter, information and referrals. Write: RAINBOWS, 2100 Golf Rd., Suite 370, Rolling Meadows, IL 60008-4231. Call 1-800-266-3206 or 847-952-1770; Fax: 847-952-1774. *Website:* http://www.rainbows.org *E-mail:* info@rainbows.org

"Clinging to the past is the problem. Embracing change is the answer."-- Gloria Steinem

SINGLE PARENTING
(see also parenting, divorce/separation and widows/widowers)

STATEWIDE

Parents Without Partners Devoted to the interests and welfare of single parents over 18 and their children. Provides recreational, educational and social activities. Rap sessions. Membership dues $25-40/yr. 18 chapters throughout NJ. Call 1-800-637-7974 (day). *Website:* http://www.parentswithoutpartners.org

ESSEX

Women Parenting Alone Mutual support for single mothers. Group starts periodically and runs for 6 weeks. Registration fee $45. Building is handicapped accessible. Meets at Linda and Rudy Slucker NCJW Center for Women, 513 W. Mount Pleasant Ave., Suite 325, Livingston. Call 973-994-4994 (peer support project). *Website:* http://www.centerforwomennj.org *E-mail:* centerforwomen@ncjwessex.org

MORRIS

Parents Without Partners Mutual support and education for single parents. Provides recreational, educational and social activities for single parents and their children. Dues $40/yr. All children's activities are subsidized. Meetings vary in Morris County. For information call Parents Without Partners 973-539-5523. *Website:* http://www.parentswithoutpartners.org

SUSSEX

Project Self-Sufficiency *Professionally-run.* Support for single parents, teen parents, displaced homemakers and low-income families. Offers peer support groups for single parents and teen parents, loss recovery groups for children, parenting skills training and support, family activities, home visitation, family stabilization, physical and emotional health educational seminars, comprehensive job training and educational services designed to promote self-sufficiency. Meetings vary. Call Deborah Berry-Toon 973-383-5129 (day). *E-mail:* pss@garden.net

"Serenity isn't freedom from the storm; it is peace within the storm." -- Author Unknown

NATIONAL

National Organization of Single Mothers *National. 3 affiliated groups. Founded 1991.* Networking system helping single mothers meet the challenges of daily life with wisdom, dignity, confidence and courage. Information and referrals. Dues $15.97/yr. Assistance in starting new groups. Write: National Organization of Single Mothers, P.O. Box 68, Midland, NC 28107. Call 704-888-5437. *Website:* http://www.singlemothers.org *E-mail:* info@singlemothers.org

Parents Without Partners *National. 225+ chapters/5 affiliates. Founded 1957.* Educational organization of single parents (either divorced, separated, widowed or never married). Online chatroom, single parent magazine, chapter development guidelines and personal growth/self-help articles from various authors. Local chapter activities for families and parents only. Annual convention. Membership dues $30-50/yr. Write: Parents Without Parents, 1650 S. Dixie Highway, Suite 510, Boca Raton, FL 33432. Call 1-800-637-7974 or 561-391-8833; Fax: 561-395-8557. *Website:* http://www.parentswithoutpartners.org

Single Mothers By Choice *National. 25 chapters. Founded 1981.* Support and information to mature single women, who have chosen or who are considering, single motherhood. "Thinkers" workshops, quarterly newsletter, brochure and list of back issues of newsletter available. Write: Single Mothers By Choice, P.O. Box 1642, Gracie Square Station, New York, NY 10028. Call 212-988-0993. *Website:* http://www.singlemothersbychoice.com c-office@pipeline.com

Single Parent Resource Center *International. 7 affiliated groups. Founded 1975.* Support and discussion group for single fathers. Refers single parents to helpful programs in New York City and nationwide. Assists new single-parent organizations in forming, offers skills-building workshops, a relapse-prevention program for single parents in recovery from substance abuse and a family reunification program for children and parents in the first year after incarceration. Write: Single Parent Resource Center, 228 East 45th St., 2nd Fl., New York, NY 10017. Call 212-951-7030; Fax: 212-951-7037. *Website:* http://www.singleparentusa.com

Can't find an appropriate group in your area? The Clearinghouse helps people start groups.
*Give us a call at **1-800-367-6274**.*

HEALTH

AIDS / HIV INFECTION
(see also toll-free helplines)

STATEWIDE

AIDS Coalition of Southern New Jersey *Professionally-run.* Helps to ensure the quality of care and continuity of vital resources for persons affected by AIDS/HIV. Provides support groups, direct services and education. Newsletter, speakers' bureau, phone help and guest speakers. Serves Burlington, Camden, Gloucester and Salem counties. Write: AIDS Coalition of Southern NJ, 100 Essex Ave., Suite 300, Bellmawr, NJ 08031. Call 856-933-9500 (day). *Website:* http://www.acsnj.org

Hyacinth AIDS Foundation Support groups and information for anyone affected by AIDS or HIV+ (patients, families, partners and friends). Advocacy, legal services, public education and training, short-term emergency services and hotline. All services are confidential. Serves Northern and Central NJ. Write: Hyacinth AIDS Foundation, 317 George St., Suite 203, New Brunswick, NJ 08901. For information call 1-800-433-0254 (9am-7pm) or Administration 732-246-0204 (day). *Website:* http://www.hyacinth.org *E-mail:* info@hyacinth.org

ATLANTIC

HIV Support Group *Professionally-run.* Support for persons with HIV. Families and friends welcome. Social group, literature and buddy system. Building is handicapped accessible. Meets 3rd Mon., 5:30-7pm, Access One, 730 Shore Rd., Somers Point. Call Michele Keenan, MSW 609-927-6662 ext. 6 (day). *E-mail:* hivaccess@aol.com

South Jersey A.I.D.S. Alliance *Professionally-run.* Support, education and information for anyone affected by AIDS (patients, families, partners, friends). Buddy system. Support centers in Atlantic City 609-347-1085, Bridgeton 856-455-6164 and Cape May County 609-523-0024 or Hotline 1-800-281-2437. *Website:* http://www.southjerseyaidsalliance.org

BERGEN

Double Jeopardy Peer Support Group *Professionally-run* Emotional support and information for men and women who have HIV/HCV and substance abuse issues. Building is handicapped accessible. Meets Thurs., 6-8pm, Buddies of New Jersey, 149 Hudson St., Hackensack. Call Susan 201-489-2900 (10am-6pm). *Website:* http://www.njbuddies.org

New Jersey Buddies *Professionally-run.* Provides support and education to people infected with or affected by HIV/AIDS. Support groups for HIV positive women, gay men, men and women, substance abusers, as well as a group for those who have engaged in risky activities, but have not been tested. Meetings vary, Buddies of New Jersey, 149 Hudson St., Hackensack. Call 201-489-2900 (9am-5pm). *Website:* http://www.njbuddies.org *E-mail:* njbuddies@aol.com

S.E.L.F. (Support, Education, Learning, Friendship) Mutual support and education for HIV+ gay men. Rap sessions and guest speakers. Building is handicapped accessible. Meets Mon., 7-8:30pm, Buddies of New Jersey, Inc., 149 Hudson St., Hackensack. Call Steve Scheuermann 201-489-2900 (day). *E-mail:* njbuddies@aol.com

CAPE MAY

South Jersey A.I.D.S. Alliance *Professionally-run.* Support, education and information for anyone affected by AIDS (patients, families, partners, friends) and prevention case management. Buddy system. Support centers in Atlantic City 609-347-1085, Bridgeton 856-455-6164 and Cape May County 609-523-0024 or Hotline 1-800-281-2437. *Website:* http:www.southjerseyaidsalliance.org

CUMBERLAND

South Jersey A.I.D.S. Alliance *Professionally-run.* Support, education and information for anyone affected by AIDS (patients, families, partners, friends and prevention case management. Buddy system. Support center in Atlantic City 609-347-1085, Bridgeton 856-455-6164 and Cape May County 609-523-0024 or Hotline 1-800-281-2437. *Website:* http://www.southjerseyaidsalliance.org

ESSEX

Co-Ed Wellness Support Group *Professionally-run. (ESSEX COUNTY RESIDENTS ONLY)* Support for men and women who are HIV+. Literature. Building is handicapped accessible. Meets Tues., 2-4pm, Hyacinth Foundation,

520 Broad St., 1st Floor, Newark. Call Exmo Gonzalez or Alexandra Cruz 973-565-0300 (day).

Double Trouble *Professionally-run*. Support for HIV+ persons who are also substance abusers. Meets Wed., noon-2pm, North Jersey Community Research Initiative, 393 Central Ave., 2nd Floor, Newark. Call 973-483-3444 ext. 122.

Men's HIV+ Support Group Offers support for men who are HIV+. Meets Tues., noon-2pm, North Jersey Community Research Initiative, 393 Central Ave., 2nd Floor, Newark. Lunch provided. Call Kendall Clark 973-483-3444 ext. 101 (day).

Our Place *Professionally-run*. Provides a safe and confidential environment to offer support for persons infected with the HIV virus, their loved ones and caregivers. Meets Tues., 6:30pm, Montclair. Pre-registration required. Before attending call Ilene Palent 973-783-6655. *Website:* http://www.copecenter.net *E-mail:* lpalent@copecenter.net

Women's HIV+ Support Group *Professionally-run*. Support for women who are HIV+. Meets Wed., noon-2pm, North Jersey Community Research Initiative, 393 Central Ave., 2nd Floor, Newark. Guests welcome. Lunch provided. Call 973-483-3444 (day). *Website:* http://www.njcri.org

Women's Wellness *Professionally-run. (ESSEX COUNTY RESIDENTS ONLY)* Support for women who are HIV+. Literature. Meets Mon., 1-3pm, Hyacinth Foundation, 520 Broad St., 1st Floor, Newark. Call Exmo Gonzalez or Alexandra Cruz 973-565-0300 (day).

HUDSON

Beacon Society Inc. Mutual support for people living with or affected by HIV/AIDS. Families are welcome. Rap sessions, guest speakers, literature and buddy system. Building is handicapped accessible. Meets Mon., 6:30-8pm, The Community Church of Hoboken, 606 Garden St., Hoboken. Call Frank Merck 201-933-1766 or Karen Manzano 201-200-0911 (day).

Hyacinth AIDS Foundation Support Group Mutual support for anyone infected by AIDS or HIV+. Patients, families, friends and partners welcome. Meets Thurs., 6:30-8:30pm, Hyacinth AIDS Foundation, 880 Bergen Ave., Suite 802, Jersey City. Pre-registration required. Call 201-432-1134 or the Hyacinth Foundation 1-800-433-0254 (10am-6pm). *Website:* http://www.hyacinth.org

Hyacinth AIDS Foundation Support Group Mutual support for persons who are infected with AIDS or HIV+. Wellness Community meets Thurs., 1-3pm; Treatment support group meets 2nd Tues., 2-4pm; Men's Wellness group meets 4th Thurs., 4-6pm; Spanish Treatment group meets last Fri., 1-3pm; Spiritual group meets 4th Tues., 2-4pm, Hyacinth AIDS Foundation, 880 Bergen Ave., Suite 802, Jersey City. Pre-registration required. Call 201-432-1134 or the Hyacinth Foundation 1-800-433-0254 (10am-6pm). *Website:* http://www.hyacinth.org

Living Beyond HIV *(HUDSON COUNTY RESIDENTS ONLY) Professionally-run.* Mutual support for gay men who are HIV+. Rap sessions, guest speakers, literature and buddy system. Meets Thurs., 7-9pm, Hudson Pride Connections, Pride Connections Center of New Jersey, 32 Jones St., Jersey City. Call Nancy Caamano 201-963-4779 ext. 111.

MIDDLESEX

HIV Infected/Affected Group *Professionally-run.* Mutual support and education for persons infected or affected by HIV. Rap sessions and literature. Building is handicapped accessible. Meets Mon., 6-8pm, Raritan Bay Medical Center, 530 New Brunswick Ave., Perth Amboy. Before attending call Sandra Nilsson or Ed Kelly, Early Intervention Program 732-324-5022.

Support Group for HIV+ Gay Men *Professionally-run.* Support for gay men who are HIV+. Rap sessions. Meets 3rd Tues., 6-7:30pm, E.B. Chandler Health Center, 277 George St., New Brunswick. Call Chas White 908-595-2674 (day).

MONMOUTH

HIV Support Group Mutual support for individuals infected/affected by HIV/AIDS. Family and friends welcome. Guest speakers. Building is handicapped accessible. Meets Thurs., 6-8pm, Riverview Medical Center, Jane Booker Building, 2nd Floor, Red Bank. Call Elise Millea 732-450-2863.

OCEAN

HIV/AIDS Infected/Affected Group *Professionally-run.* Support for persons who are infected or affected by HIV/AIDS. Members build a support network and share knowledge. Guest speakers and literature. Building is handicapped accessible. Meets Tues., 7-8pm, Ocean County Department of Health, 175 Sunset Ave., Toms River. Call Patricia Brown 732-341-9700 ext. 7603 or Anne McBride 732-341-9700 ext. 7633 (day); TTD: 1-800-852-7899. *E-mail:* amcbride@ochd.org

PASSAIC

HIV/AIDS Support Group *(SPANISH) Professionally-run.* Mutual support and education for Spanish-speaking adults with HIV/AIDS and their family members. Case management, massage therapy and grocery vouchers. Meetings vary, Paterson Division of Health, 176 Broadway, Paterson. Call Paul 973-321-1277 ext. 4365 (day).

SOMERSET

Ryan White Support Group *Professionally-run.* Provides support and education for those affected by HIV disease. Guest speakers. Building is handicapped accessible. Meets 1st and 3rd Thurs., 6-8pm, Somerset Medical Center, 110 Rehill Ave., Conference Room A and B, Somerville. Call 908-685-2814 (day).

Somerset Treatment Services Activity Group Mutual support for anyone living with HIV/AIDS. Dinner discussion group with hot meal provided. Meets Thurs., 5:30-8pm, Somerset Treatment Services, 118 W. End Ave., Somerville. Call Grace Wosu 908-722-1232 ext. 3015 (day).

NATIONAL

National Association of People With A.I.D.S. *National. Founded 1986.* Network of persons with AIDS. Sharing of information and collective voice for health, social and political concerns. Phone, mail and electronics network, speakers' bureau, quarterly newsletter and free publications. Write: National Association of People With A.I.D.S., 8401 Colesville Rd., Suite 750, Silver Spring, MD 20910. Call 240-247-0880 (day); Fax: 240-247-0574. *Website:* http://www.napwa.org *E-mail:* info@napwa.org

One Day At A Time *Model. 10 affiliated groups in Pennsylvania. Founded 1987.* Helps people with HIV infection become aware of and make use of services provided. To encourage self-empowerment by providing a source of support given by other HIV+ people. Also provides drug and alcohol addiction and homeless shelter services, community outreach, prevention and education. Newsletter and group development assistance. Write: One Day At A Time, 2532 North Broad St., Philadelphia, PA 19132. Call 215-221-1033 (24 hr.) or 215-226-7869; Fax: 215-226-7869. *Website:* http://www.odaat.us *E-mail:* info@odaat.us

PKIDs (Parents of Kids with Infectious Diseases) *National network. Founded 1996.* Provides informational and educational support for parents of children with chronic viral infectious diseases, with an emphasis on Hepatitis B and C. Opportunity for parents, children and teens to share information and experiences. Publications, advocacy and phone support. Online e-mail list, support group and other resources. Write: PKIDS, P.O. Box 5666, Vancouver, WA 98668. Call 1-877-557-5437 or 360-695-0293; Fax: 360-695-6941. *Website:* http://www.pkids.org *E-mail:* pkids@pkids.org

ALLERGY

NATIONAL

Kids with Food Allergies *National.* Organization dedicated to fostering optimal health, nutrition and well-being of children with food allergies by providing a caring support community and education for their families and caregivers. Opportunity for parents to connect with one another for food allergy management strategies, to share personal experiences and to connect with one another for emotional support. Newsletter, recipes, resources, support forums and allergy alerts. Write: Kids with Food Allergies, 73 Old Dublin Pike, Suite 10, #163, Doylestown, PA 18901. Call 215-230-5394; Fax: 215-340-7674. *Website:* http://www.kidswithfoodallergies.org

Asthma and Allergy Foundation of America *National. 100+ affiliated groups and 9 chapters. Founded 1953.* Serves persons with asthma and allergic diseases through the support of research, advocacy, patient and public education. Newsletter, support/education groups. Assistance in starting and maintaining groups. Books, videos and other educational resources. Write: Asthma and Allergy Foundation of America, 1233 20th St. NW, Suite 402, Washington, DC 20036. Call 1-800-727-8462 or 202-466-7643 (Mon.-Fri., 10am-3pm EST); Fax: 202-466-8940. *Website*: http://www.aafa.org *E-mail:* info@aafa.org

FAAN (Food Allergy and Anaphylaxis Network) *National network. 30 groups. Founded 1991.* Mission is to increase public awareness about food allergies and anaphylaxis, provides education, advance research on behalf of all those affected by food allergies and anaphylaxis, a severe life-threatening reaction that can result in hives, swelling, unconsciousness and possibly death. Information and referrals, conferences, literature, phone support, booklets, newsletters and educational videos. Guidelines available for starting a similar group. Write: Food Allergy and Anaphylaxis Network, 11781 Lee Jackson Highway, Suite 160, Fairfax, VA 22033. Call 1-800-929-4040 or 703-691-3179

(Mon.-Fri., 9am-5pm EST); Fax: 703-691-2713. *Website:* http://www.foodallergy.org *E-mail:* faan@foodallergy.org

ONLINE

TerrificKidsWFA *Online. 381 members. Founded 2002.* Support for parents, family and friends of children that have food allergies or food sensitivities. Share stories, recipes, advice and alerts of certain foods that might have hidden ingredients. *Website:* http://health.groups.yahoo.com/group/TerrificKidsWFA

ALZHEIMER'S DISEASE / DEMENTIA
(see also caregivers, toll-free helplines)

STATEWIDE

Alzheimer's Association Delaware Valley Chapter *Professionally-run.* Sponsors support groups for caregivers of persons with Alzheimer's and related dementias in southern Jersey. Information, referrals, education, newsletter, advocacy, patient and family service programs. Serves Atlantic, Burlington, Camden, Cape May, Cumberland, Gloucester and Salem counties. Write: Alzheimer's Association, Delaware Valley Chapter, 3 Eves Dr., Suite 310, Marlton, NJ 08053. Call 856-797-1212 or 1-800-272-3900 (day). *Website:* http://www.alz.org/desjsepa

Alzheimer's Association Greater NJ Chapter *Professionally-run.* Sponsors support groups throughout 14 counties in northern and central NJ. Information and referral service, education, advocacy, patient and family service programs. Write: Alzheimer's Association, 400 Morris Ave., Suite 251, Denville, NJ 07834. Call Alzheimer's Helpline 1-800-883-1180 or 973-586-4300 (day). *Website:* http://www.alznj.org

Consider passing this Directory on to a student or staff member - browsing through the Directory pages can often provide helpful education as to the wide variety of groups available.

ATLANTIC

Alzheimer's Association Caregivers Support Group *Professionally-run.* Offers support to families and caregivers coping with Alzheimer's disease. Guest speakers and literature. Call 1-800-272-3900 (day). Check website for additional meeting information. *Website:* http://www.alz.org/desjsepa

> **Atlantic City** Meets 3rd Mon., 2pm, Herman Pogachefsky Senior Services Pavilion, 1102 Atlantic Ave. Call Adrienne Epstein 609-345-5555 (day).
>
> **Brigantine** Meetings vary, Community Presbyterian Church of Brigantine, 1501 West Brigantine Ave. Before attending call 1-800-272-3900 (day).
>
> **Galloway** Meets 1st Tues., 5:30pm, Seashore Gardens, 22 West Jimmie Leeds Rd.
>
> **Galloway** Meets 2nd Tues., 6pm, Senior Care of Galloway, 76 West Jimmie Leeds Rd.
>
> **Galloway** Meets 3rd Sat., 10am, Sunrise of Galloway, 46 West Jimmie Leeds Rd.
>
> **Hammonton** Meets 3rd Thurs., 7pm, Presbyterian Church, 326 Bellevue Ave.
>
> **Linwood** Meets last Wed., 3:45pm, Brandall Estates, 432 Central Ave.
>
> **Linwood** Meets 3rd Thurs., 2pm, Linwood Care Center, New Rd. and Central Ave.
>
> **Northfield** Meets 3rd Wed., 7pm, Meadowview Nursing Home, 235 Dolphin Ave.
>
> **Somers Point** Meets 3rd Wed., 3pm, Generations Adult Day Health Center, 40 East New York Ave.

BERGEN

Alzheimer's Association Caregivers Support Group *(BILINGUAL)* Korean-speaking support for caregivers of persons with Alzheimer's disease, Parkinson's disease or other related dementia. Provides opportunity to share practical information, exchange community resources, solve problems and learn new ways to cope with dementia. Meets 2nd Wed., 1pm, Friends of Grace Seniors, 40 Bennett Rd., Englewood. Call Jaesoon Clara Choi or Jahyang Kim 201-541-1200 or 1-800-883-1180 (day). Check website for additional meeting information. *Website:* http://www.alznj.org

Alzheimer's Association Caregivers Support Group Support for caregivers of persons with Alzheimer's disease and related dementias. Group provides opportunity to share practical information, exchange community resources, solve problems and learn ways to cope with dementia-related issues. Call 1-800-

883-1180 (day). Check website for additional meeting information. *Website:* http://www.alznj.org

New Milford Meets 4th Wed., 5:30pm, Woodcrest Health Care Center, 800 River Rd. Call Kathy Frost or Karen Angrist 201-967-1700.

Norwood Meets 1st Wed., 7pm, Buckingham at Norwood, 100 McClellan St.

Paramus Meets 1st Wed., 7pm, Brighton Gardens of Paramus, 186 Paramus Rd. Before attending call Fred Meyer 201-797-3421.

Ridgewood Meets 3rd Tues., 8pm, American Red Cross Building, 74 Godwin Ave.

Rockleigh Meets 1st Wed., 10am, Gallen Adult Day Care Center, 10 Link Dr. Call Shelley Steiner 201-784-1414 ext. 5340.

Rutherford Meets 3rd Thurs., 10am (except Aug.), 55 Kip Center, 55 Kip Ave. Call Marie Fletcher 201-460-1600.

Tenafly Meets 2nd Wed., 7:30pm and 4th Thurs., 11am, Adult Reach Center, 411 E. Clinton Ave. Call Vivian Green Korner 201-569-7900 ext. 461.

Caregivers Family Support Group *Professionally-run.* Support for caregivers and family members of persons with Alzheimer's or related disorders. Meets 3rd Thurs., 1:30-3pm, Community Services Building, 327 E. Ridgewood Ave., Room 208, 2nd Floor, Paramus. Call first if requesting professional supervision of frail family member. Call Diana Shapiro 201-634-2822 (day).

BURLINGTON

Alzheimer's Association Caregivers Support Group *Professionally-run.* Offers support to families and caregivers coping with Alzheimer's disease. Guest speakers and literature. Call 1-800-272-3900 (day). Check website for additional meeting information. *Website:* http://www.alz.org/desjsepa

Delran Meets last Thurs., 7pm (no meeting Nov.; 1st Thurs. Dec.), Senior Care of Delran, 8008 Route 130 North, Building B, Suite 300.

Moorestown Meets 3rd Thurs., 5:30pm, Moorestown Estates, 1205 North Church St.

Mount Laurel Meets 2nd Thurs., 7pm, Sunrise at Mount Laurel, 400 Fernbrook Lane.

Mount Laurel Meets 2nd Wed., 5:30pm, Innova Care, 3718 Church Rd.

"With the gift of listening comes the gift of healing."—
Catherine de Hueck Doherty (Poustinia)

CAMDEN

Alzheimer's Association Support Group *Professionally-run.* Support and information for families and friends of persons with Alzheimer's disease and related disorders. Call 1-800-272-3900. Check website for additional meeting information. *Website:* http://www.alz.org/desjsepa

> **Atco** Meets last Thurs., 6pm, Fountains at Cedar Park, 114 Hayes Mill Rd.
>
> **Berlin** Meets 3rd Mon., 6pm, Virtua Health and Rehabilitation, 100 Long-A-Coming Rd.
>
> **Camden** Meets 2nd Thurs., 5:30pm, Senior Care of Camden, 1000 Atlantic Ave.
>
> **Camden** Meets 3rd Wed., noon (except Aug.), Mt. Calvary Baptist Church, 1198 Penn St.
>
> **Cherry Hill** Meets 2nd Tues., 7:30pm, Cadbury Continuing Care, Route 38 and Woods Rd.
>
> **Cherry Hill** Meets 3rd Thurs., 7pm, Arden Courts of Cherry Hill, 2700 Chapel Ave. West.
>
> **Collingswood** Meets 4th Mon., 4pm, Collingswood Manor, 460 Haddon Ave.
>
> **Runnemede** Meets 3rd Wed., 6:30pm, Runnemede Senior Center, Black Horse Pike.
>
> **Voorhees** Meets last Thurs., 7pm, Kresson View - Genesis Healthcare, 2601 Evesham Rd.
>
> **Voorhees** Meets 4th Tues., 7pm, Laurel Lakes Estates, 207 Laurel Rd.
>
> **Voorhees** Meets last Wed., 6:30pm (except July/Aug.), Senior Care of Voorhees, 1000 Voorhees Dr.
>
> **Voorhees** Meets 4th Wed., 11am, Summerville @ Voorhees, 1301 Laurel Oak Rd.
>
> **Voorhees** Meets 1st Thurs., 7pm, Voorhees Center - Genesis Healthcare, 3001 Evesham Rd.

Promise Alternative Care Support and information to Alzheimer's patients and their families. Guest speakers, literature and newsletter. Meets last Tues., 2pm (Jan., Feb., April, June and Oct.) and last Wed., 7pm (March, May, Sept. and Nov.), Promise Alternative Care, 1149 Marlkress Rd., Cherry Hill. Call Erin 856-751-4884 (day).

Need help finding a specific group? Give us a call – we're here to help!
*Call **1-800-367-6274**.*

CAPE MAY

Alzheimer's Association Caregiver Support Group Offers support for caregivers of those with Alzheimer's disease. Call 1-800-272-3900 (day). Check website for additional meeting information. *Website:* http://www.alz.org/desjsepa
> **Cape May** Meets 3rd Fri., 4pm, Oceanview Rehabilitation Center, 2721 Route 9.
> **Cape May Courthouse** Meets last Thurs., 6pm, Loyalton of Cape May, 591 Route 9 South.
> **North Cape May** Meets 4th Wed., 4pm, Victoria Commons Assisted Living, 610 Townbank Rd.
> **Rio Grande** Meets 2nd Tues., 10am, The Chapin House, 1042 Route 47. Call Marie Giansante 609-884-7670 (day).

CUMBERLAND

Alzheimer's Association Support Group Information, discussions and guest speakers for families and friends of persons with Alzheimer's disease and related disorders. Call 1-800-272-3900. Check website for additional meeting information. *Website:* http://www.alz.org/desjsepa
> **Millville** Meets 2nd Thurs., 7pm (except July/Aug.), Millville Center Genesis Elder Care, 54 Sharp St.
> **Vineland** Meets last Wed., 6pm, Senior Care of Vineland, 2695 S. Lincoln Ave.

ESSEX

Alzheimer's Association Caregivers Support Group Support for caregivers of persons with Alzheimer's disease. Provides opportunity to share practical information, exchange community resources, solve problems and learn new ways of coping with dementia. Call 1-800-883-1180 (day). Check website for additional meeting information. *Website:* http://www.alznj.org
> **East Orange** Meets 4th Wed., 5pm, Parkway Manor Health Care Center, 480 Parkway Dr. Call Grace Ann Kelly 973-674-2700 ext. 2276.
> **East Orange** Meets 1st Tues., 7pm, St. Mark AME Church, 587 Springdale Ave. Call church 973-674-5859.
> **Newark** Meets 3rd Wed., 5pm, Newark Beth Israel, 156 Lyons Ave. Call Mary Sinton 973-926-6065.
> **Nutley** Meets 3rd Wed., 7pm, Nutley Public Affairs Building, 149 Chestnut St. Call Lorraine Travers or Peggy Brodowsky 973-284-4977 ext. 2423 (day).

West Caldwell Meets 3rd Tues., 7pm, Crane's Mill Assisted Living Center, 459 Passaic Ave.

Alzheimer's Caregiver Support Group *Professionally-run.* Support for persons caring for someone with Alzheimer's or related memory impairment. Group sessions, guest speakers, literature and educational series. Building is handicapped accessible. Meets 3rd Sat., 10am, Arden Courts-Manorcare Health Services, 510 Prospect Ave., West Orange. Call Gail Kuchavik or Bill Milianes 973-736-3100 ext. 205 (day). *Website:* http://www.hcrmanorcare.com

GLOUCESTER

Alzheimer's Association Support Group Mutual support for family or friends caring for persons afflicted with Alzheimer's or dementia. Call1-800-272-3900 (day). Check website for additional meeting information. *Website:* http://www.alz.org/desjsepa

> **Glassboro** Meets 3rd Wed., 6pm, The Gardens at Cross Keys, 3152 Glassboro-Cross Keys Rd.
>
> **Sewell** Meets 3rd Thurs., 6pm, Communicare Adult Day Center, 309 Fries Mill Rd., Echo Plaza 17.
>
> **Sewell** Meets last Wed., 7pm, Senior Care, 100 Kingsway East, Building C.
>
> **Williamstown** Meets 4th Tues., 6pm, Juniper Village, 1640 Black Horse Pike.
>
> **Woodbury** Meets 1st Tues., 10am and 3rd Thurs., 11am, Sunrise of Woodbury, 752 Cooper Ave.
>
> **Woodbury** Meets 3rd Mon., 7-9pm, Underwood Memorial Hospital, 509 N. Broad St., Medical Arts Building, Suite 14. Call Karen Rodemer 856-853-2114 (day).
>
> **Woodbury** Meets 3rd Tues., 2:30pm, Woodbury Mews, 122 Greene Ave.

HUDSON

Alzheimer's Association Caregivers Support Group *Professionally-run.* support for caregivers of persons with Alzheimer's disease and related dementia. Opportunity to share practical information, exchange community resources, solve problems and learn ways to cope with dementia-related issues. Meets 4th Thurs., 2pm, Meadowlands Hospital Medical Center, Meadowlands Pkwy., Secaucus. Call Edna Mondadori 201-865-8542 (day) or 1-800-883-1180 (day). Check website for additional meeting information. *Website:* http://www.alznj.org

HUNTERDON

Alzheimer's Association Caregivers Support Group *Professionally-run.* Support for caregivers of persons with Alzheimer's disease and related dementia. Opportunity to share practical information, exchange community resources, solve problems and learn ways to cope with dementia-related issues. Meets 2nd Wed., 7pm, Hunterdon Medical Center, 2100 Westcott Dr., 4th Floor, Conference Room, Flemington. Call Chris Stevens 908-788-6401 or 1-800-883-1180 (day). Check website for additional meeting information. *Website:* http://www.alznj.org

Dementia Caregivers Group *Professionally-run.* Mutual support and education for caregivers of persons with any type of dementia. Building is handicapped accessible. Meets 2nd Tues., 1-3pm, Hunterdon County Division of Senior Services (Office on Aging), Route 31, Flemington. Call 908-788-6401 ext. 3149. *E-mail:* burgard.barbara@hunterdonhealthcare.org

MERCER

Alzheimer's Association Caregivers Support Group *Professionally-run.* Support for caregivers of persons with Alzheimer's disease and related dementia. Opportunity to share practical information, exchange community resources, solve problems and learn ways to cope with dementia-related issues. Call 1-800-883-1180 (day). Check website for additional meeting information. *Website:* http://www.alznj.org

> **Mercerville** Meets 3rd Thurs., 6:30pm, Robert Wood Johnson Center for Health and Wellness, 3100 Quakerbridge Rd. Call Cathleen Chabala 609-532-6375 (day).
> **Pennington** Meets 3rd Thurs., 6pm, Stony Brook Assisted Living, 143 West Franklin Ave. Call Michelle Curry 609-730-9922 (day).
> **Princeton** Meets 3rd Sat., 2pm, Woodlands Professional Building, Suite 6, 256 Bunn Dr. Call Louise Donnangelo 609-426-1545 (day) or Kathleen Ostertag 732-355-1300 (day).
> **Princeton** Meets 4th Thurs., 3pm, Potomac at Princeton, 181 Washington Rd. Call Cathleen Chabala 609-532-6375 (day).

Buckingham's Caregiver Connection *Professionally-run.* Support for those caring for an elderly parent, spouse or relative with memory loss. Meets 4th Wed., 5:30pm (light supper), 6-7pm (group), Buckingham Place Assisted Living and Adult Day Center, 155 Raymond Rd., Princeton. Pre-registration required. Before attending call Hilary Murray 732-329-8888 ext. 401 (day).

MIDDLESEX

Alzheimer's Association Caregivers Support Group *Professionally-run.* Support for caregivers of persons with Alzheimer's disease and related dementia. Opportunity to share practical information, exchange community resources, solve problems and learn ways to cope with dementia-related issues. Call 1-800-883-1180 (day). Check website for additional meeting information. *Website:* http://www.alznj.org

> **Monmouth Junction** Meets 3rd Thurs., 7pm, Oak Woods Senior Housing, 700 Woods Lane. Call Kathleen Ostertag 732-355-1300 (day).
>
> **Monroe Township** Meets 1st Thurs., 7pm, Cranbury Center, 292 Applegarth Rd. Call Linda Silverstein or Marilyn Magan 609-860-2500.
>
> **Monroe Township** Meets last Tues., 10am, St. Peter's University Hospital, Center for Adult Healthcare, 300 Overlook Dr. Call Beth Chassin or Rachel Kallish 609-409-1363 (day).
>
> **Old Bridge** Meets 1st Mon., 6:30pm, Raritan Bay Medical Center, Old Bridge Division, One Hospital Plaza. Call Wanda Forys 732-324-4930.
>
> **Perth Amboy** Meets 2nd Tues., 6:30pm, Raritan Bay Medical Center, Groom St. Call 732-324-4930 (day).

Alzheimer's Association Caregivers Support Group Support for caregivers of persons with Alzheimer's disease and related dementia. Opportunity to share practical information, exchange community resources, solve problems and learn ways to cope with dementia-related issues. Meets 1st Sat., 10:30am, JFK Hartwyck Adult Medical Day Center, 2050 Oak Tree Rd., Lifestyle Building, Edison. Call Mary Buglio or Michelle Charme 732-548-9770 or 1-800-883-1180 (day). Check website for additional meeting information. *Website:* http://www.alznj.org

COPSA Spouse Support Group *Professionally-run.* Mutual support and understanding for spouses of persons with any type of memory loss including Alzheimer's, Parkinson's, vascular disease, stroke, head injury and dementia. Meets 1st and 3rd Mon., 9:30-11am, University Behavioral Healthcare Center, 671 Hoes Lane, Piscataway. Call Mary Catherine Lundquist 732-235-2858 (day). *E-mail:* lundqumc@umdnj.edu

Young Wives' Support Group Mutual support and understanding for young women caring for a spouse with dementia. Meets 3rd Tues., 4:30-6pm, UBHC, 667 Hoes Lane, Piscataway. Call Sandy Egan or Meredith Doll 732-235-4519.

MONMOUTH

Alzheimer's Association Caregivers Support Group *Professionally-run.* Support for caregivers of persons with Alzheimer's disease and related dementia. Opportunity to share practical information, exchange community resources, solve problems and learn ways to deal with dementia-related issues. Call 1-800-883-1180 (day). Check website for additional meeting information. *Website:* http://www.alznj.org

> **Allenwood** Meets 3rd Wed., 6:30pm, Geraldine Thompson Care Center, Hospital Rd. Call Bonnie Lamont or Karen Hill 732-938-5250.
>
> **Colts Neck** Meets 2nd Tues., 6:30pm, Brandywine Senior Living, 3 Meridian Circle. Call Amy Willner or Kerry Hudanish 732-303-3100 (day).
>
> **Englishtown** Meets 3rd Thurs., 7pm, Assisted Living at Governor's Crossing, 49 Lasatta Ave. Call Neepa Patel 732-786-1000 (day).
>
> **Freehold** Meets 2nd Thurs., 2pm, Monmouth Crossing, 560 Iron Bridge Rd. Call Heleyne Gladstein 732-303-7416 (day).
>
> **Holmdel** Meets 3rd Tues., 7pm, Bayshore Hospital, 727 N. Beers St. Call Carol Auletto 732-914-9306.
>
> **Lincroft** Meets 4th Tues., 6:30pm, Sunrise Assisted Living, 734 Newman Springs Rd. Call Linda Gelpke 732-212-1910 (day).
>
> **Marlboro** Meets 2nd Wed., Sunrise of Marlboro, 3A South Main St. Call Lindell Ellis 732-409-6665 (day).
>
> **Tinton Falls** Meets 1st Thurs., 6:30pm (except Oct.), Atria Senior Living Group, 44 Pine St. Call Roxanne Smith 732-918-1960 (day).
>
> **Tinton Falls** Meets 3rd Wed., 6pm, Renaissance Gardens at Seabrook, 3002 Essex Rd. Call Francine Pannella 732-643-2060 (day).

Alzheimer's Association Caregivers Support Group Support for caregivers of persons with Alzheimer's disease and related dementia. Opportunity to share practical information, exchange community resources, solve problems and learn ways to cope with dementia-related issues. Call 1-800-883-1180. Check website for additional meeting information. *Website:* http://www.alznj.org

> **Freehold** Meets 3rd Tues., 7pm, First United Methodist Church, 91 West Main St.
>
> **Tinton Falls** Meets 2nd Wed., 7pm, Kensington Court, 864 Shrewsbury Ave. Call Kathleen Geren or Meghan Desmond 732-784-2404.
>
> **Wall** Meets last Thurs., 6pm, Allaire Center Senior Day Care, Wall Circle Park, Route 34 South. Call Cheryl Fenwick 732-974-7666.

Alzheimer's Caregiver Support Group *Professionally-run.* Support for caregivers and family members coping with Alzheimer's disease. Meets last Tues., 2-3:30pm, Monmouth Medical Center, Maysie Stroock Pavilion, 300 Second Ave., Geriatric Conference Room, Long Branch. Registration is required. Before attending call Robin DeNucci, CSW 732-923-7560 (day).

MORRIS

Alzheimer's Association Caregivers Support Group *Professionally-run.* Support for caregivers of persons with Alzheimer's disease and related dementia. Opportunity to share practical information, exchange community resources, solve problems and learn ways to cope with dementia-related issues. Call 1-800-883-1180. Check website for additional meeting information. *Website:* http://www.alznj.org

> **Chatham** Meets 2nd Wed., 2-3pm and 3rd Thurs., 7:30-9pm, Victorian Garden Adult Day Center, 353 Main St. Call Phyllis Flemming or Peg Tedesco, RN 973-635-2266 (day). *E-mail:* vgadc@aol.com
>
> **Denville** Meets 4th Mon., 10am, Alzheimer's Association, 400 Morris Ave., Suite 251.
>
> **Florham Park** Meets 3rd Wed., 5:30pm, Brighton Gardens of Florham Park, 21 Ridgedale Ave. Call Joan Blackwood 973-966-8999. *E-mail:* joan.beloff@chiltonmemorial.org
>
> **Morris Plains** Meets 2nd Wed., 7pm, The Country Home for Seniors, 1095 Tabor Rd., Dining Room. Call Ralph Lohr 973-538-2117. *E-mail:* joan.beloff@chiltonmemorial.org
>
> **Morristown** Meets 1st Thurs., 7pm, Morristown Memorial Hospital, 95 Madison Ave., Suite B-06. Call Peter Flemming 973-635-0899. *E-mail:* joan.beloff@chiltonmemorial.org
>
> **Morristown** Meets 2nd Thurs., 2:30pm, Care One at Madison, 151 Madison Ave. Call Carol Carlucci 973-656-2724 (day). *E-mail:* joan.beloff@chiltonmemorial.org
>
> **Pompton Plains** Meets 2nd Wed., 7-8:30pm, Chilton Health Network Building, 242 West Parkway. Call 973-831-5167 (day). *E-mail:* joan.beloff@chiltonmemorial.org

OCEAN

Alzheimer's Association Caregivers Support Group *Professionally-run.* Support for caregivers of persons with Alzheimer's disease and related dementia. Opportunity to share practical information, exchange community resources, solve problems and learn ways to cope with dementia-related issues. Call 1-800-883-1180 (day). Check website for additional meeting information. *Website:* http://www.alznj.org

Jackson Meets 1st Thurs., 7pm, Sunrise of Jackson, 390 North County Line Rd. Call Lisa Williams 732-928-5600 (day).

Jackson Meets 1st Wed., 5:30pm, The Orchards at Bartley, County Line Rd. Call Meghan Des Jardin or Debbie Carswell 732-370-4700 (day).

Jackson Meets last Tues., 10am, Bella Terra Retirement Community, 2 Kathleen Dr. Call Paula Douglass 732-730-9500.

Lakewood Meets 2nd Thurs., 7-9pm, Kimball Medical Center, River Rd., Conference Room A. Call Dolores Rosen 732-657-1656 or Jane Kirby 908-309-2583 (day).

Little Egg Harbor Meetings vary, Seacrest Village, 1001 Center St. Before attending call Rachel Bowen 609-296-9292 (day).

Manhawakin Meetings vary, Southern Ocean County Hospital, Wellness Center, 1140 Route 72 West. Before attending call Rachel Bowen 609-296-9292.

Toms River Meets 2nd and 4th Mon., 2pm, The Regency at Dover, 1311 Route 37 West, Suite 8. Call Dr. Mira Ahuja 732-286-2220.

Toms River Meets 2nd Tues., 10am, The Haven, 1700 Route 37 West. Call Linda Panarella 732-341-0880 (day).

Toms River Meets 3rd Mon., 9:15am, Visiting Homemaker Service Day Care, Conference Room. Call Michelle Mahieu 732-244-5565.

Toms River Meets 3rd Sat., 10am, Magnolia Gardens Assisted Living, 1935 Lakewood Rd. Call Cathy Vakulchik or Amy Palazzo 732-557-6500 ext. 0.

Toms River Meets 3rd Thurs., 2pm, Bey Lea Nursing Home, 1351 Old Freehold Rd. Call Edward Mount 732-240-0090.

Whiting Meets 2nd Fri., 2pm, Christ Evangelical Church, 300 Schoolhouse Rd. Call Pastor Luckenbill 732-350-0330 (day).

Whiting Meets 2nd Wed., 10:30am, St. Elizabeth Ann Seton Church, School House Rd., Parish Hall. Call Marion Ariemma 732-350-8688 (Mon.-Fri., 9am-noon).

Ocean Alzheimer's Caregivers Support Group Support for caregivers of those afflicted with Alzheimer's or dementia. Advocacy, guest speakers, mutual sharing, phone help, literature and educational information. Building is handicapped accessible. Meets Wed., 1:30-3:30pm, First Aid Squad Building, Colonial Drive, Manchester Township. Call Therese 732-818-1992.

"Alone we can do so little, together we can to so much." – Helen Keller

PASSAIC

Alzheimer's Association Caregivers Support Group *Professionally-run.* Support for caregivers of persons with Alzheimer's disease or other related dementia. Opportunity to share practical information, exchange community resources, solve problems and learn ways to cope with dementia-related issues. Call 1-800-883-1180 (day). Check website for additional meeting information. *Website:* http://www.alznj.org

> **Clifton** Meets 2nd Mon., 7pm, Clifton Family Medicine, 716 Broad St. Call Diane Lesko 973-904-6186 (day).
> **Clifton** Meets last Tues., 11am, Daughters of Miriam, 155 Hazel St., Rothenberg Bldg. Pre-registration required. Before attending call Michelle Klapper 973-253-5709.
> **Hawthorne** Meets 3rd Thurs., 7pm, Van Dyk Park Place (Assisted Living), 644 Goffle Rd. Call Jean Connolly 973-648-4062.
> **Wayne** Meets 2nd Wed., 10:30am, Christian Health Care Center of Wayne, 2000 Siena Village. Call Amanda Zunick 973-305-9155 (day).

SALEM

Alzheimer's Association Support Group Mutual support for family or friends caring for persons afflicted with Alzheimer's disease or dementia. Call 1-800-272-3900 (day). Check website for additional meeting information. *Website:* http:/www.alz.org/desjsepa

> **Elmer** Meets 3rd Mon., 2pm, Elmer Hospital, 501 West Front St., Classroom B.
> **Woodstown** Meets 4th Mon., 7pm, Friends Village, 1 Friends Dr. Hancock Center, Recreation Room.

SOMERSET

Alzheimer's Association Caregivers Support Group *Professionally-run.* Support for caregivers of persons with Alzheimer's disease or related dementia. Opportunity to share practical information, exchange community resources, solve problems and learn ways to cope with dementia-related issues. Call 1-800-883-1180 (day). Check website for additional meeting information. *Website:* http://www.alznj.org

> **Bridgewater** Meets 2nd Wed., 5pm, Harborside Healthcare Woods Edge, 875 Route 202/206 North. Call Peggy McArdle 908-895-2032.
> **Bridgewater** Meets 3rd Mon., 6pm, Brandywine Assisted Living at Middlebrook Crossing, 2005 Route 22 West. Call 732-868-8181 (day).
> **Somerville** Meets 3rd Wed., 7pm, Open Arms Day Club, 69 Grove St. Call Darlene Tranquilli 908-218-0078 (day).

SUSSEX

Alzheimer's Association Caregivers Support Group *Professionally-run.* Support for caregivers of persons with Alzheimer's disease or related dementia. Opportunity to share practical information, exchange community resources, solve problems and learn ways to cope with dementia-related issues. Call 1-800-883-1180 (day). Check website for additional meeting information. *Website:* http://www.alznj.org

> **Lafayette** Meets 4th Tues., 11:30am, Andover Sub-Acute Health Care and Rehabilitation, 99 Mulford Rd. Call Susan Herleth 973-383-6200 ext. 211.
> **Newton** Meets 2nd Fri., 7pm, Bristol Glen, 200 Bristol Glen Dr. (Route 206). Call Sherri Pizzi 973-940-6310 ext. 1112 (day) or Cindy Mendoza 973-940-6310 ext. 2101.

UNION

Alzheimer's Association Caregivers Support Group *Professionally-run.* Support for caregivers of persons with Alzheimer's disease and related dementia. Opportunity to share practical information, exchange community resources, solve problems and learn ways to cope with dementia-related issues. Call 1-800-883-1180 (day). Check website for additional meeting information. *Website:* http://www.alznj.org

> **Berkeley Heights** Meets 3rd Thurs., 1-2pm, Runnells Specialized Hospital, 40 Watchung Way, Third Floor, Room C 318. Call Liz Carabuena, LSW 908-771-5828 (day).
> **Cranford** Meets 1st Wed., 7pm, Family Resource Center, 300 North Ave. Call Ruth Adelman 201-707-5154.
> **Mountainside** Meets 1st Thurs., 7pm, Brighton Gardens at Mountainside, 1350 Route 22 West. Call Tonya Williams or Lisa Williams 908-654-4460 (day).
> **Summit** Meets 4th Thurs., 7-9pm, Overlook Hospital, 99 Beauvoir Ave.
> **Union** Meets 3rd Tues., 6pm, WISE Adult Day Services, 973A Stuyvesant Ave. Call Kerry Reilly 908-687-2995 (day).

Life is mostly froth and bubble; Two things stand like stone: Kindness in another's trouble, Courage in your own. --Adam Lindsay Gordon

WARREN

Alzheimer's Association Caregivers Support Group *Professionally-run.* Support for caregivers of persons with Alzheimer's disease and related dementia. Opportunity to share practical information, exchange community resources, solve problems and learn ways to cope with dementia-related issues. Call 1-800-883-1180 (day). Check website for additional meeting information. *Website:* http://www.alznj.org

> **Oxford** Meets 3rd Tues., 7pm, Warren Haven, 350 Oxford Rd. Call Dee Clayton 908-475-7700 (day).
> **Phillipsburg** Meets 3rd Sat., 11am, Warren Hospital, 755 Memorial Parkway, Building 302. Call Malika Brown 908-859-6700 ext. 2276.
> **Vienna** Meets 3rd Thurs., 10am and 7pm, Selah Care Center, 232 Route 46. Call Darlene Tranquilli 908-328-2744 (day).

NATIONAL

Alzheimer's Association *National. 80+ chapters. Founded 1980.* Assistance and information for caregivers of Alzheimer's patients. Quarterly newsletter and literature. Online message board. Write: Alzheimer's Association, 225 N. Michigan Ave., Suite 1700, Chicago, IL 60601. Call 1-800-272-3900 or 312-335-8700; TDD: 312-335-8882; Fax: 866-699-1246. *Website:* http://www.alz.org *E-mail:* info@alz.org

ONLINE

DASN - Dementia Advocacy and Support Network *Online. 399 members. Founded 2000.* Support for persons with early stage dementia and their supporters. Opportunity to communicate, lessen isolation and improve the lives of all people living with early stage dementia of any kind. *Website:* http://health.groups.yahoo.com/group/DASN

FTD Support Forum *Online. 358 members.* Sensitive and respectful support for people who have been diagnosed with fronto-temporal dementia, and those who care for loved ones with FTD. Encourages increased awareness of FTD within the medical community and the general public. *Website:* http://ftdsupportforum.com

Can't find an appropriate group in your area? The Clearinghouse helps people start groups. Give us a call at 1-800-367-6274.

AMYOTROPHIC LATERAL SCLEROSIS
(ALS / Lou Gehrig's Disease)

ATLANTIC

ALS Resource Group "Lou Gehrigs Disease" *Professionally-run.* Mutual support for patients and families to learn how to cope with the daily changes associated with ALS. Guest speakers and literature. Meets 2nd Tues., 6:30-8pm, Holy Redeemer Health System, 6550 Delilah Rd., Suite 501, Egg Harbor Township. Call Stephanie Hand-Kowchak 609-457-9261 (day). *Website:* http://www.alsphiladelphia.org

BERGEN

MDA/ALS Support Group *Professionally-run.* Mutual support for individuals with muscular dystrophy or ALS. Families and caregivers welcome. Sharing of information, experiences, ideas and resources. Usually meets 3rd Thurs., 4-5:30pm, Jewish Community Center on the Palisades, 411 East Clinton Ave., Tenafly. Pre-registration required. Before attending call 201-843-4452 (day).

MERCER

ALS Resource Group "Lou Gehrigs Disease" *Professionally-run.* Mutual support for patients and families to learn how to cope with the daily changes associated with ALS. Guest speakers and literature. Building is handicapped accessible. Meets 1st Sat., 1-3pm, Lawrence Township Municipal Building, Public Meeting Room, 2207 Lawrenceville Rd., Lawrenceville. Call Cathe Frierman 609-394-3556 (day) or Rick van den Heuvel 609-883-6784 (day). *Website:* http://www.alsphiladelphia.org

MIDDLESEX

A.L.S. Association *Professionally-run.* Mutual support for patients and families to learn to cope with ALS. Building is handicapped accessible. Meetings vary, Robert Wood Johnson University Hospital, New Brunswick. For meeting information call 732-710-8832. *Website:* http://www.alsa-ny.org *E-mail:* schlossberg@als-ny.org

MONMOUTH

Joan Dancy and People with ALS Support Group *Professionally-run.* Mutual support for patients and families to cope with ALS. Guest speakers. Building is handicapped accessible. Meets 1st Tues., 6:30pm, Riverview

307

Medical Center, Riverview Plaza, Administrative Board Room, Red Bank. Call Patricia Schaeffer, RN 732-450-2677 (day). *E-mail:* Pat@ALSPhiladelphia.org

NATIONAL

A.L.S. Association *National. 75+ chapters and support groups. Founded 1984.* Dedicated to finding the cause, prevention and cure of amyotrophic lateral sclerosis. Aims to enhance the quality of life for ALS patients and their families. Newsletter 3x/yr. and provides chapter development guidelines. Write: A.L.S. Association, 27001 Agoura Rd., Suite 250, Calabasas Hills, CA 91301. Call 1-800-782-4747 or 818-880-9007 for information and referral (Mon.-Fri., 7:30am-4pm PST); Fax: 818-880-9006. *Website:* http://www.alsa.org *E-mail:* alsinfo@alsa-national.org

ANEMIA

NATIONAL

Aplastic Anemia and MDS International Foundation, Inc. *International. Founded 1983.* Emotional support and worldwide support groups, free educational materials, information about current research and clinical trials, and financial assistance for persons with aplastic anemia, myelodysplastic syndromes, paroxysmal nocturnal hemoglobinuria and other bone marrow failure diseases. Financially supports research. Write: Aplastic Anemia and MDS International Foundation Inc., P.O. Box 310, Churchton, MD 20733. Call 1-800-747-2820 or 410-867-0242; Fax: 410-867-0240. *Website:* http://www.aamds.org *E-mail:* help@aamds.org

Cooley's Anemia Foundation *National. 12 chapters. Founded 1954.* Offers education and networking for families affected by Cooley's anemia (thalassemia). Fund-raising for research. Newsletter, annual seminars, research grants, patient support group, patient services, and chapter development guidelines. Write: Cooley's Anemia Foundation, 330 Seventh Ave., Suite 900, New York, NY 10001. Call 1-800-522-7222 or 212-279-8090; Fax: 212-279-5999. *Website:* http://www.cooleysanemia.org *E-mail:* info@cooleysanemia.org

ONLINE

Myelodysplastic Syndromes Foundation *Online.* Unmoderated forums for patients and professionals dealing with myelodysplastic syndromes, a group of bone marrow diseases. Also has referrals to treatment centers. Write: Myelodysplastic Syndromes Foundation, P.O. Box 353, Crosswicks, NJ 08515.

Call 1-800-637-0839 (US), 609-298-6746 (Outside US); Fax 609-298-0590. *Website:* http://www.mds-foundation.org   *E-mail:* patientliaison@mds-foundation.org

APHASIA

BERGEN

Aphasia Support Group *Professionally-run.* Support, advocacy and education for persons suffering with aphasia. Guest speakers and literature. $5 per meeting for refreshments and material. Meets 2nd and 4th Wed., 4:15-5:15pm, Kessler Institute, 300 Market St., Saddle Brook. Call Patricia Monti 201-368-6095 (day).

Aphasia Support Group Mutual support for persons suffering from aphasia and their families. Disseminates information and group discussions. Dues $12yr./$3/wk. Meets Fri., 10:30am-noon (except Aug.), Kip Center, 55 Kip Ave., Rutherford. Call Donna 201-438-2734 (eve.) or Kip Center 201-460-1600 (day).

Caregiver and Aphasia Support Group *Professionally-run.* Support for people with aphasia and their caregivers. Group is primarily for individuals who have had a stroke, but also includes those with head injury or other brain trauma. Lecture series, social group and guest speakers. Building is handicapped accessible. Meets Wed., 11:30am-12:30pm and 3rd Mon., 7-9pm, Adler Aphasia Center, 60 West Hunter Ave., Maywood. Call Karen Tucker 201-368-8585 (day). *Website:* http://www.adleraphasiacenter.org

ESSEX

Aphasia Support Group *Professionally-run.* Support, education and advocacy for persons suffering from aphasia. Guest speakers. Dues $5/mtg. for refreshments and materials. Building is handicapped accessible. Meets 1st and 3rd Wed., 4:15-5:15pm, Kessler Institute, 1199 Pleasant Valley Way, West Orange. Call Steven Labarbera 973-243-6956 (day).

We can also refer callers to over 100 individuals who are seeking others to help start new support groups throughout NJ. Give us a call for more information. ***1-800-367-6274***

MIDDLESEX

Aphasia Support Group *Professionally-run.* Support, education, discussions and information for persons with aphasia and their families. Meets Wed., 1:30pm, JFK Johnson Rehab Institute, JFK Hospital, Speech and Audiology Dept., 65 James St., 1st Floor, Edison. Pre-registration required. Before attending call Kristy Soriano 732-321-7063 (day).

UNION

Kean University Aphasia Support Group Mutual support for persons suffering from aphasia, Parkinson's and stroke. Families are welcome. Disseminates information, group discussions, rap sessions and guest speakers. Meetings vary, Kean University, 1000 Morris Ave., Union. Before attending call Wendy Greenspan 908-737-5811 (day).

NATIONAL

National Aphasia Association *National umbrella organization. 350+ groups. Founded 1987.* Educates the public about aphasia. Provides educational information to patients and their families about coping with aphasia. Listing of state representatives and support groups. Write: National Aphasia Association, 350 Seventh Ave., Suite 902, New York, NY 10001. Call 1-800-922-4622; Fax: 212-267-2812. *Website:* http://www.aphasia.org *E-mail:* naa@aphasia.org

ARTHRITIS

STATEWIDE

Arthritis Foundation NJ Chapter Mutual support and education for people with arthritis and their families. Write: Arthritis Foundation NJ Chapter, 200 Middlesex Turnpike, Iselin, NJ 08830. Call 1-888-467-3112 or 732-283-4300 (day). *Website:* http://www.arthritis.org

BERGEN

Juvenile Arthritis Group *Professionally-run.* Mutual support and education for teens with arthritis and other rheumatic conditions. Concurrent group for parents. Building is handicapped accessible. Meets regularly, Hackensack University Medical Center, Pediatric Rheumatology, 30 Prospect Ave., Hackensack. For meeting information call Katie Rosenthal 201-336-8241.

GLOUCESTER

Arthritis Support Group *Professionally-run.* Mutual support for those with arthritis. Rap sessions. Building is handicapped accessible. Meets 3rd Wed., 2-3:30pm, New Seasons Assisted Living, 600 Medical Center Dr., Washington Township. Call Tanya McKeown 1-800-522-1965 (day).

HUNTERDON

Arthritis Foundation NJ Chapter Mutual support and education for people with arthritis and osteoporosis. Families welcome. Meets 2nd Mon., 1-3pm, Hunterdon Medical Center, 2100 Wescott Drive, Flemington. Call 908-788-6373 or Arthritis Foundation 1-888-467-3112 (day).

MERCER

Arthritis Foundation NJ Chapter Support and education for people with all types of arthritis. Meets 3rd Wed., 7pm, Robert Wood Johnson University Hospital at Hamilton, 1 Hamilton Health Place, Hamilton. Call 609-584-5900 or Arthritis Foundation 1-888-467-3112 (day).

MORRIS

Arthritis and Osteoporosis Support Group *Professionally-run.* Support and education for individuals with arthritis and osteoporosis. Families welcome. Guest speakers, literature and newsletter. Building is handicapped accessible. Meets 3rd Thurs., 1-2pm, Arthritis Center, 95 Madison Ave., 3rd Floor, Suite 306, Morristown. Before attending call 1-877-973-6500 (day).

North Jersey Regional Arthritis Center Support Group *Professionally-run.* Mutual support and education for persons with arthritis, and their families. Aim is to raise quality of life for those with arthritis through group discussions, educational programs, mutual sharing, guest speakers, phone help, speakers' bureau and literature. Meets 4 times/yr., Rockaway Township Municipal Building, 65 Mt. Hope Rd., Conference Room, Rockaway. Registration required. Before attending call Kathy 973-983-2899.

"Listening is an attitude of the heart, a genuine desire to be with another which both attracts and heals." -- J. Isham

PASSAIC

Arthritis Support Group *Professionally-run.* Support and education for persons (ages 50+) with arthritis. Guest speakers and literature. Meets 4th Tues., 10:30-11:30am, Renaissance Subacute Care Center, 493 Black Oak Ridge Rd., Wayne. Call Joan Beloff 973-831-5167 (day) or Kathy Ferrara 973-831-5175 (day).

SUSSEX

North Jersey Regional Arthritis Center Support Group *Professionally-run.* Mutual support and education for persons with arthritis, and their families. Aim is to raise quality of life for those with arthritis through group discussions, educational programs, mutual sharing, and guest speakers. Offers phone help, speakers' bureau and literature. "Lunch and Chat" group meets 1st Tues., 11:30am-1:30pm, Lafayette House, Lafayette. Call NJRAC 1-877-973-6500.

NATIONAL

American Juvenile Arthritis Organization *National. 50 Chapters. Founded 1981.* Council of the Arthritis Foundation devoted to serving the special needs of children, teens and young adults with childhood rheumatic diseases (including juvenile rheumatoid arthritis, systemic lupus erythematosus and ankylosing spondylitis) and their families. Provides information, advocacy, educational materials, programs and conferences. Offers online support and local chapter locator. Dues $20/yr. (for Arthritis Foundation). Write: American Juvenile Arthritis Organization, 1330 West Peachtree St., Suite 100, Atlanta, GA 30309. Call 404-872-7100 ext. 7538; Fax: 440-872-9559. *Website:* http://www.arthritis.org

Arthritis Foundation *National. 64 chapters. Founded 1948.* Offers support groups, education and activities for people with arthritis, their families and friends. Mission is to improve lives through leadership in the prevention, control and cure of arthritis and related diseases. Self-help instruction programs. Land and water exercises. Provides community-based public health, public policy and nationwide research funding. Bimonthly magazine. Write: Arthritis Foundation, 1330 West Peachtree St. NW, Atlanta, GA 30309. Call 1-800-568-4045 or 404-872-7100. *Website:* http://www.arthritis.org *E-mail:* help@arthritis.org

BONE MARROW / STEM CELL TRANSPLANT

BERGEN

Life After Transplant Support Group *Professionally-run.* Provides emotional support and education to post-bone marrow or stem cell transplant patients, their family and friends. Guest speakers. Meets 3rd Thurs., 5-6:30pm, Hackensack University Medical Center, Sanzari Building, 360 Essex St., Suite 303, Hackensack. Parking in garage under building. Enter on Thompson St. Call Renee Stein-Goetz, LCSW 201-336-8290.

NATIONAL

Blood and Marrow Transplant Information Network *Resource. Founded 1990.* Transplant Center has information about 220 transplant programs in U.S. and Canada, a resource directory, attorney referral service and a patient-to-survivor link service. Resources include "Blood and Marrow Transplant Newsletter" for bone marrow, peripheral stem cell and cord blood transplant patients; Bone Marrow and Blood Stem Cell Transplants: A Guide for Patients" which describes the physical and emotional aspects of marrow and stem transplantation. Also a 208-page book "Autologous Stem Cell Transplant: A Handbook for Patients." Write: BMT Information Network, 2310 Skokie Valley Rd., Suite 104, Highland Park, IL 60035. Call 847-433-3313 or 1-888-597-7674; Fax: 847-433-4599. *Website:* http://www.bmtinfonet.org *E-mail:* help@bmtinfonet.org

BRAIN TUMOR
(see also toll-free helplines)

STATEWIDE

Acoustic Neuroma Association of New Jersey Support and information for pre or post-operative patients. Quarterly meetings present programs of interest to acoustic neuroma patients and their families. Dues $25/yr. Quarterly newsletter. Ongoing programs to create public awareness. Write: Acoustic Neuroma Association of NJ, Inc., 291 Nassau St., Princeton, NJ 08540. Call Wilma Ruskin 609-683-4650 (eve.); Fax: 609-279-9295. *Website:* http://www.ananj.org *E-mail:* ananjinc@aol.com

MIDDLESEX

Brain Tumor (Tu-Mor Helping Hands) Support Group Support and education for individuals and their families recovering from, or who will be undergoing, brain tumor surgery. Phone help. Building is handicapped accessible. Meets 2nd Mon., 7:00pm, Robert Wood Johnson University Hospital, One Robert Wood Johnson Place, BMSCH Conference Room, New Brunswick. Call 732-418-8110 (day).

MONMOUTH

Monmouth and Ocean County Brain Tumor Support Group Provides support for patients and family members of those affected by all types of brain tumors. Guest speakers, literature and speakers' bureau. Building is handicapped accessible. Meets 1st Sat., 3-4:45pm (Sept.-June); 1st Thurs., 7pm (July / Aug.), Monmouth County Library, Wall Township Branch, 2700 Allaire Rd., Wall. Before attending check website to confirm meeting day or call Bruce 609-758-0806. *Website:* http://www.njbt.org *E-mail:* mngioma634@aol.com

OCEAN

Brain Tumor Support Group *Professionally-run.* Emotional support and education for persons with a brain tumor, their families and friends. Meetings vary, Community Medical Center, 99 Highway 37 West, Toms River. Call Sherry 732-557-8270 (day).

SOMERSET

Brain Tumor Resources And Support Center *Professionally-run.* Support for brain tumor patients and their families. Meets 1st Thurs., 7pm, St. Luke's Church, 300 Clinton Ave., North Plainfield. Call Patty Anthony 732-321-7000 ext. 62874 (day). *Website:* http://www.njbt.org *E-mail:* info@njbt.org

NATIONAL

Acoustic Neuroma Association *National. 53 affiliated groups. Founded 1981.* Support and information for patients who have been diagnosed with acoustic neuroma, a benign tumor affecting the 8th cranial nerve. Quarterly newsletter ($40/yr), nationwide support group network, biennial national symposium and patient information booklets. Write: Acoustic Neuroma Association, 600 Peachtree Parkway, Suite 108, Cumming, GA 30041-6899. Call 1-877-200-8211 or 770-205-8211; Fax: 1-877-202-0239. *Website:* http://www.anausa.org *E-mail:* info@anausa.org

American Brain Tumor Association *National. Founded 1973.* Dedicated to supporting brain tumor patients and eliminating brain tumors by pen pal program, funding, encouraging research, providing free patient education materials, newsletter, publications and resource listings. Support group referrals and assistance in starting groups. Write: American Brain Tumor Association, 2720 River Rd., Suite 146, Des Plaines, IL 60018. Call 1-800-886-2282 or 847-827-9910 (patient services); Fax: 847-827-9918. *Website:* http://www.abta.org *E-mail:* info@abta.org

Brain Tumor Society *National. Founded 1989.* Committed to finding a cure for brain tumors. Improves the quality of life for brain tumor patients, survivors and caregivers through support programs, research, education and services. Maintains a database of brain tumor support groups, funds research, newsletter, e-newsletter, comprehensive resource guide and brain tumor fact sheets. Write: Brain Tumor Society, 124 Watertown St., Suite 3-H, Watertown, MA 02472-2500. Call 1-800-770-8287 or 617-924-9997; Fax: 617-924-9998. *Website:* http://www.tbts.org *E-mail:* info@tbts.org

Children's Brain Tumor Foundation, Inc. *(BILINGUAL) National network. Founded 1988.* Provides a Parent-to-Parent Network to link parents of a child with a brain or spinal cord tumor with another parent with similar experiences for information and support. Offers free resource guide (English/Spanish), "Parker's Brain Storm" (a book for children), Brain Tumor Week at Camp Sunshine, newsletter, annual teleconferences (available for replay on website) and funds research. Write: Children's Brain Tumor Foundation, 274 Madison Ave., Suite 1004, New York, NY 10016. Call 1-866-228-4673 or 212-448-9494 (Mon.-Fri., 9am-5pm EST); Fax: 212-448-1022. *Website:* http://www.cbtf.org *E-mail:* info@cbtf.org

Musella Foundation *National.* Provides emotional support and exchange of information for patients with various brain tumors and their families. Information on research, medication and clinical trials. Chatrooms, support groups, video library and other resources. Write: Musella Foundation, 1100 Peninsula Blvd., Hewlett, NY 11557. Call 1-888-295-4740; Fax: 516-295-2870. *Website:* http://www.virtualtrials.com *E-mail:* musella@virtualtrials.com

National Brain Tumor Foundation *National. Founded 1981.* Support and information for persons with brain tumors and their loved ones. Provides funding for research as well as client services for brain tumor patients and family members. Offers support group listings, a quarterly newsletter, conferences, literature, support line, information and referrals. Assistance in starting and maintaining support groups. Write: National Brain Tumor Foundation, 22 Battery St., Suite 612, San Francisco, CA 94111-5520.

Call 1-800-934-2873 or 415-834-9970 (Mon.-Fri., 9am-5pm PST); Fax: 415-834-9980. *Website:* http://www.braintumor.org *E-mail:* nbtf@braintumor.org

Pediatric Low Grade Astrocytoma Foundation *International. Founded 2006.* Support for families and caregivers of children suffering from low grade brain tumors (juvenile pilocytic astrocytoma, low grade glioma or pediatric brain tumor). Offers moderated message board, listserv, e-mail discussion group, phone support and international conferences. How-to materials for starting a support group are provided on website. Write: Pediatric Low Grade Astrocytoma Foundation, 98 Random Farms Dr., Chappaqua, NY 10514. Call 914-762-3494. *Website:* http://www.fightplga.org *E-mail:* contact@fightplga.org

ONLINE

BRAIN TRUST, The Healing Exchange *Online. Founded 1993.* Mission is to exchange support and information among people affected by brain tumors and related conditions including patient-survivors, families, caregivers and health professionals. Online support groups cover a large range of brain tumors, acquired injuries and other special interests. *Website:* http://www.braintrust.org *E-mail:* info@braintrust.org

Brain Tumour Foundation of Canada *Online. Founded 1982.* Virtual support group includes online chatroom, message board and moderated chat events. Support groups meet monthly in many Canadian communities. *Website:* http://www.braintumour.ca *E-mail:* braintumour@braintumour.ca

It's Just Benign *Online.* Group for survivors of benign brain tumors. The purpose is to connect with one another for support and information. *Website:* http://www.itsjustbenign.org

BREAST CANCER
(see also cancer, toll-free helplines)

ATLANTIC

AtlantiCare Breast Cancer Support Group *Professionally-run.* Support, education and advocacy for breast cancer patients and their families. Literature and buddy system. Building is handicapped accessible. Meets 2nd Thurs. 7-8pm, AtlantiCare Life Center, 2500 English Creek Ave., Building 200, Community Resource Room, Egg Harbor Township. Pre-registration required. Before attending call 1-888-569-1000 (day). *E-mail:* 1-888-569-1000@atlanticare.org

BERGEN

Gilda's Club Northern NJ *Professionally-run.* Support groups for individuals, family members and friends touched by all types of cancer. Some groups include: breast and lung cancer, men's club and living life after treatment. Entre Amigos a Spanish-speaking network. Programs for children also. Meetings vary, Gilda's Club, 575 Main St., Hackensack. Call 201-457-1670 (day). *Website:* http://www.gildasclubnnj.org

Hope Is In Your Hands *Professionally-run.* Support group for breast cancer patients. Family and friends welcome. Meets 2nd Wed., 7-8:30pm, Hackensack University Medical Center, Betty Rorricelli Breast Cancer Center, 20 Prospect Ave., 5th Floor, Conference Room, Hackensack. Call Betty, LCSW 201-336-8135.

Sisters Network Passaic/Bergen County Mutual support for female African American breast cancer survivors. Aim is to increase awareness of the impact of breast cancer. Literature and phone help. Meets 3rd Sat., 10am-noon, Gilda's Club Northern New Jersey, 575 Main St., Hackensack. Call Cheryl Walters 973-279-6070.

Support Group For Breast Cancer *(SPANISH)* Support for women with breast cancer. Mutual sharing, educational and guest speakers. Meets Tues., 7pm, Latin America Institute, 10 Banta Place, Suite 110, Hackensack. Call 201-525-1700 (day). *E-mail:* ssdeber05@hotmail.com

Tennis For Life Mutual support for women with breast cancer. Peer-led rap sessions, guest speaker and a free tennis lesson. Meets in Ridgewood. To register call Joan Monaghan 201-996-5827 (day).

BURLINGTON

Speak Easy Breast Cancer Support Group *Professionally-run.* Mutual support and information to breast cancer survivors. Guest speakers, phone help and literature. Meets 1st Tues., 7-9pm (except July/ Aug.), Lourdes Medical Center of Burlington County, 218A Sunset Rd., Willingboro. Call Maxine Mayer 856-662-5474 (day).

Women Supporting Women Through Breast Cancer *Professionally-run.* Mutual support for breast cancer patients and those currently under treatment. Meets 4th Tues., 6:30-8pm, Virtua Memorial Hospital, 175 Madison Ave., Mt. Holly. Before attending call 1-888-847-8823 (day).

CAMDEN

Pink Ribbon Poetry Breast Cancer Support Group Support for breast cancer survivors that uses poetry as a tool for reflection. Meetings vary, 7-9pm, Barry D. Brown Health Education Building, 106 Carnie Blvd., Voorhees. Before attending call 1-888-847-8823 (day).

Women Supporting Women Through Breast Cancer *Professionally-run.* Mutual support for breast cancer patients and those currently under treatment. Meets 2nd and 4th Wed., 6:30-8pm, Barry Brown Health Education Center, 106 Carnie Blvd. Voorhees. Before attending call 1-888-847-8823 (day).

ESSEX

Circle of Women *Professionally-run.* Networking group to support women diagnosed with breast cancer. Rap sessions and mutual sharing. Building is handicapped accessible. Meets 2nd and 4th Tues., 7-8:30pm (except Aug.), Mountainside Hospital, Harries Pavillion, Cancer Center, 1 Bay Ave., Montclair. Pre-registration required. Call Bridget Nash, LSW 973-429-6038 (day) or Kathy Furniss 973-259-3479 (day).

Primary Breast Cancer Support Group *Professionally-run.* Mutual support for women with breast cancer to share their concerns and experiences with other women facing the same illness and treatments. Meeting dates and times vary, St. Barnabas Medical Center, 94 Old Short Hills Rd., Livingston. Call Patti Conlin, LSW 973-322-8405 (day).

MERCER

Advanced Breast Cancer Support Group *Professionally-run.* Provides support for women living with stage IV breast cancer. Sharing of experiences, solutions, triumphs and concerns. Building is handicapped accessible. Meets 1st and 3rd Mon., 7:30-9pm, YWCA Princeton, 59 Paul Robeson Place, Bramwell House Living Room, Princeton. Call 609-497-2100 ext. 346. *Website:* http://www.bcrcnj.org *E-mail:* bcrc@ywcaprinceton.org

Beyond the Diagnosis: Survivor-to-Survivor Support Group *Professionally-run.* Support for breast cancer survivors one year out of treatment and beyond. Women assist and support each other as they address ongoing concerns. Meets 1st Tues., 6:30-8pm, Cancer Institute of New Jersey Hamitlon, 2575 Klockner Rd., Hamilton. Call Trish Tatrai 609-584-2836.

Breast Cancer Survivors Support Group *Professionally-run.* Support for breast cancer patients. Families welcome. Meets 2nd Tues., 6:30-8pm, Cancer Institute of New Jersey Hamilton, 2575 Klockner Road, Hamilton. Before attending call Lois Glasser, LCSW 1-800-813-4673 ext. 6807.

Breast Cancer Support Group Provides peer support to anyone diagnosed with breast cancer at any stage of treatment or recovery. Share questions, concerns and coping strategies in a caring, understanding environment. Building is handicapped accessible. Meets 4th Wed., 11:45am-1pm, YWCA Princeton, 59 Paul Robeson Place, Bramwell House Living Room, Princeton. Call 609-497-2100 ext. 346 or Breast Cancer Helpline 609-497-2126. *Website:* http://www.bcrcnj.org *E-mail:* bcrc@ywcaprinceton.org

Dealing with Breast Cancer Support Group *Professionally-run.* Support for women who are newly diagnosed with breast cancer, are currently in treatment or are up to one year post-treatment. Meets 3rd Tues., 6:30-8pm, Cancer Institute of New Jersey Hamilton, 2575 Klockner Rd., Hamilton. Call Trish Tatrai 609-584-2836.

Young Women's Breast Cancer Support Group *Professionally-run.* Provides support to women (under the age of 45) diagnosed with breast cancer. Addresses issues such as fertility, dating, self-image, coping with treatment side effects, raising young children and recent marriage. Building is handicapped accessible. Meets 3rd Wed., noon-1:30pm, YWCA Princeton, 59 Paul Robeson Place, Bramwell House Living Room, Princeton. Call 609-497-2100 ext. 346. *Website:* http://www.bcrcnj.org *E-mail:* bcrc@ywcaprinceton.org

MIDDLESEX

Breast Cancer Support Group Mutual support and education for women with breast cancer and their family members. Guest speakers. Meets 1st and 3rd Mon., 7-8:30pm, Cancer Institute of NJ, 195 Little Albany St., 2nd Floor, Waiting Room, New Brunswick. Call Linda Mathew, LSW 732-235-8799 (day).

Voices of Healing *Professionally-run.* Helps women with breast cancer to decrease their feelings of isolation and provides a sense of purpose and belonging. Empowerment, body image and family roles are discussed. Members are encouraged to discover the strength of their own inner resources. Meets 1st Tues., 6:30-8pm, Haven Hospice, JFK Medical Center, 65 James St., Edison. Call Tracy Grafton 732-321-7769 (day).

MONMOUTH

Breast Cancer Support Group *Professionally-run.* Support and education for mastectomy and lumpectomy patients. Peer-counseling and guest speakers. Meets 1st Tues., 7:00pm, Riverview Medical Center, 1 Riverview Plaza, Red Bank. Call 732-530-2382 (day).

Breast Cancer Support Group *Professionally-run.* Support and education for those diagnosed with breast cancer. Guest speakers. Meets Tues., 2-4pm (6 week sessions), Jersey Shore University Medical Center, Ambulatory Care Center, Cancer Center Conference Room, Neptune. Before attending call 732-776-4432 (day). *Website:* http://www.meridianhealth.com

Breast Cancer Support Group *Professionally-run.* Support, information and mutual sharing for breast cancer survivors. Rap sessions and phone help. Building is handicapped accessible. Meets 1st Mon., 7:30-9pm, Health Awareness Center, 901 W. Main St., Freehold. Call Stephanie O'Neil 732-637-6383 (day).

Living with Early Stage Breast Cancer Support Group *Professionally-run.* Opportunity for women facing a new diagnosis of breast cancer. Meets 3rd Tues., 5:30-7pm, Monmouth Medical Center, Jacqueline M. Wilentz Comprehensive Breast Center, 300 Second Ave., Library, Long Branch. Pre-registration required. Call 732-923-7582 (day).

Living with Metastatic Breast Cancer Support Group *Professionally-run.* Support for women facing the challenge of recurrent or metastic breast cancer. Meets 3rd Tues., 1-2:30pm, Monmouth Medical Center, Jacqueline M. Wilentz Comprehensive Breast Center, 300 Second Ave., Library, Long Branch. Pre-registration required. Call 732-923-7582 (day).

MORRIS

Breast Cancer Support Group *Professionally-run.* Information and support to women with breast cancer. Building is handicapped accessible. Meets 3rd Tues., 7-8:30pm, Morristown Memorial Hospital, Carol G. Simon Cancer Center, 100 Madison Ave., Conference Room, Morristown. Call Jean Marie 973-971-6514.

Together *Professionally-run.* Education and sharing for women who are undergoing or have undergone treatment for breast cancer. Rap sessions, guest speakers. Building is handicapped accessible. Before attending call 973-625-6176. *E-mail:* Bjohnson@saintclares.org

Denville Meets 1st and 3rd Wed., 7-8:30pm, Saint Clare's Hospital, 25 Pocono Rd., Urban 2 Conference Room.
Denville Meets 2nd and 4th Mon., 1-2pm, Cancer Care at Saint Clare's, Conference Room.

OCEAN

Breast Cancer Support Group *Professionally-run.* Education and sharing for women diagnosed with breast cancer. Rap sessions and occasional guest speaker. Building is handicapped accessible. Meets last Wed., 5-6:30pm, Community Medical Center, 99 Highway 37 West, Radiation Oncology, Ground Floor, Toms River. Before attending call Tracie Barberi, LCSW or Rose Cowen, CSW 732-557-8076 (day). *E-mail:* tbarberi@sbhcs.com

Breast Cancer Support Group *Professionally-run.* Support and education for persons afflicted with breast cancer. Building is handicapped accessible. Meets 2nd Tues., 7-8pm, Ocean Club, 700 Route 9 South, Stafford Township. Call 609-978-3559.

PASSAIC

Breast Cancer Support Group - Embracing Life *(SPANISH)* Self-help for women coping with breast cancer. Meets 1st and last Wed., 5-6pm, St. Joseph's Regional Medical Center, 703 Main St., Seton Bldg., Paterson. Before attending call Victoria Pacheco 973-616-0514.

Post-Mastectomy/Lumpectomy Program *Professionally-run.* Support and exercise for women who have had breast surgery. Building is handicapped accessible. Meets spring and fall, 8 week sessions, YWHA, 199 Scoles Ave., Clifton. For information call Ellen Cannel 973-890-5633 or American Cancer Society 201-457-3418. *Website:* http//www.cancer.org

SOMERSET

Advanced Breast Cancer Networking Group *Professionally-run.* Provides an opportunity for individuals with advanced breast cancer and their loved ones to discuss and exchange information. Rap sessions. Meetings vary, The Wellness Community of Central New Jersey, 3 Crossroads Dr., Bedminster. Call Ellen Levine, LCSW 908-658-5400 ext. 2. *Website:* http://www.thewellnesscommunity.org/cnj *E-mail:* elevine@thewellnesscommunity.org

Breast Cancer Networking Group *Professionally-run.* Provides an opportunity for individuals with a breast cancer diagnosis to discuss and exchange information. Meets 3rd Wed., 6:30-8pm, The Wellness Community of Central New Jersey, 3 Crossroads Dr., Bedminster. Call Karen Larsen, LCSW 908-658-5400 (day).

Post-treatment Breast Cancer Support Group *Professionally-run.* Support for women who have had surgery, radiation and/or chemotherapy. Meetings vary, 7pm, Sharing Village, 161 Main St., Peapack. Registration required. Before attending call 908-234-0334 (day).

Sisters Network of Central New Jersey Mutual support for female African American breast cancer survivors. Aim is to increase awareness of the impact of breast cancer. Literature and phone help. Meets 2nd Mon., 7-8:30pm, 1201 Hamilton St., Somerset. Call Dorothy Reed 732-246-8300 (day). *Website:* http://www.sncnj.org *E-mail:* sistercentral@sncnj.org

UNION

Breast Cancer Support Group *Professionally-run.* Support for newly diagnosed patients, as well as those who have been living with breast cancer. Meets 1st Wed., 7-8:30pm, Robert Wood Johnson Fitness and Wellness Center, 2120 Lamberts Mill Rd., Scotch Plains. Call 732-499-6193.

Facing Breast Cancer Together *Professionally-run.* Support for women with breast cancer, diagnosed at any age and at any stage of diagnosis and treatment, where resources and coping strategies are shared. Literature, newsletter and phone help. Building is handicapped accessible. Meets Wed., 7:15-8:30pm, Pathways, 79 Maple St., Summit. Pre-registration required. Before attending call 908-273-4242 ext. 154 (day).

Newly Diagnosed Breast Cancer *Professionally-run.* Mutual support and understanding for women newly diagnosed with breast cancer. Provides women the opportunity to share feelings, coping strategies, and to talk with others who truly understand. Building is handicapped accessible. Meets 2nd and 4th Wed., 7-8:30pm, Overlook Hospital, 99 Beauvoir Ave., Summit. Before attending call Joan Runfola, LCSW 908-234-0334.

Recurrent Breast Cancer Support Group *Professionally-run.* Support for women with recurrent breast cancer. Focuses on facing change while finding meaning and value in a challenging time. Literature, newsletter and phone help. Building is handicapped accessible. Meets 2nd and 4th Mon., 1-2:15pm,

Pathways, 79 Maple St., Summit. Pre-registration required. Before attending call 908-273-4242 ext. 154 (day).

WARREN

Breast Cancer Support Group *Professionally-run.* Mutual support and encouragement for women with breast cancer. Meets Mon., Joan Knechel Cancer Center at Hackettstown Regional Medical Center, 651 Willow Grove St., Hackettstown. Before attending call Joan Runfola, LCSW 908-441-1503.

Women's Cancer Group Mutual support and encouragement for women with any type of cancer and for those women in recovery from cancer. Building is handicapped accessible. Meets 1st Thurs., 7-8:30pm, Lutheran Church of the Good Shepherd, 168 Route 94, Blairstown. Call Kathy 908-362-6344.

NATIONAL

AABCA (African American Breast Cancer Alliance) *Model. 1 group in Minnesota. Founded 1990.* Support, education and advocacy for black women and men with breast cancer and their families. Provides information and referrals, education, a support group for patients and survivors to discuss issues and concerns. Open to anyone interested in supporting and working with this grass-roots organization. Write: AABCA, P.O. Box 8981, Minneapolis, MN 55408. Call 612-825-3675; Fax: 612-827-2977. *Website:* http://www.aabcainc.org *E-mail:* aabcainc@yahoo.com

Breast Cancer Network of Strength *(BILINGUAL) National. 9 affiliate groups. Founded 1978.* (formerly known as Y-ME National Breast Cancer Organization) Mission is to decrease the impact of breast cancer, create and increase breast cancer awareness, and ensure through information, empowerment and peer support that no one faces breast cancer alone. Information and peer support for breast cancer patients and their families during all stages of the disease. Offers 24-hour hotlines (English and Spanish), a Latino Outreach program, a Men's Match program for husbands and partners of women with breast cancer, support groups, a Teen Education program and Advocacy Network, publications, wig and prosthesis bank and newsletter. Group development guidelines. Write: Breast Cancer Network of Strength, 212 W. Van Buren St., Suite 1000, Chicago, IL 60607-3903. Call 1-800-221-2141 (English 24 hr.) or 1-800-986-9505 (Spanish 24 hr.); Fax: 312-294-8597. *Website:* http://www.networkofstrength.org

Breast Cancer Support and Reach to Recovery Discussion Group *National.* Local outgrowth of Reach to Recovery Program which in most areas is a one-to-one visitation program but in some areas is a support group. Contact your local or state chapter of the American Cancer Society at 1-800-227-2345 to determine availability of such groups and availability of trained volunteers. *Website:* http://www.cancer.org (click on "survivors;" then click on "support;" then click "view all message boards")

Mothers Supporting Daughters with Breast Cancer *Model. Founded 1995.* Offers emotional support to the mothers of daughters newly diagnosed with breast cancer to help them to be better "care partners" to their daughters. Helps mothers cope with stress, learn about breast cancer treatment and promote breast cancer awareness. Literature, advocacy and phone support. Write: MSDBC, c/o Charmayne Dierker, 25235 Foxchase Dr., Chestertown, MD 21620. Call 410-778-1982; Fax: 410-778-1411. *Website:* http://www.mothersdaughters.org *E-mail:* msdbc@verizon.net

SHARE: Self-Help for Women with Breast or Ovarian Cancer *(BILINGUAL) Model. 18 sites in NY Metro Area. Founded 1976.* Provides support to women with breast or ovarian cancer, their families and friends. Support groups led by trained survivors. Cutting edge educational forums and advocacy activities held throughout the five boroughs of New York City. Write: SHARE, 1501 Broadway, Suite 704A, New York, NY 10036. Call 1-866-891-2392; Fax: 212-869-3431; Breast Cancer Hotline: 212-382-2111; Ovarian Hotline: 212-719-1204; Latina Hotline (Spanish): 212-719-4454; New York State Ovarian Hotline (toll-free): 1-866-537-4273. *Website:* http://www.sharecancersupport.org

Sisters Network Inc. *National. 40 affiliated chapters. 3,000 members. Founded 1994.* A national African American breast cancer survivors organization that promotes the importance of breast health through empowerment, support, breast education programs, resource information and clinical trials. Write: Sisters Network Inc., 8787 Woodway Dr., Suite 4206, Houston, TX 77063. Call 1-866-781-1808 or 713-781-0255 (9am-5pm CST); Fax: 713-780-8998. *Website:* http://www.sistersnetworkinc.org *E-mail:* infonet@sistersnetworkinc.org

Young Survival Coalition *International. 15 affiliates. Founded 1998.* Support and education for young women (age 40 and under) living with a diagnosis of breast cancer. Addresses the concerns and issues that are unique to young women and breast cancer (such as higher mortality rates, fertility issues and early menopause). Information, resources, advocacy, one-to-one Point of Contact Program and online support forums. Write: Young Survival Coalition, 61 Broadway, Suite 2235, New York, NY 10006. Call 1-877-972-1011 (toll-free) or 646-257-3000. Fax: 646-257-3030. *Website:* http://www.youngsurvival.org *E-mail:* info@youngsurvival.org

ONLINE

FORCE (Facing Our Risk of Cancer Empowered) *Online. Founded 1999.* Support and education for women whose family history and genetic status put them at high risk of getting ovarian or breast cancer. Open to family members. Provides resources for women to determine if they are at high risk. Forums, chats, bulletin boards, member profiles and phone support network. *Website:* http://www.facingourrisk.org/ *E-mail:* info@facingourrisk.org

MaleBC *Online. Founded 1997.* Brings men together who have been diagnosed with male breast cancer so they can share experiences, gain information and support each other. *Website:* http://www.acor.org (click on A-Z cancers, then select "breast"- then "MaleBC")

CANCER
(see also breast cancer, life threatening, toll-free helplines)

ATLANTIC

Gilda's Club South Jersey *Professionally-run.* Emotional and social support for anyone touched by cancer. Separate support groups, workshops, lectures and social events for family members. Programs for children.also Building is handicapped accessible. Meetings vary, Gilda's Club South Jersey, 700 New Rd., Linwood. Before attending call 609-926-2699. *Website:* http://www.gildasclubsouthjersey.org *E-mail:* erin@gildasclubsouthjersey.org

"Man to Man" Prostate Cancer Support Group An educational, information sharing and emotional support group designed to meet the challenge of living with prostate cancer for men and their partners. Educational series, literature and guest speakers. Meets 2nd Tues., 7-9pm (except June/July/Aug.), Shore Memorial Cancer Center, Brighton Ave. and Shore Rd., 2nd Floor, Somers Point. Call Burnett Watson 609-641-7907.

BERGEN

Cancer Care *(BILINGUAL) Professionally-run.* Various support groups for cancer patients and their families. Groups also include bereavement, telephone and internet groups. Building is handicapped accessible. Groups start periodically and run for 8 weeks. Groups meet in Ridgewood. For meeting information 1-800-813-4673 or 201-444-6630 (day). *Website:* http://www.cancercare.org *E-mail:* njinfo@cancercare.org

Cancer Support Group *Professionally-run.* Support for seniors (ages 55+) coping with cancer. Rap sessions. Meetings vary, Southeast Senior Center for Independent Living, 228 Grand Ave., Englewood. Pre-registration required. Before attending call Laura Hollander 201-569-4080 (day). *E-mail:* lyd228@aol.com

CARE (Cancer Alternatives Research Exchange) Mutual support for persons with cancer and their families. Explores any type of treatment that may be of benefit with a focus on integrated medicine. Supportive environment for whichever treatment is chosen. Guest speakers and literature. Donation $5. Meets 2nd Thurs., 6:30pm (except July/Aug.), Ridgewood United Methodist Church, 100 Dayton St., Ridgewood. Call Harvey 201-664-5005 (day).

DongGueRaMee Mutual support and education for Korean patients who have cancer, as well as cancer survivors. Families welcome. Guest speakers. Meets 1st Fri., 10am-12:30pm, Holy Name Hospital, 718 Teaneck Rd., Teaneck. Pre-registration required. Before attending call Hei Young 201-833-3332 or helpline 201-833-3399 (day).

Filipino American Cancer Support Group Mutual support and encouragement for Filipino Americans with any type of cancer. Families welcome. Rap sessions, guests speakers, fundraising and community volunteer work. Meetings vary, in various members' homes. For information call Linda 201-894-3380 or 201-895-4165. *E-mail:* erubio20@aol.com

Gastrointestinal/Colorectal Cancer *Professionally-run.* Mutual support for patients, families and friends affected by gastrointestinal/colorectal cancer. Rap sessions, guest speakers and literature. Meets 2nd Thurs., 5:30-7pm, Medical Plaza, 20 Prospect Ave., Suite 200, Hackensack. Call Betty 201-336-8135 (day).

Gilda's Club Northern NJ *Professionally-run.* Support groups for individuals, family members and friends touched by all types of cancer. Some groups include: men's club, living life after treatment, breast and lung cancer. Entre Amigos a Spanish-speaking network. Programs for children also. Meetings vary, Gilda's Club, 575 Main St., Hackensack. Call 201-457-1670 (day). *Website:* http://www.gildasclubnnj.org

Living With Cancer Mutual support for patients who have completed treatment. Rap sessions, guest speakers and literature. Meets 4th Thurs., 10:30am-noon, Cancer Center, 60 2nd St., 1st Floor, Hackensack. Call Melissa Donahue 201-996-5836 (day).

Lung Cancer Support Group *Professionally-run.* Support for anyone with lung cancer. Meets 2nd Fri., Gilda's Club, 575 Main St., Hackensack. Before attending call Lenore Guido 201-457-1670 ext. 123.

Lung/Thoracic Cancer Mutual support for patients affected by lung/thoracic cancer. Rap sessions, guest speakers and literature. Meets 1st Thurs., 10:30am-noon, Cancer Center, 60 Second St., 1st Floor, Hackensack. Call Melissa Donahue 201-996-5836 (day).

Multiple Myeloma *Professionally-run.* Mutual support for patients, families and friends affected by multiple myeloma. Rap sessions, guest speakers and literature. Meets 3rd Thurs., 10:30am-noon, Sanzari Building, 369 Essex St., Hackensack. Call Ann 201-996-5983 (day).

Northern NJ Chapter Leukemia and Lymphoma Society *Professionally-run.* Emotional support and educational information for adult survivors and family members whose lives have been touched by a blood cancer diagnosis (leukemia, lymphoma, Hodgkins disease, myeloma or MDS). Building is handicapped accessible. Meets Wed., 10:30am-noon, 6 week sessions, 3 times/yr., The Hackensack University Medical Center, The Cancer Center, Hackensack Pre-registration required. Call Deborah Halpern, MSW, LCSW 908-956-6607 (day). *Website:* http://www.lls.org/nj *E-mail:* Deborah.Halpern@lls.org

On Treatment Families *Professionally-run.* Support and education for patients, parents and siblings who have cancer or serious blood disorders. Also groups for children and families who have completed treatment. Meetings vary, Hackensack University Medical Center, Reuten Clinic, Hackensack. Call Judy Solomon 201-996-5437 (day).

Prostate Cancer Support Group *Professionally-run.* Support and education for men diagnosed with prostate cancer, Meets 4th Thurs., 2-3:30pm, Regional Cancer Center, 718 Teaneck Rd., Teaneck. Call Sister Patricia Lynch 201-541-5900 ext. 2 (day).

Prostate Cancer Support Group *Professionally-run.* Support and education for prostate cancer patients and their families. Meets 3rd Wed., 10am-noon, Hekemian Conference Center, Hackensack University Medical Center, 30 Prospect Ave., Hackensack. Call Melissa Donahue 201-996-5836 (day).

Thyroid Cancer Awareness, Education and Support Network *(BILINGUAL)* Mutual support, education and awareness for individuals with thyroid cancer. Guest speakers. Meets 3rd Sat., 11:30am-1:30pm, Gilda's Club Northern NJ, 575 Main St., Hackensack. Call Wilma 973-246-1034 (day).

Us TOO Prostate Support Group *Professionally-run.* Support and education for men diagnosed with prostate cancer and their significant others. Meets 3rd Fri., 10am-noon, Daniel and Gloria Blumenthal Cancer Center, One Valley Health Plaza, 2nd Floor, Meeting Room, Paramus. Call 201-634-5339 (day).

BURLINGTON

Living with Lung Cancer *Professionally-run.* Mutual support and encouragement for anyone with lung cancer. Meets 1st Wed., 11:30am-12:30pm, Virtua Memorial Hospital at Burlington County, 175 Madison Ave., Conference Center, Mt. Holly. Before attending call Virtua Memorial Hospital 1-888-847-8823 (day).

"Man to Man" Prostate Cancer Support Group *Professionally-run.* An educational, information sharing and emotional support group designed to meet the challenge of living with prostate cancer. Meets 3rd Tues., 7-8:30pm, Virtua Memorial Hospital of Burlington County, 175 Madison Ave., Conference Room B, Mt. Holly. Call 1-800-227-2345 (day). *Website:* http://www.cancer.org

CAMDEN

Leukemia and Lymphoma Society of America Eastern Pennsylvania Chapter *Professionally-run.* Support and education for families to help cope with the emotional and personal issues of lymphoma, leukemia and multiple myeloma. Meets 4th Thurs., 7-8:30pm, Einstein Center One, Suite 206, 9880 Bustleton Ave., Philadelphia. Free parking. Call Anne Waldman 215-456-3822 (day). *E-mail:* waldmana@einstein.edu

Lung Cancer Support Group *Professionally-run.* Support for anyone with lung cancer. Meets 2nd Sat., 10am-noon, Suzanne Morgan Center at Ridgeland, Chamounix Dr., West Fairmount Park, Philadelphia, PA. Call Kathleen Coyne 215-879-7733 (day).

Us TOO (Prostate Cancer Support Group) Provides support and education for men with prostate cancer and their families. Meets 4 times/yr., 6-7:30pm, Cooper Cancer Institute, 900 Centennial Blvd., Voorhees. Pre-registration required. Before attending call 1-800-826-6737 or Frank DelRossi, CSW 856-325-6779 (day).

CUMBERLAND

ThyCa Southern New Jersey Support Group Support, education and communication for thyroid cancer survivors, families, friends and health care professionals. Guest speakers, literature, newsletter, phone help, buddy system and message board. Meets 3rd Sat., 11am-12:30pm, The Fitness Connection, Sherman Ave. and Orchard St., Vineland. Call Louise Samuel 215-742-5636 (day) or Kim Samuel 215-587-7092 (eve.). *Website:* http://www.thyca.org/sg/nj_vineland.htm *E-mail:* southernjersey@thyca.org

ESSEX

Beyond Primary Cancer *Professionally-run.* Group provides a supportive environment to share thoughts, concerns, gain practical information and emotional support for patients coping with recurrent or metastic cancer. Meeting days vary, Saint Barnabas Medical Center, 94 Old Short Hills Rd., Livingston. Before attending call Angela McCabe 973-322-2668.

Caring Arms *Professionally-run.* Opportunity for men and women who have been diagnosed with cancer to come together to offer strength, experience, and hope. Provides a supportive environment where persons can express feelings and concerns with others who share a common experience. Meditation offered after meeting. Building is handicapped accessible. Meets Mon., 11am-noon, Saint Michael's Medical Center, Cathedral Regional Cancer Center, Central Ave., Conference Room, Newark. Before attending call Joanne Rodriguez 973-877-2967 (day).

Expressive Arts Group *Professionally-run.* Support for patients who are undergoing cancer treatment. Meeting days and times vary, St. Barnabas Medical Center, 94 Old Short Hills Rd., Livingston. Call Angela 973-322-2668 (day).

"It's not enough to have lived. We should be determined to live for something. May I suggest that it be creating joy for others, sharing what we have for the betterment of personkind, bringing hope to the lost and love to the lonely."--Leo Buscaglia

Gynecological Cancer Support Group *Professionally-run.* Mutual support for women with any type of gynecological cancer. Opportunity to talk and share with one another. Building is handicapped accessible. Meets 3rd Tues., 6-7:30pm (except Aug.), Mountainside Hospital Cancer Center, 1 Bay Ave., Harries Pavillion, Conference Room, Montclair. Pre-registration required. Call Bridget Nash, LSW 973-429-6038 (day) or Kathy Morelli 973-429-6009 (day).

Healing Stitches *Professionally-run.* Mutual support for cancer patients to gather weekly to chat, knit or crochet while interacting and creating projects. Families and caregivers welcome. Building is handicapped accessible. Meets Wed., 1-3pm, Mountainside Hospital, Cancer Center, 1 Bay Ave., Montclair. Pre-registration required. Call Bridget Nash, LSW 973-429-6038 (day).

Us Too (Prostate Cancer Support Group) *Professionally-run.* Support and information for men with prostate cancer, their family and friends. Guest speakers, phone help, educational series, literature. Building is handicapped accessible. Meets 1st Thurs., 7-8:30pm (except Aug.), Mountainside Hospital, Harries Pavillion Cancer Center, Conference Room, 1 Bay Ave., Montclair. Pre-registration required. Call Bridget Nash, LSW 973-429-6038 (day).

GLOUCESTER

Leukemia and Lymphoma Support Group *Professionally-run.* Emotional support, education, and discussion of common issues for people with leukemia, lymphomas and related disorders. Families and loved ones welcome. Rap sessions and guest speakers. Building is handicapped accessible. Meets 3rd Tues., 7-9pm, Gloucester County Dept. of Education, Tanyard Rd., Sewell. Call Leukemia Society 856-869-0200 or Libby Maurer 856-468-1167.

MERCER

Cancer Support Group *Professionally-run.* Mutual support and discussion group for people living with cancer, their families and friends. Building is handicapped accessible. Meets 1st Wed., 1pm, Capital Health System at Mercer, 446 Bellevue Ave., Radiation Oncology Conference Room, Trenton. Please park across the street in parking lot A. Call Karleen Yapp, LSW 609-815-7446 (day).

"A man doesn't realize how much he can stand until he is put to the test. You can stand far more than you think you can. You are much stronger than you think you are."
--Martin Niemoller

Cancer Support Group *Professionally-run.* Support, education and empowerment for individuals with cancer and their families. Rap sessions, literature and phone help. Meets 4th Wed., 6:30-7:30pm, Princeton HealthCare System, Community Education and Outreach, 731 Alexander Rd., Suite 103, Princeton. Call Lois Glasser, LCSW 1-800-813-4673 ext. 6807 (day).

Central Laryngectomee Support Group of Central Jersey *Professionally-run.* Support and education for laryngeal cancer patients and their families. Share concerns and problems related to life after laryngeal cancer. Meets 3rd Wed., 11am-noon, Medical Society of New Jersey, 2 Princess Rd., Lawrenceville. Pre-registration required. Before attending call Karen Rust, RN 609-655-5755 (day).

Prostate Cancer Support Group *Professionally-run.* Support and education for those with prostate cancer and their families. Rap sessions, guest speakers, literature and phone help. Meets 4th Wed., noon-1:30pm, Princeton HealthCare System, Community Education and Outreach, 731 Alexander Rd., Princeton. Call Lois Glasser, LCSW 1-800-813-4673 ext. 6807 (day).

Sharing Your Journey Through Cancer *Professionally-run.* Peer support for persons with cancer to share experiences. Families welcomed. Phone help and literature. Building is handicapped accessible. Meets 1st and 3rd Thurs., 6:30-8pm, Cancer Institute of New Jersey Hamilton, 2575 Klockner Road, Conference Room, Hamilton. Call 609-584-6680 (day).

Thyroid Cancer Survivors Support Group Support group for thyroid cancer survivors. Families welcome. Literature, guest speaker and phone help. Meets 3rd Sat., 10-11:30am, Cancer Institute of New Jersey, Robert Wood Johnson Hospital @ Hamilton, One Hamilton Health Pl., Hamilton. Call Michael Dubrow 1-877-588-7904 (eve.). *E-mail:* centraljersey@thyca.org

MIDDLESEX

Coping With Cancer *Professionally-run.* Provides a safe environment for cancer patients and their families to share their feelings and concerns. Helps patients become educated partners in their healthcare through information on diagnosis and treatment. Meets 4th Tues., 2-3:30pm, JFK Medical Center, 65 James St., Edison. Call 732-321-7769 (day).

Need help finding a specific group? Give us a call – we're here to help!
Call 1-800-367-6274.

Gynecologic Cancer Support Group *Professionally-run.* Support for women facing a diagnosis of a gynecologic cancer and their loved ones. Promotes mutual problem solving and facilitates sharing. Building is handicapped accessible. Meets 2nd Tues., 7-8:30pm, Cancer Institute of NJ, 195 Little Albany St., 1st Floor, Women Center, Waiting Room, New Brunswick. Call Julie Murphy 732-235-8522 (day). *E-mail:* murphyju@umdnj.edu

Healing Journey: Relaxation for Cancer Patients/Families, The *Professionally-run.* Support for those afflicted with cancer to develop relaxation and visualization skills. Families welcome. Educational and experiential group. Building is handicapped accessible. Meets 3rd Tues., 6-7:30pm, Haven Hospice, JFK Medical Center, 65 James St., Edison. Call Erika Kolb 732-321-7769 (day).

Lesbians with Cancer Support Group *Professionally-run.* Mutual support, sharing and education. Partners welcome. Meets 3rd Mon., 6:30pm, The Cancer Institute of NJ, 195 Little Albany St., Social Work Suite, New Brunswick. Call Rose Slirzewski 732-235-6781 (day).

Living with Cancer Support Group *Professionally-run.* Mutual support for anyone who has been diagnosed with cancer, to help them gain control over their lives through better knowledge of the disease. Family and friends welcome. Meets 2nd and 4th Wed., 7pm, Cancer Institute of NJ, 195 Little Albany St., 2nd Floor Waiting Room, New Brunswick. Pre-registration required. Call 732-235-7557 (day).

Strength For Caring *Professionally-run.* Support, education and coping skills to families caring for a loved one with cancer. Building is handicapped accessible. Meets 4th Tues., 7pm, Cancer Institute, 195 Little Albany St., 2nd Floor Learning Room, New Brunswick. To register call 732-235-6027 (day).

MONMOUTH

Blood Cancer Support Group *Professionally-run.* Emotional support, education and discussion of common issues for people with leukemia, lymphomas and related disorders. Families and loved ones welcome. Rap sessions and guest speakers. Building is handicapped accessible. Meets 1st Wed., 7pm, Centra State Medical Center, 901 W. Main St., Freehold. Call Leukemia and Lymphoma Society 1-888-920-8557. *Website:* http://www.LLS.org/snj/supportgroups

Cancer Networking Groups *Professionally-run.* Separate ongoing support groups for family and friends of those with cancer, lung cancer, prostate cancer (open to partners), leukemia, lymphoma, myeloma and breast cancer. Activity groups available. Meetings vary, The Wellness Community, 613 Hope Rd., Eatontown. Before attending call 732-578-9200.

Cancer Patient and Family Support *Professionally-run.* Mutual support and education for persons with all types of cancer and their families. Exchange of coping skills. Building is handicapped accessible. Meets 2nd Mon., 3-4:30pm, CentraState Medical Center, 901 W. Main St., Freehold. Call Deb Turi-Smith, BACSW 732-294-2841 (day).

Kids Need Support, Too *Professionally-run.* Support for children and adolescents who have a family member diagnosed with cancer or other serious illness. Building is handicapped accessible. Meets 1st Wed., 7pm, Monmouth Medical Center, 300 Second Ave., Long Branch. Pre-registration required. Before attending call 732-923-6990 (day).

Ovarian Cancer Support Group Support for women with ovarian, cervical, uterine and endometrial cancer. Meets 1st and 3rd Tues., 11:30am-1:30pm, Jersey Shore University Medical Center, Ambulatory Care Center, Cancer Conference Room, 1945 Route 33, Neptune. Call 732-776-4432.

Partners in Healing Information Session *Professionally-run.* Mutual support for spouses or significant others of diagnosed with cancer. Meets 3rd Tues., 7:00-9pm, Cancer Center Conference Room, Ambulatory Care Pavilion, Jersey Shore Medical Center, Neptune. Before attending call 732-776-2380.

SPOHNC (Support for People with Oral and Head and Neck Cancer) *Professionally-run.* Support for persons with oral, head and neck cancer. Families welcome. Guest speakers, newsletter and phone help. Meets 2nd Thurs., 6-7pm, Monmouth Medical Center, 300 Second Ave., Radiation Oncology Conference Room, Long Branch. Pre-registration required. Before attending call 732-923-6575 (day).

Us TOO (Prostate Cancer Support Group) Provides support and education for men with prostate cancer and their families. Meets 1st Thurs., 7-9pm, Monmouth Medical Center, Goldsmith Wellness Center, 300 Second Ave., Long Branch. Pre-registration required. Before attending call Cancer Services 732-923-7269.

Younger Generation *Professionally-run.* Mutual support for individuals (ages 20-45) with all cancers. Rap sessions and guest speakers. Meets 1st Tues., 6-8pm, Jersey Shore Medical Center, 1945 Route 33, Neptune. Before attending call 732-776-2380.

MORRIS

Children's Group *Professionally-run.* Provides support to children (ages 6-12) dealing with family issues of cancer. Building is handicapped accessible. Group meets for 8 week sessions. Group for parents meets concurrently. For information call Brandy Johnson 973-625-6176 (day).

Head and Neck Cancer Support for any person afflicted with head and neck cancer. Meets 3rd Wed., 1:30-3pm, Carol G. Simon Cancer Center, Morristown Memorial Hospital, 100 Madison Ave., 3rd Floor, Conference Room, Morristown. Call Catherine Owens, LCSW 973-971-5169.

Living with Cancer *Professionally-run.* Support and information for people with cancer, their families and supportive friends to help them adjust. Building is handicapped accessible. Meetings vary, 7-8:30pm, Saint Clare's Hospital, 25 Pocono Rd., Urban 2 Conference Room, Denville. Before attending call Brandy 973-625-6176 (day). *E-mail:* bjohnson@saintclares.org

Lung Cancer Support Group Support for people at any stage of lung cancer. Spouses are welcome. Meets 4th Wed., 2-3:30pm, Carol G. Simon Cancer Center, Morristown Memorial Hospital, 100 Madison Ave., 3rd Floor, Conference Room, Morristown. Call Catherine Owens, LCSW 973-971-5169.

Multiple Myeloma Support Group *Professionally-run.* Mutual support for patients, families and friends affected by multiple myeloma. Guest speakers. Meets 4th Mon., 1:30-3pm, Carol G. Simon Cancer Center, Morristown Memorial Hospital, 100 Madison Ave., Cancer Center Conference Room, Morristown. Call Ruth Lin, RN 973-971-7742 (day) or Anne Kahn, LCSW 973-971-4269 (day).

Pancreatic Cancer Support Group *Professionally-run.* Support for anyone with a diagnosis of pancreatic cancer. Families welcome. Guest speakers. Building handicapped accessible. Meets 3rd Thurs., 11am-12:30pm, Morristown Memorial Hospital, Carol G. Simon Cancer Center, 100 Madison Ave., Morristown. Call 973-971-6299 (day).

Thyroid Cancer Support Group *Professionally-run.* Support and education for persons with thyroid cancer and their families. Guest speakers, rap sessions Meets 3rd Tues., 7-8:30pm, Saint Clare's Hospital, Silby cafeteria (in the back), Pocono Rd., Denville. For information call Diane Wood 973-625-6176 (day) or Candy Larkin 973-334-1006 (day). 973-334-1006.

Tri-County New Voice Laryngectomee Support Group *(Morris/Sussex/Warren counties)* Mutual support and social activities for laryngectomees. Also includes neck, head and or oral cancers. Hospital visitation for new laryngectomees. Family and friends are welcome. Building is handicapped accessible. Meeting day and time varies, 7:15pm, Saint Clare's Hospital, Silby Hall, 25 Pocono Rd., Denville. Call Tom Beneventine 973-694-8417.

Us TOO (Prostate Cancer Support Group) *Professionally-run.* Education and support for prostate cancer survivors and their supportive family members and friends. Building is handicapped accessible. Meets 2nd Tues., (except July/Aug.), 7:30-9pm, Saint Clare's Hospital, Silby Cafeteria, 25 Pocono Rd., Denville. Before attending call Diane Wood 973-625-6176.

Us TOO (Prostate Cancer Support Group) Provides support and education for those with prostate cancer and their families. Monthly speaker and individual support groups. All are welcome. Building is handicapped accessible. Meets 1st Tues., 7:30-9:30pm, Morristown Memorial Hospital, Malcolm Forbes Ampitheater, 100 Madison Ave., Morristown. Call Bill Grassmyer 973-895-2135 or Catherine Owens, LCSW 973-971-5169 (day).

Women to Women Support Group *Professionally-run.* Mutual support for women living with cancer. Meets 1st and 3rd Tues., 1-2:30pm, Chilton Memorial Hospital, 97 West Parkway, Collins Pavillion, Pompton Plains. Call 973-831-5311; TTY: 973-831-5000.

OCEAN

Cancer Concern Center Support for those coping with cancer. Family and friends welcome. Yoga, meditation and wigs. Phone help available. Meets Tues., noon-1pm and Wed., 6:30-8:30pm, Cancer Concern Center, 1101 Richmond Ave., Route 35 South, Point Pleasant. Call 732-701-0250.

"What do we live for if not to make life less difficult for each other."–George Elloit

Colorectal Cancer Support Group *Professionally-run.* Mutual support for persons with colorectal cancer. Family and friends welcome. Guest speakers and phone help. Building is handicapped accessible. Meets 2nd Wed., 3pm, Community Medical Center, 99 Route 37 West, Radiation - Oncology Dept., Toms River. Call Sherry 732-557-8270 (day).

Lung Cancer Support Group *Professionally-run.* Support and education for anyone with lung cancer. Meets 2nd Thurs., 11am-noon, Ocean Medical Center, Brick. Pre-registration required. Before attending call 1-800-560-9990 (24 hr.).

Prostate Cancer Support Group Provides support and education for men diagnosed with prostate cancer and their families. Meets 3rd Thurs., 2pm, The Lighthouse, 591 Lakehurst Rd., Toms River. Call 1-800-621-0096 (day).

SPOHNC (Support for People with Oral and Head and Neck Cancer) *Professionally-run.* Support for persons with oral, head and neck cancer. Families welcome. Guest speakers, newsletter and phone help. Meets last Thurs., 3pm, Community Medical Center, 99 Route 37 West, Radiation - Oncology Dept., Toms River. Call Sherry 732-557-8270 (day). *Website:* http://www.spohnc.org

SOMERSET

Cancer Support Group *Professionally-run.* Provides support for cancer patients to share thoughts, feelings and information with others diagnosed with cancer. Meets Thurs., 10-11:30am, The Wellness Community of Central New Jersey, 3 Crossroads Dr., Bedminster. Pre-registration required. Before attending call Karen Larsen, LCSW 908-658-5400 (day).

Caregiver Support Group *Professionally-run.* Support for family members and friends who are caring for an adult with cancer. Sharing of thoughts, feelings and information. Meetings vary, The Wellness Community of Central New Jersey, 3 Crossroads Dr., Bedminster. Pre-registration required. Before attending call Ellen Levine, LCSW 908-658-5400 (day).

Central Jersey Multiple Myeloma Support Group *Professionally-run.* Mutual support for patients, families and friends affected by multiple myeloma. Meets 1st Wed., 7pm, Steeplechase Cancer Center, 110 Rehill Ave., Somerville. Call Paula Van Riper 908-725-4948 (day).

Gynecological Cancer Networking Group *Professionally-run.* Provides an opportunity for individuals with a gynecological cancer diagnosis to discuss and exchange information. Meets 4th Wed., 11am-12:30pm, The Wellness

Community of Central New Jersey, 3 Crossroads Dr., Bedminster. Call Karen Larsen, LCSW 908-658-5400 (day).

Kidney Cancer Networking Group *Professionally-run.* Provides an opportunity for individuals with kidney cancer and their loved ones to discuss and exchange information. Rap sessions. Meetings vary, The Wellness Community of Central New Jersey, 3 Crossroads Dr., Bedminster. Call Ellen Levine, LCSW 908-658-5400 ext. 2. *Website:* http://www.thewellnesscommunity.org/cnj *E-mail:* elevine@thewellnesscommunity.org

Kids Connect/Parents Connect *Professionally-run.* Support for children (ages 7-17) to help them cope with a parent's cancer diagnosis. Children participate in creative activities to help them express their feelings. Parents develop skills to talk with children about their cancer. Meetings vary, The Wellness Community of Central New Jersey, 3 Crossroads Dr., Bedminster. Pre-registration required. Before attending call Karen Larsen, LCSW 908-658-5400 (day).

Life After Cancer Networking Group *Professionally-run.* Support for people who are well beyond day to day treatment of cancer. Building is handicapped accessible. Meets 2nd Wed., 6:30-8pm, The Wellness Community, 3 Crossroads Dr., Bedminister. Call Karen Larsen 908-658-5400 (day). *Website:* http://www.thewellnesscommunity.org/cnj

Living with Cancer Networking Group *Professionally-run.* Support for people who are newly diagnosed or currently in treatment for cancer. Building is handicapped accessible. Meets 1st Wed., 6:30-8pm, The Wellness Community, 3 Crossroads Dr., Bedminister. Call Karen Larsen 908-658-5400 (day). *Website:* http://www.thewellnesscommunity.org/cnj

SUSSEX

Blood Cancer Family Support Group *Professionally-run.* Support for patients affected by leukemia, lymphoma and myeloma. Families and friends welcome. Rap sessions and guest speakers. Building is handicapped accessible. Meets monthly, 6:30-8pm, Sparta Cancer Center, Sparta. To register call Deborah Halpern 908-956-6607 ext. 12. Before attending each session call Kathryn Cramer or Nina Sullivan 973-726-0005 (day). *Website:* http://www.lls.org/nnj *E-mail:* Deborah.Halpern@lls.org

"Man to Man" Prostate Cancer Support Group An educational, information sharing and emotional support group designed to meet the challenge of living with prostate cancer for men and their partners. Educational series, literature and guest speakers. Building is handicapped accessible. Meets 3rd Tues., 6:30-8:30pm, Sparta Health and Wellness Center, 89 Sparta Ave., Sparta. Call Michele Capossela 973-285-8010 (day). *E-mail:* Michele.capossela@cancer.org

Northern NJ Chapter Leukemia and Lymphoma Society *Professionally-run.* Emotional support and educational information for newly diagnosed adult survivors and family members whose lives have been touched by a blood cancer diagnosis. Mutual sharing, guest speakers, advocacy and literature. Meets last Wed., 6:30-8pm, The Sparta Cancer Center, 89 Sparta Ave., Sparta. Pre-registration required. Call Deborah Halpern, MSW, LCSW 908-956-6607 (day). *Website:* http://www.lls.org/nnj *E-mail:* Deborah.Halpern@lls.org

UNION

Gynecological Cancer Support Group *Professionally-run.* Support for women afflicted with gynecological cancers at any stage of diagnosis and treatment. Resources and coping strategies are shared. Building is handicapped accessible. Meets 4th Tues., noon-1:15pm, Pathways, 79 Maple St., Summit. Pre-registration required. Before attending call 908-273-4242 ext. 154.

Hearts and Hands *Professionally-run.* An open drop-in cancer support group offering patients and caregivers the opportunity to support each other. Members may knit, crochet or do other crafts during meeting. Building is handicapped accessible. Meets Thurs., 2-4pm, Overlook Hospital, 99 Beauvoir Ave., Conference Room 1, Summit. Call Lee Anne Caffrey 908-522-5349 (day) or Kristen Scarlett 908-522-5255 (day).

Insight *Professionally-run.* Support for cancer patients and their families to talk about problems and issues in dealing with cancer. Building is handicapped accessible. Meets 3rd Thurs., 7-9pm, Jewish Community Center, 1391 Martine Ave., Scotch Plains. Call Mary Aloia 732-321-7000 ext. 62355 (day) or Jewish Community Center 908-889-8800.

N.J. Chapter - Metro New York Carcinoid Support Group Provides help and education to patients and caregivers. Discusses experiences and options for those with carcinoid or other neuroendocrine tumors. Building is handicapped accessible. Meets 1st Sun., 1:30pm (except Feb., Apr., July, Aug., Oct.), Crossroads Christian Fellowship, 2815 Morris Ave., Union. Call Jim Weiveris 609-812-9294 or Judy Golz 201-891-2259 (eve.). *Website:* http://www.carcinoid.us *E-mail:* caring4noids@aol.com

Northern NJ Chapter Leukemia and Lymphoma Society *Professionally-run.* Emotional support and educational information for newly diagnosed adult survivors and family members whose lives have been touched by a blood cancer diagnosis (leukemia, lymphomia, Hodgkins disease, myeloma and MDS). Mutual sharing, guest speakers', advocacy and literature. Meets 3rd Mon., 10:30am-noon, The Leukemia and Lymphoma Society, 14 Commerce Dr., Suite 301, Cranford. Call Deborah Halpern, MSW, LCSW 908-956-6607 (day). *Website:* http://www.lls.org/nnj *E-mail:* Deborah.Halpern@lls.org

WARREN

Women's Cancer Group Mutual support and encouragement for women with any type of cancer and for those women in recovery from cancer. Building is handicapped accessible. Meets 1st Thurs., 7-8:30pm, Lutheran Church of the Good Shepherd, 168 Route 94, Blairstown. Call Kathy 908-362-6344.

NATIONAL

Cancer Care, Inc. *National. Founded 1944.* Support for cancer patients and their families. Financial assistance, information and referrals, community and professional education. On-going telephone, online and in-person support groups. Free counseling. Write: Cancer Care, Inc., 275 Seventh Ave., New York, NY 10001. Call 1-800-813-4673; Fax: 212-719-0263. *Website:* http://www.cancercare.org *E-mail:* info@cancercare.org

Candlelighters Childhood Cancer Foundation *International. 32 groups in U.S. Founded 1970.* Support for parents of children and adolescents with cancer, their families, adult survivors of childhood cancer, and the professionals working with them. Links parents, families and groups. Provides psychosocial support, educational resource materials and advocates on behalf of childhood cancer. Newsletter, youth newsletter, educational materials and publication list. Write: Candlelighters Childhood Cancer Foundation, P.O. Box 498, Kensington, MD 20895-0498. Call 1-800-366-2223 or 301-962-3520; Fax: 301-962-3521. *Website:* http://www.candlelighters.org *E-mail:* staff@candlelighters.org

Carcinoid Cancer Foundation *National. Founded 1968.* Provides support, information and educational materials to patients, caregivers and medical professionals dealing with carcinoid cancer and related neuroendocrine tumors. Support groups located throughout the United States. Online support groups, e-mail and toll-free telephone support available. Conducts conferences, supports research and maintains a carcinoid and neuroendocrine tumor database. Write: Carcinoid Cancer Foundation, 333 Mamaroneck Ave., #492, White Plains, NY

10605. Call 1-888-722-3132 or 914-683-1001 (Tues.-Thurs., 10:00am-4:00pm EST). *Website:* http://www.carcinoid.org *E-mail:* carcinoid@optonline.net

DES Action *National. Founded 1983.* Mutual support and education for DES-exposed women, with a special focus on DES cancer issues. Provides research, advocacy and medical/legal resources. Write: DES Action, 2925 Garber St., Berkeley, CA 94705. *Website:* http://descancer.org

International Myeloma Foundation *International network. 89+ groups in the US. Founded 1990.* Mission is to improve the quality of life of myeloma patients while working toward a prevention and a cure. Educational and supportive programs, information packets, phone support and newsletter. Networks patients together for mutual support. Referrals to self-help groups nationwide. Guidelines offered to assist those interested in starting a group. Write: International Myeloma Foundation, 12650 Riverside Dr., Suite 206, North Hollywood, CA 91607. Call 818-487-7455 or 1-800-452-2873 (Mon-Fri, 9am-4pm PST); Fax: 818-487-7454. *Website:* http://www.myeloma.org *E-mail:* TheIMF@myeloma.org

Intestinal Multiple Polyposis and Colorectal Cancer (IMPACC) *National network. Founded 1986.* Support network to help patients and families dealing with familial polyposis and hereditary colon cancer. Provides information and referrals, encourages research, educates professionals and public. Phone support network, correspondence and literature. Write: IMPACC, c/o Ann Fagan, P.O. Box 11, Conyngham, PA 18219. Call Ann Fagan 570-788-1818 (day) or 570-788-3712 (eve); Fax: 570-788-4046. *E-mail:* impacc@epix.net

Kidney Cancer Association *National. Founded 1990.* Provides information about kidney cancer to patients and doctors. Sponsors research and advocates on behalf of patients. E-newsletter, literature, conferences, information and referrals. Write: Kidney Cancer Association, 1234 Sherman Ave., Suite 203, Evanston, IL 60202. Call 1-800-850-9132 or 847-332-1051 (Mon.-Fri., 9am-5pm CST); Fax: 847-332-2978. *Website:* http://www.kidneycancer.org *E-mail:* office@kidneycancer.org

Kids Konnected *National. 17 affiliated groups. Founded 1993.* Opportunity for children who have a parent with cancer to connect with other children in similar situations for support and understanding. Groups are headed by youth leaders and co-facilitated by professionals. Youth Leadership program, monthly meetings, newsletter, summer camps, information and referrals. Call 1-800-899-2866 or 949-582-5443 (24 hr.). *Website:* http://www.kidskonnected.org *E-mail:* info@kidskonnected.org

Leukemia and Lymphoma Society, The *(BILINGUAL) National. 66 chapters. Founded 1949.* Educational materials, patient financial aid, support services for patients, families and friends coping with leukemia, lymphoma, myeloma and other blood cancers. Support group meetings schedule depends on location. Patients should consult local chapter. Live help online (10am-5pm EST). Write: The Leukemia and Lymphoma Society, 1311 Mamaroneck Ave., Suite 310, White Plains, NY 10605. Call 1-800-955-4572 or 914-949-5213. *Website:* http://www.lls.org

Lymphoma Research Foundation *National. 20 chapters. Founded 1991.* Devoted exclusively to funding lymphoma research and providing patients and healthcare professionals with critical information on the disease. Provides information and emotional support for lymphoma patients and their families. Offers free educational materials, lymphoma helpline, national buddy program, quarterly newsletter, annual patient educational forum and local seminars. Fundraises for research. Advocacy. Some materials available in Spanish and Chinese. Write: Lymphoma Research Foundation, 8800 Venice Blvd., Suite 207, Los Angeles, CA 90034. Call 310-204-7040 or 1-800-500-9976; Fax: 310-204-7043. *Website:* http://www.lymphoma.org *E-mail:* LRF@lymphoma.org

Man To Man Program *(BILINGUAL) National. 325 affiliated groups. Founded 1990.* Support and education for men with prostate cancer to enable them to better understand their options and to make informed decisions. Phone support, information and referrals, support group meetings, education and support visitation program. Newsletter. Some chapters invite wives and partners.; other chapters have wives and partners meet separately. Assistance available for starting new groups. Call the American Cancer Society 1-800-227-2345. *Website:* http://www.cancer.org

Mautner Project, The National Lesbian Health Organization *Model. Several groups in Washington, DC. Founded 1990.* Cancer support and survivorship groups for lesbian, bisexual and transgender women who partner with women (WPWs) their partners and caregivers. Bereavement support groups for WPWs who have lost a partner, friend or loved one. Smoking cessation groups for the lesbian, gay, bisexual and transgender community. Health self-empowerment groups for black WPWs. Provides phone and online support to WPWs outside the DC-Metro area. Provides LGBT cultural competency training to health care professionals and their staff members. Educates the lesbian/WPW community about health issues. Information and referrals, phone support, literature, newsletter and advocacy. Write: Mautner Project, 1875 Conn. Ave. NW, Suite 710, Washington, DC 20009. Call 1-866-628-8637 or 202-332-5536 (Mon-Fri, 9am-5:30pm EST); Fax: 202-332-0662; TDD: 202-332-5536. *Website:* http://www.mautnerproject.org *E-mail:* mautner@mautnerproject.org

National Cervical Cancer Coalition *International. Founded 1996. 4500+ members.* Provides on-going support system for women, family members and friends facing issues related to cervical cancer, HPV and other HPV cancers. Offers phone pal system matching women together for support, online moderated message board, newsletter, annual conferences, information and referrals. How-to materials on starting local NCCC chapter available. Write: National Cervical Cancer Coalition, 6520 Platt Ave., #693, West Hills, CA 91307. Call 1-800-685-5531 or 818-909-3849; Fax: 818-780-8199. *Website:* http://www.nccc-online.org *E-mail:* info@nccc-online.org

National Coalition for Cancer Survivorship *National network. Founded 1986.* Grassroots network that works on behalf of persons with any type of cancer. Mission is to advocate for quality of cancer care for all Americans by leading and strengthening the survivorship movement, empowering cancer survivors and advocating for policy issues affecting survivors' quality of life. Provides information on employment and insurance issues, referrals and publications. Newsletter. Guidelines available to help start a similar group. Write: National Coalition for Cancer Survivorship, 1010 Wayne Ave., Suite 770, Silver Spring, MD 20910. Call 301-650-9127 (Mon.-Fri., 8:30am-5:30pm EST); Fax: 301-565-9670. *Website:* http://www.canceradvocacy.org *E-mail:* info@canceradvocacy.org

National Ovarian Cancer Coalition *National. 80 affiliated divisions. Founded 1995.* Promotes education and awareness regarding ovarian cancer for patients, families and medical community. Information and referrals, networking, conferences, literature and phone support. Helps develop statewide divisions. Write: National Ovarian Cancer Coalition, 2501 Oak Lawn, Suite 435, Dallas TX 75219. Call 1-888-682-7426. *Website:* http://www.ovarian.org *E-mail:* nocc@ovarian.org

Patient Advocates for Advanced Cancer Treatment (PAACT) *International. 150 affiliated groups. Founded 1984.* Provides support and advocacy for prostate cancer patients, their families and the general public at risk. Information relative to the advancements in the detection, diagnosis, evaluation and treatment of prostate cancer. Information, referrals, phone help, conferences and newsletter. Group development guidelines. Write: PAACT, P.O. Box 141695, Grand Rapids, MI 49514-1695. Call 616-453-1477; Fax: 616-453-1846. *Website:* http://www.paactusa.org *E-mail:* paact@paactusa.org

People Living Through Cancer *Model. 35 groups in New Mexico. Founded 1983.* Helps cancer survivors and their loved ones make informed choices and improve the quality of life by sharing in a community of people who have "been there." Newsletter, information and referrals, support groups and advocacy.

Dues $35/yr. (includes subscription to journal). Conducts national training for American Indians and Alaskan natives who are interested in developing cancer survivorship programs based on a grassroots program serving Pueblo Indians. Write: People Living Through Cancer, 3401 Candelaria NE, Suite A, Albuquerque, NM 87107. Call 505-242-3263; Fax: 505-242-6756. *Website:* http://www.pltc.org *E-mail:* pltc@pltc.org

Pregnant with Cancer Network *National. Founded 1997.* Created by three women who were diagnosed with cancer while pregnant. Mission is to let women know that they are not alone facing cancer and pregnancy. Links women together who have a similar diagnosis. Newsletter. Write: The Pregnant with Cancer Network, P.O. Box 1243, Buffalo, NY 14220. Call 1-800-743-4471. *Website:* http://www.pregnantwithcancer.org

SHARE: Self-Help for Women with Breast or Ovarian Cancer *(BILINGUAL) Model. Founded 1976.* Provides support to women with breast or ovarian cancer, their families, and friends. Support groups led by trained survivors. Cutting edge educational forums and advocacy activities held throughout the five boroughs of New York City. Write: SHARE, 1501 Broadway, Suite 704A, New York, NY 10036. Call 1-866-891-2392; Fax: 212-869-3431; Breast Cancer Hotline: 212-382-2111; Ovarian Hotline: 212-719-1204; Latina Hotline (Spanish): 212-719-4454; New York State Ovarian Hotline (toll-free): 1-866-537-4273. *Website:* http://www.sharecancersupport.org

Support for People with Oral and Head and Neck Cancer (SPOHNC) *National. 60+ affiliated groups. Founded 1991.* Patient-directed self-help program offering information, encouragement, support, acceptance and self-expression for persons with oral, head and neck cancer. *National* Survivor Volunteer Network offering one-on-one support, phone support, educational programs and publications. Assistance in starting groups. Membership dues $25 (includes 8 newsletters). Write: SPOHNC, P.O. Box 53, Locust Valley, NY 11560-0053. Call 1-800-377-0928; Fax: 516-671-8794. *Website:* http://www.spohnc.org *E-mail:* info@spohnc.org

ThyCa: Thyroid Cancer Survivors' Association, Inc. *National.* Support, education and communication for people with all types of thyroid cancer, as well as caregivers. Outreach to the public for thyroid cancer awareness and early detection. Nine online support groups, local support groups, free online newsletter, free downloadable low-iodine cookbook, free regional workshops, annual international conference and free thyroid cancer awareness brochures. Thyroid Cancer Awareness Month, funding for research and educational website. Write: ThyCa: Thyroid Cancer Survivors' Association, Inc., P.O. Box

1545, New York, NY 10159-1545. Call 1-877-588-7904; Fax: 630-604-6078. *Website:* http://www.thyca.org *E-mail:* thyca@thyca.org

Us Too International Prostate Cancer Education and Support Network *International. 300 affiliated groups. Founded 1990.* Education and support provided for men and their families with fellowship and peer counseling. Timely, personalized, unbiased and reliable information about prostate cancer. Monthly newsletter distributed through support groups and also on website. Write: Us Too International Prostate Cancer Education and Support Network, 5003 Fairview Ave., Downers Grove, IL 60515-5286. Call 1-800-808-7866 or 630-795-1002 (Mon.-Fri., 9am-5pm CST); Fax: 630-795-1602. *Website:* http://www.ustoo.org *E-mail:* ustoo@ustoo.org

ONLINE

ACOR (Association of Cancer Online Resources) *Online.* Provides over 150 e-mail support groups for patients, caregivers and survivors to share their experiences with many different cancers – such as lung, colon, melanoma, endometrial, pancreatic, metastatic, stomach, testicular, pediatric and rare. Covers related issues like fatigue, finance and other situations. *Website:* http://www.acor.org (click on "Mailing Lists")

Bladder Cancer Advocacy Network *Online. Founded 2005.* National advocacy organization dedicated to improving public awareness of bladder cancer, increasing research directed towards the diagnosis, treatment and cure of the disease. Weekly online support chats. Plans to help local chapters nationwide. *Website:* http://www.bcan.org. *E-mail:* dzquale@bcan.org

Cancer and Careers *Online.* A resource for working women with cancer, their employers, coworkers and caregivers. Offers first-hand experiences and articles for working women with cancer. Provides resource information and publications via the website. *Website:* http://www.cancerandcareers.org *E-mail:* ksweeney@cew.org

DES Action *National. Founded 1983.* Mutual support and education for DES-exposed women, with a special focus on DES cancer issues. Provides research advocacy and medical/legal resources. Write: DES Action, 2925 Garber St., Berkeley, CA 94705. *Website:* http://descancer.org

FORCE (Facing Our Risk of Cancer Empowered) *Online. Founded 1999.* Support and education for women whose family history and genetic status put them at high risk of getting ovarian or breast cancer. Open to family members.

Provides resources for women to determine if they are at high risk. Forums, chats, bulletin boards, member profiles and phone support network. *Website:* http://www.facingourrisk.org/ *E-mail:* info@facingourrisk.org

Group Loop *Online.* Support for teens with cancer and their parents. Weekly scheduled online support groups with professionals, discussion boards, resources, information and news about many types of cancers and their affect on teens. *Website:* http://www.grouploop.org

Johns Hopkins Disease Information *Online.* Provides information and support to cancer patients and their families. Specific cancer websites include: colon, pancreas, ovarian, gallbladder and bile duct. Also has message boards for Barrett's esophagus and non-cancerous conditions. *Website:* http://www.pathology2.jhu.edu/department/patientcare.cfm (select condition from drop down menu)

CELIAC SPRUE / GLUTEN INTOLERANCE

BERGEN

American Celiac Society - Bergen County Chapter Phone support for people with celiac disease. Call Laurie Schlussel 201-573-0397. *E-mail:* fit4us1227@aol.com

Celiac Disease Support Group for Parents *Professionally-run.* Information, sharing, mutual support and education for parents of children with celiac disease. Families welcome. Rap sessions, guest speakers, literature and quarterly newsletter. Building is handicapped accessible. Meetings vary, Don Imus Pediatric Center, Hackensack University Medical Center, Hackensack. Call Joseph Chan 201-336-8840 (day).

CAMDEN

Celiac Sprue Association (Southern New Jersey Chapter) Mutual support and information to persons diagnosed with celiac sprue (gluten sensitive enteropathy), dermatitis herpetiformis and parents of celiac children. Guest speakers, rap sessions, literature and phone help. Annual dues $20/yr. new members; $15/yr./thereafter. Meets 1st Sun., 2pm (except July/Aug.), West Jersey Hospital, Barry Brown Health Education Center, Evesham Rd. and Carnie Blvd., Voorhees. Call Patti Townsend 856-854-5508 (eve) or Bill Lucas 609-387-7139. *Website:* http://www.home.earthlink.net/~celiac9/index.html *E-mail:* celiac9@earthlink.net

MIDDLESEX

Central NJ Celiac Sprue and Dermatitis Herpetiformis Group Dietary support for persons with celiac sprue and dermatitis herpetiformis. Also Cel-Kids Network. Dues $20/yr. Meeting day and time varies, East Brunswick. Before attending call Diane Paley 732-679-6566. *Website:* http://www.csaceliacs.org

MONMOUTH

ROCK (Raising Our Celiac Kids) Support Support group for parents of children with celiac sprue. Events planned and activities for school-aged children. Building is handicapped accessible. Meetings vary, 7-8:45pm, Monmouth County Library, Symmes Rd., Manalapan. Call Elissa 732-677-2700.

WARREN

Celiac Sprue Association/Gluten Free 101 Support Group Support group dedicated to helping those with celiac disease and its complication, dermatitis herpetiformis, learn to live safely on the gluten free diet. Literature, speakers bureau, advocacy, social and phone help. Building is handicapped accessible. Meets 2nd Wed., 7:30-9:30pm, Warren Hospital, Farley Education Center, Phillipsburg. Call Gary Powers 610-438-0205 (eve). *Website:* http://www.csaceliacs.org *E-mail:* gppowers14@earthlink.net

NATIONAL

American Celiac Society / Dietary Support Coalition *National. 78 affiliated chapters. Founded 1976.* Mutual support and information for celiac-sprue patients, families and health care professionals. Buddy system, visitation, phone help system, newsletter and participation in educational efforts. Also supports dermatitis herpetiformis, Crohn's disease, lactose intolerance and other food allergies. Write: American Celiac Society, c/o Mrs. Annette Bentley, P.O. Box 23455, New Orleans, LA 70183. Call Mrs. Annette Bentley 504-737-3293. *Website:* http://www.americanceliacsociety.org *E-mail:* americanceliacsociety@yahoo.com or amerceliacsoc@netscape.net (please do not send attachments)

Celiac Disease Foundation *National. Founded 1990.* Creates awareness and provides services and support for patients, their families, medical and healthcare professionals seeking information about celiac disease/dermatitis herpetiformis. Free information packets. Annual membership $35.00. Handbook "Guidelines

For a Gluten-Free Lifestyle" is included with annual membership or sold separately for $10. Members receive a quarterly newsletter and update notices of upcoming events. Brochure and quick start diet guide available in English and Spanish. Write: Celiac Disease Foundation, 13251 Ventura Blvd., Suite 1, Studio City, CA 91604. Call 818-990-2354 (day); Fax: 818-990-2379. *Website:* http://www.celiac.org *E-mail:* cdf@celiac.org

Celiac Sprue Association/United States of America, Inc. *National. 100 chapters and 60 resource units. Founded 1969.* Provides educational materials on celiac sprue, dermatitis herpetiformis and basics for the gluten-free diet for patients, parents of children with celiac sprue and professionals. Children's camp in August in Rhode Island. CelKids network. Provides opportunities for support groups and networking with patients and professionals. Newsletter and annual conference. Group development guidelines. Write: Celiac Sprue Association USA, P.O. Box 31700, Omaha, NE 68131-0700. Call 1-877-272-4272; Fax: 402-643-4108. *Website:* http://www.csaceliacs.org *E-mail:* celiacs@csaceliacs.org

Gluten Intolerance Group of North America *National network. 30+ affiliated groups. Founded 1974.* Mission is to increase awareness by providing accurate and up-to-date information, education and support to persons with gluten intolerance, celiac disease/dermatitis herpetiformis, their families, health care professionals and the public. Offers News magazine ($35), information and referral, conferences, e-mail support, guidance to those starting groups, group development guidelines and cookbooks. Write: Gluten intolerance Group, 31214 124th Ave. SE, Auburn, WA 98092. Call 253-833-6655; Fax: 253-833-6675. *Website:* http://www.gluten.net *E-mail:* info@gluten.net

CHRONIC FATIGUE SYNDROME

STATEWIDE

NJ Chronic Fatigue Syndrome Association, Inc. Support for people with chronic fatigue syndrome. All welcome. Educational series, guest speakers, speakers bureau, advocacy, social group, literature, medical conferences and phone help. Newsletter $30/yr. Call 1-888-835-3677. *Website:* http://www.njcfsa.org

Need help finding a specific group? Give us a call – we're here to help!
*Call **1-800-367-6274**.*

ATLANTIC

Atlantic County Chronic Fatigue Syndrome Support Group Offers emotional support and sharing of the latest information on chronic fatigue syndrome for those afflicted, as well as their families. Under 18 welcome. Doctor referrals available. Rap sessions, guest speakers, phone help. Meets 2nd Sun., 2-4pm (except July/Aug.), AtlanticCare Regional Medical Center, Mainland Division, Jimmie Leeds Rd., Pomona. Call Betty McConnell 609-748-3559 (eve.). *Website:* http://www.njcfsa.org

BERGEN

Chronic Fatigue Syndrome Association Support Group Support, education and mutual assistance for patients with chronic fatigue syndrome, their family, friends and interested professionals. Meets 3rd Sun., 2pm (Sept.-May; (no meeting July/Aug.); 2nd Sun., June), YWCA/YMCA of Ridgewood, 112 Oak St., Ridgewood. Call 1-888-835-3677 (voicemail - day). *E-mail:* pat.njcfsa@larosas.net

MERCER

Chronic Fatigue Syndrome Support Group of Mercer County Mutual support, education and sharing of resources for persons with chronic fatigue syndrome, their families, caregivers, and friends. Literature and some social activities. Meets 2nd Sun., 2-4pm, Robert Wood Johnson University Hospital at Hamilton, Outpatient Services Building, 1 Hamilton Health Place, Auditorium, Hamilton. Call 609-584-5900 (ext. 1).

MONMOUTH

Chronic Fatigue Syndrome/ Epstein-Barr/ Fibromyalgia Support *Professionally-run.* Provides support for chronic fatigue syndrome, Epstein-Barr and fibromyalgia patients, their families, friends and significant others. Guest speakers. Building is handicapped accessible. Meets 3rd Sun., 10-11:30am, Monmouth Medical Center, 300 Second Ave., Long Branch. Pre-registration required. Call 732-923-6990 (day).

MORRIS

Morris County Chronic Fatigue Syndrome Support Group Mutual support and encouragement for persons diagnosed with chronic fatigue syndrome. Meets 2nd Sat., 2-3:30pm, Morris County Library, Conference Room, Hanover

Township. Call Peggy 973-765-0577 or Patty 973-335-7357. *E-mail:* pstrunck@optonline.net

WARREN

Fibromyalgia and Chronic Fatigue Support Group Provides education and support for those with fibromyalgia or chronic fatigue syndrome. Meets 1st Thurs., 7pm (Jan., Apr., July and Oct.), Warren Hospital, 185 Roseberry St., Farley Education Center, Phillipsburg. Before attending call 908-859-6735 (day).

NATIONAL

CFIDS Association, Inc. *National. Founded 1987.* Encouragement, information and advocacy for persons with chronic fatigue immune dysfunction syndrome. Publishs CFIDS Chronicle Newsletter ($35/US; $45/Canada; $60/Overseas/Air) and Research Newsletter. Write: CFIDS Association, P.O. Box 220398, Charlotte, NC 28222-0398. Call 704-365-2343 (resources). *Website:* http://www.cfids.org *E-mail:* cfids@cfids.org

CLEFT PALATE

MIDDLESEX

Craniofacial Girls/Guys Support Group *Professionally-run.* Separate mutual sharing support groups for girls (ages 11-16) and boys (ages 10-15) with cleft lip/palate. Also includes ear microtia and other facial syndromes. Guest speakers, education, social, phone help and buddy system. Building is handicapped accessible. Meets various Sun., Saint Peter's University Hospital, 254 Easton Ave., New Brunswick. Before attending call Helene Knee, LCSW 732-745-7943 (day).

MONMOUTH

Cleft Palate Support Group *Professionally-run.* Support group for parents of children with a cleft palate and/or cleft lip. Provides a forum for discussing shared concerns and exploring resources. Building is handicapped accessible. Meets 2nd Thurs., various times, Monmouth Medical Center, Long Branch. Registration required. Call Helene Henkel 732-923-7653.

NATIONAL

Cleft Palate Foundation *National network. Founded 1973.* Provides information and referrals to individuals with cleft lip and palate or other craniofacial anomalies. Referrals to local cleft palate/craniofacial teams for treatment and to local parent support groups. Free information on various aspects of clefting for parents and individuals. Write: Cleft Palate Foundation, 1504 E. Franklin St., Suite 102, Chapel Hill, NC 27514. Call 1-800-242-5338 or 919-933-9044; Fax: 919-933-9604. *Website:* http://www.cleftline.org *E-mail:* info@cleftline.org

Prescription Parents, Inc. *Model. Founded 1973.* Support group for families of children with cleft lip and palate. Education for parents of newborns. Family social events and phone support network. Write: Prescription Parents, Inc., P.O. Box 920554, Needham, MA 02492. Call 617-499-1936. *Website:* http://www.prescriptionparents.org *E-mail:* info@prescriptionparents.org

ONLINE

cleftAdvocate *Online.* Resource for educational materials, cleft/craniofacial team information, emotional support and more. Local and regional family networking for parents, kids, teens and adults. cleftAdvocate hosts the North American Craniofacial Family Conference for individuals and families dealing with all craniofacial conditions, including acquired facial differences (trauma, illness and disease). Write: cleftAdvocate, P.O. Box 751112 Las Vegas, NV 89136. Call 702-769-9264; Fax: 702-341-5351. *Website:* http://www.cleftadvocate.org *E-mail:* debbie@cleftadvocate.org

CYSTIC FIBROSIS

STATEWIDE

New Jersey CF Family Network Telephone network that provides mutual support for parents of children with cystic fibrosis. Up-to-date news regarding all aspects of CF including new treatments, equipment and physicians. Call Jean Gaito 973-492-3868 or Carol Russo 201-265-3503. *E-mail:* jcgaito@msn.com

NATIONAL

Cystic Fibrosis Foundation *National. 80 affiliated groups. Founded 1955.* Provides information and referrals to patients, families, caregivers and the general public. Accredits more than 115 care centers throughout the United

States. Newsletter, literature, fundraising, provides grants to researchers and conferences. Write: Cystic Fibrosis Foundation, 6931 Arlington Rd., Bethesda, MD 20814. Call 1-800-344-4823 or 301-951-4422; Fax: 301-951-6378. *Website:* http://www.cff.org *E-mail:* info@cff.org

DIABETES
(see also transplants)

STATEWIDE

American Diabetes Association (Northern NJ Area Office) *Professionally-run.* Support and educational programs for persons with diabetes, their families, professionals and public. Referrals to local groups and education programs. Adult and youth discussion groups. Fundraising for research. Write: American Diabetes Association, Center Point II, 1160 Route 22 East, Suite 103, Bridgewater, NJ 08807. Call 732-469-7979. *Website:* http://www.diabetes.org

Juvenile Diabetes Research Foundation Support and educational programs for parents of children with type 1 diabetes. Referrals to local chapter support groups. *Website:* http://www.jdrf.org

> **Central Jersey Chapter** Covers Essex, Union, Monmouth and Ocean. Write: Juvenile Diabetes Research Foundation, 740 Broad St., Suite 4, Shrewsbury, NJ 07702. Call 732-219-6654. *E-mail:* centraljersey@jdrf.org

> **Mid-Jersey Chapter** Covers Hudson, Hunterdon, Mercer, Middlesex, Morris and Somerset. Write: C.A.R.E.S., c/o Juvenile Diabetes Research Foundation, 28 Kennedy Blvd., Suite 180, East Brunswick, NJ 08816-1248. Call Erika Ferrigno 732-296-7171.

> **Northern NJ Chapter** Covers Bergen, Passaic, Sussex, Warren and Rockland. Write: Juvenile Diabetes Research Foundation, 560 Sylvan Ave., Englewood Cliffs, NJ 07632. Call 201-568-4838. *E-mail:* rockland@jdrf.org

"All of us are born for a reason, but all of us don't discover why. Success in life has nothing to do with what you gain in life or accomplish for yourself. It's what you do for others." --Danny Thomas

ATLANTIC

AtlantiCare Adult Diabetes Support Group *Professionally-run.* Support and education for adults with diabetes. Families welcome. Building is handicapped accessible. Rap sessions and guest speakers. Pre-registration required. Before attending call 1-888-569-1000 (day). *E-mail*: 1-888-569-1000@atlanticare.org

> **Atlantic City** Meetings vary, 7-8pm (Jan., Mar., May, July, Sept., Nov.), AtlantiCare Regional Medical Center, 1925 Pacific Ave.
> **Pomona** Meets 2nd Tues., 7-8pm, AtlantiCare Regional Medical Center, 65 West Jimmie Leads Rd.

BERGEN

Diabetes Support for Children and Their Families *Professionally-run.* Support for children up to age 18 with diabetes. Family members welcome. Discusses nutrition, school issues, new treatments, guest speakers, rap sessions and education. Meets 2nd Tues., 7-9pm (except July/Aug.), Valley Home Care, 15 Essex Rd., Paramus. Call Leslie Schifrien, MS, 201-291-6000 ext. 7116 (day) or Judy Brewer 201-447-6293 (day). *E-mail:* j.brewer.cde@gmail.com

Diabetes Support Group of Englewood Hospital and Medical Center *Professionally-run.* Support and education for persons with diabetes, their families and significant others. Teaches members to become self-sufficient in the daily management of their diabetes. Building is handicapped accessible. Meets 4th Tues., 7-8:30pm, Englewood Hospital and Medical Center, 350 Engle St., Englewood. Call Diabetes Educator 201-894-3335 (day).

Holy Name Hospital Diabetes Program *Professionally-run.* Provides support and education for people with diabetes and their families. Building is handicapped accessible. Meets 1st Wed., 7:30-9pm, Holy Name Hospital, 718 Teaneck Rd., Teaneck. Call Community Health Services 201-833-3371 (day).

Molly Diabetes Center Support Group *Professionally-run.* Mutual support for individuals with diabetes. Building is handicapped accessible. Meets 1st Mon., 6-7pm (except July/Aug.), Hackensack University Medical Center, Diabetes Center, 211 Essex St., Suite 101, Hackensack. Pre-registration required. Call Judith Shanberg 201-968-0585 (day).

BURLINGTON

Diabetes Friends Support and education for those who have diabetes. Guest speakers, weight management, stress management, nutrition and mutual aid. Meets 1st Tues., 7-8:30pm (except Dec., July, Aug.), Virtua Memorial Hospital,

Conference Center, 175 Madison Ave., Mt. Holly. Before attending call 1-888-847-8823 (day).

CAMDEN

Diabetes Friends Voorhees Support and education for people with diabetes. Guest speakers, weight management, stress management, nutrition and mutual aid. Meets 2nd Tues., 7-8:30pm (except Jan., July, Aug.), Virtua Health's Education Center, 106 Carnie Blvd., Voorhees. Before attending call 1-888-847-8823 (day).

Diabetes Support Group *Professionally-run.* Group deals with daily life challenges related to having diabetes (both type 1 and 2). Building is handicapped accessible. Meets 4th Mon., 1:30-3:00pm, Kennedy Center, 1099 White Horse Road, Voorhees. Call Tanya McKeown 856-566-2096 (day) or 1-800-522-1965.

Diabetes Support Group *Professionally-run.* Support for adults with diabetes to express their concerns, ask questions and get information. Guest speakers and literature. Building is handicapped accessible. Meets 2nd Wed., 7-8:30pm (Jan., Mar., May, Sept., Nov.), Cooper Community Health Education Center, 931 Centennial Blvd., Voorhees. Pre-registration required. Before attending call 1-800-826-6737 (day).

Teen Diabetes Support Group Support for teens (ages 13-19) with diabetes. Meets 4 times/yr., Virtua Health's Barry D. Brown Health Education Center, 106 Carnie Blvd., Voorhees. Before attending call 1-888-847-8823 (day).

CUMBERLAND

Adult Diabetes Support Group *Professionally-run.* Mutual support for people with type 1 or type 2 diabetes, their families, friends and caregivers. Phone help and guest speakers. Meets 1st Wed., 2pm, South Jersey Healthcare, 1505 West Sherman Ave., Vineland. Call Cathy Giovinazzi 856-641-7542. *E-mail:* giovinazzic@sjhs.com

ESSEX

Diabetes at Newark Beth Israel Medical Center Support Group *Professionally-run.* Support group for people of all ages with any type of diabetes. Offers an open format for educational and emotional concerns. Meets last Fri., noon, Newark Beth Israel Medical Center, 201 Lyons Ave., Newark. Pre-registration required. Call 973-926-3218 (day).

GLOUCESTER

Diabetes Support Group *Professionally-run.* Support and education for those who have diabetes. Families welcome. Guest speakers, literature and phone help. Building is handicapped accessible. Meets 4th Thurs. (3rd Thurs., Nov.; 2nd Thurs., Dec.), 6:45-8:45pm, Underwood-Memorial Hospital, 509 N. Broad St., Woodbury. Call Nancy Edwards 856-845-2476 (day).

HUDSON

Diabetes Support Group of Bayonne *Professionally-run.* Support and education for people of all ages and ethnic backgrounds with type 1 and type 2 diabetes, as well as their families. Rap sessions and guest speakers. Meets 2nd Tues., 7pm, Bayonne Medical Center, 29 East 29th St., Cafeteria, Bayonne. Before attending call 201-858-5219 (day). *E-mail:* mwilliams@bayonnemedicalcenter.org

HUNTERDON

Diabetes Education Series - "Diabetes After Dark" *Professionally-run.* Support and education in a comfortable environment for those with diabetes and their families to share feelings, listen and learn. Literature and guest speakers. Building is handicapped accessible. Meets 2nd Thurs., 7-8pm (except July/Aug.), Center for Nutrition and Diabetes Management, Wescott Medical Arts Center, 9100 Wescott Dr., Suite 102, Flemington. Call Alicia Dougherty 908-237-6920 ext. 7303 (day). *Website:* http://www.hmcdiabetes.org

Insulin Pump Support Group *Professionally-run.* Support for anyone, including friends and family, interested in or using insulin pump therapy as a treatment for diabetes. Building is handicapped accessible. Meets 3rd Tues., 6-7pm, Center for Nutrition and Diabetes Management, Wescott Medical Arts Center, 9100 Wescott Dr., Suite 102, Flemington. Call 908-237-6920 (day). *Website:* http://www.hmcdiabetes.org

Sugar Babies *Professionally-run.* Support for children with Type 1 diabetes and their families. Building is handicapped accessible. Meets 3rd Wed., 6:30pm, Center for Nutrition and Diabetes Management, Wescott Medical Arts Center, 9100 Wescott Dr., Suite 102, Flemington. Call Mary Waitlock RN, CDE 908-237-6920 ext. 7313 (day).

MERCER

Diabetes Support Group *Professionally-run.* Support and education for anyone living with diabetes. Families and friends welcome. Guest speakers, literature and phone help. Meetings vary, 7-8pm, Robert Wood Johnson University Hospital Hamilton, One Hamilton Health Pl., Hamilton. Before attending call 609-584-5900 (day).

MIDDLESEX

Adults with Diabetes *Professionally-run.* Support and education for persons with diabetes, their families and friends. Meets 1st Wed., 5:30-6:30pm, St. Peter's University Hospital, CARES Building, 4th Floor, Conference Room A, New Brunswick. Call Raquel Roland 732-745-8600 ext. 6667 (day).

Diabetes Type 2 Support Group *Professionally-run.* Support for people affected with type 2 diabetes. Meets 1st Wed., 1:30pm and 7pm; weight management meets 2nd and 4th Wed., 1:30pm; insulin pump group meets 2nd Tues., 7:15pm, Diabetes Center of New Jersey, 308 Talmadge Rd., Edison. Registration required. Before attending call 1-800-991-6668 (day).

MONMOUTH

Central Jersey Chapter Juvenile Diabetes Foundation Mutual support for insulin-dependent children and their parents to discuss solutions to the problems of day-to-day living with the disease. Phone help and peer counseling. Meets 3rd Wed. (every other month except July/Aug.), 7-8:30pm, Jersey Shore Medical Center, 2nd Floor, Ackerman Bldg., Conference Room 4, Neptune. For meeting information call 732-219-6654 (day). *Website:* http://www.jdrf.org

Diabetes Insulin Pump Support Group *Professionally-run.* Support and mutual aid for any person on an insulin pump or contemplating using a pump. Building is handicapped accessible. Meets 1st Wed. (Jan., Mar., May, July, Sept., Nov.), 7:30-9pm, Monmouth Medical Center, 300 Second Ave., Long Branch. Pre-registration required. Before attending call 732-923-5025.

Diabetes Support Group *Professionally-run.* Mutual support and education for people with diabetes. Family and friends welcome. Building is handicapped accessible. Meets 3rd Thurs., 5-6pm (except Nov.), Monmouth Medical Center, Long Branch. Pre-registration required. Before attending call 732-923-5025 (day).

Diabetes Support Group *Professionally-run.* Support and education for adults with diabetes. Families welcome. Guest speakers. Building is handicapped accessible. Meets 2nd Thurs., 6:30-8pm, Jersey Shore University Medical Center, 1945 Route 33, Room B-104, Neptune. Call Rosemary McCabe 732-776-4084 (day).

Pediatric Insulin Pump Support Group *Professionally-run.* Support group for children using an insulin pump. Families and caregivers welcome. Building is handicapped accessible. Meets 1st Wed., 6:30-7:30pm (Jan., Mar., May, July, Sept., Nov.), Monmouth Medical Center, 300 Second Ave., Long Branch. Pre-registration required. Before attending call 732-923-6990.

MORRIS

Diabetes Support Group *Professionally-run.* Mutual support for adults with diabetes and their families. Rap sessions, guest speakers, phone help and literature. Building is handicapped accessible. Meets 1st and 3rd Wed., 7:30-9pm and last Thurs., 10-11am, Saint Clare's Regional Diabetes Center, 400 W. Blackwell St., Dover. Before attending call 973-989-3603 (day).

Diabetes Type 2 Support Group *Professionally-run.* Education and support for people (ages 60+) with type 2 diabetes. Guest speakers and literature. Building is handicapped accessible. Meets 1st Fri., 10-11am, Chilton Memorial Hospital, 97 West Parkway, Collins Pavillion, Pompton Plains. Call Joyce Carlino 973-831-5216 (day).

Insulin Pump Support Group *Professionally-run.* Mutual support for diabetics who use an insulin pump. Families and professionals are welcome. Rap sessions, phone help, literature and guest speakers. Building is handicapped accessible. Meets last Mon., 7:30-9pm, Saint Clare's Regional Diabetes Center, 400 W. Blackwell St., Dover. Before attending call 973-989-3603 (day).

Pump Continuing Education Group *Professionally-run.* Support for people living with diabetes. Mutual sharing, educational and updates on current medical treatments. Meets 1st Thurs., every other month, 7-8pm, Morristown Hospital Diabetes Center, Morristown. Call Donna Naturale 973-971-5524.

Type 2 Continuing Education *Professionally-run.* Support for people living with diabetes. Mutual sharing, education and updates on current medical treatments. Meets 3rd Wed., 7-8pm, Morristown Hospital Diabetes Center, Bldg. B, Morristown. Call Donna Naturale 973-971-5524.

OCEAN

Center for Diabetes Support Group *Professionally-run.* Support, on-going education and social interaction for adults with type 1 or 2 diabetes and their caretakers. Rap sessions and guest speakers. Building is handicapped accessible. Meets once per month, Center for Diabetes, 731 Lacey Rd., Suite 1, Forked River. Call Kathleen Siciliano 732-349-5757.

Diabetic Support Group *Professionally-run.* Education and sharing for people with diabetes and their families. Meets 1st Thurs., 2pm, Ocean Club, 700 Route 9 South, Stafford Township. Call Eddi 609-978-3491 (day). *Website:* http://www.soch.org

PASSAIC

St. Joseph's Wayne Hospital Diabetes Support *Professionally-run.* Provides support and education for those with diabetes and their families. Monthly lectures by health professionals related to diabetes. Building is handicapped accessible. Meets 3rd Thurs. (except July, Aug., Dec.), St. Joseph's Wayne Hospital, 224 Hamburg Turnpike, Wayne. For meeting time call Mary Schneider 973-720-6733 (day). *E-mail:* diabetes@sjwh.org

SOMERSET

Living Well With Diabetes Support Group *Professionally-run.* Mutual support and information for adults with diabetes, type 1 or 2. Building is handicapped accessible. Meets quarterly, Somerset Medical Center, 110 Rehill Ave., Somerville. For meeting information call 908-685-2846 (day).

SUSSEX

Support Group for Those with Diabetes *Professionally-run.* Provides educational enrichment and emotional support for those with diabetes. Also offers rap sessions and guest speakers. Meets 1st Wed., 10am, Newton Memorial Hospital, 175 High St., Newton. Before attending call Chris Orr 973-579-8340 (day). *E-mail:* corr@nmhnj.org

Consider passing this Directory on to a student or staff member - browsing through the Directory pages can often provide helpful education as to the wide variety of groups available.

UNION

Diabetes Support Group *Professionally-run.* Mutual support and education for persons with diabetes, their family and friends. Occasional guest speakers and rap sessions. Building is handicapped accessible. Meets 1st Tues., 7-8:30pm, Robert Wood Johnson University Hospital at Rahway, 865 Stone St., 1st Floor Conference Room, Rahway. Call 732-499-6109 (day).

Diabetes Support Group *Professionally-run.* Share personal experiences and discuss new ideas for living well with diabetes. Families welcome. Meets 3rd Thurs., 7-8:30pm (except July/Aug.), Overlook Hospital, 99 Beauvoir Ave., Conference Room #1, Summit. Call 908-522-5277.

WARREN

Diabetes Support Group *Professionally-run.* Mutual support for adults with diabetes. Guest speakers. Meets 4th Mon., 7pm, Hackettstown Regional Medical Center, 651 Willow Grove St., Conference Dining Room, Hackettstown. Before attending call Donna Kendrick 908-850-6937 (day).

Diabetes Support Group *Professionally-run.* Support and education for people with diabetes, their friends, family and caregivers. Usually meets last Tues., 3pm (except Dec.), Warren Hospital, Farley Education Center, 185 Roseberry St., Phillipsburg. Call Education Dept. 908-859-6777 (day).

NATIONAL

American Diabetes Association *(BILINGUAL) National. 100+ affiliates. Founded 1940.* Seeks to prevent and cure diabetes, to improve the lives of people affected by diabetes and fundraising for research. Referrals to local support groups, offices and chapters. Dues $28 (includes magazine). Write: American Diabetes Association, 1701 N. Beauregard St., Alexandria, VA 22311. Call 1-800-342-2383 (Mon.-Fri., 8:30am-8pm EST); Fax: 703-549-6995. *Website:* http://www.diabetes.org *E-mail:* askADA@diabetes.org

Juvenile Diabetes Research Foundation International *International. 110 chapters in North America; 11 international affiliates. Founded 1970.* Supports and funds research to find a cure for diabetes and its complications. Individual chapters offer support groups and other activities for families affected by diabetes. Awards research grants and sponsors a variety of career development and research training programs. International conferences and workshops for researchers. Chapter development guidelines. Online listing of local chapters. Write: Juvenile Diabetes Research Foundation International, 120 Wall St., 19th

Floor, New York, NY 10005-4001. Call 1-800-533-2873 or 212-785-9500 (Mon-Fri, 9am-5pm EST); Fax: 212-785-9595. *Website:* http://www.jdrf.org *E-mail:* info@jdrf.org

ONLINE

Diabetic Mommies *Online.* Support for all women with diabetes (type 1, type 1.5, type 2, gestational and pre-diabetes) at all stages of life whether already a mom, during pregnancy or trying to conceive. Articles, forum, chatroom, surveys, networking and newsletters. *Website:* http://www.diabeticmommy.com *E-mail:* editor@diabeticmommy.com

EATING DISORDERS
(see also overeating, overweight, toll-free helplines)

STATEWIDE

Eating Disorders Association of New Jersey *Professionally-run.* Support for persons with eating disorders, their families, friends and interested professionals. Dues $5/mtg. Membership $50/yr. Various meeting locations throughout NJ. Call 1-800-522-2230 (voice mail). *Website:* http://www.edanj.org

BERGEN

Eating Disorders Association of New Jersey *Professionally-run.* Support for persons with anorexia, bulimia or compulsive overeating and their families. Newsletter. Donation $5 per family. Meets 3rd Sat., 10-11:30am, Hackensack Medical Center, Hekemian Conference Center Building, Hackensack. Call Pia Jacangelo, ACSW 973-882-4099 (day). *Website:* http://www.edanj.org

Food Addicts in Recovery Anonymous 12-Step. Fellowship of those recovering from the disease of food addiction, obesity, anorexia and bulimia. *Website:* http:/www.foodaddicts.org
> **Maywood** Meets Mon. and Tues., 10:30am-noon, St. Martin's Episcopal Church, 29 Parkway. Call Deb 201-843-1667.
> **Paramus** Meets Thurs., 6:30-8pm, Kraft Center, 15 Essex Rd. Call Joe S. 973-243-8807.

"Those who walk together strengthen each other."-- a thousand-year-old proverb from the Swahili people of eastern Africa

ESSEX

ANAD (Anorexia Nervosa and Associated Disorders) of Northern NJ *Professionally-run.* Support for people with anorexia, bulimia or compulsive overeating. Concurrent groups for family and friends. Under 18 welcome. National newsletter. Donation $5 (optional). Meets 1st Sat. (2nd Sat. for major holidays), 9:30-11am, Saint Barnabas Ambulatory Care Center, 200 S. Orange Ave. (across from the Livingston Mall), Livingston. Call Barbara Reese, MSW, LCSW 973-783-2292 (mailbox #3). *Website:* http://www.anad.org

Eating Disorders Association of NJ *Professionally-run.* Support group for people with anorexia, bulimia or compulsive overeating. Donation $5. Meets 2nd Sun., 10-11:30am, Mountainside Hospital, Main Bldg., 1st Floor, Montclair. Call Maureen Kritzer-Lange, MSW, LCSW 973-313-1691, Ilene Fishman, MSW, LCSW 973-509-1400 or 1-800-522-2230 (day). *Website:* http://www.edanj.org

Food Addicts Anonymous 12-Step. Fellowship to recover from food addiction. Primary purpose is to maintain abstinence from sugar, flour and wheat. Meets Sun., 7:30-8:30pm, St. Peter's Episcopal Church, 94 East Mount Pleasant Ave., Livingston. Call Roger 908-403-6535 or Lisa 973-403-0333 (day).

MIDDLESEX

Eating Disorders Association of NJ *Professionally-run.* Support group for people with anorexia, bulimia or compulsive overeating. Meets 2nd Sat., 10:30am-noon, East Brunswick Library, Ryders Lane and Civic Center Dr., East Brunswick. Call Ann Chicchi, MS, RD 732-254-7896 or 1-800-522-2230 (day). *Website:* http://www.edanj.org

SMART Recovery (Self-Management And Recovery Training) *Professionally-run.* Self-help group for individuals wanting to gain their independence from addictive behaviors (drugs, alcohol, nicotine and other compulsive behaviors including gambling and eating disorders). SMART is an abstinence program based on cognitive-behavioral education and principles, especially those of rational-emotive behavior therapy. Meets Thurs. 6-7:30pm, Rutgers University, 152 Frelinghuysen Rd., Busch Campus, Psychology Building, Room A340, 2nd Floor, Piscataway. Call Ayelet Kattan 732-445-6111 ext. 871 (day). *Website:* http://www.smartrecovery.org *E-mail:* Rutgers.smart@gmail.com

MONMOUTH

Eating Disorders Support Group *Professionally-run.* Support group for people with anorexia or bulimia and their families. Under 18 welcome. Meets 4th Sat., 10:30am-noon, Riverview Medical Center, 1 Riverview Plaza, Board Room, Red Bank. Call Monmouth Psychological Associates 732-530-9029 (Mon.-Fri. 9am-5pm, ask for free support group).

MORRIS

Food Addicts in Recovery Anonymous 12-Step. Fellowship of those recovering from the disease of food addiction, obesity, anorexia and bulimia. Meets Sat., 9-10:30am, Saint Clare's Hospital, 400 W. Blackwell St., Conference Room C, Dover. Call Joe 201-704-0931 (day). *Website:* http://www.foodaddicts.org

SMART Recovery (Self-Management And Recovery Training) Self-help group for individuals wanting to gain their independence from addictive behaviors (alcohol, drugs, nicotine and other compulsive behaviors including gambling and eating disorders). SMART is an abstinence program based on cognitive-behavioral education and principles, especially those of rational-emotive behavior therapy. Meets Thurs., 7-8:30pm, Family Services, 62 Elm St., Morristown. Call Rich 973-983-8755 or Glenn 973-255-7296. *Website:* http://www.smartrecovery.org

OCEAN

Food Addicts Anonymous 12-Step. Fellowship to recover from food addiction. Primary purpose is to maintain abstinence from sugar, flour and wheat.
> **Brick** Meets Mon., 11am and Thurs., 7:30pm, First Baptist Church of Laurelton, 1824 Route 88 East. Call Phyllis 732-244-4324 (Mon. group) or Barbara 732-864-9611 (Thurs. group).
> **Toms River** Meets Thurs., 11am, Presbyterian Church of Toms River, Hooper Ave. and Chestnut St. (use back entrance). Call Barbara 732-864-9611 or Phyllis 732-244-4324.

"Refusing to ask for help when you need it is refusing someone the chance to be helpful."
-- Ric Ocasek

Overcomers In Christ Recovery program that deals with every aspect of addiction and dysfunction (spiritual, physical, mental, emotional and social). Uses Overcomers goals which are Christ-centered. *Resources*, literature, information and referrals. Meets Mon., 7-8:30pm, America's Keswick, 601 Route 530, Whiting. Separate groups for men and women. Women's group call Diane Hunt 732-350-1187 ext. 47. Men's group call Chaplain Jim Freed 732-350-1187 ext. 43. *Website:* http://www.americaskeswick.org

PASSAIC

Food Addicts in Recovery Anonymous 12-Step. Fellowship of those recovering from the disease of food addiction, obesity, anorexia and bulimia. Meets Sun., 8-9:30am, Eva's Village, 393 Main St., Paterson. Call Naomi 201-265-6917. *Website:* http://www.foodaddicts.org

SOMERSET

Anorexia/Bulimia Family and Friend Support Group *Professionally-run.* Support and education for family and friends of those with anorexia or bulimia to help understand the disorder. Guest speakers and quarterly newsletter. Building is handicapped accessible. Meets Tues., 7:30-9pm, Somerset Medical Center, 110 Rehill Ave., Somerville. Call Eating Disorders Unit 908-685-2847 (day).

Eating Disorders Association of New Jersey *Professionally-run.* Support for those with anorexia, bulimia or compulsive eating and their families. Under 18 welcome. Rap sessions. Membership $50/yr. or $5/mtg. Building is handicapped accessible. Meets 4th Sat., 10-11:30am, Clarence Dillon Library, 2336 Lamington Rd., Bedminister. Call Kim Leatherdale 908-256-4779. *Website:* http://www.edanj.org

Eating Disorders Support Group *Professionally-run.* Provides mutual support for those suffering from an eating disorder. Under 18 welcome. Members share information and experiences. Meets Tues., 7:30-9pm, Somerset Medical Center, 110 Rehill Ave., Eating Disorder Conference Room, 1st Floor, Room 197, Somerville. Call Eating Disorders Unit 908-685-2847 (day).

UNION

Eating Disorders Association of New Jersey *Professionally-run.* Support for those with anorexia, bulimia or compulsive eating and their families. Under 18 welcome. Rap sessions. Membership $50/yr. or $5/mtg. Meets 1st Sun., 10-

11:30am, Summit Medical Group, 1 Diamond Hill Rd., Berkeley Heights. Call Jeannie Gedeon 908-542-0060 (day).

Food Addicts Anonymous 12-Step. Fellowship to recover from food addiction. Primary purpose is to maintain abstinence from sugar, flour and wheat. Meets Mon., 8pm, Clark Public Library, 303 Westfield Ave., Board Room, 2nd Floor, Clark. Call Phyllis 732-244-4324.

NATIONAL

Eating Addictions Anonymous - SANE Fellowship *National. 6 affiliated chapters.* 12-Step. Recovery program for men and women recovering from all forms of eating and body image addictions. Includes anorexia, bulimia, binge eating, overeating, exercise bulimics, etc. Focuses on internal growth and reclaiming bodies rather than weight or appearance. Write: Eating Addictions Anonymous, P.O. Box 8151, Silver Spring, MD 20907-8151. Call 202-882-6528. *Website:* http://www.eatingaddictionsanonymous.org *E-mail:* 12n12@tidalwave.net

Eating Disorders Anonymous *International. Founded 2000.* Fellowship of men and women who share their experience, strength and hope with each other that they may solve their common problems and help others to recover from their eating disorders. Focuses on the solution; not the problem. Eating Disorders Anonymous endorses sound nutrition. Pen pals, phone support, literature, information and referrals. Assistance in starting groups. Offers online referrals to local groups. Write: General Service Board of EDA, P.O. Box 55876, Phoenix, AZ 85078-5876. *Website:* http://www.eatingdisordersanonymous.org

National Association of Anorexia Nervosa and Associated Disorders, Inc. *(BILINGUAL) International. Founded 1976.* Telephone hotline for victims of eating disorders, their families and friends. Provides information on over 250+ free ANAD support groups, referrals to therapists and treatment centers that specialize in eating disorders. Quarterly newsletter. Assistance with insurance discrimination and parity issues. Free eating disorders education program for middle and high schools. Write: National Association of Anorexia Nervosa and Associated Disorders, Inc., P.O. Box 7, Highland Park, IL 60035. Call 847-831-3438 (Mon.-Fri., 9am-5pm CST); Fax: 847-433-4632. *Website:* http://www.anad.org or Spanish *Website:* http://www.anadenespanol.org *E-mail:* anadhelp@anad.org

Overcomers In Christ *International. Founded 1987.* Recovery program that deals with every aspect of addiction and dysfunction (spiritual, physical, mental, emotional and social). Uses Overcomers goals which are Christ-centered. Resources, literature, information and referrals. Assistance in starting new groups. Write: Overcomers In Christ, P.O. Box 34460, Omaha, NE 68134-0460. Call 1-866-573-0966 or 402-573-0966. *Website:* http://www.OvercomersInChrist.org *E-mail:* OIC@OvercomersInChrist.org

Overcomers Outreach, Inc. *International. 700 affiliated groups. Founded 1985.* 12-Step. Christ-centered support group for anyone affected by addictions, as well as their families and friends. Uses 12-steps of A.A. and applies them to the Scriptures. Uses Jesus Christ as "higher power." Supplements involvement in other 12-step groups. Newsletter, group development guidelines and conferences. Write: Overcomers Outreach, Inc., P.O. Box 2204, Oakhurst, CA 93644. Call 1-800-310-3001. *Website:* http://www.overcomersoutreach.org *E-mail:* info@overcomersoutreach.org

Recoveries Anonymous *International. 50 chapters.* Spiritual recovery group for anyone seeking a solution from any kind of addiction, problem or behavior. Family and friends welcome. "How To Begin..." guides and "Start A Group" kit can be downloaded free from the website. Write: R.A. Universal Services, P.O. Box 1212, East Northport, NY 11731. *Website:* http://www.r-a.org *E-mail:* raus@r-a.org

ONLINE

BDD Central *Online.* Provides resources, information and support for body dysmorphic disorder (BDD). Support through two e-mail lists, chatroom and a message board. Information available for family, friends and professionals. DVD, newsletter and doctor lists available. *Website:* http://www.bddcentral.com

ECZEMA

National Eczema Association *National network. Founded 1988.* Provides support for persons with atopic dermatitis as well as other forms of eczema. Promotes education and research. Offers networking, newsletter, information and referrals. Write: National Eczema Association, 4460 Redwood Highway, Suite 16-D, San Rafael, CA 94903-1953. Call 1-800-818-7546 or 415-499-3474; Fax: 415-472-5345. *Website:* http://www.nationaleczema.org *E-mail:* info@nationaleczema.org

ENDOMETRIOSIS

NATIONAL

Endometriosis Association *International. 170 groups. Founded 1980.* Offers group support to those affected by endometriosis. Educates the public and medical community about the disease. Funds and promotes research projects. Newsletters, books, literature, support group information, teen programs and network. Brochures in 29 languages. Chapter development guidelines. Online support group, crisis call listeners, and e-mail support. Write: Endometriosis Association, 8585 N. 76th Pl., Milwaukee, WI 53223. Call 1-800-992-3636 (for an information packet) or 414-355-2200; Fax: 414-355-6065. *Website:* http://www.endometriosisassn.org or http://www.killercramps.org *E-mail:* endo@EndometriosisAssn.org

Endometriosis Research Center *International. 50+ support groups worldwide. Founded 1997.* Maintains and offers a vast database of materials on every aspect of endometriosis to all those interested in the disease. Education, research and advocacy. Write: Endometriosis Research Center, 630 Ibis Dr., Delray Beach, FL 33444. Call 1-800-239-7280 or 561-274-7442; Fax: 561-274-0931. *Website:* http://www.endocenter.org *Network Listserv:* http://groups.yahoo.com/group/erc *E-mail:* EndoFL@aol.com Support

EPILEPSY / CONVULSIVE DISORDERS
(see toll-free helplines)

STATEWIDE

Epilepsy Foundation of New Jersey Support, information and referrals for people of any age with epilepsy and their families. Support groups, employment services, pharmaceutical plan, respite care, camp, family services and education. Write: Epilepsy Foundation of NJ, 429 River View Plaza, Trenton, NJ 08611-3420. Call Trenton: 609-392-4900 (day); Westmont: 856-858-5900 (day); Parsippany: 973-244-0850 (day); Brick: 732-262-8020 (day); Manasquan: 1-800-372-6510 (day); Bordentown: 1-877-265-6360 (day) or 1-800-336-5843. *Website:* http://www.efnj.com

ATLANTIC

Epilepsy Foundation Support Group - Atlantic/Cape *Professionally-run.* Mutual support and education for persons with epilepsy or related seizure disorder. Open to parents, caregivers and other interested persons. Rap sessions.

365

Building is handicapped accessible. Meets 4th Sat., 10am-noon, Shore Memorial Hospital, New York Ave., Jenkins Room, 2nd Room, Somers Point. Call Marian 609-822-8783. *E-mail:* marianrein@juno.com

BERGEN

Epilepsy Adult Group *Professionally-run.* Mutual support for adults with epilepsy and their caregivers. Share experiences on how to best live with this sometimes puzzling disorder. Guest speakers, literature, phone help and buddy system. Meets 3rd Thurs., 6:30-8pm, Hackensack University Medical Center, 20 Prospect Ave., Main Conference Room, Suite 800, Hackensack. Call Lindsey Davis 908-522-2092 (day). *Website:* http://www.epilepsygroup.com *E-mail:* ldavis@epilepsygroup.com

GLOUCESTER

Epilepsy Foundation Support Group Mutual support and education for anyone with epilepsy, their families and friends. Guest speakers, advocacy and literature. Meets 2nd Tues., 7-9pm, Wedgewood Country Club, Hurffville Rd., Dining Room, Turnersville. Call Shelby Myers 856-401-0445. *Website:* http://www.claytonshope.org

MIDDLESEX

Pediatric Epilepsy Support Group Provides support, encouragement and acceptance for children and families affected by epilepsy, to increase awareness and knowledge of issues relating to epilepsy. Building is handicapped accessible. Meets 2nd Wed., 6:30-8pm, JFK Medical Center, 65 James St., NJ Neuroscience Conference Room, Edison. Call Diane Poracky 732-321-7000 ext. 67245 (day). *E-mail:* cnrc@solarishs.org

MORRIS

Pediatric Epilepsy Support Group *Professionally-run.* Provides support network and education for parents of children with epilepsy. Guest speakers and literature. Meets 2nd Thurs., 7pm (Jan., Mar., May, July, Nov.), Saint Clare's Hospital, 25 Pocono Rd., Denville. Pre-registration required. Before attending call 973-625-6199 (day).

"All that matters is what we do for each other." – *Lewis Carroll*

UNION

Epilepsy Adult Group *Professionally-run.* Mutual support for adults with epilepsy and their caregivers. Share experiences on how to best live with this sometimes puzzling disorder. Guest speakers, literature, phone help and buddy system. Meets 2nd Thurs., 6:30-8pm, Overlook Hospital, Neuroscience Conference Center, 99 Beauvoir Ave., Summit. Call Lindsey Davis 908-522-2092 (day). *Website:* http://www.epilepsygroup.com *E-mail:* ldavis@epilepsygroup.com

NATIONAL

Epilepsy Foundation *(BILINGUAL) National. 60+ affiliates. Founded 1967.* Information and support for people with epilepsy, their families and friends. Publishes Epilepsy USA magazine and a wide range of informational materials for people of all ages. Referrals to local affiliates (many of which have employment related programs). Write: Epilepsy Foundation, 8301 Professional Place East, Landover, MD 20785. Call 301-459-3700; Professional Library: 1-800-332-4050; Consumer Infoline: 1-888-886-3745; Fax: 301-577-4941. *Website:* http://www.epilepsyfoundation.org *E-mail:* postmaster@efa.org

ONLINE

Pyridoxine Dependent Kids *Online. 149 members. Founded 1998.* Support group for parents of children with pyridoxine dependency or parents who are using B6 as an anticonvulsant. Offers public and subscribers only message boards. *Website:* http://groups.yahoo.com/group/b6children

FIBROMYALGIA

GLOUCESTER

FibroMyalgia of Gloucester County Support Group Support for people with fibromyalgia. Information and resource sharing. Rap sessions, guest speakers, literature and phone help. Meetings vary, 6-8pm, Turnersville. Call JD 856-227-2260 (day).

"Expect to have hope rekindled. Expect your prayers to be answered in wondrous ways. The dry seasons in life do not last. The spring rains will come again."
--Sarah Ban Breathnach

MONMOUTH

Chronic Fatigue Syndrome/Epstein-Barr/Fibromyalgia Support *Professionally-run.* Provides support for chronic fatigue syndrome, Epstein-Barr and fibromyalgia patients, their families, friends and significant others. Guest speakers. Building is handicapped accessible. Meets 3rd Sun., 10-11:30am, Monmouth Medical Center, 300 Second Ave., Long Branch. Pre-registration required. Call 732-923-6990 (day).

MORRIS

Fibromyalgia Support Group of Morris County *Professionally-run.* Support, education and coping skills for those with fibromyalgia. Families welcome. Rap sessions, literature and pen pals. Meets 4th Thurs., 1-3pm, 60-1 Morris Turnpike, Randolph. Pre-registration required. Before attending call Chris Gerken 973-252-7851 (eve.). *E-mail:* chrisgerken@optonline.net

UNION

Union County Fibromyalgia Support Connection Support and sharing of information for individuals with fibromyalgia syndrome and related illnesses. Families and caregivers welcome. Provides understanding of fibromyalgia syndrome, its symptoms and daily pain management. Message board. Meets 3rd Sat., 10:30am, Doctor's Care Offices, 901 N. Wood Ave., 2nd Floor Waiting Room, Linden. Call Lily 732-499-9028. *Website:* http://www.cafemom.com/group/16615 *E-mail:* lendaed@aol.com

WARREN

Fibromyalgia and Chronic Fatigue Support Group Provides education and support for those with fibromyalgia or chronic fatigue syndrome. Meets 1st Thurs., 7pm (Jan., Apr., July and Oct.), Warren Hospital, 185 Roseberry St., Farley Education Center, Phillipsburg. Before attending call Health Education Dept. 908-859-6735 (day).

NATIONAL

National Fibromyalgia Association *National network.* Develops and executes programs dedicated to improving the quality of life for people with fibromyalgia by increasing the awareness of the public, media, government and medical communities. Patient assistance, information programs, awareness outreach, support group directory and quarterly magazine. Write: National Fibromyalgia Association, 2121 South Towne Centre Place, Suite 300, Anaheim, CA 92806. Call 714-921-0150; Fax: 714-921-6920. *Website:* http://www.fmaware.org *E-mail:* sbennett@fmaware.org

ONLINE

Men With Fibromyalgia *Online. 172 members.* Support, fellowship and information for men with fibromyalgia. Opportunity to learn, share, listen, offer and receive support. Spouses and loved ones welcome. Offers forum and chatroom. *Website:* http://www.menwithfibro.com

GRAVES' DISEASE

National Graves' Disease Foundation *National. 32 affiliated groups in 25 states. Founded 1990.* Aim is to establish patient-based Graves' exclusive support groups to provide better treatment and to increase public awareness. Participates in research. Newsletter, information and referrals, phone support, national conferences, internet bulletin board and weekly online chatroom. Each group has medical back-up/resource. Guidelines available to assist in starting a similar group. Write: National Graves' Disease Foundation, c/o Dr. Nancy Patterson, P.O. Box 1969, Brevard, NC 28712. Call 828-877-5251. *Website:* http://www.ngdf.org *E-mail:* nancyngdf@yahoo.com

HEADACHES
NATIONAL

National Headache Foundation *National. 30+ affiliated groups. Founded 1970.* Mutual support for chronic headache sufferers and their families. Education on how to deal with chronic head pain. Group meetings, phone support, e-mail pen pals and group development guidelines. Public awareness seminars, funds research, newsletter, brochures and information on diets. Write: National Headache Foundation, 820 N. Orleans, Suite 217, Chicago, IL 60610-3132. Call 1-888-643-5552 (day); Fax: 312-640-9049. *Website:* http://www.headaches.org *E-mail:* sbarron@headaches.org

OUCH (Organization for Understanding Cluster Headaches) *National.* Offers information and support for cluster headache suffers worldwide. Provides message board, newsletter and informative links. Support research to improve treatments. Holds annual conference. Write: OUCH-US, 3225 Winding Way, Round Rock, TX 78664. *Website:* http://www.ouch-us.org *E-mail:* contact_ouch@ouch-us.org

New Daily Persistent Headache Support Group *Online.* Community of patients, family members and friends dedicated to dealing with new daily persistent headaches, together. Chance to find support, help others, share personal experiences and ask questions. *Website:* http://www.mdjunction.com/ndph

HEART DISEASE / MITRAL VALVE PROLAPSE
(see specific disorder, toll-free helplines, transplants)

BERGEN

It's My Heart New Jersey Chapter Provides support, education, awareness and advocacy for parents with a child affected by congenital heart defects. Families welcome. Guest speakers, phone help, online message board and online e-mail discussion group. Building is handicapped accessible. Meets 2nd Thurs., 7-9pm, Don Imus WFAN Building, 30 Prospect Ave., Hackensack. Call Kim Shadek 973-291-4676. *Website:* http://www.itsmyheart.org *E-mail:* newjersey@itsmyheart.org

Mended Hearts, Inc. Help, encouragement and education for those anticipating or recovering from heart surgery and/or other heart disease. Family and friends welcome. Professional speakers. Meets 3rd Thurs., 7pm, Hackensack Medical Center, 30 Prospect Ave., Cafeteria, Hackensack. Call Barbara Cecco 201-265-9296 (day). *E-mail:* bobbi0530@aol.com

BURLINGTON

Zapper Club *Professionally-run.* Support group for patients with implantable defibrillators and their families. Building is handicapped accessible. Meets 1st Wed., 10am, Deborah Heart and Lung Center, 200 Trenton Rd., Browns Mills. Call Dianna Barker 609-893-1200 ext. 5256 (day). *Website:* http://www.deborah.org

Zipper Club Mutual support for persons coping with heart disease or heart surgery. Building is handicapped accessible. Meets 9 times/yr., Thurs., 10am-noon, Deborah Heart and Lung Center, 200 Trenton Rd., Browns Mills.

Registration required. For meeting information call 609-893-1200 ext. 5618. *Website:* http://www.zipperclub.com

CAMDEN

Heart and Soul Cardiac Support Group Mutual support and education for persons with any type of heart disease. Meets 2nd Thurs., 7:30-8:30pm (except July/Aug.), Virtua Health, Barry D. Brown Health Education Center, 106 Carnie Blvd., Voorhees. Before attending call 1-888-847-8823 (day).

Second Chance Heart Transplant Support Group Mutual support for pre- and post-heart transplant patients, their families, friends and caregivers. Rap sessions and guest speakers. Meets 2nd Tues., 11am, Hahnemann University Hospital, Broad and Vine, Philadelphia, PA. Call Renard 856-346-9030.

MIDDLESEX

COPSA Spouse Support Group *Professionally-run.* Mutual support and understanding for spouses of persons with any type of memory loss including Alzheimer's, Parkinson's, vascular disease, stroke, head injury and dementia. Meets 1st and 3rd Mon., 9:30-11am, University Behavioral Healthcare Center, 671 Hoes Lane, Piscataway. Call Mary Catherine Lundquist 732-235-2858 (day). *E-mail:* lundqumc@umdnj.edu

MONMOUTH

Cardiac Support Group *Professionally-run.* Mutual support and education for cardiac patients. Families and friends welcome. Literature. Meets 3rd Wed., 2-3pm, Centra State Medical Center, Cardiac Rehab Center, 901 West Main St., 1st Floor, Ambulatory Campus, Freehold. Before attending call 732-294-2918 (day).

Cardiac Support Group *Professionally-run.* Provides mutual support, education and encouragement for people who are coping with cardiac disease and their families. Meets 3rd Mon., 7pm, Monmouth Medical Center, 300 Second Ave., Cardiac Rehab, Long Branch. Registration is required. Before attending call 1-888-724-7123 (day).

*Can't find an appropriate group in your area? The Clearinghouse helps people start groups. Give us a call at **1-800-367-6274**.*

ICD Patient/Family Support and Education Group *Professionally-run.* Provides support, education and a mechanism for networking for patients and families having implantable cardioverter defibrillators. Rap sessions, guest speakers, phone help and literature. Building is handicapped accessible. Meetings vary, Jersey Shore Medical Center, Neptune. Call 732-775-5500 ext. 55249. *E-mail:* nbowe@meridianhealth.com

Mended Hearts Support and encouragement for heart patients and their families. Visitation, guest speakers, newsletter and phone help. Dues $22 1st yr.; $17/yr. thereafter. Building is handicapped accessible. Meetings vary, Brick, Neptune and Red Bank. For meeting information call Bill 732-367-3648 (day). *Website:* http://www.heartsofjersey.org

OCEAN

Mended Hearts Support and encouragement for heart patients and their families. Visitation, guest speakers, newsletter and phone help. Dues $22 1st yr.; $17/yr. thereafter. Meetings vary, Brick, Neptune and Red Bank. For meeting information call Bill 732-367-3648 (day). *Website:* http://www.heartsofjersey.org

SOMERSET

Cardiac Heart Support Group *Professionally-run.* Support and education for heart patients and their families. Meets 1st and 3rd Tues., 10:30am, Somerset Hills YMCA, 140 Mt. Airy Rd., Basking Ridge. Pre-registration required. Before attending call Carol Carlson, PhD 973-627-4087 (day).

UNION

Cardiac Support Group *Professionally-run.* Support and education for cardiac patients and their families. Building is handicapped accessible. Meets 1st Mon., 7-8:30pm, Robert Wood Johnson University Hospital at Rahway, 865 Stone St., Rahway. Call Helen Peare 732-499-6073 (day).

NATIONAL

Adult Congenital Heart Association *National. Founded 1998.* Seeks to improve the quality of life and extend the lives of adults with congenital heart defects. Education, outreach, advocacy and promotion of research. Online support, quarterly newsletter and national conferences. Write: Adult Congenital Heart Association, 6757 Greene St., Suite 335, Philadelphia, PA 19119. Call

1-888-921-2242 or 215-849-1260; Fax: 245-849-1261. *Website:* http://www.achaheart.org *E-mail:* info@achaheart.org

Arrhythmia Alliance (The Heart Rhythm Charity) *International network. Founded 2004.* A network of sufferers, medical professionals, various UK based charities and related industry promoting better understanding, diagnosis, treatment and quality of life for individuals with cardiac arrhythmias. Write: Arrhythmia Alliance, P.O. Box 3697, Stratford upon Avon Warwickshire CV37 8YL United Kingdom. Call: +44 (0) 17890450787; Fax: +44 (0) 17890450682. *Website:* http://www.heartrhythmcharity.org.uk *E-mail:* info@arrhythmiaalliance.org.uk

Congenital Heart Anomalies-Support, Education, Resources (CHASER) *National network. Founded 1992.* Opportunity for parents of children born with heart defects to network with other parents with similar needs and concerns. Education on hospitalization, surgeries, medical treatments, etc. Newsletter, phone support, information and referral. Heart surgeons and facilities directory. Write: CHASER, 2112 N. Wilkins Rd., Swanton, OH 43558. Call Jim and Anita Myers 419-825-5575 (day).

It's My Heart *National. 15 groups. Founded 2005.* Mutual-aid support provided via family matching program (matches families with others that have a similar CHD diagnosis or by proximity), moderated online message board and listserv. Provides support, education and advocacy for those affected by congenital heart defects by creating alliances with fellow families, hospitals, support groups and the community. Newsletter, online support group and assistance in starting local support groups available. Call 1-888-432-7807; Fax: 866-222-0334. Write: It's My Heart, 19728 Saums Rd., PMB #137, Houston, TX 77084. *Website:* http://www.itsmyheart.org *E-mail:* info@itsmyheart.org

Kids With Heart *National. 3 affiliated groups. Founded 1985.* Mutual support for families and adults affected by congenital or acquired heart defects. Also provides bereavement services. Matches parents together for support, referrals to local support groups nationwide. Promotes public awareness of congenital heart defects. Books, awareness products, advocacy assistance and assistance in starting groups. Write: Kids With Heart NACHD, Inc., 1578 Careful Dr., Green Bay, WI 54304. Call 1-800-538-5390 or 920-498-0058 (voice/fax) (Mon.-Fri., 8am-3pm CST). *Website:* http://www.kidswithheart.org *E-mail:* michelle@kidswithheart.org

Little Hearts, Inc. *National.* Provides support, resources, networking and hope to families affected by congenital heart defects. Provides newsletter, literature, phone support, annual picnic and advocacy. Call 1-866-435-4673; Fax: 860-635-0006. *Website:* http://www.littlehearts.org *E-mail:* info@littlehearts.org

Mended Hearts *National. 285 chapters. Founded 1951.* Mutual support for persons who have heart disease, their families, friends and other interested persons. Quarterly magazine and chapter development kit. Write: Mended Hearts, 7272 Greenville Ave., Dallas, TX 75231. Call 1-888-432-7899 or 214-360-6149; Fax: 214-360-6145. *Website:* http://www.mendedhearts.org *E-mail:* info@mendedhearts.org

National Society for MVP and Dysautonomia *National. 54 affiliated groups. Founded 1987.* Assists individuals suffering from Mitral Valve Prolapse syndrome and dysautonomia to find support and understanding. Education on symptoms and treatment. Newsletter and literature. Write: National Society for MVP and Dysautonomia, 880 Montclair Rd., Suite 370, Birmingham, AL 35213. Call 1-800-541-8602 or 205-592-5765; Fax: 205-592-5707. *Website:* http://www.mvprolapse.com *E-mail:* staff@MVProlapse.com

SADS Foundation *International. 5 affiliated groups. Founded 1992.* International organization working to save the lives of young persons who are predisposed to sudden death due to cardiac arrhythmia. Offers networking, newsletter, literature, advocacy, information, phone support and referrals. Write: SADS Foundation, 508 E. South Temple, Suite 20, Salt Lake City, UT 84102. Call 1-800-786-7723 or 801-531-0937; Fax: 801-531-0945. *Website:* http://www.sads.org *E-mail:* sads@sads.org

Society for Mitral Valve Prolapse Syndrome *International. 23 affiliated groups. Founded 1991.* Provides support and education to patients, families and friends about mitral valve prolapse syndrome. Newsletter, phone support, literature, conferences and support group meetings. Publishes "Survival Guide." Offers guidelines to start similar groups. Write: Society for MVP Syndrome, P.O. Box 431, Itasca, IL 60143-0431. Call 630-250-9327; Fax: 630-773-0478. *Website:* http://www.mitralvalveprolapse.com *E-mail:* bonnie0107@aol.com

ONLINE

Children's Cardiomyopathy Foundation *Online.* Provides support and information on pediatric cardiomyopathy. Offers website discussion forum and biannual newsletter. Working on plans to start community support groups. *Website:* http://www.childrenscardiomyopathy.org *E-mail:* info@childrenscardiomyopathy.org

Congenital Heart Information Network *Online.* Offers support, information and resources to families of children with congenital heart defects, acquired heart disease and adults with congenital heart defects. Also open to interested professionals. *Website:* http://www.tchin.org

Pacemaker Club *Online. Founded 2000.* Regular exchange of messages, listserv and newsgroup. Chat meetings. E-mail pen pal program to support new members. Offers support, information and encouragement in a fun and interactive environment. Also information on local groups. *Website:* http://www.pacemakerclub.com *E-mail:* info@pacemakerclub.com

Sudden Cardiac Arrest Association Online Community *Online.* Support community connecting those who have suffered sudden cardiac arrest, have an implantable defibrillator, are family or caregivers of someone who suffered a cardiac arrest and all who want to interact with others interested in reducing sudden cardiac arrest. *Website:* http://www.suddencardiacarrest.org (click "Online Community" link on bottom left corner of Home page)

SVT (Supra Ventricular Tachycardia) Support *Online. Founded 2002.* E-mail list support. Mutual aid support from and for persons with supra ventricular tachycardia or any type of arrhythmia. Newsletter. *Website:* http://groups.yahoo.com/group/SVTSupport/

HEPATITIS

CAMDEN

South Jersey Liver Opportunity for persons with any liver disease, including hepatitis C, to share coping skills. Buddy system, guest speakers and phone help. Dues $3/mtg. Building is handicapped accessible. Meets 2nd Tues., 7-9:30pm (except June, July, Aug. and Dec.), West Jersey Hospital, Barry Brown Health Education Center, 316 Carnie Blvd., Voorhees. Call Harry Hagar Jr. 856-983-8247 or Marlene Reid 856-468-2883. *Website:* http://www.geocities.com/SJLDSG

"There are only two ways to approach life – as a victim or as a gallant fighter – and you must decide if you want to act or react." –Anonymous

MERCER

Mercer County Survivors of Liver Disease/Hepatitis Support and education for those afflicted with liver disease or hepatitis. Family, friends and professionals welcome. Lectures, guest speakers, advocacy, rap sessions and social group. Building is handicapped accessible. Meets 1st and 3rd Sun., 7-9pm, Robert Wood Johnson at Hamilton, 1 Hamilton Place, Hamilton. Call Peggy Goodale 609-903-8524 or Tammy Leigh 609-584-2166 (day).

NATIONAL

Hepatitis B Foundation *International network. Founded 1991.* Mutual support and information for persons affected by Hepatitis B. Dedicated to finding a cure for Hepatitis B. Supports research, advocacy, information and referrals, educational literature, newsletter, conferences, confidential phone and e-mail support. Referrals to liver specialists. Suggested donation $40. Write: Hepatitis B Foundation, 3805 Old Easton Rd., Doylestown, PA 18902. Call 215-489-4900; Fax: 215-489-4313. *Website:* http://www.hepb.org *E-mail:* info@hepb.org

Hepatitis Foundation International *International network. Founded 1995.* Grassroots support network for persons with viral hepatitis. Provides education about the prevention, diagnosis and treatment of viral hepatitis. Phone support network, quarterly newsletter and literature. Referrals to local support groups. Some materials available in Spanish, Mandarin and Vietnamese. Write: Hepatitis Foundation International, 504 Blick Dr., Silver Springs, MD 20904. Call 1-800-891-0707; Fax: 301-622-4702. *Website:* http://www.hepatisfoundation.org *E-mail:* hfi@comcast.net

PKIDs (Parents of Kids with Infectious Diseases) *National network. Founded 1996.* Provides informational and educational support for parents of children with chronic viral infectious diseases, with an emphasis on Hepatitis B and C. Opportunity for parents, children and teens to share information and experiences. Publications, advocacy and phone support. Online e-mail list, support group and other resources. Write: PKIDS, P.O. Box 5666, Vancouver, WA 98668. Call 1-877-557-5437 or 360-695-0293; Fax: 360-695-6941. *Website:* http://www.pkids.org *E-mail:* pkids@pkids.org

ONLINE

HCV: Hepatitis C Anonymous *Online. 12-Step.* Provides support through message board and regularly scheduled chats. Has articles, newsletters and matching program. Offers packets containing information on starting local groups. Write: HCV Anonymous, Inc., 129 W. Canada, San Clemente, CA 92672. Call 949-264-4175 (hotline and general information). *Website:* http://www.hcvanonymous.com

Hepatitis Neighborhood *Online.* An online educational resource to help individuals understand hepatitis, treatment options, find support, message boards and chatrooms. *Website:* http://www.hepatitisneighborhood.com *E-mail:* mycommunity@curascript.com

HERPES / SEXUALLY TRANSMITTED DISEASES
(see also toll-free helplines)

NATIONAL

ASHA's STI Resource Center *National network. 85+ groups. Founded 1914.* Emotional support and education for persons with herpes and other sexually transmitted infections. Referrals to HELP (herpes) support groups, which provide a safe, confidential environment in which to obtain accurate information and share experiences with others. Support group development guidelines. Book ($26.95); quarterly journal ($25). Write: ASHA's STI Resource Center, P.O. Box 13827, Research Triangle Park, NC 27709. Call 919-361-8488 (hotline: Mon.-Fri., 8am-8pm EST); 919-361-8486 (for starting groups) or 919-361-8400 (ASHA); Fax: 919-361-8425. *Website:* http://www.ashastd.org *E-mail:* hsvnet@ashastd.org

ONLINE

PickingUpThePieces *Online. Founded 1998.* Support and educational group open to anybody interested in learning more about Herpes Simplex Virus (HSV) or Human Papillomavirus (HPV). Group message board available to share your story and ask questions. *Website:* http://health.groups.yahoo.com/group/pickingupthepieces/

You have it easily in your power to increase the sum total of this world's happiness now. How? By giving a few words of sincere appreciation to someone who is lonely or discouraged. -- Dale Carnegie

HIP REPLACEMENT

ONLINE

Totally Hip *Online. Founded 1997.* Support to help relieve the fear of total hip replacement surgery, share experiences and offer morale as well as spiritual support to patients. Helps answer questions on hip replacement. Also discuss other joint problems. Click on bulletin board at website for message exchange. Fax: 601-249-2065. *Website:* http://www.totallyhip.org *E-mail:* Linda@totallyhip.org

HUMAN PAPILLOMA VIRUS

ONLINE

Club HPV *Online. 1877 members. Founded 2005.* Opportunity for people with human papilloma virus (genital warts) to share experiences and information with others. *Website:* http://groups.yahoo.com/group/clubhpv

HUNTINGTON'S DISEASE

STATEWIDE

Huntington's Disease Society of America *Professionally-run.* Education and support for afflicted families. Fund-raising, visitation and phone help. Meets various times at various locations throughout NJ. Call HDSA 973-784-4965. *Website:* http://www.hdsanj.org *E-mail:* hdsanjoffice@aol.com

CAMDEN

Huntington's Disease Support Group *Professionally-run.* Support and education for persons who have Huntington's disease, their caregivers, relatives and those at risk. Building is handicapped accessible. Meets 3rd Tues., 6:30-8pm, University Doctors Pavilion, 42 E. Laurel Rd., Room 1013, Stratford. Call Nancy Alterman, LCSW 856-566-7078.

MIDDLESEX

Huntington's Disease Support Group *Professionally-run.* Support and education for persons who have Huntington's disease, caregivers, relatives and those at risk. Building is handicapped accessible. Meets 4th Wed., 6:30-8pm,

UMDNJ, UBHC Building, 671 Hoes Lane, Room A108, Piscataway. Call Christine Hogan 732-235-5993 (day).

OCEAN

Huntington's Disease Support Group *Professionally-run.* Support and education for persons who have Huntington's Disease, their caregivers, relatives and those at risk. Meets 2nd Wed., 6:30-8pm, Leisure Chateau, 962 River Ave., Lakewood. Call Judy 732-370-8600.

UNION

Huntington's Disease Support Group *Professionally-run.* Support for caregivers of individuals with Huntington's disease. Guest speakers, literature and phone help. Meetings vary, 6:30-7:30pm, Hartwyck at Cedar Brook, 1340 Park Ave., Plainfield. Registration required. Call Kathy Little 908-754-3100 (day).

NATIONAL

Huntington's Disease Society of America *National. 28 chapters/10 affiliates. Founded 1967.* Provides information and referrals to local chapters, support groups, social workers, local health care professionals and other resources. Supports and funds research for treatment and cure of Huntington's disease. Provides written and audiovisual materials. Publishes three newsletters. Write: Huntington's Disease Society of America, 505 8th Ave., Suite 902, New York, NY 10018. Call 1-800-345-4372 or 212-242-1968. *Website:* http://www.hdsa.org *E-mail:* hdsainfo@hdsa.org

HYPERTENSION / HIGH BLOOD PRESSURE

ONLINE

High Blood Pressure (Hypertension) Online Support *Online. 1715 members. Founded 1999.* E-mail list for those suffering from high blood pressure/hypertension who are looking for others suffering from the same situation. *Website:* http://health.groups.yahoo.com/group/hypertension

---

"They may forget what you said, but they will never forget how you made them feel." -- *Carl W. Buechner*

INCONTINENCE

NATIONAL

Continence Restored Inc. *International. 8 affiliated groups. Founded 1984.* Forum where persons with incontinence, their families and friends can express concerns and receive assistance. Disseminates information on bladder control. Phone support. Assistance in starting groups. Write: Continence Restored Inc., 407 Strawberry Hill Ave., Stamford, CT 06902. Call 203-348-0601. *E-mail:* as4young@optonline.net

National Association For Continence (NAFC) *National.* Dedicated to improving the quality of life of people with incontinence by providing support and information about the causes, prevention, diagnosis, treatments and management alternatives for incontinence. Offers telephone support network, moderated message board and listserv. Newsletter, literature (some available in Spanish), regional conferences, information and referrals. Membership dues $25/yr. Write: National Association For Continence, PO Box 1019, Charleston, SC 29402. Call 1-800-252-3337; Fax: 843-377-0905. *Website:* http://www.nafc.org *E-mail:* memberservices@nafc.org

Pull-thru Network, The *International network. Founded 1988.* Support and information for the families with children born with anorectal, colorectal or urogenital disorder and any of the associated diseases. Disorders include cloaca, bladder exstrophy, imperforate anus, VATER/VACTERL association, anal stenosis, cloacal exstrophy and Hirschsprung's Disease. Maintains a database for personal networking. Quarterly magazine, online discussion group, weekly chat for members, phone support and literature. Dues $30/year - can be waived upon request. Write: Pull-thru Network, 2312 Savoy St., Hoover, AL 35226-1528. Call 205-978-2930. *Website:* http://www.pullthrunetwork.org *E-mail:* ptnmail@charter.net

Simon Foundation for Continence *National. 500+ affiliated groups. Founded 1983.* Support and advocacy for people suffering from incontinence. Quarterly newsletter, pen pals, books, videos and group development guidelines. Write: Simon Foundation for Continence, P.O. Box 835, Wilmette, IL 60091. Call 1-800-237-4666; Fax: 847-864-9758. *Website:* http://www.simonfoundation.org *E-mail:* cbgartley@simonfoundation.org

"Do your little bit of good where you are; it's those little bits of good put together that overwhelm the world." -- Desmond Tutu

INFERTILITY / CHILDLESSNESS
(see also women's health)

STATEWIDE

RESOLVE *Professionally-run.* Provides education, support and resources (medical, therapeutic, and adoption professionals) for individuals and couples experiencing infertility. Information on current medical treatments and adoption. Bi-monthly newsletter. Membership dues $55/yr. Educational meetings. Support group meetings also held throughout NJ counties. Call 1-888-765-2810. *Website:* http://www.northeast.resolve.org *E-mail:* info@resolve.org

NATIONAL

NINE (National Infertility Network Exchange) *National. Founded 1988.* Support for persons and couples with impaired fertility and the professionals who serve them. Support system to help understand, cope and reach a resolution. Monthly educational meetings, newsletter, talk line and professional referral. Guidelines to assist others start a similar group. Dues $40/yr. Write: NINE, P.O. Box 204, East Meadow, NY 11554. Call 516-794-5772; Fax: 516-794-0008. *Website:* http://www.nine-infertility.org *E-mail:* NINE204@aol.com

No Kidding! *International. 50 chapters in five countries. Founded 1984.* Mutual support and social activities for married and single people who either have decided not to have children, are postponing parenthood, are undecided or are unable to have children. Chapter development guidelines. Write: No Kidding!, Box 2802, Vancouver, BC, Canada V6B 3X2. Call 604-538-7736 (24 hr). *Website:* http://www.nokidding.net *E-mail:* info@nokidding.net

Organization of Parents Through Surrogacy *National. Founded 1988.* Educational, support and advocacy organization for families built through surrogate parenting. Members work together to address legislative bills on surrogacy. Information, networking, referrals, e-mail chatroom, phone support and literature. Dues $50/parents and surrogates. $100/professionals. Write: OPTS, P.O. Box 611, Gurnee, IL 60031. Call 847-782-0224; Fax: 847-782-0240. *Website:* http://www.opts.com *E-mail:* bzager@msn.com

RESOLVE, The National Infertility Association *National. 50+ chapters. Founded 1974.* Provides emotional support and medical referrals for infertile couples. Support groups, education for members and public. Quarterly magazine and publications. Chapter development guidelines. Write: RESOLVE, Inc., 8405 Greensboro Dr., Suite 800, McLean, VA 22102. Call 703-556-7172; Fax: 703-506-3266. *Website:* http://www.resolve.org *E-mail:* Info@Resolve.org

ONLINE

Cyster Connection *Online. 531 members.* Support for women with polycystic ovarian syndrome (PCOS), a condition in which ovaries create an abundance of follicles each month without producing an egg. PCOS usually goes hand-in-hand with insulin resistance. It is also the most common cause of infertility among women in the United States. *Website:* http://pcostcc.proboards83.com

Fertile Thoughts *Online.* Provides support for infertile couples through chatrooms and forums. Issues include: general infertility, primary vs. secondary infertility, over 35, overweight, grief, polycystic ovarian syndrome, male infertility, adoption and parenting. *Website:* http://www.fertilethoughts.net

International Council on Infertility Info. Dissemination (INCIID) *Online.* Dedicated to helping infertile couples find their best family-building options. Includes treatment and prevention of infertility and pregnancy loss. Guidance for those seeking to adopt. Provides free in-vitro fertilization scholarships to couples in need. Offers message boards on a variety of issues including fertility after forty, men, recurrent pregnancy loss, legal and insurance-related issues, grief, alternative therapies, medical issues and other online resources. *Website:* http://www.inciid.org

Parent Soup Message Boards *Online.* Offers a large variety of message boards which deal with parenting issues including infertility, pregnancy, parenting challenges, parents of disabled, pregnancy loss, newborn babies, toddlers, adoption, family issues, etc. *Website:* http://www.parentsoup.com/messageboards

TASC (The American Surrogacy Center) *Online.* Cybercommunity of friends and acquaintances who have a personal interest or experience concerning surrogacy issues. Various e-mail discussions, password protected bulletin boards, live chats and monthly virtual seminars. Topics include: surrogate parents, egg donation, multiple miscarriages, DES daughters, sperm donation and Mayer-Rokitansky-Kustur-Hauser syndrome. *Website:* http://www.surrogacy.com *E-mail:* info@surrogacy.com

"In about the same degree as you are helpful, you will be happy" – Karl Reilan

INFLAMMATORY BOWEL DISEASE / IRRITABLE BOWEL SYNDROME / CROHN'S

STATEWIDE

Crohn's and Colitis Foundation of America, Inc. Greater NJ Chapter *Professionally-run.* Provides support and education for persons with inflammatory bowel disease, Crohn's or ulcerative colitis and their families. Does not include irritable bowel syndrome. Membership dues $30/yr. Various meeting locations throughout NJ. Write: NJ Chapter CCFA, 45 Wilson Ave., Manalapan, NJ 07726. Call 732-786-9960 (Mon.-Fri., 9am-5pm). *Website:* http://www.ccfa.org *E-mail:* newjersey@ccfa.org

BERGEN

Crohn's and Colitis Foundation of America, Inc. Greater NJ Chapter *Professionally-run.* Provides support and education for persons with inflammatory bowel disease, Crohn's or ulcerative colitis. Families welcome. Does not include irritable bowel syndrome. Meets 2nd Wed., 7:30-9pm, Valley Hospital, 223 N. Van Dien Ave., Bergen Conference Room (main floor off lobby), Ridgewood. Pre-registration required. Before attending call 732-786-9960 (day). *Website:* http://www.ccfa.org *E-mail:* newjersey@ccfa.org

Inflammatory Bowel Disease Support for Parents *Professionally-run.* Provides support and education for parents of children with inflammatory bowel disease. Families welcome. Rap sessions, guest speakers, literature and quarterly newsletter. Building is handicapped accessible. Meetings vary, Don Imus Pediatric Center, Hackensack University Medical Center, Hackensack. Call Joseph Chan, LCSW 201-336-8840 (day).

MERCER

Crohn's and Colitis Support Group *Professionally-run.* Support and education for people with Crohn's and colitis. Family and friends welcome. Guest speakers, literature, phone help, buddy system and educational series. Meetings 4 times/yr., Robert Wood Johnson Hospital, Hamilton. For meeting information call Bill 609-587-7215.

MONMOUTH

Children with Irritable Bowel Disease Support Group Support for children and teenagers with irritable bowel disease. Parents welcome. Meets 4th Thurs., 7pm, (Feb., Apr., June, Aug., Oct., Dec.), Monmouth Medical Center, 300

Second Ave., Long Branch. Pre-registration required. Before attending call 732-786-9960 (day).

Crohn's and Colitis Foundation of America, Inc. Greater NJ Chapter *Professionally-run.* Provides support and education for persons with inflammatory bowel disease, Crohn's or ulcerative colitis. Families welcome. Does not include irritable bowel syndrome. Meets 3rd Tues., 6:30-8:30pm, Monmouth County Library, 125 Symmes Dr., Manalapan. Call Helene 732-536-8251 (eve.). *Website:* http://www.ccfa.org *E-mail:* hdortheimer@aol.com

MORRIS

Crohn's and Colitis Foundation of America, Inc. Greater NJ Chapter *Professionally-run.* Provides support and education for persons with inflammatory bowel disease, Crohn's or ulcerative colitis. Families welcome. Does not include irritable bowel syndrome. Meets 1st Tues., 7-9pm, Morristown. Pre-registration required. Before attending call 732-786-9960 (day). *Website:* http://www.ccfa.org *E-mail:* newjersey@ccfa.org

OCEAN

Crohn's and Colitis Foundation of America, Inc. Greater NJ Chapter *Professionally-run.* Provides support and education for persons with inflammatory bowel disease, Crohn's or ulcerative colitis. Families welcome. Does not include irritable bowel syndrome. Meets 2nd Wed., 7-9pm, Ocean Medical Center, 425 Jack Martin Blvd., Conference Room (across from employee cafeteria on 2 West), Brick. Pre-registration required. Before attending call 732-786-9960 (day). *Website:* http://www.ccfa.org *E-mail:* newjersey@ccfa.org

NATIONAL

American Celiac Society / Dietary Support Coalition *National. 78 affiliated chapters. Founded 1976.* Mutual support and information for celiac-sprue patients, families and health care professionals. Buddy system, newsletter, visitation, phone help system and participation in educational efforts. Also supports dermatitis herpetiformis, Crohn's disease, lactose intolerance and other food allergies. Write: American Celiac Society, c/o Mrs. Annette Bentley, P.O. Box 23455, New Orleans, LA 70183. Call Mrs. Annette Bentley 504-737-3293. *Website:* http://www.americanceliacsociety.org *E-mail:* americanceliacsociety@yahoo.com or amerceliacsoc@netscape.net (please do not send attachments)

Crohn's and Colitis Foundation of America (CCFA) *National. Founded 1967.* Support groups and educational programs for people with Crohn's disease or ulcerative colitis, as well as their family and friends. Membership benefits include: newsletter, a national magazine, discounts on books and brochures. Dues: $30yr./individual, $60yr./family. Write: CCFA, 386 Park Ave. South, 17th Fl., New York, NY 10016. Call 1-888-694-8872. (Mon-Fri, 9am-5pm EST). *Website:* http://www.ccfa.org (to find support groups on website: click on "chapters and events"; then select your state; then click on the "support groups" icon) *E-mail:* info@ccfa.org

International Foundation for Functional Gastrointestinal Disorders *International network. Founded 1990.* Educational and research organization that provides support, information, and assistance for people affected by functional gastrointestinal disorders, IBS, GERD and bowel incontinence. Publishes quarterly journal addressing digestive disorders in adults and children. Many other fact sheets and educational publications are available. Write: International Foundation for Functional Gastrointestinal Disorders, P.O. Box 170864, Milwaukee, WI 53217-8076. Call 1-888-964-2001 or 414-964-1799; Fax: 414-964-7176. *Website:* http://www.iffgd.org *E-mail:* iffgd@iffgd.org

Irritable Bowel Syndrome Self-Help and Support Group *International. Groups in USA and Canada. Founded in 1987.* Mutual support for persons with irritable bowel syndrome, their families and health care professionals. Literature, advocacy and assistance in starting similar groups. Write: IBS Self-Help and Support Group, 1440 Whalley Ave., #145, New Haven, CT 06515. *Website:* http://www.ibsgroup.org *E-mail:* ibs@ibsgroup.org

Reach Out for Youth with Ileitis and Colitis, Inc. *Model. 2 local groups. Founded 1979.* Provides support and education to patients and their families. Networking, literature, advocacy, information and referrals, phone support, conferences, regular group meetings and pen pals. Promotes research and sponsors fund raising activities. Write: Reach Out for Youth with Ileitis and Colitis, Inc., 84 Northgate Circle, Melville, NY 11747. Call 631-293-3102; Fax: 631-293-3103. *Website:* http://www.reachoutforyouth.org *E-mail:* reachoutforyouth@reachoutforyouth.org

ONLINE

Diverticulosis Support Group *Online. 551 members. Founded 2000.* Provides support and information for those with diverticulosis or diverticulitis. Weekly scheduled support meeting room chats. *Website:* http://health.groups.yahoo.com/group/diverticulosis/

385

INTERSTITIAL CYSTITIS

CAMDEN

South Jersey Interstitial Cystitis Support Group Support and information for persons with interstitial cystitis or painful bladder, their families and friends. Rap sessions, guest speakers and phone help. National ICA newsletter ($40). Building is handicapped accessible. Meets bi-monthly, Sat., 1-3pm, West Jersey Hospital, Voorhees. Before attending call Linda Benecke 856-667-5842 (day) or Virtua 1-888-847-8823 (day). *Website:* http://www.ichelp.org

MIDDLESEX

Interstitial Cystitis Support Group of Central NJ Mutual support for persons with interstitial cystitis. Families are welcome. Guest speakers. Meets 3rd Tues, 7-8:30pm (Feb., Apr., Aug., Oct., Dec.; 4th Tues., June), St. Peter's University Hospital, 254 Easton Ave., CARES Building, 3rd Floor, New Brunswick. Call Michelle 732-390-0422 (day). *E-mail:* brillo4@aol.com

NATIONAL

Interstitial Cystitis Association *National. Founded 1984.* Provides education, information and support for persons with interstitial cystitis, their spouses and families. Quarterly newsletter. Dues $45/yr. Write: Interstitial Cystitis Association, 110 N. Washington St., Suite 340, Rockville, MD 20850-2239. Call 1-800-435-7422 or 301-610-5300 (Mon.-Fri., 8am-5pm EST); Fax: 301-610-5308. *Website:* http://www.ichelp.org *E-mail:* icamail@ichelp.org

ONLINE

Interstitial Cystitis Heroes *Online. 163 members. Founded 2007.* Support for all who suffer from interstitial cystitis, a painful bladder disease. A place to come together to talk about symptoms, treatments and to encourage one another. *Website:* http://www.revolutionhealth.com/groups/interstitial-cystitis-heroes

KIDNEY DISEASE
(see also transplants)

ESSEX

Parents' Night Out *(BILINGUAL) Professionally-run.* Support for families of young children (up to age 8) with kidney disease. Group includes families with children on dialysis, pre- or post-kidney transplant. Guest speakers, phone help and buddy system. Meetings vary, 4 times/yr., St. Barnabas Medical Center, Livingston. For meeting day and time call Jennifer Bronsnick, MSW 973-322-2249 (day). *E-mail:* jbronsnick@sbhcs.com

MORRIS

Kidney Korner, The *Professionally-run.* Support and education for dialysis and transplant patients. Building is handicapped accessible. Meets every other month, 7pm, Roxbury Library, Main St., Succasunna. Call 973-584-1117 ext. 4.

NATIONAL

American Association of Kidney Patients *National. 14 chapters. Founded 1969.* Patient organization dedicated to helping renal patients and their families deal with the physical, emotional and social impact of kidney disease. Aim is to inform and inspire patients and their families to better understand their condition, adjust more readily to their circumstances and assume more normal, productive lives. Provides education and support for kidney patients, including those with reduced kidney function, on dialysis and transplant patients. Offers various educational materials, a bimonthly and quarterly magazine, two electronic newsletters and an annual convention. Write: American Association of Kidney Patients, 3505 East Frontage Rd., Suite 315, Tampa, FL 33607. Call 1-800-749-2257 or 813-636-8100 (Mon.-Fri., 8:30am-4:30pm EST); Fax: 813-636-8122. *Website:* http://www.aakp.org *E-mail:* info@aakp.org

PKD Foundation for Research in Polycystic Kidney Disease *International. 65 volunteer Friends chapters. Founded 1982.* Funds research and provides emotional support and education for persons with polycystic kidney disease and their families. Promotes public awareness. Holds medical seminars and fund-raisers. Conferences, phone support, newsletter and assistance in starting new groups. Write: PKD Foundation, 9221 Ward Parkway, Suite 400, Kansas City, MO 64114-3367. Call 1-800-753-2873 or 816-931-2600; Fax: 816-931-8655. *Website:* http://www.pkdcure.org *E-mail:* daves@pkdcure.org

"It is possible to be standing on one side of a door and perceive the world as a dark and lonely place, while on the other side of that very same door are countless people just waiting to lend support and cheer you on. All that is required is that you turn the knob."
Author Unknown

LARYNGECTOMY

CAMDEN

Laryngectomy Club (Nu-Voice Program) Support group for laryngectomy patients and their families. Meets 2nd Mon., 7pm, American Cancer Society, 1851 Old Cuthbert Rd., Cherry Hill. Before attending call 1-800-227-2345 (day).

MERCER

Central Laryngectomee Support Group of Central Jersey *Professionally-run.* Support and education for laryngeal cancer patients and their families. Share concerns and problems related to life after laryngeal cancer. Meets 3rd Wed., 11am-noon, Medical Society of New Jersey, 2 Princess Rd., Lawrenceville. Pre-registration required. Before attending call Karen Rust, RN 609-655-5755 (day).

MIDDLESEX

Laryngectomee Support Group *Professionally-run.* Support for patients who have undergone a laryngectomee. Families welcome. Guest speakers. Building is handicapped accessible. Meets 3rd Tues., 2-3pm (except July/Aug.), JFK Medical Center, Dept. of Speech and Audiology, 65 James St., Edison. Pre-registration required. Before attending call Patricia 732-321-7063 (Tues., Wed., Fri.).

MORRIS

Tri-County New Voice Laryngectomee Support Group *(Morris/Sussex/Warren counties)* Mutual support and social activities for laryngectomees. Also includes anyone with neck, head and/or oral cancers. Hospital visitation for new laryngectomees. Family and friends are welcome. Building is handicapped accessible. Meeting day and time varies, Saint Clare's Hospital, Silby Hall, 25 Pocono Rd., Denville. Call Tom Beneventine 973-694-8417.

OCEAN

Nu-Voice Self-help for people who have had a laryngectomy. Newsletter. Dues $3. Meets Fri., 10am, The Lighthouse, 591 Lakehurst Rd., Toms River. Call 1-800-621-0096.

SOMERSET

Somerset County Miracle Voice Club *Professionally-run.* Support, education and encouragement for laryngectomy patients their families and/or caregivers. Building is handicapped accessible. Meets 1st Thurs., 1pm, The Wellness Community of Central New Jersey, 3 Crossroads Dr., Bedminster. Call Roy 908-850-3702. *Website:* http://somersetmiraclevoiceclub.org/

NATIONAL

International Association of Laryngectomees *International. 200 chapters. Founded 1952.* Acts as a bridge starting before laryngectomy surgery through rehabilitation. Provides practical and emotional support. Newsletter. Chapter development guidelines. Write: International Association of Laryngectomees, 1203 Wolf Swamp Rd., Jacksonville, NC 28546. Call 1-866-425-3678; Fax: 910-455-1855. *Website:* http://www.larynxlink.com *E-mail:* ialhq@larynxlink.com or minergl@ec.rr.com

LIFE THREATENING / CHRONIC ILLNESS
(see also cancer, specific illness, toll-free helplines)

BERGEN

Nutrition and Chronic Illness Support Group *Professionally-run.* Mutual support and education for persons with any type of chronic illness who are interested in healthy lifestyles. Topics include nutrition, healthy living, eating correctly, etc. Meets 3rd Thurs., 7-8:30pm, Community Seventh Day Adventist Church, 245 Tenafly Rd., Englewood. Call Claudine 201-724-4852.

MONMOUTH

Art Therapy for Children with a Chronically Ill Loved One *Professionally-run.* Support for children (ages 4 1/2-13) who have a family member with a chronic or terminal illness. Uses art therapy to help children express their feelings. Building is handicapped accessible. Meets periodically for 7 weeks, Riverview Medical Center, 1 Riverview Plaza, Red Bank. For information call Jane Weinheimer 732-530-2382 (day).

"Kind words can be short and easy to speak but their echoes are truly endless."
--*Mother Teresa*

NATIONAL

CorStone *National. Founded 1975.* Emotional and spiritual support programs for children, youth and adults facing their own or a family member's life-threatening illness, long-term diagnosis or bereavement. Offers group guidelines for starting a local group. Also open to anyone wishing to change their perception of their lives. Workshops and trainings. Website contains information on centers and contacts around the world. Write: Center for Attitudinal Healing, 33 Buchanan Dr., Sausalito, CA 94965. Call 415-331-6161; Fax: 415-331-4545. *Website:* http://www.attitudinalhealing.org *E-mail:* info@attitudinalhealing.org

Project DOCC-Delivery Of Chronic Care *International. 28 chapters. Founded 1994.* Provides education regarding the impact of chronic illness and/or disability on a family. Information, referrals, phone support, e-mail correspondence and "how to" guides on developing a local group. Write: Project DOCC, 18 Dunster Rd., Great Neck, NY 11021-4640. Call 516-829-0786; Fax: 516-498-1899. *Website:* http://projectdocc.org *E-mail:* projdocc@aol.com

Rest Ministries *National. 300 affiliated groups. Founded 1997.* Christian ministry for people who live with chronic pain or illness and their families. Quarterly magazine, daily devotionals, Hope Endures radio podcast, share and prayer e-mail support mailing list and online chat. Encouragement and resources for starting groups (approximately $15). Write: Rest Ministries, Inc., P.O. Box 502928, San Diego, CA 92150. Call 1-888-751-7378 or 858-486-4685; Fax: 1-800-933-1078. *Website:* http://www.restministries.org *E-mail:* rest@restministries.org

ONLINE

Ability Online Support Network *Online.* A family friendly monitored electronic message system that enables children and adolescents with disabilities or chronic illness (also parents/caregivers/siblings) to share experiences, information, encouragement, support and hope through messages. Registration is free. Call 1-866-650-6207 *Website:* http://www.abilityonline.org *E-mail:* information@ableline.org

Need help finding a specific group? Give us a call – we're here to help!
*Call **1-800-367-6274**.*

LIVER DISEASE
(see also hepatitis, specific illness)

STATEWIDE

American Liver Foundation (Greater NY Chapter covers northern NJ counties) *Professionally-run.* Support for persons with hepatitis or any other liver disease. Advocacy, education, guest speakers, phone help and literature. Family, friends and concerned professionals welcome. Meeting day and times vary. Call 1-877-307-7507 (Mon.-Fri., 9am-5pm). *Website:* http://www.liverfoundation.org/chapters/greaterny *E-mail:* greaterny@liverfoundation.org

CAMDEN

South Jersey Liver Opportunity for persons with any liver disease, including hepatitis C, to share coping skills. Buddy system, guest speakers and phone help. Dues $3/mtg. Building is handicapped accessible. Meets 2nd Tues., 7-9:30pm (except June, July, Aug., Dec.), West Jersey Hospital, Barry Brown Health Education Center, 316 Carnie Blvd., Voorhees. Call Harry Hagar Jr. 856-983-8247 or Marlene Reid 856-468-2883.

MERCER

Mercer County Survivors of Liver Disease/Hepatitis Support and education for those afflicted with liver disease or hepatitis. Family, friends and professionals welcome. Lectures, guest speakers, advocacy, rap sessions and social group. Building is handicapped accessible. Meets 1st and 3rd Sun. 7-9pm, Robert Wood Johnson University Hospital, 1 Hamilton Place, Hamilton. Call Peggy Goodale 609-903-8524 (day) or Tammy Leigh 609-584-2166 (day).

NATIONAL

American Liver Foundation *National. 25 chapters. Founded 1976.* Dedicated to the prevention, treatment and cure of liver disease (including hepatitis) through research, education and advocacy. Members include patients, families, professionals and supporters. Chapters organized and operated by lay volunteers and staff. Offers guidelines for starting groups. Online local chapter locator. Write: American Liver Foundation, 75 Maiden Lane, Suite 603, New York, NY 10038-4810. Call 1-800-465-4837; Fax: 212-483-8179. *Website:* http://www.liverfoundation.org

Children's Liver Association for Support Services (CLASS) *Model. Founded 1995.* Dedicated to addressing the emotional, educational and financial needs of families with children with liver disease or liver transplantation. Telephone hotline, newsletter, parent matching, literature and financial assistance. Supports research and educates public about organ donations. Write: Children's Liver Association for Support Services, 27023 McBean Pkwy., Suite 126, Valencia, CA 91355. Call 1-877-679-8256 or 661-263-9099; Fax: 661-263-9099. *Website:* http://www.classkids.org

ONLINE

Autoimmune Liver Disease Support Group *Online.* Support and sharing for those who have been afflicted with autoimmune liver disease of all forms. Message board. *Website:* http://health.groups.yahoo.com/group/LiverSupport-L/

PSC-Support *Online. 1444 members. Founded 1998.* Support for patients or family members of patients with primary sclerosing cholangitis, a chronic cholestatic liver disease characterized by periductal inflammation of both intrahepatic and extrahepatic bile ducts. *Website:* http://health.groups.yahoo.com/group/psc-support

LUPUS

STATEWIDE

Lupus Foundation of America, Inc. - North Jersey Chapter *Professionally-run.* Monthly support group meetings in various counties. Professional staff, volunteers and peer counselors assist and support lupus patients and their families. Information and referral, resource library, pen pals and seminars. Quarterly newsletter to members. Dues $20/individual, $30/family. Provides speakers for public and professional education. Write: Lupus Foundation of America, Inc., NJ Chapter, 150 Morris Ave., P.O. Box 1184, Suite 102, Springfield, NJ 07081. Call 1-800-322-5816. *Website:* http://www.lupusnj.org *E-mail:* info@lupusnj.org

BERGEN

Lupus Foundation of America Support and information for lupus patients and their families. Promotes education and public awareness. Dues $20yr/individual, $30yr/family. Building is handicapped accessible. Meets 4th Mon., 7:30pm (except Jan., July, Aug., Dec.), Kessler Institute for Rehabilitation, 300 Market

St., 4th Floor, Saddle Brook. Call 1-800-322-5816. *Website:* http://www.lupusnj.org

ESSEX

Lupus Foundation of America Support and information for lupus patients and their families. Promotes education and public awareness. Dues $20yr/individual, $30yr/family. Building is handicapped accessible. Meets 1st Sat., 11am, (except Jan., Feb., July, Aug., Nov. and Dec.), Newark Beth Israel, 201 Lyons Ave., Newark. Call 1-800-322-5816. *Website:* http://www.lupusnj.org

HUDSON

Lupus Foundation of America Support and information for lupus patients and their families. Promotes education and public awareness. Dues $20yr/individual, $30yr/family. Meets 3rd Thurs., 7:30pm (except Jan., Feb., July, Aug., Nov., Dec.), St. Anne's Church, 3545 Kennedy Blvd., Centennial Hall, Jersey City. Call 1-800-322-5816. *Website:* http://www.lupusnj.org

MERCER

Lupus Foundation of America Support and information for lupus patients and their families. Promotes education and public awareness. Dues $20yr/individual, $30yr/family. Meets 3rd Wed., 7:30pm (except Jan., July, Aug., Nov., Dec.), Mercer County Library, 2751 Brunswick Pike, Lawrenceville. Call 1-800-322-5816. *Website:* http://www.lupusnj.org

MIDDLESEX

Lupus Foundation of America Support and information for lupus patients and their families. Promotes education and public awareness. Dues $20yr./individual, $30yr./family. Call 1-800-322-5816. *Website:* http://www.lupusnj.org

> **Edison** Meets 2nd Sat. (except Jan., July, Aug.), Haven Hospice, JFK Medical Center, 65 James St., Haven Conference Room, 3rd Floor.
> **Old Bridge** Meets 3rd Sat., 11am (except Jan., July, Aug.), Old Bridge Library, Main Branch, One Old Bridge Plaza, Municipal Center (Route 516 and Cottrell Rd.).

MONMOUTH

Lupus Foundation of America Support and information for lupus patients and their families. Promotes education and public awareness. Dues $20yr/individual, $30yr/family. Building is handicapped accessible. Meets 1st Sat., 11am (except Jan., July, Aug.), Jersey Shore University Medical Center, 1945 Route 33, Neptune. Call 1-800-322-5816. *Website:* http://www.lupusnj.org

MORRIS

Lupus Foundation of America Support and information for lupus patients and their families. Promotes education and public awareness. Dues $20yr/individual, $30yr/family. Building is handicapped accessible. Meets 2nd Wed., 7:30pm (except Jan., Feb., Apr., July, Aug., Sept., Oct.), Saint Clare's Hospital, 400 W. Blackwell St., 1st Floor, Conference Room C, D and E, Dover. Call 1-800-322-5816. *Website:* http://www.lupus.org

OCEAN

Lupus Foundation of America Support and information for lupus patients and their families. Promotes education and public awareness. Dues $20yr/individual, $30yr/family. Building is handicapped accessible. Meets 2nd Tues., 7:30pm, Ocean Medical Center, 425 Jack Martin Blvd., Brick. Call 1-800-322-5816. *Website:* http://www.lupus.org

NATIONAL

Lupus Foundation of America, Inc., The *(BILINGUAL) National. 40 chapters. Founded 1977.* Provides information and materials about lupus, and services to people with lupus and their families. Conducts education and supports research programs. Membership and national magazine (Lupus Now) available by subscription and through local chapters. Write: Lupus Foundation of America, Inc., 2000 L St. NW, Suite 710, Washington, DC 20036. Call 1-800-558-0121 or 202-349-1155; Spanish: 1-800-558-0231; Fax: 202-349-1156. *Website:* http://www.lupus.org *E-mail:* info@lupus.org

"You cannot hope to build a better world without improving the individuals. To that end each of us must work for our own improvement, and at the same time share a general responsibility for all humanity, our particular duty being to aid those to whom we think we can be most useful."-- Marie Curie

LYME DISEASE

MORRIS

Long Valley Lyme Disease Association *Professionally-run.* Support, information and networking for people with Lyme disease. Social group, educational series and advocacy. Meets 3rd Wed., 7-9pm (except Dec.), Our Lady Of The Mountain Church, Springtown and Schooley's Mountain Rd., Long Valley. Call Nancy Braithwaite 908-852-5937 (eve). *E-mail:* dabrai@comcast.net

Morristown Lyme Support Group Support and education for Lyme disease patients and their families. Building is handicapped accessible. Meets 3rd Tues., 7pm, The Presbyterian Parish House, 65 South St., Morristown. Call Anita Glick 973-267-8858.

NATIONAL

Lyme Disease Network *National network. Founded 1991.* Support, information and referrals for victims of Lyme disease and their families. Maintains computer information system. Write: Lyme Disease Network, 43 Winton Rd., East Brunswick, NJ 08816. *Website:* http://www.lymenet.org *E-mail:* webmaster@lymenet.org

LYMPHEDEMA

ATLANTIC

Living with Lymphedema *Professionally-run.* Support for any type of lymphedema. Families welcome. Guest speakers, education and literature. Building is handicapped accessible. Meets 2nd Thurs., 7-8:30pm, Shore Memorial Hospital, Cancer Center, Shore Rd. and Brighton Ave., Somers Point. Call Jennifer Brooks 609-653-3512 (day).

NATIONAL

National Lymphedema Network Inc. *National. Founded 1988.* Support groups and information regarding primary and secondary lymphedema for patients and professionals. Newsletter, telephone infoline, conferences, pen pal program, referrals to treatment centers and physicians. Assistance in starting new groups. Dues $45. Write: National Lymphedema Network, 1611 Telegraph Ave., Suite 1111, Oakland, CA 94612. Call 1-800-541-3259 (recording) or 510-208-3200;

Fax: 510-208-3110. *Website:* http://www.lymphnet.org *E-mail:* nln@lymphnet.org

MULTIPLE MYELOMA

BERGEN

Multiple Myeloma *Professionally-run.* Mutual support for patients, families and friends affected by multiple myeloma. Rap sessions, guest speakers and literature. Meets 3rd Thurs., 10:30am-noon, Sanzari Building, 369 Essex St., Hackensack. Call Ann 201-996-5983 (day).

MORRIS

Multiple Myeloma Support Group *Professionally-run.* Mutual support for patients, families and friends affected by multiple myeloma. Guest speakers. Meets 4th Mon., 1:30-3pm, Carol G. Simon Cancer Center, Morristown Memorial Hospital, 100 Madison Ave., Cancer Center Conference Room, Morristown. Call Ruth Lin, RN 973-971-7742 (day) or Anne Kahn, LCSW 973-971-4269 (day).

SOMERSET

Central Jersey Multiple Myeloma Support Group *Professionally-run.* Mutual support for patients, families and friends affected by multiple myeloma. Meets 1st Wed., 7pm, Steeplechase Cancer Center, 110 Rehill Ave., Somerville. Call Paula Van Riper 908-725-4948 (day).

NATIONAL

International Myeloma Foundation *International network. 89 groups. Founded 1990.* Goal is to improve the quality of life of myeloma patients while working toward prevention and a cure. The IMF operates a Myeloma Hotline, disseminates comprehensive printed and online information about myeloma, treatment options and disease management. Seminars and workshops for the patient community and medical professionals. Write: International Myelome Foundation, 12650 Riverside Dr., Suite 206, North Hollywood, CA 91607. Call 818-487-7455 or 1-800-452-2873 (Mon-Fri, 9am-4pm PST); Fax: 818-487-7454. *Website:* http://www.myeloma.org *E-mail:* TheIMF@myeloma.org

MULTIPLE SCLEROSIS
(see also physical disability, toll-free helplines)

STATEWIDE

Multiple Sclerosis Association of America Mutual support and education for persons with multiple sclerosis. Offers phone support, information and referrals, networking program, support group meetings, lending library, home modification program, equipment distribution program and more. Assistance in starting local support groups. Write: MSAA, 706 Haddonfield Rd., Cherry Hill, NJ 08002. Call 1-800-532-7667 (Mon.-Thurs., 8:30am-7pm; Fri., 8:30am-5pm EST); Fax: 856-488-8257. *Website:* http://www.msassociation.org *E-mail:* webmaster@msassociation.org

National Multiple Sclerosis Society Local support groups, resource centers and lending library information, educational programs, national research and much more.

> **Greater Delaware Valley** Serving South Jersey, Greater Delaware Valley Area, Lehigh Valley and Reading. Write: National Multiple Sclerosis Society/Greater Delaware Valley, 1 Reed St., Suite 200, Philadelphia, PA 19147. Call 1-800-548-4611 or 215-271-1500. *Website:* http://www.nationalmssociety.org/pae/home *E-mail:* pae@nmss.org
>
> **New Jersey Metro Chapter** Serving Bergen, Essex, Hudson, Hunterdon, Mercer, Middlesex, Monmouth, Morris, Ocean, Passaic, Somerset, Sussex, Union and Warren counties. Write: National Multiple Sclerosis Society, 1 Kalisa Way, Suite 205, Paramus, NJ 07652-3550. Call 1-800-344-4867 or 201-967-5599 (day). *Website:* http://www.nationalmssociety.org/njb *E-mail:* pat@njb.nmss.org

ATLANTIC

Pomona MS Group Provides support and education for persons with multiple sclerosis. Rap sessions, guest speakers and literature. Building is handicapped accessible. Meets 1st Tues., 6-8pm, Galloway Library, 306 East Jimmie Leeds Rd., Galloway. Call Barbara 609-264-1916 (day), Phyllis 609-266-1497 (day) or Linda 609-484-0991 (day).

"No one is useless in the world who lightens the burden of others."--Charles Dickens

BERGEN

National MS Society Support Group - "COPE" Peer support, information and socialization for persons with multiple sclerosis. Meets last Thurs., 11am, Cornell Medical Supply Company, 30 New Bridge Rd., Bergenfield. Before attending call Joan 201-837-7790. *Website:* http://www.njbnmss.org *E-mail:* pat@njb.nmss.org

National MS Society Support Group - (Faith Is Our Pathway) Support and education for African Americans diagnosed with multiple sclerosis, their families and friends. Guest speakers. Meets 3rd Sat., 10am, Ebenezer Baptist Church, 216 4th St., Englewood. Call Irvina 201-569-3613. *Website:* http://www.njbnmss.org *E-mail:* pat@njb.nmss.org

National MS Society Support Group - "Friends" Support group for persons with multiple sclerosis and their families. Occasional guest speakers. Meets 1st Thurs., 7pm, Holy Name Hospital, Teaneck. Call Sister Mary Morris 201-967-5599. *Website:* http://www.njbnmss.org *E-mail:* pat@njb.nmss.org

National MS Society Support Group - T.M. (Twice Monthly) Support and education for persons diagnosed with multiple sclerosis, their families and friends. Guest speakers. Meets 1st and 3rd Mon., 7pm, Trinity Presbyterian Church, 650 Pascack Rd., Paramus. Call Joe 201-797-3386. *Website:* http://www.njbnmss.org *E-mail:* pat@njb.nmss.org

ESSEX

National MS Society - Gay/Lesbian Support Group *Professionally-run.* Mutual support for gay/lesbians with multiple sclerosis. Family and friends welcome. Rap sessions. Meets 2nd Thurs., 7pm (except June, July, Aug.), Vincent United Methodist Church, 100 Vincent Place, Nutley. Call Nancy 201-788-3663. *Website:* http://www.njbnmss.org *E-mail:* pat@njb.nmss.org

National MS Society Support Group *Professionally-run.* Mutual support for individuals with multiple sclerosis. Rap sessions. Meets 4th Mon., 10:30am (except June, July, Aug.), St. Barnabas Ambulatory Care Center, Dr. Herbert's office, 1st Floor, 200 South Orange Ave, Livingston. Call Roseanne 973-334-8434. *Website:* http://www.njbnmss.org *E-mail:* pat@njb.nmss.org

National MS Society Support Group Support group for persons with multiple sclerosis and their families. *Website:* http://www.njbnmss.org *E-mail:* pat@njb.nmss.org

Livingston Meets 2nd Mon., 7pm, Livingston Community Center, 204 Hillside Ave. Guest speaker. Call Marlene 973-992-5313.

Newark Meets 3rd Thurs., 11:30am (except June, July, Aug.), University of Medicine and Dentistry, DOC Building, 8th Floor Conference Room. Lunch provided. Before attending call Linda 973-923-6912.

Nutley Meets 3rd Thurs., 7pm, Vincent United Methodist Church, 100 Vincent Pl. Call Gary 973-667-5209.

GLOUCESTER

Gloucester County MSAA Client Support *Professionally-run.* Provides fellowship and support to persons with multiple sclerosis. Education, guest speakers, rap sessions and socials. Meets 4th Wed., 6:30-8:30pm, Deptford Library, Highland Ave., Deptford. Call Shirley 856-228-8474.

Washington-Gloucester Twp. MS Self-Help Mutual support for persons with multiple sclerosis, their families and friends. Rap sessions and guest speakers. Building is handicapped accessible. Meets 3rd Mon., 11am-1pm, Cardinal Retirement Home, 455 Hurffville-Crosskey Rd, Sewell. Call Denise Savarese 856-627-6401. *Website:* http://www.greaterdelvalnmss.org *E-mail:* sewell@greaterdelvalnmss.org

HUDSON

National MS Society Support Group Mutual support and education for persons with multiple sclerosis, their families and friends. Guest speakers, phone help and social activities. Meets 1st Wed., 7:30pm (except June, July, Aug.), Newport Nursing and Rehabilitation Center, 198 Stevens Ave., Jersey City. For meeting information call Christine 201-332-3417 (day). *Website:* http://www.njbnmss.org *E-mail:* pat@njb.nmss.org

MERCER

National MS Society Support Group Support, information and open discussions on living and managing the physical and emotional aspects of multiple sclerosis. *Website:* http://www.njbnms.org *E-mail:* pat@njb.nmss.org

> **Lawrenceville** Meets 4th Sun., 2-4pm (except July/Aug.), Morris Hall, 1 Bishop's Court and Route 546. Also open to family members. Call Mike 609-588-0902.

> **Robbinsville** Meets 1st Tues., 7-9pm, Mercer County Library, 42 Robbinsville-Allentown Rd. Call Stephanie H. 609-647-7357 or Steve B. 609-799-9585.

MIDDLESEX

National MS Society Support Group Mutual help for persons with multiple sclerosis. Building is handicapped accessible. Meets 3rd Tues., 10am-1pm (except July/Aug.) First Presbyterian Church, Social Center, Woodbridge Ave. and Home St., Metuchen. Call Sonya 732-826-7754 or Camille H. 732-634-4104. *Website:* http://www.nationalmssociety.org

National MS Society Support Group Mutual support for people with multiple sclerosis, their families and friends. Transportation available. Meets 3rd Wed., 7-9pm, East Brunswick Public Library, 2 Civic Center Dr., East Brunswick. Before attending call Elihu 732-613-5080 or Katie O. 732-651-1232. *Website:* http://www.njbnmss.org *E-mail:* pat@njb.nmss.org

MONMOUTH

Disability Support Group Support for men and women with any type of physical disability including MS. Guest speakers and phone help. Meets Wed., 11am-2pm, St. Anselm's Church, 1028 Wayside Rd., Wayside. Call Rhoda 732-462-0401 (day).

Eastern Monmouth County Multiple Sclerosis Self-Help Phone support and networking for persons with multiple sclerosis and their families. Call Evelyn Wilson 732-229-2027 (day).

Multiple Sclerosis Support Group Mutual support for persons with multiple sclerosis. Families and friends welcome. Meetings vary, Marlboro Public Library, Library Ct. and Wyncrest Cr., Marlboro. Call Lorraine 732-671-9384 or Diane 732-536-3033. *E-mail:* lolo391064@aol.com

Multiple Sclerosis Support Group Mutual support for persons with multiple sclerosis. Families, friends and caregivers welcome. Meets 3rd Sat., 10am-noon, St. Anselm's Church, 1028 Wayside Rd., Wayside. Call Dennis 732-531-7570.

National MS Society Support Group *Professionally-run.* Support, information, discussions on living, managing the physical and emotional aspects of multiple sclerosis. Families welcome. Meets 3rd Mon., 1-3pm (except Jan., Feb., July, Aug.), Centra State Hospital, Fitness and Wellness Center, 901 West Main St., Freehold. Call 732-294-2505 ext. 3 (day). *Website:* http://www.njbnmss.org *E-mail:* pat@njbnmss.org

National MS Society Support Group Mutual support for person with multiple sclerosis. Meets 2nd Tues., noon-2pm, MS Society, 246 Monmouth Rd., Oakhurst. Call Nancy M. 732-531-6758 or Dawn D. 732-335-4477. *Website:* http://www.njbnmss.org *E-mail:* pat@njbnmss.org

MORRIS

National MS Society Support Group Fellowship of multiple sclerosis patients that meet for information, networking and creative exchange of ideas. All ages welcome. Guest speakers, discussions and socials. Meets 1st Tues., 7pm (except June, July, Aug.), Presbyterian Parish House, 65 South St., Morristown. Call Mary Ellen 973-299-1778. *Website:* http://www.njbnmss.org *E-mail:* pat@njb.nmss.org

National MS Society Support Group *Professionally-run.* Fellowship of persons with multiple sclerosis. Provides information, networking and a creative exchange of ideas. All ages welcome. Meets 2nd Thurs. (except June, July, Aug.), 10am, Montville Youth Center, Changebridge Rd., Montville. Call Roseann 973-334-8434. *Website:* http://www.njbnmss.org *E-mail:* pat@njb.nmss.org

OCEAN

National MS Society Support Group Provides education, rap sessions, guest speakers, phone help, support and camaraderie for people with multiple sclerosis. Building is handicapped accessible. Meets 4th Fri., 7-9pm (except July/Aug.), Presbyterian Church of Toms River, 1070 Hooper Ave., Toms River. Call Pat 732-244-7523 or Dianne 732-892-2230. *Website:* http://www.njbnmss.org *E-mail:* pat@njb.nmss.org

National MS Society Support Group Support group for persons with multiple sclerosis and their families. Occasional guest speakers. *Website:* http://www.njbnmss.org *E-mail:* pat@njb.nmss.org
> **Brick** Meets last Mon., 10:30am-noon, Ocean Medical Center, Jack Martin Blvd., 1st Floor Atrium. Call Marcy 732-840-5269, Alice 732-244-8332 or Jan 732-840-2186.
> **Manahawkin** Meets 3rd Fri., 10:30am-12:30pm (except July, Aug., Dec.), Lutheran Church of the Holy Spirit, 333 N. Main St. Call Jill 609-607-8720 or Gail 609-978-1268.

Multiple Sclerosis Support Group (Sponsored by MSAA) Mutual support for multiple sclerosis patients, their families and friends. Meets 3rd Sat., 1pm (except June, July, Aug.), Epiphany Roman Catholic Church, All Purpose

Room, Thiele Rd., Brick. Before attending call Gene Van Severen 732-920-3641 (day).

PASSAIC

National MS Society Support Group - "OUI Group" Support group for persons with multiple sclerosis and their families. Guest speakers. Meets 3rd Mon., 7pm, Packanack Lake Church, 120 Lake Drive East, Wayne. Call Michael 973-628-8991. *Website:* http://www.njbnmss.org *E-mail:* pat@njb.nmss.org

National MS Society Support Group - "Squeaky Wheels" Caring and sharing support group for persons with multiple sclerosis and their families. Information and advocacy. Meets 4th Wed., noon (except June, July, Aug.), Hillcrest Center, Macopin Rd., West Milford. Call Janice 973-728-1282 (day) or Mary 973-835-2565. *Website:* http://www.njbnmss.org *E-mail:* pat@njb.nmss.org

National MS Society Support Group - "Working with MS" Support group for persons with multiple sclerosis who are still working. Guest speakers, rap sessions, literature and buddy system. Meets 2nd Thurs., 7pm (except June, July, Aug.), Clifton Public Library, 291 Piaget Ave., Clifton. Call Susan 973-667-1416. *Website:* http://www.njbnmss.org *E-mail:* pat@njb.nmss.org

SOMERSET

National MS Society Support Group Information and open discussions on living with and managing physical and emotional aspects of multiple sclerosis for both the person with MS and their significant others. *Website:* http://www.njbnmss.org *E-mail:* pat@njb.nmss.org

> **Bridgewater** Meets 4th Tues., 7-9pm, The People Care Center, 120 Finderne Ave. Call Doug 908-334-9212 or John 908-295-1401.
> **Hillsborough** Meets 4th Thurs., 7-9pm (except July/Aug.), Summerville at Hillsborough Assisted Living Complex, 600 Auten Rd. Building is handicapped accessible. Call Wendy 908-359-4514 (day).

SUSSEX

National MS Society Support Group Fellowship of multiple sclerosis patients meeting for information, networking and creative exchange of ideas. Guest speakers, discussions and socials. Meets 1st Wed., 7pm (except June, July, Aug.), Catholic Charities Family Services, Adult Day Care Center, 55 Mill St., Newton. Call Debbie 973-948-6586 or Marie 973-209-2420. *Website:* http://www.njbnmss.org *E-mail:* pat@njb.nmss.org

UNION

Building Bridges: A Group for Minorities Peer support, information and socialization for people with multiple sclerosis. Meets 2nd Sat. (except June, July, Aug.), 1pm, Muhlenberg Medical Center, Park Ave. and Randolph Rd., Plainfield. Call Tennille 973-207-4191. *Website:* http://www.njbnmss.org *E-mail:* pat@njb.nmss.org

National MS Society Support Group Peer support, information and socialization for people with multiple sclerosis. Meets 1st Tues., 7pm (except June, July, Aug.), Clark Town Hall, 430 Westfield Ave., Clark. Call Anne Marie 908-925-0677. *Website:* http://www.njbnmss.org *E-mail:* pat@njb.nmss.org

WARREN

National MS Society Support Group Mutual support for persons with multiple sclerosis. Guest speakers. Meets 2nd Mon., 7:30pm, Hackettstown Hospital, 651 Willow Grove St., Hackettstown. Call Cynthia 973-786-5382 or Helen 908-979-0984. *Website:* http://www.njbnmss.org *E-mail:* pat@njb.nmss.org

National MS Society Support Group Peer support, information and socialization for people with multiple sclerosis. *Website:* http://www.njbnmss.org *E-mail:* pat@njb.nmss.org
> **Alpha** Meets 4th Thurs., (except June, July, Aug.), 7-9pm, Alpha Municipal Building, 1001 East Blvd. Call Klara T. 908-454-7770 or 908-619-3150.
> **Phillipsburg** Meets 4th Thurs., (except June, July, Aug.), 7pm, Warren Hospital, 185 Roseberry St. Call Neil 908-454-6448.

NATIONAL

Multiple Sclerosis Association of America *National. 6 regional U.S. offices. Founded 1970.* Mutual support and education for persons with multiple sclerosis. Offers phone support, information and referrals, networking program, support group meetings, MRI funding, lending library, home modification program, cooling equipment program and more. Write: MSAA, 706 Haddonfield Rd., Cherry Hill, NJ 08002. Call 1-800-532-7667 (Mon.-Thurs., 8:30am-8pm; Fri., 8:30am-5pm EST); Fax: 856-488-8257. *Website:* http://www.msaa.com *E-mail:* msaa@msaa.com

National Multiple Sclerosis Society *(BILINGUAL) National. 1800 groups. Founded 1946.* Funds research in multiple sclerosis, provides information and referrals, support groups for patients and families, professional education and newsletter. Write: National Multiple Sclerosis Society, 733 Third Ave., New York, NY 10017. Call 1-800-344-4867 or 212-986-3240 (administration). *Website:* http://www.nationalmssociety.org

ONLINE

MS Moms (Managing Our Multiple Sclerosis) *Online.* Support for mothers living, parenting and managing with their multiple sclerosis. *Website:* http://www.msmoms.com

MUSCULAR DYSTROPHY

BERGEN

MDA/ALS Support Group *Professionally-run.* Mutual support for individuals with muscular dystrophy or ALS. Families and caregivers welcome. Sharing of information, experiences, ideas and resources. Usually meets 3rd Thurs., 4-5:30pm, Jewish Community Center on the Palisades, 411 East Clinton Ave., Tenafly. Pre-registration required. Before attending call 201-843-4452 (day).

NATIONAL

Muscular Dystrophy Association *National. 200+ chapters. Founded 1950.* Provides comprehensive medical services to persons with neuromuscular disease. Supports research into the causes, cures and treatments of neuromuscular disorders. Support programs include self-help groups, phone friends, pen pals and scheduled online chat sessions. Write: Muscular Dystrophy Association, 3300 E. Sunrise Dr., Tucson, AZ 85718-3299. Call 1-800-572-1717; Fax: 520-529-5454. *Website:* http://www.mda.org *E-mail:* mda@mdausa.org

Parent Project for Muscular Dystrophy Research, Inc. *International network. Founded 1994.* Support for parents of children with Duchenne and Becker muscular dystrophy. To improve the treatment, quality of life and long-term outlook for all individuals affected by DMD through research, advocacy, education and compassion. Provides user-friendly website with online forums, scientific and legislative conferences, newsletters, information on newest diagnosis, standards of care and research strategies. Write: Parent Project Muscular Dystrophy Research, Inc., 158 Linwood Plaza, Fort Lee, NJ 07024.

Call 1-800-714-5437 or 201-944-9985; Fax: 201-944-9987. *Website:* http://www.parentprojectmd.org *E-mail:* info@parentprojectmd.org

SMDI (Society for Muscular Dystrophy International) *International network. Founded 1983.* Purpose is to share and encourage the exchange of non-technical, neuromuscular and disability-related information. Referrals to support groups via networking website. Write: SMDI International, P.O. Box 479, Bridgewater, NS Canada B4V 2X6. Call 902-685-3961; Fax: 902-685-3962.

NEUROPATHY

BERGEN

Northern New Jersey Peripheral Neuropathy Support Group Support, information and advocacy to persons with peripheral neuropathy. Guest speakers, educational series, phone help and literature. Building is handicapped accessible. Meets 3rd Thurs., 7:30-9:30pm, (except Jan., Feb., July, Aug., Dec.), Englewood Hospital, 350 Engle St., Englewood. Call Tom 201-692-9313. For directions to Englewood Hospital call 201-894-3000. *E-mail:* mcculluma@optonline.net

MERCER

Peripheral Neuropathy Support Group Support for person with nerve damage as a result of neuropathy. Family and friends are welcome. Offers guest speakers, mutual sharing, educational series, rap sessions, literature, and phone help. Meets 4 times/yr., Robert Wood Johnson Hospital, Hamilton Square. For meeting information call Bill 609-587-7215.

MONMOUTH

Monmouth/Ocean Neuropathy Support Group Support and information to those afflicted with neuropathy. Mutual sharing, guest speakers, literature and phone help. Dues $15 yr. Meets 3rd Sat. (Sept., Nov., Jan., Mar., May), 1-3pm, Rehabilitation Hospital of Tinton Falls, 2 Centre Plaza, Tinton Falls. Call Fontaine 908-233-9709. *E-mail:* FontaineGatti@msn.com

NATIONAL

Neuropathy Association *International. 214 affiliated groups. Founded 1995.* Provides support, education and advocacy for persons with peripheral neuropathy. Promotes and funds research into the cause and cure. Information and referrals, newsletter, literature, phone support, online bulletin board, referrals to support groups and doctors. Write: Neuropathy Association, 60 E. 42nd St., Room 942, New York, NY 10165. Call 212-692-0662; Fax: 212-692-0668. *Website:* http://www.neuropathy.org *E-mail:* info@neuropathy.org

OSTEOPOROSIS

ESSEX

Osteoporosis Support Group *Professionally-run.* Support and education for people with osteoporosis, their families and friends. Discussions, guest speakers and literature. Meets 2nd Thurs., 11:30am-1pm, St. Barnabas Ambulatory Care Center, 200 S. Orange Ave., Conference Room A/B, Livingston. Call Joan Petersen 973-322-7417 (day). *E-mail:* jpetersen@sbhcs.com

HUNTERDON

Arthritis Foundation NJ Chapter Mutual support and education for people with arthritis or osteoporosis and their families. Building is handicapped accessible. Meets 2nd Mon., 1-3pm, Hunterdon Medical Center, Meeting Room A and B, 2100 Wescott Drive, Flemington. Call 908-788-6373.

MORRIS

Arthritis and Osteoporosis Support Group *Professionally-run.* Support and education for individuals with arthritis and osteoporosis. Families welcome. Guest speakers, literature and newsletter. Building is handicapped accessible. Meets 3rd Thurs., 1-2pm, Arthritis Center, 95 Madison Ave., 3rd Floor, Suite 306, Morristown. Before attending call 1-877-973-6500 (day).

Osteoporosis Support Group *Professionally-run.* Provides those with osteoporosis, their family, and friends an opportunity to discuss their problems, offers mutual respect and exchange ideas to help cope with the disease. Building is handicapped accessible. Meets 3rd Thurs., 10:30am-noon, Madison YMCA, 111 Kings Rd., Madison. Call Angele Thompson 908-898-0055 (day).

NATIONAL

National Osteoporosis Foundation *National. 80+ affiliated support groups. Founded 1984.* Dedicated to reducing the widespread prevalence of osteoporosis through programs of research, education and advocacy. Provides referrals to existing support groups, educational materials, as well as free resources and materials to assist people to start groups. Newsletter, conferences, information and referrals. Write: NOF, 1232 22nd St., NW, Washington, DC 20037-1202. Call 202-223-2226 or 1-800-223-9994; Fax: 202-223-2237. *Website:* http://www.nof.org *E-mail:* jeffrey@nof.org

OSTOMY

BURLINGTON

United Ostomy Association of America Education and encouragement for ostomy patients, those with related surgery. Families are welcome. Visitation, peer-counseling and newsletter. Building is handicapped. Dues $10/yr. Meets 3rd Mon., 7-9pm, Virtua Memorial Hospital of Burlington County, 175 Madison Ave., Conference Center, Mt. Holly. Call Ken Aukett 856-854-3737 (1-10pm). *Website:* http://www.ostomysnj.org *E-mail:* kenaukett@uoaa.org

ESSEX

United Ostomy Association of America Education and encouragement for ostomy patients and their families. Outreach, peer-counseling, phone help and newsletter. Meets Jan., Mar., May, Sept., Nov., 8pm, St. Barnabas Ambulatory Care Center, 200 S. Orange Ave., Livingston. Call Paula Von Rosendahl 973-239-1616 or Margaret Tretola 973-743-9550.

HUNTERDON

Ostomy Support Group *Professionally-run.* Education and support for ostomy patients and their families. Guest speakers, lecture series and literature. Building is handicapped accessible. Meets 3rd Tues., 7-9pm, Hunterdon Medical Center, 2100 Wescott Dr., Flemington. Call Beverly Phillips 908-237-5427.

MIDDLESEX

United Ostomy Association of America Education and encouragement for ostomy patients and their families. Outreach, visitation, phone help, newsletter. Dues $15/yr. Meets 1st Wed., 6:30pm (except Jan., July, Aug., Sept.), American Cancer Society, 2600 U.S. Route 1 North, North Brunswick. Call 732-572-3298. *E-mail:* medicamm@verizon.net

MORRIS

North Jersey Ostomates *Professionally-run.* Mutual support and education for ostomy patients and their families. Provides outreach, visitation and peer-counseling. Meets 1st Mon., 7:30-9pm (except Jan./Feb.), Chilton Memorial Hospital, 97 West Parkway, Collins Pavilion, 2nd Floor, Pompton Plains. Call Chuck 973-633-9840 or Sue Becker, RN 973-831-5303 (day).

United Ostomy Association of America Education and encouragement for ostomy patients and their families. Provides outreach, visitation, peer-counseling and newsletter. Meets 3rd Wed., 7:30-9:00pm, Morristown Memorial Hospital, Carol G. Simon Cancer Center, 100 Madison Ave., Conference Room, Morristown. Call Toni McTigue, RN 973-971-5522 (day).

OCEAN

United Ostomy Association Education and encouragement for ostomy patients and their families. Visitation, peer-counseling and newsletter. Dues $10/yr. Building is handicapped accessible. Meets 4th Fri., 7pm (except July/Aug.), Toms River Presbyterian Church, 1070 Hooper Ave., Toms River. Call Tom 732-901-9411 (day) or American Cancer Society 732-914-1000.

SOMERSET

United Ostomy Association Education and encouragement for ostomy patients and their families. Outreach visitation, guest speakers, phone help and newsletter. Building handicapped accessible. Meets 3rd Tues., 7:30-9pm (except June, July, Aug., Dec.), Somerset Medical Center, Conference Room C and D, 110 Rehill Ave., Somerville. Call Monica Smith 908-685-2814 (day).

WARREN

Warren County Ostomy Club (United Ostomy Association) *Professionally-run.* Dedicated to serving and educating persons before and after surgery for a colostomy, ileostomy or urostomy. Families welcome. Education, visitation and socials. Building is handicapped accessible. Meets 3rd Sun., 2pm, Warren Hospital, 185 Roseberry St., Farley Education Room, Warren. Dues $15/yr. Call Cathy Kiley 610-252-4777.

NATIONAL

Pull-thru Network, The *International network. Founded 1988.* Support and information for families with children born with anorectal, colorectal or urogenital disorders and any of the associated diagnoses. Disorders include bladder exstrophy, imperforate anus, VATER/VACTERL association, anal stenosis, cloacal exstrophy, Hirschsprung's disease and associated diagnoses. Maintains a database for member networking. Quarterly magazine, online discussion group, weekly chat for members, phone support and literature. Dues $30/year - free membership upon request. Write: The Pull-thru Network, 2312 Savoy St., Hoover, AL 35226-1528. Call 205-978-2930. *Website:* http://www.pullthrunetwork.org *E-mail:* ptnmail@charter.net

United Ostomy Association of America *National. 240 affiliates. Founded 2005.* Dedicated to helping every person with an ostomy and related surgeries return to normal living. Also has support groups for parents of children with ostomies, teens, young adults, gay, lesbian and transgenders and those who have had a continent diversion. Provides education, support to local groups, national identity and affiliate development help, visitation program and quarterly magazine. Chapter development help. Local group directory on website. Write: United Ostomy Associations of America., P.O. Box 66, Fairview, TN 37062. Call 1-800-826-0826; Fax: 615-799-5915. *Website:* http://www.uoaa.org *E-mail:* info@uoaa.org

PAIN, CHRONIC

ATLANTIC

Atlantic Chronic Pain Support Group Mutual support for individuals dealing with a chronic pain situation. Meets 2nd and 4th Wed., 6:30-8:30pm, Bacharach Institute for Rehabilitation, 61 West Jimmie Leeds Rd., Board Room, Pomona. Call Bob 609-266-1198 (day).

BURLINGTON

Reflex Sympathetic Dystrophy and Chronic Pain Support Group 12-Step. Support for persons with reflex sympathetic dystrophy or chronic pain, their families and friends. Helps members maintain as normal and pain free life as possible. Guest speakers, educational programs, pen pals, rap sessions, literature, phone help and advocacy.
> **Mt. Holly** Meets 3rd Wed., 7-9pm, Virtua Hospital, 175 Madison Ave., Conference Room, 1st Floor. Building is handicapped accessible. Call Kathy Henson 609-268-1565 (day). *E-mail:* bepainfree2000@aol.com
> **Mt. Laurel** Meets 4th Tues., 6-8pm, YMCA, 5001 Centerton Rd. Call Ursula Weed 856-304-6682 or Lisa Vasey 609-877-0213 *E-mail:* sula252000@yahoo.com

CAMDEN

American Chronic Pain Association Support for those suffering from chronic pain and their families. A helping hand and friendly ear for those chronic pain sufferers willing to help themselves. Rap sessions, guest speakers and literature. Building is handicapped accessible. Meets the last Thurs., 7:30-8:30pm, New Seasons Assisted Living Facility, 501 Laurel Oak Rd., 3rd Floor Library, Voorhees. Call Philip 856-489-4383.

Chronic Pain Support Group *Professionally-run.* Provides support for those living with chronic pain. Building is handicapped accessible. Meets 2nd Fri., 10:30-11:30am, New Seasons Assisted Living, 501 Laurel Oak Rd., Voorhees. Call Elder Med 1-800-522-1965.

MORRIS

American Chronic Pain Association Support Group *Professionally-run.* Support and education for people and their families living with chronic pain. Rap sessions, guest speakers and literature. Meets last Thurs., 1-2:30pm, Sister Catherine Health Center (bldg. adjacent to St. Clares - Dover General Hospital, 400 West Blackwell St., Dover. Pre-registration required. Before attending call Pat Merritt 973-347-7470 or Pat Santoro 973-366-8765. *Website:* http://www.theacpa.org *E-mail:* merrittspnb@optonline.net

New Hope and Healing *Professionally-run.* Support for adults experiencing pain in their lives. Offers mutual support, sharing coping skills, guest speakers, education workshops, seminars and retreats. Meets in Morris County. Call Christine 973-927-4719 (day).

NATIONAL

American Chronic Pain Association, Inc. *National. 200+ affiliated chapters. Founded 1980.* Provides peer support and education for individuals with chronic pain and their families so that they may live more fully in spite of their pain. Workbooks for self-help recovery, quarterly newsletter, group development guidelines, phone network and outreach program to clinics. At website, click on "About Us" to access locations of "Groups." Write: American Chronic Pain Association, P.O. Box 850, Rocklin, CA 95677. Call 1-800-533-3231 or 916-632-0922; Fax: 916-632-3208. *Website:* http://www.theacpa.org *E-mail:* ACPA@pacbell.net

Rest Ministries *National. 275 affiliated groups. Founded 1997.* Christian ministry for people who live with chronic pain or illness and their families.

Quarterly magazine, daily devotionals, share and prayer e-mail support mailing list, online chat, etc. Encouragement and resources for starting groups (approximately $15). Write: Rest Ministries, Inc., P.O. Box 502928, San Diego, CA 92150. Call 1-888-751-7378 or 858-486-4685; Fax: 1-800-933-1078. *Website:* http://www.restministries.org *E-mail:* rest@restministries.org

PARKINSON'S DISEASE
(see also toll-free helplines)

STATEWIDE

American Parkinson's Disease Association NJ Chapter Provides literature, speakers' bureau, educational programs and physician referrals. Referrals to support groups. Write: NJ APDA Information and Referral Center, Robert Wood Johnson University Hospital, 1 Robert Wood Johnson Place, New Brunswick, NJ 08901. Call 732-745-7520.

BERGEN

Northern Valley Parkinson's Support Group Mutual support and education for individuals diagnosed with Parkinson's disease. Families and caregivers welcome. Rap sessions, guest speakers, literature and phone help. Building is handicapped accessible. Meets 1st Sat., 1-2:30pm (except July/Aug., easy yoga exercise at 12:15pm) First Congregational Church, Haworth Ave., Haworth. Call Ilse Heller 201-265-4946.

Parkinson's Support Group Mutual support and exercise for persons with Parkinson's disease. Rap sessions, guest speakers and phone help. Meets Fri., 1-3pm, Englewood Southeast Center for Independent Living, 228 Grand Ave., Englewood. Call Ilse Heller or Kevin Kyle 201-747-9096 or 201-265-4946 (day). *E-mail:* kxkyle@aol.com

Parkinson's Support Group of the Greater Ridgewood Area *Professionally-run.* Mutual support and exchange of information for persons with Parkinson's, their families and caregivers. Rap sessions and guest speakers. Building is handicapped accessible. Entrance on side of building. Meets 1st Thurs., (separate groups for patients and caregivers), 7pm; lecture and educational series meets 3rd Thurs., 7:30pm (except July, Aug., Dec.), Cedar Hill Christian Reformed Church, 422 Cedar Hill Ave., Wyckoff. Call Marion Arenas 201-670-0083 (day) or Gene Provost 973-875-8429 (day).

BURLINGTON

Virtua Parkinson's Support Group *Professionally-run.* Self-help and support for persons with Parkinson's disease and their families. Meets 3rd Wed., 7-8:30pm (except Dec.), Virtua Health and Rehab Center, 62 Richmond Ave., Mt. Holly. Call Virtua Health 1-888-847-8823 (day) or Amy Gallagher 609-267-0700 ext. 23080 (day). *Website:* http://www.virtua.org

CAPE MAY

Parkinson's Support Group of Cape May County Mutual support for Parkinson's disease patients and their families. Building is handicapped accessible. Meets 2nd Thurs., 1pm (except July/Aug.), Victoria Commons, Town Bank Rd., North Cape May. Call Rita 609-886-2455 (day).

ESSEX

Parkinson's Support Group of North Jersey Mutual support and exchange of information for persons with Parkinson's, families and caregivers. Discussions and guest speakers. Building is handicapped accessible. Meets 3rd Sat., 10am-noon, Mountainside Hospital, Bay Ave., Montclair. Call Ginnie 862-210-8388 or Betty 973-376-3365.

GLOUCESTER

Parkinson's Support Group of Southern New Jersey *Professionally-run.* Support, education and social events for Parkinson's patients and their families. Occasional guest speakers. Meets 1st Wed., 7pm, Woodbury Mews, 122 Green Ave., Woodbury. Call Diane 609-254-3096 (day).

HUNTERDON

Hunterdon County Parkinson's Support Group *Professionally-run.* Support for persons with Parkinson's and their caregivers. Patients and caregivers meet both together and separately. Building is handicapped accessible. Meets 4th Fri., 1:30-3:30pm, Hunterdon County Div. of Senior Services, Office on Aging, Route 31 South, Flemington. Call Barbara Burgard 908-788-6401 ext. 3149 (day).

MERCER

Parkinson's Support Group of Central Delaware Valley Support and information for Parkinson's patients and families. Guest speakers and educational programs. Building is handicapped accessible. Meets 3rd Wed., 1pm (except Jan., Feb., July, Aug.), Lawrenceville Presbyterian Church, 2688 Main St., Route 206, Lawrenceville. Call John Wicoff 609-737-3364.

MIDDLESEX

COPSA Spouse Support Group *Professionally-run.* Mutual support and understanding for spouses of persons with any type of memory loss including Alzheimer's, Parkinson's, vascular disease, stroke, head injury and dementia. Meets 1st and 3rd Mon., 9:30-11am, University Behavioral Healthcare Center, 671 Hoes Lane, Piscataway. Call Mary Catherine Lundquist 732-235-2858 (day). *E-mail:* lundqumc@umdnj.edu

JFK Johnson Rehab Institute Parkinson's Group Support, education and coping skills for individuals with Parkinson's disease. Families welcome. Literature, rap sessions and guest speakers. Meets 1st Wed., 1-2:30pm, Monroe Township Office on Aging, Municipal Complex, Perrineville Rd., Monroe Township. Pre-registration required. Call Jennifer 732-521-6111 (day) or Janice Dibling 732-321-7063 (day).

Parkinson's Disease Patient and Family Support Group Mutual support and education for those with Parkinson's, their families and caregivers. Patients and caregivers meet both separately and together. Meets 3rd Thurs., 12:30pm, New Brunswick. Call NJ Parkinson's Disease Information and Referral Center 732-745-7520 (day).

Young Onset Parkinson's Patient and Family Support Group *Professionally-run.* Support and education for Parkinson's patients under 60 years old, their families and caregivers. Meets 3rd Wed., 7pm, New Brunswick. For meeting location call NJ Parkinson's Disease Information and Referral Center 732-745-7520 (day).

MONMOUTH

Parkinson's Support Group Mutual support for Parkinson's patients and their families. Guest speakers. Building is handicapped accessible. Meets 3rd Tues., 11:15am-12:15pm, Manalapan Senior Center, Route 522, Manalapan. Call Seniors First 732-780-3013 (day).

"The deepest need of man is the need to overcome his separateness, to leave the prison of his aloneness." –Eric Fromm, PhD

MORRIS

Parkinson's Disease Support Group *Professionally-run.* Provides emotional support and education for those diagnosed with Parkinson's disease, their family members and caregivers. Guest speakers. Building is handicapped accessible. Meets 3rd Mon., 1:00pm, Care One at Morris, 200 Mazda Brook Rd., Parsippany. Before attending call Carol Carlson, PhD 973-627-4087 (day).

Parkinson's Support Group *Professionally-run.* Provides emotional support and education for those diagnosed with Parkinson's disease, their families and caregivers. Meets 2nd Tues., 1:30pm, Madison YMCA, 111 Kings Rd., Madison. Pre-registration required. Before attending call Carol Carlson, PhD 973-627-4087 (day).

UNION

Kean University Aphasia Support Group Mutual support for persons suffering from aphasia, Parkinson's and stroke. Families are welcome. Disseminates information, group discussions, rap sessions and guest speakers. Meetings vary, Kean University, 1000 Morris Ave., Union. Before attending call Wendy Greenspan 908-737-5811 (day).

Parkinson's Support Group *Professionally-run.* Support and education for patients of all ages with Parkinson's disease. Literature, buddy system and guest speakers. Meets 2nd Wed., 1-3pm, Robert Wood Johnson University Hospital at Rahway, Stone St., Rahway. Call Debbie Hargiss 908-272-2362 (day).

Parkinson's Support Group In Westfield Provides support and education to persons with Parkinson's disease as well as their caregivers, including former caregivers who have lost a family member to Parkinson's. Handicapped accessible. Meets 2nd Mon., 1:30-3pm, (except July, Aug., Oct.), Presbyterian Church in Westfield, 140 Mountain Ave., Westfield. Call Barbara 908-322-9214 (day).

WARREN

Lehigh Valley Parkinson's Support Group, The Mutual support and encouragement for Parkinson's patients, their families and friends. Guest speakers. Building is handicapped accessible. Meets 4th Tues., 10:30am-noon, Muhlenberg Hospital, Banko Building, Schoenersville Rd., Bethlehem, PA. Call Gerry 610-868-3510.

NATIONAL

American Parkinson Disease Association, Inc. *National. 59 chapter, 300 support groups. Founded 1961.* Offers support, online booklets and referrals. Chapter development guidelines and quarterly newsletter. Promotes research. Fifty-nine information and referral centers nationwide. Write: American Parkinson Disease Association, 135 Parkinson Ave., Staten Island, NY 10305. Call 1-800-223-2732 or 718-981-8001 (Mon-Fri, 8:30am-4:30pm EST); Fax: 718-981-4399. *Website:* http://www.apdaparkinson.org

National Parkinson Foundation *National. 1000 groups.* Provides support, information and education for persons with Parkinson's, their families and health care professionals. Funds research. Seeks to improve quality of life for both patients and their caregivers. Includes Young Onset Parkinson network. Helps to start groups. Write: National Parkinson Foundation, 1501 N.W. Ninth Ave., Miami, FL 33136. Call 1-800-327-4545 or 305-547-6666 (Mon-Fri, 9am-5pm EST); Fax: 305-243-5595. *Website:* http://www.parkinson.org *E-mail:* contact@parkinson.org

POLIO

STATEWIDE

Polio Network of NJ Support and information for NJ polio survivors and their families. Optional $15/yr donation. For information on support groups in your area call the Polio Network of NJ 201-845-6860 (day). *Website:* http://www.njpolio.org *E-mail:* info@njpolio.org

ATLANTIC

Atlantic County Post-Polio Support Group Support and information on the late effects of polio, for post-polio survivors, their families and friends. Dues $15/yr. Meets 3rd Sat., 9:30-11:30am (except Jan., Feb., July, Aug.), Atlantic Township Library, Mays Landing. Before attending call Marge 609-909-1518 (day). *E-mail:* kittystamp@comcast.net

"From what we get, we can make a living;
from what we give, however, makes a life." – Arthur Ashe

BERGEN

Bergen County Polio Support Group *Professionally-run.* Support network and information on late effects of polio and polio survivors. Peer-counseling, phone network and guest speakers. Building is handicapped accessible. Meets 1st Sat., 11:30am, Maywood Senior Center, 145 West Magnolia Ave., Maywood. Call Heather Broad 201-845-6317. *E-mail:* hbroad@netzero.com

CAMDEN

South West Jersey Polio Support Group Support and information on the late effects of polio for post-polio survivors and their families and friends. Dues $15/yr. Building is handicapped accessible. Meets 4th Sat., 11am-12:30pm, New Seasons at Voorhees Assisted Living, 501 Laurel Oak Rd., 2nd Floor Dining Room, Voorhees. Elevator available. Before attending call Anna 856-740-1106 (day).

ESSEX

New Jersey Polio Network - Essex/Union Chapter Mutual support for persons with post-polio. Provides an opportunity to discuss problems and solutions. Family members welcome. Rap sessions, education, guest speakers and literature. Building is handicapped accessible. Meets various Sat., noon-2pm, East Orange General Hospital, East Pavilion, 6th Floor, Conference Room, East Orange. Call Edwina Jackson 973-673-0380.

MONMOUTH

Monmouth County Post-Polio Support Group Support for persons suffering from post-polio syndrome, in need of pain management, or who need help controlling their lives, through meetings, referrals, discussions, guest speakers, social events and networking. Families and friends welcome. Phone help. Dues $15/yr. Building is handicapped accessible. Meets 3rd Mon., Seabrook Village, 300 Essex Rd., Tinton Falls. Before attending call Antoinette Wilczewski 732-229-9343 (day). *Website:* http://www.njpolio.org

MORRIS

Morris County Polio Network Mutual support for post-polio survivors, their families and friends. Information on the late-effects of polio. Rap sessions and newsletter. Dues $10/yr. Building is handicapped accessible. Meets 3rd Sat., 11am (Apr., May, June, Sept., Oct. and Nov.), St. Clare's Hospital, 25 Pocono Rd., Silby Cafeteria, Denville. Also meets 3rd Wed., 7pm (Mar., July and

Dec.), Zeris Inn, Route 46, Mountain Lakes. Before attending call Dr. Vincent Avantagiato 973-769-0075 (day). *E-mail:* drvince@njpolio.org

OCEAN

Ocean County Post-Polio Support Group Support and information sharing for polio survivors. Networking with professionals and other groups. Phone help, guest speakers, literature, newsletter and buddy system. Meets 5 times per year, 3rd Sat., Health South, 14 Hospital Dr., Toms River. For meeting information call Susan Payne Gato 732-864-0998 (day) or Jerry Bojko 732-505-0151 (day). *Website:* http://www.tomsrivernjpolio.org

SOMERSET

Raritan Valley Post-Polio Support Group Support, information and sharing for post-polio survivors. Anyone with a physical disability is also welcome to attend. Networking with professionals and other groups. Phone help, speakers and monthly newsletter. Dues $10/yr. Meets 1st Sat. (Oct., Nov., Dec., Mar., Apr.), Manville Library, Manville. Call Arthur Siegfried 908-722-7212 (eve.). *Website:* http://www.njpolio.org/rvppsg

NATIONAL

Post-Polio Health International *National network. Founded 1958.* Information on late effects of polio for survivors and health professionals. International conferences. Membership $30/yr. Guidelines and workshops for support groups. Handbook on late effects ($11.50). Write: Post-Polio Health International, 4207 Lindell Blvd., Suite 110, St. Louis, MO 63108-2930. Call 314-534-0475; Fax: 314-534-5070. *Website:* http://www.post-polio.org *E-mail:* info@post-polio.org

POLYCYSTIC OVARIAN SYNDROME

NATIONAL

Polycystic Ovarian Syndrome Association *International. Founded 1997.* Provides emotional support and information for women with polycystic ovarian syndrome. Provides information on various treatments and diagnosis. Newsletter, phone support, literature, conferences, regional symposiums and advocacy. Online chats and e-mail lists. Assistance in starting local groups. Dues $40. Write: Polycystic Ovarian Syndrome Association, P.O. Box 3403, Englewood, CO 80111. *Website:* http://www.pcosupport.org *E-mail:* info@pcosupport.org

ONLINE

Cyster Connection *Online. 531 members.* Support for women with polycystic ovarian syndrome (PCOS), a condition in which ovaries create an abundance of follicles each month without producing an egg. PCOS usually goes hand-in-hand with insulin resistance. It is also the most common cause of infertility among women in the United States. *Website:* http://pcostcc.proboards83.com

PSORIASIS

National Psoriasis Foundation *National. Founded 1968.* Support and information for people who have psoriasis and psoriatic arthritis, their families and friends. Education to increase public awareness of these disorders. Fundraising for research, quarterly magazine for members, educational booklets and physician directory. Offers online message board and chatrooms. Write: National Psoriasis Foundation, 6600 SW 92nd Ave., Suite 300, Portland, OR 97223. Call 503-244-7404 or 1-800-723-9166 (free packet of information); Fax: 503-245-0626. *Website:* http://www.psoriasis.org *E-mail:* getinfo@psoriasis.org

REFLEX SYMPATHETIC DYSTROPHY

STATEWIDE

Reflex Sympathetic Dystrophy Syndrome Association - Southern NJ Chapter Aims to meet the practical and emotional needs of reflex sympathetic dystrophy syndrome patients and their families. Promotes research into the cause and cure of RSDS. Offers education to the public and professionals. Call Jim Everett 609-828-4980 (day).

BURLINGTON

Reflex Sympathetic Dystrophy and Chronic Pain Support Group 12-Step. Support for persons with reflex sympathetic dystrophy or chronic pain, their families and friends. Helps members maintain as normal and pain free life as possible. Guest speakers, educational programs, pen pals, rap sessions, literature, phone help and advocacy. Building is handicapped accessible.
　　　Mt. Holly Meets 3rd Wed., 7-9pm, Virtua Hospital, 175 Madison Ave., Conference Room, 1st Floor. Call Kathy Henson 609-268-1565 (day). *E-mail:* bepainfree2000@aol.com

Mt. Laurel Meets 4th Tues., 6-8pm, YMCA, 5001 Centerton Rd. Call Ursula Weed 856-304-6682 or Lisa Vasey 609-877-0213 *E-mail:* sula252000@yahoo.com

SOMERSET

Living with RSDA/CRPS, Inc. Offers education and support for persons afflicted with reflex sympathetic dystrophy (chronic regional pain syndrome). Families and friends are welcome. Building is handicapped accessible. Meets 1st Tues., 7-9pm, Somerset Medical Center, 110 Rehill Ave., Somerville. Call 908-575-7737 (answering machine). *Website:* http://www.livingwithrsds.com *E-mail:* slweiner@hotmail.com

NATIONAL

Reflex Sympathetic Dystrophy Syndrome Association *National. 100 independent groups. Founded 1984.* Aims to meet the practical and emotional needs of reflex sympathetic dystrophy syndrome (aka complex regional pain syndrome) patients and their families. RSDS is a disabling disease involving nerve, skin, muscle, blood vessels and bones. The only common symptom in all patients is pain. Promotes research, educates public and professionals. Quarterly newsletter. Group development guidelines available. Write: Reflex Sympathetic Dystrophy Syndrome Association, P.O. Box 502, Milford, CT 06460. Call 1-877-662-7737 (8:30am-4:30pm EST). *Website:* http://www.rsds.org *E-mail:* info@rsds.org

RESPIRATORY DISEASE / EMPHYSEMA

STATEWIDE

American Lung Association of New Jersey *Professionally-run.* Refers callers to regional resources for information on lung health, asthma, smoking and environment. Referrals to support groups for persons with chronic lung disorders (emphysema, chronic bronchitis, asthma, pulmonary problems, etc.). Write: American Lung Association of New Jersey, 1600 Route 22 East, Union, NJ 07083. Call 908-687-9340 (day); Fax: 908-851-2625. *Website:* http://www.lungusa.org

BURLINGTON

Better Breathers Club *Professionally-run.* Support for those with lung disease and their families. Building is handicapped accessible. Meets 1st Wed., 10am, Deborah Heart and Lung Center, 200 Trenton Rd., Browns Mills. Call Dianna Barker 609-893-1200 ext. 5256 (day). *Website:* http://deborah.org

CAMDEN

Better Breathers Club Mutual support for people with chronic obstructive pulmonary disease (bronchitis, emphysema, fibrosis, asthma, post-lung cancer, etc.) their family and friends. Rap sessions and guest speakers. Building is handicapped accessible. Meets 4 times/yr., NBN Infusion and Respiratory, 2 Pin Oak Lane, Unit 250, Cherry Hill. Call 856-669-6441. *Website:* http://www.betterbreathersclub.org *E-mail:* nbnbetterbreathersclub.org

MERCER

Better Breathers Club *Professionally-run.* Mutual support for people with chronic obstructive pulmonary disease (bronchitis, emphysema, fibrosis, asthma, post-lung cancer, etc.) their family and friends. Rap sessions and guest speakers. Meetings vary, 4 times/yr., Capital Health System, Mercer Campus, 446 Bellevue Ave., Trenton. Before attending call 609-394-4340 (day). *Website:* http://www.betterbreathersclub.org

MONMOUTH

Monmouth Medical Center Adult Pulmonary Support Group *Professionally-run.* Support group for adults (ages 60 and over) with COPD, emphysema, chronic asthma, asthma or bronchitis. Families welcome. Building is handicapped accessible. Meets 2nd Thurs., 10:30am-noon (except June, July, Aug.), Monmouth Medical Center, Elizabeth Benjamin Care Center, 300 Second Ave., Conference Room, Long Branch. Pre-registration required. Before attending call 732-923-6990 (day).

MORRIS

IPF Support Group Mutual support for patients with idiopathic pulmonary fibrosis and their caregivers. Family members welcome. Rap sessions and phone help. Building is handicapped accessible. Meets last Wed., 7-9pm, Morristown Memorial Hospital, 100 Madison Ave., Morristown. Before attending call Barbara Murphy 908-276-3394 (eve). *E-mail:* bjmurphy21@comcast.net

Lung Talk *Professionally-run.* Support group for patients with chronic lung disease (COPD). Families welcome. Educational series, rap sessions, literature and guest speakers. Building is handicapped accessible. Meets 3rd Fri., 2-3pm, Chilton Memorial Hospital, 97 West Parkway, Board Room, Pompton Plains. Call William McCarthy 973-831-5070 (day).

NATIONAL

Alpha 1 Association *International. 54 affiliated groups. Founded 1988.* Support, advocacy and information for persons with alpha-1 antitrypsin deficiency and their families. Networking of members through newsletter and support groups across the country. Sharing of current information on treatments and research. Newsletter, group development guidelines, educational materials and advocacy information. Write: Alpha-1 Association, 2937 SW 27th Ave., Suite 106, Miami, FL 33133. Call 1-800-521-3025 or 305-648-0088; Fax: 305-648-0089. *Website:* http://www.alpha1.org *E-mail:* info@alpha1.org

American Lung Association *(BILINGUAL) National. Founded 1904.* Refers callers to regional resources for information on lung health, smoking and environment. Local chapters can provide referrals to support groups for persons with chronic lung disorders (emphysema, chronic bronchitis, asthma, pulmonary problems, etc.) if available. These groups use names such as "Easy Breathers" or "Family Asthma Support Group." Write: American Lung Association, 61 Broadway, 6th Floor, New York, NY 10006. Call 1-800-586-4872 or 212-315-8700. *Website:* http://www.lungusa.org

Asthma and Allergy Foundation of America *National. 100+ affiliated groups and 9 chapters. Founded 1953.* Serves persons with asthma and allergic diseases through advocacy, the support of research, patient and public education. Newsletter and support/education groups. Assistance in starting and maintaining groups. Books, videos and other educational resources. Write: Asthma and Allergy Foundation of America, 1233 20th St. NW, Suite 402, Washington, DC 20036. Call 1-800-727-8462 or 202-466-7643 (Mon.-Fri., 10am-3pm EST); Fax: 202-466-8940. *Website:* http://www.aafa.org *E-mail:* info@aafa.org

Coalition for Pulmonary Fibrosis *National. 40 affiliated groups. 12,000 members. Founded 2001.* Information, resources, educational materials and support for patients with pulmonary fibrosis. Write: Coalition for Pulmonary Fibrosis, 1659 Branham Lane, Suite F, #227, San Jose, CA 95118. Call 1-888-222-8541. *Website:* http://www.coalitionforpf.org *E-mail:* info@coalitionforpf.org

ONLINE

Bronchiectasis Support and Information *Online. 192 members. Founded 2005.* Provides information and support to fellow sufferers and caregivers. Bronchiectasis is a condition where some bronchi and smaller bronchioles in lungs are permanently dilated. Message board. *Website:* http://health.groups.yahoo.com/group/ Bronchiectasis_support/

COPD-Support, Inc. *Online.* Provides a variety of online self-help support programs for chronic obstructive pulmonary disease patients, caregivers and interested medical personnel. Programs include: moderated mailing lists, forums, chats, a weekly newsletter "COPD-Watch" for those living alone, "Smoke No More" for help in quitting smoking and "Let's Get Fit" exercise program. *Website:* http://copd-support.com

EFFORTS *Online.* Support for persons afflicted with emphysema. Offers information on local support groups. Forum for sharing ideas and help in dealing with emphysema. Advocacy for research. Listserv. Write: EFFORTS, 239 NE Hwy 69, Suite D, Claycomo, MO 64119. Fax: 816-413-0176. *Website:* http://www.emphysema.net/bindex.html

Huff-n-Puff *Online. 1000+ members.* Provides support for people with any type of interstitial lung disease (including pulmonary fibrosis). Opportunity to meet others with similar conditions, experiences and knowledge. *Website:* http://www.huff-n-puff.net

SCLERODERMA

STATEWIDE

Scleroderma Foundation of the Delaware Valley (Serves southern/central NJ/Delaware/PA) *Professionally-run.* Support and education for persons with scleroderma. Funds research. Seeks to increase public awareness, provides patient education and support programs. Phone support, networking, newsletter, information and referral. Membership dues $25/yr. Meetings are free. Several meeting locations. Write: Scleroderma Foundation, Cherry Professional Building, 385 Kings Highway North, Cherry Hill, NJ 08034. Call 856-779-7225 (day) or 1-866-675-5545 (Mon.-Fri., 9am-5pm). *Website:* http://www.scleroderma.org/chapter/delaware_valley/

Scleroderma Foundation of Tri-State Chapter (Serves northern NJ, NY, CT) *Professionally-run.* Promotes the welfare of scleroderma patients and their families. Provides education, support groups, phone help, referrals. Fund-raising for research. Newsletter, resource library and other educational materials. Group development guidelines. Annual dues $25. Several meeting locations in the tri-state area. Write: Scleroderma Foundation, 59 Front St., Binghamton, NY 13905. Call 1-800-867-0885; Fax: 607-723-2039. *Website:* http://www.scleroderma.org *E-mail:* sdtristate@scleroderma.org

CAMDEN

Scleroderma Foundation Support Group Provides support and education to scleroderma patients, their families and friends. Rap sessions, guest speakers and literature. Meets 2nd Thurs., Cherry Professional Building, Cherry Hill. Before attending call Laurie Rabin 856-231-0221.

HUDSON

Scleroderma Foundation, Inc. Provides support and education to scleroderma patients and their families. Building is handicapped accessible. Rap sessions. Meets 4th Mon., 1:30pm, Hunterdon Medical Center, Route 31, Flemington. Call Mary 908-284-1332.

MORRIS

Northern New Jersey Scleroderma Support Group Provides support and education to scleroderma patients, their families and friends. Guest speakers, rap sessions and literature. Building is handicapped accessible. Meets 2nd Tues., 7-9pm (Mar., May, Sept., Nov.), St. Clare's Hospital, Route 46 West, Dover. Call Kitsa Jobeless 973-328-2627 (eve.) or 1-800-867-0885.

SOMERSET

Scleroderma Foundation Support Group Provides support and education to scleroderma patients, their families and friends. Rap sessions, guest speakers and literature. Meets 1st Wed., 7pm, Trinity United Church, 118 King George Rd., Warren. Call Ellen Waldstein 908-647-7266 or Chris Frascella 908-604-6054. For directions call church 732-469-5044. *E-mail:* ellw@optonline.net

NATIONAL

Juvenile Scleroderma Network *International. Founded 1999.* Support network connecting children with juvenile scleroderma with each other to help them feel less isolated and less frightened. Provides comfort and reassurance to families. Membership $20/yr. Newsletter, information and referrals, literature, advocacy, telephone support network and pen pal program. Moderated message board and e-mail discussion group. Provides assistance and materials on starting new groups. Write: Juvenile Sclerderma Network, 1204 W. 13th St., San Pedro, CA 90731. Call 310-519-9511. *Website:* http://www.jsdn.org

Scleroderma Foundation *National. 22 chapters, 170 affiliated groups. Founded 1998.* Mission is support, education and research. Dedicated to providing emotional support to people with scleroderma, their families and caregivers. Sponsors scleroderma education and public awareness events and funds research. Referrals to local support groups and physicians. Advocacy program and annual conference. Online message board. Dues $25/yr. Write: Scleroderma Foundation, 300 Rosewood Dr., Suite 105, Danvers, MA 01923. Call 1-800-722-4673 or 978-463-5843 (Mon.-Fri., 8:30am-5pm EST); Fax: 978-463-5809. *Website:* http://www.scleroderma.org *E-mail:* sfinfo@scleroderma.org

Scleroderma Research Foundation *National. Founded 1987.* Mission is to find a cure for scleroderma by funding and facilitating the most promising research. Provides scleroderma information online and via "Insights" scleroderma newsletter. Write: Scleroderma Research Foundation, 220 Montgomery St., Suite 1411, San Francisco, CA 94104. Call 1-800-441-2873; Fax: 415-834-9177. *Website:* http://www.sclerodermaresearch.org *E-mail:* info@sclerodermaresearch.org

SCOLIOSIS

NATIONAL

National Scoliosis Foundation *International. 5 affiliated groups. Founded 1976.* Dedicated to helping children, parents, adults and health care providers deal with the complexities of spinal deformities such as scoliosis. Whether the issue is early detection and screening programs, treatment methods, pain management or patient care, NSF strives to promote public awareness, provide reliable information, encourage on-going research and educate and support the scoliosis community. Bi-annual newsletter, information packets, pen pals, conferences and phone support. Assistance in starting local groups. Write: National Scoliosis Foundation, 5 Cabot Pl., Stoughton, MA 02072. Call 1-800-673-6922 or 781-341-6333 (Mon.-Thurs., 9am-5pm EST); Fax: 781-341-8333. *Website:* http://www.scoliosis.org *E-mail:* NSF@scoliosis.org

Scoliosis Association, Inc. *National. 50 chapters. Founded 1974.* Information support network for scoliosis patients and parents of children with scoliosis. Establishes local patient and parent self-help groups. Encourages school screening programs. Supports research. Newsletter. Membership contribution $20. Guidelines for starting chapters. Write: Scoliosis Association Inc., c/o Stanley Sacks, Chair and C.E.O., P.O. Box 811705, Boca Raton, FL 33481-1705. Call 1-800-800-0669. *Website:* http://www.scoliosis-assoc.org

SLEEP APNEA

CAMDEN

South Jersey A.W.A.K.E. Support Group *Professionally-run.* Support and education to individuals and their families suffering from sleep apnea. Rap sessions, guest speakers and phone help. Building is handicapped accessible. Meets 4 times/yr., Cooper University Hospital at Voorhees, 900 Centennial Rd., Conference Room A, Voorhees. Before attending call 856-669-6440. *Website:* http://www.sjawake.com

MERCER

A.W.A.K.E. (American Sleep Apnea Association) Network Group *Professionally-run.* Support and education to individuals and their families suffering from sleep apnea. Rap sessions, guest speakers and phone help. Building is handicapped accessible. For meeting information call Sharon Puglisi 609-584-5150 (day). *E-mail:* spuglisi@chsnj.org

MORRIS

Sleep Apnea Support Group of Northwest New Jersey Support group for persons afflicted by sleep apnea. Family members welcome. Exchange information and experiences. Guest speakers, educational and mutual sharing. Meetings vary, 7:30-9pm, St. Clare's Hospital, 1st Floor Cafeteria, Dover. Call Sleep Center 973-989-3477 (option #2).

NATIONAL

A.W.A.K.E. (American Sleep Apnea Association) Network Groups *National. 200+ affiliated groups. Founded 1990.* Provides support, education and social interaction for persons with sleep apnea, their families and friends. Membership dues $25/year. Assistance and guidelines for starting groups ($30).

Write: A.W.A.K.E. Network Groups, 1424 K St. NW, Suite 302, Washington, DC 20005. Call 202-293-3650; Fax: 202-293-3656. *Website:* http://www.sleepapnea.org *E-mail:* asaa@sleepapnea.org

SPINA BIFIDA
(see also disabilities general, parents of children with disabilities)

STATEWIDE

Spina Bifida Association Support for persons with spina bifida and their families. Peer-counseling, advocacy, newsletter, conferences, family support coordination and continence management assistance. Various meeting times and places. Also has several telephone support groups. Write: Spina Bifida Association, 84 Park Ave., Suite G-106, Flemington, NJ 08822. Call 908-782-7475 (8:30am-4:30pm); Fax: 908-782-6102. *Website:* http://www.sbatsr.org *E-mail:* info@sbatsr.org

NATIONAL

Spina Bifida Association of America *(BILINGUAL) National. 62 chapters. Founded 1972.* Encourages educational and vocational development of patients. Promotes public awareness, advocacy and research. Newsletter, chapter development guidelines, national resource center, scholarships and film/videotapes. Write: Spina Bifida Association of America, 4590 MacArthur Blvd. NW, Suite 250, Washington, DC 20007. Call 1-800-621-3141 or 202-944-3285; Fax: 202-944-3295. *Website:* http://www.sbaa.org *E-mail:* sbaa@sbaa.org

STROKE
(see also caregivers, physical disabilities)

ATLANTIC

AtlantiCare Stroke Support Group *Professionally-run.* Support, education and advocacy for stroke patients, their families and friends. Building is handicapped accessible. Meets 1st Wed., 2-3pm (Jan., Mar., May, July, Sept., Nov.), Bacharach Institute for Rehabilitation, 61 West Jimmie Leeds Rd., Room 210, 2nd Floor, Pomona. Pre-registration required. Before attending call 1-888-569-1000 (day). *E-mail:* 1-888-569-1000@altanticare.org

AtlantiCare Stroke Support Group *Professionally-run.* Support, education ad advocacy for stroke patients, their families and friends. Building is handicapped accessible. Meets 1st Wed., 2-3pm (Feb., Apr., June, Aug., Oct., Dec.), AtlantiCare Life Center, 2500 English Creek Ave. Building 200, Egg Harbor Township. Pre-registration required. Before attending call 1-888-569-1000 (day). *E-mail:* 1-888-569-1000@atlaticare.org

BERGEN

New Jersey Stroke Activity Center Support and recovery of long-term stroke survivors, sound and movement therapy, networking and socialization. Families welcome. Rap sessions, guest speakers, phone help, newsletter and speakers' bureau. Call Mary Jo Schreiber 973-450-4114. *Website:* http://www.njsac.org *E-mail:* maryjo@njsac.org

> **Paramus** Meets 2nd and 4th Tues., 11:30am, Care One at the Cupola, 100 West Ridgewood Ave.
> **Saddle Brook** Meets 1st and 3rd Tues., Kessler Institution for Rehabilitation, 300 Market St.

Post-Stroke and Disabled Adult Program *Professionally-run.* (BERGEN COUNTY RESIDENTS ONLY) Mutual support for post-stroke patients and disabled adults. Program functions include group discussions, various activities that promote physical fitness, arts and crafts, games, exercises and occasional recreational events. Meets various times and days, E. Rutherford, Englewood, Paramus and Maywood. Call Anika Davis 201-336-6502 (day); TTY/TDD: 201-336-6505.

Post-Stroke Support Group *Professionally-run.* Mutual support for post-stroke individuals. Building is handicapped accessible. Meets Fri., 9am-12:30pm, 228 Grand Ave., Englewood. Before attending call Frieda Wells 201-569-4080 (day). *E-mail:* sth1smlh@aol.com

Stroke Club *Professionally-run.* Support and education for stroke survivors, their families and friends. Building is handicapped accessible. Meets Tues., 11:15am-noon. Kessler Institute for Rehabilitation, 300 Market St., Saddle Brook. Before attending call Anne Marie Chesterman, CTRS 201-368-6012 (day).

Under 60 Stroke Support Group *Professionally-run.* Support for stroke survivors under the age of 60, their families and friends. Building is handicapped accessible. Meets 4th Wed., 6-7:30pm, Kessler Institute for Rehabilitation, 300 Market St., Saddle Brook. Before attending call Anne Marie Chesterman, CTRS 201-368-6012 (day).

BURLINGTON

Stroke Club *Professionally-run.* Promotes the well-being of stroke patients and families through educational and social programs and sharing of concerns. Building is handicapped accessible. Meets 4th Tues., 7-9pm (except Nov./Dec.), Virtua Health and Rehabilitation Center, 62 Richmond Ave., Mt. Holly. Before attending call 1-888-847-8823 (day).

Stroke Support Group Mutual support for stroke patients and their families. Meets 2nd Fri., 10-11:30am (except July/Aug.), Lourdes Health System, 218 A Sunset Rd., Willingboro. Call 609-835-5813 (day).

CAMDEN

Stroke Support Group *Professionally-run.* Provides emotional support and sense of community for stroke survivors and caregivers. Rap sessions, lecture series, guest speakers and literature. Building is handicapped accessible. Meets 3rd Thurs., 1:30-3pm (except Jan., Feb., July), Our Lady of Lourdes Medical Center, 1600 Haddon Ave., 2nd Floor, North Building, Rehab Solarium, Camden. Call Kim Campion 856-757-3793 (day). *E-mail:* campionk@lourdesnet.org

MERCER

St. Lawrence Stroke Support Group *Professionally-run.* Promotes the well-being of stroke patients and families through educational and social programs and sharing of concerns. Discussions and guest speakers. Building is handicapped accessible. Meets 1st Wed., 6:30-8pm, St. Lawrence Rehab Center, 2381 Lawrenceville Rd., Cafeteria, Lawrenceville. Call Pat Foltz, MSW, LSW 609-896-9500 ext. 2303 (day). *E-mail:* pfoltz@slrc.org

MIDDLESEX

COPSA Spouse Support Group *Professionally-run.* Mutual support and understanding for spouses of persons with any type of memory loss including Alzheimer's, Parkinson's, vascular disease, stroke, head injury or dementia. Meets 1st and 3rd Mon., 9:30-11am, University Behavioral Healthcare Center, 671 Hoes Lane, Piscataway. Call Mary Catherine Lundquist 732-235-2858 (day). *E-mail:* lundqumc@umdnj.edu

JFK Stroke Wives Group Support for women who are married to men who have had strokes. Mutual sharing, rap sessions and social group. Building is handicapped accessible. Meets 3rd Tues., 7-8:30pm, JFK Hospital, James St., Edison. Call Rosemarie 732-752-2644. *E-mail:* crossingladynj@aol.com

Middlesex County Stroke Support Group *Professionally-run.* Promotes the well-being of stroke patients and families through educational programs and sharing of concerns. Dues $1 mtg. Building is handicapped accessible. Meets 2nd Wed., 7:15pm, JFK Rehab Institute, 65 James St., Edison. Before attending call Frank Roche 732-969-2097 (day).

Stroke Club Support Group Support and education for stroke patients, their families and friends. Guest speakers. Building is handicapped accessible. Meets last Fri., 12:30-2pm (except July, Aug., Nov.), Robert Wood Johnson University Hospital, New Brunswick. Call 732-418-8110 (day).

MONMOUTH

New Jersey Stroke Activity Support and recovery of long-term stroke survivors, sound and movement therapy, networking and socialization. Families welcome. Rap sessions, guest speakers, phone help, newsletter and speakers' bureau. Meets 1st and 3rd Wed., 2pm, Health South Rehabilitation Hospital, 2 Centre Plaza, Tinton Falls. Call Mary Jo Schreiber 973-450-4114. *Website:* http://www.njsac.org *E-mail:* maryjo@njsac.org

Stroke Support Group Mutual support for stroke patients and their families. Education, guest speakers, lecture series and literature. Building is handicapped accessible. Meets 2nd Wed., 2-4pm (except July/Aug.), Rehabilitation Hospital of Tinton Falls, 2 Centre Plaza, Tinton Falls. Call Shirley Maguire 732-460-6743 (day).

MORRIS

North Jersey Stroke Discussion Group Support group promotes the well-being of stroke patients and families through educational programs and sharing of concerns in a living room setting. Donation $2. Building is handicapped accessible. Meets 2nd and 4th Tues., 1pm (call for meeting place July/Aug.), Grace Episcopal Church, Route 24, Library, Madison. Call George 973-543-6386. *E-mail:* grbwitt@patmedia.net

Stroke Discussion Group *Professionally-run.* Mutual support and education for stroke survivors and their families. Exchange of coping skills. Meets 1st and 3rd Tues., 1-2:30pm, Care One, 151 Madison Ave., Morristown. Pre-registration required. Before attending call 973-714-7652.

OCEAN

Stroke of Luck *Professionally-run.* Mutual support for stroke survivors and caregivers. Family and friends welcome. Lecture series, guest speakers and literature. Building is handicapped accessible. Meets 4th Wed., 2pm, Health South Rehabilitation Hospital, 14 Hospital Dr., Toms River. Before attending call Marianne Harms 732-505-5293 (day).

Stroke Support Group *Professionally-run.* Mutual support and education for stroke patients, their families and caregivers. Guest speakers. Building is handicapped accessible. Meets 2nd Mon., 2-4pm, West Lake Community Club House, 1 Pine Lake Circle, Jackson. Call 732-780-3013 (day).

Stroke Support Group *Professionally-run.* Purpose of group is to educate and support individuals and families associated with stroke related issues. Rap sessions and guest speakers. Under 18 welcome. Building is handicapped accessible. Meets 4th Tues., 2pm, Shore Rehab Institute, 425 Jack Martin Blvd., Brick. Call Tami Pindulic 732-836-4527.

SOMERSET

Stroke Club of Somerset County *Professionally-run.* Mutual support for stroke patients and their families. Building is handicapped accessible. Meets 1st Thurs., 2-3:30pm (except Dec.), Somerset Medical Center, Somerset Family Practice, 110 Rehill Ave., Conference Room, Somerville. Call 908-685-2814 (day).

SUSSEX

Stroke Support Group *Professionally-run.* Offers support for persons recovering from a stroke. Caretakers welcomed. Meets 4th Tues., 6-7pm, Newton Memorial Hospital, 175 High St., Rehabilitation Dining Room, Newton. Call Social Services Dept. 973-579-8620.

UNION

Kean University Aphasia Support Group Mutual support for persons suffering from aphasia, Parkinson's and stroke. Families are welcome.

Disseminates information, group discussions, rap sessions and guest speakers. Meetings vary, Kean University, 1000 Morris Ave., Union. Before attending call Wendy Greenspan 908-737-5811 (day).

Stroke Club, The *Professionally-run.* Support and socialization for stroke survivors and their families. Rap sessions, guest speakers and educational series. Optional $1 donation. Building is handicapped accessible. Meets 2nd Thurs., 12:30-2pm, Rahway Hospital, 865 Stone St., Rahway. Pre-registration required. Before attending call Rehabilitation Dept. 732-499-6012 (day). *E-mail:* bmorgan@rwjuhr.com

NATIONAL

American Stroke Association, Division of American Heart Association *(BILINGUAL) National. 1800 groups. Founded 1979.* Maintains a listing of support groups for stroke survivors, their families, friends and interested professionals. Publishes bimonthly magazine. Provides information and referrals to groups and general resources. Write: Stroke Connection, 7272 Greenville Ave., Dallas, TX 75231-4596. Call 1-888-478-7653. *Website:* http://www.StrokeAssociation.org *E-mail:* strokeconnection@heart.org

National Stroke Association *National. 9 chapters. Founded 1984.* Dedicated to reducing the incidence and impact of stroke through prevention, medical treatment, rehabilitation, family support and research. Professional publications, *Stroke Smart* magazine, information and referrals to local groups. Guidance for starting stroke clubs and groups. Write: National Stroke Association, 9707 E. Easter Lane, Suite B, Englewood, CO 80112-3747. Call 1-800-787-6537 or 303-649-9299; Fax: 303-649-1328. *Website:* http://www.stroke.org *E-mail:* info@stroke.org

THYROID CONDITIONS

BERGEN

Thyroid Cancer Awareness, Education and Support Network *(BILINGUAL)* Mutual support, education and awareness for individuals with thyroid cancer. Guest speakers. Meets 3rd Sat., 11:30am-1:30pm, Gilda's Club Northern NJ, 575 Main St., Hackensack. Call Wilma 973-246-1034 (day). *Website:* http://www.steviejoelliescancercarefund.org

CUMBERLAND

ThyCa Southern New Jersey Support Group Support, education and communication for thyroid cancer survivors, families, friends and health care professionals. Guest speakers, literature, newsletter, phone help, buddy system and message board. Meets 3rd Sat., 11am-12:30pm, The Fitness Connection, Sherman Ave. and Orchard St., Vineland. Call Louise Samuel 215-742-5636 (day) or Kim Samuel 215-587-7092 (eve.). *Website:* http://www.thyca.org/sg/nj_vineland.htm *E-mail:* southernjersey@thyca.org

MERCER

Thyroid Cancer Survivors Support Group Support group for thyroid cancer survivors. Families welcome. Literature, guest speaker and phone help. Meets 3rd Sat., 10-11:30am, Cancer Institute of New Jersey Hamilton, Robert Wood Johnson Hospital @ Hamilton, One Hamilton Health Pl., Hamilton. Call Michael Dubrow 1-877-588-7904 (eve.). *E-mail:* centraljersey@thyca.org

OCEAN

Thyroid Support Group Support for anyone affected by a thyroid problem. Mutual support, mutual sharing, guest speakers and video viewing. Building is handicapped accessible. Meets 3rd Mon., 10am, St. Stephen's Episcopal Church, 180 Route 539, Whiting. Call Stefanie 732-350-2904.

NATIONAL

ThyCa: Thyroid Cancer Survivors' Association, Inc. *National.* Support, education and communication for people with all types of thyroid cancer, as well as caregivers. Outreach to the public for thyroid cancer awareness and early detection. Nine online support groups, more than 60 local support groups, free online newsletter, free downloadable low-iodine cookbook, free regional workshops, annual international conference and free thyroid cancer awareness brochures. Thyroid Cancer Awareness Month, funding for research and educational website. Write: ThyCa: Thyroid Cancer Survivors' Association, Inc., P.O. Box 1545, New York, NY 10159-1545. Call 1-877-588-7904; Fax: 630-604-6078. *Website:* http://www.thyca.org *E-mail:* thyca@thyca.org

"If someone listens, or stretches out a hand, or whispers a word of encouragement, or attempts to understand a lonely person, extraordinary things begin to happen."
-- Loretta Girzartis

TRANSPLANT, ORGAN

BERGEN

Life After Transplant Support Group *Professionally-run.* Provides emotional support and education to post-bone marrow or stem cell transplant patients, their family and friends. Facilitator is a transplant recipient. Guest speakers. Meets 3rd Thurs., 5-6:30pm, Hackensack University Medical Center, Cancer Center, Hackensack. Call Renee Stein-Goetz, LCSW 201-336-8290 or Deborah Halpern, MSW 908-956-6607 (day). *E-mail:* Deborah.Halpern@lls.org

CAMDEN

Second Chance Heart Transplant Support Group Mutual support for pre- and post-heart transplant patients, their families, friends and caregivers. Rap sessions and guest speakers. Meets 2nd Tues., 11am, Hahnemann University Hospital, Broad and Vine St., Philadelphia, PA. Call Renard 856-346-9030. *E-mail:* repetron@aol.com

MERCER

Circle of Hope Support and education for organ transplant recipients, candidates, donor families and spouses. Guest speakers, advocacy, literature, and phone help. Building is handicapped accessible. Meets 3rd Wed., 7-8:30pm (except July/Aug., holidays), Robert Wood Johnson University Hospital at Hamilton, One Hamilton Health Place, Third Floor, Tele North Conference Room #303, Hamilton. Call Dick Harbourt 609-799-1498 (day). *E-mail:* raharbourt@aol.com

MIDDLESEX

Kidney and Pancreas Support Group *Professionally-run.* Mutual support for pre- and post-kidney and pancreas transplant patients. Family and relatives welcome. Guest speakers, literature, educational series and social group. Building is handicapped accessible. Meets 3rd Mon., 7pm, Robert Wood Johnson University Hospital, 1 Robert Wood Johnson Place, Board Room, New Brunswick. Call 732-235-8987 (day).

Second Chance Mutual support for heart transplant patients and their families. Building is handicapped accessible. Meets 1st Thurs., 2pm, Robert Wood Johnson University Hospital, 1 Robert Wood Johnson Place, BMSCH Conference Room, New Brunswick. Call 732-418-8110.

MONMOUTH

Central Jersey Transplant Lifeline Support for persons who have had, or are waiting for, an organ transplant. Open to family, friends or anyone interested in organ donations. Rap sessions, mutual sharing and phone help. Building is handicapped accessible. Meets 2nd Tues., 7-9pm, Riverview Medical Center, 1st Floor, Red Bank. Call Virginia O'Keefe 732-450-1271.

MORRIS

Lung Transplant Support Group Mutual support for persons who have received a lung transplant or are considering it. Sharing of information and concerns. Families welcome. Rap sessions. Meetings vary, 2:30-4pm, St. Clares Hospital/Dover General, 400 West Blackwell St., Dover. Before attending call Carmella Thomas, RRT 973-989-3128 (day).

Organ Transplant Recipient Support Group Provides mutual support and education to persons who have undergone an organ transplant or are considering having one. Family and friends welcome. Meets 1st Thurs., 10-11:30am, Denville Library, Meeting Room, 121 Diamond Spring Rd., Denville. Call Betty 973-683-0727 (day).

NATIONAL

Second Wind Lung Transplant Association, Inc. *International network. Founded 1995.* Developed by transplant patients. Opportunity for persons who have undergone, or who will undergo, lung transplants to share their stories on a web page. Newsletter available. Write: Second Wind Lung Transplant Association, c/o Kathryn Flynn, Vice President, 2509 Old NC 10, Hillsborough, NC 27278. Call 1-888-855-9463 or 919-732-0851. *Website:* http://www.2ndwind.org *E-mail:* sarika@mindspring.com or tea3440@sbcglobal.net

TRIO (Transplant Recipients International Organization) *International. 43 chapters. Founded 1983.* Works to improve the quality of life of transplant candidates, recipients, donors and their families. TRIO serves its members in the areas of donor awareness, support, education and advocacy. Annual conference, bi-monthly newsletter, monthly membership update, support network and chapter development assistance. Offers information online on finding local chapters. Write: TRIO, 2100 M St., NW, Suite 170-353, Washington, DC 20037. Call 1-800-874-6386. *Website:* http://www.trioweb.org *E-mail:* info@trioweb.org

VACCINE

OCEAN

NJ Alliance for Informed Choice in Vaccination Provides support, research aid and information on the freedom of vaccine choice. Mutual sharing, guest speakers, telephone support network and literature. Dues $3/family. For information call Cathy Millet 732-892-4852 (eve). *Website:* http://www.njaicv.org *E-mail:* email@njaicv.org

NATIONAL

National Vaccine Information Center *National. 20 affiliated groups. Founded 1982.* Support, information and advocacy group for parents whose children were adversely affected by vaccines. Advocates for safety reforms in the mass vaccination system and safer vaccines. Promotes education for parents and professionals. Various literature available. Dues $25/yr. Write: National Vaccine Information Center, 204 Mill St., Suite B-1, Vienna, VA 22180. Call 703-938-3783; Fax: 703-938-5768. *Website:* http://www.nvic.org *E-mail:* nvicinfo@gmail.com

WOMEN'S HEALTH
(see also breast cancer, specific illness, toll-free helplines)

BURLINGTON

Midpoint *Professionally-run.* Support and discussion for women to share their feelings, fears and concerns in coping with menopause, mid-life and beyond issues. Phone help and speakers. Building is handicapped accessible. Meets 4th Wed., 7:30-9:30pm (except July/Aug.), Lourdes Medical Center of Burlington County, Wellness Center, 218A Sunset Rd., Willingboro. Call Lorraine 856-663-7862 (eve.) or hospital 609-835-5813.

NATIONAL

Black Women's Health Imperative *International. 15 chapters. Founded 1981.* Grassroots organization aimed at improving the health of black women by providing wellness education, services, self-help group development, leadership development, health information and advocacy. Assists in the development of new local affiliate groups. Self-help brochure, quarterly newsletter and annual news magazine. Membership dues vary. Write: Black Women's Health Imperative, 1420 K St., NW, Suite 1000, 10th Fl., Washington, DC 20005. Call

202-548-4000; Fax: 202-543-9743. *Website:* http://www.blackwomenshealth.org *E-mail:* nbwhp@nbwhp.org

DES Action *National. Founded 1983.* Mutual support and education for DES-exposed women, with a special focus on DES cancer issues. Provides research advocacy and medical/legal resources. Write: DES Action, 2925 Garber St., Berkeley, CA 94705. Call 1-800-337-9288. *Website:* http://descancer.org

International Premature Ovarian Failure Foundation *National network. 8 affiliated groups. Founded 1995.* Mutual support for women who have prematurely entered menopause. Phone support, literature, information and referrals. Assistance in starting groups. Write: International Premature Ovarian Failure Foundation, c/o Catherine Corp, P.O. Box 23643, Alexandria, VA 22304. Call 703-913-4787. *Website:* http://www.pofsupport.org *E-mail:* info@pofsupport.org

ONLINE

Cyster Connection *Online. 531 members.* Support for women with polycystic ovarian syndrome (PCOS), a condition in which ovaries create an abundance of follicles each month without producing an egg. PCOS usually goes hand-in-hand with insulin resistance. It is also the most common cause of infertility among women in the United States. *Website:* http://pcostcc.proboards83.com

iVillage Health Message Boards *Online.* Provides various message boards concerning all aspects of health, including menopause, breast cancer, addictions, allergies, arthritis, heart, immune disorders, vision, disabilities, diabetes, caregivers, brain disorders, infertility, respiratory, mental health, pain, parenting, thyroid and medications. Mailing lists, message boards, chats and newsletters. *Website:* http://www.ivillage.com/boards

Mullerian Anomalies of the Uterus *Online.* Support and information for those with mullerian anomalies of the uterus such as bicornuate, septate, unicornauate, hypoplastic and didelphys uteria. Weekly chat, e-mail list and message board. *Website:* http://health.groups.yahoo.com/group/MullerianAnomalies/

Postpartum Hemorrhage Survivors *Online.* E-mail list for women who are supporting each other after a postpartum hemorrhage and hysterectomy. *Website:* http://health.groups.yahoo.com/group/pph-survivors

Power Surge *Online.* Provides support and information for women going through menopause. Online interactive chats, message boards, newsletters and weekly gab sessions. Some pages require flash. *Website:* http://power-surge.com

ANXIETY ATTACKS / PHOBIAS / AGORAPHOBIA
(see also mental health general, mental health consumers, toll-free helplines)

STATEWIDE

DOROT/University Without Walls Telephone Support Teleconference support groups for persons with limited mobility who are coping with vision loss, anxiety, aging issues, etc. There is a $10 registration fee and $15 tuition per support group. Scholarships are available. Write: DOROT, 171 W. 85th St., New York, NY 10024. For more information call 1-877-819-9147 or Fran Rod 973-763-1511. *Website:* http://www.dorotusa.org

GROW Mutual self-help group to prevent and recover from depression, anxiety and other mental health problems. Caring and sharing community to attain emotional maturity, personal responsibility and recovery. Meets in various counties in NJ. Write: GROW Center, 4A Iowa Dr., Whiting, NJ 08759. Call 732-350-4800.

BERGEN

Emotions Anonymous 12-Step. Fellowship sharing experiences, hopes and strengths in order to gain better emotional health. Deals with anxiety, fears, anger, depression, etc. Donation $2/mtg.
> **Hackensack** Meets Tues. and Thurs., 7:30pm, First Presbyterian Church, 64 Passaic St. (use right side entrance), 1st Floor. Call Sam 201-962-8038 (day).
> **Hillsdale** Meets Mon., 7:30pm, Holy Trinity Episcopal Church, 326 Hillsdale Ave. Call Lea 201-666-1009 (day).

Recovery, Inc. Self-help method of will training. Offers techniques for controlling temperamental behavior and changing attitudes toward nervous symptoms, anxiety, depression and fears. Call 201-612-8153. *Website:* http://www.recovery-inc.org *E-mail:* inquiries@recovery-inc.org
> **Hasbrouck Heights** Meets Wed., 8pm, First Reformed Church, Washington Place and Burton Ave. Call Philip 201-261-7044.
> **Ridgewood** Meets Fri., 1:30pm, Christ Church, Cottage Place and Franklin Ave.

BURLINGTON

Recovery, Inc. Self-help method of will training. Offers techniques for controlling temperamental behavior and changing attitudes toward nervous symptoms, anxiety, depression and fears. Call Barry 856-848-8715 or John 856-983-7291. *Website:* http://www.recovery-inc.org *E-mail:* 155@recovery-inc.org

> **Marlton** Meets Mon. and Thurs., 7pm, Prince of Peace Lutheran Church, 61 Route 70 East.
>
> **Westampton** Meets Tues., 7pm, Hampton Hospital, Rancocas Rd. and Route 295, Cafeteria.

CAMDEN

Depression / Anxiety Support Group Support for anyone suffering from anxiety and/or depression to help one another in an effort to remain healthy, to share common problems and concerns. Under 18 welcome. Rap sessions, phone help and literature. Meets 3rd Mon., 7:15-9pm, Marie Fleche Library, White Horse Pike, Berlin. Call Nancy 856-768-1258 (eve.) or Rhonda 856-768-2030.

New Beginnings Support Group - A Chapter of DBSA Mutual support and education for persons with mood disorders. Separate group for families and friends. Also open to persons with anxiety, dual diagnosis and schizo-affective disorder. Opportunity to discuss successes in dealing with various symptoms. Meets Mon., 7-9pm (separate group for family and friends meets 1st and 3rd Mon.); Wed., 11am-1pm and Thurs., 7-9pm, Holy Trinity Lutheran Church, North Warwick Rd. and Evesham Rd., Magnolia. Call 1-877-313-5050 or Doug 856-451-1240. Family and friends group call Karen 856-451-1240. *Website:* http://www.nbgroup.org *E-mail:* newbeginningsnj@gmail.com

Recovery, Inc. Self-help method of will training. Offers techniques for controlling temperamental behavior and changing attitudes toward nervous symptoms, anxiety, depression and fears. *Website:* http://www.recovery-inc.org *E-mail:* 155@recovery-inc.org

> **Magnolia** Meets Wed., 9:30am, Holy Trinity Lutheran Church, North Warwick Rd. and Evesham Rd. Call Stacy 856-931-1411 or Barry 856-848-8715.
>
> **Westmont** Meets Sat., 11:30am, Starting Point, 215 Highland Ave. Call Ann 856-853-2724 or Rob 609-413-6959.

CUMBERLAND

GROW Mutual self-help group to prevent and recover from depression, anxiety and other mental health problems. Caring and sharing community to attain emotional maturity, personal responsibility and recovery. Before attending call Ninfa 732-575-5766.

Vineland Meets Thurs., 7pm, Church of Christian/Missionary Alliance, Main Rd. and Harding Ave., Board Room.

Vineland Meets Thurs., 7pm, New Horizons Self-Help Center, 63 S. Myrtle St.

Overcomer's Outreach Christian 12-Step. Fellowship to overcome any type of addiction or compulsive behavior, anxiety, depression or loneliness using God's word as a basis of recovery. Bible study, discussion, prayer and phone help. Meets Thurs., 7-8pm, Shiloh Seventh Day Baptist Church, East Ave., Shiloh. Call Frank B. Mulford 856-451-8698 (day) or Rev. Chroniger 856-455-0488 (day). *E-mail:* ahfarm@hotmail.com

ESSEX

GROW Mutual self-help group to prevent and recover from depression, anxiety and other mental health problems. Caring and sharing community to attain emotional maturity, personal responsibility and recovery. Meets Mon., 4:30pm, Pleasant Moments Self-Help Center, 465-475 Broadway, Newark. Before attending call Caroline 732-575-5765.

Phobia Support Group *Professionally-run.* Support for those with agoraphobia or any other type of phobia. Families welcome. Guest speakers, literature and phone help. Childcare available. Building is handicapped accessible. Meetings vary, Brandt Life Therapy Center, 15 Bloomfield Ave., Suite 2, Verona. Before attending call 973-239-0954. *E-mail:* dougbrandt@comcast.net

Recovery, Inc. Self-help method of will training. Offers techniques for controlling temperamental behavior and changing attitudes toward nervous symptoms, anxiety, depression and fears. Meets Tues., 8pm, Prospect Presbyterian Church, 646 Prospect St., Maplewood. Call Hal 973-762-0764 or 201-612-8153. *Website:* http://www.recovery-inc.org *E-mail:* inquiries@recovery-inc.org

A little boy was having difficulty lifting a heavy stone.
His father came along just then. Noting the boy's failure, he asked, "Are you using all your strength?"
"Yes, I am," the little boy said impatiently.
"No, you are not," the father answered. "I am right here just waiting, and you haven't asked me to help you." -- Author Unknown

GLOUCESTER

Recovery, Inc. Self-help method of will training. Offers techniques for controlling temperamental behavior and changing attitudes toward nervous symptoms, anxiety, depression and fears. Families welcome. Call Barry 856-848-8715. *Website:* http://www.recovery-inc.org *E-mail:* 155@recovery-inc.org.
Deptford Meets Fri., 10-11am, James Johnson Library, 670 Ward Dr.
Woodbury Heights Meets Wed., 7pm, First Presbyterian Church, 4th and Elm Ave. Call Ann 856-853-2724.

MERCER

GROW Mutual self-help group to prevent and recover from depression, anxiety and other mental health problems. Caring and sharing community to attain emotional maturity, personal responsibility and recovery. Meets Thurs., 6pm, Reach Out/Speak Out, 2100 E. State St., Hamilton. Before attending call Caroline 732-575-5765.

New Perspectives Mutual support for persons with depression, bipolar disorder, anxiety or panic disorder. Meets every other Mon., 7:30pm, Unitarian Universalist Church, Washington Crossing. Call David Hughes 609-818-0177 (eve.). *E-mail:* David.Hughes419@att.net

P.U.S.H. (Phobics Using Self-Help) Mutual support and encouragement for persons suffering from agoraphobia or panic attacks. Donation $1/week. Meets Mon., 7pm, St. Mark's United Methodist Church, Paxson Ave., Hamilton Square. For information call 609-291-0095 (answering machine).

MIDDLESEX

Overcomer's Outreach Christian 12-Step. Fellowship to overcome any type of addiction or compulsive behavior, anxiety, depression or loneliness using God's word as a basis of recovery. Bible study, discussion, prayer and phone help. Meets Tues., 6:30-7:30pm, Metuchen Assembly of God, 130 Whitman St., Metuchen. Call Janet 732-388-2856 (eve.).

MONMOUTH

Emotions Anonymous 12-Step. Fellowship sharing experiences, hopes and strengths in order to gain better emotional health. Deals with anxiety, fears, anger, depression, etc. Donation $1-2/mtg. Meets Sat., noon, Port Monmouth. Call Chris or Lillian 732-495-7453 (day). *E-mail:* graye22@netzero.net

GROW Mutual self-help group to prevent and recover from depression, anxiety and other mental health problems. Caring and sharing community to attain emotional maturity, personal responsibility and recovery.

>**Freehold** Meets Wed., 5:30pm, Freehold Self-Help Center, 17 Bannard St. Before attending call Nancy 732-350-4800.

>**Ocean Grove** Meets Thurs., 6:45pm, St. Paul's Methodist Church, 80 Enbury St., Stokes Room. Before attending call Caroline 732-575-5765.

MORRIS

Anxiety Support Group Mutual support and encouragement for people suffering from anxiety and phobias. Building is handicapped accessible. Meets 1st and 3rd Mon., 7-8:30pm, United Methodist Church, 903 South Beverwyck Rd., Parsippany. Call Flora 973-257-7023 (eve.).

OCEAN

GROW Mutual self-help group to prevent and recover from depression, anxiety and other mental health problems. Caring and sharing community to attain emotional maturity, personal responsibility and recovery.

>**Brick** Meets Tues., 6:30pm, Brick Presbyterian Church, 111 Drum Point Rd. Before attending call Caroline 732-575-5765.

>**Toms River** Meets Thurs., 4pm, Presbyterian Church of Toms River, Hooper Ave. and Chestnut St., River Room. Before attending call Ninfa 732-575-5766.

>**Toms River** Meets Tues., 6:30pm, Brighter Days Self-Help Center, S and F Plaza, 2008 Route 37 East, Suite 6. Before attending call Nancy 732-350-4800.

P.H.O.B.I.A.(People Helping Others Become Independent Again) Support group for people with panic attacks, anxiety, phobias, depression and agoraphobia. Families welcome. Guest speakers, literature and phone help. Meets Wed., 7-9pm, St. Stephen's Church, Route 9, Waretown. Call Cathy 609-971-9110. *Website:* http://www.moodgarden.org/phobia *E-mail:* phobia@comcast.net

Recovery, Inc. Self-help method of will training. Offers techniques for controlling temperamental behavior and changing attitudes toward nervous symptoms, anxiety, depression and fears. Meets Mon., 7:30pm, Presbyterian Church of Toms River, Hooper Ave. and Chestnut St., Toms River. Call Delores 732-557-5466 or 201-612-8153. *Website:* http://www.recovery-inc.org *E-mail:* inquiries@recovery-inc.org

UNION

GROW Mutual self-help group to prevent and recover from depression, anxiety and other mental health problems. Caring and sharing community to attain emotional maturity, personal responsibility and recovery. Before attending call Caroline 732-575-5765.

Elizabeth Meets Wed., 4pm, New Beginnings Self-Help Center, 516 Morris Ave.

Plainfield Meets Wed., 3:30pm, Park Avenue Self-Help Center, 333 Park Ave.

Recovery, Inc. Self-help method of will training. Offers techniques for controlling temperamental behavior and changing attitudes toward nervous symptoms, anxiety, depression and fears. Call 201-612-8153.*Website:* http://www.recovery-inc.org *E-mail:* inquiries@recovery-inc.org

Summit Meets Wed., 7:45pm, Central Presbyterian Center, Morris Ave. and Maple St., (parking lot entrance).

Westfield Meets Fri., 8pm, Union County Community Building, 300 North Ave. East (parking lot entrance), 2nd Floor, Conference Room. Call Dorothy 732-381-3712.

NATIONAL

Agoraphobics In Motion *National. 7 groups. Founded 1983.* Self-help group that uses specific behavioral and cognitive techniques, along with an adapted 12-Steps of AA to help people recover from anxiety disorders. Relaxation techniques, small group discussions and field trips. Group development guidelines ($2.50). Informative facilitator's manual ($15). Subscription available for weekly handouts ($30/yr). Write: AIM, 1719 Crooks, Royal Oak, MI 48067-1306. Call 248-547-0400. *Website:* http://www.aim-hq.org *E-mail:* anny@ameritech.net

Anxiety Disorders Association of America *National network. 197 groups. Founded 1980.* Promotes the diagnosis and treatment of all anxiety and related disorders including obsessive compulsive disorder, post-traumatic stress disorder, panic disorder, specific phobia, social anxiety disorder and generalized anxiety disorder. Listing of state-by-state local support groups, brochures, information about anxiety disorders, local listing of healthcare professionals providing treatment for anxiety disorders and a national listing of clinical trails provided free. Write: Anxiety Disorders Association of America, 8730 Georgia Ave., Suite 600, Silver Spring, MD 20910. Call 240-485-1001; Fax: 240-485-1035. *Website:* http://www.adaa.org

GROW in America *International. 143 groups. Founded in 1957.* 12-Step. Group offers mutual help, friendship, community, education and leadership. Focuses on recovery and personal growth. Open to all including those with mental health issues, depression, anxiety, grief, fears, etc. Write: GROW in America, P.O. Box 3667, Champaign, IL 61826. Call 1-888-741-4769. *E-mail:* growil@sbcglobal.net

International Paruresis Association, Inc. *International network. 35 affiliated groups. Founded 1996.* Provides emotional support and information for persons with paruresis (shy or bashful bladder). Supports research to develop effective treatments. Information, referrals, literature, phone support, workshops, conferences and advocacy. Assistance in starting similar groups. Write: International Paruresis Association, P.O. Box 65111, Baltimore, MD 21209. Call 1-800-247-3864 or 410-367-1253; Fax: 410-367-1254. *Website:* http://www.paruresis.org *E-mail:* ssoifer@ssw.umaryland.edu

Recovery, Inc. *International. 640+ groups. Founded 1937.* Mental health self-help organization that offers weekly group meetings for people suffering from various emotional and mental conditions. Principles parallel those found in cognitive-behavioral therapy. Teaches people how to change their thoughts, reactions and behaviors that cause their physical and emotional symptoms. Write: Recovery, Inc., 802 N. Dearborn St., Chicago, IL 60610. Call 312-337-5661; Fax: 312-337-5756. *Website:* http://www.recovery-inc.org

Selective Mutism Foundation, Inc. *National. Founded 1992.* Pioneering group that offers mutual support for professionals and parents of children with selective mutism or social phobia (a psychiatric anxiety disorder in which children are unable to speak in social situations). Includes social anxiety and shyness. Also open to adults who have or outgrew, the disorder. Provides information and online support. Website contains DSM revisions, research studies, printable brochures, literature and publications. Write: Carolyn Miller, P.O. Box 13133, Sissonville, WV 25360 or Sue Newman Mercado, P.O. Box 25972, Tamarac, FL 33320. *Website:* http://www.selectivemutismfoundation.org *E-mail:* carolyn@selectivemutismfoundation.org or sue@selectivemutismfoundation.org

Social Phobics Anonymous *International. 8 groups.* 12-Step. Both face-to-face and telephone support groups that provides support for people who suffer from social phobia or social anxiety. Assists others in starting local groups. Meeting information available on website. Call Phil 720-882-8976 for telephone meeting log-in procedure. *Website:* http://www.healsocialanxiety.com *E-mail:* healsocialanxiety@hotmail.com

ONLINE

Dental Fear Central *Online. Founded 2004.* Support for anyone with an extreme phobia of dentists or specific dental fears. Information for dental professionals and dental students with an interest in dental anxiety management. Various message boards, including one for mutual support and another to "Share Your Success Story." "Ask the Dentist" section and information on coping with different fears associated with dentistry. *Website:* http://www.dentalfearcentral.org/

Gift From Within *Online. (WOMEN ONLY)* Offers a one-on-one post-traumatic stress disorder e-mail/pen pal support network, where female victims of specific trauma can be matched with survivors of similar PTSD. Audio-visual resources available. *Website:* http://www.giftfromwithin.org *E-mail:* joyceb3955@aol.com

International Emetophobia Society Forums *Online.* Support for people who suffer from emetophobia - an irrational fear of vomiting, to help them with their fears and share their experiences with others. Several topics are addressed, such as: social isolation, obsession, travel issues, morning sickness and eating strategies. *Website:* http://www.emetophobia.org

Panic Center, The *Online.* Offers online scheduled support group meetings, forums and e-mail list. Addresses various types of anxiety, panic attacks and phobias. *Website:* http://www.paniccenter.net

Panic Survivor *Online.* Support group for persons who suffer from anxiety, panic attacks, social anxiety, generalized anxiety, post-traumatic stress disorder, obsessive compulsive disorder, hypochondria or any other form of anxiety. Focus is on recovery and day-to-day survival with a "can do" attitude. *Website:* http://panicsurvivor.com

Selective Mutism Group, The *Online.* Devoted to educating and promoting awareness on selective mutism and other related childhood anxiety disorders. Online support group for parents, teachers and professionals dealing with selective mutism. *Website:* http://selectivemutism.org *E-mail:* sminfo@selectivemutism.org

"Taking Flight" Fear of Flying Support *Online.* Mutual self-help group created by and for fearful fliers for their own recovery. Message boards, information and a variety of resources. *Website:* http://www.takingflight.us *E-mail:* info@takingflight.us

DEPRESSION / BIPOLAR DISORDER / POSTPARTUM DEPRESSION

(see also mental health consumers)

STATEWIDE

DBSA (Depression and Bipolar Support Alliance) of NJ *16 chapters throughout New Jersey.* Education and support for persons with depression or bipolar disorder, their families and friends. Peer support groups and educational programs. Call 908-377-5245. *Website:* http://www.dbsanewjersey.org

GROW Mutual self-help group to prevent and recover from depression, anxiety and other mental health problems. Caring and sharing community to attain emotional maturity, personal responsibility and recovery. Meets in various counties in NJ. Write: GROW Center, 4A Iowa Dr., Whiting, NJ 08759. Call 732-350-4800.

NAMI NJ (National Alliance on Mental Illness New Jersey) Dedicated to improving the quality of life for people diagnosed with a mental illness and their families. Provides self-help groups, education and advocacy. Provides an array of public education and mental illness awareness activities to create understanding and eradicate the stigma associated with a mental illness. For information call 732-940-0991 (day) or 1-866-626-4437. *Website:* http://www.naminj.org *E-mail:* info@naminj.org

ATLANTIC

Bipolar Support Group Mutual support and encouragement for persons with bipolar disorder. Meets Mon., 6-7pm, First Presbyterian Church, 1311 Main St., Pleasantville. Call 609-272-1700 ext. 303 (day).

Depression Support Group Mutual support and encouragement for persons with depression. Rap sessions. Call 609-272-1700 ext. 303 (day).
> **Atlantic City** Meets Tues., 6pm, AtlantiCare Behavioral Health, 13 North Hartford Ave.
> **Atlantic City** *(SPANISH)* Meets Tues., 6pm, AtlantiCare Behavioral Health, 13 North Hartford Ave.

Persons with Depression and Bipolar Disorder Support Group Mutual support and encouragement for persons suffering from depression or bipolar disorder and their families. Meets Fri., 7-9pm, St. Mark All Saints Episcopal Church, Pitney Rd., Galloway. Call Barbara 609-404-1984.

TLC for Moms (Postpartum Depression Support Group) *Professionally-run.* Mutual support and education for women experiencing postpartum depression and for expectant mothers experiencing depression. Babies are welcome. Meets Mon., 1-2:30pm (except Nov.), Shore Memorial Hospital, Jenkins Room, Somers Point. Call 609-926-4229 (day).

BERGEN

DBSA (Depression and Bipolar Support Alliance) Mutual support for persons with depression or bipolar disorder. Families and friends welcome. Phone help, guest speakers, rap sessions and literature. Donation $1. Meets Thurs., 7:15pm, Bergen Regional Medical Center, 230 E. Ridgewood Ave., Psych Pavilion, Room E007, Paramus. Call 1-888-622-3272.

Emotions Anonymous 12-Step. Fellowship sharing experiences, hopes and strengths in order to gain better emotional health. Deals with anxiety, fears, anger, depression, etc.
> **Hackensack** Meets Tues. and Thurs., 7:30pm, First Presbyterian Church, 64 Passaic St. (use right side entrance). Call Sam 201-962-8038 (day).
> **Hillsdale** Meets Mon., 7:30pm, Holy Trinity Episcopal Church, 326 Hillsdale Ave. Donation $2/mtg. Call Lea 201-666-1009.

Postpartum Depression Support Group *Professionally-run.* Mutual support and encouragement for women who are suffering from postpartum depression. Meets 1st and 3rd Wed., 11am or 2nd and 4th Tues., 7pm, Valley Hospital, 223 N. Van Dien Ave., Ridgewood. Call Trudy Heerema 201-447-8539 (day).

Recovery, Inc. Self-help method of will training. Offers techniques for controlling temperamental behavior and changing attitudes toward nervous symptoms, anxiety, depression and fears. *Website:* http://www.recovery-inc.org *E-mail:* inquiries@recovery-inc.org
> **Hasbrouck Heights** Meets Wed., 8pm, First Reformed Church, Washington Place and Burton Ave. Call Philip 201-261-7044 or 201-612-8153.
> **Ridgewood** Meets Fri., 1:30pm, Christ Church, Cottage Place and Franklin Ave. Call 201-612-8153.

BURLINGTON

DBSA (Depression and Bipolar Support Alliance) Support and education for persons with depression or bipolar disorder. Family and friends welcome. Literature, phone help and buddy system. Building handicapped accessible.

Meets 2nd Tues. and 4th Wed., 7-9pm, Virtua Hospital, Madison Ave., Conference Center, Main Floor, Mt. Holly. Call Steve 609-784-8131 (day).

Recovery, Inc. Self-help method of will training. Offers techniques for controlling temperamental behavior and changing attitudes toward nervous symptoms, anxiety, depression and fears. Call Barry 856-848-8715 or John 856-983-7291. *Website:* http://www.recovery-inc.org *E-mail:* 155@recovery-inc.org

> **Marlton** Meets Mon. and Thurs., 7pm, Prince of Peace Lutheran Church, 61 Route 70 East.
>
> **Westampton** Meets Tues., 7pm, Hampton Hospital, Rancocas Rd., Cafeteria.

CAMDEN

Depression / Anxiety Support Group Support for anyone suffering from anxiety and/or depression to support one another in an effort to remain healthy, share common problems and concerns. Under 18 welcome. Rap sessions, phone help and literature. Meets 3rd Mon., 7:15-9pm, Marie Fleche Library, Berlin. Call Nancy 856-768-1258 (eve.) or Rhonda 856-768-2030 (day).

New Beginnings Support Group - A Chapter of DBSA Mutual support and education for persons with mood disorders. Separate group for families and friends. Also open to persons with anxiety, dual diagnosis and schizo-affective disorder. Opportunity to discuss successes in dealing with various symptoms. Meets Mon., 7-9pm (separate group for families and friends meets 1st and 3rd Mon.); Wed., 11am-1pm and Thurs., 7-9pm, Holy Trinity Lutheran Church, North Warwick Rd. and Evesham Rd., Magnolia. Call 1-877-313-5050 or Doug 856-451-1240. Family and friends call Karen 856-451-1240. *Website:* http://www.nbgroup.org *E-mail:* newbeginningsnj@gmail.com

Recovery, Inc. Self-help method of will training. Offers techniques for controlling temperamental behavior and changing attitudes toward nervous symptoms, anxiety, depression and fears. *Website:* http://www.recovery-inc.org *E-mail:* 155@recovery-inc.org

> **Magnolia** Meets Wed., 9:30am, Holy Trinity Lutheran Church, North Warwick Rd. and Evesham Rd. Call Stacy 856-931-1411 or Barry 856-848-8715.
>
> **Westmont** Meets Sat., 11:30am, Starting Point, 215 Highland Ave. Call Ann 856-853-2724 or Rob 609-413-6959.

South Jersey Depression, Bipolar and PTSD Group Support for persons with depression, bipolar disorder or post-traumatic stress disorder who want to take the next step towards wellness and recovery. Meets Fri., 7pm, St. Andrew's

United Methodist Church, 327 Marlton Pike West, Cherry Hill. Call Richard 609-980-6980.

TLC for Moms (Postpartum Depression Support Group) *Professionally-run.* Mutual support and education for women experiencing postpartum depression and for expectant mothers experiencing depression. Babies are welcome. Meets Wed., noon-1:30pm, Virtua Health, Barry D. Brown Health Education Center, 106 Carnie Blvd., Voorhees. Pre-registration required. Before attending call 1-866-380-2229 (day).

CUMBERLAND

Depression Support Group *Professionally-run.* Mutual support for persons suffering from depression or any other mental illness. Provides a safe and comfortable environment where persons can share with others who also suffer from depression. Building is handicapped accessible. Meets Thurs., 6:30-9pm, in Millville. For meeting information call 856-825-3521 (after 10am).

GROW Mutual self-help group to prevent and recover from depression, anxiety and other mental health problems. Caring and sharing community to attain emotional maturity, personal responsibility and recovery. Before attending call Ninfa 732-575-5766.
> **Vineland** Meets Thurs., 7pm, Church of Christian/Missionary Alliance, Main Rd. and Harding Ave., Board Room.
> **Vineland** Meets Thurs., 7pm, New Horizons Self-Help Center, 63 S. Myrtle St.

Overcomer's Outreach Christian 12-Step. Fellowship to overcome any type of addiction or compulsive behavior, anxiety, depression or loneliness using God's word as a basis of recovery. Bible study, discussion, prayer and phone help. Meets Thurs., 7-8pm, Shiloh Seventh Day Baptist Church, East Ave., Shiloh. Call Frank B. Mulford 856-451-8698 (day) or Rev. Chroniger 856-455-0488 (day). *E-mail:* ahfarm@hotmail.com

ESSEX

Comfort Zone, The Provides mutual support for people suffering from depression and bipolar disorder. Meets Fri., noon-1:30pm, Mental Health Association of Essex County, 33 South Fullerton Ave., Montclair. Call Mary Ann Forster 973-509-9777 (day). *E-mail:* mforster@mhaessex.org

DBSA (Depression and Bipolar Support Alliance) Mutual support and sharing of information for individuals diagnosed with depression or bipolar disorder. Family members welcome. Rap sessions, guest speakers, educational programs, literature, phone help and e-mail. Meets Thurs., 7:30-9pm, First Congregational Church, 40 South Fullerton Ave. (enter via side door on Crescent St.), Montclair. Call Tom B. 201-998-5751. *Website:* http://www.dbsanewjersey.org/essexcounty

GROW Mutual self-help group to prevent and recover from depression, anxiety and other mental health problems. Caring and sharing community to attain emotional maturity, personal responsibility and recovery. Meets Mon., 4:30pm, Pleasant Moments Self-Help Center, 465-475 Broadway, Newark. Before attending call Caroline 732-575-5765.

New Moms' Circle *Professionally-run.* Support group for new mothers to openly discuss the ups and downs of adjusting to motherhood. Topics to be covered include: myths of motherhood, shifting identity, postpartum depression, attempting to balance it all, marriage and the transition to parenthood. Meets Tues., 10-11:30am, Saint Barnabas Ambulatory Care Center, 200 South Orange Ave. (across from the Livingston Mall), Livingston. For information call Saint Barnabas Women's Health Education 973-322-5360 or Dr. Lauren Meisels, PhD 973-762-4147. Infants in strollers or car seats are welcome to attend and free childcare is available, if needed, by calling 973-322-7309 at least 24 hours in advance.

Recovery, Inc. Self-help method of will training. Offers techniques for controlling temperamental behavior and changing attitudes toward nervous symptoms, anxiety, depression and fears. Meets Tues., 8pm, Prospect Presbyterian Church, 646 Prospect St., Maplewood. Call Hal 973-762-0764 or 201-612-8153. *Website:* http://www.recovery-inc.org *E-mail:* inquiries@recovery-inc.org

GLOUCESTER

Recovery, Inc. Self-help method of will training. Offers techniques for controlling temperamental behavior and changing attitudes toward nervous symptoms, anxiety, depression and fears. Families welcome. *Website:* http://www.recovery-inc.org *E-mail:* 155@recovery-inc.org

> **Deptford** Meets Fri., 10-11am, James Johnson Library, 670 Ward Dr. Call Barry 856-848-8715.

> **Woodbury Heights** Meets Wed., 7pm, First Presbyterian Church, 4th and Elm Ave. Call Ann 856-853-2724 or Barry 856-848-8715.

TLC for Moms (Postpartum Depression Support Group) *Professionally-run.* Mutual support and education for women experiencing postpartum depression and for expectant mothers experiencing depression. Babies are welcome. Meets Wed., 11am-12:30pm, Kennedy Health System, 400 Medical Center Dr., Suite C, Turnersville. Pre-registration required. Before attending call 856-582-3098 (day).

HUDSON

DBSA (Depression and Bipolar Support Alliance) Mutual support for persons with depression or bipolar disorder. Meets 2nd and 4th Mon., 5pm, Hudson County Self-Help Center, 880 Bergen Ave., Suite 605, Jersey City. Call Wayne 201-420-8013 (day).

HUNTERDON

DBSA (Depression and Bipolar Support Alliance) Mutual support for persons suffering from depression or bipolar disorder. Rap sessions and literature. Suggested donation $1 or $2 for DBSA literature. Meets Mon., 7:30pm, Clinton Church of the Nazarene, 80 Beaver Ave., Clinton. Before attending call Lyn Siegel, LCSW 908-586-3254 (day). *Website:* http://www.dbsalliance.org (click on "Find support") *E-mail:* lynsiegel@embarqmail.com

Postpartum Depression Support Group *Professionally-run.* Mutual support and education for women experiencing postpartum depression. Babies welcome. Building is handicapped accessible. Meets 1st and 3rd Mon., 1-2:30pm, Hunterdon Medical Center, 2100 Westcott Dr., Flemington. Before attending call Jean Jamele, RN 908-788-6634 (day).

MERCER

DBSA (Depression and Bipolar Support Alliance) An informal forum for support, education and socialization among patients diagnosed with depression, bipolar disorder or related disorders. Families, friends and interested others welcome. Building is handicapped accessible. Meets Tues., 7:30-9:15pm, Lambert House, 253 Witherspoon St., Room 1, Princeton. Call Emily 908-788-5270 or David 609-912-0273. *Website:* http://www.dbsanewjersey.org/princeton

GROW Mutual self-help group to prevent and recover from depression, anxiety and other mental health problems. Caring and sharing community to attain emotional maturity, personal responsibility and recovery. Meets Thurs., 6pm, Reach Out/Speak Out, 2100 East State St., Hamilton. Before attending call Caroline 732-575-5765.

New Perspectives Mutual support for persons with depression, bipolar disorder, anxiety or panic disorder. Meets every other Mon., 7:30pm, Unitarian Universalist Church, Washington Crossing. Call David Hughes 609-818-0177 (eve.). *E-mail:* David.Hughes419@att.net

Pregnancy and Postpartum Support Group *Professionally-run.* Support for pregnant women, new mothers and all women adjusting to emotional issues such as blues, depression, obsessive compulsive disorder and anxiety. Building is handicapped accessible. Meets 3rd Sat., 10:30am-noon, Mary Jacobs County Library, Route 518, Rocky Hill. Pre-registration required. Before attending call Joyce 609-921-3555 (day), Terry 908-752-3797, Leah 732-255-6896 (eve.) or Gail 732-248-4921 (eve.).

MIDDLESEX

DBSA (Depression and Bipolar Support Alliance) Support and information for persons suffering from depression or bipolar disorder.
> **Metuchen** Meets Mon., 7:30-9pm, Metuchen YMCA, 65 High St., Pre-school Room, 2nd Floor. Families, friends and interested others welcome. Call John 908-217-3845. *Website:* http://health.groups.yahoo.com/group/bipolardepressionsupport
> **New Brunswick** Meets Fri., 7:30pm, Robert Wood Johnson University Hospital, Auditorium, Main Floor. Call 1-888-226-6437. *Website:* http://www.dbsanewjersey.org/middlesex   *E-mail:* dbsacentralnj@yahoo.com

Overcomer's Outreach Christian 12-Step. Fellowship to overcome any type of addiction or compulsive behavior, anxiety, depression or loneliness using God's word as a basis of recovery. Bible study, discussion, prayer and phone help. Meets Tues., 6:30-7:30pm, Metuchen Assembly of God, 130 Whitman St., Metuchen. Call Janet 732-388-2856 (eve.).

MONMOUTH

DBSA (Depression and Bipolar Support Alliance) Support for persons affected by depression or bipolar disorder. Families and interested professionals are welcome. Guest speakers, phone help and mutual sharing. Building is handicapped accessible. Meets Mon. and Thurs., 7:30-9pm, St. Mary's Church, Route 34 and Phalanx Rd., Colts Neck. Call Tom Mahoney 732-264-8363 or Maureen Falkowitz 732-536-5326. *Website:* http://www.dbsanewjersey.org/coltsneck

Emotions Anonymous 12-Step. Fellowship sharing experiences, hopes and strengths in order to gain better emotional health. Deals with anxiety, fears, anger, depression, etc. Donation $1-2 per week. Meets Sat., noon, Port Monmouth. Call Chris or Lillian 732-495-7453 (day). *E-mail:* graye22@netzero.net

GROW Mutual self-help group to prevent and recover from depression, anxiety and other mental health problems. Caring and sharing community to attain emotional maturity, personal responsibility and recovery.

> **Freehold** Meets Wed., 5:30pm, Freehold Self-Help Center, 17 Bannard St. Before attending call Nancy 732-350-4800.
>
> **Ocean Grove** Meets Thurs., 6:45pm, St. Paul's Methodist Church, 80 Enbury St., Stokes Room. Before attending call Caroline 732-575-5765.

New Babies - New Emotions *Professionally-run.* Support for moms-to-be and new moms with any kind of postpartum related depression and/or baby blues. Babies 12 months and under are welcome. Guest speakers, literature, newsletter and phone help. Call Pat Vena 732-363-5400 ext. 22 (day)

> **Eatontown** Meets 1st Wed., 7pm, Babies R Us, 70 Route 36 East. Call Douge Beagle 732-935-9366.
>
> **Long Branch** Meets 1st Mon., 11am-noon, Monmouth Medical Center, 300 Second Ave., Ronald McDonald Family Room. Call Jean Bonn 732-923-6990.
>
> **Long Branch** *(SPANISH) Professionally-run.* Meets 2nd Fri., 2-3pm, Monmouth Family Health Center, 300 Second Ave., BBR3, 3rd Floor, OB/GYN Dept. Call Marti Eisner 732-923-7102.
>
> **Manalapan** Meets last Wed., 7:30pm, Babies R Us, 7 Route 9 South. Call Antoinette Urciouli 732-845-2861.
>
> **Neptune** Meets 3rd Tues., 7pm, Jersey Shore University Medical Center, 1945 Route 33, 2nd Floor Conference Room #3, Ackerman Wing. Call Linda Caroll 732-776-4282.
>
> **Red Bank** *(SPANISH)* Meets 3rd Wed., 12:30-1:30pm, Saint Anthony's of Padua Church, 121 Bridge Ave. Call Lourdes Montoya 732-747-5790 or Claudia Major 732-363-5400 ext. 21 (day).
>
> **Sea Girt** *(SPANISH)* Meets 1st Sun., 6:30-7:30pm, St. Mark's Roman Catholic Church, 215 Crescent Parkway. Before attending call Pat Vena 732-363-5400 ext. 22 (day).

Can't find an appropriate group in your area? The Clearinghouse helps people start groups.
*Give us a call at **1-800-367-6274**.*

MORRIS

DBSA (Depression and Bipolar Support Alliance) Support and education for persons with depression or bipolar disorder. Family and friends welcome. Free literature and tape library.

> **Morristown** Peer support group meets Tues. (except holidays), 7:30-9pm, suggested donation $2; lecture/educational series meets last Wed. (earlier dates in Nov./Dec.), 7:30pm, suggested donation $3 non-members, Morristown Unitarian Fellowship, 21 Normandy Heights Rd. Call Ron 908-377-5245 (after 6pm) for peer support group meeting and weather cancellation. Call Linda 973-994-1143 for lecture schedule and weather cancellation of meeting. *Website:* http://www.dbsanewjersey.org/morristownarea *E-mail:* lsb1@panix.com or ireklein@aol.com

> **Succasunna** Meets 2nd Tues., 7:15-9pm, First Presbyterian Church, 99 Main St. Call Paulette 973-590-1042. *Website:* http://www.dbsalliance.org/ledgewood *E-mail:* how2cope@yahoo.com

> **Succasunna** Rap group meets 1st and 3rd Thurs., 7:15-9pm; educational and lecture series meets 2nd Thurs., 7:15pm, Temple Shalom, 215 South Hillside Ave. Call 973-647-8082 or Bonnie 973-361-5456. Literature and lending library. Building is handicapped accessible. *Website:* http://www.dbsasuccasunna.org *E-mail:* info@dbsasuccasunna.org

Postpartum Support Group *Professionally-run.* Provides support for new mothers experiencing postpartum mood disorders. Meets 1st and 3rd Tues., 7-8pm, Saint Clare's Behavioral Health Center, 50 Morris Ave., Denville. Before attending call 1-888-626-2111 (ask for mom's support group).

OCEAN

Bipolar and Depression Self-Help Group Mutual support and understanding for persons with bipolar disorder or depression in an energetic, caring and informal environment. Group meets Wed., 7-9pm, Saint Stephen's Church, Route 9, Waretown. Call Lynn 609-607-8696.

"In helping others, we shall help ourselves, for whatever good we give out completes the circle and comes back to us." --- Flora Edwards

DBSA (Depression and Bipolar Support Alliance) Mutual support and education for persons diagnosed with depression or bipolar disorder, their families and friends.

> **Brant Beach** Meetings vary, St. Francis Community Center, Seniors' Luncheon Room, Long Beach Blvd. Call Gary 609-384-5124 or Pat 609-296-5920 about families and friends.

> **Lakewood** Meets Mon. and Wed., 7-8:45pm, Preferred Behavioral Health, 725 Airport Rd. Guest speakers, rap sessions and literature. Call Cecilia 732-600-9573 or Sharon 732-849-5401. *Website:* http://www.dbsanewjersey.org/lakewood

> **Stafford** Meets 1st and 3rd Fri., 7:15-9pm, Ocean Club, Family Resource Center, Route 9. Building is handicapped accessible. Call Salvina 609-812-5219 or Josephine 609-661-4910. *E-mail:* sivan710@comcast.net

> **Toms River** Meets Wed. and Fri., 7:30-9:30pm, Community Medical Center, 99 Route 37 West, Auditorium B (Wed.) and Auditorium C (Fri.). Call 1-888-226-6437 or Bonnie 732-505-1231 (day). *Website:* http://www.dbsanewjersey.org/ocean *E-mail:* singtune@yahoo.com

GROW Mutual self-help group to prevent and recover from depression, anxiety and other mental health problems. Caring and sharing community to attain emotional maturity, personal responsibility and recovery.

> **Brick** Meets Tues., 6:30pm, Brick Presbyterian Church, 11 Drum Point Rd. Before attending call Caroline 732-575-5765.

> **Toms River** Meets Thurs., 4pm, Presbyterian Church of Toms River, Hooper Ave. and Chestnut St., River Room. Before attending call Ninfa 732-575-5766.

> **Toms River** Meets Tues., 6:30pm, Brighter Days Self-Help Center, S and F Plaza, 2008 Route 37 East, Suite 6. Before attending call Nancy 732-350-4800.

New Babies - New Emotions *Professionally-run.* Support for moms-to-be and new moms with any kind of postpartum related depression and/or baby blues. Babies 12 months and under are welcome. Guest speakers, literature, newsletter and phone help.

> **Brick** Meets 2nd Mon., 3:30-4:30pm, Ocean Medical Center, 425 Jack Martin Blvd., Community Room (use main entrance). Call Pat Vena 732-363-5400 ext. 22 (day).

> **Toms River** Meets 2nd Wed., 10:30am-noon, Babies R Us, 1220 Hooper Ave. Call Pat Vena 732-363-5400 ext. 22 (day) or Jackie Hay 732-244-8880.

New Mothers' Group *Professionally-run.* Support for new moms with any kind of postpartum related depression and/or baby blues. Babies 12 months and under are welcome. Guest speakers, literature, newsletter and phone help. Meets 4th Tues., 10-11:30am, Holy Spirit Episcopal Church, 220 Main St., Tuckerton. Call Lynne A. Virginia 609-296-8300 or Pat Vena 732-363-5400 ext. 22 (day).

Recovery, Inc. Self-help method of will training. Offers techniques for controlling temperamental behavior and changing attitudes toward nervous symptoms, anxiety, depression and fears. Meets Mon., 7:30pm, Presbyterian Church of Toms River, Hooper Ave. and Chestnut St., Toms River. Call Delores 732-557-5466 or 201-612-8153. *Website:* http://www.recovery-inc.org *E-mail:* inquiries@recovery-inc.org

SUSSEX

DBSA (Depression and Bipolar Support Alliance) Support and education for persons suffering from depression or bipolar disorder. Rap sessions and guest speakers. Family and friends welcome. Building is handicapped accessible. Meets Wed., 7:30-9pm, Redeemer Lutheran Church, 37 Newton-Sparta Rd., Newton. Call Dan 973-948-6999. *Website:* http://www.scdbsa.org *E-mail:* dan@scdbsa.org

Depression Support Group Support for anyone with depression. Exchange experiences and resources. Rap sessions and phone help. Meets 1st and 3rd Mon., 10:30am-12:30pm, Andover. Call Betty 973-347-3873.

UNION

DBSA (Depression and Bipolar Support Alliance) Support and education for persons with depression or bipolar disorder, their families and friends. Rap sessions. Call Theldora Hawkins 908-233-7074 (day).

> **Summit** Meets 1st and 3rd Thurs., 7:30-9pm, Overlook Hospital, Conference Room #1.
> **Westfield** Meets Tues., 7:30-9pm and Sat., 1-3pm, First Baptist Church (accessible by bus # 59), 170 Elm St.

"Remember there's no such thing as a small act of kindness. Every act creates a ripple with no logical end." -- Scott Adams

GROW Mutual self-help group to prevent and recover from depression, anxiety and other mental health problems. Caring and sharing community to attain emotional maturity, personal responsibility and recovery. Before attending call Caroline 732-575-5765.

> **Elizabeth** Meets Wed., 4pm, New Beginnings Self-Help Center, 516 Morris Ave.
>
> **Plainfield** Meets Wed., 3:30pm, Park Avenue Self-Help Center, 333 Park Ave.

Recovery, Inc. Self-help method of will training. Offers techniques for controlling temperamental behavior and changing attitudes toward nervous symptoms, anxiety, depression and fears. *Website:* http://www.recovery-inc.org *E-mail:* inquiries@recovery-inc.org

> **Summit** Meets Wed., 7:45pm, Central Presbyterian Center, Morris Ave. and Maple St. (parking lot entrance). Call 201-612-8153.
>
> **Westfield** Meets Fri., 8pm, Union County Community Building, 300 North Ave. East (parking lot entrance), 2nd Floor, Conference Room. Call Dorothy 732-381-3712 or 201-612-8153.

WARREN

Depression and Bipolar Disorder Support Group Mutual support and encouragement for persons with depression and bipolar disorder. Rap sessions. Meets Tues., 6-8pm (except 1st Tues., 7-8pm), Better Futures Self-Help Center, 21 W. Washington Ave., Washington. Call Bruce 908-835-0055 or Better Future Self-Help Center 908-835-1180.

NATIONAL

DBSA (Depression and Bipolar Support Alliance) *National. 1000+ affiliated groups. Founded 1986.* Mutual support and information for persons with depression and bipolar disorder and their families. Provides education on the nature of depressive illnesses. Advocacy for research and improved access to care. Scheduled online support group meetings (Mon., Tues. and Wed.), annual conference, chapter development guidelines and quarterly newsletter. Write: DBSA, 730 N. Franklin St., Suite 501, Chicago, IL 60610. Call 1-800-826-3632 or 312-642-0049 (Mon.-Fri., 8:30am-5pm CST); Fax: 312-642-7243. *Website:* http://www.dbsalliance.org

Dep-Anon *National. Founded 1999.* 12-Step. Fellowship for men, women and children whose lives have been affected by a family member's depression. Members share hope, strength and experience in order to grow emotionally and spiritually. Write: Dep-Anon, P.O. Box 17414, Louisville, KY 40217. Call

Hugh S. 502-569-1989. *Website:* http://www.depressedanon.com *E-mail:* info@depressedanon.com

Depressed Anonymous *International. 50 affiliated groups. Founded 1985.* 12-Step. Program to help depressed persons believe and hope they can feel better. Newsletter, phone support, workshops, conferences, seminars, information and referrals. Information packet and assistance starting a similar group available. Write: Depressed Anonymous, Box 17414, Louisville, KY 40217. Call Hugh 502-569-1989. *Website:* http://www.depressedanon.com *E-mail:* info@depressedanon.com

GROW in America *International. 143 groups. Founded in 1957.* 12-Step. Group offers mutual help, friendship, community, education and leadership. Focuses on recovery and personal growth. Open to all including those with mental health issues, depression, anxiety, grief, fears, etc. Write: GROW in America, P.O. Box 3667, Champaign, IL 61826. Call 1-888-741-4769. *E-mail:* growil@sbcglobal.net

Postpartum Support International *International. 600+ members; support networks in 48 states and 25 countries. Founded 1987.* Goal is to increase the awareness of the emotional changes women often experience during pregnancy and after the birth of a baby. Information on diagnosis and treatment of postpartum depression. Provides education, advocacy and annual conference. Encourages formation of support groups. Helps strengthen existing groups. Phone support, referrals, literature and newsletter. Write: Postpartum Support International, P.O. Box 60931, Santa Barbara, CA 93160. Call 1-800-944-4773; Fax: 805-967-0608. *Website:* http://www.postpartum.net *E-mail:* psioffice@postpartum.net

Recoveries Anonymous *International. 50 chapters.* Spiritual recovery group for anyone seeking a solution for any kind of addiction, problem or behavior. Family and friends welcome. "How To Begin..." guides and "Start A Group" kit can be downloaded free from the website. Write: R.A. Universal Services, P.O. Box 1212, East Northport, NY 11731. *Website:* http://www.r-a.org *E-mail:* raus@r-a.org

Recovery, Inc. *International. 640 groups. Founded 1937.* Mental health self-help organization that offers weekly group meetings for people suffering from various emotional and mental conditions. Principles parallel those found in cognitive-behavioral therapy. Teaches people how to change their thoughts, reactions and behaviors that cause their physical and emotional symptoms. Write: Recovery, Inc., 802 N. Dearborn St., Chicago, IL 60610. Call 312-337-5661; Fax: 312-337-5756. *Website:* http://www.recovery-inc.org

ONLINE

Bipolar Dream *Online. 191 members. Founded 2003.* Offers support, encouragement and education geared toward lifestyle changes for bipolar people. Recovery, healing and goal achievement are discussed by caring people who provide suggestions and constructive criticisms. Aim is to help people face themselves and the illness, and accept responsibility for improvement through alternatives which are presented and discussed to stimulate self-determination. *Website:* http://health.groups.yahoo.com/group/Bipolar_Dream

BPSO (Bipolar Significant Others) Bulletin Board *Online.* Provides support and information for families and friends of persons with bipolar disorder (aka manic-depression). Opportunity to communicate online with others in similar situations. Website offers chatroom, forums, e-mail list and over 3000 pages of information. *Website:* http://www.bipolarworld.net/ *E-mail:* bipolarworld@yahoo.com

Child and Adolescent Bipolar Foundation *Online.* Site provides information posted by members to provide support to families of children or teens with bipolar disorder. Offers message boards, support group information, community center and general information. *Website:* http://www.bpkids.org

Conduct Disorders Parent Message Board *Online. 7080 members. Founded 1995.* Support for parents living with a child with one of the many behavior disorders including: attention deficit hyperactivity disorder, oppositional defiance disorder, conduct disorder, depression and substance abuse. Parents with children of all ages welcome. *Website:* http://www.conductdisorders.com

Mood Garden *Online.* Community of people dealing with mood disorders (e.g. depression, bipolar disorder and related conditions like anxiety/panic disorder), who share their experiences, strengths, coping skills, practical resources and hopes through the message boards. Also has chatroom. Provides interested members with opportunity to have their own blog for journaling and resources like mood charts. *Website:* http://www.moodgarden.org *E-mail:* admin@moodgarden.org

"We can't help everyone, but everyone can help someone." – Dr. Loretta Scott

MENTAL HEALTH CONSUMERS
(see also other mental health sections)

STATEWIDE

COMHCO (Coalition Of Mental Health Consumer Organizations) Information, support and advocacy on mental health issues. Speakers and workshops. Membership $5/yr. For meeting time and location, call Annette Wright 973-778-8810 (after 1pm). *E-mail:* comhco@aol.com

Consumer Connections Support Network Regional support group meetings for consumers who work in mental health/social services. Groups focus on work-related issues only. Write: Consumer Connections - MHA in NJ, 88 Pompton Ave., Verona, NJ 07044. Call Ray Cortese 973-571-4100 (day). *Website:* http://www.mhanj.org

CSP (Collaborative Support Programs) of NJ, Inc. Assists statewide in the development and networking of mental health consumer/psychiatric survivor groups. Workshops, quarterly newsletter, conferences, system advocacy, funding of consumer-run self-help centers, community services, technical assistance and supportive housing. Brochures available. Write: CSP, 11 Spring St., Freehold, NJ 07728. Call 1-800-227-3729 or 732-780-1175; Fax: 732-780-8977. *Website:* http://www.cspnj.org

NAMI CARE (Consumers Advocating Recovery through Empowerment) Support for anyone afflicted with any type of psychiatric disorder. Follows a national model, based upon shared insights and empathy. Groups are affiliated with local NAMI groups for education and advocacy. Offers trained peer facilitators. Help in forming CARE groups. Call Jay Yudof, NAMI NJ Consumer Outreach Liaison 1-866-464-3267. *E-mail:* jyudof@hotmail.com

ATLANTIC

ICE Self-Help Center Consumer-run self-help center provides an environment of support, recreational activities and empowerment that provides wellness for mental health consumers. For information call ICE Self-Help Center or Jaime Angelini 609-272-1700 ext. 308.

Need help finding a specific group? Give us a call – we're here to help!
Call 1-800-367-6274.

Peer to Peer Support Group An informal forum where consumers may get together to discuss problems of daily living or pertinent current information in a supportive non-judgmental environment. Rap sessions, literature, guest speakers, advocacy, discussion, recreation, trips and phone help. Meets Mon., 7pm, First Presbyterian Church, 1311 Main St., Pleasantville. Call 609-272-1700 ext. 303.

BERGEN

For Us/By Us Self-Help Center Consumer-run self-help center that brings together consumers of mental health services. Center provides support, socializing, recreational activities and advocacy. Open Mon.-Fri., 3-6pm and Sun., noon-5pm, For Us/By Us Self-Help Drop-In Center, 40 North Van Brunt St., Englewood. Call 201-541-1221.

Mental Health Support Group *Professionally-run.* Support for mental health consumers. Meets 1st Thurs., 7pm, Community Services Building, 327 East Ridgewood Ave., Paramus. Call 201-635-9595 (day).

On Our Own Self-Help Center Consumer-run self-help center that offers support groups, socializing, recreational activities and advocacy to bring together consumers of mental health services. Open Mon.-Fri., noon-7pm; Sat. and Sun., 1-6pm; support group meets 1st and 3rd Thurs., 6-8:30pm, On Our Own Self-Help Center, 179 Main St., 2nd Floor (entrance on Mercer St.), Suite 3, Hackensack. Call 201-489-8402.

BURLINGTON

RITE (Realizing Independence Through Empowerment) Center, The Consumer-run self-help center that provides opportunities for sharing, recreation and advocacy. Offers rap sessions, literature, socialization and outside activities. Open Tues., Wed., Thurs., Fri., 1-6:30pm and Sat., 10:30am-4pm, The RITE Center, 693 Main St., Bldg. C, Lumberton. Call 609-518-7292.

Riverbank Self-Help Center Consumer-run self-help center that provides mutual support, advocacy and social activities for mental health consumers. Open Wed., 5-9pm; Thurs., 6:30-9pm; Fri., 6:30-9pm and Sun., noon-4pm, Riverbank Self-Help Center, 114 Delaware Ave., Burlington. Call 609-239-1786. *E-mail:* riverhelps@comcast.net

Youth Partnership Group Adult supervised activities for youth (ages 13-21) with complex emotional, mental health or behavioral issues to help them express what they have been through and share concerns. Rap sessions. Meets Thurs.,

6:30-8:30pm, Family Support Organization of Burlington County, 774 Eayrestown Rd., Lumberton. Call Jamison Gsell 609-265-8838 (day).

CAMDEN

Donald Mays Jr. Self-Help Center, The Consumer-run center that offers support, recreational activities and advocacy for mental health consumers. Open Mon., 2-8pm; Wed., 1-7pm; Fri., 1-8pm and Sat., 11am-6pm, The Donald Mays Jr. Self-Help Center, 1 Colby Ave., Suite 12, Stratford. Call 856-346-9043.

Independent Survivors Support group to help consumers socialize, help one another and advocate for each other. Phone help, literature, buddy system and pen pals. Meeting times and location vary. Call 609-506-7987 or 856-625-4798 for details. *E-mail:* Izzie996@hotmail.com

New Beginnings Support Group - A Chapter of DBSA Mutual support and education for persons with mood disorders. Separate group for families and friends. Also open to persons with anxiety, dual diagnosis and schizo-affective disorder. Opportunity to discuss successes in dealing with various symptoms. Meets Mon., 7-9pm (separate group for families and friends meets 1st and 3rd Mon.); Wed., 11am-1pm and Thurs., 7-9pm, Holy Trinity Lutheran Church, North Warwick Rd. and Evesham Rd., Magnolia. Call 1-877-313-5050 or Doug 856-451-1240. Family and friends call Karen 856-451-1240. *Website:* http://www.nbgroup.org *E-mail:* newbeginningsnj@gmail.com

Pink and Blues Peer Support Group (LGBT) Support group for lesbian, gay, bisexual and transgender people living with a mental illness. Building is handicapped accessible. Meets Wed., 7pm, St. Luke's and the Epiphany Church, 330 S. 13th St., Philadelphia, PA. Call 215-627-0424 (eve.). *E-mail:* madpride1988@yahoo.com

Wellness Self-Help Center Consumer-run organization designed to empower consumers. Provides environment for learning and growth in a supportive and comfortable setting. Offers support groups, social activities and educational programs. Open Wed.-Fri., 3-7pm; Sat. and Sun., 11:30am-3:30pm, Wellness Self-Help Center, 415 Federal St., Camden. Call Pat Mincey 856-757-0385 (day). *E-mail:* pmincey@mhaswnj.org

Youth Partnership Group Adult supervised activities for youth (ages 13-21) with complex emotional, mental health or behavioral issues to help them express what they have been through and share concerns. Rap sessions, guest speakers, literature and phone help. Building is handicapped accessible. Meets Thurs., 6:30-8pm, Camden County Family Support Organization, 23 W. Park Ave.,

Suite 103-104, Merchantville. Call Susan A. Doherty-Funke or Peter Burgos 856-662-2600 (day). *Website:* http://www.camdenfso.org *E-mail:* sdoherty-funke@camdenfso.org

CAPE MAY

Learning Recovery Center Consumer-run self-help center that provides mutual support, advocacy, social and recreational activities for mental health consumers. Open Wed., 4-8pm; Thurs., 1-7pm; Fri., 3-9pm and Sat., 11am-4pm, Learning Recovery Center, 4404 Pacific Ave., Wildwood. For meeting information call 609-523-7100.

CUMBERLAND

New Horizons Self-Help Center Consumer-run self-help center providing mutual support, special events, socializing, recreational activities and advocacy for mental health care consumers. Open Mon., Wed., Fri., 11am-4pm and Tues., 11am-8pm, New Horizons Self-Help Center, 63 S. Myrtle St., Vineland. For information call 856-696-8921.

Youth Partnership Group Adult supervised activities for youth (ages 13-21) with complex emotional, mental health or behavioral issues to help them express what they have been through and share concerns. Rap sessions. Meets Thurs., 6-8pm, Family Support Organization of Cumberland, Gloucester and Salem counties, 1226 East Landis Ave., Elmer. Call Renisha O'Donnell 856-507-9400 (day).

ESSEX

Pleasant Moments Self-Help Center Consumer-run self-help center that offers support and advocacy for mental health consumers. Provides resources, socialization, recreational activities and literature. Open Mon.-Wed., 3-7pm; Fri., 3-6pm; Sat. and Sun., 1-4pm, Pleasant Moments Self-Help Center, 465 Broadway, Newark. Call 973-991-2773.

Spirituality Group Support for mental health consumers fostering an awareness of spirituality and a sense of being a part of a much larger powerful entity. Offers mutual sharing, education, rap sessions, social, phone help and advocacy. Meets Tues., 4:30pm, Where Peaceful Waters Flow, 47 Cleveland St., Orange. Call Richard 973-677-7700 (eve.) or 973-651-7382.

Thursdays *Professionally-run.* Drop-in center that provides mutual support for mental health care consumers. Opportunity to socialize, guest speakers and trips.

Building is handicapped accessible. Meets Thurs., 6:30-9pm, MHA of Essex, 33 South Fullerton Ave., Montclair. Call Judi Fiederer 973-509-9777.

Where Peaceful Waters Flow Self-Help Center Consumer-run self-help center that offers support and advocacy for mental health consumers. Provides resources, socialization, rap sessions, recreational activities, literature and phone help. Open Mon.-Thurs., 2-7pm and Sat., 9am-4pm, Where Peaceful Waters Flow Self-Help Center, 47 Cleveland St., Orange. Call 973-677-7700.

Youth Partnership Group Adult supervised activities for youth (ages 13-21) with complex emotional, mental health or behavioral issues to help them express what they have been through and share concerns. Rap sessions, guest speakers, literature, newsletter and phone help. Meets Wed., 6-8pm, Family Support Organization of Essex County, 60 Evergreen Place, East Orange. Call Jacquelyn Oliver or Hazeline Pilgrim 973-395-1441 (day).

GLOUCESTER

Independent Survivors Support group to help consumers socialize, help one another and advocate for each other. Phone help, literature, buddy system and pen pals. Meeting times and location vary. Call 609-506-7987 or 856-625-4798 for details. *E-mail:* Izzie996@hotmail.com

Schizophrenics Anonymous Mutual support for persons with schizophrenia. Literature. Meets 1st Sat., 10am-noon, Underwood Memorial Hospital, Broad St. and Red Bank Ave., Dining Room B, Woodbury. Before attending call Community Relations 856-853-2011.

Up Your Alley Self-Help Center Consumer-run self-help center that provides socialization, support, advocacy, rap sessions and guest speakers. Open Mon. and Tues., 3-8pm, Wed., 1-6pm and Sat., 11am-4pm, Up Your Alley Self-Help Center, 8 Liberty St., Glassboro. Call 856-881-2204.

HUDSON

Hudson County Self-Help Center Consumer-run self-help center that provides socialization, recreation and advocacy for mental health consumers. Open Mon., Tues., Wed., Fri., 2-7pm and Sat., noon-5pm, Hudson County Self-Help Center, 880 Bergen Ave., Suite 605, Jersey City. Call 201-420-8013.

NAMI NJ en Espanol of Hudson County *(SPANISH)* Support and advocacy for family and friends of those diagnosed with a mental illness and for mental health consumers who attend. Building is handicapped accessible. Meets 1st Wed., 6:30-8pm (except Aug.), Catholic Community Service Office, 2201 Bergenline Ave., 2nd Floor, Union City. Call Martha Silva 1-888-803-3413. *Website:* http://www.naminj.org *E-mail:* naminjenespanol@msn.com

Schizophrenics Anonymous Fellowship for persons diagnosed with any schizophrenia-related disorder. Focuses on recovery, using a 6-step program, along with medication and professional help. Meets 1st and 3rd Tues., 4-5pm, Hudson County Self-Help Center, 880 Bergen Ave., Suite 605, 6th Floor, Jersey City. Call Anthony or Barbara 201-420-8013 (eve).

Youth Partnership Group Adult supervised activities for youth (ages 13-21) with complex emotional, mental health or behavioral issues to help them express what they have been through and share concerns. Rap sessions. Meets Tues. and Fri., 5:30-8pm, Family Support Organization of Hudson County, 705 Bergen Ave., Jersey City. Call 201-915-5140 (day).

HUNTERDON

Getting Together Self-Help Center Consumer-run drop-in center for mental health consumers. Educational series, support groups, social and advocacy. Open Sun., noon-4pm; occasional Mon.; Tues., 4:30-6pm; Wed., 5-8pm; 2nd and 4th Thurs. 3-4:30pm (drop-in) and 5-6:30pm (drumming circle); Fri., 4-8pm and 1st and 3rd Sat., 5-8pm, Getting Together Self-Help Center, 52 E. Main St., Flemington. Call Eileen 908-806-8202.

Living Your Life Opportunity for persons with a mental illness to work on life goals and learn the steps necessary to achieve them. Focus is not on mental illness but on what members want and can do with their lives. Meets Tues., 4:30-6pm, Getting Together Self-Help Center, 52 E. Main St., Flemington. Before attending call Eileen 908-806-8202.

NAMI Hunterdon Support, information and systems advocacy for anyone affected by mental illness (individuals, families, friends). Spring and Fall classes for families: Family-Family (12 week course for families of adults with mental illness); NAMI Basics (6 week course for families of youth/adolescents with mental illness). General meeting 2nd Wed., 7pm and families meeting 3rd Thurs., 7pm, Hunterdon Medical Center, Wescott Dr. and Route 31, Flemington. For more information about meetings or classes call 908-284-0500.

Youth Partnership Group Adult supervised activities for youth (ages 13-21) with complex emotional, mental health or behavioral issues to help them express what they have been through and share concerns. Rap sessions. Building is handicapped accessible. Meets every other Fri., 6-8pm, Family Support Organization, 11 Minneakoning Rd., Flemington. For meeting information call Stanley Croughter 908-213-9932 (day). *Website:* http://www.fsohsw.org

MERCER

NAMI CARE (Consumers Advocating Recovery through Empowerment) Self-help group run by and for consumers. Building is handicapped accessible. Meets 2nd and 3rd Mon., 6-7:30pm, NAMI Mercer, Lawrence Commons, 3371 Brunswick Pike, Suite 124, Lawrenceville. Pre-registration required. Before attending call 609-799-8994 (day). *E-mail:* home@namimercer.org

Reach Out / Speak Out Self-Help Center Consumer-run self-help center that offers mutual support and socialization for mental health consumers. Advocacy, education, social activities and referrals. Open Tues., Wed. and Thurs., 2-8pm; Fri., 5-8pm and Sat., 10am-4pm, Reach Out / Speak Out Self-Help Center, 2100 East State St. Extension, Hamilton. Call 609-586-2551.

Wellness and Recovery *Professionally-run.* Opportunity for mental health consumers to share wellness and recovery techniques. Meets 1st Mon., 6-7:30pm, Lawrence Commons, 3371 Brunswick Pike, Suite 124, Lawrenceville. Use entrance in back of building. Pre-registration required. Before attending call 609-799-8994 (day).

MIDDLESEX

CAMHOP-NJ (Chinese Mental Health Self-Help Group) *(MANDARIN and CANTONESE)* Mutual support group for families and individuals of Chinese origin diagnosed with mental illnesses. Call Maggie Luo 732-940-0991 (day). *E-mail:* namichinesegroup@yahoo.com

> **Edison** Meets 1st Thurs., 7-8:20pm, University Behavioral Healthcare, 100 Metroplex Dr., Suite 200. Building is handicapped accessible.
> **North Brunswick** Meets 3rd Tues., 7-8:30pm, NAMI NJ, 1562 Route 130.

"Although the world is full of suffering, it is also full of overcoming it."-- Helen Keller

Moving Forward Self-Help Center Consumer-run self-help center that offers support and socialization for adults with a mental health issue or other special needs. Includes peer employment, wellness and recovery support groups and others. Handicapped accessible. Open Mon.-Thurs., 3-7pm; Fri., 3-8pm and Sat., 1-5pm, Moving Forward Self-Help Center, 35 Elizabeth Street, 2nd Floor, Suite 2-B, New Brunswick. Call 732-317-3893. *Website:* http://www.cspnj.com

Peer to Peer Group Support and confidential discussion of concerns for mental health consumers. Meetings vary, Moving Forward Self-Help Center, 35 Elizabeth St., 2nd Floor, Suite B, New Brunswick. Call Moving Forward 732-317-3893 (day). *Website:* http://www.cspnj.org

SAMHAJ Support for South Asians Mutual support for South Asian (Indians, Pakistanis, Bangladeshi, Sri Lankan) families affected by mental illness. Educational series, guest speakers and literature. Meets 1st Thurs., 7-9pm, 1562 Route 130, North Brunswick. Call Anu Singh 732-940-0991 (day). *E-mail:* samhaj@naminj.org

Youth Partnership Group Adult supervised activities for youth (ages 13-21) with complex emotional, mental health or behavioral issues to help them express what they have been through and share concerns. Educational series, advocacy, social group, newsletter, phone help and buddy system. Meets Fri., 6-8pm, Family Support Organization of Middlesex County, 1 Ethel Rd., Edison. Call Dylys Koney or Sam Hartman 732-287-8701 (day). *E-mail:* dkfsomiddlesex9@msn.com

MONMOUTH

C.A.R.E. Center, The (Consumer Advocacy Recreation Exchange) Consumer-run self-help center for mental health consumers to provide support and socialization. Open Mon., Wed. and Thurs., noon-7pm; Tues. and Fri., noon-4pm; Sat., noon-5pm, C.A.R.E. Center, 80 Steiner Ave., Neptune City. Call 732-774-0288 (day).

Freehold Self-Help Center Consumer-run support group and drop-in center for mental health consumers. Resource center, rap sessions, social, educational and employment resources for persons with disabilities. Open Mon., noon-7:30pm; Wed.-Fri., 2-8pm and Sat., 1-7pm, Freehold Self-Help Center, 17 Bannard St., Suite 22, Freehold. Call 732-625-9485.

NAMI CARE (Consumers Advocating Recovery through Empowerment) Support and advocacy group for mental health consumers. Meets 2nd and 4th Thurs., 6:30-7:30pm, Freehold Self-Help Center, 17 Bannard St., Freehold. Call Jay 732-531-7624. *E-mail:* jyudof@hotmail.com

NAMI Greater Monmouth Support and advocacy for both consumers and families of those living with a mental illness. Meeting starts with a 30 minute talk for families and consumers, then breaks into separate groups: a family meeting, which may break off into a "families of youngsters" session; and a CARE consumers group, which may break off into a "teen/young adult" session. Also offers separate Family-to-Family educational sessions on mental illness, treatment options and family communications. Optional dues $3/mtg, $30/yr. Meets 3rd Tues., 7pm, Colts Neck Community Church, 25 Merchants Way, Colts Neck. Call 732-462-6448 or 732-4NAMI-4U.

Youth Partnership Group Peer support and advocacy to empower youth (ages 13-21) with emotional or behavioral challenges. Rap sessions, guest speakers, literature, phone help and newsletter. Meets Tues., 6-8pm, Family Based Services Association, 279 Broadway, Suite 400, Long Branch. Before attending call Florene Grant 732-571-3272 (day).

MORRIS

CAP (Consumer Advocacy Program) *(MORRIS COUNTY RESIDENTS ONLY)* Self-help and advocacy group for mental health consumers. Building is handicapped accessible. Meetings vary, Mental Health Association, 100 Route 46 E., Bldg. C, Mountain Lakes. Call Tracy Cappiccille 973-334-3496 (day).

M.O.M.M.I.E.S. (Mothers Overcoming Medical Mental Illnesses Eternal Support) Group, The Support for mothers with mental illnesses who have children of all ages. Rap sessions, education, guest speakers, newsletter, literature, buddy system and phone help. Meets Fri., 6-8pm, Saint Clare's Hospital, 130 Powerville Rd., Community Room, Boonton Township. Call Kim-Marie Ptashinski 973-257-9585 (day).

Morris Self-Help Center Consumer-run drop-in center for mental health consumers that provides socialization. Handicapped accessible. Open Mon.-Fri., 3-7pm; Sat. and Sun., 1-5pm, Morris Self-Help Center, 1259 Route 46 East, Bldg. 4, Entrance 4D, Parsippany. Call 973-334-2470.

Schizophrenics Anonymous Fellowship, support and information for persons with schizophrenia or related disorders. Focuses upon recovery, using a 6-step program, along with medication and professional help. Building is handicapped accessible. Meets 1st and 3rd Wed., 7pm, Mental Health Association, 100 Route 46 E., Bldg. C, Mountain Lakes. Call Tracy 973-334-3496.

OCEAN

Brighter Days Self-Help Mutual Aid Center Consumer-run self-help center that offers mutual support and discussion for mental health consumers. Rap sessions, advocacy, socials and special celebrations. Open Mon., 2-9pm; Tues., 2-9pm; Wed., 4-9pm; Thurs., 2-9pm and Sat., 11am-7pm, Brighter Days Self-Help Center, 268 Bennetts Mills Rd., Jackson. Call Brighter Days 732-534-9960.

Journey to Wellness Self-Help Center Peer-run self-help center offers mutual support, advocacy and WRAP trainings. Journey to Wellness Self-Help Center, 575 N. Main St., Barnegat. For hours of operation call Michele Green 609-698-8889 (day).

Youth Partnership Group Adult supervised activities for youth (ages 13-18) with complex emotional, mental health or behavioral issues to help them express what they have been through and share concerns. Rap sessions. Building is handicapped accessible. Meets 2nd and 4th Thurs., 6:30-8pm, Ocean County Family Support Organization, Inc., 44 Washington St., Suite 2A, Toms River. Call Annie Hercules 732-281-5770 ext. 16. *Website:* http://www.ocfso.org *E-mail:* info@ocfso.org

PASSAIC

Our House Self-Help Center Consumer-run self-help center that provides support for mental health consumers. Open Mon., Tues., Wed., Fri., 3-7pm and Sat., noon-6pm, Our House Self-Help Center, 750 Broadway, Paterson. Call 973-553-1101.

Social Connections Self-Help Center Consumer-run self-help center that provides support for mental health consumers. Rap groups, social activities and meeting new friends. Open Tues. and Thurs., 2-6pm; Wed. and Fri., 4-9:30pm and Sun., 11am-5pm, Social Connections Self-Help Center, 1 Westervelt Ave., Vanderhoef House, Clifton. Call Annette Wright 973-778-8810.

Youth Partnership Group Adult supervised activities for youth (ages 13-21) with complex emotional, mental health or behavioral issues to help them express what they have been through and share concerns. Rap sessions, guest speakers, literature, newsletter and phone help. Meets Wed., 7-8:30pm, Family Support

Organization of Passaic County, 810 Belmont Ave., 2nd Floor, North Haledon. Call Kaity Rodriguez 973-427-0100 (day).

SALEM

NAMI CARE (Consumers Advocating Recovery through Empowerment) Support and advocacy group for mental health consumers. Meets 1st Wed., 7pm, Union Presbyterian Church, 254 Shell Rd., Carney's Point. Call Virginia 856-769-2492. *E-mail:* jyudolf@hotmail.com

New Dimensions Self-Help Center Consumer-run self-help center that offers socialization for mental health consumers. Handicapped accessible. MICA (Mentally Ill Chemically Addicted) group, arts and crafts, mental health education and lending library. Open Tues., Wed., Thurs. and Sat., 3:30-9pm, New Dimensions Self-Help Center, 316A Merion Ave., Carneys Point. Call 856-351-9100 (day).

SOMERSET

Freedom Trail Self-Help Center Consumer-run self-help center that provides support, socializing, and advocacy for mental health consumers. Open Mon., Wed., Fri., 10am-3pm; Tues. and Thurs., 5-10pm and Sat., 6-11pm, Freedom Trail Self-Help Center, 166 W. Main St. (rear of building), Somerville. Before attending call 908-722-5778.

Youth Partnership Group Adult supervised activities for youth (ages 13-21) with complex emotional, mental health or behavioral issues to help them express what they have been through and share concerns. Rap sessions. Building is handicapped accessible. Meeting day and time varies in Somerset. For meeting information call Stanley Croughter 908-788-8585 (day). *Website:* http://www.fso-hsw.org

SUSSEX

A Way To Freedom Self-Help Center Consumer-run drop-in center where mental health consumers can support each other. Advocacy, education, socialization and recreation. Mutual sharing, rap sessions, literature, guest speakers, phone help, depression/bipolar support group and part-time consumer training and employment opportunities. Meets Mon., Wed., Thurs. and Fri., 3-7:30pm and Sat., 11am-4pm, A Way To Freedom Self-Help Center, 29 Trinity St., Newton. Call Betty 973-300-0830.

UNION

Esperanza Self-Help Center *(SPANISH)Professionally-run.* Mutual support, social and recreational activities for Latino mental health consumers to provide positive interpersonal relationships. Building is handicapped accessible. Open Mon.-Thurs., 9am-1pm, Esperanza Self-Help Center, 361-363 Monroe Ave., Kenilworth. Call Jose or Marta 908-272-5296.

NAMI NJ en Espanol of Union County *(SPANISH)* Support, education and advocacy for families of persons diagnosed with a mental illness. Meets 4th Thurs., 6:30pm (except Aug.), Trinitas Hospital, 225 Williamson St., Room 7 South, Elizabeth. Call Martha Silva 1-888-803-3413. *Website:* http://www.naminj.org *E-mail:* naminjenespanol@msn.com

New Beginnings Self-Help Center Consumer-run self-help center that offers support for mental health consumers to establish a social network to share experiences, resource information, encouragement and companionship. Self-help group discussions, recreational and social activities. Open Mon., Wed., Thurs. and Fri., 3-8pm and Sun., 2-7pm, New Beginnings Self-Help Center, 516 Morris Ave., 1st Floor, Elizabeth. Call Joyce Haberer or Kenneth Quigley 908-352-7830 (day).

Park Avenue Self-Help Center Consumer-run self-help center for mental health consumers to provide support and socialization. Offers a peer employment support group, among others. Open Mon., 1-5pm; Wed. and Thurs., 3-7pm and Sat., 12:30-4pm, Park Avenue Self-Help Center, 333 Park Ave., Plainfield. Call 908-757-1350.

Youth Partnership Group Adult supervised activities for youth (ages 13-21) with complex emotional, mental health or behavioral issues to help them express what they have been through and share concerns. Rap sessions. Meets 2nd and 4th Mon., 6:30-8:30pm, Family Support Organization, 143 Elmer St., 1st Floor, Westfield. Call 908-789-7625 (day). *Website:* http://www.fso-union.org

WARREN

Better Future Self-Help Center Consumer-run self-help drop-in center for persons with a mental illness and/or clinical depression. Various support groups are offered. Meals offered. Transportation provided. Open Mon.-Fri., 3-9pm; Sat. and Sun., 1-5pm, Better Future Self-Help Center, 21 West Washington Ave., Washington. Call 908-835-1180. *E-mail:* betterfutureshc@yahoo.com

NATIONAL

CONTAC (Consumer Organization and Networking Technical Assistance Center) *Resource.* Center for mental health consumers and consumer-run organizations nationwide that promotes self-help, recovery and empowerment. Provides technical assistance for organizing and maintaining self-help groups. Conducts leadership training. listserv, electronic library and online peer support. Write: CONTAC, P.O. Box 11000, Charleston, WV 25339. Call 1-888-825-8324 or 304-342-4881 (Mon.-Fri., 8:30am-4:30pm EST); Fax: 304-345-7303. *Website:* http://www.contac.org *E-mail:* usacontac@contac.org

NAMI Connection Support Groups *National. 160 groups. Founded 2007.* Provides weekly recovery support groups for consumers living with mental illness where members learn from each others' experiences, share coping strategies and offer each other encouragement and understanding. Helps anyone interested in starting a group. Call 1-800-950-6264. *Website:* http://www.nami.org (click on "Find Support," then "Consumer Support")

National Mental Health Consumers Self-Help Clearinghouse *(BILINGUAL) Resource. Founded 1986.* Provides information and recovery-oriented services for mental health consumers. Assistance in self and system advocacy, on-site consultations, training and educational events. Assistance in starting groups. Also provides technical assistance to consumer-run groups. Maintains a database of consumer support and advocacy groups. Write: National Mental Health Consumers Self-Help Clearinghouse, 1211 Chestnut St., Suite 1207, Philadelphia, PA 19107-4103. Call 1-800-553-4539 (Mon.-Fri., 9am-5pm EST); TDD: 215-751-9655; Fax: 215-636-6312. *Website:* http://www.mhselfhelp.org *E-mail:* info@mhselfhelp.org

Schizophrenics Anonymous *International. 175 groups. Founded 1985.* Organized and run by people with a schizophrenia-related disorder. Offers support, fellowship and information. Focuses on recovery, using a 6-step program, along with medication and professional help. Weekly meetings and newsletters. Provides assistance in starting and maintaining groups. Call Joanne 248-477-1983. *Website:* http://www.sardaa.org/sa_main.html

ONLINE

BPDWORLD (Borderline Personality Disorder) *Online.* Mutual support for individuals with borderline personality disorder (BPD) provided through message boards. Started by a person with BPD in England, who has developed the online organization as a non-profit. *Website:* http://www.bpdworld.net

PsychCentral Dissociative Disorders Forum *Online.* Provides mutual support for persons with dissociative identity disorder (DID, formerly known as multiple personality disorder) and other dissociative disorders. Members share ideas and pool information on resources through the Forum's message boards. *Website:* http://forums.psychcentral.com (under the "Mental Health" heading, click on "Dissociative Disorders")

Voice-hearers *Online. 468 members. Founded 2002.* Support for people who hear, or who have heard voices. Opportunity to share concerns, ideas and coping strategies for living with voices with others in similar situations. Message board and e-mail discussion group. *Website:* http://groups.yahoo.com/group/voice-hearers

MENTAL HEALTH FAMILY SUPPORT
(see also mental health consumers, general mental health, toll-free helplines)

STATEWIDE

DBSA (Depression and Bipolar Support Alliance) of NJ *16 chapters throughout New Jersey.* Education and support for persons with depression or bipolar disorder, their families and friends. Peer support groups and educational programs. Call 908-377-5245. *Website:* http://www.dbsanewjersey.org

NAMI NJ (National Alliance on Mental Illness New Jersey) Dedicated to improving the quality of life for people diagnosed with a mental illness and their families. Provides self-help groups, education and advocacy. Provides an array of public education and mental illness awareness activities to create understanding and eradicate the stigma associated with a mental illness. For information call 732-940-0991 (day) or 1-866-626-4437. *Website:* http://www.naminj.org *E-mail:* info@naminj.org

New Jersey Parents' Caucus *(BILINGUAL)* Statewide coalition of families of children with special emotional and behavioral needs. Works to ensure youth's needs are met through parent support groups, parent education and training, advocacy efforts and direct services at local offices. Helps parents to start local groups. Training and materials also in Spanish. Write: New Jersey Parents' Caucus, 236 South Salem St., Randolph, NJ 07869. Call 1-866-560-6572 or 973-989-8866. *Website:* http://www.newjerseyparentscaucus.org *E-mail:* info@njparentcaucus.org

ATLANTIC

Family Support Group *Professionally-run.* Mutual support for parents and families of persons diagnosed with both a mental illness and alcohol or chemical addiction. Sharing of emotional and practical coping skills. Guest speakers. Meets 2nd Thurs., 10:30am and 4th Thurs., 5:30pm, Mental Health Association, 1127 North New Rd., Absecon. Call Christine Gromadzyn, MSW 609-272-1700 (day). *Website:* http://www.mhaac.org

Family Support Organization (Parents Supporting Parents) Provides support, education and advocacy for parents and caregivers of children with emotional, mental and behavioral challenges. Guest speakers, literature, speakers' bureau, newsletter and phone help. Building is handicapped accessible. Meets 1st and 3rd Wed., 6:30-8:30pm, Atlantic Cape Family Support Organization, 1601 Tilton Rd., Unit #1, Northfield. Call Laura Marcy 609-485-0575 (day). *Website:* http://www.acfamsupport.org *E-mail:* lmarcy@acfamsupport.org

NAMI Atlantic County Support and advocacy for families of persons with chronic psychiatric disorders. Offers a 12 week "Family-to-Family" education series. Meets 3rd Tues., 7pm, Pleasantville Presbyterian Church, 1311 S. Main St., Pleasantville. Call Gail 609-927-0215 (eve.) or Gary 609-748-9558 (eve.).

BERGEN

Family Support Organization *Professionally-run.* Provides support, education and advocacy to families and caregivers of children with complex emotional and behavioral challenges. Childcare available. Meets Wed., 7-8:30pm, Family Support Organization of Bergen County, 0-108 29th St., Fair Lawn. Before attending call 201-796-6209 (day). *Website:* http://www.fsobergen.org

Intensive Family Support Services (IFFS) *Professionally-run.* Support, education and advocacy for family members of those with a mental illness. Building is handicapped accessible. Family education workshops held 3 times/yr. Meets Thurs., 7-9pm, Care Plus, 610 Valley Health Plaza, Paramus. Call Lara Zucker 201-646-0333 (day). *Website:* http://www.cbhcare.com

NAMI Bergen County Support, education, advocacy, information and referrals for families of those diagnosed with a mental illness. Newsletter. Membership $20/yr./individual; $30/yr./family. Meets 1st Mon., 8pm, Community Services Building (Museum Building), 327 Ridgewood Ave., Paramus. Call 201-635-9595 (day). *Website:* http://www.namibergen.org *E-mail:* namibergen@optonline. net

NAMI Family Organization of Bergen County *Professionally-run.* Provides support, information, education and advocacy to families of those diagnosed with mental illness. Membership $30/year. Guest speakers. Meets 1st Wed., 7-9pm, Care Plus Mental Health Center Inc., 610 Valley Health Plaza, Paramus. Call 201-797-3579 (day).

NAMI NJ en Espanol of Bergen County *(SPANISH)* Advocacy and support for family and friends of those with a mental illness. Building is handicapped accessible. Meets 3rd Mon., 6:30-8pm (except Aug.), Latin America Institute, 10 Banta Pl., Suite 101, Hackensack. Call Martha Silva 1-888-803-3413. *Website:* http://www.naminj.org *E-mail:* naminjenespanol@msn.com

SMG ~ CAN Connections *Professionally-run.* Provides support and education for parents and professionals involved with a selectively mute child. Rap sessions, guest speakers, literature and phone help. Building is handicapped accessible. Meets 4th Mon., 12:45-2:30pm, Franklin Lakes Library, 470 DeKorte Dr., Franklin Lakes. Call Gail Kervatt 973-208-1848. *Website:* http://www.selectivemutism.org *E-mail:* kervatt@optonline. net

BURLINGTON

B.I.L.Y. (Because I Love You) Mutual support to help parents with children, of any age, who have behavioral challenges. Guest speakers. Meets 1st and 3rd Thurs., 6:30-8:30pm, Sisterhood, Inc., 132-136 E. Broad St., Burlington. Call 609-265-8838 (day). *E-mail:* familyvoices@fsoburlco.org

Family Support Organization of Burlington/Mercer Counties *Professionally-run.* Provides support and advocacy to families and caregivers of children with complex emotional and behavioral challenges. Educational lectures offered. Meets Tues., 7-9pm, Family Support Organization of Burlington/Mercer Counties, 774 Eayrestown Rd., Lumberton. Call Russ or Terry 609-265-8838 (day).

Intensive Family Support Services (IFSS) *Professionally-run.* Support, information and advocacy for family members and caregivers of those with an adult relative diagnosed with mental illness. Call Charlene McNichol 609-386-8653 (day).
> **Burlington** Meets 3rd Thurs., 1:30-3pm, Riverbank Building, Catholic Charities, 114 Delaware Ave.
> **Mt. Holly** Meets 1st Wed., 6-7:30pm, Virtua Memorial Hospital of Burlington County, 175 Madison Ave.

NAMI FACE of Burlington County (National Alliance for Mental Illness) Mutual support for families and friends of those diagnosed with a mental illness. Education, information and referrals. Dues $25 (includes newsletter). Meets 2nd and 4th Mon., 7:30pm, First Presbyterian Church, Moorestown. Call Lucille Klein 609-877-4260, Larry Joyce 856-461-3339 (day) or 609-914-0933 (office). *E-mail:* namifacenj@aol.com

NAMI NJ: AACT-NOW (African American Community Takes New Outreach Worldwide) Support, education and advocacy for African-American families affected by the mental illness of a loved one. Sponsored by NAMI-NJ. Meets 3rd Wed., 7:30-9:30pm, Parkway Baptist Church, 4 Pennypacker Dr., Willingboro. Call Winifred 609-265-0746 (day).

CAMDEN

Grandparents Raising Grandchildren Support and education for women and men who are caring for their grandchildren struggling with emotional, behavioral and mental challenges. Guest speakers, literature, social, advocacy and buddy system. Meets 4th Mon., 6:30-8:30pm, Holy Trinity Lutheran Church, 325 South Whitehorse Pike, Audubon. Call Marge Varneke 856-547-1620 (eve.) or Susan A. Doherty-Funke 856-662-2600 (day). *Website:* http://www.camdenfso.org *E-mail:* sdoherty-funke@camdenfso.org

NAMI of Camden County Support for families and friends of those diagnosed with a mental illness. Advocacy, phone help and guest speakers. Meets 2nd and 4th Tues., 7pm, Steininger Behavioral Care Services, 19 East Ormond Ave., Cherry Hill. Call Barbara 856-783-2518 (day) or Harriet 856-424-0030.

New Beginnings Support Group - A Chapter of DBSA Mutual support and education for families of persons with mood disorders. Opportunity to discuss successes in dealing with various symptoms. Meets 1st and 3rd Mon., 7-9pm, Holy Trinity Lutheran Church, 214 N. Warwick Rd., Magnolia. Call Karen 856-451-1240 or 1-877-313-5050.

NJ Parents' Caucus Support Group *(BILINGUAL)* Mutual support and help provided for and by parents or caregivers of children with special emotional/behavioral needs. Guest speakers, phone help and speakers' bureau. Before attending call 1-866-560-6572 or 856-964-5155.

> **Camden** Meets 2nd Wed., noon-2pm, Ferry Avenue Branch Library, 852 Ferry Ave.
> **Camden** Meetings vary, 6-8pm, New Jersey Parents' Caucus of Camden County, 1419 Baird Blvd.

Parents Empowering Parents Provides support and advocacy for parents and caregivers of children with complex emotional and behavioral challenges. Rap sessions, guest speakers, literature and phone help. Childcare provided. Meets Tues. and Thurs., 6:30-8:30pm, Family Support Organization of Camden County, 23 West Park Ave., Suite 103-104, Merchantville. Call 856-662-2600. *Website:* http://www.camdenfso.org

CAPE MAY

Families First Problem Solving Group *Professionally-run.* Support for those coping with an adult family member who suffers from a mental illness. Rap sessions. Meets 2nd Thurs., 6-7:30pm, Cape Counseling, 217 N. Main St., Suite 202, Cape May Courthouse. Call Jodi Hynes 609-463-0014 ext. 33 or Sally Barlow 609-463-0014 ext. 17.

Family Support Organization (Parents Supporting Parents) Support, education and advocacy for parents and caregivers of children with emotional and behavioral challenges. Rap sessions, guest speakers, buddy system, newsletter and phone support. Meets 4th Wed., 6:30-8:30pm, The Court House Church of Christ, 102 East Pacific Ave., Cape May Court House. Call Chris Haas 609-729-2034 (day). *Website:* http://www.acfamsupport.org *E-mail:* chaas@acfamsupport.org

Heart to Heart Spousal Support Group *Professionally-run.* Mutual support for members to share ideas on communicating positively with their spouse or significant other who has a mental illness. Rap sessions. Meets 3rd Mon., 9:30-11am, Cape Counseling, 217 N. Main St., Suite 202, Cape May Courthouse. Call Jodi Hynes 609-463-0014 ext. 33.

Intensive Family Support Services (IFSS) *Professionally-run.* Support and advocacy for families and friends of those diagnosed with a mental illness. Rap sessions and guest speakers. Building is handicapped accessible. Meets 2nd Thurs., 6-7:30pm, Cape Counseling Services, 217 N. Main St., Suite 202, Cape May Court House. Call Jodi Hynes 609-463-0014 ext. 33.

CUMBERLAND

Intensive Family Support Services (IFSS) *Professionally-run.* Support, information and advocacy for family members and caregivers of an adult with a major mental illness. Guest speakers and phone help. Meets Thurs., 10am-noon or 2nd, 4th and 5th Tues., 7-9pm, Cumberland County Guidance Center, 2038 Carmel Rd., Millville. Call Daniel Rickets 856-825-6810 ext. 278 (day), Mary

Sauceda 856-825-6810 ext. 256 (day) or Rebecca Rodriguez 856-825-6810 (day).

NAMI Cumberland County *Professionally-run.* Support for families and friends of persons diagnosed with a mental illness. Mutual sharing, education, advocacy, literature, phone help and guest speakers. Dues $23/yr. Meets 3rd Mon., 7-9pm, Chestnut Assembly of God, 2554 East Chestnut Ave., Vineland. Call 856-691-9234 or 856-794-9987.

ESSEX

Family Resource Center, The *Professionally-run.* Support for family members and significant others of persons with chronic mental/emotional illness. Groups for parents of adults with mental illness. Support groups for siblings and adult offspring meet on a time limited basis. Children and adolescents who have a family member diagnosed with mental illness attend Kids Cope in age appropriate groups at various locations. Meet various times and days. Call 973-509-9777 (day). *Website:* http://www.namiessex-familysupport.org

NAMI Essex County Support and advocacy for families of persons diagnosed with a mental illness by sharing ideas and experiences in a caring atmosphere. Guest speakers, phone help and newsletter. Dues $30/yr. Meets 4th Mon., 7pm, 60 S. Fullerton Ave., Montclair. Before attending call Regina 973-731-6113 or Mental Health Association 973-509-9777 (day). *Website:* http://www.namiessex-familysupport.org

NAMI NJ en Espanol of Essex County *(SPANISH and PORTUGUESE)* Advocacy and support for family and friends of those with a mental illness. Meets 3rd Tues., 6:30-8pm, Ironbound Community Corp., 317 Elm St., Newark. Call Martha Silva 1-888-803-3413. *Website:* http://www.naminj.org *E-mail:* naminjenespanol@msn.com

GLOUCESTER

NAMI Gloucester County Mutual support and education for families and friends of persons diagnosed with a mental illness. Advocacy, phone help, literature and professional speakers. Dues $30/yr. Meets 2nd Wed., 7pm, Newpoint Behavioral Health, 1070 Main St., Sewell. Call Domenica 856-423-1217.

HUDSON

F.S.O. "I Need You, You Need Me" Parent Group *Professionally-run.* Support for parents raising a child with emotional and/or behavioral challenges. Educational series, advocacy, guest speakers, phone help, literature and buddy system. Building is handicapped accessible. Meets 2nd Sat., 10am-noon, Family Support Organization of Hudson County, 705 Bergen Ave., Jersey City. Call Roslyn Gibbs-Muse 201-915-5140 (day). *Website:* http://www.fsohc.org *E-mail:* rgibbs-muse@fsohc.org

NAMI Hudson County Support and advocacy for family and friends of those diagnosed with a mental illness. Meets 2nd Tues., 6:30-9pm (except Aug.), Catholic Community Service Center, 3040 Kennedy Blvd. (entrance on Huron Ave., behind St. John's Church), Jersey City. Before attending call Martha Silva 201-861-0614 or 1-888-803-3413. *Website:* http://www.naminj.org *E-mail:* naminjenespanol@msn.com

NAMI NJ en Espanol of Hudson County *(SPANISH)* Support and advocacy for family and friends of those diagnosed with a mental illness and for mental health consumers who attend. Building is handicapped accessible. Meets 1st Wed., 6:30-8pm (except Aug.), Catholic Community Service Office, 2201 Bergenline Ave., 2nd Floor, Union City. Call Martha Silva 1-888-803-3413. *Website:* http://www.naminj.org *E-mail:* naminjenespanol@msn.com

HUNTERDON

Families of Persons with Mental Illness Opportunity for families of persons diagnosed with a mental illness to share experiences. Rap sessions, mutual sharing, psycho-education and encouragement. Meets 1st Wed., 1pm, Flemington. Before attending call Cris Maglione 908-788-6401 ext. 3006 or Elaine Howe 908-788-6401 ext. 3029.

Family Support Group *Professionally-run.* Support for parents and caregivers raising a child with emotional and behavioral challenges. Building is handicapped accessible. Meetings vary, Family Support Organization, 11 Minneakoning Rd., Flemington. Call Stanley Croughter 908-213-9932 (day). *Website:* http://www.fsohsw.org

Intensive Family Support Services (IFFS) *Professionally-run.* Support, education, caring and advocacy for family members of those with a mental illness. Sharing of experiences. Building is handicapped accessible. Meets 1st Wed., 1-3pm, Perkins Restaurant, Church St., Back Room, Flemington. Registration required. Before attending call Chris Maglione 908-788-6401 ext.

3006 (day). *Website:* http://www.hunterdonhealthcare.org *E-mail:* maglione.christine@hunterdonhealthcare.org

NAMI Hunterdon Support, information and systems advocacy for anyone affected by mental illness (individuals, families, friends). Spring and Fall classes for families: Family-Family (12 week course for families of adults with mental illness); NAMI Basics (6 week course for families of youth/adolescents with mental illness). General meeting 2nd Wed., 7pm and families meeting 3rd Thurs., 7pm, Hunterdon Medical Center, Wescott Dr. and Route 31, Flemington. Call 908-284-0500 for more information about meetings or classes.

MERCER

Intensive Family Support Services (IFSS) *Professionally-run.* Support for family members and caregivers of any adult with a mental illness. Guest speakers, phone help and literature. Call Amy Layng 609-396-6788 ext. 236.
> **Lawrenceville** Meets Mon., 5:30-7pm, Lawrence Road Presbyterian Church, 1039 Lawrence Rd.
> **Lawrenceville** Meets Tues., 5:30-7pm, Lawrence Commons, 3371 Brunswick Pike, Suite 124. Use entrance in back of building.

Parent Support Group *Professionally-run.* Support for parents whose children are experiencing emotional and behavioral problems. Meets last Sat., 3:30-5pm, Lawrence Commons, 3371 Brunswick Pike, Suite 124, Lawrenceville. Use entrance in back of building. Call Joanna Harrison-Smith 609-799-8994 (day).

Parent Support Group *Professionally-run.* Support and information for parents of adolescents. Opportunity to share ideas, concerns, strategies, learn helpful parenting skills and techniques. Meets Mon., 6-7pm, Anchor House, 482 Centre St., Trenton. Call 609-396-8329.

MIDDLESEX

B.I.L.Y. (Because I Love You) Mutual support to help parents with children (of any age) who have behavioral challenges. Meets Wed., 6-8pm, Family Support Organization of Middlesex County, 1 Ethel Rd., Suite 108A, Edison. Pre-registration required. Before attending call 732-287-8701 (day).

We can also refer callers to over 100 individuals who are seeking others to help start new support groups throughout NJ. Give us a call for more information. ***1-800-367-6274***

CAMHOP-NJ (Chinese Mental Health Self-Help Group) *(MANDARIN and CANTONESE)* Mutual support group for families and individuals of Chinese origin diagnosed with mental illnesses. Call Maggie Luo 732-940-0991 (day). *E-mail:* namichinesegroup@yahoo.com

>**Edison** Meets 1st Thurs., 7-8:20pm, University Behavioral Healthcare, 100 Metroplex Dr., Suite 200. Building is handicapped accessible.
>**North Brunswick** Meets 3rd Tues., 7-8:30pm, NAMI NJ, 1562 Route 130.

NAMI Middlesex County Support for those diagnosed with mental illness and their families to promote improved quality of life for people with severe mental illness. Dues $25yr./person and $35yr./family. Education and advocacy program meets 1st Mon., 7pm, University Behavioral Mental Health Center, 671 Hoes Lane, Room C 101, Piscataway. Coping meeting meets 2nd Thurs., 7pm, Intensive Family Support Services, 151 Centennial Ave., Piscataway. Call Elizabeth Golden 732-745-0709 or Carol Piekarski 732-297-4959 (eve.). *Website:* http://www.naminj.org

NAMI NJ en Espanol of Middlesex County *Professionally-run.* Support and advocacy for families of those diagnosed with a mental illness. Before attending call Martha Silva 1-888-803-3413. *Website:* http://www.naminj.org

>**New Brunswick** *(SPANISH)* Meets last Thurs., 6:30-8pm, First Baptist Church of New Brunswick, 226 Hale St. *E-mail:* mceisner@optonline.net
>**Perth Amboy** *(SPANISH)* Meets 4th Tues., 6:30-8pm (except Aug.), Christian Centers Ministry, 299 Barclay St. *E-mail:* naminjenespanol@naminj.org

P.A.C.E.S. (Parent And Caregivers Emotional Support) *Professionally-run.* Mutual support to help parents and caregivers with children of any age, who have behavioral, emotional or mental health challenges. Educational series, advocacy and coping skills. Meets Mon., 6:30-8:30pm, Family Support Organization of Middlesex County, 1 Ethel Rd., Suite 108, Edison. Before attending call Bryn Schain 732-287-8701 (day). *E-mail:* brynschain1325@msn.com

SAMHAJ Support for South Asians Mutual support for South Asian (Indians, Pakistanis, Bangladeshi, Sri Lankan) families affected by mental illness. Educational series, guest speakers and literature. Meets 1st Thurs., 7-9pm, 1562 Route 130, North Brunswick. Call Anu Singh 732-940-0991 (day). *E-mail:* samhaj@naminj.org

MONMOUTH

Family Support Group Support group for family members of persons (ages 18+) with a psychiatric diagnosis. Meets 2nd and 4th Mon., 6-7:30pm (except July/Aug.), Community Connections, 75 N. Bath Ave. and Second Ave., Long Branch. Registration required. Before attending call Ron Collier 732-923-5226.

Monmouth Family and Friends Group *Professionally-run.* Mutual support for families and friends of adults who have a mental illness. Discussions, educational workshops, learning and advocacy for improved services. Building is handicapped accessible. Meets 1st and 3rd Tues., noon-1:30pm or 2nd and 4th Tues., 7:30-9pm, Mental Health Association, 119 Avenue at the Commons, Shrewsbury. Call 732-542-6422 (day). *Website:* http://www.mentalhealthmonmouth.org *E-mail:* mhamonmouth@verizon.net

NAMI Greater Monmouth Support and advocacy for both consumers and the families of those living with a mental illness. Meeting starts with a 30 minute talk for families and consumers. Then breaks into separate groups: a family meeting, which may break off into a "families of youngsters" session; and a CARE consumers group, which may break off into a "teen/young adult" session. Also offers separate Family-to-Family educational sessions on mental illness, treatment options and family communications. Optional dues $3/mtg, $30/yr. Meets 3rd Tues., 7pm, Colts Neck Community Church, 25 Merchants Way, Colts Neck. Call 732-462-6448 or 732-4NAMI-4U.

Parent Support Group Mutual support for parents with children experiencing emotional and behavioral problems. Rap sessions, guest speakers, literature, phone help and newsletter. Childcare and limited transportation.

> **Keansburg** Meets Mon., 6:30pm, First United Methodist Church, 21 Church St. Building is handicapped accessible. Pre-registration required. Before attending call 732-571-3272 (day).
> **Long Branch** Meets Thurs., 7-9pm, Family Based Services Association, 279 Broadway, Suite 400. Before attending call 732-571-3272 (day).
> **Long Branch** *(SPANISH)* Meets Wed., 7-9pm, Family Based Services Association, 279 Broadway, Suite 400. Pre-registration required. Before attending call Luz Velasquez 732-546-1996 (day).

SAMHAJ Support for South Asians Mutual support for South Asian (Indians, Pakistanis, Bangladeshi, Sri Lankan) families affected by mental illness. Educational series, guest speakers and literature. Meets 1st Tues., 7-9pm, Girl Scouts of Jersey Shore, Monmouth Service Center, 242 Adelphia Rd., Farmingdale. Call Anu Sing 732-940-0991 (day). *E-mail:* samhaj@naminj.org

MORRIS

Family Support Group *Professionally-run.* Support and education for families of individuals with substance abuse and/or mental health issues. Literature. Meets Thurs., 6pm, Morristown Memorial Hospital, Atlantic Rehabilitation Institute, 95 Mt. Kemble Ave., 6th Floor, Morristown. Call Diana Krafcik 973-971-4742 (day).

Family Support Organization *Professionally-run.* Provides support and advocacy to families and caregivers of children with complex emotional and behavioral challenges. Educational lectures offered. Building is handicapped accessible. Meets 2nd Wed., 10:30am-noon and 1st Mon., 7-8:30pm, Family Support Organization, 200 Valley Rd., Suite 405, Mt. Arlington. Childcare and refreshments provided. Call Norma 973-770-2700 (day). *Website:* http://www.fso-ms.org

Intensive Family Support Services (IFSS) *Professionally-run.* Support and education for family members or caretakers of individuals with a mental illness.
> **Denville** Meets 2nd Wed., 7pm, Saint Clare's Behavioral Health Center, 50 Morris Ave., Room 320. Call 973-625-7131 (day).
> **Denville** Meets 4th Thurs., 7pm, Saint Clare's Behavioral Health Center, 50 Morris Ave., Room 320. Call 973-625-7095 (day).

Kids Cope *Professionally-run.* Support for children (ages 5-17) whose lives have been impacted by a family member with a mental illness. Children groups are separated into different age groups. Groups provide mutual sharing, art and games to encourage social interaction. Groups are time limited. Building is handicapped accessible. Meetings vary, St. Clare's Behavioral Health Center, 50 Morris Ave., Room 320, Denville. Call 973-625-7069.

NAMI Concerned Families of Greystone *Professionally-run.* Support and advocacy for family and friends of persons diagnosed with a mental illness. Provides literature, advocacy, guest speakers and mutual sharing. Dues $5/yr. Meets 4th Tues., 6:30-8:30pm (except July/Aug.), Greystone Hospital, 59 Koch Ave., Board Room, Morris Plains. Call Dorothy 973-386-1845. *E-mail:* louis724ferraro@netscape.net

NAMI Morris County Support and advocacy for families of persons with chronic psychiatric disorders. Educational series. Meets 3rd Mon., 7:30pm, St. Clare's Behavioral Health Center, 50 Morris Ave., Room 320, Denville. Call Eileen Griffith 908-879-5687.

New Bridge Family Support Group *Professionally-run.* Support and education for families of individuals diagnosed with a mental illness. Meets Thurs., 7-8pm, New Bridge, 640 Newark-Pompton Turnpike, Pompton Plains. Call 973-839-2520 (day).

OCEAN

Intensive Family Support Services (IFSS) *Professionally-run.* Support and education for family members or caretakers of individuals with a mental illness. Call Maureen Giacobbe 732-606-9573 ext. 1013 (day).

> **Bayville** Meets last Wed., 7-9pm, Ocean Mental Health Services, 160 Route 9.
> **Lakewood** Meets 2nd and 4th Mon., 7-9pm, Preferred Behavioral Health, 725 Airport Rd.
> **Manahawkin** Meets 3rd Thurs., 9:30-11am, Ocean Mental Health Services, 81 Nautilus Rd.

NAMI Ocean County *Professionally-run.* Support, education, socialization, advocacy, coping and support for families and friends of those diagnosed with a mental illness. Dues $23/yr. (can be waived). Meets 2nd Wed., 6:30pm (speaker) and 8-9pm (group), Ocean County Complex, Hooper Ave. and Madison Ave., 2nd Level Cafeteria, Toms River. Call 732-244-4401 (day).

Parents Empowering Parents Support, education and advocacy for parents and caregivers of children with emotional and behavioral challenges. Rap sessions and guest speakers. Meets 2nd and 4th Tues., 7-9pm, Ocean County Family Support Organization, 44 Washington St., Suite 2A, Toms River. Call Annie Hercules 732-281-5770 ext. 16 (day). *Website:* http://www.ocfso.org *E-mail:* annie.hercules@ocfso.org

PASSAIC

Behavioral Support Group *Professionally-run.* Support for parents raising a child with behavioral challenges. Literature and phone help. Meets last Tues., 7pm, Hillcrest Community Center, 1810 Macopin Rd., Room 25, West Milford. Before attending call Julie Rikon 973-728-0999 (day).

"Have the courage to act instead of react." -- *Earlene Larson Jenks*

Family Circle Support Group *Professionally-run.* Mutual support for families living with a relative diagnosed with a mental illness. Provides an opportunity to share experiences with others. Meets 2nd and 4th Wed., 7-8:30pm, Mental Health Association, 404 Clifton Ave. (use back entrance), Clifton. Call Julia Miller 973-478-4444 ext. 13. *Website:* http://www.mhapc.com *E-mail:* jmiller@mhapc.com

Family Support Organization of Passaic County Support for parents and caregivers raising a child with emotional and behavioral challenges. Building is handicapped accessible. Pre-registration required. Before attending call 973-427-0100. *Website:* http://www.fso-pc.org

> **North Haledon** Meets Wed., 7-8:30pm, Family Support Organization of Passaic County, 810 Belmont Ave., 2nd Floor.
> **North Haledon** *(SPANISH)* Meets Tues., 7-8:30pm, Family Support Organization of Passaic County, 810 Belmont Ave., 2nd Floor.

Intensive Family Support Services (IFFS) *Professionally-run.* Support, education and advocacy for family members of those with a mental illness. Share about experiences and caring. Meets 2nd and 4th Wed., 7-9pm, Mental Health Association of Passaic County, 404 Clifton Ave., 1st Floor (entrance in back of building), Clifton. Pre-registration required. Before attending call Lorraine 973-478-444 ext. 10 (day).

NAMI - Families In Quest *Professionally-run.* Mutual support for families and friends of persons diagnosed with a mental illness. Mutual support, advocacy and exchange of information. Meets 1st Tues., 7:30pm, Mental Health Association, 404 Clifton Ave. (use back entrance), 1st Floor, Clifton. Call 973-478-4444 (day) or Edward 973-773-5112. *Website:* http://www.naminj.org/affiliates/passaic.html

NAMI NJ en Espanol of Passaic County *(SPANISH)* Mutual support for Latino families of persons diagnosed with a mental illness. Meets 3rd Tues., 6:30pm (except Aug.), St. Anthony of Padua Church, 101-103 Myrtle Ave, Passaic. Call Martha Silva 1-888-803-3413. *Website:* http://www.naminj.org *E-mail:* naminjenespanol@msn.com

SALEM

NAMI Salem County Mutual sharing, understanding, discussion of problems and education for families of those diagnosed with a mental illness. All welcome. Building is handicapped accessible. Meets 1st Wed., 7pm, Union Presbyterian Church, Carneys Point. Call Virginia 856-769-2492. *E-mail:* saullnami@aol.com

SOMERSET

AACT-NOW! of Central Jersey (African American Community Takes New Outreach Worldwide) Support, education and advocacy for African-American families affected by the mental illness of a loved one. Sponsored by NAMI-NJ. Meets 4th Thurs., 6-8pm, First Baptist Church of Lincoln Gardens, 771 Somerset St., Somerset. Call Cynthia Miles 732-940-0991 (day).

Fathering Support Group *Professionally-run.* Support for fathers of children (ages 5-18) with mental health and behavioral issues in the Hunterdon, Somerset or Warren county area only. Meets twice a month in Branchburg. Fathers must initially speak with Dr. Richard Horowitz prior to group enrollment. Call 908-526-3900 ext. 114. *E-mail:* rhorowitz@tricountycmo.org

NAMI Somerset County Mutual support, education and advocacy for families of persons diagnosed with a mental illness. Dues $25/yr. Meets 1st Thurs., 7pm (business meeting) and 7:30pm (coping meeting), Richard Hall Mental Health Center, 500 North Bridge St., Bridgewater. Call Sonja Peterson 908-781-2071 (day) or Helen Campbell 908-359-0321.

SUSSEX

Family Support Organization *Professionally-run.* Provides support and advocacy to families and caregivers of children with complex emotional and behavioral challenges. Educational lectures offered. Childcare and refreshments provided. Meets 1st and 3rd Thurs., 6:30-8pm, Family Support Organization, 67A Spring St., Newton. Call Bessy 973-940-3194 (day).

Kids Cope *Professionally-run.* Support for children (ages 5-17) whose lives have been impacted by a family member with a mental illness. Children are separated into different age groups. Groups provide mutual sharing, art and games to encourage social interaction. Groups are time limited. Building is handicapped accessible. Meetings vary, St. Clare's Hospital, 20 Walnut St., Sussex. Call 973-702-7069 (day).

NAMI Sussex County Support for families dealing with a loved one's mental illness. Dues $25/yr. Meets 1st Mon., 7pm, Newton Memorial Hospital, Sussex House, Meeting Room, Newton. Call Jane Blackburn 973-875-7802.

"Medicines may be necessary. Flowers lift the heart. But your smile is the best restorative of all." --Pam Brown

UNION

Family Support Group *Professionally-run.* Provides support, information and education for families of adults diagnosed with a mental illness. Meets 1st and 3rd Wed., 7:30pm, Mental Health Association in NJ, 363 Monroe Ave., Kenilworth. Call Joyce Benz 908-272-5309 ext. 106 (day). *Website:* http://www.mhanj.org *E-mail:* jbenz@mhanj.org

NAMI NJ en Espanol of Union County *(SPANISH)* Support, education and advocacy for families of persons diagnosed with a mental illness. Meets 4th Thurs., 6:30pm (except Aug.), Trinitas Hospital, 225 Williamson St., Room 7 South, Elizabeth. Call Martha Silva 1-888-803-3413. *Website:* http://www.naminj.org *E-mail:* naminjenespanol@msn.com

NAMI Union County Support, education, information and advocacy for persons diagnosed with a mental illness, their families and friends. Building is handicapped accessible. Meets 4th Mon., 7:30-9:30pm, Osceola Presbyterian Church, 1689 Raritan Rd., Clark. Call NAMI Union 908-233-1628. *Website:* http://nami-nj-uc.org *E-mail:* nami.union.nj@nami.org

NJ Parents' Caucus Support Group *(BILINGUAL)* Mutual support and help provided for and by parents or caregivers of children with special emotional/behavioral needs. Guest speakers, phone help and speakers' bureau. Childcare provided. Building is handicapped accessible. Meets 2nd Mon., 7-9pm, Trinitas Hospital, 655 East Jersey St., Grassman Hall (basement), Elizabeth. Call Linda McConneyhead or Jainette Tiru 908-994-7471.

Sibling Support Group *Professionally-run.* Support, information and education for siblings of adults diagnosed with a mental illness. Meets 2nd Wed., 7:30-9pm, Mental Health Association in NJ, 363 Monroe Ave., Kenilworth. Call Joyce Benz 908-272-5309 ext. 106 (day). *Website:* http://www.mhanj.org *E-mail:* jbenz@mhanj.org

Spouse and Partner Support Group Support, information and education for spouses and partners of people diagnosed with a mental illness. Meets 4th Wed., 7:30-9pm, Mental Health Association in NJ, 363 Monroe Ave., Kenilworth. Call Joyce Benz 908-272-5309 ext. 106 (day). *Website:* http://www.mhanj.org *E-mail:* jbenz@mhanj.org

TARA-NJ Confidential support and education for families of those with borderline personality disorder (BPD), who learn and share what treatments and communication techniques are helpful, e.g., how they can apply Dialectical Behavior Therapy (DBT) coping skills. Meets monthly, 6:30-8:45pm, First

Baptist Church of Westfield, 170 Elm St., Westfield. Meeting days and times via e-mail. *E-mail:* taranj@verizon.net

WARREN

Intensive Family Support Services (IFSS) *Professionally-run.* Provides support, mutual sharing and education for families and friends of adults with a mental illness. Guest speakers. Call Darrell 908-689-1000 ext. 331 (day).

> **Phillipsburg** Meets 1st and 3rd Tues., 6:30-8pm, Family Guidance Center, 550 Marshall St.
> **Washington** Meets 2nd and 4th Tues., 7-8:30pm, Family Guidance Center, 492 Route 57 West.

NAMI Warren County Mutual support and advocacy for families and friends of persons diagnosed with a mental illness. Dues $25/yr. (can be waived). Meets 1st Thurs., 7:30-9pm, St. Joseph Church, 200 Carlton Ave., Washington. Call 908-859-4368 (eve./weekend). *E-mail:* NAMI_Warren_county@NAMI.org

NATIONAL

Adult Children of Multiplicity *Model. Founded 1998.* Provides companionship and back-up support for adult children (ages 18+) who had or have a parent with Multiple Personality Disorder or Dissociative Identity Disorder (MPD/DID). Write: Children of Multiplicity, P.O. Box 12376, San Francisco, CA 94112. Call 415-585-6352 (11am-11:30pm PST).

Attachment and Trauma Network *National network. Founded 1997.* Support and information for parents and professionals dealing with children with attachment issues or reactive attachment disorder. Newsletter, referrals, phone and online support. Dues $25 (includes newsletter). Call 240-357-7369; Fax: 641-453-1778. *Website:* http://www.radzebra.org *E-mail:* lorraine@radzebra.org

Federation of Families for Children's Mental Health *National. 137 affiliated groups. Founded 1989.* Parent-run organization focused on the needs of children and youth with emotional, behavioral or mental disorders and their families. Provides information, advocacy, newsletter and conferences. For local support group information, click on "Who We Are" on top of menu bar: then click on "Local Chapters and State Organizations." Write: Federation of Families for Children's Mental Health, 9605 Medical Center Dr., Suite 280, Rockville, MD 20850. Call 240-403-1901; Fax: 240-403-1909. *Website:* http://www.ffcmh.org *E-mail:* ffcmh@ffcmh.org

NAMI (National Alliance on Mental Illness) *(BILINGUAL) National. 1100 groups. Founded 1979.* Dedicated to improving the lives of persons living with serious mental illness and their families. Has local self-help and educational groups for family members and mental health consumers. Online community message boards, e-newsletters, blogs and online fact sheets. Quarterly magazines. Focuses on support, education, advocacy and research. Provides online veterans resource center. Write: NAMI, Colonial Place Three, 2107 Wilson Blvd., Suite 300, Arlington, VA 22201-3042. Call 1-800-950-6264 (helpline) or 703-524-7600 (day); Fax: 703-524-9094. *Website:* http://www.nami.org

Schizophrenia Society of Canada *(ENGLISH and FRENCH) National. 110 societies. Founded 1979.* Information, support and advocacy for families and friends of persons with schizophrenia. Public awareness campaigns, advocacy and fund-raising. Newsletters. Guidelines and assistance for starting self-help groups. Information and referrals, phone help, conferences, brochures, handbooks and videos. Write: Schizophrenia Society of Canada, 100-4 Fort Street, Winnapeg, WA R3C1C4, Canada. Call 204-786-1616; Fax: 204-783-4898. *Website:* http://www.schizophrenia.ca *E-mail:* info@schizophrenia.ca

Selective Mutism Foundation, Inc. *National. Founded 1992.* Pioneering group that offers mutual support for professionals and parents of children with selective mutism or social phobia (a psychiatric anxiety disorder in which children are unable to speak in social situations). Includes social anxiety and shyness. Also open to adults who have or outgrew, the disorder. Provides information and online support. Website contains DSM revisions, research studies, printable brochures, literature and publications. Write: Carolyn Miller, P.O. Box 13133, Sissonville, WV 25360 or Sue Newman Mercado, P.O. Box 25972, Tamarac, FL 33320. *Website:* http://www.selectivemutismfoundation.org *E-mail:* carolyn@selectivemutismfoundation.org or sue@selectivemutismfoundation.org

Sibling Support Project *National. 200 affiliated groups. Founded 1990.* Organization dedicated to the life long concerns of brothers and sisters of children with special health, developmental and mental health concerns. Provides training and technical assistance regarding Sibshops and workshops for school-age siblings. Write: Sibling Support Project, c/o Donald Meyer, 6512 23rd Ave. NW, Suite 213, Seattle, WA 98117. Call 206-297-6368; Fax: 509-752-6789. *Website:* http://www.siblingsupport.org *E-mail:* donmeyer@siblingsupport.org

ONLINE

Adult Children of Narcissists *Online.* E-mail-based support group for children of narcissistic parents. Offers a safe, supportive, nurturing environment to discuss past and present concerns about being raised with a narcissistic parent. *Website:* http://health.groups.yahoo.com/group/adultchildrenofnarcissists

Attachment Disorder Support Group *Online.* Provides an interactive supportive website for parents, families friends and professionals concerned with a child's troublesome behavior. Offers message forum, e-mail listserv, general information, educational material and helpful links. *Website:* http://adsg.syix.com

BPD Central *Online.* Provides links to online groups for persons dealing with a loved one with borderline personality disorder. Several mailing lists given for parents, siblings, grandparents and others close to someone with BPD. Group for persons with BPD themselves (BorderPD). *Website:* http://www.bpdcentral.com

Conduct Disorders Parent Message Board *Online. 7080 members. Founded 1995.* Support for parents living with a child with one of the many behavior disorders including: attention deficit hyperactivity disorder, oppositional defiance disorder, conduct disorder, depression and substance abuse. Parents with children of all ages welcome. *Website:* http://www.conductdisorders.com

North American Society for Childhood Onset Schizophrenia (NASCOS) *Online. Founded 2004.* Provides families of children with childhood-onset schizophrenia (onset before age 13) with access to information, discussion forum, e-mail list and a geographical locator in order to find other members in your region. Families and caregivers of older patients, whose onset was during childhood, as well as interested professionals are welcome to join. Write: NASCOS, 88 Briarwood Drive East, Berkeley Heights, NJ 07922. *Website:* http://www.nascos.org *E-mail:* info@nascos.org

paranoidpersonalitydisorderforum *Online. 562 members. Founded 2001.* Support, understanding and information for anyone affected by a loved one or friend with paranoid personality disorder. Meeting place to come together to share daily struggles and teach one another from individual experiences. *Website:*
http://health.groups.yahoo.com/group/paranoidpersonalitydisorderforum

Schizophrenia-parents *Online. 294 members. Founded 2000.* Support group of people who have children (of any age) or other loved ones that have a schizophrenia disease. Warm, supportive, caring and educational environment for sharing experiences, feelings, research and resources. *Website:* http://groups.yahoo.com/group/schizophrenia-parents

Selective Mutism Group, The *Online. Founded 1999.* Devoted to educating and promoting awareness on selective mutism and other related childhood anxiety disorders. Online forums and "Expert Chats" in addition to the Connections Program that links individuals and provides state support group meeting information. *Website:* http://selectivemutism.org *E-mail:* sminfo@selectivemutism.org

SibNet *Online. 1157 members. Founded 1998.* Listserv for and about adult brothers and sisters of people with special health, developmental and emotional needs. Opportunity for young adults and adult brothers and sisters to share information and discuss issues of common interest. Subscribers can connect with their peers, seek information about local services, create connections for their siblings and discuss the proper policies agencies should have toward brothers and sisters. *Website:* http://groups.yahoo.com/group/sibnet

MENTAL HEALTH (GENERAL)
(see also mental health consumers, specific disorder, toll-free helplines)

STATEWIDE

GROW Mutual self-help group to prevent and recover from depression, anxiety and other mental health problems. Caring and sharing community to attain emotional maturity, personal responsibility and recovery. Meets in various counties in NJ. Write: GROW Center, 4A Iowa Dr., Whiting, NJ 08759. Call 732-350-4800.

BERGEN

Emotions Anonymous 12-Step. Fellowship sharing experiences, hopes and strengths in order to gain better emotional health. Deals with anxiety, fears, anger, depression, etc.
> **Hackensack** Meets Tues. and Thurs., 7:30pm, First Presbyterian Church, 64 Passaic St. (use right side entrance). Call Sam 201-962-8038 (day).
> **Hillsdale** Meets Mon., 7:30pm, Holy Trinity Episcopal Church, 326 Hillsdale Ave. Donation $2/mtg. Call Lea 201-666-1009.

Recovery, Inc. Self-help method of will training. Offers techniques for controlling temperamental behavior and changing attitudes toward nervous symptoms, anxiety, depression and fears. *Website:* http://www.recovery-inc.org *E-mail:* inquiries@recovery-inc.org

> **Hasbrouck Heights** Meets Wed., 8pm, First Reformed Church, Washington Place and Burton Ave. Call Philip 201-261-7044 or 201-612-8153.
>
> **Ridgewood** Meets Fri., 1:30pm, Christ Church, Cottage Place and Franklin Ave. Call 201-612-8153.

BURLINGTON

Recovery, Inc. Self-help method of will training. Offers techniques for controlling temperamental behavior and changing attitudes toward nervous symptoms, anxiety, depression and fears. Call Barry 856-848-8715 or John 856-983-7291. *Website:* http://www.recovery-inc.org *E-mail:* 155@recovery-inc.org

> **Marlton** Meets Mon. and Thurs., 7pm, Prince of Peace Lutheran Church, 61 Route 70 East.
>
> **Westampton** Meets Tues., 7pm, Hampton Hospital, Rancocas Rd., Cafeteria.

CAMDEN

Recovery, Inc. Self-help method of will training. Offers techniques for controlling temperamental behavior and changing attitudes toward nervous symptoms, anxiety, depression and fears. *Website:* http://www.recovery-inc.org *E-mail:* 155@recovery-inc.org

> **Magnolia** Meets Wed., 9:30am, Holy Trinity Lutheran Church, 501 North Warwick Rd. Call Stacy 856-931-1411 or Barry 856-848-8715.
>
> **Westmont** Meets Sat., 11:30am, Starting Point, 215 Highland Ave. Call Ann 856-853-2724 or Rob 609-413-6959.

CUMBERLAND

GROW Mutual self-help group to prevent and recover from depression, anxiety and other mental health problems. Caring and sharing community to attain emotional maturity, personal responsibility and recovery. Before attending call Ninfa 732-575-5766.

> **Vineland** Meets Thurs., 7pm, Church of Christian/Missionary Alliance, Main Rd. and Harding Ave., Board Room.
>
> **Vineland** Meets Thurs., 7pm, New Horizons Self-Help Center, 63 S. Myrtle St.

ESSEX

GROW Mutual self-help group to prevent and recover from depression, anxiety and other mental health problems. Caring and sharing community to attain emotional maturity, personal responsibility and recovery. Meets Mon., 4:30pm, Pleasant Moments Self-Help Center, 465-475 Broadway, Newark. Before attending call Caroline 732-575-5765.

Recovery, Inc. Self-help method of will training. Offers techniques for controlling temperamental behavior and changing attitudes toward nervous symptoms, anxiety, depression and fears. Meets Tues., 8pm, Prospect Presbyterian Church, 646 Prospect St., Maplewood. Call Hal 973-762-0764 or 201-612-8153. *Website:* http://www.recovery-inc.org *E-mail:* inquiries@recovery-inc.org

GLOUCESTER

Recovery, Inc. Self-help method of will training. Offers techniques for controlling temperamental behavior and changing attitudes toward nervous symptoms, anxiety, depression and fears. Families welcome. *Website:* http://www.recovery-inc.org *E-mail:* 155@recovery-inc.org

> **Deptford** Meets Fri., 10-11am, James Johnson Library, 670 Ward Dr. Call Barry 856-848-8715.
> **Woodbury Heights** Meets Wed., 7pm, First Presbyterian Church, 4th and Elm Ave. Call Ann 856-853-2724 or Barry 856-848-8715.

MERCER

GROW Mutual self-help group to prevent and recover from depression, anxiety and other mental health problems. Caring and sharing community to attain emotional maturity, personal responsibility and recovery. Meets Thurs., 6pm, Reach Out/Speak Out, 2100 E. State St., Hamilton. Before attending call Caroline 732-575-5765.

MONMOUTH

Emotions Anonymous 12-Step. Fellowship sharing experiences, hopes and strengths in order to gain better emotional health. Deals with anxiety, fears, anger, depression, etc. Meets Sat., noon, Port Monmouth. Call Chris or Lillian 732-495-7453 (day). *E-mail:* graye22@netzero.net

GROW Mutual self-help group to prevent and recover from depression, anxiety and other mental health problems. Caring and sharing community to attain emotional maturity, personal responsibility and recovery.

>**Freehold** Meets Wed., 5:30pm, Freehold Self-Help Center, 17 Bannard St. Before attending call Nancy 732-350-4800.

>**Ocean Grove** Meets Thurs., 6:45pm, St. Paul's Methodist Church, 80 Embry St., Stokes Room. Before attending call Caroline 732-575-5765.

MORRIS

Antidote to Anger, The *Professionally-run.* Support for those with personal issues of anger or dealing with an angry individual. Group focuses on understanding anger, expressing and managing it appropriately, resolving disputes calmly, restoring peace and harmony. Literature. Meets 1st and 3rd Wed., 7-8:30pm, St. Simon the Apostle Church, 1010 Green Pond Rd., Green Pond. Call Janet 973-697-1904 or church 973-697-4699 (day).

OCEAN

GROW Mutual self-help group to prevent and recover from depression, anxiety and other mental health problems. Caring and sharing community to attain emotional maturity, personal responsibility and recovery.

>**Brick** Meets Tues., 6:30pm, Brick Presbyterian Church, 111 Drum Point Rd. Before attending call Caroline 732-575-5765.

>**Toms River** Meets Thurs., 4pm, Presbyterian Church of Toms River, Hooper Ave. and Chestnut St., River Room. Before attending call Ninfa 732-575-5766.

>**Toms River** Meets Tues., 6:30pm, Brighter Days Self-Help Center, Sand F Plaza, 2008 Route 37 East, Suite 6. Before attending call Nancy 732-350-4800.

Recovery, Inc. Self-help method of will training. Offers techniques for controlling temperamental behavior and changing attitudes toward nervous symptoms, anxiety, depression and fears. Meets Mon., 7:30pm, Presbyterian Church of Toms River, Hooper Ave. and Chestnut St., Toms River. Call Delores 732-557-5466 or 201-612-8153. *Website:* http://www.recovery-inc.org *E-mail:* inquiries@recovery-inc.org

"The greatest gift we can give one another is rapt attention to one another's existence."
–Sue Atchley Ebaugh

SUSSEX

Self-Enhancement Support Group *Professionally-run.* Support for men and women who want to make improvements in their personal lives. Donation $5. Meets Thurs., 7-9pm (except June/July/Aug.), Partnership for Social Services Family Center, 48 Wyker Rd., Franklin. Pre-registration required. Before attending call Dr. Thomasina Gebhard 973-827-4702 (day).

UNION

GROW Mutual self-help group to prevent and recover from depression, anxiety and other mental health problems. Caring and sharing community to attain emotional maturity, personal responsibility and recovery.

> **Elizabeth** Meets Wed., 4pm, New Beginnings Self-Help Center, 516 Morris Ave. Before attending call Caroline 732-575-5765.
> **Plainfield** Meets Wed., 3:30pm, Park Avenue Self-Help Center, 333 Park Ave. Before attending call Caroline 732-575-5765.

Recovery, Inc. Self-help method of will training. Offers techniques for controlling temperamental behavior and changing attitudes toward nervous symptoms, anxiety, depression and fears. *Website:* http://www.recovery-inc.org *E-mail:* inquiries@recovery-inc.org

> **Summit** Meets Wed., 7:30pm, Central Presbyterian Center, Morris Ave. and Maple St., (use glass doors from rear parking lot). Call 201-612-8153.
> **Westfield** Meets Fri., 8pm, Union County Community Building, 300 North Ave. East (parking lot entrance), 2nd Floor, Conference Room. Call Dorothy 732-381-3712 or 201-612-8153.

NATIONAL

C.A.I.R. (Changing Attitudes In Recovery) *Model. 30 groups. Founded 1990.* Self-help "family" sharing a common commitment to gain healthy esteem. Includes persons with relationship problems, addictions, mental illness, etc. Offers new techniques and tools that lead to better self-esteem. Assistance in starting groups. Handbook ($12.95) and CDs available. Write: CAIR, c/o Psychological Associates Press, 706 13th St., Modesto, CA 95354. Call 209-577-1667; Fax: 209-577-3805. *Website:* http://www.cairforyou.com

Emotions Anonymous *International. 823 chapters. Founded 1971.* Fellowship for people experiencing emotional difficulties. Uses the 12-step program sharing experiences, strengths and hopes in order to improve emotional health. Books and literature available to new and existing groups. Guidelines available to help start a similar group. Write: Emotions Anonymous International, P.O. Box 4245, St. Paul, MN 55104-0245. Call 651-647-9712; Fax: 651-647-1593. *Website:* http://www.emotionsanonymous.org *E-mail:* info@emotionsanonymous.org

GROW in America *International. 143 groups. Founded in 1957.* 12-Step. Group offers mutual help, friendship, community, education and leadership. Focuses on recovery and personal growth. Open to all including those with mental health issues, depression, anxiety, grief, fears, etc. Write: GROW in America, P.O. Box 3667, Champaign, IL 61826. Call 1-888-741-4769. *E-mail:* growil@sbcglobal.net

International Association for Clear Thinking *International. 100 chapters. Founded 1970.* Support for people interested in living their lives more effectively and satisfactorily. Uses principles of clear thinking and self-counseling. Offers group handbook, chapter development kit, audio tapes, facilitator leadership training and self-help materials. Write: International Association for Clear Thinking, P.O. Box 1011, Appleton, WI 54912. Call 920-739-8311; Fax: 920-582-9783.

Pathways To Peace, Inc. *International. 11 groups. Founded 1998.* Self-help group program for anger management. Also offers education and assistance with starting groups. Write: Pathways To Peace, Inc., P.O. Box 259, Cassadaga, NY 14718. Call 1-800-775-4212; Fax: 716-595-3886. *Website:* http://www.pathwaystopeaceinc.com *E-mail:* transfrm@netsync.net

Recovery, Inc. *International. 640 groups. Founded 1937.* Mental health self-help organization that offers weekly group meetings for people suffering from various emotional and mental conditions. Principles parallel those found in cognitive-behavioral therapy. Teaches people how to change their thoughts, reactions and behaviors that cause their physical and emotional symptoms. Write: Recovery, Inc., 802 N. Dearborn St., Chicago, IL 60610. Call 312-337-5661; Fax: 312-337-5756. *Website:* http://www.recovery-inc.org

"There is more than anger, there is more than sadness, more than terror. There is hope."
--L. Davis & E. Bass, from their book, The Courage to Heal

OBSESSIVE-COMPULSIVE DISORDER

STATEWIDE

NJ Affiliate of the Obsessive Compulsive Foundation, Inc. Mutual support for anyone concerned with obsessive compulsive disorder. Provides quarterly newsletter, referrals to professionals, speakers' bureau, fund-raising, education, socials, support group network, phone help and literature. Provides assistance in starting new groups. Call Ina Spero 732-828-0099 or Dr. Allen Weg 732-390-6694. *Website:* http://www.njocf.org

NJ TTM Support for Children, Teens and Parents Support primarily for kids and teens who have trichotillomania (compulsive hair pulling) and their parents. Assistance available for starting local trichotillomania support groups. Call Marc 201-670-4192. *E-mail:* mfoner@optonline.net

BERGEN

NJ TTM Support Group for Children, Teens and Parents Support primarily for kids and teens who have trichotillomania (compulsive hair pulling) and their parents. Meets monthly, Glen Rock Public Library, 315 Rock Rd., Basement Meeting Room, Glen Rock. For meeting information call Marc 201-670-4192. *E-mail: m*foner@optonline.net

BURLINGTON

OCD Support Group Support for persons who suffer from obsessive compulsive disorder. Family members and friends are welcome to attend. Meets 2nd Mon., 7:30-9pm, Virtua West Hospital, 90 Brick Rd., Marlton. Before attending call Betty 856-751-1957.

ESSEX

Obsessive-Compulsive Support Group Support for persons with obsessive compulsive disorder. Meets 1st and 3rd Thurs., 8-9:30pm, Mountainside Hospital, 1 Bay Ave., Schering-Plough Conference Room 3, Montclair. Call Nancy 973-472-8215 (eve.).

Northern Jersey TTM Support Group, The Provides support, compassion and even laughter for adults trichotillomania. Meets monthly on Thurs., 7:30-9:30pm, in Essex, Morris and Union counties. E-mail Lisa for meeting information. *E-mail:* ljp_edc@hotmail.com

GLOUCESTER

OCD Families Support Group Mutual support and coping skills for families and friends of children and adolescents who suffer from obsessive compulsive disorder. Rap sessions. Meets 1st Sun., 6:30-7:30pm, Underwood Memorial Hospital, 509 North Broad St., Medical Arts Building, Suite 14, Woodbury. Call Rich Bellamente 856-853-2011 (day).

MERCER

Tuesday Night Group, The Mutual support for women with trichotillomania (compulsive hair pulling). Also welcomes women with other body-focused repetitive behaviors such as skin-picking. Meets Tues., 7:30-9pm, Princeton YWCA Library, 59 Paul Robeson Pl., Princeton. E-mail Audrey for additional information. *E-mail:* mercertrich@yahoo.com

MIDDLESEX

Central NJ Affiliate of the Obsessive Compulsive Foundation Support for any person concerned with OCD. Provides guest speakers, phone help, literature, newsletter and annual conference. Building is handicapped accessible. Meets 2nd Mon., 7:30-9pm (Mar., June, Sept., Dec.), Robert Wood Johnson Hospital, Medical Education Building, New Brunswick. For meeting information call Ina Spero 732-828-0099 (9am-9pm).

Overcomer's Outreach *Christian 12-Step.* Fellowship to overcome any type of addiction or compulsive behavior, anxiety, depression and loneliness using God's word as a basis of recovery. Bible study, discussion, prayer and phone help. Meets Tues., 6:30-7:30pm, Metuchen Assembly of God, 130 Whitman St., Metuchen. Call Janet 732-388-2856 (eve.).

Rutgers OCD Support Group *Professionally-run.* Provides support and education for individuals with obsessive compulsive disorder, their families and friends. Donation $1. Meets 1st and 3rd Wed., 7-8:30pm, Rutgers University, 797 Hoes Lane West, Piscataway. Call 732-445-5384 (day).

MONMOUTH

OCA Obsessive-Compulsive Anonymous 12-Step. Fellowship for persons affected by obsessive compulsive disorder. Offers mutual sharing, rap sessions and stories from the Big Book. Building is handicapped accessible. Meets Wed., 8:15-9:45pm, Southard Grange #218, 4860 Highway 9 South, Howell. Call Ron 848-702-5044. *E-mail:* Ronnyhugs@aol.com

MORRIS

Northern Jersey TTM Support Group, The Provides support, compassion and even laughter for adults trichotillomania. Meets monthly on Thurs., 7:30-9:30pm, in Essex, Morris and Union counties. E-mail Lisa for meeting information. *E-mail:* ljp_edc@hotmail.com

OCD Support Group Mutual support for persons with obsessive compulsive disorder. Family members are welcome to attend. Opportunity to discuss techniques and solutions to overcome the disorder. Rap sessions, phone help and literature. Building is handicapped accessible. Meets 2nd and 4th Wed., 7:30pm, Saint Clare's Hospital, 130 Powerville Rd., Boonton. Call Diane Walker 862-268-6397. *E-mail:* dianewalker25@yahoo.com

OCEAN

Obsessive Compulsive Anonymous 12-Step. Provides mutual support for individuals recovering from obsessive compulsive disorder.
> **Brick** Meets Fri., 8-9:30pm, St. Paul's United Methodist Church, 714 Herbertsville Rd., Norcross Memorial Library. Call Mary S. 908-675-2627.
> **Jackson Township** Meets Sun., 8-9:30pm, Debows United Methodist Church, 509 Monmouth Rd. Call Kathy 732-644-3291.

SOMERSET

Obsessive - Compulsive Disorder Support Group *Professionally-run.* Support, education and coping skills for persons suffering with, or recovering from, obsessive compulsive disorder including trichotillomania. Families are welcome. Building is handicapped accessible. Meets 3rd Thurs., 7:30pm, Somerset Medical Center, Hamilton Wing, Conference Room, Somerville. Call Joseph Donnellan, MD 908-725-5595 (day).

UNION

Northern Jersey TTM Support Group, The Provides support, compassion and even laughter for adults trichotillomania. Meets monthly on Thurs., 7:30-9:30pm, in Essex, Morris and Union counties. E-mail Lisa for meeting information. *E-mail:* ljp_edc@hotmail.com

Obsessive Compulsive Anonymous 12-Step. Provides relief or recovery from obsessive compulsive disorder. Fellowship and support through sharing of experiences, strength and hope. Must have obsessive compulsive disorder to attend meetings. Donations optional. Meets Mon., 7:45-9:15pm, Diamond Hill United Methodist Church, Diamond Hill Rd., Berkley Heights. Call Altagracia 908-456-0711. *Website:* http://www.obsessivecompulsiveanonymous.org

NATIONAL

Anxiety Disorders Association of America *National network. 197 groups. Founded 1980.* Listing of state-by-state local support groups, brochures, information about anxiety disorders, local listing of healthcare professionals providing treatment for anxiety disorders and a national listing of clinical trails provided free. Promotes the diagnosis and treatment of all anxiety and related disorders including obsessive compulsive disorder, post-traumatic stress disorder, panic disorder, specific phobia, social anxiety disorder and generalized anxiety disorder. Write: Anxiety Disorders Association of America, 8730 Georgia Ave., Suite 600, Silver Spring, MD 20910. Call 240-485-1001; Fax: 240-485-1035. *Website:* http://www.adaa.org

Eating Addictions Anonymous - SANE Fellowship *National. 6 affiliated chapters.* 12-Step. Recovery program for men and women recovering from all forms of eating and body image addictions. Includes anorexia, bulimia, binge eating, overeating, exercise bulimics, etc. Focuses on internal growth and reclaiming bodies rather than weight or appearance. Write: Eating Addictions Anonymous, P.O. Box 8151, Silver Spring, MD 20907-8151. Call 202-882-6528. *Website:* http://www.eatingaddictionsanonymous.org *E-mail:* 12n12@tidalwave.net

Obsessive-Compulsive Anonymous *(BILINGUAL) National. 50 affiliated groups. Founded 1988.* 12-Step. Self-help group for people with obsessive-compulsive disorders. Online meetings, assistance and guidelines available for starting groups. Write: OCA, P.O. Box 215, New Hyde Park, NY 11040. Call 516-739-0662. *Website:* http://www.obsessivecompulsiveanonymous.org

Obsessive-Compulsive Foundation, Inc. *International. 9 chapters. Founded 1986.* Support and assistance for people with OCD and related disorders, their families, friends, professionals and other concerned individuals. Educates the public and professional communities about OCD and related disorders, publishes a quarterly newsletter, annual summer conference, behavior therapy training institutes for mental health professionals, and a speakers bureau for public speaking events. Call 617-973-5801; Fax: 617-973-5803. Write: Obsessive-Compulsive Foundation, P.O. Box 961029, Boston, MA 02196. *Website:* http://www.ocfoundation.org *E-mail:* info@ocfoundation.org

Trichotillomania Learning Center *International. Founded 1991.* Support and information to patients, families and professionals about trichotillomania (compulsive hair pulling). Information and referrals, newsletter, annual retreat, conferences, phone support, pen pals and literature. Assistance in starting similar groups. Write: TLC, 207 McPherson St., Santa Cruz, CA 95060. Call 831-457-1004; Fax: 831-426-4383. *Website:* http://www.trich.org *E-mail:* info@trich.org

ONLINE

OCD and Parenting List *Online. Over 1400 members.* Mutual support and information for parents of children with obsessive compulsive disorder through an e-mail discussion group and professional advisors who respond to questions. Also has an extensive listing of web links. *Website:* http://health.groups.yahoo.com/group/ocdandparenting *E-mail:* louisharkins@yahoo.com or louisharkins@gmail.com

Panic Survivor *Online.* Support group for persons who suffer from anxiety, panic attacks, social anxiety, generalized anxiety, post-traumatic stress disorder, obsessive compulsive disorder, hypochondria or any other form of anxiety. Focus is on recovery and day-to-day survival with a "can do" attitude. *Website:* http://panicsurvivor.com

"The truth is that our finest moments are most likely to occur when we are feeling deeply uncomfortable, unhappy, or unfulfilled. For it is only in such moments, propelled by our discomfort, that we are likely to step out of our ruts and start searching for different ways or truer answers."-- M. Scott Peck

MISCELLANEOUS

ACCIDENT VICTIMS

NATIONAL

ACCESS (AirCraft Casualty Emotional Support Services) *National network. Founded 1996.* Matches persons who have lost a loved one in an aircraft related tragedy to volunteers who previously experienced a similar loss. Goal is to help fill the void that occurs when the emergency and disaster relief organizations disband, the initial shock subsides and the natural grieving process intensifies. Offers guidelines to help start a similar group. Persons communicate through e-mail or by phone. Online newsletter. Write: ACCESS, 1202 Lexington Ave., Suite 335, New York, NY 10028. Call 1-877-227-6435. *Website:* http://www.accesshelp.org *E-mail:* info@accesshelp.org

Wings of Light, Inc. *National. 3 support networks. Founded 1995.* Support and information network for individuals whose lives have been touched by aviation accidents. Separate networks for airplane accident survivors, families and friends of persons killed in airplane accidents. Helps individuals involved in the rescue, recovery and investigation of crashes. Phone support, information and referrals. Write: Wings of Light, P.O. Box 1097, Sun City, AZ 85372. Call 623-516-1115. *Website:* http://www.wingsoflight.org

ONLINE

Accidents Support Group *Online.* Supportive community dedicated to recovering from, and dealing with, the long-term stress of accidents and unexpected events (bicycle accidents, car and motorcycle accidents, workplace accidents, etc.). Deals with both the emotional and physical distress. *Website:* http://dailystrength.org/support/traumas_injuries/accidents/

CRASH Foundation (Citizens for Reliable And Safe Highways) *Online.* Dedicated to providing immediate compassionate support to truck crash survivors and families of truck crash victims. Referrals to grief counseling, medical services and truck crash experts. Phone support, conferences, advocacy, First Response Program and survivors network. Write: CRASH, 2020 N. 14th St., Suite 710, Arlington, VA 22201. Call 1-888-353-4572; Fax: 703-294-6406. *Website:* http://www.trucksafety.org/ *E-mail:* crash@trucksafety.org

AGING / OLDER PERSONS
(see also caregivers, specific disorder, toll-free helplines)

STATEWIDE

AARP A membership organization for people age 50 and over. Provides information, resources, advocacy, newsletter, offers a wide range of benefits and services for our members. National membership $12.50/yr. Write: AARP - NJ State Office, 101 Rockingham Row, Princeton, NJ 08540-5739. Call 1-866-542-8165 (Mon.-Fri., 9am-5pm). *Website:* http://www.aarp.org/nj

DOROT/University Without Walls Telephone Support Teleconference support groups for persons age 59+ who are coping with vision loss, aging issues, anxiety, etc. There is a $10 registration fee and $15 tuition per support group. Scholarships are available. Write: DOROT, 171 W. 85th St., New York, NY 10024. For more information call 1-877-819-9147 or Fran Rod 973-763-1511. *Website:* http://www.dorotusa.org

BERGEN

As Life Changes *(Professionally-run)* Support for seniors (ages 55+) to discuss emotional and physical changes as they age and how it impacts their daily life, family and future. Building is handicapped accessible. Meets Tues., 1pm, Southeast Senior Center for Independent Living, 228 Grand Ave., Englewood. Pre-registration required. Before attending call Laura Hollander, MSW 201-569-4080 (day).

Transitions Discussions *(Professionally-run)* Support for seniors age 60+ to discuss problems of aging, relocation, loss of spouse, friends, health, relationships and children. Building is handicapped accessible.
> **Midland Park** Meets Mon., 12:30-2pm, Northwest Senior Center, 46-50 Center St. Call 201-445-5690 (day).
> **Wallington** Meets Mon., 10-11:30am, Wallington Senior Center, 24 Union Blvd. Call 973-777-5815 (day).

HUDSON

Healthy Aging in Jersey City *(Professionally-run)* Education, discussion, socialization and wellness workshops for women and men age 55 and over. Building is handicapped accessible. Meets Wed., 10:30am, Christ Hospital, Jersey City. Call Michele Bernstein 201-795-8416 (day) or Crystal 201-795-8178 (day).

OCEAN

Senior Support Group *(Professionally-run)* Mutual support to share experiences, resources, coping skills and topics of interest for the elderly. Social and guest speakers. Call Rita Sason or Arlene 732-363-8010 (Mon.-Thurs.). *E-mail:* jfcs@ocjf.org

> **Brick** Meets Thurs., 10-11:30am, Temple Beth Or, 200 Van Zile Rd.
> **Lakewood** Meets Wed., 1-2:30pm, Jewish Family and Children's Services, 301 Madison Ave.

NATIONAL

AARP *(BILINGUAL) National. 4000 chapters. Founded 1958.* Organization for people age 50 and older. Addresses needs and interests through information, education, advocacy and community service which are provided by a network of local chapters and experienced volunteers throughout the country. Offers members a wide range of special benefits and services, including "AARP Magazine" and the monthly "Bulletin." Write: AARP, 601 E St., NW, Washington, DC 20049. Call 1-888-687-2277 (Mon-Fri, 7am-midnight EST). *Website:* http://www.aarp.org

Gray Panthers *National. 47 chapters. Founded 1970.* Multigenerational education and advocacy movement/organization which works to bring about fundamental social changes including a national health care system, elimination of all forms of discrimination and economic justice. Newsletter and newspaper. Chapter development guidelines. Dues $20/US; $35/Organization; $40/International. Online site offers referrals to local chapters and useful links. Write: Gray Panthers, 733 15th St., NW, Suite 437, Washington, DC 20005. Call 1-800-280-5362 or 202-737-6637; Fax: 202-737-1160. *Website:* http://www.graypanthers.org *E-mail:* info@graypanthers.org

Older Women's League *National. 60+ chapters. Founded 1980.* Membership organization that advocates on behalf of various economic and social issues for midlife and older women (social security, pension rights, employment, caregiver support, elder abuse, etc.). Newsletter and chapter development guidelines. Dues $25/yr. Write: Older Women's League, 3300 North Fairfax Dr., Suite 218, Arlington, VA 22201. Call 1-800-825-3695; Fax: 703-812-0687. *Website:* http://www.owl-national.org *E-mail:* owlinfo@owl-national.org

*Can't find an appropriate group in your area? The Clearinghouse helps people start groups. Give us a call at **1-800-367-6274**.*

ARTISTIC CREATIVITY

CAPE MAY

ARTS Anonymous (Artists Recovering Through the Twelve Steps) A spiritual program based on the 12-steps and 12-traditions of A.A. The only requirement for membership is a desire to fulfill creative potential. Meets Thurs., 9:30am, Cape May County Lower Branch Library, 2600 Bayshore Rd., Villas. Call Mary 609-884-0827. *Website:* http://www.artsanonymous.org

ESSEX

ARTS Anonymous (Artists Recovering Through the Twelve Steps) A spiritual program based on the 12-steps and 12-traditions of A.A. The only requirement for membership is a desire to fulfill creative potential. Meets Mon., 6:30pm, St. James Episcopal Church, 581 Valley Rd. and Bellevue Ave. (parking area in back of church on Bellevue), Montclair. Call Joyce 973-943-3670. *Website:* http://www.artsanonymous.org

MONMOUTH

ARTS Anonymous (Artists Recovering Through the Twelve Steps) A spiritual program based on the 12-steps and 12-traditions of A.A. The only requirement for membership is a desire to fulfill creative potential. Meets Fri., 10:30am, Monmouth Beach Cultural Center, 128 Ocean Ave., Rte. 36, Monmouth Park. For additional information call Dawn 732-840-3532. *Website:* http://www.artsanonymous.org

NATIONAL

ARTS Anonymous (Artists Recovering Through the Twelve Steps) *International. 150 affiliated groups. Founded 1984.* Supports individuals in identifying and overcoming challenges to their artistic expression. Through a mix of traditional 12-Step tools, literature, weekly meetings, artist-to-artist fellowship, innovative ArtShares and Annual Fellowship Convention. ARTS establishes a safe haven in which to grow, explore, take risks and celebrate the many facets of creativity. Meeting start-up guidelines available. Include self-addressed stamped envelope. Write: ARTS Anonymous, P.O. Box 230175, New York, NY 10023. (For requests outside of NY/NJ/CT area, include $2 with name of nearby cities). For NY/NJ/CT group information, call 212-873-7075 (need a touch tone phone). *Website:* http://www.artsanonymous.org *E-mail:* artseasternregion@yahoo.com

BULLYING

ONLINE

Nineveh *Online. 930 members. Founded 2001.* Lay Christian support group whose mission is to provide support, validation, education and empowerment to individuals who feel they are experiencing bullying, mobbing and scapegoating in work and other organizational environments. *Website:* http://groups.yahoo.com/group/nineveh/

CAREGIVERS / FAMILIES OF NURSING HOME RESIDENTS
(see also Alzheimer's, specific illness, toll-free helplines)

ATLANTIC

AtlantiCare Caregivers Support Group *(Professionally-run)* Support, education and advocacy for caregivers who are caring for family members. Building is handicapped accessible. Meets 2nd Mon., 2-4pm, Bacharach Institute for Rehabilitation, 61 West Jimmie Leeds Rd., Room 210, 2nd floor, Pomona. Pre-registration required. Before attending call 1-888-569-1000 (day). *E-mail:* 1-888-569-1000@atlanticare.org

BERGEN

ARC (Adult Reach Center) *(Professionally-run)* Provides emotional support, information and referrals for caregivers. Guest speakers. Building is handicapped accessible. Meets 2nd Wed., 7:30pm (except Aug.), and 4th Thurs., 11am, JCC on the Palisades, 411 E. Clinton Ave., Tenafly. Call Vivian Green Korner 201-569-7900 ext. 461 (day). *E-mail:* Vkorner@jcconthepalisades.org

Caregiver Support Group *(Professionally-run)* Provides mutual support for people caring for an ill relative (ages 60+). Building is handicapped accessible. Meets Tues., 10-11am, Northwest Senior Center, 46-50 Center St., Midland Park. Call Sheila Brogan 201-447-5695 (Tues. and Wed., 9am-3pm).

Caregivers of the Disabled or Elderly *(Professionally-run)* Mutual support, sharing of coping skills and education for persons who are caregivers of elderly or disabled adults. Meets 1st Wed., 1pm, Day-A-Way, Holy Name Hospital, Community Services Building, 725 Teaneck Rd., Teaneck. Call Maryellen Doran 201-833-3757.

CAMDEN

Promised Partners Support Group *(Professionally-run)* Support for any caregiver focused on their ongoing needs. Rap sessions, guest speakers, literature and mutual sharing. Meets last Tues., 2pm and last Wed., 7pm (except July/Aug.), Promise Adult Day Health Center, 1149 Marlkress Rd., Cherry Hill. Before attending call Kathy Licardo or Erin O'Donnell 856-751-4884 (day).

Senior Care of Voorhees Caregiver Support Group *(Professionally-run)* Offers information and support for families or caregivers of any senior. Lecture series, mutual sharing, education and guest speakers. Meets last Thurs., 6:30-7:30pm, Senior Care at Voorhees, 1000 Voorhees Dr., Voorhees. Call 856-784-4000 (day).

Well Spouse Association, The Support for a spouse or partner who cares for a chronically-ill spouse (MS, Parkinson's, emphysema, diabetes, etc.) to share common feelings and concerns. Building is handicapped accessible. Meets 2nd Thurs., 7:30pm, Kennedy Memorial Hospital, Chapel Ave. and Cooper Landing Rd., Cherry Hill. Call Judy Baumbach 609-654-5618. *E-mail:* jebaumbach@verizon.net

CAPE MAY

Caring for You, Caring for Me *(Professionally-run)* Support for those who provide care for family or friends. Discussion, activities, speakers and refreshments. Building is handicapped accessible. Meets 1st Tues., 1-3pm, Cape Regional Medical Center, Two Stone Harbor Blvd., Maruchi Room, Cape May Courthouse. Call Bonnie Kratzer, RN 609-463-4043 (day).

ESSEX

Caregiver Support Group Mutual support for caregivers. Meets 1st Wed., 10-11am, First Presbyterian Church, 10 Fairview Ave., Verona. Call Erik Spencer 973-239-3561 (day). *E-mail:* firstpresbyterian@att.net

Caregivers Support Group *(Professionally-run)* Mutual support for caregivers. Mutual support for caregivers. Meets 1st Mon., 1pm, Livingston Care One, 76 Passaic Ave., Livingston. Pre-registration required. Before attending call Carol Carlson, PhD 973-627-4087 (day).

Senior Care and Activities Center Support Group *(Professionally-run)* Support, education and training for caregivers. Also various special activities. Meets 1st Mon., 7-9pm, Senior Care and Activities Center, 110 Greenwood

Ave., Montclair. Call Ruth Rothbart-Mayer 973-783-5589 (day). *Website:* http://www.seniorcarecenter.org

GLOUCESTER

Circle of Caring *(Professionally-run)* Promotes the well-being of caregivers through emotional support and information. Families welcome. Phone help, guest speakers and literature. Meets last Fri., 9:30am-noon, Division of Senior Services, 115 Budd Blvd., West Deptford. Call 856-686-8331 (day).

HUNTERDON

Caregivers Support Group *(Professionally-run)* Support for family caregivers of the frail elderly. Call 908-788-6401 ext. 3149.
> **Flemington** Meets 1st Thurs., 1-3pm and 3rd Wed., 7-9pm, Hunterdon Medical Center, 2100 Westcott Drive, 4th Floor Conference Room. Building is handicapped accessible.
> **Clinton** Meets 3rd Thurs., 1-3pm, Hunterdon County Library. 65 Halstead St.

Caregivers Support Group *(Professionally-run)* Support for family caregivers of the frail elderly with dementia. Building is handicapped accessible. Meets 2nd Tues., 1-3pm, Hunterdon County Division of Senior Services, Office on Aging, Route 31 South, Flemington. Call 908-788-6401 ext. 3149.

MERCER

Caregiver Support Group *(Professionally-run)* Support for those caring for an older adult. Any type of care, including Alzheimer's, Parkinson's, stroke, heart, COPD or other illnesses of aging. Building is handicapped accessible. Meets 2nd Mon., 1-2:30pm, Princeton Senior Resource Center, Suzanne Patterson Building (behind Borough Hall), 45 Stockton St., Princeton. Call Susan Hoskins 609-924-7108 (day).

Caregivers Support Group *(Professionally-run) (MERCER COUNTY RESIDENTS ONLY)* Provides support and education for caregivers who are caring for family members or friends with a serious chronic disease. On-going and short term groups. For meeting day, time and location call Barbara Stender 609-396-6788 ext. 241 (day). *E-mail:* bstender@gtbhc.org

Children of Aging Parents *(Professionally-run)* Information, education and peer support for adult children who are caring for aging parents near or far. Literature and guest speakers. Building is handicapped accessible. Meets 2nd Wed., 4:30-6pm, Princeton Senior Resource Center, Suzanne Patterson Building (behind Borough Hall), 45 Stockton St., Princeton. Call Susan Hoskins 609-924-7108 (day).

MIDDLESEX

Caregivers Support Group *(Professionally-run)* Support and education for caregivers of elderly and disabled adults. Building is handicapped accessible. Pre-registration required.

> **Milltown** Meets 4th Wed., 6:30-8pm, Jewish Family and Vocational Service of Middlesex County, 32 Ford Ave. Before attending call 732-777-1940 (day).
> **Monroe** Meets 3rd Tues., 10-11:30am, Jewish Family and Vocational Service of Middlesex County, 52 Concordia Shopping Center, Prospect Plains Rd. Before attending call 609-395-7979 (day).

EARS (Educate, Advocate, Reduce Stress for Caregivers) *(Professionally-run)* Mutual support for caregivers of the elderly. Rap sessions, guest speakers, educational series and phone help. Meets 2nd Wed., 1-3pm, University Behavioral Healthcare, 100 Metroplex Dr., Suite 200, Edison. Call Susan Schwartz 1-866-300-3277 or 732-235-8424 (day).

Spouses Caregiver Support Group *(Professionally-run)* Mutual support for elderly persons caring for a spouse. Building is handicapped accessible. Meets 2nd Thurs., 1:30-3pm, St. Peter's Adult Daycare Center, Pondview Plaza, 200 Overlook Dr., Monroe. Call Stephanie Fitzsimmons 1-800-269-7508 ext. 8662 (day).

Strength For Caring *(Professionally-run)* Provides support and education to families coping with the emotional strain of caring for a loved one with cancer. Offers literature and mutual sharing. Meets 4th Tues., Cancer Institute of NJ, 195 Little Albany St., New Brunswick. Registration required. Call Brenda Bly 732-235-6027.

MONMOUTH

Well Spouse Association Provides peer-to-peer emotional support for spousal caregivers or significant others who care for a chronically ill or disabled spouse. Quarterly newsletter. Dues $25/yr. Meets 2nd Tues., 7pm, Freehold. Call Donna

732-577-8899   or   1-800-838-0879   (Mon.-Fri.,   10am-3pm).   *Website:* http://www.wellspouse.org *E-mail:* info@wellspouse.org

MORRIS

Evening Caregivers Support Group *(Professionally-run)* Provides mutual support, information and education to caregivers of dependent adults. Meets 2nd Wed., 7-9pm, Time Out Adult Care Center, 4 Division Ave., Madison. Call Ellen Brody 973-822-8006 (day). *Website:* http://www.fsmc.org

Well Spouse Support Group *(Professionally-run)* Mutual support and encouragement for wives, husbands and partners of the chronically ill and/or disabled. Building is handicapped accessible. Meets 2nd Mon., 1:30-3pm, Chilton Memorial Hospital, 97 West Parkway, Collins Pavilion, Pompton Plains. Call Elisa DiChristine, LSW 973-831-5311 (day). *E-mail:* elisa_dichristine@chiltonmemorial.org

Your Aging Parent and You *(Professionally-run)* Support and education for those caring for their aging parents. Mutual sharing, education, guest speakers and literature. Fee $15. Building is handicapped accessible. Meets evenings for 5 week sessions, 2 times per year, Chilton Memorial Hospital, 97 West Parkway, Pompton Plains. Call Joan Beloff 973-831-5167 (day). *Website:* http://www.chiltonmemorial.org

OCEAN

Caregiver Support Group Mutual support and encouragement for caregivers of any kind. Provides an opportunity for caregivers to share problems and solutions with others in the same circumstances. Families are welcome. Meets 3rd Tues., 4pm, Sunrise Leisure Village, 1400 Route 70 East, Lakewood. Call Rita Sason 732-363-8010 (Mon.-Thurs.). *E-mail:* jfcs@ocjf.org

Caregiver Support Group *(Professionally-run)* Mutual support for persons who are caring for the elderly or disabled. Literature available. Building is handicapped accessible. Meets 4th Mon., 7pm, Adult Day Care Center, 591 Lakehurst Rd., Toms River. Call Lisa 732-505-9420 (day).

Caregivers Support Group *(Professionally-run)* Mutual support and encouragement for caregivers. Meets 3rd Wed., 10am, Ambassador Medical Day Care, 619 River Ave., Lakewood. Call Rita Sason, LCSW 732-363-8010 (Mon.-Thurs.).

SOMERSET

F.A.R.E. (Friends And Relatives of the Elderly) *(Professionally-run)* Mutual support for emotional and practical concerns facing those taking care of an elderly or chronically disabled adult. Call FARE Hotline 908-766-0180 ext. 241. *Website:* http://www.visitingnurse.org

> **Basking Ridge** Meets 4th Mon., 1:30pm, Somerset Hills Adult Day Center, 200 Mt. Airy Rd. Building is handicapped accessible.
> **Bridgewater** Meets 2nd Wed., 6-7:30pm, Arbor Glen, 100 Monroe St. Bring your own dinner, dessert and drinks provided.

Well Spouse Group Mutual support group for spouses or partners of those with a chronic illness or disability. Rap sessions. Meetings vary, 7:30pm, Warren. Call Mary 908-212-1921 (day).

SUSSEX

Caregiver Support Group *(Professionally-run)* Emotional and social support for caregivers of the elderly. Families welcome. Guest speakers. Building is handicapped accessible. Meets last Tues., 5:30-6:30pm, Sussex County Homestead, 129 Morris Turnpike, Frankford. Call Donna Green 973-948-5400 ext. 3122 (day).

UNION

Caregivers Support Mutual sharing and support for caregivers of the elderly. Meetings vary, Muhlenberg Campus, Adult Day Health Program, Park Ave. and Randolph Rd., Plainfield. Call MRMC Adult Day Health Center 908-668-2328.

Caretakers of the Elderly Support Group Mutual support for people responsible for caring for an elderly family member. Assists through group discussions. Meets 1st Mon., 8pm, St. Helen's Parish Center, 1600 Rahway Ave., Westfield. Call Marilyn Ryan 908-232-1867 (day).

C.O.O.P. (Caregivers Of Older Parents) Mutual support for adult children of elderly persons. Information, sharing, discussions of feelings and problems. Guest speakers and phone help. Meets last Wed., 7pm, Cranford Community Center, Walnut Ave., Cranford. Call 908-276-9206 (day) or Reggi Bleemer 908-272-6731. *E-mail:* regmel@aol.com

Engel Center Support Group *(Professionally-run)* Support group for caregivers of the elderly. Sharing of information and experiences. Building is handicapped accessible. Meets 2nd Wed., noon-1:30pm, 505 South Ave. East, Cranford. Call 908-497-3944 (day).

P.R.E.P. (People Responsible for Elderly Persons) *(Professionally-run)* Mutual support and education for caregivers of elderly people. Building is handicapped accessible. Meets 3rd Wed., 7-9pm, SAGE Eldercare, 290 Broad St., Summit. Call Ellen McNally 908-598-5509 (day). *Website:* http://www.sageeldercare.org *E-mail:* emcnally@sageeldercare.org

NATIONAL

CAPS (Children of Aging Parents) *National. 65 groups. Founded 1977.* Non-profit membership organization dedicated to the needs of caregivers of the elderly. National network of support and offers information, referral and counseling. Write: CAPS, P.O. Box 167, Richboro, PA 18954. Call 1-800-227-7294 or 215-355-6611 *Website:* http://www.CAPS4caregivers.org

ElderCare Rights Alliance *Statewide model. Founded 1972.* Promotes the principles of justice and dignity in the long-term care system through education, advocacy and action. Individual advocacy and advocacy training, crime victim support, community education, family caregiver training, support and training for nursing home Resident and Family Councils education. Write: ElderCare Rights Alliance, 2626 E. 82nd St., Suite 230, Bloomington, MN 55425. Call 1-800-893-4055 or 952-854-7304; Fax: 952-854-8535. *Website:* http://www.eldercarerights.org *E-mail:* mwandersee@eldercarerights.org

National Family Caregivers Association *National. Founded 1992.* Dedicated to improving the quality of life for family caregivers through support and validation, education, information, public awareness and advocacy. Information and referrals, quarterly newsletter, resources and literature. Write: National Family Caregivers Association, 10400 Connecticut Ave., Suite 500, Kensington, MD 20895-3944. Call 1-800-896-3650 or 301-942-6430. *Website:* http://www.thefamilycaregiver.org *E-mail:* info@thefamilycaregiver.org

Well Spouse Association *International. 60+ groups. Founded 1988.* Provides emotional support to spousal caregivers of the chronically ill and/or disabled through support groups, round robins, mentor programs, online chat forum, respite weekends, national conference and a quarterly newsletter. $25/yr but minimum $5 for financial hardship cases. Guidelines and assistance available for starting new groups. Write: Well Spouse Association, 63 West Main St.,

Suite H, Freehold, NJ 07728. Call 1-800-838-0879 or 732-577-8899 (Mon.-Fri., 10am-3pm EST); Fax: 732-577-8644. *Website:* http://www.wellspouse.org *E-mail:* info@wellspouse.org

ONLINE

ElderCare Online *Online. Founded 1997.* Provides daily support for caregivers. Biweekly e-mail newsletter includes articles, news releases, self-care tips, etc. Online chats and message boards covering a broad range of topics. Some chatrooms are run by authors and professionals. Free caregivers book. Offers software for medical planners, taxes, etc. *Website:* http://www.ec-online.net

Family Caregiver Alliance *Online.* Unmoderated listservs for caregivers to share strategies, information, education, support and ideas with each other. Provides free fact sheets and newsletter. Write: Family Caregiver Alliance, 180 Montgomery St., Suite 1100, San Francisco, CA 94104. Call 1-800-445-8106; Fax: 415-434-3508. *Website:* http://www.caregiver.org *E-mail:* info@caregiver.org

CRIME VICTIMS / OFFENDERS
(see also bereavement, spouse abuse, sexual abuse, toll-free helplines)

STATEWIDE

MADD (Mothers Against Drunk Driving) NJ Mission is to stop drunk driving and prevent underage drinking. Offers support for the victims of this violent crime. Has 11 chapter locations in NJ. Call 609-409-1220 (day) or 1-866-623-3165 (24 hr. hotline). Write: MADD NJ, 2008 East Park Blvd., Cranbury, NJ 08512. *Website:* http://www.madd.org/nj

ATLANTIC

Atlantic City Grief Support Group *(Professionally-run)* Mutual support for anyone who has lost a loved one due to natural causes, suicide, homicide or sudden death. Meets 2nd Wed., 6:30-8:30pm, AtlantiCare Healthplex, 1401 Atlantic Ave., Atlantic City. Pre-registration is required. Before attending call AtlantiCare Hospice 609-272-2424 or AtlantiCare Access 1-888-569-1000 (day).

BERGEN

END DWI Support for victims of drunk driving crashes in Bergen/Hudson counties. Aims to prevent drunk driving crashes. Helps victims through the court system. Phone support. Regular membership dues $20yr./individual; $35yr./family; $10yr./senior citizens; free for victims. Meets 1st Thurs., 7pm, Elm Ave., Bogota. Pre-registration required. Call 201-525-5414 (day). *Website:* http://www.enddwi.com

BURLINGTON

Helping Hand Grief Support Group Christian-based support for someone bereaving the loss of a loved one (including death of a child, loss to homicide or suicide) through education, encouragement, counseling and understanding. Families welcome. Meets 1st and 3rd Mon., 7-9pm, Fellowship Alliance Chapel (log house in back of church), 199 Church Rd., Medford. Call Wanda and George Stein 609-953-7333 ext. 309.

ESSEX

Mothers of Murdered Sons and Daughters Support and advocacy for mothers and families of murdered children. Rap sessions and guest speakers. Meets 3rd Sun., 5pm (except Nov. and Dec.), East Orange General Hospital, 300 Central Ave., East Orange. Before attending call Christine Johnson 973-399-5029.

RAP (Reality After Prison) Group *(Professionally-run)* Rap group for ex-offenders to discuss issues relating to re-entry struggles and living healthy lives in the community. Guest speakers and literature. Meets 2nd Wed., 5-7pm, Hyacinth Foundation, Newark. Before attending call 1-800-433-0254 (day).

Survivors of Murdered Children *(Professionally-run)* Mutual support and understanding for families and friends who have lost a loved one to murder. Guest speakers, advocacy, speakers' bureau, social and buddy system. Meets 2nd Fri., 6:30pm, ECHOES, The Grief Center, 116 Main St., Orange. Call Beverly Henderson 973-675-1199.

UNION

Homicide Survivors *(Professionally-run)* Provides support to family members and friends of homicide victims. Rap sessions and guest speakers. Building is handicapped accessible. Meets 3rd Mon., 7-8:30pm (except July/Aug.), Robert Wood Johnson Hospital, Rahway. Call Elaine O'Neal 908-527-4596 (day).

NATIONAL

Cleptomaniacs And Shoplifters Anonymous (CASA) *National. Founded 1992.* Secular 12-step support group for recovering shoplifters, kleptomaniacs and other persons suffering from dishonesty related to fraud, stealing or cheating. Pen pals, information, referrals and phone support. Offers online chat room and e-group. Assistance in starting similar groups. When writing, include self-addressed stamped envelope. Write: CASA, c/o Terry S., P.O. Box 250008, Franklin, MI 48025. Call 248-358-8508. *Website:* http://www.shopliftersanonymous.com/support.htm *E-mail:* info@shopliftersanonymous.com

Molesters Anonymous *Model. Founded 1985.* Provides support with anonymity and confidentiality for men who molest children. Use of "thought stoppage" technique and buddy system. Groups are initiated by a professional but become member-run. Group development manual $9.95. Write: Jerry Goffman, 1040 S. Mt. Vernon Ave., G-306, Colton, CA 92324. Call Jerry Goffman 951-312-1041. *E-mail:* jerrygoffman@hotmail.com

Mothers Against Drunk Driving (MADD) *National. 600+ chapters. Founded 1980.* The mission of MADD is to stop drunk driving, support victims of this violent crime and prevent underage drinking. Write: MADD, 511 E. John Carpenter Freeway, Suite 700, Irving, TX 75062-8187. Call 1-800-438-6233 (general information); 1-877-623-3435 (victim/survivor hotline); Fax: 972-869-2206. *Website:* http://www.madd.org

National Center for Missing Adults (NCMA) *National.* Operates as the national clearinghouse for missing adults, providing services and coordination between various government agencies, law enforcement, media and most importantly - the families of missing adults. Write: National Center for Missing Adults, 4641 North 12th St., Suite 100, Phoenix, AZ 85014. Call 602-749-2000. *Website:* http://www.missingadults.org

National Organization for Victim Assistance *National. 2300 members. Founded 1975.* Support and advocacy for victims and survivors of violent crimes and disasters. Newsletter, information, referrals, phone help, conferences, crisis response training and group development guidelines. Referrals to local self-help groups. Dues $50/indiv.; $200/org. Write: National Organization for Victim Assistance, 510 King St., Suite 424, Alexandria, VA 22314. Call 1-800-879-6682 or 703-535-6682 *Website:* http://www.try-nova.org *E-mail:* nova@try-nova.org

Parents of Murdered Children, Inc. (POMC) *National. 230 chapters in the US, Canada and Costa Rica. Founded 1978.* Provides self-help groups to support persons who survived the violent death of someone close. Newsletter and guidelines for starting local chapters. Court accompaniment also provided in many areas. Parole Block Program and Second Opinion Service also available. Write: Parents of Murdered Children, 100 E. 8th St., Suite 202, Cincinnati, OH 45202. Call 1-888-818-7662 or 513-721-5683 (office) (Mon.-Fri., 8am-5pm EST); Fax: 513-345-4489. *Website:* http://www.pomc.org *E-mail:* natlpomc@aol.com

Remove Intoxicated Drivers (RID) *National. 152 chapters in 41 states. Founded 1978.* Citizens' project organized to advocate against drunk driving, educate the public, reform legislation and aid victims of drunk driving. Newsletter. Chapter information kit ($20). To receive descriptive pamphlet, send self-addressed stamped envelope. Write: Remove Intoxicated Drivers, c/o Doris Aiken, P.O. Box 520, Schenectady, NY 12301. Call 1-888-283-5144 or 518-372-0034; Fax: 518-370-4917. *Website:* http://www.rid-usa.org *E-mail:* dwi@rid-usa.org

Stalking Victims Sanctuary *National. 2582 members.* Mutual-aid support and information for people who have fallen victim to individuals who have obsessively focused on them. Online support group provides the opportunity to share and gain invaluable information from others. Offers resources for identifying stalking, suggestions for dealing with it and regaining control. Write: Stalking Victims Sanctuary, P.O. Box 400, Angels Camp, CA 95222. *Website:* http://www.stalkingvictims.com

ONLINE

Families-of-Inmates *Online. 752 members. Founded 1998.* E-mail list for people with loved ones in jail or prison, who "support each other through the rough times." Offers public and subscribers-only chatrooms. *Website:* http://groups.yahoo.com/group/Families-of-inmates

Prison Talk *Online.* Support for families of inmates. Also offers support to the incarcerated. Offers mutual support, education and advocacy. *Website:* http://www.prisontalk.com/forums/

"People who share a common direction and sense of community can get where they are going quicker and easier because they're traveling on the strength of one another."
-- Great Northern Geese, Lesson One

CULTS

STATEWIDE

Cult Information Service Public education about destructive mind control cults. Mutual support for families and friends of cult members. Helps cult members return to society. Write: Cult Information Service, P.O. Box 867, Teaneck, NJ 07666. Call 201-833-1212 (day) or 201-833-0817.

NATIONAL

reFOCUS (recovering FOrmer CUltists Support) *National network. Founded 1984.* Support for former members of closed, high demand groups, relationships or cults. Referrals to other former cult members by group and/or area, support groups, therapists and services. Literature, free internet newsletter, recovery workshops and conferences. Write: reFOCUS, P.O. Box 2180, Flagler Beach, FL 32136. Call 386-439-7541; Fax: 386-439-7537. *Website:* http://www.refocus.org *E-mail:* refocuscarol@att.net

DEBT AND FAMILY FINANCES

ESSEX

Economic Downturn Support Group *(Professionally-run)* Support for those who are suffering from the loss of a job, fear of losing a job, struggling to pay bills and surviving during these difficult times. Meets Wed., 12:30pm, University of Medicine and Dentistry of New Jersey, University Behavioral HealthCare, 183 South Orange Ave., Newark. Call 1-800-969-5300 (day).

MIDDLESEX

Economic Downturn Support Group *(Professionally-run)* Support for those who are suffering from the loss of a job, fear of losing a job, struggling to pay bills and surviving during these difficult times. Call 1-800-969-5300 (day).

> **Edison** Meets Thurs., 3pm, University of Medicine and Dentistry of New Jersey, University Behavioral HealthCare, 100 Metroplex Dr., 2nd Floor, Suite 200.
> **Monmouth Junction** Meets Tues., noon, University of Medicine and Dentistry of New Jersey, University Behavioral HealthCare, 4326 US Highway 1.

New Brunswick Meets Wed., 3pm, University of Medicine and Dentistry of New Jersey, University Behavioral HealthCare, 303 George St., 2nd Floor.

UNION

Economic Downturn Support Group *(Professionally-run)* Support for those struggling with issues related to paying their bills and surviving during these difficult times. Group examines ways to cope and learn from each other.

> **Cranford** Meets Wed., 7-8pm, Family Resource Center, 300 North Ave. East. Call 908-276-2244.
> **Elizabeth** Meets Mon., 11am-noon, Trinitas Hospital, 654 E. Jersey St., Plaza Building, Elizabeth. Call Monica 908-994-7559.

EMPLOYMENT / RETIREMENT
(see also toll-free helplines, women)

BERGEN

Employment Peer Support Provides support to those that are unemployed. Meets last Mon., 8pm (except holidays), Church of the Presentation, 271 West Saddle River Rd., Library, Upper Saddle River. Call 201-327-1313.

Job Support Group *(Professionally-run)* Exchange of job hunting experience, "hands-on" skills of resume development, networking, interviewing and prayer support. Meets Thurs., 7:30-9pm, 228 Vittorio Court, Park Ridge. Call Bob Miller 201-391-0657. *E-mail:* RJJMiller@optonline.net

Professional Service Group *(Professionally-run)* Mutual support to help unemployed and underemployed professional-level job seekers develop leads, learn effective job search techniques and network. Meets various times, NJ State Employment Service, 60 State St., Hackensack. Call Bruce Lauber 201-329-9600 ext. 5755 (day). *Website:* http://wnjpin.net

ESSEX

Job Seekers of Montclair Mutual support and education for people seeking a new job or in career transition. Meets Wed., 7:30-9:15pm, St. Luke's Church, 73 South Fullerton Ave., Montclair. Call 973-783-3442 (leave message). *Website:* http://www.jobseekersofmontclair.org

HUDSON

Women's Project Groups *(Professionally-run)* Support, education, workshops and groups to help women on subjects such as self-esteem, separation/divorce, domestic violence, employment and stress management. Meetings vary, Christ Hospital, 176 Palisade Ave., Jersey City. Before attending call Michele Bernstein 201-795-8375 ext. 8416 (day).

MERCER

Jobseekers Education, support and networking for unemployed people and those who are changing jobs or careers. Meets Tues., 7:30pm, Trinity Church, 33 Mercer St., Princeton. Call 609-924-2277 (day). *Website:* http://www.trinityprinceton.org (click on "Job Seekers")

SOMERSET

JANUS Bereavement Group *(Professionally-run)* Support and education for anyone who has experienced a loss such as a loss of a job, retirement, relocation, separation/divorce or death. Helps individuals accept and adjust to the loss. Building is handicapped accessible. Meets 2nd Tues., 7:30-9pm, Bridgewater and Raritan. Call Barbara Ronca, LCSW, PhD 908-218-9062 (Mon.-Fri., 9am-3pm).

Jobseekers *(Professionally-run)* Mutual support and encouragement for persons who are unemployed, underemployed or seeking a career change. Guest speakers and literature. Building is handicapped accessible. Meets monthly, 7-9pm, Jewish Family Service, 150A West High St., Somerville. Call Elise Prezant 908-725-7799 (day). *Website:* http://www.jewishfamilysvc.org *E-mail:* elise.prezant@verizon.net

Somerset Hills YMCA - Career Forum Mutual support for individuals seeking a career/job change or early retirement. For those who are underemployed or unemployed. Building is handicapped accessible. Meets Tues., 7:30pm, Somerset Hills YMCA, 140 Mt. Airy Rd., Basking Ridge. Call 908-766-7898 (day).

NATIONAL

9 to 5, National Association of Working Women *(BILINGUAL) National. 24 chapters. Founded 1973.* Support, advocacy and legislative assistance on issues that affect women who work. Job problem counselors can advise women on how to make changes on their jobs. Dues $25/yr. Phone support, conferences, newsletters and referrals to local groups. Group development guidelines. Write: 9 to 5, 501 Pulliam St., Suite 344, Atlanta, GA 30312. Call 1-800-522-0925; Fax: 404-222-0006. *Website:* http://www.9to5.org *E-mail:* 9to5@9to5.org

Business and Professional Women/USA *National. 1300 chapters. Founded 1919.* Organization comprised of working women, who promote workplace equity and provide networking opportunities. Lobbying efforts, tri-annual magazine, periodic publications, resource center and grassroots community action projects. Annual national convention. Local group information available online. Write: Business and Professional Women/USA, 1900 M St. NW, Suite 310, Washington, DC 20036. Call 202-293-1100; Fax: 202-861-0298. *Website:* http://www.bpwusa.org *E-mail:* memberservices@bpwusa.org

Quintessential Careers *Online resource.* Website includes "For Networking and Support, Join or Start a Job Club" article which provides helpful information and links for job seekers - including links which provide information on local job support groups, accessible by state. If no local support group exists, the article offers practical suggestions on how anyone can join with others to start and run their own job club self-help support group.

FOOD BORNE INFECTIOUS DISEASES

ONLINE

S.T.O.P. (Safe Tables Our Priority) *Online. Founded 1993.* Offers support, education and advocacy for victims and the family of victims of food borne infectious diseases (E.coli, Salmonella, Listeria, Shigella, Vibrio and many others). Phone and online networking, newsletter and annual meeting. Call 1-800-350-7867 (helpline) or 301-585-7867; *Website:* http://www.safetables.org *E-mail:* mail@safetables.org

"Always remember, there is more strength in you than you ever realized or even imagined. Certainly nothing can keep you down if you are determined to get on top of things and stay there"--Norman Vincent Peale

HOLOCAUST SURVIVORS

BERGEN

Second Generation: Children of Holocaust Survivors Support for children of survivors to discuss and share common experiences. New topic focus every month, discussion and occasional guest speaker. Building is handicapped accessible. Meets 2nd or 3rd Thurs., 7-8:30pm, Jewish Family Service, 1485 Teaneck Rd., Teaneck. Before attending call Amy Bolton 201-837-9090 (day). *E-mail:* thelivingroom@jfsbergen.org

HOLISTIC HEALTH

BERGEN

Nutrition and Chronic Illness Support Group *(Professionally-run)* Mutual support and education for persons with any type of chronic illness who are interested in healthy lifestyles. Topics include nutrition, healthy living, eating correctly, etc. Meets 3rd Thurs., 7-8:30pm, Community Seventh Day Adventist Church, 245 Tenafly Rd., Englewood. Call Claudine 201-724-4852.

HOUSING

STATEWIDE

New Jersey Tenants Organization Works for pro-tenant state legislation. Helps organize local tenants associations. Gives legal guidance to members and fights for tenants rights, including in the event of foreclosure. Membership dues $22/individual; different for groups. Membership meeting once a year in alternating towns. Call 201-342-3775 (day). *Website:* http://www.njto.org *E-mail:* info@njto.org

UNION

Economic Downturn Support Group *(Professionally-run)* Support for those struggling with issues related to paying their bills and surviving during these difficult times. Group examines ways to cope and learn from each other.
> **Cranford** Meets Wed., 7-8pm, Family Resource Center, 300 North Ave. East. Call 908-276-2244.
> **Elizabeth** Meets Mon., 11am-noon, Trinitas Hospital, 654 E. Jersey St., Plaza Building, Elizabeth. Call Monica 908-994-7559

LIGHTNING / SHOCK SURVIVORS

NATIONAL

Lightning Strike and Electric Shock Survivors International, Inc. *International network. Founded 1989.* Mutual support for survivors of lightning or electric shock, their families and families of non-survivors. Studies the long-term after-effects. Phone support, annual conferences, help in starting a support group, newsletter, information and referrals. Books and tapes available. Write: Lightning Strike and Electric Shock Survivors International, Inc., P.O. Box 1156, Jacksonville, NC 28541-1156. Call Steve 910-346-4708; Fax: 910-346-4708. *Website:* http://www.lightning-strike.org *E-mail:* smarshburnsr@yahoo.com or info@lightning-strike.org

ONLINE

Lightning Strike Survivor List *Online. Founded 1999.* An on-line e-mail support group whose members have been affected by a lightning strike. Group members include survivors, family members of survivors, caregivers, doctors and others who want or need a way to share with people who can understand because they have been there. *Website:* http://health.groups.yahoo.com/group/lightningstrike/

MEN'S ISSUES
(see also separation/divorce)

MIDDLESEX

Men's Group Offers mutual support for men. Opportunity for men to discuss issues that are important in their lives. Meets twice a month in various members' homes in Southern Middlesex County. Call Frank Foulkes 609-655-0059 (eve).

MORRIS

Men-To-Men Mutual support for men in transition. Topics include divorce, anger, parenting, health, aging, relationships, etc. Offers networking, phone support and guest speakers. Donation $10 per meeting. Meets Wed., Xavier Center, College of St. Elizabeth, Convent Station. Before attending call Richard Oates 201-501-8442 or Brad Nelson 973-993-8628. *Website:* http://www.men-to-men.themenscenter.com

SOMERSET

Men Mentoring Men A men's center dedicated to the sharing of a man's unique experience in a complex world through organizing and facilitating peer led men's discussion groups. Literature. Suggested donation $15/mtg. Meets twice a month, 7:30pm, 125 West End Ave., Somerville. Call Richard Horowitz or Jerry Zipkin 908-707-0774. *Website:* http://www.menmentoringmen.org *E-mail:* questions@mthree.org

NATIONAL

NORM (National Organization of Restoring Men) *International. 20 affiliated groups. Founded 1989.* (meetings for MEN ONLY; information for all) Provides a safe environment in which men can, without fear of being ridiculed, share their concerns about circumcision/restoration and their desire to be intact and whole again. Confidential discussions of goals and methods of foreskin restoration. Information and referrals, phone support, assistance in starting new groups. Write: NORM, c/o R. Wayne Griffiths, 3205 Northwood Dr., #209, Concord, CA 94520-4506. Call 925-827-4077 (eve). *Website:* http://www.norm.org *E-mail:* waynerobb@aol.com

ONLINE

Menstuff *Online Resource. Founded 1982.* Provides information on variety of local men's support groups in USA, Canada and a few other countries. Provides references for guides to starting a group, other resources and links. *Website:* http://www.menstuff.org (Click on "Groups" within menu list on left side. Then click on "Men's Groups - Peer Led") *E-mail:* gordonclay@aol.com

MESSINESS

BERGEN

Clutterers Anonymous 12-Step. Support for persons who have a problem with clutter. Opportunity to share experience, strength and hope with one another in the hope of solving this common problem and helping each other to recover. Building is handicapped accessible. Meets Mon., 7:30pm, St. Mark's Episcopal Church, 118 Chadwick Rd. (side entrance on Grange St.), Room 3, Teaneck. Call Laraine 201-836-5149.

BURLINGTON

Clutterers Anonymous 12-Step. Support for persons who have a problem with clutter. Opportunity to share experience, strength and hope with one another in the hope of solving this common problem and helping each other to recover. Building is handicapped accessible. Meets 1st and 3rd Tues., 7pm, Virtua Hospital, Route 73 and Brick Rd., Howe Room, Marlton. Call Bobbi 609-654-9603 (day).

ESSEX

Clutterers Anonymous 12-step. Support to help overcome compulsive saving, pack ratting, procrastination and cluttering. Donation. Meets Mon., 7:30pm, 58 Dodd St., Bloomfield. Call Aloma 973-748-0423 (day).

MIDDLESEX

Clutterers Anonymous 12-Step. Support for persons who have a problem with clutter. Opportunity to share experience, strength and hope with one another in the hope of solving this common problem and helping each other to recover. Meets Sun., 5pm, St. Luke's Episcopal Church, Middlesex Ave. and Oak Ave., Parish Hall, Metuchen. Call church 732-548-4309.

UNION

Clutter Club *(Professionally-run)* Mutual support for persons who have a problem with clutter. Rap sessions, literature, phone help, newsletter and buddy system. Building is handicapped accessible. Meetings vary, 7:30-9pm, Barnes and Noble, Raritan Rd., Clark. Call Jamie 1-866-294-9900. *E-mail:* jamie@jamienovak.com

NATIONAL

Clutterers Anonymous *National. 59 affiliated chapters.* 12-Step. 12-Traditions. Fellowship of individuals who share experience, strength and hope with each other that they may solve their common problem with clutter and help others recover. Based on suggestion, interchange of experience, rotation of leadership and service. The only requirement for membership is a desire to eliminate clutter and bring order into your life. Call 1-866-800-3881 or 908-875-3881. *E-mail:* cla@clutterfreeworld.net

Clutterless Recovery Groups, Inc. *National. 4 affiliated groups. Founded 2000.* Support for those persons that find it difficult to discard unwanted possessions. Group uses psychological principles to change behavior. Provides newsletter, referrals and group meeting locations. Also offers online networking. Offers information on starting similar groups. Write: Clutterless, 5413 N. 32nd St., McAllen, TX 78504. Call 512-351-4058. *Website:* http://www.clutterless.org

Messies Anonymous *(MULTILINGUAL) National. 100 groups. Founded 1981.* 12-Step. Group aims to improve the quality of life of disorganized homemakers. Provides motivation and a program for change to help members improve self-image as control of house and life is obtained. Optional donation at meetings. Online newsletter: "The Organizer Lady." Interactive online group. Books and materials available in English, German and Spanish. Send a self-addressed stamped envelope when writing. Write: Messies Anonymous, 5025 SW 114th Ave., Miami, FL 33165. Call Sandra 305-271-8404; Fax and automated order line: 786-243-2793. *Website:* http://www.messies.com *E-mail:* nestbuilder@earthlink.net

NEAR DEATH EXPERIENCE

NATIONAL

International Association for Near-Death Studies *International. 43 affiliated groups. Founded 1981.* Support and interest groups for anyone who has had a near-death or near-death-like experience or who has personal or professional interest in such experiences. Newsletter, group development guidelines. Write: International Association for Near-Death Studies, 2741 Campus Walk Ave., Bldg. 500, Durham, NC 27705. Call 919-383-7940 (voice/fax). *Website:* http://www.iands.org

NETWORKING FOR ILL / DISABLED
(see also disabilities, specific disorder)

NATIONAL

MUMS National Parent-to-Parent Network *National. 36 affiliated groups. Founded 1979.* Mutual support and networking for parents or care providers of children with any disability, rare disorder, chromosomal abnormality or health conditions using a database of over 23,000 families from 54 countries, covering 3500 disorders, very rare syndromes or undiagnosed conditions. Provides referrals to support groups and assistance in starting groups. Newsletter ($15/parents; $25/professionals). Matching services $5. Hyperbaric Oxygen Therapy as a Treatment For Brain Damage packet, $25 USA/$35 other countries. Various literature available. Write: MUMS National Parent-to-Parent Network, 150 Custer Court, Green Bay, WI 54301-1243. Call 1-877-336-5333 (parents only) or 920-336-5333 (day); Fax: 920-339-0995. *Website:* http://www.netnet.net/mums *E-mail:* mums@netnet.net

PATIENTS' RIGHTS

NATIONAL

New England Patients' Rights Group *Model. Founded 1992.* Mutual support for health care consumers, many of whom are suffering because of deficiencies or negligence in the system. Advocates for consumer empowerment, quality, accurate information, informed consent, insurance needs, patients' rights and protection. Newsletter. Write: New England Patients Rights Group, P.O. Box 141, Norwood, MA 02062. Call 781-769-5720. *Website:* http://www.newenglandpatientsrights.org *E-mail*: neprg@verizon.net

POLICE OFFICERS

ESSEX

Wounded Officers Support Group of NJ *(Professionally-run)* Provides support to officers who were wounded in the line of duty. Guest speakers and buddy system. Meets 3rd Wed., 9:30-11:30am, Fraternal Order of Police Building, 51 Rector St., Lodge #12, Newark. Call Fred Mitchell 1-866-267-2267 (day).

PREJUDICE

NATIONAL

Recovering Racists Network *National. Groups in CA, MO and MI. Founded 1997.* Mutual support to help people overcome their everyday racism and prejudice. Newsletter, literature, phone support, conferences, advocacy, anti-racism training, high school Race Awareness Program, online support, information and referral. Assistance in helping others to start similar groups. Write: Recovering Racists Network, c/o John McKenzie, 34628 Hood Canal Dr.

NE, Kingston, WA 98346. Call 360-881-0274. *Website:* http://www.rrnet.org *E-mail:* john@jmckenzie.com

PROSTITUTION / SEX INDUSTRY

NATIONAL

PRIDE (PRostitution to Independence, Dignity and Equality) *Model. One group in Minnesota. Founded 1978.* Provides PRIDE support groups and other services to assist women and children in escaping the sex industry (including prostitution, pornography and stripping). Write: PRIDE, c/o Family and Children Service, 4123 E. Lake St., Minneapolis, MN 55406. Call 612-728-2080. *Website:* http://www.everyfamilymatters.org/pride/

SELF-ABUSE / SELF-MUTILATION

MORRIS

Beyond Bandages Support group for those who cut, burn or harm their body as a way of coping with overwhelming emotions, thoughts and circumstances. Purpose is to realize that a life can be lived without self-injurious behavior. Guest speakers, discussions and literature. Meets 1st and 3rd Fri., 8-9:30pm, Living Praise Church, 37 Vreeland Rd., Room 205 (Launching Point - upper level of church), Florham Park. Call Vicki Duffy 973-224-4144. *Website:* http://www.launchingpoint.org *E-mail:* info@launchingpoint.org

NATIONAL

Self-Mutilators Anonymous (SMA) *National. 18 affiliated groups.* 12-step fellowship of men and women who share their experience, strength and hope with each other, that they may solve their common problem and help others recover from physical self-mutilation. Information resources. Online self-help group meetings available. *Website:* http://www.selfmutilatorsanonymous.org

ONLINE

Secret Shame: Self-Injury Information and Support *Online.* Offers web board and separate e-mail lists for self-injurers, their family and friends. (e-mail lists are named BUS for "bodies under siege" and are located in the left hand column). Extensive information resource on self-injury and self-abuse.

Resources for how to deal with self-abuse and the self-abuse of family members or friends. *Website:* http://www.selfharm.net

SEPTEMBER 11TH
(see also bereavement, crime victims)

STATEWIDE

WTC United Family Group, Inc. Support for families who lost a loved one in the World Trade Center attacks and for WTC survivors. Online e-mail groups for both. Families and survivors can register online or write: WTC United Family Group, Inc., 321 Mantoloking Rd., Suite 2B, Brick, NJ 08723. Call 732-262-9600. *Website:* http://www.wtcufg.org

BERGEN

WTC Bereavement Support Group *(Professionally-run)* Provides emotional support for working through the mourning process of those directly affected by the WTC disaster. Open to anyone affected. Guest speakers, mutual sharing, phone help and literature. Meets Fri., 7-9pm, Pastoral Center, 2nd Floor, Conference Room, St. Catherine's Church, 905 South Maple Ave., Glen Rock. Call Deborah Van Alstine, MA 201-444-4915 (eve). *Website:* http://mysite.verizon.net/vze8lw19/ *E-mail:* debvanalstine@optonline.net

MERCER

Sept. 11th Family Support Group Mutual support for adults who lost a family member in the September 11th attacks. Meetings vary, Princeton Junction. Call Carol 609-259-3455.

OCEAN

World Trade Center Disaster Victims Support Group Offers support to help focus on the grief process, recovery skills and how recovery is impacted by being a victim of terrorism. Building is handicapped accessible. Meetings vary, St. Francis Center, 4700 Long Beach Blvd., Brant Beach. Registration required. Call Sue Crane 609-494-1554.

> *"We are all dependent on one another, every soul of us on earth."*
> *-- George Bernard Shaw*

NATIONAL

Concerns of Police Survivors, Inc. (COPS) *National. 48 chapters. Founded 1984.* Provides resources for the surviving families of law enforcement officers killed in the line of duty according to federal criteria. Also offers law enforcement training. Quarterly newsletter, departmental guidelines and peer support. Provides annual National Police Survivors' Conference each May during National Police Week. Special hands-on programs for survivors. Summer camp for children (ages 6-14) and their parent/guardian, parents' retreats, spouse get-aways, Outward Bound experiences for young adults (ages 15-20), sibling retreat and adult children retreat. Write: COPS, P.O. Box 3199, South State Highway 5, Camdenton, MO 65020. Call 573-346-4911; Fax: 573-346-1414. *Website:* http://www.nationalcops.org *E-mail:* cops@nationalcops.org

Wings of Light, Inc. *National. 3 support networks. Founded 1995.* Support and information network for individuals whose lives have been touched by aviation accidents. Separate networks for airplane accident survivors, families and friends of persons killed in airplane accidents and persons involved in the rescue, recovery and investigation of crashes. Information, referrals and phone support. Write: Wings of Light, P.O. Box 1097, Sun City, AZ 85372. Call 623-516-1115. *Website:* http://www.wingsoflight.org

ONLINE

Gift From Within *Online. (WOMEN ONLY)* Offers a one-on-one e-mail/pen pal support network for women who are experiencing post-traumatic stress disorder. Female victims of specific trauma can be matched with survivors of similar PTSD. Audio-visual resources available. *Website:* http://www.giftfromwithin.org *E-mail:* Joyceb3955@aol.com

SEXUAL ORIENTATION / GENDER IDENTITY
(see also toll-free helplines)

STATEWIDE

Gay and Lesbian Political Action and Support Group Provides opportunity for individuals in isolated areas to be politically active and establish support groups where they are needed. Write: GLPASC, P.O. Box 11406, New Brunswick, NJ 08906-1406. For information call 732-744-1370 (day). *Website:* http://www.gaypasg.org

Rainbow Families of New Jersey Provides support, advocacy and education for gay and lesbian parents, their families and prospective parents. Social activities and quarterly newsletter. Membership dues $35/yr. Write: Rainbow Families of NJ, P.O. Box 1385, Maplewood, NJ 07040. For further information call 973-763-8511. *Website:* http://www.rainbowfamiliesofnj.org *E-mail:* info@rainbowfamiliesnj.org

BERGEN

PFLAG (Parents, Families and Friends of Lesbians and Gays) Support and discussion groups to help people understand and accept homosexuality. Educates society and advocates for full human rights for all, regardless of sexual orientation. Speakers, newsletter and phone help. Membership dues $40/yr. (includes monthly newsletter). All welcome. Building is handicapped accessible. Meets 3rd Tues., 8pm (7:30pm newcomers), Washington Twp. Call 201-287-0318 (eve). *Website:* http://www.bergenpflag.org *E-mail:* info@bergenpflag.org

BURLINGTON

Straight Spouse Support Network Supports anyone whose current or former partner/spouse is gay, lesbian, transgender or bisexual. Meets 3rd Fri., 7:30pm, Mt. Laurel. For meeting information call Mary 856-751-0337. *Website:* http://www.straightspouse.org

CAMDEN

Keeping It Safe Support for gay, lesbian, bisexual, transgender and questioning individuals under the age of 20 to discuss social, educational, health and sexuality issues in a relaxed environment. Building is handicapped accessible. Meets Mon., 4-7pm, Camden Area Health Education Center, 514 Cooper St., Camden. Call William Gray or Jonathan Ruberte 856-963-2432 (day). *Website:* http://www.camden-ahec.org

Pink and Blues Peer Support Group Support group for lesbian, gay, bisexual and transgender people living with a mental illness. Building is handicapped accessible. Meets Wed., 7pm, St. Luke's and the Epiphany Church, 330 S. 13th St., Philadelphia, PA. Call Mark Davis 215-627-0424 (eve.). *E-mail:* madpride1988@yahoo.com

Need help finding a specific group? Give us a call – we're here to help!
Call 1-800-367-6274.

CAPE MAY

GABLES of Cape May County Provides support to gays, lesbians and bisexuals, as well as their family and friends. Rap sessions, guest speakers, Rainbow directory and newsletter. Dues $20/yr. Building is handicapped accessible. Meets 1st and 3rd Mon., Cape May. Call 609-861-1848 (answer machine). *Website:* http://www.gablescapemay.com *E-mail:* gables00@email.com

ESSEX

Dignity Organization of lesbian, gay and bisexual Catholics, their family and friends. Socials and rap sessions. Building is handicapped accessible. Meets 1st and 3rd Sun., 4pm, St. George's Episcopal Church, 550 Ridgewood Rd., Maplewood. Call 973-857-4040 (day). *E-mail:* dignitymetronj@msn.com

P-FLAG (Parents, Families and Friends of Lesbians and Gays) Support and discussion groups to help people understand and accept homosexuality. Educates society and advocates for full human rights for all, regardless of sexual orientation. Speakers, newsletter and phone help. All welcome. Membership dues $25/yr./individual; $35/yr./family. Meets 2nd Sun., 2:30-4:30pm (newcomers 1:30pm), First Presbyterian and Trinity Church, 111 Irvington Ave., South Orange. Call P-FLAG hotline 973-267-8414. *Website:* http://www.pflagnorthjersey.org

HUDSON

GLITZ (Girls Living In the Transgender Zone) Peer support for women dealing with transgender issues. Rap sessions, guest speakers, literature and phone help. Meets Tues. and Thurs., 6-9pm, Hudson Pride Connections, Pride Connections Center of New Jersey, 32 Jones St., Jersey City. Call Nancy Caamano 201-963-4779 ext. 111 (day).

Youth Connect *(Professionally-run)* Support groups and drop-in hours for lesbian, gay, bisexual, transsexual and questioning youth. Guest speakers, social activities, mutual support, rap sessions and literature. Online e-mail discussion group. Meets Tues., Wed. and Thurs., 3-5pm; Fri. and Sat., 3-8pm, Hudson Pride Connections, Pride Connections Center of New Jersey, 32 Jones St., Jersey City. Call Nancy Caamano 201-963-4779 ext. 111(day). *Website:* http://www.hudsonpride.org

MERCER

"First and Third" *(Professionally-run)* Educational and social support for gay, lesbian, bisexual, and transgender youth. Rap sessions, phone help, guest speakers and mutual sharing. Building is handicapped accessible. Meets 1st and 3rd Sat., 2:30-4:30pm, 21 Wiggins St., Princeton. Call Corrine 609-683-5155 ext. 217 (day). *Website:* http://www.hitops.org *E-mail:* corrine@hitops.org

MIDDLESEX

Gay Dad's Group Mutual support and discussion group for gay dads. Discussions range from how to raise kids as a gay dad, how to come out to your kids and how to deal with your spouse or ex-spouse in relation to your kids. Meets 1st and 3rd Wed., 7:30-9pm, The Pride Center, 321 Raritan Ave., Highland Park. Call Joel 908-507-2204. *E-mail:* explorejoel@yahoo.com

Men's Coming Out Rap Group Assists men dealing with issues pertaining to coming out. Dues $2. Meets Wed., 7:30-9pm, The Pride Center, 321 Raritan Ave., Highland Park. Call Gary P. 732-846-2232 (day). *Website:* http://www.pridecenter.org *E-mail:* info@pridecenter.org

Orthodykes - NJ *(Professionally-run)* Mutual support for Orthodox Jewish lesbians as they attempt to integrate these two identities. Rap sessions and newsletter. Dues $3. Meets 3rd Sun., 7:30-8:30pm, North Brunswick. Call Elissa 732-650-1010. *E-mail:* info@njhav.org

OWLs (Older Wilder Lesbians) Group of mature lesbians who meet for support and socialization. Meets 3rd Fri., 7:30pm, The Pride Center, 321 Raritan Ave., Highland Park. Call 732-846-2232 (day). *Website:* http://www.pridecenter.org *E-mail:* info@pridecenter.org

Youth Drop-In Center Support and socials for lesbian, gay, bisexual, transgendered, intersexed and questioning youth (ages 17 and under) and their allies. Meets 2nd and 4th Sat., 1pm, The Pride Center, 321 Raritan Ave., Highland Park. Call 732-846-2232 (day). *Website:* http://www.pridecenter.org *E-mail:* info@pridecenter.org

MORRIS

Gay Activist Alliance in Morris County Educates the lesbian and gay community through speakers and programs, socials and political involvement. Monthly newsletter and speakers' bureau. Publishes resource book. Membership $40/yr. Dues $4/member; $6/non-member. Meets Mon., 7pm, Morristown

Unitarian Fellowship, 21 Normandy Heights Rd., Morristown. *Website:* http://www.gaamc.org *E-mail:* info@gaamc.org

Transgender (Female to Male) Support *(Professionally-run)* Support for transgenders, crossdressers, those with gender identity disorder and those questioning their gender identity. Building is handicapped accessible. Meets 2nd Sat., 2:30pm, (Jan., Mar., May, July, Sept. and Nov.), Colonial Professional Park, 1390 Valley Rd., Suite 1E, Stirling. Call Lisa O'Connor, MD, Maureen McGuire or Carly 908-647-1688 (day). *Website:* http://www.healthytransitions.md *E-mail:* DrLisa@healthytransitions.md

Transgender (Male to Female) Support *(Professionally-run)* Support for transgenders, crossdressers, those with gender identity disorder and those questioning their gender identity. Building is handicapped accessible. Meets 2nd Sat., 2:30pm (Feb., Apr., June, Aug., Oct. and Dec.), Colonial Professional Park, 1390 Valley Rd., Suite 1E, Stirling. Call Lisa O'Connor, MD, Maureen McGuire or Carly 908-647-1688 (day). *Website:* http://www.healthytransitions.md *E-mail:* DrLisa@healthytransitions.md

OCEAN

PFLAG (Parents, Families, and Friends of Lesbians and Gays) Jersey Shore Chapter Support and discussion group to help people understand and accept variance in sexual orientation and gender identity. Educates and advocates for full human rights for all, including sexual minorities. Speakers, literature and phone help. All welcome. Meets 2nd Wed., 7-9pm, United Church of Christ, 1681 Ridgeway Rd. (Route 571), Toms River. Call 908-814-2155 (day). *Website:* http://www.jerseyshorepflag.org or http://www.tomsriverucc.org/directions.htm (for directions) *E-mail:* jerseyshorepflag@yahoo.com

NATIONAL

COLAGE (Children Of Lesbians And Gays Everywhere) *International. 40 affiliated groups. Founded 1990.* Mission of COLAGE is to connect and empower people to make the world better for children of lesbian, gay, bisexual and transgender parents. Information and referrals, conferences, pen pals, literature and newsletter. Various online programs. Write: COLAGE, 1550 Bryant St., Suite 830, San Francisco, CA 94103. Call 415-861-5437; Fax: 415-255-8345. *Website:* http://www.colage.org *E-mail:* colage@colage.org

COURAGE *International. Over 95 groups. Founded 1980.* Provides spiritual support and fellowship for men and women with same-sex attractions who are striving to live chaste lives in accordance with the Roman Catholic Church's teachings. The companion group, EnCourage, is for families and friends of persons with same-sex attractions. Newsletter, phone help, conferences and assistance in starting groups. Write: COURAGE, c/o St. John the Baptist, 210 W. 31st St., New York, NY 10001. Call 212-268-1010. *Website:* http://www.couragerc.net *E-mail:* NYCourage@aol.com

Dignity/USA *National. 50 chapters. Founded 1969.* Organization of gay, lesbian, bisexual and transgendered Catholics, their families and friends. Concerned with spiritual development, feminism, education and advocacy. Newsletter and chapter development guidelines. Write: Dignity/USA, P.O. Box 15373, Washington, DC 20003. Call 1-800-877-8797. *Website:* http://www.dignityusa.org *E-mail:* info@dignityusa.org

Family Equality Council *National. 160+ local groups. Founded 1979.* Support, education and advocacy for gay, lesbian or transgendered parents, prospective parents and their families. Information and referrals, phone support, family events, literature and newsletter. Assistance in starting groups. Write: Family Equality Council, P.O. Box 206, Boston, MA 02133. Call 617-502-8700; Fax: 617-502-8701. *Website:* http://www.familyequality.org *E-mail:* info@familyequality.org

Homosexuals Anonymous *National. 40 chapters. Founded 1980.* Christian fellowship of men and women who have chosen to help each other to live free from homosexuality. Group support through weekly meetings. Online groups. Newsletter and chapter manual. Write: Homosexuals Anonymous, P.O. Box 7881, Reading, PA 19603. Call 610-779-2500.

International Foundation for Gender Education *International. Founded 1978.* Support and educational services for and about gender variant persons (including transsexuals, cross-dressers, intersex, androgynes, non-gendered and multi-gendered persons). Services include referrals to local support groups and to medical and psychological professionals. Speakers program, publication of "Transgender Tapestry" magazine, Synchronicity Bookstore and national outreach. Write: International Foundation for Gender Education, P.O. Box 540229, Waltham, MA 02454-0229. Call 781-899-2212; Fax: 781-899-5703. *Website:* http://www.ifge.org *E-mail:* info@ifge.org

Mautner Project, The National Lesbian Health Organization *Model. Several groups in Washington, DC. Founded 1990.* Cancer support and survivorship groups for lesbian, bisexual and transgender women who partner with women (WPWs), their partners and caregivers. Bereavement support groups for WPWs who have lost a partner, friend or loved one. Smoking cessation groups for the lesbian, gay, bisexual and transgender community. Health self-empowerment groups for black WPWs. Provides phone and online support to WPWs outside the DC-Metro area. Provides LGBT cultural competency training to health care professionals and their staff members. Educates the lesbian/WPW community about health issues. Information and referrals, phone support, literature, newsletter, advocacy. Write: Mautner Project, 1875 Conn. Ave. NW, Suite 710, Washington, DC 20009. Call 1-866-628-8637 or 202-332-5536 (Mon-Fri, 9am-5:30pm EST); Fax: 202-332-0662; TDD: 202-332-5536. *Website:* http://www.mautnerproject.org *E-mail:* mautner@mautnerproject.org

National Gay and Lesbian Task Force *National. Founded 1973.* Advocates and organizes for the rights of gay, lesbian, bisexual and transgendered people. Technical assistance for state and local organizers. Publications, materials and newsletter. Write: National Gay and Lesbian Task Force, 1325 Massachusetts Ave., NW, Suite 600, Washington, DC 20005. Call 202-393-5177; Fax: 202-393-2241. *Website:* http://www.thetaskforce.org *E-mail:* ngltf@ngltf.org

PFLAG (Parents, Families and Friends of Lesbians and Gays) *International. 490 chapters worldwide. Founded 1981.* Helps families understand and accept gay, lesbian, bisexual and transgendered family members. Offers help in strengthening families, support groups for families and friends, educational outreach, newsletter, chapter development guidelines, grassroots advocacy, information and referrals. Also has a Transgender Network (PFLAG TNET). Write: P-FLAG, 1726 M Street NW, Suite 400, Washington, DC 20036. Call 202-467-8180; Fax: 202-467-8194. For information about TNET call Karen Gross 216-691-4357 or e-mail: imatmom@aol.com *Website:* http://www.pflag.org *E-mail:* info@pflag.org

Rainbow Room *Model. Founded 1979.* Adult-facilitated support group for gay, lesbian, bisexual, transgender and questioning youth (ages 13-21). Provides a safe space for youth to talk about the issues that affect their daily lives. Write: Rainbow Room, c/o Hartford Gay and Lesbian Health Collective, P.O. Box 2094, Hartford, CT 06145-2094. Call 860-278-4163; Fax: 860-278-5995. *E-mail:* info@hglhc.org

Society for the Second Self (Tri-Ess International) *National. 30 chapters. Founded 1976.* Provides informational and educational resources to promote the understanding of crossdressing. Offers support equally for heterosexual crossdressers, their spouses, partners and families. Emphasizes security and confidentiality, full expression of both masculine and feminine elements, the balance and integration of these traits into the whole personality and relationship-building. Pen pals and Big Sister programs, quarterly journal and newsletter and membership directory. Online forums. Annual conventions for crossdressers, spouses, partners and couples. Write: Society for Second Self, P.O. Box 980638, Houston, TX 77098-0638. Call 713-349-9910. *Website:* http://www.tri-ess.org *E-mail:* TRIESSINFO@aol.com

Straight Spouse Network (SSN) *International network. 75 groups and 61 state/country contacts. Founded 1986.* Confidential personal support network serving current or former heterosexual spouses or partners, of gay, lesbian, bisexual or transgender mates and mixed-orientation couples. Empowers straight spouses or partners to cope constructively and promotes understanding between spouses, within families and with the larger community through education and collaboration. Resource information, research-based publications, referrals, newsletter, reading and media references. Guideline available for starting new groups. Numerous confidential internet lists. Write: Straight Spouse Network, P.O. Box 507, Mahwah, NJ 07430. Call 201-825-7763. *Website:* http://www.straightspouse.org *E-mail:* dir@straightspouse.org (Support media, research information: call 510-595-1005. *E-mail:* founder@straightspouse.org)

SHORT / TALL
(see also specific disorder)

STATEWIDE

Little People of America - Garden State Chapter Mutual support for short-statured people (infants - adults) and parents of short-statured children. Guest speakers, social get-togethers and fund-raisers. Spring and Fall regional conferences and national conventions. Dues $50/yr. per household. Call Helen Finkle 732-780-3827 or Robin Thibault 973-822-3665. *Website:* http://www.lpaonline.org

NATIONAL

Adult Growth Hormone Deficiency *National network. Founded 1989.* Provides public education and networking for adults with growth-related disorders. Information and referrals, phone support, pen pals, annual convention and conferences. Newsletter. Write: Adult Growth Hormone Deficiency, c/o The MAGIC Foundation, 6645 W. North Ave., Oak Park, IL 60302. Call 1-800-362-4423; Fax: 708-383-0899. *Website:* http://www.magicfoundation.org *E-mail*: mary@magicfoundation.org

Growth Hormone Deficiency Support Network *National network of MAGIC. Founded 1989.* Network and exchange of information for families of children with growth hormone deficiency disorders. Information and referrals, phone support, pen pals, conferences, literature, annual convention and membership newsletter ($35/US, $40/Canada, $45/overseas). Write: Growth Hormone Deficiency Support Network, c/o MAGIC Foundation, 6645 W. North Ave., Oak Park, IL 60302. Call 1-800-362-4423 or 708-383-0808 (Mon-Fri, 9am-4pm CST); Fax: 708-383-0899. *Website:* http://www.magicfoundation.org *E-mail:* mary@magicfoundation.org

Human Growth Foundation *National. 31 chapters. Founded 1965.* Local groups provide members the opportunity to meet other parents of children with growth related disorders. Mutual sharing of problems, research and public education. Monthly and quarterly newsletter. Parent-to-parent support and networking program. Annual conference. Also offers internet support list for parents and adults. Write: Human Growth Foundation, 997 Glen Cove Ave., Glen Head, NY 11545-1564. Call 1-800-451-6434 or 516-671-4041; Fax: 516-671-4055. *Website:* http://www.hgfound.org *E-mail:* hgf1@hgfound.org

Little People of America *(BILINGUAL) National. 68 chapters. Founded 1957.* Provides mutual support to people of short stature (4 ft. 10 inches and under) and their families. Information on physical and developmental concerns, employment, education, disability rights, medical issues, adaptive devices, etc. Newsletter. Provides educational scholarships and medical assistance grants, access to medical advisory board and assistance in adoption. Local, regional and national conferences and athletic events. Online chatroom and e-mail list serve. Dues $50/year, $10/year seniors, $500/lifetime. Write: Little People of America, 250 El Camino Real, Suite 201, Tustin, CA 92780. Call 1-888-572-2001 or 714-368-3689; Fax: 714-368-3367. *Website:* http://www.lpaonline.org *E-mail:* info@lpaonline.org

MAGIC Foundation for Children's Growth *National network. Founded 1989.* Provides public education and networking for families of children with growth-related disorders. MAGIC Foundation has 11 divisions including: growth hormone deficiency, congenital adrenal hyperplasia, Turner's syndrome, precocious puberty, McCune Albright syndrome, panhypopituitarism, adult growth hormone deficiency, Russell Silver Syndrome, thyroid disorders, chronic renal insufficiencies and septo optic dysplasia. Information and referrals, phone support, pen pals, annual convention and conferences. Newsletters for children and adults. Write: The MAGIC Foundation, 6645 W. North Ave., Oak Park, IL 60302. Call 1-800-362-4423 (Mon-Fri, 9am-4pm CST); Fax: 708-383-0899. *Website:* http://www.magicfoundation.org *E-mail:* mary@magicfoundation.org

Tall Clubs International *International. 65+ groups. Founded 1938.* Social support for tall persons (men at least 6 ft. 2 inches, women at least 5 ft. 10 inches). Also advocacy for clothing and other special needs of tall people.

Skywriters and TALLrific for persons under 21. Group development guidelines, information and referrals, conferences, newsletters and social gatherings. Write: Tall Clubs International, P.O. Box 1811, Cincinnati, OH 45201. Call 1-888-468-2552. *Website:* http://www.tall.org *E-mail:* admin@tall.org

SINGLES

(see also separation/divorce, widowhood)

MIDDLESEX

ETZ Chaim Sociable Singles Support and social group for men and women (ages 50+) who are divorced, separated, widowed or never married. Open to people of any faith. Dues $5/month. Rap sessions and guest speakers. Building is handicapped accessible. Meets Sun., 1-4pm, ETZ Chaim Jewish Center, 11 Cornell Ave., Monroe. Before attending call Eli 609-655-5137 (day) or Fran Solomon 609-395-8707 (day).

SOMERSET

Single Senior Women Support for women (ages 60+) who are divorced, separated, widowed, never married or have a spouse who is ill. Recreational activities. Meets 2nd and 4th Thurs., 10am-noon, Office on Aging, 27 Warren St., Somerville. Call Erin 908-704-6339 (day).

SPEECH / STUTTERING

(see also toll-free helplines)

STATEWIDE

Toastmasters International Mutual help for people to improve speaking skills, express themselves more effectively and to gain confidence. For those who are hesitant to speak before an audience. Membership fees. Monthly magazine. Check website for nearest group. *Website:* http://www.toastmasters.org

BERGEN

Speak Easy International Foundation, Inc. Self-help group for people who stutter. Must have speech dysfunction or phobia. Phone network, peer-counseling, newsletter and yearly conference. Dues $85/yr. Meets alternate Tues., 7:30pm, Cerebral Palsy Center, Fair Lawn. Call Bob 201-262-0895. *E-mail:* speakezusa@optonline.net

Toastmasters International Fairleigh Early Birds Support and education to improve communication, leadership, social and public speaking skills. Dues $33/semi-yearly. Meets Sat., 9-11am (except July and Aug.), Rutherford Public Library, Park Ave. and Chestnut St., Rutherford. Call Sylvia 973-773-4998 (day). *Website:* http://www.toastmaster.org

CAMDEN

National Stuttering Association - New Jersey Division Provides support and promotes fluency for stutters. Meets 2nd and 4th Thurs., 7-9pm, John F. Kennedy Hospital, Stratford. Call Kathy Filer 609-706-4098. *Website:* http://www.nsastutter.org *E-mail:* katfiler@aol.com

CAPE MAY

Toastmasters International Boardwalk Chapter Support and education to improve communication, leadership, social and public speaking skills. Dues $74/yr.; $25 initiation. Meets 1st and 3rd Wed., Chatterbox Restaurant, Ninth and Central Ave., Ocean City. Call Dennis Emerick 609-926-0415 or Rich 609-296-7048. *Website:* http://www.boardwalktoastmasters.com *E-mail:* denniscemerick@aol.com or rfcatando@aol.com

NATIONAL

International Foundation for Stutterers, Inc. *International. Founded 1980.* Aims to eliminate stuttering through speech therapy in conjunction with support groups. Education for public and professionals about stuttering and support. Speakers, phone help system and guidelines on forming support groups. Write: International Foundation for Stutterers, 2414 Romano Court, East Norriton, PA 19401. Call Elliot Dennis 610-272-1771 or Ed Riordan 908-359-6469 (eve.). *E-mail:* elliotdennis@yahoo.com

National Stuttering Association *National. 80 groups. Founded 1977.* Provides information about stuttering. Self-help chapter meetings provide supportive environment where people who stutter can learn to communicate more effectively. Network of groups. Referrals, advocacy, monthly newsletter and group development guidelines. Dues $35; $20 (senior, student, low income). Write: National Stuttering Association, 119 West 40th St., 14th Floor, New York, NY 10018. Call 1-800-364-1677; Fax: 212-944-8244. *Website:* http://www.WeStutter.org *E-mail:* info@WeStutter.org

Speak Easy International Foundation, Inc. *International. 6 chapters. Founded 1977.* Self-help group for adult and adolescent stutterers. Must have speech dysfunction or phobia. Phone network, peer counseling and newsletter. Offers assistance starting new groups. Annual national symposium and fall retreat in Madison, CT (contact Brian Baik 860-292-2040). Dues $85/yr. Write: Speak Easy International Foundation, c/o Bob Gathman, 233 Concord Dr., Paramus, NJ 07652. Call Bob 201-262-0895. *E-mail:* speakezusa@optonline.net

Toastmasters International *International. 11,000+ chapters. Founded 1924.* Mutual help for people to improve speaking and leadership skills to express themselves more effectively and to gain confidence. For those who are hesitant to speak before an audience. Leadership training. Dues $54/yr. One time membership kit $20. Monthly magazine. Write: Toastmasters International, P.O. Box 9052, Mission Viejo, CA 92690-7052. Call 949-858-8255; Fax: 949-858-1207. *Website:* http://www.toastmasters.org *E-mail:* tminfo@toastmasters.org

U.S. Society for Augmentative and Alternative Communication *National. 30 affiliated groups. Founded in 1986.* Addresses the needs of persons who are severely speech impaired or unable to speak. Works to improve services and products. Dues $63 (includes newsletter). Networking, conferences, advocacy, literature, networking, information and referrals. Write: U.S. Society for Augmentative and Alternative Communication, P.O. Box 1195, Burlingame, CA 94011. Fax: 928-585-8525. *Website:* http://ussaac.org *E-mail:* info@ussaac.org

ONLINE

Latetalkers *Online.* E-mail group to discuss developmental speech delays caused by apraxia, dyspraxia, phonological disorders, autism spectrum disorders, learning disabilities or other causes. Aim is to help children attain intelligible speech. Open to families, speech language pathologists, medical professionals, students and educators. *Website:* http://groups.yahoo.com/group/latetalkers

Stuttering Chat *Online. 3862 members. Founded 2000.* Mutual-aid support group for people who stutter - friends, relatives and speech therapists welcome. Mission is to provide support to people who stutter in the form of information about stuttering, therapy/treatment and the sharing of experiences. *Website:* http://health.groups.yahoo.com/group/stutteringchat/

"I get by with a little help from my friends." -- John Lennon

SPIRITUALITY / MEDITATION

ESSEX

Spirituality Group Support for mental health consumers fostering an awareness of spirituality and a sense of being a part of a much larger powerful entity. Offers mutual sharing, education, rap sessions, social, phone help and advocacy. Meets Tues., 4:30pm, Where Peaceful Waters Flow, 47 Cleveland St., Orange. Call Richard 973-677-7700 (eve).

TRAUMA
(see also specific trauma, toll-free helplines)

STATEWIDE

Vet Center Support Groups *(Professionally-run)* Four Veteran Centers. Support groups and related services for both combat veterans of all wars (Iraq, Afghan, Vietnam, WWII) and their families to deal with PTSD and other readjustment issues. Write: Ann Talmage, Vet Center, 2 Broad St., Suite 703, Bloomfield, NJ 07003. For group types and times, contact the closest center: Bloomfield (Essex) 973-748-0980; Secaucus (Hudson) 201-223-7787; Ewing (Mercer) 609-882-5744; Ventnor (Atlantic) 609-487-8387. *Website:* http://www.vetcenter.va.gov *E-mail:* ann.talmage@va.gov

CAMDEN

South Jersey Depression, Bipolar and PTSD Group Support for persons with depression, bipolar disorder or post-traumatic stress disorder who want to take the next step towards wellness and recovery. Meets Fri., 7pm, St. Andrew's United Methodist Church, 327 Marlton Pike West, Cherry Hill. Call Richard 609-980-6980.

ONLINE

Gift From Within *Online. (WOMEN ONLY)* Offers a one-on-one PTSD e-mail/pen pal support network, where female victims of specific trauma can be matched with survivors of similar PTSD. Audio-visual resources available. *Website:* http://www.giftfromwithin.org *E-mail:* joyceb3955@aol.com

VETERANS / MILITARY
(see also toll-free helplines)

STATEWIDE

Vet Center Support Groups *(Professionally-run)* Four Veteran Centers. Support groups and related services for both combat veterans of all wars (Iraq, Afghan, Vietnam, WWII) and their families to deal with PTSD and other readjustment issues. Write: Ann Talmage, Vet Center, 2 Broad St., Suite 703, Bloomfield, NJ 07003. For group types and times, contact the closest center: Bloomfield (Essex) 973-748-0980; Secaucus (Hudson) 201-223-7787; Ewing (Mercer) 609-882-5744; Ventnor (Atlantic) 609-487-8387. *Website:* http://www.vetcenter.va.gov *E-mail:* ann.talmage@va.gov

BERGEN

Military Family Support Group Mutual support for families who have a loved one currently serving in the armed forces. Sharing of thoughts, fears, anxieties, bravery, love and strength felt towards loved ones while they are at war, going to war, or back from war. Meets Tues., 7:30pm, Community Hall, 500 Third St., Carlstadt. For information call 201-438-5526.

HUNTERDON

Balkan and Persian Gulf Military Support Group Informal support network for families and friends of American troops in Persian Gulf, Bosnia and Kosovo. For information call 908-782-6722. *E-mail:* tmuller08551@yahoo.com

MIDDLESEX

Army and Air National Guard Family Support Offers support for any family member of military personnel. Mutual support to discuss or share any issues of concern. Family member does not have to be on active duty. For meeting information call 732-937-6290.

NATIONAL

Blinded Veterans Association *National. 53 regional groups. Founded 1945.* Support, information and outreach to blinded veterans, including those who were blinded in combat and those suffering from age-related macular degeneration and other eye diseases. Help in obtaining prosthetic devices and accessing the latest technological advances to assist the blind. Information on benefits and rehabilitation programs. Quarterly newsletter. Regional meetings.

Write: BVA, 477 H St., NW, Washington, DC 20001. Call 1-800-669-7079 or 202-371-8880; Fax: 202-371-8258. *Website:* http://www.bva.org *E-mail:* bva@bva.org

EX-P.O.SE (Ex-Partners of Servicemembers for Equality) *National membership. Founded 1980.* Primary information resource for spouses facing separation and divorce from a service member, active duty or retired. Lawyer referral service. Quarterly newsletter. Publishes a New Member Information Letter. Membership dues $25. Write: EX-P.O.SE, P.O. Box 11191, Alexandria, VA 22312. Call 703-941-5844 (Tues.-Thurs., 11am-3pm EST); Fax: 703-212-6951. *Website:* http://www.ex-pose.org *E-mail:* ex-pose@juno.com

National Gulf War Resource Center, Inc. *National. 61 affiliated groups. Founded 1995.* Supports the efforts of grassroots organizations that assist veterans affected by the Persian Gulf War illnesses. Also provides advocacy and support for Gulf War veterans, veterans of Afghanistan and Iraq and their families. Conducts research into the causes of Gulf War Syndrome. Self-help guides, media assistance, provides congressional testimony, advocacy, literature, information and referrals. Write: National Gulf War Resource Center, 1403 Southwest Blvd., Kansas City, KS 66103. Call 1-866-531-7183; Fax: 913-831-7184. *Website:* http://www.ngwrc.org *E-mail:* ngwrc@sbcglobal.net

Paralyzed Veterans of America *National. 34 chapters and 58 field service offices.* Aim is to ensure that spinal cord injured or diseased veterans achieve the highest quality of life possible. Membership is available solely to individuals who are American citizens with spinal cord dysfunction as a result of trauma or disease. Must have served on active duty and had an other than dishonorable discharge. Support groups, publications, VA benefits counseling, magazine, information and referrals. Write: Paralyzed Veterans of America, 801 18th St. NW, Washington, DC 20006. Call 1-800-424-8200 or 202-872-1300 (Mon.-Fri., 8:30am-5pm EST). *Website:* http://www.pva.org *E-mail:* info@pva.org

Society of Military Widows *National. 24 chapters. Founded 1968.* Support and assistance for widows of members of all U.S. uniformed services. Help in coping with adjustment to life on their own. Promotes public awareness. Bimonthly magazine/journal. Dues $12/yr. Chapter development guidelines. Online listing on local chapters. Write: Society of Military Widows, 5535 Hempstead Way, Springfield, VA 22151. Call 1-800-842-3451 ext. 1005 or 253-750-1342. *Website:* http://www.militarywidows.org *E-mail:* president@militarywidows.org or patschecter@earthlink.net

Student Veterans of America (SVA) *National. 80 groups. Founded 2008.* A coalition of student groups for military veterans on college campuses. Local groups have informal social meetings that serve as peer support groups. Also connects student groups with resources, helps those wishing to start new groups, advocates at the state and national levels. Has regional and national conferences. Write: Student Veterans of America, P.O. Box 77673, Washington, D.C. 20013. Call 202-470-6100. *Website*: http://www.studentveterans.org

Tragedy Assistance Program for Survivors (TAPS) *National network.* Provides support for persons who have lost a loved one while serving in the armed forces (Army, Air Force, Navy, Marine Corps, National Guard, Reserves, Service Academies, Coast Guard or contractors serving beside the military). Offers networking, crisis information, problem solving assistance and liaison with military agencies. Also TAPS youth programs. Annual seminar. Write: TAPS, 910 17th Street NW, Suite 800, Washington, DC 20006. Call 1-800-959-8277 or 202-588-8277; Fax: 202-457-8278. *Website:* http://www.taps.org *E-mail:* info@taps.org

United Spinal Association *National. Founded 1946.* Aim is to provide support and improve the quality of life for all Americans with spinal cord injuries and disorders. Write: United Spinal Association, 75-20 Astoria Blvd., Jackson Heights, NY 11370-1177. Call 718-803-3782 ext. 1203.

Vietnam Veterans of America, Inc. *National. 600+ chapters. Founded 1978.* Devoted to the needs and concerns of Vietnam era veterans and their families. Provides leadership and advocacy in all areas that have an impact on veterans, with an emphasis on Agent Orange related problems and post traumatic stress disorder. Bimonthly newspaper. Write: VVA, 8605 Cameron St., Suite 400, Silver Spring, MD 20910-3710. Call 1-800-882-1316 or 301-585-4000 (Mon.-Fri. 9am-5:30pm, EST); Fax: 301-585-0519. *Website:* http://www.vva.org

ONLINE

Marine Moms Online *Online.* Discussion forum offers support, information, questions, answers and chatroom. There is also a forum for dads. *Website:* http://mmo.proboards10.com/index.cgi

Need help finding a specific group? Give us a call – we're here to help!
*Call **1-800-367-6274**.*

WOMEN'S ISSUES
(see also separation/divorce, toll-free helplines)

STATEWIDE

National Organization for Women of NJ (NOW – NJ) Political advocacy for women's equality in society. Dedicated to eliminating sexism and racism. Political advocacy for reproductive rights, older women's rights, homemakers' rights, women in the work force, lesbian rights, etc. Information and referrals about chapters, groups and services throughout NJ. Dues $35/yr. Write: N.O.W - NJ, 110 W. State St., Trenton, NJ 08608. Call 609-393-0156 (day). *Website:* http://www.nownj.org *E-mail:* now-nj@nownj.org

ESSEX

Peer Support Various support groups dealing with women's issues (including separation/divorce, parenting, widows, etc.). Groups start periodically and run for 6 weeks. Registration fee $45. Meets at Linda and Rudy Slucker NCJW Center for Women, 513 West Mt. Pleasant Ave., Suite 325, Livingston. Call 973-994-4994. *Website:* http://www.centerforwomennj.org *E-mail:* centerforwomen@ncjwessex.org

GLOUCESTER

Center for People in Transition *(Professionally-run)* Assists displaced homemakers whose major source of financial support has been lost due to separation/divorce, death or disability of a spouse. Helps individuals to become emotionally and economically self-sufficient through life skills training, career decision making, education or vocational training and supportive services. Evening divorce and bereavement support groups for men and women. For information call 856-415-2222 (Mon.-Fri.). *E-mail:* peopleintransition@gccnj.edu

HUDSON

Women's Project Groups *(Professionally-run)* Support, education, workshops and groups to help women on subjects such as self-esteem, separation/divorce, domestic violence, employment and stress management. Meetings vary, Christ Hospital, 176 Palisade Ave., Jersey City. Before attending call Michele Bernstein 201-795-8375 ext. 8416 (day).

MONMOUTH

Women's Support Group Helps women who are displaced homemakers (facing the loss of their primary source of income due to separation, divorce, disability or death of spouse). Issues addressed include self-sufficiency, career development, assertiveness, self-esteem, divorce, separation, widowhood and other related topics. Meets Fri., Brookdale Community College, Lincroft. Pre-registration required. Before attending call Robin Vogel 732-495-4496 ext. 4007 (day) or Mary Ann O'Brien 732-229-8675.

MORRIS

Familias en Paz *(Professionally-run)* Support group for Latino women who want to improve their personal life through education, insight and self-empowerment. Discusses issues such as domestic abuse, relationships and other issues of interest to women. Education, advocacy, guest speakers, literature and buddy system. Meets Mon., 7-9pm, Morris County Organization for Hispanic Affairs, 9597 Bassett Highway, Dover, 07801. Call Alberto Olarte 201-919-4742 or 973-366-4770. *E-mail:* user9398@optonline.net

Morris County National Organization For Women Goals are to bring women into full participation in the mainstream of American society. Dues $35/yr. (sliding scale $15-34). Meets 1st Tues., 7:30-9pm, Morris Plains Community Center, Jim Fear Dr., Morris Plains. Call 973-285-1200 (day). *Website:* http://www.morriscountynow.org *E-mail:* morriscountynow@hotmail.com

WARREN

Career and Life Transitions Center for Women *(Professionally-run)* Provides support services, vocational counseling and career training for displaced homemakers who have lost their primary source of income due to divorce, separation, death, active military deployment or disability of her spouse. Meets various times, 108 East Washington Ave., Rt. 57, Washington. Call 908-835-2624. *Website:* http://www.norwescap.org *E-mail:* transitions@norwescap.org

NATIONAL

Business and Professional Women/USA *National. 1300 chapters. Founded 1919.* Organization comprised of working women, to promote workplace equity and provide networking opportunities. Lobbying efforts, tri-annual magazine, periodic publications, resource center and grassroots community action projects. Annual national convention. Local group information available online. Write:

Business and Professional Women/USA, 1900 M St. NW, Suite 310, Washington, DC 20036. Call 202-293-1100 (Mon.-Fri., 9am-5pm EST); Fax: 202-861-0298. *Website:* http://www.bpwusa.org *E-mail:* memberservices@bpwusa.org

National Organization for Women (NOW) *National. 500 chapters. Founded 1966.* NOW is an action organization that seeks social, political, economic and legal equity between women and men through grassroots organizing, lobbying, litigation, protests and demonstrations. Educational meetings, national newsletter and chapter development guidelines. Write: National Organization for Women, 1100 H Street NW, 3rd Floor, Washington, DC 20005. Call 202-628-8669; TDD: 202-331-9002; Fax: 202-785-8576. *Website:* http://now.org *E-mail:* now@now.org

Older Women's League *National. 60+ chapters. Founded 1980.* Membership organization that advocates on behalf of various economic and social issues for midlife and older women (social security, pension rights, employment, caregiver support, elder abuse, etc.). Newsletter and chapter development guidelines. Dues $25/yr. Write: Older Women's League, 3300 North Fairfax Dr., Suite 218, Arlington, VA 22201. Call 1-800-825-3695; Fax: 703-812-0687. *Website:* http://www.owl-national.org *E-mail:* owlinfo@owl-national.org

SOWN (Supportive Older Women's Network) *Model. 32 groups in Philadelphia area. Founded 1982.* Helps women (ages 60+) cope with their specialized aging concerns. Support groups, leadership training, consultation, telephone support, outreach and networking. Newsletter. Write: SOWN, 4100 Main Street, Suite 200, Philadelphia, PA 19127. Call 215-487-3000; Fax: 215-487-3111. *Website:* http://www.sown.org *E-mail:* info@sown.org

WORKAHOLICS

NATIONAL

Workaholics Anonymous World Service Organization, Inc. *International. 100+ groups. Founded 1983.* 12-step fellowship for men and women who feel their work lives have gotten out of control. Also for affected family members and friends. Provides mutual support in solving problems of compulsive overworking. Available phone and online support and information for those wishing to start a chapter. Write: Workaholics Anonymous, P.O. Box 289, Menlo Park, CA 94026-0289. Call 510-273-9253. *Website:* http://www.workaholics-anonymous.org

YOUTH / STUDENTS
(see also toll-free helplines)

BURLINGTON

Youth Partnership Group Adult supervised activities for youth (ages 13-21) with complex emotional, mental health or behavioral issues to help them express what they have been through and share concerns. Rap sessions. Meets Thurs., 6:30-8:30pm, Family Support Organization of Burlington County, 774 Eayrestown Rd., Lumberton. Call Jamison Gsell 609-265-8838 (day).

CAMDEN

Youth Partnership Group Adult supervised activities for youth (ages 13-21) with complex emotional, mental health or behavioral issues to help them express what they have been through and share concerns. Rap sessions, guest speakers, literature and phone help. Building is handicapped accessible. Meets Thurs., 6:30pm, Camden County Family Support Organization, 23 W. Park Ave., Suite 103-104, Merchantville. Call Susan A. Doherty-Funke or Peter Burgos 856-662-2600 (day). *Website:* http://www.camdenfso.org

CUMBERLAND

Youth Partnership Group Adult supervised activities for youth (ages 13-21) with complex emotional, mental health or behavioral issues to help them express what they have been through and share concerns. Rap sessions. Meets Thurs., 6-8pm, Family Support Organization of Cumberland, Gloucester and Salem County, 1226 East Landis Ave., Elmer. Call Renisha O'Donnell 856-507-9400 (day). *E-mail:* rodonnell@cgsfso.com

ESSEX

Youth Partnership Group Adult supervised activities for youth (ages 13-21) with complex emotional, mental health or behavioral issues to help them express what they have been through and share concerns. Rap sessions, guest speakers, literature, newsletter and phone help. Meets Wed., 6-8pm, Family Support Organization of Essex County, 60 Evergreen Place, East Orange. Call Jacqueline Oliver or Hazeline Pilgrim 973-395-1441 (day).

"It is good to have an end to journey toward, but it is the journey that matters in the end."
--Ursula K. Leguin

HUDSON

Youth Partnership Group Adult supervised activities for youth (ages 13-21) with complex emotional, mental health or behavioral issues to help them express what they have been through and share concerns. Rap sessions. Meets Tues. and Fri., 5:30-8pm, Family Support Organization of Hudson County, 705 Bergen Ave., Jersey City. Call 201-915-5140 (day).

HUNTERDON

Youth Partnership Group Adult supervised activities for youth (age 13-21) with complex emotional, mental health or behavioral issues to help them express what they have been through and share concerns. Rap sessions. Building is handicapped accessible. Meets every other Fri., 6-8pm, Family Support Organization, 4 Minneakoning Rd., Flemington. For meeting information call Stanley Croughter 908-788-8585 (day). *Website:* http://www.fsohsw.org

MIDDLESEX

Youth Partnership Group Adult supervised activities for youth (ages 13-21) with complex emotional, mental health or behavioral issues to help them express what they have been through and share concerns. Educational series, advocacy, social group, newsletter, phone help and buddy system. Meets Fri., 6-8pm, Family Support Organization of Middlesex County, 1 Ethel Rd., Edison. Call Dylys Koney or Sam Hartman 732-287-8701 (day). *E-mail:* dkfsomiddlesex9@msn.com

MONMOUTH

Youth Partnership Group Peer support and advocacy to empower youth (ages 13-21) with emotional or behavioral challenges. Rap sessions, guest speakers, literature, phone help and newsletter. Meets Tues., 6-8pm, Family Based Services Association, 279 Broadway, Suite 400, Long Branch. Before attending call Florene Grant 732-571-3272 (day).

OCEAN

Spectrum *(Professionally-run)* Support and information for any youth in junior high or high school who have questions on human sexuality. Including straight, gay, lesbian, bisexual or transgendered issues. Meetings vary, 5:30pm, Toms River. For information call Mother Jacquelyn 848-333-3977.

Youth Partnership Group Adult supervised activities for youth (ages 13-18) with complex emotional, mental health or behavioral issues to help them express what they have been through and share concerns. Rap sessions. Building is handicapped accessible. Meets 2nd and 4th Thurs., 6:30-8pm, Ocean County Family Support Organization, Inc., 44 Washington St., Suite 2A, Toms River. Call Annie Hercules 732-281-5770 ext. 16. *Website:* http://www.ocfso.org *E-mail:* info@ocfso.org

PASSAIC

Youth Partnership Group Adult supervised activities for youth (ages 13-21) with complex emotional, mental health or behavioral issues to help them express what they have been through and share concerns. Rap sessions, guest speakers, literature, newsletter and phone help. Meets Wed., 7-8:30pm, Family Support Organization of Passaic County, 810 Belmont Ave., 2nd Floor, North Haledon. Call Kaity Rodriguez 973-427-0100 (day).

SOMERSET

Youth Partnership Group Adult supervised activities for youth (ages 13-21) with complex emotional, mental health or behavioral issues to help them express what they have been through and share concerns. Rap sessions. Building is handicapped accessible. Meeting day and time varies in Somerset. For meeting information call Stanley Croughter 908-788-8585 (day). *Website:* http://www.fso-hsw.org

SUSSEX

Teen Support Group *(Professionally-run)* Sharing and encouragement for teenagers dealing with everyday stress. Donation $5 towards refreshments, literature and space rental. Meets Mon., 3:30-4:30pm, Partnership for Social Services Family Center, 48 Wyker Rd., Franklin. Call 973-827-4702. *E-mail:* psocserv@catholicharities.org

UNION

Youth Partnership Group Adult supervised activities for youth (ages 13-21) with complex emotional, mental health or behavioral issues to help them express what they have been through and share concerns. Rap sessions. Meets 2nd and 4th Mon., 6:30-8:30pm, Family Support Organization, 143 Elmer St., 1st Floor, Westfield. Call 908-789-7625 (day). *Website:* http://www.fso-union.org

NATIONAL

National Students of Ailing Mothers and Fathers Support Network *International.* Network of university students helping each other cope with the serious illness or death of a parent or loved one. Campus-based mutual support groups, online newsletter, online chats and service projects. Website provides information, group development guidelines and a listing of universities currently interested in group development. Write: National Students of AMF, 514 Daniels St., Suite 356, Raleigh, NC 27605. *Website:* http://www.studentsofamf.org

Students Against Destructive Decisions (SADD) *National. 10,000 chapters. Founded 1981.* Provides prevention and intervention tools to eliminate impaired driving, end underage drinking, drug abuse and other destructive decisions. Offers community awareness programs, literature, sponsors SADD chapters and group development guidelines. Write: SADD, 255 Main St., Marlborough, MA 01752. Call 1-877-723-3462 or 508-481-3568; Fax: 508-481-5759. *Website:* http://www.sadd.org *E-mail:* info@sadd.org

ONLINE

Conduct Disorders Parent Message Board *Online. 7080 members. Founded 1995.* Support for parents living with a child with one of the many behavior disorders including: attention deficit hyperactivity disorder, oppositional defiance disorder, conduct disorder, depression and substance abuse. Parents with children of all ages welcome. *Website:* http://www.conductdisorders.com

Pregnant Teen Support *Online.* E-mail list support group for teens (ages 12-20) who are facing an unplanned, unexpected or unwanted pregnancy. *Website:* http://health.groups.yahoo.com/group/Pregnant_Teen_Support

TeenHelp *Online. Founded 1998.* Support for young people on any issue they have through a network of peers and volunteer support staff. Online community of e-mail support, scheduled real-time chat meetings, blogging journal system and moderated message board. Resources, articles and assistance in starting new groups available. *Website:* http://www.teenhelp.org

---

"Too often we underestimate the power of a touch, a smile, a kind word, a listening ear, an honest compliment, or the smallest act of caring, all of which have the potential to turn a life around." --Leo Buscaglia

49XXXXY SYNDROME

49XXXXY *National network. Founded 1990.* Mutual support and networking for families affected by 49XXXXY disorder. Information, pen pals, phone support and newsletter. Write: 49XXXXY, c/o Elise Watzka, 870 Miranda Green, Palo Alto, CA 94306. Call 650-941-2408. *Website:* http://klinefeltersyndrome.org/49er.htm *E-mail:* epqatzka@iname.com

AARSKOG SYNDROME

Aarskog Syndrome Parents Support Group, The *International network. Founded 1993.* Support provided via e-mail or letter writing (regular mail delivery) for families of children and adults affected with Aarskog syndrome. Letter writing club, e-mail club for families and pen pal club for children 12 years old and up. Free complimentary information packet for any person in the United States. Write: The Aarskog Syndrome Parents Support Group, c/o Shannon Caranci, 62 Robin Hill Lane, Levittown, PA 19055-1411. Call 215-943-7131 (leave a brief message with your name, e-mail address, phone number) *E-mail:* shannonfaith49@msn.com or aarskogsyndrome52@msn.com

ACID MALTASE DEFICIENCY / POMPE DISEASE

Acid Maltase Deficiency Association (AMDA) *International network. Founded 1995.* Support and information for persons affected by Pompe disease (acid maltase deficiency). Newsletter, literature, phone support, information and referrals. Supports research into the cause and cure. Write: Acid Maltase Deficiency Association, P.O. Box 700248, San Antonio, TX 78270. Call 210-494-6144; Fax: 210-490-7161. *Website:* http://www.amda-pompe.org *E-mail:* tianrama@aol.com

ACIDEMIA, ORGANIC

Organic Acidemia Association, Inc. *International. Founded 1982.* Support, information and networking for families affected by organic acidemia and related disorders. Dues $25/yr. Internet listserv, family conferences, research information and tri-annual newsletter. Write: Organic Acidemia Association, c/o Kathy Stagni, 13210 35th Ave. North, Plymouth, MN 55441. Call 763-559-1797. *Website:* http://www.oaanews.org *E-mail:* oaanews@aol.com

ACNE SCARS

ONLINE

Acne Support Group in Cyberspace *Online. Founded 2000.* Support forum to talk, listen, share and help those interested in acne recovery, healing, surgery and non-surgical acne cosmetic procedures. *Website:* http://asgic.proboards26.com/index.cgi

ADDISON'S DISEASE / ADRENAL DISEASE

CAMDEN

Addison's Support Group Mutual support and information for those with Addison's disease. Rap sessions, literature, phone help and guest speakers. Meets Sat., 4 times/yr., St. Pius Parish Center, Kresson Rd., Cherry Hill. Call Janice Judge 856-354-6029. *E-mail:* JanPT@aol.com

NATIONAL

National Adrenal Diseases Foundation *National. 32 affiliated groups. Founded 1984.* Dedicated to serving the needs of those with adrenal disease and their families, especially through information, education and support groups. Quarterly newsletters, pamphlets and group development guidelines. Write: National Adrenal Diseases Foundation, 505 Northern Blvd., Suite 200, Great Neck, NY 11021. Call 516-487-4992. *Website:* http://www.nadf.us *E-mail:* nadfmail@aol.com

AGENESIS OF THE CORPUS CALLOSUM

ACC Network, The *International network. Founded 1989.* Helps individuals with agenesis (or other anomaly) of the corpus callosum, their families and professionals. Opportunity to network with others who are experiencing similar issues and to share information and support. Phone support, information, newsletter and referrals. Coordinates listserv, an electronic discussion group on the internet. Write: ACC Network, University of Maine, 5749 Merrill Hall, Room 118, Orono, ME 04469-5749. Call 207-581-3116. Fax: 207-581-3120. *Website:* http://www.umaine.edu/edhd/research/accnetwork.htm

"The greatest good you can do for another is not just share your riches, but reveal to them their own." -- Disraeli

AICARDI SYNDROME / INFANTILE SPASMS
(see also epilepsy/seizure disorders)

NATIONAL

Aicardi Syndrome Newsletter, Inc. *International network. Founded 1983. 5 regional chapters.* Support for families with daughters who have Aicardi syndrome, a rare seizure disorder that affects primarily females and is characterized by seizures and retinal lesions. Resources, research projects, biennial conferences, phone support network, research group, newsletters, information and referrals. Dues $25/year. Write: Aicardi Syndrome Newsletter, Inc., c/o Denise Park Parsons, 1510 Polo Fields Ct., Louisville, KY 40245. Call 502-244-9152. *Website:* http://www.aicardisyndrome.org *E-mail:* aicnews@aol.com

ONLINE

Infantile Spasms List *Online. 1300+ members. Founded 1998.* Support and information for parents and caregivers of children with infantile spasms. Opportunity to discuss their children, treatment options and offer support. Professionals welcomed. *Website:* http://health.groups.yahoo.com/group/infantilespasms

ALAGILLE SYNDROME

Alagille Syndrome Alliance *National network. Founded 1993.* Support network for anyone who cares about people with Alagille syndrome, a rare, multi-symptom genetic disorder. Disseminates information. Aims to increase awareness in general public as well as health professionals. Newsletter, phone support, medical advisory board, information and referrals. Write: Alagille Syndrome Alliance, c/o Cindy L. Hahn, President, 10500 S.W. Starr Dr., Tualatin, OR 97062. Call 503-885-0455. *Website:* http://www.alagille.org *E-mail:* alagille@earthlink.net

ALBINISM

NOAH (National Organization for Albinism and Hypopigmentation) *National. Local chapters and contact people. Founded 1982.* Support and information for individuals, families and professionals dealing with albinism (a lack of melanin pigment). Encourages research leading to improved diagnosis and treatment. Newsletter, chapter development guidelines, national conference, online community and regional gatherings. Dues $20/individual; $25/family. Write: NOAH, P.O. Box 959, East Hampstead, NH 03826-0959. For information call 1-800-473-2310 or 603-887-2310; Fax: 1-800-648-2310. *Website:* http://www.albinism.org/ *E-mail:* info@albinism.org

ALOPECIA AREATA

MIDDLESEX

Alopecia Support Group Mutual support and encouragement for persons with alopecia and their families. Building is handicapped accessible. Meets 6 sessions a year, Robert Wood Johnson University Hospital, 1 Robert Wood Johnson Place, BMSCH Conference Room, New Brunswick. Call 732-418-8110.

NATIONAL

National Alopecia Areata Foundation *National. Founded 1981.* Support network for people with alopecia areata, totalis, and universalis. Goals are to set up support groups around the country, educate the public and fund raise for research. Quarterly newsletter and support group guidelines. Write: National Alopecia Areata Foundation, 14 Mitchell Blvd., San Rafael, CA 94903. Call 415-472-3780; Fax: 415-472-5343. *Website:* http://www.naaf.org *E-mail:* info@naaf.org

ALSTROMS SYNDROME

Alstrom Syndrome International *International network. 5 affiliated groups (Canada, France, Brazil, Japan and UK). Founded 1995.* Provides support and networking for families affected by Alstrom syndrome. Supports medical research initiatives to more fully understand the complexities of Alstrom syndrome and develop better therapies for Alstrom patients. Publishes a quarterly newsletter. Provides information resources to families, educators, researchers and physicians. Write: Alstrom Syndrome International, 14 Whitney Farm Rd., Mount Desert, ME 04660. Call 1-800-371-3628 or 207-288-6385; Fax: 207-244-7678. *Website:* http://www.jax.org/alstrom *E-mail:* jdm@jax.org

ALVEOLAR CAPILLARY DYSPLASIA

Alveolar Capillary Dysplasia Association *International network. Founded 1996.* Mutual support for families who have lost a child to alveolar capillary dysplasia (ACD), a congenital lung disorder. Aim is to share information while offering supportive environment to share fears and concerns. Encourages research into cause and cure. Literature, networking, information newsletter and referrals. Write: Alveolar Capillary Dysplasia Association, c/o Steve and Donna

Hanson, 5902 Marcie Court, Garland, TX 75044-4958. *Website:* http://www.acd-association.com *E-mail:* sdesj@verizon.net

AMYLOIDOSIS

Amyloidosis Support Groups, Inc. *National. 21 regional groups. Founded 2005.* Support for patients, caregivers, families, those who lost loved ones to amyloidosis and friends of amyloidosis patients. Also deals with multiple myeloma, peripheral neuropathy, familial amyloidosis and protein misfolding. Telephone support network, pen pal program, educational materials, national conference, advocacy, information and referrals. Online mutual aid activities include message board, mailing list and scheduled real-time chat meetings. Assistance in starting and maintaining groups. Write: Admyloidosis Support Groups, Inc., 232 Orchard Drive, Wood Dale, IL 60191. Call 1-866-404-7539 (24 hr.); Fax: 847-350-0577. *Website:* http://www.amyloidosissupport.com *E-mail:* muriel@finkelsupply.com

ANDROGEN INSENSITIVITY

AISSG-USA (Androgen Insensitivity Syndrome Support Group) *Founded 1995.* Provides information and support to people affected by androgen insensitivity syndrome (AIS) and similar disorders of sex development/intersex conditions. Support for affected adults, parents and teens (including online chat forums). Information and referrals, phone support, regional and national support group meetings, literature, advocacy and newsletters. Write: AISSG-USA, P.O. Box 2148, Duncan, OK 73534-2148. *Website:* http://www.aissgusa.org *E-mail:* aissgusa@hotmail.com

ANENCEPHALY

ONLINE

Anencephaly Support Foundation *Online. Founded 1992.* Provides support for families who have had a baby born with anencephaly or couples who are continuing a pregnancy after being diagnosed with anencephaly. Information and resources for parents and professionals. Phone support, member discussion board, chatroom and pregnancy message board. Registration required. Write: Anencephaly Support Foundation, 20311 Sienna Pines Court, Spring, TX 77379. *Website:* http://www.asfhelp.com *E-mail:* help@asfhelp.com

ANGELMAN SYNDROME

Angelman Syndrome Foundation, Inc. *National network. Founded 1992.* Mission is to advance the awareness and treatment of Angelman syndrome through education, information, research and support for individuals with Angelman syndrome, their families and other concerned persons. Write: Angelman Syndrome Foundation, 4255 Westbrook Dr., Suite 219, Aurora, IL 60504. Call 1-800-432-6435 or 630-978-4245; Fax: 630-978-7408. *Website:* http://www.angelman.org *E-mail:* info@angelman.org

ANKYLOSING SPONDYLITIS

MORRIS

Spondylitis Support Group of New Jersey Support for people who have been diagnosed with ankylosing spondylitis and related diseasess. Provides information and education on managing the disease. Families welcome. Rap sessions, guest speakers, newsletter, phone help, speakers' bureau and visitation program. Building is handicapped accessible. Meets 1st Sat., 10am-noon (Jan., Mar., May, July, Sept., Nov.), Atlantic Rehabilitation Institute, 95 Mt. Kembel Ave., Room 577, Morristown. Call Craig Gimbel 973-476-8976 or Barbara Schiller 973-966-1736. *Website:* http://www.njssg.org

NATIONAL

Spondylitis Association of America *International network. 25 affiliated groups. Founded 1983.* Support, research, advocacy, education for patients, families, friends and health professionals concerned with ankylosing spondylitis and related diseases (reactive arthritis/Reiter's syndrome, psoriatic arthritis, and inflammatory bowel disease). Publications, videotapes and newsletter. Guidelines available to start support groups. Write: Spondylitis Association of America, P.O. Box 5872, Sherman Oaks, CA 91413. Call 1-800-777-8189 or 818-981-1616 (in CA); Fax: 818-981-9826. *Website:* http://www.spondylitis.org *E-mail:* info@spondylitis.org

ONLINE

KickAS.org *Online. 4864+ members.* Support and information for persons with ankylosing spondylitis and related disorders. Provides inspiration, friendship and humor. Message board. Separate forums for affected persons, families, friends and affected teens. *Website:* http://www.kickas.org

ANORCHIDISM

STATEWIDE

Anorchidism Support Group - USA Provides support and information for families and persons affected by anorchidism (absence of the testes) whether congenital or acquired. Phone support, information and referrals, newsletter, pen pals and literature. Write: Anorchidism Support Group - USA, c/o Marianne Bittle, 4 Funny Bone Court, Sicklerville, NJ 08081. Call 856-740-1748 (eve.). *Website:* http://freespace.virgin.net/asg.uk/ *E-mail:* asg.uk@virgin.net

NATIONAL

Anorchidism Support Group *International network. Founded 1995.* Information and support for families and persons affected by anorchidism (absence of the testes), whether congenital or acquired (aka testicular regression syndrome, anorchia, vanishing testes syndrome or absent testes). Newsletter. Provides information and support via phone, letter or e-mail. An information leaflet available on request. Write: Anorchidism Support Group, P.O. Box 3025, Romford, Essex RM3 8GX, England. Call 44(0)1708 372597 (will return phone calls outside of UK; please allow for time difference when calling, please telephone between 9am-5pm GMT/BST). *Website:* http://freespace.virgin.net/asg.uk

ANORECTAL MALFORMATIONS

Pull-thru Network, The *International. Founded 1988.* Support and information for the families with children born with anorectal, colorectal or urogenital disorder and any of the associated diagnoses. Disorders include, but are not limited to cloaca, bladder exstrophy, imperforate anus, VACTERL/VATER association, anal stenosis, cloacal exstrophy and Hirschsprung's disease. Maintains a database for member networking. Quarterly magazine, online discussion group, weekly chat for members, phone support and literature. Dues $30/year - free membership available upon request. Write: The Pull-Thru Network, 2312 Savoy St., Hoover, AL 35226-1528. Call 205-978-2930. *Website:* http://www.pullthrunetwork.org *E-mail:* ptnmail@charter.net

"Don't be afraid if things seem difficult in the beginning. That's only the initial impression. The important thing is not to retreat; you have to master yourself."
-- Olga Korbut

ANOSMIA / PAROSMIA

ONLINE

Anosmia *Online. Founded 1999.* Provides mailing list and resources for people with anosmia (lacking the sense of smell). *Website:* http://groups.yahoo.com/group/anosmia

Congenital Anosmia Forums *Online.* Forum for persons who suffer from congenital anosmia (born without a sense of smell). Provides support and information. *Website:* http://www.anosmia.net/

Parosmia Smelling Disorder *Online.* Provides mutual support and information for persons who have distortions of their sense of smell. *Website:* http://health.groups.yahoo.com/group/parosmia/

ANTIPHOSPHOLIPID ANTIBODY SYNDROME

APS Foundation of America, Inc. *Founded 2005.* Dedicated to fostering and facilitating joint efforts in the areas of education, support, public awareness, research and patient services for those affected by Antiphospholipid Antibody Syndrome (APS), the major cause of multiple miscarriages, thrombosis, young strokes and heart attacks. Online support forum. Write: APS Foundation of America, Inc., P.O. Box 801, La Crosse, WI 54602-0801. Call 608-782-2626, Fax: 608-782-6569. *Website:* http://www.apsfa.org *E-mail:* apsfa@apsfa.org

APERT SYNDROME

Apert Syndrome Pen Pals *National network. Founded 1992.* Group correspondence program for persons with Apert syndrome to share experiences. Pen pals, phone help, information and referrals. Write: Apert Syndrome Pen Pals, P.O. Box 115, Providence, RI 02901. Call 401-952-1353. *E-mail:* christinebucci2001@yahoo.com

APRAXIA / DYSPRAXIA
(see also speech)

BERGEN

Apraxia Network of Bergen County Support for parents and caregivers of children with apraxia. Mutual sharing, socials, guest speakers, literature and education. Membership dues $10/yr. Building is handicapped accessible. Meets

4 times/yr., River Edge. Call Jeanne 201-741-4035 (afternoon, evenings and weekends). *Website:* jbmistletoe@optonline.net

CAMDEN

South Jersey Apraxia Support Group Support for parents of children with apraxia of speech and/or dyspraxia. Families welcome. Guest speakers, education and literature. Building is handicapped accessible. Meets last Thurs., 7-9pm, Cherry Hill Public Library, 1100 Kings Highway N., Cherry Hill. Call Susan 856-310-9792 (day). *E-mail:* susan.m.bunnell@att.net

NATIONAL

Apraxia-Kids (a program of The Childhood Apraxia of Speech Association) *National. Founded 2000.* Information and support for parents of children with apraxia of speech, speech-language pathologists and others interested in apraxia. Provides encouragement for parents to start support groups. Education, multimedia educational products, newsletter, literature, conferences, research, information, listserv, message boards, e-mail and help desk referrals to self-help groups nationwide. Write: Apraxia Kids, 1151 Freeport Rd., Suite 243, Pittsburgh, PA 15238. *Website:* http://www.apraxia-kids.org *E-mail:* helpdesk@apraxia-kids.org

ARACHNOIDITIS

ONLINE

Circle Of Friends With Arachnoiditis (COFWA) *Online. 1758 members. Founded 1998.* Support group which communicates primarily through the use of e-mail. Provides avenue for support, caring, sharing of information and friendly conversations with someone who knows what you are going through on a daily basis. *Website:* http://health.groups.yahoo.com/group/cofwa/

ARNOLD-CHIARI MALFORMATION

ONLINE

World Arnold Chiari Malformation Association *Online. 7000+ members. Founded 1996.* Provides information, support and understanding to persons concerned with Arnold Chiari malformation. Separate adult and children's online support groups. Write: World Arnold Chiari Malformation Association, c/o Bernard Meyer, 31 Newtown Woods Rd., Newtown Square, PA 19073. Call 610-353-4737. *Website:* http://www.pressenter.com/~wacma or http://wacma.com *E-mail:* chip@pressenter.com

ARTERIO VENOUS MALFORMATION / BRAIN ANEURYSM

MIDDLESEX

Kathleen McCriskin Brain AVM/Aneurysm Support Group *Professionally-run.* Provides mutual support and encouragement for persons with brain aneurysms, arterio-venous malformations (AVM) or subarachnoid hemorrhage. Rap sessions and guest speakers. Meets 4th Wed., 6-8pm, Jan., Mar., May, July, Sept., Nov., JFK Medical Center, NJ Institute Neuroscience Building, 65 James St., Edison. Call Nancy Vassallo 732-321-7000 ext. 68973.

ARTHROGRYPOSIS

NATIONAL

Arthrogryposis Multiplex Congenita *International. 700 members. Founded 2005.* Provides and encourages understanding and mutual support among anyone affected with the diagnosis of Arthrogryposis Multiplex Congenita (AMC). Aim is to increase awareness, provide educational material to new parents, or soon-to-be parents, and provide resource information to the medical field so to assist them in the treatment of a child or person with the diagnosis of AMC. Write: Arthrogryposis Multiplex Congenita Support Inc., P.O. Box 1883, Salyersville, KY 41465. *Website:* http://www.amcsupport.org *E-mail:* admin@amcsupport.org

ONLINE

Adults with AMC *Online. 178 members. Founded 2001.* Offers support for adults with arthrogryposis to come together and communicate with others affected by AMC. *Website:* http://groups.yahoo.com/group/amc_adults/

Arthrogryposis Support Group *Online. 184 members. Founded 2000.* Offers an online support group for children, adults and family members of people with arthrogryposis. *Website:* http://groups.yahoo.com/group/arthrogryposissupportgroup/

*Can't find an appropriate group in your area? The Clearinghouse helps people start groups. Give us a call at **1-800-367-6274**.*

ASHERMANS SYNDROME

ONLINE

Asherman's Syndrome Online Community *Online.* *(MULTILINGUAL)* Community of women worldwide who have been diagnosed with Asherman's syndrome (aka intrauterine or uterine synechiae). Provides support by sharing of information and knowledge. *Website:* http://www.ashermans.org *E-mail:* ashermansbook@yahoo.com

ATAXIA

NATIONAL

National Ataxia Foundation *International. 73 groups. Founded 1957.* Assists families with ataxia. Provides education for professionals and the public. Encourages prevention of ataxia through genetic counseling. Promotes research into causes and treatment. Newsletter, assistance in starting support groups, information and referrals. Group development guidelines. Write: National Ataxia Foundation, c/o Michael Parent, 2600 Fernbrook Lane, Suite 119, Minneapolis, MN 55447. Call 763-553-0020; Fax: 763-553-0167. *Website:* http://www.ataxia.org *E-mail:* naf@ataxia.org

ONLINE

A-T Children's Project *(BILINGUAL) Online. Founded 1993.* Enables families of children affected by ataxia telangiectasia to seek information and share thoughts with other families. Family online forum, information and workshops. Write: A-T Children's Project, 668 S. Military Trail, Deerfield Beach, FL 33442. Call 1-800-543-5728 or 954-481-6611. *Website:* http://www.atcp.org *E-mail:* info@atcp.org

ATRESIA / MICROTIA
(see also facial disfigurement)

ONLINE

Atresia-Microtia Group *Online. 1200+ members.* Forum for people, and parents of children, with aural atresia and/or microtia. Issues addressed include emotional support, hearing aids, ear reconstruction and insurance. *Website:* http://health.groups.yahoo.com/group/AtresiaMicrotia/ *E-mail:* AtresiaMicrotia-owner@yahoogroups.com

AUTOIMMUNE DISORDERS
(see also specific disorder)

OCEAN

Autoimmune Information Network Mutual support for patients with any one of over 140 autoimmune diseases and myasthenia gravis. Family members welcome. Rap sessions, literature, phone help, advocacy, guest speakers and buddy system. Building is handicapped accessible. Meets 4th Sun., 1-3pm, Ocean Medical Center, 425 Jack Martin Blvd., Conference Room A and B, Brick. Call Barbara Yodice 732-664-9259. *Website:* http://www.aininc.org *E-mail:* autoimmunehelp@aol.com

NATIONAL

American Autoimmune Related Diseases Association, Inc. *National. 2 affiliated groups. Founded 1991.* Mutual support and education for patients with any type of autoimmune disease. Advocacy, referrals to support groups, literature, conferences and quarterly newsletter. Supports research and physician symposium. Dues/newsletter subscription $34/yr. Write: American Autoimmune Related Diseases Association, 22100 Gratiot Ave., Eastpointe, MI 48021-2227. Call 586-776-3900 or 1-800-598-4668 (for a packet of information about autoimmunity); Fax: 586-776-3903. *Website:* http://www.aarda.org *E-mail:* aarda@aarda.org

ONLINE

National Eosinophilia-Myalgia Syndrome Network *Online.* Peer support and educational information for EMS survivors and their families. Supports research into L-trytophan induced EMS and other similar auto-immune disorders. Newsletter, phone help and online e-mail discussion group. Write: National Eosinophilia-Myalgia Syndrome Network, 767 Tower Blvd., Lorain, OH 44052. *Website:* http://www.nemsn.org/ *E-mail:* elveevee@aol.com

BARTH SYNDROME

Barth Syndrome Foundation, The *International. Founded 2000. (MULTILINGUAL)* Offers support to affected individuals and their families. Provides information, support awareness, medical database, diagnostic and clinical descriptions, fact sheets, moderated listserv information available on website, research, outreach, newsletter, referrals, pen pals and biennial conference. Peer-to-peer mentoring program. Write: The Barth Syndrome Foundation, P.O. Box 974, Perry, FL 32348. Call 850-223-1128. *Website:* http://www.barthsyndrome.org

BATTEN DISEASE

Batten Disease Support and Research Association *International. 20 affiliated groups. Founded 1987.* Emotional support for persons with Batten disease. Information and referrals, support group meetings, phone support, conferences and newsletter. Assistance provided for starting new groups. Write: Batten Disease Support and Research Association, 166 Humphries Dr., Suite 2, Reynoldsburg, OH 43068. Call 1-800-448-4570. *Website:* http://www.bdsra.org *E-mail:* bdsra1@bdsra.org

BECKWITH WIEDEMANN

ONLINE

Beckwith Wiedemann Family Forum *(MULTILINGUAL) Online. 250 members. Founded 2000.* Promotes support and the lively exchange of Beckwith Wiedemann information and support. Membership is open to anyone interested in BWS. *Website:* http://groups.yahoo.com/group/bwschat/

BEHCET'S SYNDROME

American Behcet's Disease Association *National network. Founded 1978.* Mutual support and information for Behcet's patients, their families and professionals. Newsletter (transcribed on tape for visually impaired), phone support, pen pals, conferences, medical advisory board, pamphlets, literature, press kit, information and referrals. Write: American Behcet's Disease Association, P.O. Box 869, Smithtown, NY 11787-0869. Call 1-800-723-4238 (9am-9pm EST). *Website:* http://www.behcets.com *E-mail:* cfornabaio@behcets.com

BELL'S PALSY

ONLINE

Bell's Palsy InfoSite and Forums *Online.* Offers several forums for support and discussion (pregnancy, treatment experiences, emotional aspect, Facial Palsy, parents, etc.). Chatroom offers weekly scheduled Bell's Palsy and facial paralysis chats. *Website:* http://www.bellspalsy.ws/

"The greatest gift we can give one another is rapt attention to one another's existence."--Sue Atchley Ebaugh

BENIGN ESSENTIAL BLEPHAROSPASM

Benign Essential Blepharospasm Research Foundation, Inc. *National. 170 groups. Founded 1981.* Provides information and emotional support to persons with benign essential blepharospasm (BEB). Networks people together with similar symptoms. Doctor referrals and education. Supports research, bimonthly newsletter and local group development guidelines. Voluntary contributions. Write: B.E.B. Foundation, P.O. Box 12468, Beaumont, TX 77726-2468. Call 409-832-0788; Fax: 409-832-0890. *Website:* http://www.blepharospasm.org *E-mail:* bebrf@sbcglobal.net or bebrf@blepharospasm.org

BLADDER EXSTROPHY

Association for the Bladder Exstrophy Community *International network. Founded 1991.* Mutual support for persons affected by bladder exstrophy including: parents of children with bladder exstrophy, adults, healthcare professionals and others interested in exstrophy. Newsletter, literature, information and referrals, informal pen pal program, conferences, advocacy and directory of members. Informal kids e-mail exchange. Dues $25/yr. Write: Association for the Bladder Exstrophy Community, 3075 First St., La Salle, MI 48145. Call Cindy 1-866-300-2222. *Website:* http://www.bladderexstrophy.com *E-mail:* admin@bladderexstrophy.com

BRACHIAL PLEXUS INJURY / ERB'S PALSY

Brachial Plexus Palsy Foundation, The *International. 4 affiliated groups. Founded 1994.* Support, information, resources and education for families and individuals affected by brachial plexus palsy (also known as brachial plexus injury or Erb's palsy). Online support message board and annual family event. Write: Brachial Plexus Palsy Foundation, 210 Springhaven Circle, Royersford, PA 19468. *Website:* http://www.brachialplexuspalsyfoundation.org

BRONCHIECTASIS

ONLINE

Bronchiectasis Support Group *Online.* E-mail support group for people who have bronchiectasis and their loved ones. *Website:* http://health.groups.yahoo.com/group/bronchiectasis

CANAVAN DISEASE
(see also leukodystrophy, Tay-Sachs)

Canavan Foundation *International. Founded 1992.* Provides information and education for persons affected by Canavan's. Offers literature, phone support, conferences and advocacy. Supports research. Online support available. Write: Canavan Foundation, 450 West End Ave., New York, NY 10024. Call 212-873-4640 or 1-877-422-6282; Fax: 212-873-7892. *Website:* http://www.canavanfoundation.org *E-mail:* info@canavanfoundation.org

CAVERNOUS ANGIOMA

ONLINE

Angioma Alliance *Online. Founded 2002.* Support and information for any person affected by cavernous angioma of the brain and spine. Educational materials, support via a community forum, listserv, chats and contact information for research studies. Maintains tissue/DNA bank and patient registry. Site available in Spanish and (in a limited way) Portuguese. Hosts annual national family conferences and scientific workshops for researchers. Works to increase physician and public awareness of the illness. Call 1-866-432-5226 or 757-623-0615. *Website:* http://www.angiomaalliance.org *E-mail:* info@angiomaalliance.org

CEREBROCOSTOMANDIBULAR SYNDROME

Cerebrocostomandibular Syndrome Support Group *National network. Founded 1998.* Provides support and guidance to families of children with cerebrocostomandibular syndrome (recessed lower mandible and rib anomalies). Exchange of messages through e-mail. Guidelines and help available for starting new groups. Write: Tara Montague, 7 Primrose Dr., Burlington, NJ 08016. Call 609-239-7831. *E-mail:* tara@marysplacerehab.com

CFC SYNDROME

CFC International *International network. Incorporated in 1999.* Mutual support for parents and healthcare providers of children with cardiofaciocutaneous syndrome. Strives to find and disseminate information on CFC syndrome. Offers newsletter, information, referrals, online listserv and phone support. Information on medical advisors and genetic testing. International clinic and family conferences every two years. Write: CFC International, c/o Brenda Conger, 183 Brown Rd., Vestal, NY 13850. Call 607-

772-9666 (eve.). *Website:* http://www.cfcsyndrome.org *E-mail:* bconger@cfcsyndrome.org

CHARCOT-MARIE-TOOTH DISEASE / PERONEAL MUSCULAR ATROPHY / HEREDITARY MOTOR SENSORY NEUROPATHY

NATIONAL

Charcot-Marie-Tooth Association *National. 25 affiliated groups. Founded 1983.* Information and support for patients and families affected by Charcot-Marie-Tooth disorders (also known as peroneal muscular atrophy or hereditary motor sensory neuropathy). Referrals, newsletter, phone help, support groups and conferences. Assistance starting similar groups. Write: Charcot-Marie-Tooth Association, 2700 Chestnut St., Chester, PA 19013. Call 1-800-606-2682 or 610-499-9264 (Mon.-Fri., 9am-5pm EST); Fax: 610-499-9267. *Website:* http://www.charcot-marie-tooth.org *E-mail:* info@charcot-marie-tooth.org

Hereditary Neuropathy Foundation *International network. Founded 2001.* Sharing and caring for those with Charcot-Marie-Tooth disease and other hereditary neuropathies. Extensive library of support materials and resources available. Publishes informational brochures. Write: Hereditary Neuropathy Foundation, 1751 2nd Ave., Suite 103, New York, NY 10128. Call 212-722-8396. *Website:* http://www.hnf-cure.org *E-mail:* info@hnf-cure.org

CHARGE SYNDROME

CHARGE Syndrome Foundation, Inc. *International network. Founded 1993.* Networking of families affected by CHARGE Syndrome (coloboma of the eye, heart malformations, atresia of the nasal passages, retardation of growth and/or development, genital hypoplasia, ear malformations). Publications include CHARGE syndrome brochure, New Parent packet (12+ pgs.), "CHARGE Syndrome: A Management Manual for Parents" (270 pgs.), Professional packet (35+ pgs.) and conference papers. Membership ($15/families; $20/professionals; $30/organizations) includes quarterly newsletter and parent-to-parent support. Moderated online support activities. Conferences in odd years (e.g. 2005). Write: Marion A. Norbury, c/o CHARGE Syndrome Foundation Inc., 2004 Parkade Blvd., Columbia, MO 65202-3121. Call 1-800-442-7604 or 573-499-4694. *Website:* http://www.chargesyndrome.org *E-mail:* marion@chargesyndrome.org

CHEMICAL HYPERSENSITIVITY / ENVIRONMENTAL ILLNESS
(see also allergies)

NATIONAL

H.E.A.L. (Human Ecology Action League, Inc.) *International. Founded 1977.* Education and information for persons concerned about the health effects of environmental exposures. Quarterly newsletter. Other publications include: back issues of "The Human Ecologist," information sheets, resource list, directories, reading list and book "Fragrance and Health." Referrals to local and regional chapters and support services. Dues $28/yr (US); $34/yr (Canada); $40/yr (Int'l). Write: HEAL, P.O. Box 509, Stockbridge, GA 30281. Call 770-389-4519; Fax: 770-389-4520. *Website:* http://www.healnatl.org or http://members.aol.com/HEALNatnl/index.html *E-mail:* HEALNatnl@aol.com

National Center for Environmental Health Strategies *National network. Founded 1984.* Fosters the development of creative solutions to environmental health problems with a focus on indoor environmental quality, chemical and electrical sensitivities and environmental disabilities. Clearinghouse and technical services, educational materials, workshops, community outreach, policy development, research, support and advocacy for persons injured by chemical/environment exposures. Special projects on school-related exposures and Gulf War Veterans. Books and publications. Focuses on access, accommodation and disability rights. Write: National Center for Environmental Health Strategies, 1100 Rural Ave., Voorhees, NJ 08043. Call Mary Lamielle 856-429-5358 or 856-816-8820. *E-mail:* marylamielle@ncehs.org

ONLINE

sickbuildings: Sick Buildings Information and Support *Online. 2062 members. Founded 1998.* Mutual-aid support and information regarding toxic mold exposure in homes, offices and schools. Discussions on mold-induced illnesses, building-related illnesses and health problems associated with mold exposure. *Website:* http://health.groups.yahoo.com/group/sickbuildings

CHROMOSOME 9P-

Chromosome 9P- Network *International network. Founded 1983.* Provides information, parent-to-parent networking and technical support to parents of children with 9P- and other deletions of 9P, mosaic, translocations, inverted 9P, etc. Facilitates research to further understand monosomy 9P. Information, referrals, phone support and yearly conferences. Write: Chromosome 9P-Network, P.O. Box 54, Stanley, ID 83278. *Website:* http://www.9pminus.org

CHROMOSOME 18 DISORDERS

Chromosome 18 Registry and Research Society *International network. Founded 1990.* Provides support and education concerning disorders of chromosome 18. Encourages and conducts research into areas that impact families. Links affected families and their physicians to the research community. Newsletter, phone support, annual conference, information and referrals. Dues $20/US; $25/Int'l. Write: Chromosome 18 Registry and Research Society, c/o Gloria Ellwanger, 7155 Oakridge Dr., San Antonio, TX 78229. Call 210-657-4968 (voice/fax). *Website:* http://www.chromosome18.org *E-mail:* office@chromosome18.org

CHROMOSOME 22 DISORDERS

NATIONAL

Chromosome 22 Central *International network. Founded 1996.* Networking and support for parents of children with any chromosome 22 disorder. Supports research. Offers literature, phone support, newsletter and e-mail support lists. Online bulletin boards. Write: Chromosome 22 Central, 237 Kent Ave., Timmins, Ontario, Canada P4N 3C2. Call 705-268-3099 (voice/fax). *Website:* http://www.c22c.org *E-mail:* a815@c22c.org or c22c@ntl.sympatico.ca

ONLINE

22q13 Family Discussion List *Online. 546 members. Founded 2000.* Support for families whose children are affected by abnormalities involving the 22q13 region of the 22nd chromosome, including terminal and interstitial deletions, mutations and other problems which lead to Phelan-McDermid syndrome. *Website:* http://health.groups.yahoo.com/group/22q13

"There is great comfort and inspiration in the feeling of close human relationships, and its bearing on our mutual fortunes – a powerful force, to overcome the 'tough breaks' which are certain to come to most of us from time to time." -- Walt Disney

CHROMOSOME DISORDERS

NATIONAL

Chromosome Deletion Outreach *National network. Founded 1992.* Provides support and information to families affected by rare chromosome disorders. Membership is free. Write: Chromosome Deletion Outreach, P.O. Box 724, Boca Raton, FL 33429-0724. Call 561-395-4252. Fax: 561-395-4252. *Website:* http://www.chromodisorder.org *E-mail:* info@chromodisorder.org

National Center for Chromosome Inversions *National network. Founded 1992.* Mutual support for families affected by chromosome inversions. Phone support, pen pal program, information and referrals. Write: National Center for Chromosome Inversions, 213 SE Charmont Lane, Lake City, FL 32025. Call 386-752-1548 (voice/fax). *E-mail:* ncfci@msn.com

CLUB FOOT

ONLINE

Clubfoot Support Group *Online. 420 members. Founded 1998.* Support group for parents of children with clubfoot/feet, persons with clubfoot/feet or anyone needing support on this topic. Goal is to provide support, friendship and encouragement. Operates through an e-mail mailing list. Must subscribe to list to join group. *Website:* http://health.groups.yahoo.com/group/clubfoot/

COBALAMIN
(see also metabolic disorders)

Cobalamin Network, The *International network. 2 chapters. Founded 1985.* Emotional support and information for families of children affected by inborn errors of cobalamin metabolism. Referrals to pediatric metabolic practitioners. Write: Cobalamin Network, P.O. Box 174, Thetford Center, VT 05075 or Cobalamin Network, 207 E. 14th Pl., Cut Off, LA 70345. Call 802-785-4029. *E-mail:* SueBee18@valley.net or menta@mobiletel.com

COCKAYNE SYNDROME

Share and Care Cockayne Syndrome Network *(MULTILINGUAL) International network. Founded 1981.* Mutual support and networking for families affected by Cockayne syndrome. Sharing of information between families and professionals. Maintains registry of families. Information, referrals, newsletter and phone support. Website and pamphlet available in Spanish,

569

Japanese, German and Portugese. Write: Share and Care Cockayne Syndrome Network, P.O. Box 282, Waterford, VA 20197. Call 703-727-0404. *Website:* http://www.cockaynesyndrome.org *E-mail:* JackieClark@aol.com

COFFIN-LOWRY SYNDROME

Coffin-Lowry Syndrome Foundation, The *International network. Founded 1991.* Serves as a clearinghouse for information on Coffin-Lowry syndrome. Forum for exchanging experiences, advice and information with other CLS families. Seeks to become a visible group in the medical, scientific, educational and professional communities in order to facilitate referrals of newly diagnosed individuals and to encourage medical and behavioral research. Maintains mailing list of families and professionals. Provides newsletter, family support and informational packet. Write: The Coffin-Lowry Syndrome Foundation, c/o Mary Hoffman, 675 Kalmia PI NW, Issaquah, WA 98027. Call 425-427-0939 (after 5:30pm PST). *Website:* http://groups.yahoo.com/group/clsfoundation/ *E-mail:* CoffinLowry@Gmail.com

COGAN'S SYNDROME

ONLINE

Cogan's Contact Network *Online network. Founded 1989.* Mutual support and sharing of experiences and strategies for persons with Cogan's syndrome. Aim is to help people understand Cogan's, a rare disorder that affects hearing, eyes, balance, etc. Networking, pen pals and literature. Online dues $12/yr. Write: YUPPA/Cogan's Contact, P.O. Box 145, Freehold, NJ 07728-0145. *Website:* http://www.cogansyndrome.info *E-mail:* uscogans@juno.com

CONGENITAL ADRENAL HYPERPLASIA

NATIONAL

CARES Foundation Inc. *International. 48 regional support groups. Founded 2001.* Goal is to educate the public and professionals about all types of congenital adrenal hyperplasia, the symptoms, diagnostic protocol, treatment, genetic frequency and the necessity for early intervention through newborn screening. Offers information and support to affected individuals and their families. Write: CARES Foundation, 2414 Morris Ave., Suite 110, Union, NJ 07083. Call 1-866-227-3737 or 973-912-3895; Fax: 973-912-8990. *Website:* http://www.caresfoundation.org *E-mail:* info@caresfoundation.org

Congenital Adrenal Hyperplasia *National division of MAGIC. Founded 1989.* Offers educational and emotional support to families of children with congenital adrenal hyperplasia. Provides information and referrals, kids program, phone support, annual convention, networking and quarterly newsletter. Assistance in starting new groups. Write: Mary Andrews, CAH Division of MAGIC Foundation, 6645 W. North Ave., Oak Park, IL 60302. Call 1-800-362-4423; Fax: 708-383-0899. *Website:* http://www.magicfoundation.org *E-mail:* mary@magicfoundation.org

CONGENITAL CENTRAL HYPOVENTILATION / ONDINE'S CURSE

WARREN

CCHS Family Network Support for families of children with congenital central hypoventilation syndrome (under 18 welcome). Phone help, advocacy, pen pals and literature. Family conference every three years. Communication via phone, letters and quarterly newsletters. Call Desiree Cougle 908-852-2082; Fax: 908-850-9537. *Website:* http://www.cchs.org

ONLINE

Congenital Central Hypoventilation Network (CCHS) *Online. Founded 1990.* Mutual support for families caring for a child who has congenital central hypoventilation syndrome (aka Ondine's curse). Provides family newsletter, physician directory, equipment information, moderated online mutual help activities, information and referrals. Facilitates and supports CCHS research. Holds family educational conferences every three years. Provides online referrals to local support groups. Family directory for CCHS families in the US and around the world available to families via website. Directory contains phone and other contact information. Write: CCHS Network, c/o Mary Vanderlaan, 71 Maple St., Oneonta, NY 13820. Fax: 607-431-4351. *Website:* http://www.cchsnetwork.org *E-mail:* vanderlaanm@hartwick.edu

Consider passing this Directory on to a student or staff member - browsing through the Directory pages can often provide helpful education as to the wide variety of groups available.

CONGENITAL CYTOMEGALOVIRUS DISEASE

National Congenital Cytomegalovirus Disease Registry *National network. Founded 1990.* Parent support network that provides support to families of children with congenital cytomegalovirus disease (CMV). Information, referrals, newsletter and literature. Write: National Congenital Cytomegalovirus Disease Registry, c/o Feigin Center, Suite 1150, MC3-2371, Houston, TX 77030-2399. Call Carol Griesser, RN 832-824-4387; Fax: 832-825-4347. *Website:* http://www.bcm.tmc.edu/pedi/infect/cmv *E-mail:* cmv@bcm.edu

CORNELIA DE LANGE

Cornelia de Lange Syndrome Foundation, Inc. *National. 2500+ member families. Founded 1981.* Provides support and education to families affected by Cornelia de Lange syndrome. Supports research. Newsletter. Annual meetings. Professional network. Write: Cornelia de Lange Syndrome Foundation, 302 West Main St., Suite 100, Avon, CT 06001. Call 1-800-223-8355 or 860-676-8166; Fax: 860-676-8337. *Website:* http://cdlsusa.org *E-mail:* info@cdlsusa.org

CORTICOBASAL GANGLIONIC DEGENERATION
(see also dementia, movement disorders)

ONLINE

CBGD (Corticobasal Ganglionic Degeneration) Support Network *Online. 1093 members. Founded 1998.* Support for anyone affected by corticobasal ganglionic degeneration (a rare neurological disorder characterized by cell loss in the brain). Offers education, information and newsletter. Networks members together for emotional support. Write: CBGD Support Network, c/o Theresa Roberts, 519 Loma Ave., Long Beach, CA 90814. *Website:* http://health.groups.yahoo.com/group/cbgd_support *E-mail:* theresa.roberts@housingpartners.com

COSTELLO SYNDROME

International Costello Syndrome Support Group *International network. Founded 1996.* Mutual support for parents of children with Costello syndrome. Phone support, literature, pen pals, international conference twice a year, information and referrals. Write: Colin and Cath Stone, 90 Parkfield Rd. North, New Moston, M40 3RQ, United Kingdom. Call +44 161 682 2479. *Website:* http://costellokids.com or http://forum.costellokids.com (message board) *E-mail:* c.stone8@ntlworld.com

CREUTZFELDT-JAKOB DISEASE

ONLINE

CJD Voice *Online.* Provides emotional support and information to persons who have lost a loved one to Creutzfeldt-Jakob disease, a fatal brain-deteriorating disorder. E-mail discussion group, message board and scheduled chatroom sessions. *Website:* http://www.cjdvoice.org *E-mail:* tunket60@sbcglobal.net

CRI DU CHAT (5P) SYNDROME

5P- Society *International network. Founded 1987.* Support organization for families having a child with 5P- syndrome (aka cri du chat), a genetic disorder characterized by a high-pitched cry. Dedicated to facilitating flow of information among affected families and medical professionals. Listing of families in U.S. and Canada. Newsletter. Annual meeting. Write: 5P-Society, P.O. Box 268, Lakewood, CA 90714-0268. Call 1-888-970-0777; Fax: 562-920-5240. *Website:* http://www.fivepminus.org *E-mail:* director@fivepminus.org

CROUZON SYNDROME

ONLINE

Crouzon Support Network *Online. 201 members. Founded 2001.* Support group for individuals and families who are dealing with Crouzon syndrome and other craniofacial anomalies. A place to share experience, mutual support, inspiration and information. *Website:* http://health.groups.yahoo.com/group/crouzons

CUSHING'S DISEASE

NATIONAL

Cushing's Help and Support *International. Founded 2000.* Support and information for persons with Cushing's disease. Offers support to family and friends. Message boards, literature, chatroom, guest speakers, annual national conference, pen pals, phone support network and advocacy. Write: Cushing's Help and Support, 13222 Point Pleasant Dr., Fairfax, VA 22033-3515. Call 1-877-825-0128; Fax: 703-378-8517. *Website:* http://www.cushings-help.com *E-mail:* CushingsSupport@aol.com

Cushing's Support and Research Foundation, Inc. *International. Founded 1995.* Provides support and information to patients with Cushing's. Networking and newsletter so patients can contact others with Cushing's. Write: Cushing's Support and Research Foundation, Inc., 65 East India Row, #22B, Boston, MA 02110. Call 617-723-3674 (voice/fax); *Website:* http://CSRF.net *E-mail:* cushinfo@csrf.net

CUTIS LAXA

Cutis Laxa Internationale *International. Founded 2001.* Support group for those afflicted with any type of cutis laxa, a rare genetic disorder. Networking, promotes research and advocacy. Dues $55/yr. or L25/yr. Write: Cutis Laxa Internationale, 35 route des Chaignes, 17740 Sainte Marie de Re, France. Call 33 (0)5 46 55 00 59. *Website:* http://www.orpha.net/nestasso/cutislax *E-mail:* mcjlboiteux@aol.com

CYSTINOSIS

ONLINE

Cystinosis Research Network *Online. Founded 1996.* Dedicated to supporting and advocating for continued research, providing family support and education programs. Professionals and caregivers are welcome to join. Promotes and supports research that will lead to a better understanding, improved treatments and a cure for cystinosis. Dedicated to improving awareness and education of cystinosis and to be utilized as a resource for families and public. Programs include support group, networking, toll-free number, website, newsletter and family conferences. Website to improve awareness and education of cystinosis for patients, families and physicians. Non-moderated but members must be pre-approved by CRN. Write: Cystinosis Research Network, 302 Whyegate Court, Lake Forest, IL 60045. Call 1-866-276-3669 or 847-735-0471; Fax: 847-235-2773. *Website:* http://www.cystinosis.org *E-mail:* CRN@cystinosis.org

DANCING EYE SYNDROME / KINSBOURNE SYNDROME / MYOCLONIC ENCEPHALOPATHY / OPOCLONUS-MYOCLONUS SYNDROME

NATIONAL

Dancing Eye Syndrome *International network. Founded 1988.* Support and information for families of children with dancing eye syndrome (aka Kinsbourne syndrome, opsoclonus myoclonus, or myoclonic encephalopathy of infants), a disorder consisting of loss of balance, irregular eye movements and muscle jerking. Newsletter and phone help. Write: Dancing Eye Syndrome, c/o J. Stanton-Roberts, 78 Quantock Rd., W. Sussex BN13 2HQ England. Call 1903-532383 (voice/fax). *E-mail:* support@dancingeyes.org.uk

Opsoclonus-Myoclonus Support Network *National network. Founded 1994.* Networking for parents of children with opsoclonus-myoclonus syndrome through phone and online messages. Doctor referrals, consultation, literature and current research information. Write: Sandra Greenberg, 2116 Casa Linda Dr., West Covina, CA 91791. Call 626-919-2448 or 626-315-8125. *Website:* http://www.OMSupportNetwork.org *E-mail:* sandragreenberg@hotmail.com

DANDY WALKER SYNDROME

Dandy-Walker Syndrome Network *International network. Founded 1993.* Provides mutual support, information and networking for families affected by Dandy-Walker syndrome. Phone support. Write: Dandy-Walker Syndrome Network, c/o Desiree Fleming, 5030 142nd Path, Apple Valley, MN 55124. Call 952-423-4008.

DEGOS DISEASE / MALIGNANT ATROPHIC PAPULOSIS / KOHLMEIER-DEGOS DISEASE

ONLINE

Degos Patients Support Network *Online.* Support and information for those affected by or dealing with Degos disease (aka malignant atrophic papulosis or Kohlmeier-Degos disease), an extremely rare thrombotic vasculopathy affecting people of all ages all over the world. Message board for patients, their families and caregivers. Secure section with access to discussion forum and other information for medical professionals only. *Website:* http://www.degosdisease.com *E-mail:* judith@degosdisease.com

DENTATORUBRAL PALLIDOLUYSIAN ATROPHY

Dentatorubral Pallidoluysian Atrophy (DRPLA) Network *International network. Founded 1999.* Support and information for persons affected by dentatorubral pallidoluysian atrophy, a rare genetic disorder, that leads to physical and cognitive problems. Phone support, pen pals, online and e-mail discussions. Write: DRPLA, c/o Frank J. Marone, Ph.D., 1426 46th Ave., San Francisco, CA 94122-2903. Call 415-753-5695. *E-mail:* bmsca@juno.com

DUANE'S RETRACTION SYNDROME

ONLINE

Duane's Retraction Syndrome *Online. 1150 members. Founded 1999.* A place for those affected by Duane's retraction syndrome (an eye mobility disorder) to share experiences and information with others. *Website:* http://health.groups.yahoo.com/group/duanes/

DUBOWITZ SYNDROME

NE Dubowitz Syndrome Support *National. Founded 1997.* Information, education, support and networking for parents of children with Dubowitz syndrome and concerned professionals. Information on assistive technology and educational issues. Referrals, pen pals, advocacy and information on geneticists. Write: NE Dubowitz Syndrome Support, c/o Sharon Terzian, 106 Verndale St., Warwick, RI 02889. Call 401-737-3138. *Website:* http://www.dubowitzsyndrome.net *E-mail:* dubowitzsyndrome@netzero.net

DYSAUTONOMIA
(see also neurocardiogenic synacope)

NATIONAL

Dysautonomia Foundation, Inc., The *International. 13 chapters. Founded 1951.* Provides peer support, information and referrals for families affected by familial dysautonomia. Raises funds for medical and clinic research. Aim is to raise public awareness about the disease. Testing for all Ashkenazi Jewish individuals is now available. Newsletter. Write: Dysautonomia Foundation, Inc., 315 West 39th St., Suite 701, New York, NY 10018. Call 212-279-1066; Fax: 212-279-2066. *Website:* http://www.familialdysautonomia.org *E-mail:* info@familialdysautonomia.org

Dysautonomia Youth Network of America, Inc. (DYNA) *International network. Founded 2002.* Provides young patients (under 21) with a support and outreach network focused on positive peer support. Strives to heighten awareness of dysautonomia conditions (postural orthostatic tachycardia syndrome, neurally mediated hypotension, neurocardiogenic syncope, vasovagal syncope, generalized dysautonomis, birth dysautonomia, non-familial dysautonomia, post-viral dysautonomia) within the pediatric and adolescent medical communities. Newsletter, literature (English, Spanish, Italian), pen pal program, moderated message board and national conference. Membership is free. Write: DYNA, 1301 Greengate Court, Waldorf, MD 20601. Call 301-705-6995; Fax: 301-638-3962. *Website:* http://www.dynakids.org

FD Now *National.* Provides parent support to families, networking and funding for familial dysautonomia research. Information and newsletter. Write: Ann Slaw, c/o FD Now, 1170 Green Knolls Dr., Buffalo Grove, IL 60089. Call 847-913-0455.

National Dysautonomia Research Foundation *National network. Founded 1996.* Provides support, educational material and medical referrals for persons who have dysautonomia (a disorder of the autonomic nervous system). Networking, literature, advocacy, phone support and conferences. Encourages research. Online e-mail and discussion support forum, groups and free downloadable online Patient Handbook. Write: National Dysautonomia Research Foundation, P.O. Box 301, Red Wing, MN 55066-2108. Call 651-267-0525 (Mon.-Fri., 8am-6pm CST) Fax: 651-267-0524. *Website:* http://www.ndrf.org *E-mail:* ndrf@ndrf.org

National Society For MVP and Dysautonomia *National. 59 affiliated groups. Founded 1987.* Assists individuals suffering from Mitral Valve Prolapse and dysautonomia to find support and understanding. Education on symptoms and treatment. Newsletter and literature. Write: National Society for MVP and Dysautonomia, 880 Montclair Rd., Suite 370, Birmingham, AL 35213. Call 1-800-541-8602 or 205-592-5765; Fax: 205-592-5707. *Website:* http//www.mvprolapse.com *E-mail:* staff@MVProlapse.com

DYSGRAPHIA

ONLINE

Dysgraphia *Online. 583 members. Founded 1999.* Support for parents that have children with dysgraphia (written expression disorder characterized by distorted or incorrect writing), and adults who have dysgraphia. *Website:* http://groups.yahoo.com/group/dysgraphia/

DYSTONIA
(see also movement disorders)

MONMOUTH

Central Jersey Dystonia Support Group Support and education for persons with dystonia. Newsletter. Meets Sat., 4 times per/yr., Centra State Medical Center, Freehold. Call Janice and Len 732-409-1112 (day). *E-mail:* cjdystonia@aol.com

NATIONAL

Dystonia Medical Research Foundation *International. 110 chapters. Founded 1976.* Provides education, awareness and support groups for persons with dystonia. Fundraises for research. Newsletter, information and referrals to local groups. Also offers guidelines for starting similar groups. Write: Dystonia Medical Research Foundation, 1 E. Wacker Dr., Suite 2810, Chicago, IL 60601-1905. Call 312-755-0198 (US), 1-800-361-8061 (Canada); Fax: 312-803-0138. *Website:* http://www.dystonia-foundation.org/ *E-mail:* dystonia@dystonia-foundation.org

DYSTROPHIC EPIDERMOLYSIS BULLOSA

DEBRA of America (Dystrophic Epidermolysis Bullosa Research Association) *National network. Founded 1980.* Support and information for families affected by epidermolysis bullosa. Promotes research, provides education for patients, families and professionals, emergency financial support, emergency wound care supplies, New Family Advocate program, newsletter, biennial national conference, information and referrals. Write: DEBRA of America, 16 E. 41st St., 3rd Floor, New York, NY 10017. Call 212-868-1573 or 1-866-332-7276; Fax: 212-868-9296. *Website:* http://www.debra.org *E-mail:* staff@debra.org or nurse@debra.org

ECTODERMAL DYSPLASIAS

National Foundation for Ectodermal Dysplasias *National network. Founded 1981.* Distributes information on ectodermal dysplasia syndrome and treatments. Provides support programs for families and funds research projects. Quarterly newsletter. Annual family conference and regional conferences, dental implant program and scholarship opportunities. Directory of members for informal contacts among families. Write: National Foundation for Ectodermal Dysplasias, 410 E. Main St., Box 114, Mascoutah, IL 62258-0114. Call 618-566-2020; Fax: 618-566-4718. *Website:* http://www.nfed.org *E-mail:* info@nfed.org

EHLERS-DANLOS SYNDROME

Ehlers-Danlos National Foundation *National. 35 local groups. Founded 1985.* Provides resources for Ehlers-Danlos syndrome patients, families and health care professionals. Mission is to disseminate accurate information, provide a network of support and communication and to foster and support research. Online message boards for EDNF members. Write: Ehlers-Danlos National Foundation, 3200 Wilshire Blvd., Suite 1601, South Tower, Los Angeles, CA

90010. Call 213-368-3800; Fax: 213-427-0057. *Website:* http://www.ednf.org
E-mail: staff@ednf.org

ELLIS VAN CREVELD SYNDROME /
CHONDROECTODERMAL DYSPLASIA
(see also growth disorders)

Ellis Van Creveld Support Group *International network. Founded 1997.*
Provides support and information for families affected by Ellis Van Creveld
syndrome (aka chondroectodermal dysplasia), an extremely rare form of
dwarfism. Networks families together for support. Literature, advocacy, phone
support, information and referrals. Connects with medical community to find
ways to save the lives of infants born with this genetic disorder. Write: Ellis Van
Creveld Support Group, 17 Bridlewood Trail, Honeoye Falls, NY 14472. Call
585-624-8277 or 585-737-1500. *E-mail:* PattiMO44@aol.com or
evc@crydee.plus.com

ENCEPHALITIS

NATIONAL

Encephalitis Society Resource Centre, The *International network. Founded
1994.* Provides support and information for persons with encephalitis
(inflammation of the brain) and their families. Aims to educate public and
professionals about the condition. Newsletter, information and referrals. Write:
Encephalitis Society Resource Centre, 7b Saville St., Malton, North Yorkshire,
Y017 7LL UK. Call +44 (0) 653 699 599 (voice/fax). *Website:*
http://www.encephalitis.info *E-mail:* mail@encephalitis.info

ONLINE

Encephalitis Global *Online.* Provides support and information for encephalitis
survivors, caregivers and loved ones and for interested persons. Includes a guide
for newly diagnosed persons, links, downloadable information pamphlet, group
discussions and live chats. *Website:* http://www.encephalitisglobal.org *E-mail:*
admin@encephalitisglobal.org

Encephgroup *Online. 527 members. Founded 2000.* Support group for
survivors of all types of encephalitis and their family members, caregivers and
friends. *Website:* http://health.groups.yahoo.com/group/encephgroup/

ERYTHROMELALGIA

Erythromelalgia Association, The (TEA) *International network. Founded 1999.* Provides support and information to those diagnosed with erythromelalgia. Offers education to increase awareness of this rare condition within the medical profession and the general public. Fundraises to promote research into the causes, diagnostic methods and treatments. Write: The Erythromelalgia Association, 200 Old Castle Lane, Wallingford, PA 19086. Call 610-566-0797. *Website:* http://www.burningfeet.org or http://www.erythromelalgia.org *E-mail:* memberservices@erythromelalgia.org

ESSENTIAL TREMOR
(see also movement disorders, neurological disorders)

International Essential Tremor Foundation *International. 77 affiliated groups. Founded 1989.* Provides information and support for persons affected by essential tremor. Literature, quarterly newsletter, research updates, information and referrals. Dues $30/yr. Write: International Essential Tremor Foundation, P.O. Box 14005, Lenexa, KS 66285. Call 1-888-387-3667 or 913-341-3880; Fax: 913-341-1296. *Website:* http://www.essentialtremor.org/ *E-mail:* STAFF@essentialtremor.org

FABRY DISEASE

Fabry Support and Information Group (FSIG) *National network. Founded 1996.* Dedicated to dispensing information and encouraging mutual self help as a means of emotional support to Fabry patients and family members. Networking of members, discussion page, newsletter, information and referrals. Write: Fabry Support and Information Group, P.O. Box 510, Concordia, MO 64020. Call 660-463-1355; Fax: 660-463-1356. *Website:* http://www.fabry.org *E-mail:* info@fabry.org

FACIAL DIFFERENCES
(see also accidents, burn victims, specific disorder)

NATIONAL

AmeriFace *National. Founded 1991.* Provides emotional support and information to persons with facial differences and their families. Network database of 900+ families who have similar concerns. Promotes public education and awareness. Also has cleft advocate program which provides online parent-patient support network. Newsletter, information and referrals. Write: AmeriFace, P.O. Box 751112, Las Vegas, NV 89136. Call 1-888-486-

1209 or 702-769-9264; Fax: 702-341-5351. *Website:* http://www.aboutfaceusa.org *E-mail:* info@ameriface.org

Forward Face *Model. 1 group in New York. Founded 1978.* Mutual support for people with craniofacial disfigurement and their families. Strongly advocates educating members and the public in the quest for understanding and acceptance. Liaison with medical personnel. Newsletter and videotapes. Dues $30. Teen/young adult support group called The Inner Faces. Write: Forward Face, 317 E. 34th St., 9th Floor, Suite 901A, New York, NY 10016. Call 212-684-5860; Fax: 212-684-5864. *Website:* http://www.forwardface.org *E-mail:* info@forwardface.org

Let's Face It *Resource.* Provides information and resources for persons with facial differences, their families, professionals and the public. Write: Let's Face It, c/o University of Michigan, School of Dentistry / Dentistry Library, 1011 N. University, Ann Arbor, MI 48109-1078. *Website:* http://www.dent.umich.edu/faceit/ *E-mail:* faceit@umich.edu

FACIOSCAPULOHUMERAL DISEASE / LANDOUZY-DEJERINE
(see also muscular dystrophy)

NATIONAL

FSH Society, Inc. (Facioscapulohumeral Disease) *National network. Founded 1991.* Support, information, education, networking and advocacy for individuals with facioscapulohumeral disease (aka Landouzy-Dejerine muscular dystrophy). Purpose is to increase awareness, understanding and conduct research and education on the second most prevalent muscular dystrophy in adults. Funds research through grants to researchers. Acts as a clearinghouse for information on the FSHD disorder and on potential drugs and devices designed to alleviate the effects of the disease. Newsletter, support group meetings, conferences and literature. Write: Nancy VanZant, c/o BBRI, R353, 64 Grove St., Watertown, MA 02472. Call 617-658-7878 or 781-860-0501; Fax: 617-658-7879. *Website:* http://www.fshsociety.org

"And should you ever begin to feel that you are becoming separated from the world, you are simply self-deceived, for you could no more do this than a wave could separate itself from the ocean and still be a wave."--Gerald Jampolsky

FACTOR V LEIDEN / THROMBOPHILIA

ONLINE

Factor V Leiden Mailing List and Digest *Online. 1300 members.* Mailing list that offers support and information for persons affected by Factor V Leiden (thrombophilia), a hereditary blood coagulation disorder. Daily digest (condensed version of the mailing list) also available. *Website:* http://www.fvleiden.org

FATTY OXIDATION DISORDER
(see also metabolic disorders)

FOD Family Support Group *International network. Founded 1991.* Opportunity for families dealing with fatty oxidation disorders (i.e. MCAD, LCHAD, VLCAD, SCAD, etc.) to network with others dealing with these rare, genetic metabolic disorders. Phone support, e-mail list, information and referrals. Write: FOD Family Support Group, c/o Deb Lee Gould, MEd, Dir., 2041 Tomahawk, Okemos, MI 48864. Call 517-381-1940; Fax: 866-290-5206. *Website:* http://www.fodsupport.org *E-mail:* deb@fodsupport.org

FETAL ALCOHOL SYNDROME / DRUG-AFFECTED

OCEAN

Parents Of Adoptive Children with Fetal Alcohol Syndrome Mutual support and information for parents who have adopted a child with fetal alcohol syndrome. Group meets various days and times. For meeting information call Shannon 732-600-7657.

NATIONAL

FEN (Family Empowerment Network) *National network. Founded 1992.* Support, education, advocacy and training for families of children and adults with fetal alcohol spectrum disorders or fetal alcohol effects and interested professionals. Family retreats. Fetal alcohol spectrum disorder (FASD) resources, education and referrals for diagnosis. Networks families together for support. Membership is free. Assistance in starting support groups. Monthly parent teleconferences. Write: Family Empowerment Network, c/o University of Wisconsin Department of Family Medicine, 777 S. Mills St., Madison, WI 53715. Call 1-800-462-5254 or 608-262-6590; Fax: 608-263-5813. *Website:* http://www.fammed.wisc.edu/fen *E-mail:* fen@fammed.wisc.edu

Fetal Alcohol Syndrome Family Resource Institute *International. Founded 1990.* Coalition of families and professionals concerned with fetal alcohol syndrome/effects. Educational programs, brochures and information packets. Support group meetings. Advocacy, information and referrals, phone support and conferences. Write: Fetal Alcohol Syndrome Family Resource Institute, P.O. Box 2525, Lynnwood, WA 98036. Call 1-800-999-3429 (in WA) or 253-531-2878 (outside WA); Fax: 425-640-9155. *Website:* http://fetalalcoholsyndrome.org *E-mail:* vicky@fetalalcoholsyndrome.org

FG SYNDROME

ONLINE

FG Syndrome Homepage *Online. Founded 1998.* Support network for persons interested in FG syndrome, a genetic condition resulting in multiple congenital anomalies. Newsletter, listserv, conferences, fundraising and general family support. Write: FG Syndrome Family Alliance, 946 NW Circle Blvd., Suite 290, Corvallis, OR 97330. Call 617-577-9050. *Website:* http://www.fg-syndrome.org *E-mail:* info@fg-syndrome.org

FIBRODYSPLASIA OSSIFICANS PROGRESSIVA

International Fibrodysplasia Ossificans Progressiva Association *International network. Founded 1988.* Serves as a support network for families dealing with fibrodysplasia ossificans progressiva (FOP). Supports education, communication and medical research. Newsletter. Write: International FOP Association, Box 196217, Winter Springs, FL 32719-6217. Call 407-365-4194; Fax: 407-365-3213. *Website:* http://www.ifopa.org *E-mail:* together@ifopa.org

FLOATING HARBOR SYNDROME

Floating Harbor Syndrome Support Group *National network. Founded 1999.* Provides mutual support and networking for parents of children with Floating Harbor syndrome. Newsletter, literature, phone support and photos of children with FHS. Write: Floating Harbor Syndrome Support Group, c/o Deana Swanson, 1964 Sheffield Rd., Harmony, NC 28634. *Website:* http://www.floatingharborsyndromesupport.com *E-mail:* littleflock@yadtel.net

Can't find an appropriate group in your area? The Clearinghouse helps people start groups. Give us a call at 1-800-367-6274.

FRAGILE X SYNDROME

STATEWIDE

Fragile X Association Organization of parents and professionals dedicated to improving the lives of individuals and families affected by fragile X syndrome. For information call Jennifer Keenan 856-985-3257. *Website:* http://www.fragilex.org

NATIONAL

FRAXA Research Foundation *International. 30 affiliated groups. Founded 1994.* Support and information on fragile X syndrome. Funds medical research, investigator-initiated grants and postdoctoral fellowships. Newsletter and literature. Some chapters have support group meetings. Guidelines available on starting a similar group. Write: FRAXA Research Foundation, 45 Pleasant St., Newburyport, MA 01950. Call 978-462-1866; Fax: 978-463-9985. *Website:* http://www.fraxa.org *E-mail:* info@fraxa.org

National Fragile X Foundation, The *International. 55 groups. Founded 1984.* Mission includes phone and e-mail support, promoting awareness, education, research and legislative advocacy regarding fragile X syndrome, a hereditary condition which is the most common known cause of inherited mental impairment. Services also include a quarterly journal, research grants, local, national and international conferences and educational resources (books and videotapes for a fee). Write: National Fragile X Foundation, P.O. Box 34, Walnut Creek, CA 94597. Call 1-800-688-8765 (Mon.-Fri., 8:30am-5pm PST); Fax: 925-938-9315. *Website:* http://www.FragileX.org *E-mail:* NATLFX@FragileX.org

FREEMAN-SHELDON SYNDROME

Freeman-Sheldon Parent Support Group *International network. Founded 1982.* Provides emotional support for parents of children with Freeman-Sheldon syndrome and for adults with this syndrome. Sharing of helpful medical literature. Provides information on growth and development of individuals affected. Participates in research projects. Members network by phone, mail and through a members-only listserv. Write: Freeman-Sheldon Parent Support Group, 509 E. Northmont Way, Salt Lake City, UT 84103. Call 801-364-7060. *Website:* http://www.fspsg.org *E-mail:* info@fspsg.org

GALACTOSEMIA

Parents of Galactosemic Children, Inc. *National network. Founded 1985.* Information and mutual support for parents of galactosemic children. Publications, pen pals, conferences, phone support and online message board. Write: Parents of Galactosemic Children, c/o Michelle Fowler, P.O. Box 2401 Mandeville, LA 70470. Call 1-866-900-7421. *Website:* http://www.galactosemia.org *E-mail:* president@galactosemia.org

GASTROESOPHAGEAL REFLUX

PAGER **(Pediatric/Adolescent Gastroesophageal Reflux Association)** *National network. Founded 1992.* Offers support and information for parents whose children suffer from gastroesophageal reflux (GER), an inappropriate backwash of stomach contents into the esophagus that affects millions of children and adults. Educates the public on this disorder. Newsletter, literature and telephone support network. Website with 300+ information pages and 20,000+ messages from parents. Helps new chapters start when leaders are identified. Extensive free information is available via website and mail. Write: PAGER, P.O. Box 486, Buckeystown, MD 21717. Call 301-601-9541. *Website:* http://www.reflux.org *E-mail:* pagervol1@reflux.org

GAUCHER DISEASE

National Gaucher Foundation *National. 2 chapters. Founded 1984.* Provides information and assistance for those affected by Gaucher disease. Provides education and outreach to increase public awareness. Operates the Gaucher Disease Family Support Network. Quarterly newsletter, phone support and medical board. Guidelines to help start similar groups. Write: National Gaucher Foundation, 61 General Early Dr., Harpers Ferry, WV 25425. Call 1-800-428-2437; Fax: 304-725-6429. *Website:* http://www.gaucherdisease.org *E-mail:* ngf@gaucherdisease.org

GENETIC DISORDERS
(see also specific disorder)

Genetic Alliance, The *International network. Founded 1986.* Provides technical assistance to genetic disorder support groups and disseminates information to the public on available resources and referrals. Fosters a partnership among consumers and professionals to enhance education and service for the needs of individuals affected by genetic disorders. Supports networking efforts of members of government agencies, professional groups, service providers and organizations. Write: Genetic Alliance, 4301 Connecticut Ave., NW, Suite 404,

Washington, DC 20008. Call 202-966-5557; Fax: 202-966-8553. *Website:* http://www.geneticalliance.org *E-mail:* info@geneticalliance.org

GLYCOGEN STORAGE DISEASE

Association For Glycogen Storage Disease *U.S. and Canadian network. 3 affiliated groups. Founded 1979.* Mutual support and information sharing among parents of children and patients with glycogen storage disease. Fosters communication between parents, patients and professionals, creates public awareness and encourages research. Offers GSDnet support group via e-mail. Newsletter, phone support and conference. Write: Association for Glycogen Storage Disease, P.O. Box 896, Durant, IA 52747. Call 563-785-6038 (voice/fax). *Website:* http://www.agsdus.org *E-mail:* maryc@agsdus.org

GORLIN SYNDROME / NEVOID BASAL CELL CARCINOMA / BASAL CELL CARCINOMA NEVUS SYNDROME

NATIONAL

Basal Cell Carcinoma Nevus Syndrome Life Support Network *National network.* Provides support services to patients, families and medical professionals dealing with the many manifestations of basal cell carcinoma nevus syndrome (aka Gorlin syndrome or nevoid basal cell syndrome). Offers online forum, quarterly newsletter, annual retreat and conference and periodic regional meetings. Write: Sheila LaRosa, Basal Cell Carcinoma Nevus Syndrome Life Support Network, P.O. Box 321, Burton, OH 44021. Call 1-866-834-1895 or 440-834-0011; Fax: 440-834-0132. *Website:* http://www.bccns.org *E-mail:* info@bccns.org

Gorlin Syndrome Group, The *International network. 3 affiliated groups. Founded 1992.* Provides support and information for individuals with Gorlin (aka nevoid basal cell carcinoma) and their families. Information on coping skills, treatments and current research. Helpline, newsletter, meetings and networking. Write: The Gorlin Syndrome Group, c/o Margaret Costello, 11 Blackberry Way, Penwortham, Preston, Lancashire PR1 9LQ England. Call +440 1772 496849. *Website:* http://www.gorlingroup.co.uk *E-mail:* info@gorlingroup.org

"Action conquers fear." -- *Peter Nivio Zarlenga*

GRANULOMATOUS DISEASE

Chronic Granulomatous Disease Association, Inc. *International network. Founded 1982.* Support and information for persons with chronic granulomatous disease, their families and physicians. Networks patients with similar CGD-related illnesses. Support through correspondence and phone. Publishes medical and research articles semi-annually. International registry of patients. Referrals to physicians. Write: Chronic Granulomatous Disease Association, 2616 Monterey Rd., San Marino, CA 91108. Call 626-441-4118. *Website:* http://www.cgdassociation.org *E-mail:* cgda@socal.rr.com

GUILLAIN-BARRE SYNDROME / CHRONIC INFLAMMATORY DEMYELINATING POLYNEUROPATHY

GBS/CIDP Foundation International *International. 160 chapters. Founded 1980.* Emotional support, hospital visitation and education for people affected by Guillain-Barre syndrome, CIDP (chronic inflammatory demyelinating polyneuropathy) and its variants. Promotes support, education and research. Newsletter, pen pals, phone network and online chat room. Group development guidelines and international symposium. Write: GBS/CIDP Foundation International, International Office, The Holly Building, 104 1/2 Forrest Ave., Narberth, PA 19072. Call 610-667-0131 (9am-3:30pm EST); Fax: 610-667-7036. *Website:* http://www.gbs-cidp.org *E-mail:* info@gbsfi.com

HALLEREVORDEN-SPATZ SYDROME / NEURODEGERATION WITH BRAIN IRON ACCUMULATION

NBIA Disorders Association *International network. Founded 1996.* Provides emotional support to families affected by Neurodegeration with Brain Iron Accumulation - a rare progressive neurological disorder resulting in iron deposits in the brain that causes loss of muscle control. Formerly Hallervorden-Spatz syndrome. Educates public on neurodegenerations with brain iron accumulation, supports and monitors research through grants and BioBank. Newsletter, literature, bi-annual conferences, on-line listserv, family networking program and advocacy efforts. Write: NBIA Disorders Association, 2082 Monaco Ct., El Cajon, CA 92019-4235. Call 619-588-2315; Fax: 619-588-4093. *Website:* http://www.NBIAdisorders.org *E-mail:* info@NBIAdisorders.org

HELLP SYNDROME

HELLP Syndrome Society, The *International network. Founded 1996.* Mission is to provide support to affected families, raise awareness about HELLP syndrome (hemolysis, elevated liver enzymes and low platelet count) and to support research. This syndrome affects pregnant mothers and is usually in tandem with pre-eclampsia. Brochure, newsletter and online message board. Write: The HELLP Syndrome Society, P.O. Box 44, Bethany, WV 26032. *Website:* http://www.hellpsyndrome.org *E-mail:* HELLP1995@aol.com

HEMANGIOMA

NATIONAL

Hemangioma Support System *National network. Founded 1990.* Provides parent-to-parent support for families with children affected by hemangiomas. Write: Hemangioma Support System, c/o Cynthia Schumerth, 1484 Sand Acres Dr., DePere, WI 54115. Call 920-336-9399 (after 8pm CST).

NOVA (National Organization of Vascular Anomalies) *National.* Provides support for patients and their families in the diagnosis of hemangioma and vascular malformations. Networks families together for support. Offers videos, doctor referrals, free medical conferences, educational and support materials. Online newsletter. Holds international conferences. Contact K. Hall at khall@mail.novanews.org for more conference information. Write: NOVA, P.O. Box 0358, Findlay, OH 45840 or NOVA 8711-104 Six Forks Road PMB 126, Raleigh, NC 27615. Call 419-425-1589. *Website:* http://www.novanews.org *E-mail:* admin@mail.novanews.org

HEMIFACIAL SPASM

ONLINE

Hemifacial Spasm Association *Online. 805 members. Founded 2001.* An international support community of individuals who had or are presently suffering from hemifacial spasm (HFS) and are eager to provide information, understanding and support to other individuals and their families when coping with hemifacial spasm. *Website:* http://www.hfs-assn.org

We can also refer callers to over 100 individuals who are seeking others to help start new support groups throughout NJ. For more information call 1-800-367-6274.

HEMIPLEGIA

CHASA (Children's Hemiplegia And Stroke Association) *International network. Founded 1996.* Offers support and information to families of children who have hemiplegia due to stroke or other causes. Support groups, annual family retreat and medical conference, college scholarships, online resources and "Hemi-Kids" e-mail support group. Write: Children's Hemiplegia and Stroke Association, 4101 W. Green Oaks, Suite 305, PMB 149, Arlington, TX 76016. Call 817-492-4325. *Website:* http://www.chasa.org or http://www.kidshavestrokes.org *E-mail:* info437@chasa.org

HEMOCHROMATOSIS / IRON OVERLOAD

Iron Overload Diseases Assoc., Inc. *International network. Founded 1980.* A clearinghouse of support and information for hemochromatosis and other iron overload disease patients, their families and physicians. Encourages research and public awareness. Bi-monthly newsletter "Ironic Blood." Membership dues $50/yr. Write: Iron Overload Diseases Association, Write: 525 Mayflower Rd., W. Palm Beach, FL 33405. Call 561-586-8246. *Website:* http://www.ironoverload.org *E-mail:* iod@ironoverload.org

HEMOPHILIA

STATEWIDE

Hemophilia Association of New Jersey *Professionally-run.* Self-help support for persons with hemophilia and their families. Provides information and referrals, advocacy, educational seminars, phone networking, peer counseling, guest speakers, financial assistance and vocational counseling. Dues $20/yr. Write: Hemophilia Association of New Jersey, 197 Route 18 South, Suite 206 North, E. Brunswick, NJ 08816. Call Julie Frenkel 732-249-6000 (day). *Website:* http://www.hanj.org *E-mail:* mailbox@hanj.org

NATIONAL

National Hemophilia Foundation *National. 48 chapters. Founded 1948.* Dedicated to finding better treatments and a cure for bleeding and clotting disorders. Aim is to preventing the complications of these disorders through education, advocacy and research. Write: National Hemophilia Foundation, 116 W. 32nd St., 11th Floor, New York, NY 10001. Call 1-800-424-2634; Fax: 212-328-3777. *Website:* http://www.hemophilia.org *E-mail:* info@hemophilia.org

HEREDITARY HEMORRHAGIC TELANGIECTASIA / OSLER-WEBER-RENDU SYNDROME

HHT Foundation International, Inc. *International. Founded 1991.* Mutual support and education for persons interested in hereditary hemorrhagic telangiectasia (aka Osler-Weber-Rendu syndrome). Supports clinical and genetic research. Counseling and advice for patients. Referrals to appropriate treatment centers. Annual patient/doctor conference. Tri-annual newsletter "Direct Connection." Aims to protect all members under the Right To Privacy Act. Dues $45/yr. Write: HHT Foundation International, P.O. Box 329, Monkton, MD 21111. Call 1-800-448-6389 (U.S.) or 410-357-9932 (International); Fax: 410-357-9931. *Website:* http://www.hht.org *E-mail:* hhtinfo@hht.org

HERMANSKY-PUDLAK SYNDROME / CHEDIAK HIGASHI SYNDROME

Hermansky-Pudlak Syndrome Network *International network. 2 affiliated groups. Founded 1992.* Mutual support and education for families affected by Hermansky-Pudlak Syndrome and Chediak Higashi Syndrome. Networks families together for support. Newsletter and annual conference. Supports research. Write: Hermansky-Pudlak Syndrome Network, c/o Donna Jean Appell, 1 South Rd., Oyster Bay, NY 11771-1905. Call 1-800-789-9477 (voice/fax) or 516-922-4022; Fax: 516-624-0640. *Website:* http://www.hpsnetwork.org, http://www.hermansky-pudlak.org or http://www.chediak-higashi.org *E-mail:* rmcevoy@hpsnetwork.org

HISTIOCYTOSIS-X

Histiocytosis Association of America *International network. Founded 1985.* Mutual support and information for parents and patients with this group of rare disorders. Includes Erdheim-Chester disease, sinus histiocytosis Rosai Dorfman, xanthogranuloma, hemophagocytic lymphohistiocytosis, pulmonary eosinophilic granuloma, histiocytosis and familial erythrophagocytic lymphohistiocytosis. Provides parent-patient directory to facilitate networking and communication. Funds research. Literature and pamphlets (some available in Spanish) and newsletter. Write: Histiocytosis Association of America, 332 North Broadway, Pitman, NJ 08071. Call Jeff Toughill, President 856-589-6606; Fax: 856-589-6614. *Website:* http://www.histio.org *E-mail:* histiocyte@aol.com

HOLOPROSENCEPHALY

NATIONAL

Families for HoPE, Inc. Offers support and education to families of infants and children diagnosed with holoprosencephaly (HPE), a congenital brain malformation. Offers support for all stages of the HPE journey. Write: Leslie Harley, President, Families for HoPE, Inc., 1219 N. Wittfield St., Indianapolis, IN 46229. Call 317-898-5556. *Website:* http://www.familiesforhope.com *E-mail:* info@familiesforhope.com

ONLINE

Holoprosencephaly Support Group *Online. 554 members. Founded 1999.* Mutual support for parents and families of children with holoprosencephaly (HPE). HPE is a rare birth disorder caused by the failure of the forebrain of the embryo to properly divide, causing defects in the development of the face and brain structure and function. *Website:* http://health.groups.yahoo.com/group/holoprosencephaly/

HYDROCEPHALUS

MIDDLESEX

Pediatric Hydrocephalus Support Group *Professionally-run.* Provides support and help for children up to age 21 and their parents dealing with hydrocephalus. Guest speakers, newsletter and buddy system. Building is handicapped accessible. Meets 3rd Sat., 10am-noon, JFK Medical Center, 65 James St., Neuroscience Conference Room, Edison. Call Nancy Vassallo, RN 732-321-7000 ext. 65362 (day).

NATIONAL

Hydrocephalus Association *(BILINGUAL) National network. Founded 1984.* Provides support, education and advocacy for people with hydrocephalus and their families. Provides a wealth of resource materials on hydrocephalus for all age groups, quarterly newsletter, directory of neurosurgeons, bi-annual national conference and scholarships for young adults. Support and information available in English and Spanish. Write: Hydrocephalus Association, 870 Market St., Suite 705, San Francisco, CA 94102. Call 1-888-598-3789 or 415-732-7040; Fax: 415-732-7044. *Website:* http://www.hydroassoc.org *E-mail:* info@hydroassoc.org

National Hydrocephalus Foundation (NHF) *International network. Founded 1979.* Mission is to establish and facilitate a communication network amongst families or adult-to-adult, provide informational and educational assistance to individuals and families affected by hydrocephalus and increase public awareness. Promote and support research on the cause, prevention and treatment of hydrocephalus. Guidelines to help start support groups available. Help Sheets, brochures, physician referrals and quarterly newsletter. Write: National Hydrocephalus Foundation, 12413 Centralia Rd., Lakewood, CA 90715-1623. Call 1-888-857-3434 or 562-924-6666. *Website:* http://nhfonline.org *E-mail:* hydrobrat@Earthlink.net or debbifields@nhfonline.org

HYPERACUSIS / SENSITIVE HEARING / MISOPHONIA

Hyperacusis Network, The *National network. Founded 1991.* Mutual support, education and sharing of information for individuals with hyperacusis, recruitment (hypersensitive hearing), hyperacute hearing and misophonia. Resources for family members as well. Promotes research into cause and cure. Newsletter, phone support, pen pals, information and referrals. Write: The Hyperacusis Network, P.O. Box 8007, Green Bay, WI 54308. Call 920-866-3377 (eve). *Website:* http://www.hyperacusis.net *E-mail:* earhelp@yahoo.com

HYPOPARATHYROIDISM

Hypoparathyroidism Association Inc. *(MULTILINGUAL) International network. 2500+ members from 64 countries. Founded 1994.* Dedicated to improving the lives of people with all forms of hypoparathyroidism, a rare medical disorder. Guidelines available for starting a similar group. Association promotes awareness of this disorder through quarterly newsletter and website. Online newsletter, member gallery, a forum, chatroom and extensive compilation of links and various articles. Write: Hypoparathyroidism Association Inc., c/o James E. Sanders, P.O. 2258, Idaho Falls, ID 83406. Call 208-524-3857. *Website:* http://www.hpth.org *E-mail:* hpth@cableone.net or hpth@hpth.org or jsanders@hpth.org

ICHTHYOSIS

F.I.R.S.T. (Foundation for Ichthyosis and Related Skin Types) *National network. Founded 1981.* Provides support for people with ichthyosis through networking with others. Public and professional education. Supports research on treatment and cure. Advocacy issues, quarterly newsletter, publications and bi-annual conference. Dues US/$40; Int'l/$50. Write: FIRST, 1364 Welsh Rd., G2, North Wales, PA 19454. Call 1-800-545-3286 or 215-619-0670; Fax: 215-619-0780. *Website:* http://www.scalyskin.org *E-mail:* info@scalyskin.org

IDIOPATHIC THROMBOCYTOPENIC PURPURA

Platelet Disorder Support Association *National. Founded 1998. 19 affiliated groups.* Provides information and support to persons who have ITP (idiopathic thrombocytopenic purpura) and related blood disorders. Members regularly exchange messages. Support group meetings, conferences, advocacy, newsletter and written material. Online and printed information and support on ITP and pregnancy, children with ITP and adults with ITP. Spanish language books available. Write: Platelet Disorder Support Association, 133 Rollins Ave., Suite 5, Rockville, MD 20852. Call 1-877-528-3538. *Website:* http://www.pdsa.org *E-mail:* pdsa@pdsa.org

IMMUNE DEFICIENCY

NATIONAL

Immune Deficiency Foundation *National. Founded 1980.* Provides support and education for families affected by primary immune deficiency diseases. Newsletter, handbook, videotape and educational materials for public and medical professionals. Networks individuals and family members affected by immune deficiency. Scholarships and fellowship program. Group development guidelines. Write: Immune Deficiency Foundation, 40 W. Chesapeake Ave., Suite 308, Towson, MD 21204. Call 1-800-296-4433 (Mon.-Fri., 9am-5pm EST). *Website:* http://www.primaryimmune.org *E-mail:* idf@primaryimmune.org

ONLINE

SCID Mailing Group *Online network. Founded 1997.* Online self-help group for families afflicted with severe combined immune deficiency or who have lost a child to this very rare genetic disorder which results in severe infections. Provides opportunity for families to share information and resources with one another. *Website:* http://www.scid.net *E-mail:* SCIDemail@scid.net

INCONTINENTIA PIGMENTI

Incontinentia Pigmenti International Foundation *International network. Founded 1995.* Dedicated to family support, research and physician awareness on incontinentia pigmenti. Maintains international database of patients. Write: Incontinentia Pigmenti International Foundation, 30 East 72nd St., 16th Floor, New York, NY 10021. Call 212-452-1231; Fax: 212-452-1406. *Website:* http://www.ipif.org *E-mail:* ipif@ipif.org

INFECTIOUS ILLNESS, GENERAL
(see also specific illness)

PKIDs (Parents of Kids with Infectious Diseases) *National network. Founded 1996.* Provides informational and educational support for parents of children with chronic viral infectious diseases, with an emphasis on Hepatitis B and C. Opportunity for parents, children and teens to share information and experiences. Publications, advocacy and phone support. Online e-mail list, support group and other resources. Write: PKIDS, P.O. Box 5666, Vancouver, WA 98668. Call 1-877-557-5437 or 360-695-0293; Fax: 360-695-6941. *Website:* http://www.pkids.org *E-mail:* pkids@pkids.org

INTESTINAL MULTIPLE POLYPOSIS
(see also cancer)

Intestinal Multiple Polyposis and Colorectal Cancer (IMPACC) *National network. Founded 1986.* Support network to help patients and families dealing with familial polyposis and hereditary colon cancer. Information and referrals, encourages research, educates professionals and public. Phone support network, correspondence and literature. Write: IMPACC, c/o Ann Fagan, P.O. Box 11, Conyngham, PA 18219. Call Ann Fagan 570-788-1818 (day) or 570-788-3712 (eve); Fax: 570-788-4046. *E-mail:* impacc@epix.net

ISODICENTRIC / CHROMOSOME 15 Q DUPLICATION

IDEAS (IsoDicentric 15 Exchange, Advocacy and Support) *International network. Founded 1994.* Support, information and advocacy for people affected by isodicentric and chromosome 15q duplication. Information and referrals, phone support, literature, newsletter, international conferences and parent match program. Write: IDEAS, 18 Kings Rd., Canton, MA 02021. Call 503-253-2872. *Website:* http://www.idic15.org *E-mail:* info@idic15.org

JOUBERT SYNDROME

ONLINE

Joubert Syndrome Support Group *Online. 768 members. Founded 1999.* Support for parents that have children diagnosed with Joubert syndrome (a rare, genetic disorder that affects the area of the brain that controls balance and coordination). Forum for sharing stories, therapy experience, behavioral and social issues. *Website:* http://health.groups.yahoo.com/group/joubertsyndrome/

KABUKI SYNDROME / NIIKAWAKUROKI SYNDROME

Kabuki Syndrome Network *(BILINGUAL) International network. Founded 1997.* Provides mutual support and information for families affected by Kabuki syndrome (aka Niikawakuroki syndrome). Coordinates family directory. Literature, phone support, pen pals, moderated listserv and newsletter. Brochure in English and Spanish available. Write: Kabuki Syndrome Network, c/o Dean and Margot Schmiedge, 8060 Struthers Cr., Regina, Saskatchewan, Canada S4Y 1J3. Call Margot and Dean Schmiedge 306-543-8715. *Website:* http://www.kabukisyndrome.com *E-mail:* margot@kabukisyndrome.com

KALLMANN SYNDROME / HYPOGONADOTROPHIC HYPOGONADISM

ONLINE

Kallmann Syndrome Organization *Online.* Provides support, information and encouragement to patients with Kallmann syndrome and other forms of hypogonadotrophic hypogonadism. Promotes awareness of the causes, symptoms and treatments for these disorders. Open to families and friends. *Website:* http://www.kallmanns.org *E-mail:* kallmann-syndrome@hotmail.co.uk or neilsmith38@hotmail.com

KAWASAKI DISEASE

ONLINE

Kawasaki Families' Network *E-mail listserv. Founded 1996.* Provides a means of circulating information and support for families affected by Kawasaki disease, an inflammatory illness which primarily threatens the cardiovascular system. Members can exchange messages online. Write: Kawasaki Families' Network, c/o Vickie Machado, 46-111 Nahewai Place, Kaneohe, HI 96744. Call 808-525-8027. *E-mail:* vicki.machado@verizon.net

KENNEDY'S DISEASE / BULBAR MUSCULAR ATROPHY
(see also spinal muscular atrophy)

Kennedy's Disease Association, Inc. *National network. Founded 2000.* Mutual support and information for persons with Kennedy's disease (aka spinal and bulbar muscular atrophy), their families and caregivers. Opportunity to share personal experiences to help alleviate the feeling of aloneness and to engender hope and a positive attitude. Sharing of information regarding diagnosis, treatment and current research. Online chat room every two weeks. Write: Kennedy's Disease Association, Inc., P.O. Box 1105, Coarsegold, CA 93614-1105. Call 559-658-5950. *Website:* http://www.kennedysdisease.org *E-mail:* info@kennedysdisease.org

KLINEFELTER SYNDROME

NATIONAL

Klinefelter Syndrome and Associates *National network. 4 affiliated groups. Founded 1990.* Mission is to educate, encourage research and foster treatment and cures for symptoms of sex chromosome variations. These include, but are not limited to: XXY, XXX, XYY, XXXY, XXXXY and XXYY. Brochures are available that describe basic symptoms, diagnoses and treatments. Newsletter ($25/US; $27/Canada; $30/Int'l). Write: Klinefelter Syndrome and Associates, 11 Keats Court, Coto de Caza, CA 92679. Call 1-888-999-9428; Fax: 949-858-3443. *Website:* http://www.genetic.org *E-mail:* help1@genetic.org

ONLINE

Klinefelter Syndrome Support Group *Online.* Offers online support group information. Provides e-mail list to chat with others, information on variations of the disorder, conferences and information on local support group meetings. *Website:* http://klinefeltersyndrome.org

KLIPPEL-TRENAUNAY

Klippel-Trenaunay Support Group *National network. Founded 1986.* Provides mutual support and sharing of experiences among families of children with KT, and adults with KT. Newsletter, phone support, meetings every two years. Online mailing list. Write: KT Support Group, 5404 Dundee Rd., Edina, MN 55436. Call 952-925-2596. *Website:* http://www.k-t.org *E-mail:* ktnewmembers@yahoo.com

LEAD POISONING

United Parents Against Lead *National. 7 chapters and affiliates. Founded 1996.* Organization which supports parents of lead poisoned children and who work to end the continuing threat of lead poisoning through education, advocacy, resource referral and legislative action. Membership $10/individual, $25/family and $100/organization. Write: United Parents Against Lead, P.O. Box 24773, Richmond, VA 23224. Call 804-308-1518; Fax: 804-562-5031. *Website:* http://www.upal.org *E-mail:* info@upal.com

LEUKODYSTROPHY

United Leukodystrophy Foundation, Inc. *National network. Founded 1982.* Provides information and resources for leukodystrophy patients and their families. Communication network among families. Promotes research, public and professional awareness. National conference and quarterly newsletter. Dues $25/family; $50/professional. Write: United Leukodystrophy Foundation, 2304 Highland Dr., Sycamore, IL 60178. Call 1-800-728-5483 or 815-895-3211; Fax: 815-895-2432. *Website:* http://www.ulf.org *E-mail:* office@ulf.org

LOIN PAIN HEMATURIA SYNDROME

Hearts and Hands *Model. 1 group in NC. Founded 1993.* Emotional, spiritual and educational support for persons with either rare or undiagnosed illnesses and their families. Has a registry for loin pain hematuria syndrome. Write: Hearts and Hands, c/o Winoka Plummer, 1648 Oliver's Crossing Circle, Winston-Salem, NC 27127. Call 336-785-7612. *Website:* http://www.geocities.com/hotsprings/spa/2464/index.html

LOWE SYNDROME

Lowe Syndrome Association *International network. Founded 1983.* For parents, friends, professionals and others who are interested in Lowe syndrome. Provides medical and educational information and online discussion. Supports medical research. Offers booklet, newsletter and international conference. Dues $15 (can be waived if parents are in need). Write: Lowe Syndrome Association, 18919 Voss Rd., Dallas, TX 75287. Call 972-733-1338. *Website:* http://www.lowesyndrome.org *E-mail:* info@lowesyndrome.org

LYMPHANGIOLEIOMYOMATOSIS

LAM Foundation, The *International network. Founded 1995.* Provides education for doctors, patients and support for women and their families who have LAM (lymphangioleiomyomatosis). LAM is a rare lung disease affecting only women, where smooth muscle cells grow throughout the lungs. A newsletter for general distribution and patient listserv, Personal Journeys, Lung Transplantation Booklet, advocacy program and newsletter solely for patients. Write: The LAM Foundation, c/o Leslie Sullivan-Stacey, 4015 Executive Park, Suite 320, Cincinnati, OH 45241. Call 513-777-6889; Fax: 513-777-4109. *Website:* http://www.thelamfoundation.org *E-mail:* info@thelamfoundation.org

MALIGNANT HYPERTHERMIA

Malignant Hyperthermia Association of the U.S. (MHAUS) *National network. Founded 1981.* Support, information and education for malignant hyperthermia-susceptible patients, their physicians and health care professionals. Conducts limited research. Newsletter, literature and regional conferences. Write: MHAUS, 11 E. State St., P.O. Box 1069, Sherburne, NY 13460-1069. Call 1-800-644-9737 (hotline) or 1-800-986-4287 (administration) Mon.-Fri. 8:30am-4:30pm EST; Fax: 607-674-7910. *Website:* http://www.mhaus.org *E-mail:* info@mhaus.org

MANNOSIDOSIS / GLYCOPROTEIN STORAGE DISEASE

International Advocate for Glycoprotein Storage Disease (ISMRD) *International network. Founded 1999.* Provides emotional support for families affected by any glycoprotein storage disease. Offers educational resources for medical community. Promotes research to develop treatments. Phone support, literature, pen pals, newsletter, advocacy, online message boards, chatrooms, e-mail discussions, information and referrals. Write: ISMRD, P.O. Box 328, Dexter, MI 48130. Call 734-449-8222. *Website:* http://www.ismrd.org

MAPLE SYRUP URINE DISEASE

Maple Syrup Urine Disease Family Support Group *National network. Founded 1982.* Opportunity for support and personal contact for those with maple syrup urine disease and their families. Provides information on MSUD. Aims to strengthen the liaison between families and professionals. Encourages research and newborn screening for MSUD. Newsletter ($10/yr), phone support, conferences and advocacy. Write: MSUD Family Support Group, c/o Sandra Bulcher, 82 Ravine Rd., Powell, OH 43065. Call 740-548-4475. *Website:* http://www.msud-support.org *E-mail:* dbulcher@aol.com

MARFAN SYNDROME

National Marfan Foundation *National network. Founded 1981.* Network includes chapters, support groups and volunteer telephone support contacts. Provides information on Marfan syndrome and related connective tissue disorders to patients, families, medical professionals and the public. Provides a means for patients and relatives to share experiences and support one another. Supports and fosters research. Conference, newsletter and publications. Write: National Marfan Foundation, 22 Manhasset Ave., Port Washington, NY 11050. Call 1-800-862-7326 ext. 10 or 516-883-8712; Fax: 516-883-8040. *Website:* http://www.marfan.org *E-mail:* staff@marfan.org

MARINESCO-SJOGREN SYNDROME

Marinesco-Sjogren Syndrome Support Group *National network. Founded 2000.* Support for families affected by Marinesco-Sjogren syndrome (MSS) a rare, genetic disorder characterized by ataxia, cataracts, small stature and retardation. Encourages research into the cause and cure. Information and referrals. Write: MSS Support Group, 1640 Crystal View Circle, Newbury Park, CA 91320. Call 805-499-7410. *Website:* http://www.marinesco-sjogren.org *E-mail:* mss@marinesco-sjogren.org

MASTOCYTOSIS

Mastocytosis Society, The *International network. Founded 1994.* Mutual support through a newsletter for persons with mastocytosis (a proliferation of mast cells), their families, friends and professionals working with them. E-mail discussion group for patients and researchers. Fundraising for research and phone support. Write: TMS, c/o Rita Barlow, P.O. Box 284, Russell, MA 01071. Call 413-862-4556. *Website:* http://www.tmsforacure.org *E-mail:* jbar5@verizon.net

MCCUNE-ALBRIGHT SYNDROME

McCune-Albright Syndrome/Fibrous Dysplasia Division *International network. Founded 1990.* Provides support for families of McCune-Albright syndrome patients. Newsletters, updated medical information, phone support and annual conventions. Dues $35/yr. Write: McCune-Albright Syndrome/Fibruous Dysplasia Division, c/o MAGIC Foundation, 6645 West North Ave., Oak Park, IL 60302. Call 1-800-362-4423; Fax: 708-383-0899. *Website:* http://www.magicfoundation.org *E-mail:* mary@magicfoundation.org

MENKES KINKY HAIR SYNDROME / STEELY HAIR DISEASE

ONLINE

Menkes Kinky Hair Syndrome *Online. Founded 1999.* Support and information for those affected with Menkes kinky hair syndrome (related to deficient levels of copper in the cells). Also known as kinky hair disease and steely hair disease. Message boards and chatrooms. *Website:* http://groups.yahoo.com/group/menkes_kinky_hair/

METABOLIC DISORDERS
(see also specific disorder)

NATIONAL

CDG Family Network Foundation *International network. Founded 1996.* Support for parents of children diagnosed with congenital disorders of glycosylation, an inherited metabolic disease affecting all body parts, especially the central and peripheral nervous systems. Support is attained primarily online. Group also provides bi-annual newsletter, phone support, advocacy, information and referrals. Bulletin board for families to interact with questions, comments and updates. Write: CDG Family Network, c/o Cynthia Wren-Gray, President, P.O. Box 860847, Plano, TX 75074. Call 1-800-250-5273; Fax: 903-640-8254. *Website:* http://www.cdgs.com *E-mail:* cdgaware@aol.com

CLIMB – National Information and Advice Centre for Metabolic Disease *International network.* Provides support and information for individuals and their families dealing with over 700 metabolic conditions. Newsletter, phone support, pen pals, annual conference, and befriender network. Small administration fee required for posts. Write: Climb Building, 176 Nantwich Rd., Crewe, CW2 6BG UK. Call 0044 870 77 00 326 (day); Fax: 0044 870 77 00 327. *Website:* http://www.climb.org.uk

Purine Research Society *National. Founded 1986.* Supports DNA research, looking for mutations in DNA, both nuclear and mitochondrial, that might cause autistic/epileptic symptoms in patients. Purine metabolic diseases include gout, purine autism, Lesch-Nyhan syndrome, ADA deficiency and others. Offers publications and reference information including a purine-restricted diet. Write: Purine Research Society, c/o Tahma Metz, 5424 Beech Ave., Bethesda, MD 20814. Call Tahma Metz 301-530-0354; Fax: 301-564-9597. *Website:* http://www.PurineResearchSociety.org *E-mail:* purine@erols.com

ONLINE

Trimethylaminuria Support Group *Online. 759 members. Founded 2000.* Mutual support via discussion forum for those affected by the metabolic disorder trimethyaminuria (also known as fish odor syndrome, fish malodor syndrome and stale fish syndrome). Trimethylaminuria is an inability of the body to break down trimethylamine, consequently trimethylamine accumulates in the body and is then released in a person's sweat, urine and breath. When released, Trimethylaminuria gives off a strong fishy odor. *Website:* http://health.groups.yahoo.com/group/trimethylaminuria

METATROPIC DYSPLASIA DWARFISM
(see also growth disorders, short/tall)

Metatropic Dysplasia Dwarf Registry *National network. Founded 1980.* Support and information for persons affected by metatropic dwarfism. Networks families and shares information. Offers phone support, limited literature, information and referrals. Write: Metatropic Dysplasia Dwarf Registry, 3393 Geneva Dr., Santa Clara, CA 95051. Call 408-244-6354; Fax: 408-296-6317. *Website:* http://www.lpbayarea.org/metatrophic *E-mail:* figone@netgate.net

MILLER'S SYNDROME

Foundation for Nager and Miller Syndromes *International. Founded 1989.* Networking for families that are affected by Nager or Miller syndromes. Provides referrals, library of information, phone support, newsletter, brochures and scholarships for Camp About Face. Write: Foundation for Nager Miller Syndrome, c/o De De Van Quill, 13210 South East 342nd St., Auburn, WA 98092. Call 1-800-507-3667 or 253-333-1483; Fax: 253-288-7679. *Website:* http://www.fnms.net *E-mail:* ddfnms@aol.com

MITOCHONDRIAL DISORDERS

United Mitochondrial Disease Foundation (UMDF) *National network. 13 chapters. 17 affiliated groups. Founded 1995.* Provides support to affected individuals and families, and promotes research and education for the diagnosis, treatment and cure of mitochondrial disorders. Chapter and support groups. Networking for families affected by mitochondrial disease, a genetic degenerative disease. Quarterly newsletter, information and referrals, library of medical publications, patient registry, phone help and annual symposium. Awards research grants. Write: UMDF, 8085 Saltsburg Rd., Suite 201, Pittsburgh, PA 15239. Call 412-793-8077; Fax: 412-793-6477. *Website:* http://www.umdf.org *E-mail:* info@umdf.org

MOEBIUS SYNDROME

Moebius Syndrome Foundation *International network. Founded 1994.* Communication and support network for persons with Moebius syndrome, (a paralysis of the 6th and 7th cranial nerves) and their families. Information, education and fund raising for research. Newsletter, phone support, informal meetings and national conference. Help with starting groups. Write: Moebius Syndrome Foundation, P.O. Box 147, Pilot Grove, MO 65276. Call Vicki McCarrell 660-834-3406 (eve.) or 660-882-5576 ext. 120 (day); Fax: 660-834-3407. *Website:* http://www.moebiussyndrome.com *E-mail:* vickimc@iland.net

MOTILITY DISORDERS
(see also specific disorder)

Association of Gastrointestinal Motility Disorders, Inc. *International network. Founded 1991.* Support and education for persons affected by digestive motility disorders. Serves as educational resource and information base for medical professionals. Physician referrals, video tapes, large variety of educational materials, networking support, symposiums and several publications. General membership dues $35/US; $42/Int'l (can be waived). Write: AGMD International Corp. Headquarters, 12 Roberts Dr., Bedford, MA 01730. Call 781-275-1300; Fax: 781-275-1304. *Website:* http://www.agmd-gimotility.org *E-mail:* digestive.motility@gmail.com

MOVEMENT DISORDERS
(see also specific disorder)

ONLINE

WE MOVE *Online.* Support and exchange of information and ideas among various movement disorder communities for patients, families and caregivers. Includes forums for such disorders as Parkinson's disease, essential tremor, myoclonus, dystonia, corticobasal degeneration, Rett syndrome and many more. Write: WE MOVE, 204 West 84th St., New York, NY 10024. *Website:* http://www.wemove.org *E-mail:* wemove@wemove.org

MUCOLIPIDOSES / MUCOPOLYSACCHARIDOSES / MORQUIO'S SYNDROME

NATIONAL

International Morquio Support Group, The *International network. Founded 1999.* Provides support and education for families of children with Morquio Type A. Helps educate health care professionals about this lysosomal storage disease. Funds research. Maintains database of families. Referrals to physicians and medical information, pen pals, phone support, conferences and newsletter, online guestbook and helpful links. Write: Morquio Support Group, P.O. Box 64184, Tucson, AZ 85728-4184. Call 520-744-2531; Fax: 520-744-2535. *Website:* http://www.morquio.com *E-mail:* mbs85705@yahoo.com

National MPS Society *National. Founded 1974.* Provides support and hope for individuals with mucopolysaccharidoses or mucolipidoses (and their families) through research, advocacy, public education and parent referral service for support networking. Write: National MPS Society, 4220 NC Highway 55, Suite

140, Durham, NC 27713. Call 919-806-0101. *Website:* http://www.mpssociety.org *E-mail:* info@mpssociety.org

MUCOLIPIDOSIS TYPE 4

ML4 Foundation *National network. Founded 1983.* Support network for families of children diagnosed with mucolipidosis type 4, a genetic disorder characterized by variable psychomotor retardation that primarily affects Ashkenazi Jews. Supports fund-raising for research. Offers phone support, information and referrals. Write: ML4 Foundation, 719 E. 17th St., Brooklyn, NY 11230. Call 718-434-5067; Fax: 718-859-7371. *Website:* http://www.ml4.org *E-mail:* www@ml4.org

MULLERIAN ANOMALIES

ONLINE

Mullerian Anomalies of the Uterus *Online.* Support and information for those with mullerian anomalies of the uterus such as bicornuate, septate, unicornauate, hypoplastic and didelphys uteria. Weekly chat, e-mail list and message board. *Website:* http://health.groups.yahoo.com/group/MullerianAnomalies/

MULTIPLE ENDOCRINE NEOPLASM

NATIONAL

Multiple Endocrine Neoplasia Society (MENS) *International network. 21 affiliated groups. Founded 1995.* Mutual support to persons afflicted with familial multiple endocrine neoplasia type 1 (MEN1) and their families. MEN1 affects the endocrine glands. Literature, phone support, pen pals, information and referrals. Access to doctors and current research. Write: MENS, 1432 107th St., N. Battleford SK, Canada S9A 1Z9. Call 306-445-8436 or 306-892-2080 (voice/fax). *E-mail:* hockey_freak99@hotmail.com

ONLINE

Pheochromocytoma Information Group *Online.* Offers support through information for persons affected by pheochromocytoma or multiple endocrine neoplasia syndrome. *Website:* http://www.pheochromocytoma.org

MULTIPLE HEREDITARY EXOSTOSES

ONLINE

MHE and Me: A Support Group for Kids with MHE *(a member of The MHE Coalition) Online. Founded 1999.* Provides peers and a supportive community to children suffering from multiple hereditary exostoses (a genetic disorder in which benign cartilage-capped bone tumors grow from growth plates of long bones or on the surface of flat bones). Develops information and literature to assist children and their families in dealing with the disease. Offers free Bumpy Bone Club membership to patients and their siblings. Provides We Care packages to children having surgery and their siblings. Advocacy, information and referrals, phone and e-mail support. Write: MHE and Me, c/o Susan Wynn, P.O. Box 651, Pine Island, NY 10969. Call 845-258-6058. *Website:* http://www.mheandme.com *E-mail:* mheandme@yahoo.com

MHE Coalition, The *Online. 3 affiliated groups. Founded 2000.* Support and information for persons and their families affected by multiple hereditary exostoses, a skeletal disorder characterized by the formation of abnormal bony growths. Promotes and encourages research to find the cause, treatment and cure. Newsletter, networking, literature, advocacy, online groups, information and referrals, phone support, pen pals. Write: MHE Coalition, 6783 York Road, Apt. #104, Parma Heights, OH 44130-4596. Call Chele Zelina, President 440-842-8817. *Website:* http://www.mhecoalition.org *E-mail:* CheleZ1@yahoo.com

MYASTHENIA GRAVIS

OCEAN

Myasthenia Gravis Support Group *Professionally-run.* Support and education for patients with myasthenia gravis and over 140 autoimmune diseases. Families, friend and caregivers welcome. Guest speakers, buddy system and phone help. Meets 4th Sun., 1pm, Ocean Medical Center, 425 Jack Martin Blvd., Brick. Call Barbara Yodice 732-262-0450. *Website:* http://www.aininc.org *E-mail:* autoimmunehelp@aol.com

NATIONAL

Myasthenia Gravis Foundation of America, Inc. *National. 27 chapters. Founded 1952.* Promotes research and education into myasthenia gravis, a chronic neuromuscular disease. Provides supportive services for patients and families. Information and referral. Newsletter, support groups, various web-based services, annual and scientific meetings. Write: Myasthenia Gravis

Foundation, 1821 University Ave. W, Suite S256, St. Paul, MN 55104. Call 1-800-541-5454 or 651-917-6256; Fax: 651-917-1835. *Website:* http://www.myasthenia.org *E-mail:* mgfa@myasthenia.org

ONLINE

Myasthenia Gravis Patient-To-Patient *Online.* Offers e-mail support and chatrooms. Share problems, solutions and support. *Website:* http://pages.prodigy.net/stanley.way/myasthenia/patient.htm

MYELIN DISORDERS

ONLINE

Myelin-Mail *Online. 268 members. Founded 1998.* Support and information for families, friends and professionals dealing with children's myelin related disorders. Write: Myelin-Mail, 228 Draper Ave., Warwick, RI 02889. Call 401-262-5305. *Website:* http://health.groups.yahoo.com/group/myelin-mail/ *E-mail:* myelin-mail@yahoogroups.com

PML Survivors and Supporters *Online. 26 members. Founded 2006.* Support forum to educate, inform and inspire persons with progressive multifocal leukoencephalopathy and their families. Opportunity to share treatment information and support to any person affected with or by PML. *Website:* http://health.groups.yahoo.com/PMLSurvivors

MYELOPROLIFERATIVE DISEASE

ONLINE

MPD-Net *Online. International network. Founded 1989. 1800 members.* Support network enabling persons with myeloproliferative disease to share their experiences and problems. Supports research. Publishes materials pertaining to MPD. Professional involvement. Newsletter, phone support, conferences, information and referrals. Online listserv to exchange e-mails about the disease. Write: MPD-Net, c/o Joyce Niblack, 115 E. 72nd St., New York, NY 10021. *Website:* http://www.mpdinfo.org *E-mail:* JNiblack@mpdinfo.org

Need help finding a specific group? Give us a call – we're here to help!
*Call **1-800-367-6274.***

MYOSITIS

Myositis Association, The *International network. 65 groups. Founded 1993.* Dedicated to serving those with polymyositis, dermatomyositis, juvenile myositis and inclusion body myositis. Provides education and support. Also serves as a clearinghouse between patients and scientists. Newsletter, research reviews, literature and phone support. Area meetings available, as well as annual conference. Guidelines available for starting similar groups. Fundraising for research. Dues $35/yr. Write: The Myositis Association, 1233 20th St. NW, #402, Washington, DC 20036. Call 202-887-0088 (day); Fax: 202-466-8940. *Website:* http://www.myositis.org *E-mail:* tma@myositis.org

MYOTONIA CONGENITA

ONLINE

Myotonia Congenita *Online. Founded 2001.* Forum for people with myotonia congenita as well as their friends and families. Ask questions and share tips for living with myotonia congenita. *Website:* http://www.myotoniacongenita.org (click on forum) *E-mail:* jan@accessfitness.com

MYOTUBULAR MYOPATHY

Myotubular Myopathy Resource Group *International network. Founded 1993.* Information for patients, parents and doctors regarding myotubular myopathy, a family of three rare muscle disorders usually causing low muscle tone and diminished respiratory capacity. Exchanging of successes with other affected families. Phone support, literature, information and referrals. Write: Myotubular Myopathy Resource Group, c/o Pam Scoggin, 2602 Quaker Dr., Texas City, TX 77590. Call 409-945-8569; Fax: 409-452-2162. *Website:* http://www.mtmrg.org *E-mail:* pam@scoggin.com

NAGER SYNDROME

Foundation for Nager and Miller Syndromes *International. Founded 1989.* Networking for families affected by Nager or Miller syndromes. Provides phone support, newsletter, brochures, information and referrals. Write: FNMS, c/o DeDe Van Quill, 13210 South East 342nd St., Auburn, WA 98092. Call 1-800-507-3667 or 253-333-1483. *Website:* http://www.fnms.net

NAIL PATELLA SYNDROME

Nail Patella Syndrome Networking/Support Group *International network.* *Founded 1995.* Support network for persons with nail patella syndrome to exchange information. Links to a research study and other NPS-related sites. Provides information and online chat. Write: Nail Patella Syndrome Networking/Support Group, 67 Woodlake Dr., Holland, PA 18966. *Website:* http://hometown.aol.com/PACALI/npspage.html or (discussion group) http://health.groups.yahoo.com/group/Nail_Patella_Syndrome *E-mail:* PACALI@aol.com

NARCOLEPSY / HYPERSOMNIAS

Narcolepsy Network *National. 100 affiliated support groups. Founded 1986.* Support for persons with narcolepsy or other hypersomnias seeking to optimize their quality of life. Offers communication, advocacy, research, education, support, help with coping skills, family and community problems. Newsletter, yearly conference, phone support and support group development guidelines. Individual dues $35/yr. Write: Narcolepsy Network, 79A Main St., North Kingston, RI 02852. Call 1-888-292-6522 or 401-667-2523; Fax: 401-633-6567. *Website:* http://www.narcolepsynetwork.org *E-mail:* narnet@narcolepsynetwork.org

NECROTIZING FASCIITIS / FLESH-EATING BACTERIA

ONLINE

National Necrotizing Fasciitis Foundation *Online.* Provides support and education for persons affected by necrotizing fasciitis (aka flesh-eating bacteria). Aim is to educate public and advocate for research. Provides literature, phone support, newsletter, pen pals, conferences and information and referrals. Publishes "Surviving the Flesh-Eating Bacteria: Understanding, Preventing, Treating And Living With the Effects of Necrotizing Fasciitis." *Website:* http://www.nnff.com

"I have learned two lessons in my life: first, there are no sufficient literary, psychological, or historical answers to human tragedy, only moral ones. Second, just as despair can come to one another only from other human beings, hope, too, can be given to one only by other human beings." --Elie Wiesel

NEMALINE MYOPATHY, CONGENITAL

Nemaline Myopathy Support Group *International network. Founded 1999.* Grassroots group that networks families affected by pediatric/adult Nemaline Myopathy for support and information. Pen pals, literature, phone support, information and referrals available through several Yahoo e-groups targeting age groups and English, Spanish and German speaking families. NM Conventions organized to meet researchers and other families. Write: Nemaline Myopathy Support Group, c/o 5 Cairnbank Gardens, Penicuik, Midothian, EH26 9EA, UK. *Website:* http://www.nemaline.org *E-mail:* davidmcd_@hotmail.com

NEUROCARDIOGENIC SYNCOPE
(see also dysautonomia)

ONLINE

Neurocardiogenic Syncope Fainting List *Online. 323 members. Founded 2005.* Support and understanding for those suffering from neurocardiogenic syncope, dysautonomia, orthostatic hypotension, neurally mediated hypotension, low blood pressure and other diseases that can cause fainting, heat sensitivity, nausea or dizziness. Open to families and friends. Sharing of stories, struggles, triumphs and information. *Website:* http://health.groups.yahoo.com/group/NCS_F/

NEUROFIBROMATOSIS
(see also specific disorder)

STATEWIDE

Neurofibromatosis, Inc. - Mid-Atlantic Region *Founded 1979.* Serves District of Columbia, Delaware, New Jersey, North Carolina, Pennsylvania, Virginia and West Virginia. Provides support and advocacy for those with neurofibromatosis. Provides free printed materials, conducts meetings with a real time captionist for the hearing impaired, publishes 5 newsletters a year; videos on NF and Camp New Friends, provides peer-counseling, appropriate medical education, social referrals and speakers. Promotes research and funds some clinical studies. Write: Neurofibromatosis, Inc. Mid-Atlantic, 8855 Annapolis Rd #110, Lanham, MD 20706. Call 1-866-261-1271. Fax: 301-577-0016. *Website:* http://www.nfmidatlantic.org *E-mail:* nfmidatlantic@aol.com

NATIONAL

Children's Tumor Foundation *(BILINGUAL) National. 50 chapters. Founded 1978.* For patients with neurofibromatosis and their families. Promotes and supports research on the causes of, and cure for NF. Provides information, quarterly newsletter, assistance and education. Dues $40/year. Professional grants awarded for research. Write: Children's Tumor Foundation, 95 Pine St., 16th Floor, New York, NY 10005. Call 1-800-323-7938 or 212-344-6633; Fax: 212-747-0004. *Website:* http://www.ctf.org *E-mail:* info@ctf.org

Neurofibromatosis, Inc. *National. 10 regional groups. Founded 1988.* Dedicated to individuals and families affected by the neurofibromatoses (NF-1, NF-2 and Schwannomatosis) through education, support, a summer camp, clinical and research programs. Newsletter, networking, printed materials, phone support, information and referrals. Assistance in starting groups. Write: Neurofibromatosis, Inc., P.O. Box 66884, Chicago, IL 60666. Call 630-627-1115 or 1-800-942-6825 (patient inquiries). *Website:* http://www.nfinc.org *E-mail:* nfinfo@nfinc.org

NEVUS, CONGENITAL / NEUROCUTANEOUS MELANOSIS

NATIONAL

Nevus Network *(MULTILINGUAL) International network. Founded 1983.* Provides a network of support and information for people with a large brown birthmark called a giant congenital nevus and/or an associated condition called neurocutaneous melanosis. Write: Nevus Network, P.O. Box 305, West Salem, OH 44287. Call 419-853-4525. *Website:* http://www.nevusnetwork.org *E-mail:* info@nevusnetwork.org

Nevus Outreach, Inc. *International network. Founded 1997.* Dedicated to improving awareness and providing support for people affected by congenital pigmented nevi and finding a cure. Literature, 24-hour support hotline and international conferences. Write: Nevus Outreach, Inc., 600 SE Delaware, Suite 200, Bartlesville, OK 74003. Call 918-331-0595 or toll-free hotline 1-877-426-3887; Fax: 281-417-4020. *Website:* http://www.nevus.org

NIEMANN-PICK DISEASE

National Niemann-Pick Disease Foundation, Inc. *International network. Founded 1992.* Provides support for families affected by Niemann-Pick disease type A, B and C. Promotes and supports research. Provides newsletter, family directory, networking, family conference, phone support, information and referrals. Guidelines available to help start similar groups. Write: National Niemann-Pick Disease Foundation, P.O. Box 49, 401B Madison Ave., Fort Atkinson, WI 53538. Call 920-563-0930; Fax: 920-563-0931. *Website:* http://www.nnpdf.org *E-mail:* nnpdf@idcnet.com

NONKETOTIC HYPERGLYCINEMIA

NKH International Family Network *International. Founded 1995.* Support and networking for parents of children with nonketotic hyperglycinemia (NKH), an inherited metabolic disorder. Newsletter, online network, discussion board, phone support, information and referrals. Write: NKH International Family Network, 481 Canisteo St., Hornell, NY 14843. Call 607-324-3804. *Website:* http://www.nkh-network.org *E-mail:* catrosenkh@yahoo.com

NOONAN SYNDROME

Noonan Syndrome Support Group *International network. Founded 1996.* Provides information for persons with Noonan syndrome, their families and interested others. Networks individuals together for peer support. Speakers' bureau, phone help, information and referrals. Write: Noonan Syndrome Support Group, P.O. Box 145, Upperco, MD 21155. Call 1-888-686-2224 or 410-374-5245. *Website:* http://www.noonansyndrome.org *E-mail:* info@noonansyndrome.org

NYSTAGMUS

American Nystagmus Network *National. Founded 1999.* Network of persons affected by nystagmus, an involuntary, rapid movement of the eyeball. Open to parents of affected children, adults with nystagmus and interested professionals. Provides general information. Promotes research into cause and cure. E-mail discussion group, discussion board and biannual newsletter and conferences. Write: American Nystagmus Network, Inc., 303-D Beltline Place #321, Decatur, AL 35603. *Website:* http://www.nystagmus.org *E-mail:* webmaster@nystagmus.org

ODOR (BODY / BREATH) / TRIMETHYLAMINURIA

NATIONAL

NARA (Not A Rose Assoc.) / BOSS (Body Odor Support Service) *Model. 1 group in GA. Founded 1998.* Mutual support for persons suffering from "odorous" conditions of the body, breath or unknown sources. Offers coping skills. Write: NARA/BOSS, 1492 Baron Count, Stone Mountain, GA 30087. For emergency call 770-279-0200 after 7pm EST. *E-mail:* annhenry99@yahoo.com

ONLINE

Trimethylaminuria Support Group *Online. 759 members. Founded 2000.* Mutual support via discussion forum for those affected by the metabolic disorder trimethyaminuria (also known as fish odor syndrome, fish malodor syndrome and stale fish syndrome). Trimethylaminuria is an inability of the body to break down trimethylamine, consequently trimethylamine accumulates in the body and is then released in a person's sweat, urine and breath, giving off a strong fishy odor. *Website:* http://health.groups.yahoo.com/group/trimethylaminuria

OPITZ-G/BBB SYNDROME

Opitz-G/BBB Family Network *International. Founded 1994.* Support, encouragement, education and sharing of successes and ideas for families affected by Opitz-G/BBB syndrome. Maintains database of members, literature, information, e-group, phone support and newsletter. Referrals to other families. Family conferences. Write: Opitz-G/BBB Family Network, P.O. Box 515, Grand Lake, CO 80447. Call 970-627-8935; Fax: 970-627-8818. *Website:* http://www.opitznet.org *E-mail:* opitznet@mac.com

ORTHOPEDIC
(see also movement disorders)

ONLINE

Totally Hip *Online. Founded 1997.* Support to help relieve the fear of total hip replacement surgery, share experiences and offer morale as well as spiritual support to patients. Helps answer questions on hip replacement. Also, forum to discuss other joint problems. Click on bulletin board at website for message exchange. Fax: 601-249-2065. *Website:* http://www.totallyhip.org *E-mail:* Linda@totallyhip.org

OSTEOGENESIS IMPERFECTA

ESSEX

NJ Osteogenesis Imperfecta Support Group Purpose is to share information, support and improve the quality of life for people affected by osteogenesis imperfecta. Rap sessions, guest speakers, summer picnic, fundraiser and phone help. Information and referrals. Building is handicapped accessible. For meeting information call Rosemarie or JoAnn 201-489-9232 (day). *E-mail:* rdkoif@verizon.net

NATIONAL

Osteogenesis Imperfecta Foundation *National. 30 affiliated support groups. Founded 1970.* Support and resources for families dealing with osteogenesis imperfecta. Provides information for medical professionals. Supports research. Literature, quarterly newsletter and phone support network. Write: Osteogenesis Imperfecta Foundation, 804 W. Diamond Ave., Suite 210, Gaithersburg, MD 20878-3836. Call 1-800-981-2663 or 301-947-0083; Fax: 301-947-0456. *Website:* http://www.oif.org *E-mail:* bonelink@oif.org

OSTEONECROSIS / AVASCULAR NECROSIS

ONLINE

ON/AVN Support Group International Association, Inc. *Online.* Support for persons who suffer from ostenecrosis (aka avascular necrosis). Goal is to inform and educate the world about osteonecrosis and offer emotional support to both those with ON/AVN and their families. Provides information and referrals. Also has special section for youth with ON/AVN. Open to those with other chronic bone, joint or muscular conditions and persons with joint replacements. Write: ON/AVN Support Group International Association Inc., 8500 Henry Ave., Box 118, Philadelphia, PA 19128. Call 267-235-8750. *Website:* http://www.avnsupport.org *E-mail:* avninfo@avnsupport.org

Osteonecrosis Self-Help Group Listserv *Online. 1200 members. Founded 1998.* Designed as an open forum for those having experience with the chronic bone disorder osteonecrosis (aka avascular necrosis). All are welcome to join in and share successes and frustrations in getting diagnosed and treated. Exchange of coping skills dealing with this "on again off again" chronic disease. *Website:* http://health.groups.yahoo.com/group/osteonecrosis/

OXALOSIS / HYPEROXALURIA

Oxalosis and Hyperoxaluria Foundation *National network. Founded 1989.* Provides support and current information for patients, families and medical professionals in the field of primary hyperoxaluria and oxalate stone disease. Educates the public, newsletter, phone support, pen pals, conferences, funds research, information and referrals. Yearly dues $25/ind.; $50/prof.; $100/business. Write: Oxalosis Hyperoxaluria Foundation, 201 East 19th St.,

#12E, New York, NY 10003. Call 1-800-643-8699 or 212-777-0470; Fax: 212-777-0471. *Website:* http://www.ohf.org *E-mail:* info@ohf.org

PAGET'S DISEASE

National Association for the Relief of Paget's Disease *Model. 5 regional groups in UK. 2500 member network. Founded 1973.* Offers support to persons with Paget's disease. Aims to raise awareness of this disorder through newsletter and publications. Sponsors research, phone support, literature, information and referrals. Guidelines available for starting similar groups. Write: National Association for the Relief of Paget's Disease, 323 Manchester Rd., Walkden, Worsley, Manchester M28 3HH, UK. Call +44-161-799-4646. *Website:* http://www.paget.org.uk *E-mail:* director@paget.org.uk

PANCREATITIS

ONLINE

Pancreatitis Association International *Online. Founded 1999.* Online internet discussion group which serves as a means of support and information. *Website:* http://health.groups.yahoo.com/group/pancreatitis

PANHYPOPITUITARISM

Panhypopituitarism Division *International network. Founded 1990.* Provides support for families affected by panhypopituitarism. Newsletters, updated medical information, phone support, annual conventions and Kids Program. Online assistance available in finding or forming local support groups. Dues: US $35/yr.; Canada $40/yr.; overseas $45/yr. Write: Panhypopituitarism Division, MAGIC Foundation, 6645 W. North Ave., Oak Park, IL 60302. Call 1-800-362-4423; Fax: 708-383-0899. *Website:* http://www.magicfoundation.org *E-mail:* mary@magicfoundation.org

PANNICULITIS / ERYTHEMA NODOSUM

ONLINE

Erythema Nodosum Support Group *Online. Founded 2003.* Mutual support and resources for erythema nodosum and pyoderma gangreblosum patients. *Website:* http://health.groups.yahoo.com/group/erythema_nodosum_group/

Panniculitis Support Group *Online. 300+ members. Founded 1999.* Support for persons afflicted with any form of panniculitis (Weber Christian, erythema nodosum, mesenteric panniculitis, erythema induratum, lupus panniculitis, subcutaneous sarcoid, etc.) Offers message boards, information and chatrooms. *Website:* http://groups.yahoo.com/group/Panniculitis

PAPILLOMATOSIS

STATEWIDE / NATIONAL

Recurrent Respiratory Papillomatosis Foundation Networking for families affected by recurrent respiratory papillomatosis. Interested professionals are welcome. Newsletter, phone support, online support and referrals to local support groups. Write: Recurrent Respiratory Papillomatosis Foundation, P.O. Box 6643, Lawrenceville, NJ 08648-0643. Call Bill Stern 609-530-1443; Fax: 1-866-498-7559. *Website:* http://www.rrpf.org *E-mail:* bills@rrpf.org

PARRY-ROMBERG SYNDROME / PROGRESSIVE FACIAL HEMIATROPHY

ONLINE

Romberg's Connection, The *Online. Founded 1997.* Offers mutual support for persons affected by Parry Romberg's syndrome (aka progressive facial hemiatrophy or Romberg's syndrome), and their families. Parry-Romberg syndrome is a rare disorder causing atrophy to usually one half of the face. *Website:* http://www.geocities.com/HotSprings/1018/ *E-mail:* rombergs@hotmail.com

PEMPHIGUS

International Pemphigus Foundation *International network. 16 affiliated groups. Founded 1994.* Provides support and information on pemphigus and related autoimmune blistering diseases for patients, families, friends and the medical community. Literature, newsletter, information, referrals, advocacy and phone support. Online support group and listserv. Write: International Pemphigus Foundation, 1540 River Park Dr., Suite 208, Sacramento, CA 95815. Call 916-922-1298; Fax: 916-922-1458. *Website:* http://www.pemphigus.org *E-mail:* info@pemphigus.org

PERIODIC PARALYSIS / NON-DYSTROPHIC MYOTONIAS

ONLINE

Periodic Paralysis Association *Online.* Provides information and support to individuals with periodic paralysis and non-dystrophic myotonias (disorders characterized by episodic paralysis and weakness), their families and health care professionals. Offers links to online specialist referrals, private e-mail listserv, Ask-the-experts, online newsletter and patient advocacy. Write: Periodic Paralysis Association, 1101 Douglas Dr., Tracy, CA 95304-5879. Call 626-638-3326; Fax: 626-698-0789. *Website:* http://www.periodicparalysis.org *E-mail:* inquire@periodicparalysis.org

PETER'S ANOMALY

ONLINE

Peter's Anomaly Support Group *Online.* Support for families of children with Peter's anomaly. Offers message board and forum. Also many useful links. *Website:* http://www.petersanomaly.org (click link "enter forum click here") *E-mail:* rmcginn66@yahoo.com

PEUTZ-JEGHERS SYNDROME / JUVENILE POLYPOSIS SYNDROME

ONLINE

Peutz-Jeghers Syndrome and Juvenile Polyposis Support Group *Online. 250+ members. Founded 2000.* Provides no-cost information and support for individuals with Peutz-Jeghers syndrome and juvenile polyposis syndrome, their families and interested medical professionals and researchers. Provides peer support and matching of individuals and their families. *Website:* http://peutz-jeghers.com or http://listserv.acor.org/archives/pjs.html *E-mail:* pj4steph@aol.com

Need help finding a specific group? Give us a call – we're here to help!
Call 1-800-367-6274.

PHEOCHROMOCYTOMA

ONLINE

Pheochromocytoma Information Group *Online.* Offers support through information for persons affected by pheochromocytoma or multiple endocrine neoplasia syndrome. *Website:* http://www.pheochromocytoma.org

PIERRE ROBIN

Pierre Robin Network *National network. Founded 1999.* Support and education for individuals, parents, caregivers and professionals dealing with Pierre Robin syndrome or sequence. Literature, newsletter, information, advocacy, online e-mail group and bulletin board. Outreach committee comprised of families worldwide available to correspond via mail, phone, in person or e-mail. Write: Pierre Robin Network, 3604 Biscayne, Quincy, IL 62305. Fax: 217-224-6659. *Website:* http://www.pierrerobin.org *E-mail:* info@pierrerobin.org

PINK DISEASE / MERCURY TOXICITY

Pink Disease Support Group *International network. Founded 1989.* Support group for people who had Pink disease (babyhood mercury toxicity) and their relatives. Provides information, support and newsletters by mail and e-mail. Online chat group. Dues $15 yr.(Australia) or $25yr.(int'l). Write: Pink Disease Support Group, P.O. Box 134, Gilgandra NSW, Australia 2827. *Website:* http://www.pinkdisease.org *E-mail:* pinkdisease@bigpond.com

PITUITARY DISORDERS
(see also specific disorders)

Pituitary Network Association *International network. Founded 1992.* Mutual support for persons with all types of pituitary disorders and diseases. Promotes early diagnosis, medical and public awareness along with continued research to find a cure. Phone support, newsletter, information and referrals, resource guide and patient conferences. Write: Pituitary Network Association, P.O. Box 1958, Thousand Oaks, CA 91358. Call 805-499-9973; Fax: 805-480-0633. *Website:* http://www.pituitary.org *E-mail:* PNA@pituitary.org

"Life is so precious. Please, please, let's love one another, live each day, reach out to each other, be kind to each other." – Julia Roberts

PITYRIASIS RUBRA PILARIS

ONLINE

Pityriasis Rubra Pilaris (PRP) Support Group *Online. Founded 1997.* An online discussion forum for anyone diagnosed with the rare skin disease pityriasis rubra pilaris (PRP). Discussion forum members include caregivers and interested family members, spouses, children, parents, friends and partners. Registration is required to participate. *Website:* http://www.prp-support.org *E-mail:* jeremyb@pcug.org.au or rgreene@temple.edu

PORPHYRIA

NATIONAL

American Porphyria Foundation *National network. Founded 1981.* Supports research, provides education and information to the public, patients and physicians, networks porphyria patients and support groups. Quarterly newsletter, pen pal program, phone network. Group development guidelines available. Donation $35/yr. Write: America Porphyria Foundation, P.O. Box 22712, Houston, TX 77227. Call 713-266-9617 (Mon-Fri, 9am-4pm CST); Fax: 713-840-9552. *Website:* http://www.porphyriafoundation.com *E-mail:* porphyrus@aol.com

Canadian Association for Porphyria *International. Founded 1988.* Dedicated to improving the quality of life for people affected by porphyria, a group of rare genetic disorders characterized by disturbances of porphyria metabolism. Offers programs of awareness, education, service, advocacy and support. Promotes awareness of porphyria through educational literature, articles, newsletters, information and referrals. Offers support groups, advocacy and assistance in starting groups. Encourages and supports research. Write: Canadian Association for Porphyria, Inc., P.O. Box 1206, Neepawa, Manitoba, Canada R0J 1H0. Call 1-866-476-2801 or 204-476-2800. *Website:* http://www.cpf-inc.ca *E-mail:* porphyria@cpf-inc.ca

"A man doesn't realize how much he can stand until he is put to the test. You can stand far more than you think you can. You are much stronger than you think you are."
--Martin Niemoller

PRADER-WILLI SYNDROME

STATEWIDE

NJ Chapter Prader-Willi Syndrome Association *Professionally-run.* Parents meet twice a year to provide support and education. This uncommon birth defect results in initial hypotonia, hypogenitalism and central nervous system performance dysfunction which includes an insatiable appetite leading to obesity if not controlled. Write: NJ Chapter, Prader-Willi Syndrome Association, c/o Douglas Taylor, 16 Gettysburg Way, Lincoln Park, NJ 07035. Call Douglas Taylor 973-628-6945. *Website:* http://www.pwsausa.org/nj *E-mail:* pwsa.nj@gmail.com

NATIONAL

Prader-Willi Syndrome Association *National. 38+ chapters. Founded 1975.* Support and education for anyone impacted by Prader-Willi syndrome. Bi-monthly newsletter. Membership dues $35. Many publications available. Chapter development kits available. Write: Prader-Willi Syndrome Association, 8588 Potter Park. Dr., Suite 500, Sarasota, FL 34238. Call 1-800-926-4797 or 941-312-0400; Fax: 941-312-0142. *Website:* http://www.pwsausa.org

PRECOCIOUS PUBERTY

Precocious Puberty Support Network *National network. Founded 1989.* Network and exchange of information for children who are experiencing precocious puberty and their families. Information and referrals, phone support, pen pals, annual convention, conferences and literature. Newsletter. Yearly membership: $35 US; $40 Canada; $45 overseas. Write: Precocious Puberty Support Network, c/o MAGIC Foundation, 6645 W. North Ave, Oak Park, IL 60302. Call 1-800-362-4423 or 708-383-0808; Fax: 708-383-0899. *Website:* http://www.magicfoundation.org *E-mail:* mary@magicfoundation.org

PRIMARY LATERAL SCLEROSIS / HEREDITARY SPASTIC PARAPLEGIA

NATIONAL

Spastic Paraplegia Foundation, Inc. *National. Founded 2002.* Offers support and information to those affected by primary lateral sclerosis and hereditary spastic paraplegia. Supports research. Offers regional and e-mail support groups, online chat group, newsletter and information. Write: Spastic Paraplegia

Foundation, Inc., 11 Douglas Green, Woburn, MA 01801. Call 1-877-773-4483. *Website:* http://www.sp-foundation.org

ONLINE

PLS Friends *Online.* Opportunity for persons with primary lateral sclerosis, a progressive neuromuscular disease, to share information and support via an online discussion group. Fosters support and an exchange of ideas among PLS patients, their relatives, caregivers and health care professionals. *Website:* http://www.geocities.com/freyerse/ *E-mail:* synapsePLS@comcast.net

PROGRESSIVE MULTIFOCAL LEUKOENCEPHALOPATHY

ONLINE

PML Survivors and Supporters *Online. Members 26. Founded 2006.* Support forum to educate, inform and inspire persons with progressive multifocal leukoencephalopathy and their families. Opportunity to share treatment information and support to any person affected with or by PML. *Website:* http://health.groups.yahoo.com/group/PMLSurvivors *E-mail:* PMLSurvivors@yahoo.com

PROGRESSIVE OSSEOUS HETEROPLASIA

Progressive Osseous Heteroplasia Association *National network. Founded 1995.* Support network for patients and families affected by progressive osseous heteroplasia. Fundraising for research. Write: Progressive Osseous Heteroplasia Association, 14031 S. Tamarack Drive, Plainfield, IL 60544-6356. Call 815-524-5849. *Website:* http://www.pohdisease.org *E-mail:* info@pohdisease.org

PROGRESSIVE SUPRANUCLEAR PALSY

Cure PSP (Society for Progressive Supranuclear Palsy, Inc.) *International network. 75 affiliated groups. Founded 1990.* Provides support and advocacy for patients with progressive supranuclear palsy and their families. Offers newsletter, phone support, conferences, listserv, educational materials, assistance in starting support groups, information and referrals. Write: Society for Progressive Supranuclear Palsy, Executive Plaza III, 11350 McCormick Rd., Suite 906, Hunt Valley, MD 21031. Call 1-800-457-4777 or 410-785-7004; Fax: 410-785-7009. *Website:* http://www.curepsp.org *E-mail:* info@curepsp.org

PROTEUS SYNDROME

Proteus Syndrome Foundation *International network. Founded 1991.* Provides support and education for families of children with Proteus syndrome. Supports research into cause and cure of this disorder. Newsletter, pen pals, literature and database of families. Fundraising. Write: Proteus Syndrome Foundation, 4915 Dry Stone Dr., Colorado Springs, CO 80918. Call Kim 719-375-3005 (day) or Barbara 901-756-9375 (day). *Website:* http://www.proteus-syndrome.org *E-mail:* kimhoag01@comcast.net or jakebabs@aol.com

PSEUDOXANTHOMA ELASTICUM

STATEWIDE

NY-NJ Chapter of PXE International Promotes support, education, advocacy and research for those with pseudoxanthoma elasticum and their families. Patient tissue registry, listserv and e-mail connection. Guest speakers, pen pals, phone help and literature. Meets quarterly in various locations. Call Judy Roller 732-297-7055. *Website:* http://www.pxe.org *E-mail:* jroller123@aol.com

NATIONAL

National Association for Pseudoxanthoma Elasticum *National network. Founded 1988.* Support, education, research and advocacy for persons with PXE, their families, interested others and professionals. Phone support, newsletter, information and referrals. Donations appreciated and tax deductible. Write: National Association for Pseudoxanthoma Elasticum, 8760 Manchester Rd., St. Louis, MO 63144-2724. Call 314-962-0100 (voice/fax). *Website:* http://www.pxenape.org *E-mail:* napestlouis@sbcglobal.net

PXE International, Inc. *International. 41 affiliated groups. Founded 1995.* Initiates, funds and manages research, supports patients and educates clinicians. Offers support groups, listservs, literature, semi-annual newsletter, phone and mail contacts. Offers assistance in starting similar groups. Write: PXE International, Inc., 4301 Connecticut Ave. NW, Suite 404, Washington, DC 20008-2369. Call 202-362-9599; Fax: 202-966-8553. *Website:* http://www.pxe.org *E-mail:* info@pxe.org

PULMONARY HYPERTENSION

Pulmonary Hypertension Association *National network. 130 support groups. Founded 1990.* Support and information for patients with pulmonary hypertension (a cardio-vascular disease), their families and medical professionals. Encourages research, promotes awareness and provides resource referrals. Networking, phone help, pen pals, newsletter and assistance in starting groups. Membership $15. Write: Pulmonary Hypertension Association, 801 Roeder Rd., Suite 400, Silver Spring, MD 20910. Call 1-800-748-7274 or 301-565-3004; Fax: 301-565-3994. *Website:* http://www.phassociation.org *E-mail:* pha@phassociation.org

RARE DISORDERS, GENERAL
(see also specific disorder)

NATIONAL

Hearts and Hands *Model. 1 group in NC. Founded 1993.* Emotional, spiritual and educational support for persons with either rare or undiagnosed illnesses and their families. Also has a registry for loin pain hematuria syndrome. Write: Hearts and Hands, c/o Winoka Plummer, 1648 Oliver's Crossing Circle, Winston-Salem, NC 27127. Call 336-785-7612. *Website:* http://www.geocities.com/hotsprings/spa/2464/index.html

National Organization for Rare Disorders *National network. Founded 1983.* Information and networking for persons with any type of rare disorder. Literature, information and referrals. Advocacy for orphan diseases. Networks persons or families with the same disorder for support. Guidelines available for starting similar groups. Write: NORD, 55 Kenosia Ave., P.O. Box 1968, Danbury, CT 06813-1968. Call 1-800-999-6673 or 203-744-0100; TDD: 203-797-9590; Fax: 203-798-2291. *Website:* http://www.rarediseases.org *E-mail:* orphan@rarediseases.org

RAYNAUD'S DISEASE

Raynaud's Association, Inc. *National. Founded 1992.* Mutual support group to help Raynaud's sufferers cope with day-to-day activities to maintain or improve their quality of life. Aims to increase awareness of the disease among public and medical communities. Assists in supporting treatment research efforts. Newsletter, special event meetings, literature, information and referrals. Dues $20 (optional). Write: Raynaud's Association, 94 Mercer Ave., Hartsdale, NY 10530. Call Lynn Wunderman 1-800-280-8055; Fax: 914-946-4685. *Website:* http://www.raynauds.org *E-mail:* info@raynauds.org

*We can also refer callers to over 100 individuals who are seeking others to help start new support groups throughout NJ. For more information call **1-800-367-6274.***

REFLEX ANOXIC SEIZURE DISORDER / STEPHENSON'S SEIZURE / WHITE BREATH HOLDING SYNCOPE / PALLID INFANTILE SYNCOPE

STARS-US (Syncope Trust And Reflex Anoxic Seizures) *National. Founded 2007.* Network of parents and sufferers of syncope and reflex anoxic seizure (characterized by temporary heart stoppage and a seizure-like response to any unexpected stimuli), also known as Stephenson's seizure, white breath holding or pallid infantile syncope. Newsletter, networking, literature, phone support, conferences, information and referrals. Online e-bulletin and moderated message board. Support system and education for sufferers, their families, medical community and general public. Offers assistance in starting local chapters. Dues: $25/yr. Write: STARS-US, P.O. Box 5507, Hilton Head Island, SC 29938. Call 843-785-4101. *Website:* http://www.stars-us.org *E-mail:* rsmith@stars-us.org

RESTLESS LEG SYNDROME

MIDDLESEX

Central New Jersey Restless Legs Syndrome Support Group Opportunity for RLS patients and medical professionals to help raise awareness of RLS and share in the latest information, research and medical break throughs regarding RLS. Families welcome. Discussion, guest speakers, literature, newsletter and phone help. Meets 4 times/yr., Sat., JFK Medical Center, 65 James St., Auditorium, Edison. Call Elizabeth Visone 973-715-3868. *E-mail:* elizabethvis@aol.com

NATIONAL

Restless Legs Syndrome Foundation *National network. 100 affiliated groups. Founded 1992.* Promotes awareness and information about restless legs syndrome. Offers network of support and educational groups nationwide. Publishes a free information booklet. Members receive a quarterly newsletter. Write: RLS Foundation, 1610 14th St. NW, Suite 300, Rochester, MN 55901. Call 507-287-6465 or 1-877-463-6757 (to request information); Fax: 507-287-6312. *Website:* http://www.rls.org *E-mail:* rlsfoundation@rls.org

"You have it easily in your power to increase the sum total of this world's happiness now. How? By giving a few words of sincere appreciation to someone who is lonely or discouraged." -- Dale Carnegie

RETT SYNDROME
(see also movement disorders)

International Rett Syndrome Foundation *International. 17 affiliated groups. Founded 1985.* For parents, interested professionals and others concerned with Rett syndrome. Provides information and referral, peer support among parents and funds research. Quarterly newsletter. Dues: free/corresponding partner; $30/active partner; $40/int'l; $125 organization. Write: International Rett Syndrome Foundation, 4600 Devitt Dr., Cincinnati, OH 45246. Call 1-800-818-7388 or 513-874-3020; Fax: 513-874-2520. *Website:* http://www.rettsyndrome.org *E-mail:* admin@rettsyndrome.org

REYE'S SYNDROME

National Reye's Syndrome Foundation *National. 4 affiliated chapters, 189 representatives in 45 states. Founded 1974.* Devoted to spreading the awareness of Reye's syndrome, a disease affecting the liver and brain which affects persons of all ages and races. Provides support, information and referrals. Encourages research. Representatives are usually a parent, sibling or survivor, but is open to any interested person. Write: National Reye's Syndrome Foundation, P.O. Box 829, Bryan, OH 43506. Call 1-800-233-7393; Fax: 419-924-9999. *Website:* http://www.reyessyndrome.org *E-mail:* nrsf@reyessyndrome.org

ROBINOW SYNDROME / FETAL FACE SYNDROME
(see also growth disorders)

Robinow Syndrome Foundation *National network. Founded 1994.* Aim is to locate, educate and support persons affected by Robinow syndrome (also known as fetal face syndrome) a very rare, genetic dwarfing syndrome. Online support, newsletter, bi-annual conventions and family networking. Write: Robinow Syndrome Foundation, P.O. Box 1072, Anoka, MN 55303. Call Karla Kruger 763-434-1152 (voice/fax). *Website:* http://www.robinow.org *E-mail:* kmkruger@comcast.net

ROSACEA

ONLINE

Rosacea Support Group *Online. 680+ members. Founded 1998.* E-mail support group for rosacea sufferers, their family and friends. *Website:* http://health.groups.yahoo.com/group/rosacea-support

RUBINSTEIN-TAYBI SYNDROME

Rubinstein-Taybi Parent Group USA *National network. 465 member families. Founded 1984.* Mutual support, information and sharing for parents of children with Rubinstein-Taybi syndrome. Phone contact, parent contact list, chatroom and listserv. Write: Rubinstein-Taybi Parent Group, c/o Garry and Lorrie Baxter, P.O. Box 146, Smith Center, KS 66967. *Website:* http://www.rubinsteintaybi.com *E-mail:* lbaxter@ruraltel.net

RUSSELL-SILVER SYNDROME

Russell-Silver Syndrome Support Network *National network. Founded 1989.* Network and exchange of information for parents of children with Russell-Silver syndrome. Information and referrals, phone support, pen pals, conferences, annual convention and literature. Membership dues $35/yr./US; $40/yr./Canada;$45/yr./overseas. Write: Russell-Silver Syndrome Support Network, c/o MAGIC Foundation, 6645 W. North Ave., Oak Park, IL 60302. Call 1-800-362-4423 or 708-383-0808; Fax: 708-383-0899. *Website:* http://www.magicfoundation.org *E-mail:* mary@magicfoundation.org

SARCOIDOSIS

NATIONAL

Foundation for Sarcoidosis Research, The *National network. Founded 2000.* Provides information, resources and research news on sarcoidosis (a multi-system disease that causes inflammation of the body's tissues) to patients, their families and their physicians. Online support offers patients a safe environment to share their stories and participate in discussion groups. Write: Foundation for Sarcoidosis Research, Suite 1700, 122 S. Michigan Ave, Chicago, IL 60603. Call Debbie Durrer 312-341-0500; Fax: 312-322-9808. *Website:* http://www.stopsarcoidosis.org/ *E-mail:* info@stopsarcoidosis.org

Sarcoid Networking Association *National network. 3 chapters. Founded 1992.* Provides support and education for sarcoidosis patients, their families and friends through newsletter, correspondence, phone and e-mail. Publication "Sarcoidosis Networking" published 4 times/yr. Provides information on local groups. Offers seminars, conferences, research, advocacy and meetings. Assistance in starting new groups. Write: Sarcoid Networking Association, 5302 Sheridan Ave., Tacoma, WA 98408. Call 253-826-7737 (voice/fax). *Website:* http://www.sarcoidosisnetwork.org *E-mail:* sarcoidosis_network@prodigy.net

SELECTIVE MUTISM
(see also anxiety)

BERGEN

SMG ~ CAN Connections *Professionally-run.* Provides support and education for parents and professionals involved with a selectively mute child. Rap sessions, guest speakers, literature and phone help. Building is handicapped accessible. Meets 4th Mon., 12:45-2:30pm, Franklin Lakes Library, 470 DeKorte Dr., Franklin Lakes. Call Gail Kervatt 973-208-1848. *Website:* http://www.selectivemutism.org *E-mail:* kervatt@optonline.net

NATIONAL

Selective Mutism Foundation, Inc. *National. Founded 1992.* Pioneering group that offers mutual support for professionals and parents of children with selective mutism or social phobia (a psychiatric anxiety disorder in which children are unable to speak in social situations). Includes social anxiety and shyness. Also open to adults who have, or outgrew, the disorder. Provides information and online support. Website contains DSM revisions, research studies, printable brochures, literature and publications. Write: Carolyn Miller, P.O. Box 13133, Sissonville, WV 25360 or Sue Newman Mercado, P.O. Box 25972, Tamarac, FL 33320. *Website:* http://www.selectivemutismfoundation.org *E-mail:* carolyn@selectivemutismfoundation.org or sue@selectivemutismfoundation

ONLINE

Selective Mutism Group, The *Online. Founded 1999.* Devoted to educating and promoting awareness on selective mutism and other related childhood anxiety disorders. Online forums and "Expert Chats" in addition to the Connections Program that links individuals and provides state support group meeting information. *Website:* http://selectivemutism.org *E-mail:* sminfo@selectivemutism.org

SEMANTIC-PRAGMATIC DISORDER

ONLINE

Semantic-Pragmatic Disorder Forum *Online.* Opportunity for persons affected by semantic-pragmatic disorder, a communication disorder and their families. SPD is characterized by problems in processing the meaning of language. *Website:* http://forums.delphiforums.com/pragma/start

SEPTO OPTIC DYSPLASIA / OPTIC NERVE HYPOPLASIA / DEMORSIER SYNDROME

NATIONAL

Septo Optic Dysplasia Division - MAGIC Foundation *National network. Founded 1989.* Provides public education and networking for families of children with septo optic dysplasia. Information and referrals, phone support, pen pals, annual convention and conferences. Membership is $35/US, $40/Canada, $45/International. Write: Septo Optic Dysplasia Division, c/o The MAGIC Foundation, 6645 W. North Ave., Oak Park, IL 60302. Call 1-800-362-4423; Fax: 708-383-0899. *Website:* http://www.magicfoundation.org *E-mail:* mary@magicfoundation.org

ONLINE

Focus Families *Online.* E-mail support group for parents of children with septo-optic dysplasia and optic nerve hypoplasia (aka deMorsier syndrome). Opportunity to share experiences. Online newsletter and annual conference. *Website:* http://www.focusfamilies.org

SHINGLES

STATEWIDE

Shingles Telephone Support Group Telephone network to provide support and encouragement to people suffering with shingles. Contact Laura 732-928-7696 (day/early eve.) or Barbara 201-447-5978 (day).

SHWACHMAN-DIAMOND SYNDROME

Shwachman Diamond Syndrome Foundation *National network. Founded 1994.* Patient advocacy organization whose goals are to support research towards a cure and improve medical management of symptoms. Links families for emotional support and provides them with the most current medical information available which is provided through the knowledge and cooperation of a professional medical advisory board. Write: Shwachman Diamond Syndrome Foundation, 710 Brassie Drive, Grand Junction, CO 81506. Call 1-877-737-4685 or 614-939-2324; Fax: 970-255-8293. *Website:* http://www.shwachman-diamond.org

SICKLE CELL DISEASE

Sickle Cell Disease Association of America, Inc. *National. 60 chapters. Founded 1971.* Education for the public and professionals about sickle cell disease. Support and information for persons affected by the disease. Supports research, quarterly newsletter, chapter development guidelines, phone network, videos, online network, research updates and forum. Write: Sickle Cell Disease Association of America, 231 E. Baltimore St., Suite 800, Baltimore, MD 21202. Call 1-800-421-8453 (Mon.-Fri., 8:30am-5pm EST); Fax: 410-528-1495. *Website:* http://www.sicklecelldisease.org

SJOGREN'S SYNDROME

NATIONAL

Sjogren's Syndrome Foundation, Inc. *National. 78 groups. Founded 1983.* Information and education for Sjogren's syndrome patients, families, health professionals and the public. Opportunities for patients to share ways of coping. Stimulates research for treatments and cures. Newsletter "Moisture Seekers," chapter development assistance, video tapes, annual symposium and Sjogren's handbook. Write: Sjogren's Syndrome Foundation, Inc., 6707 Democracy Blvd., Suite 325, Bethesda, MD 20817. Call 1-800-475-6473 or 301-530-4420; Fax: 301-530-4415. *Website:* http://www.sjogrens.org

ONLINE

Sjogren's World *Online. 826 members. Founded 1999.* Caring internet community built for people who have Sjogren's Syndrome (a chronic, slowly progressive autoimmune disease that affects the exocrine glands) to meet and share experiences, personal knowledge and to disseminate information to improve quality of life and thwart loneliness. Support available via E-Pals, discussion forums, instant messaging, live chats and e-mail lists. *Website:* http://www.sjogrensworld.org *E-mail:* sjogrens@sjogrensworld.org

SMITH-LEMLI-OPITZ SYNDROME

Smith-Lemli-Opitz/RSH Foundation *International network. Founded 1988.* Support for families, medical professionals and others dealing with individuals that have Smith-Lemli-Opitz (RSH) syndrome. Research funding also available via a grant process. Phone and e-mail support. Newsletter 2X/yr. Bi-annual conferences and newsletter. Write: Smith-Lemli-Opitz/RSH Foundation, c/o Cynthia Gold, P.O. Box 212, Georgetown, MA 01833. Call 978-352-5885. *Website:* http://www.smithlemliopitz.org *E-mail:* sloinfo@smithlemliopitz.org

SMITH-MAGENIS SYNDROME

PRISMS (Parents & Researchers Interested in Smith-Magenis) *International network. Founded 1993.* Parent-to-parent program offering support, advocacy and education for families affected by Smith-Magenis syndrome. Information, referrals, literature, phone support and newsletter. Dues $30. Write: PRISMS, Inc,. 21800 Town Center Plaza, Suite 266A-663, Sterling, VA 20164. Call 972-231-0035. *Website:* http://www.prisms.org *E-mail:* info@prisms.org

SOTOS SYNDROME

Sotos Syndrome Support Association *International network. Founded 1984.* Provides information and mutual support for families of children with Sotos syndrome. Newsletter, phone support, pen pals, annual conferences, information and referrals. Write: Sotos Syndrome Support Association, P.O. Box 4626, Wheaton, IL 60189. Call 1-888-246-7772. *Website:* http://www.well.com/users/sssa *E-mail:* sssa@well.com

SPASMODIC DYSPHONIA

NATIONAL

National Spasmodic Dysphonia Association *National. 35 affiliated support groups. Founded 1990.* Dedicated to advancing medical research into the causes and treatments for spasmodic dysphonia. Promotes physician and public awareness of the disorder through outreach and sponsoring support activities for people with SD and their families. Educational materials, annual symposiums, support groups, newsletter and on-line resources. Offers assistance in starting similar groups. Write: National Spasmodic Dysphonia Association, 300 Park Blvd., Suite 301, Itasca, IL 60143. Call 1-800-795-6732. *Website:* http://www.dysphonia.org *E-mail:* kkuman@dysphonia.org

Spasmodic Dysphonia Support Group *National. 20 groups. Founded 1987.* Provides members with the latest information regarding spasmodic dysphonia, as well as emotional and practical support. Offers workshops and discussions. Encourages education for the public and physicians. Guest speakers, information and referrals. Write: Spasmodic Dysphonia Support Group of NY, c/o A. Simons, 67-33 152 St., Flushing, NY 11367. Call 718-793-2442. *E-mail:* ahsimons@verizon.net

SPASMODIC TORTICOLLIS

National Spasmodic Torticollis Association *National. 75 chapters. Founded 1983.* Advocacy group providing information and support to spasmodic torticollis patients and their families. Network of support groups and volunteers on-call to talk with other patients. Quarterly magazine, annual symposium, supports research, e-mail support, educates the public and medical community. Write: National Spasmodic Torticollis Association, 9920 Talbert Ave., Fountain Valley, CA 92708. Call 1-800-487-8385 or 714-378-7837 (Mon.-Fri., 9am-5pm PST); Fax: 714-378-7830. *Website:* http://www.torticollis.org *E-mail:* nstamail@aol.com

SPASTIC PARAPLEGIA

Spastic Paraplegia Foundation, Inc. *National. Founded 2002.* Offers support and information to those affected by primary lateral sclerosis and hereditary spastic paraplegia. Supports research. Offers regional and e-mail support groups, online chat group, newsletter and information. Write: Spastic Paraplegia Foundation, Inc., 11 Douglas Green, Woburn, MA 01801. Call 1-877-773-4483. *Website:* http://www.sp-foundation.org

SPINAL MUSCULAR ATROPHY
(see also Kennedy's disease)

Families of S.M.A. (Spinal Muscular Atrophy) *(MULTILINGUAL) International. 31 chapters. Founded 1984.* Funding of research, support and networking for families affected by spinal muscular atrophy types I, II, III, adult onset and Kennedy's. Educational resources, group development guidelines, quarterly newsletter, pen pals, phone support and videotapes. Online message boards and kids corner support. Write: Families of SMA, P.O. Box 196, Libertyville, IL 60048-0196. Call 1-800-886-1762 or 847-367-7620 (Mon-Fri, 7am-3pm CST); Fax: 847-367-7623. *Website:* http://www.fsma.org or http://www.curesma.com *E-mail:* info@fsma.org

STEVENS JOHNSON SYNDROME

NATIONAL

Aniridia Foundation International *International. Founded 2002.* Offers support, data studies, research and education to the public, medical community and members. Provides information, referrals, literature, newsletter, phone support, pen pals and conferences. Online e-mail support and chatrooms. Also supports those with low vision or blindness who experience the same associated conditions such as glaucoma, corneal disease and cataracts. OPTIC program helps those with Stevens-Johnson syndrome, chemical and thermal burns to the eyes and other corneal dystrophy patients. Write: Aniridia Foundation International, c/o Hamilton Eye Institute, 930 Madison Ave., Suite 314, Memphis, TN 38163. Call 901-448-2380; Fax: 901-448-2382 *Website:* http://www.aniridia.net *E-mail:* info@aniridia.net

Stevens Johnson Syndrome Foundation *International network. Founded 1995.* Provides to the public and medical communities information on adverse allergic drug reactions. Aim is to quicken diagnoses to avoid permanent damage. Literature, phone support, chatroom, moderated discussion group, information and referrals. Write: Stevens Johnson Syndrome Foundation, P.O. Box 350333, Westminster, CO 80035. Call 303-635-1241. *Website:* http://www.sjsupport.org *E-mail:* sjsupport@aol.com

STICKLER SYNDROME

Stickler Involved People *International network. Founded 1995.* Network that offers support and education for persons affected by Stickler syndrome. This genetic disorder affects connective tissues, including the joints, eyes, palate and hearing. Phone support, annual conference, literature, DVD, online listserv, quarterly newsletter, information and referrals. Write: Stickler Involved People, 15 Angelina, Augusta, KS 67010. Call 316-259-5194. *Website:* http://www.sticklers.org *E-mail:* sip@sticklers.org

STREP, GROUP B

Canadian Strep B Foundation *International network. Founded 2003.* Educates the public about group B streptococcal infections during pregnancy. Information and referrals, advocacy and phone support. Group development guidelines available. Write: Patricia Normand, President, The Canadian Strep B Foundation, 1712 Montee Sauvage, Prevost, Quebec JOR 1TO. Call 1-877-873-7424 or 450-224-7718. *Website:* http://www.strepb.ca *E-mail:* info@strepb.ca

STURGE-WEBER SYNDROME / PORT WINE STAINS
(see also Klippel Trenaunay syndrome)

Sturge-Weber Foundation, The *International network. Members in 50 states and internationally. Founded 1987.* Mutual support network for families and professionals involved with Sturge-Weber syndrome, Port Wine Stains or Klippel Trenaunay syndrome. Disseminates information, funds and facilitates research. Newsletter, E-news monthly, phone support, bi-annual conference, pen pals and active e-mail support group. Educational materials for schools, parents and clinicians. Write: Sturge-Weber Foundation, P.O. Box 418, Mt. Freedom, NJ 07970. Call 1-800-627-5482 or 973-895-4445; Fax: 973-895-4846. *Website:* http://www.sturge-weber.org *E-mail:* swf@sturge-weber.org

SYRINGOMYELIA / CHIARI MALFORMATION

American Syringomyelia Alliance Project *International network. Founded 1988.* Support, networking and information for people affected by syringomyelia and chiari malformation, their families and friends. Newsletter, phone support, pen pals and conferences. Also offers online message boards and chatrooms. Write: American Syringomyelia Alliance Project, P.O. Box 1586, Longview, TX 75606-1586. Call 1-800-272-7282 or 903-236-7079; Fax: 903-757-7456. *Website:* http://www.asap.org *E-mail:* info@asap.org

TAKAYASU'S ARTERITIS

Takayasu's Arteritis Association *Model. Founded 1995.* Education and support for persons with Takayasu's arteritis (an inflammation of the large elastic arteries and aorta), their families and health professionals. Network program, information, phone and online support, literature, newsletters, research conferences and resources. Write: Takayasu's Arteritis Association, 2030 County Line Rd., Suite 199, Huntingdon Valley, PA 19006. Call 1-800-575-9390 (access code 00). *Website:* http://www.takayasus.org *E-mail:* admin@takayasus.org

TAY-SACHS DISEASE
(see also Canavan disease)

National Tay-Sachs and Allied Diseases Association *(MULTILINGUAL) International. Founded 1957.* Dedicated to the treatment and prevention of Tay-Sachs, Canavan and related genetic diseases. Provides information and support services to individuals of all ages and families affected by these disorders as well as caregivers and the public at large. The strategies for achieving these goals include public and professional education, research, genetic screening, support services (i.e. peer support group for parents, grandparents, extended family members) and advocacy. Translations available in Spanish, Russian, Hebrew and French. Write: National Tay-Sachs and Allied Diseases Association, 2001 Beacon St., Suite 204, Boston, MA 02135. Call 1-800-906-8723 or 617-277-4463; Fax: 617-277-0134. *Website:* http://www.ntsad.org *E-mail:* info@ntsad.org

TEMPOROMANDIBULAR JOINT DYSFUNCTION (TMJ)

TMJ Association *International. Founded 1986.* Created by two patients suffering from temporomandibular joint and muscle disorders (TMJDs) which cause pain and dysfunction in and around the temporomandibular or jaw joint. Resource and advocacy organization for TMJ sufferers and their families, as well as a resource for researchers and health professionals. Write: TMJ Association, P.O. Box 26770, Milwaukee, WI 53226-0770. Call 262-432-0350; Fax: 262-432-0375. *Website:* http://www.tmj.org *E-mail:* info@tmj.org

TOURETTE SYNDROME

STATEWIDE

Tourette Syndrome Association of NJ, Inc. Mission is to support the needs of families of persons with Tourette syndrome, as well as adults with TS. Offers advocacy for persons with Tourette syndrome. Provides education to the public and professionals. Offers peer-counseling. Support group meetings in Atlantic, Bergen, Burlington, Hunterdon, Mercer, Middlesex, Monmouth, Morris and Somerset counties. Write: Tourette Syndrome Association of NJ, Inc., 50 Division St., Suite 205, Somerville, NJ 08876. Call 908-575-7350 or 732-972-4459 (helpline); Fax: 908-575-8699. *Website:* http://www.njcts.org *E-mail:* info@tsanj.org or info@njcts.org

ATLANTIC

Tourette Family Support Group *Professionally-run.* Provides support network and education for parents of children with Tourette syndrome. Guest speakers and literature. Meets 1st Thurs., 7pm (Feb., Apr., June, Oct., Dec.), AtlantiCare Regional Medical Center, Jimmie Leeds Rd., New Cafe, Pomona. Call 908-575-7350 (day). *Website:* http://www.njcts.org

CAMDEN

Tourette Family Support Group *Professionally-run.* Provides support network and education for parents of children with Tourette syndrome. Guest speakers and literature. Meets 1st Mon., 7:30pm (Feb., Apr., June, Oct., Dec.), West Jersey Hospital, 101 Carnie Blvd., Voorhees. Call 908-575-7350 (day). *Website:* http://www.njcts.org

CUMBERLAND

Tourette Family Support Group *Professionally-run.* Provides support network and education for parents of children with Tourette syndrome. Guest speakers and literature. Meets 3rd Thurs., 7pm (Feb., Apr., June, Oct., Dec.), South Jersey Regional Hospital, Fitness Connection, 1430 West Sherman Ave., Board Room, Vineland. Call 908-575-7350 (day). *Website:* http://www.njcts.org

MERCER

Tourette Family Support Group *Professionally-run.* Provides support network and education for parents of children with Tourette syndrome. Guest speakers and literature. Meets 3rd Thurs., 7pm (Jan., Mar., May, Sept., Nov.), RWJ Hamilton Center for Health and Wellness, 3100 Quakerbridge Rd., Mercerville. Call 908-575-7350 (day). *Website:* http://www.njcts.org

MIDDLESEX

Tourette Family Support Group *Professionally-run.* Provides support network and education for parents of children with Tourette syndrome. Guest speakers and literature. Meets 2nd Tues., 7pm (Jan., Mar., May, Sept.), JFK Hospital Neuroscience Institute, 65 James St., Edison. Call 908-575-7350 (day). *Website:* http://www.njcts.org

MONMOUTH

Tourette Family Support Group *Professionally-run.* Provides support network and education for parents of children with Tourette syndrome. Guest speakers and literature. Meets 3rd Tues., 7pm (Jan., Mar., May, Sept., Nov.), Jersey Shore University Hospital, Meridian Life Fitness, 2020 Highway 33, Neptune. Call 908-575-7350 (day). *Website:* http://www.njcts.org

MORRIS

Tourette Family Support Group *Professionally-run.* Provides support network and education for parents of children with Tourette syndrome. Guest speakers and literature. Building is handicapped accessible. Meets 1st Thurs., 7pm (Feb., Apr., June, Aug., Oct., Dec.), Saint Clare's Hospital, 25 Pocono Rd., Auditorium, Denville. Pre-registration required. Before attending call 973-625-6199 (day).

SOMERSET

Tourette Family Support Group *Professionally-run.* Provides support network and education for parents of children with Tourette syndrome. Guest speakers and literature. Meets 4th Mon., 7pm (Jan., Mar., Sept., Nov.); May meets 3rd Mon., Somerset Medical Center, 110 Rehill Ave., Conference Room A and B, Somerville. Call 908-575-7350 (day). *Website:* http://www.njcts.org

NATIONAL

Tourette Syndrome Association *National. 35 chapters. Founded 1972.* Dedicated to identifying the cause, finding the cure, and controlling the effects of Tourette syndrome through education, research and service. Provides support services to families and professionals to enable patients to achieve optimum development. Chapter development guidelines and newsletter. Dues $45. Write: Tourette Syndrome Association, 42-40 Bell Blvd., Suite 205, Bayside, NY 11361-2820. Call 718-224-2999; Fax: 718-279-9596. *Website:* http://tsa-usa.org *E-mail:* ts@tsa-usa.org

TRACHEOESOPHAGEAL FISTULA / ESOPHAGEAL ATRESIA

NATIONAL

TEF/VATER Support Network *International. 6 groups. Founded 1990.* Offers support and encouragement for parents of children with tracheoesophageal fistula, esophageal atresia and VATER. Aims to bring current information to parents and the medical community. Newsletter, information and referrals and phone support. Write: TEF/VATER Support Network, c/o Greg and Terri Burke, 15301 Grey Fox Rd., Upper Marlboro, MD 20772. Call 301-952-6837; Fax: 301-952-9152. *E-mail:* tefvater@ix.netcom.com

ONLINE

EA/TEF Child and Family Support Connection, Inc. *Online.* Provides information and support for families of children with esophageal atresia and tracheoesophageal fistula. Offers pamphlets, brochures and discussion forum. *Website:* http://eatef.org *E-mail:* info@eatef.org

---

"Confront your fears, list them, get to know them, and only then will you be able to put them aside and move ahead."--Jerry Gillies

TRACHEOSTOMY

ONLINE

Aaron's Tracheostomy Page *Online. Founded 1998.* Mutual support and information sharing for persons who have, or anticipate having, a tracheostomy. Open to parents of children, patients, families, caregivers and professionals. Through a listserv, members are given a chance to support each other, ask questions and offer coping tips. Write: Trachties, 102 Morene Ave., Waxahachie, TX 75165. *Website:* http://www.tracheostomy.com

TRANSVERSE MYELITIS

Transverse Myelitis Association *National. Over 6000 members in 80 countries.* Offers support and education to persons with transverse myelitis and other neuroimmunologic diseases of the central nervous system (e.g. acute disseminated encephalomyelitis, optic neuritis and neuromyelitis optica, Devic's disease) and their families. Networks families together for support. Provides research literature, newsletter and membership directory. Investigates, advocates for and supports research and treatment efforts. Provides a support forum for communication. Bulletin board. Assists in the development of local support groups. Fund-raises for research. Conducts symposia and workshops. Write: Tranverse Myelitis Association, c/o Sandy Siegel, 1787 Sutter Parkway, Powell, OH 43065-8806. Call 614-766-1806. *Website:* http://www.myelitis.org *E-mail:* ssiegel@myelitis.org

TREACHER COLLINS SYNDROME

Treacher Collins Connection *National network. Founded 2001.* Provides support, networking and education for individuals who are affected by Treacher Collins syndrome. Write: Treacher Collins, P.O. Box 120416, Boston, MA 02112. Call Judy 704-545-1921. *Website:* http://www.tcconnection.org *E-mail:* judy@tcconnection.org

TRIGEMINAL NEURALGIA / TIC DOULOUREUX

Trigeminal Neuralgia Association *National. 65+ groups. Founded 1990.* Provides information, mutual support and encouragement to persons with trigeminal neuralgia and related facial pain disorders. Families are welcome. Helps to reduce the isolation of those affected. Aims to increase awareness, promotes research into the cause and cure. Quarterly newsletter, phone support, educational information and patient advocacy. Write: Trigeminal Neuralgia Association, 925 Northwest 56th Terrace, Suite C, Gainesville, FL 32605. Call

1-800-923-3608 or 352-331-7009; Fax 352-331-7078. *Website:* http://www.endthepain.org *E-mail:* info@fpa-support.org

TRIPLE-X SYNDROME

Triple X Support Group *International network. Founded 1997.* Provides support, resources and informational materials to parents of children with triple X syndrome (aka trisomy X or 47, XXX syndrome). Aims to educate professionals and the public on this syndrome. Networks parents together for support. Literature, referrals and phone support. Write: Triple X Support Group, c/o Helen Clements, 32 Francemary Rd., Brockley, London, England SE4 1JS. Call (020)86909445. *Website:* http://www.triplo-x.org *E-mail:* helenclements@hotmail.com

TRISOMY

STATEWIDE

S.O.F.T. (Support Organization For Trisomy) Support for families of children with trisomy 18 and 13 and related disorders. Education about trisomy, implications to families and community. Meets various times and locations. Call Colleen Frazier 609-567-4151, Pat O'Toole 215-663-9652 or Kathleen Johnson 215-489-2678. *E-mail:* kathy.johnson.1sw@verizon.net

NATIONAL

SOFT (Support Organization For Trisomy) *National. 50 chapters. Founded 1979.* Support and education for families of children with trisomy 18 and 13 and related genetic disorders (including trisomy 9). Education for professionals. Quarterly newsletter, pen pal program, phone network, regional gatherings, annual international conference and booklets. Online information on finding a local support group. Dues $25. Write: SOFT, c/o Barbara Van Herreweghe, 2982 S. Union St., Rochester, NY 14624. Call Barbara Van Herreweghe 585-594-4621 or 1-800-716-7638 (for families); Fax: 585-594-1957. *Website:* http://www.trisomy.org *E-mail:* barbsoft@rochester.rr.com

TUBE FEEDING

Oley Foundation, Inc. *National. 51 affiliated groups. Founded 1983.* Provides information and psychosocial support for home nutrition support (intravenous or tube-feeding) patients, their families, caregivers and professionals. Programs include bi-monthly newsletter, national network of volunteers providing patient support, annual summer conference, regional meetings, patient-to-patient networking and information clearinghouse. Write: Oley Foundation, c/o Albany Medical Center, 214 HUN Memorial, MC-28, Albany, NY 12208. Call 1-800-776-6539 (day) or 518-262-5079; Fax: 518-262-5528. *Website:* http://www.oley.org *E-mail:* bishopj@mail.amc.edu

TUBEROUS SCLEROSIS

Tuberous Sclerosis Alliance *National. Founded 1974.* Dedicated to finding a cure for tuberous sclerosis while improving the lives of those affected. Provides research, support and education among individuals, families and the helping professionals. Newsletter, peer networking programs, conferences and information. Write: Tuberous Sclerosis Alliance, 801 Roeder Rd., Suite 750, Silver Spring, MD 20910-4467. Call 1-800-225-6872 or 301-562-9890; Fax: 301-562-9870. *Website:* http://www.tsalliance.org

TURNER SYNDROME

HUDSON

Turner Syndrome Society of the U.S. – NJ Chapter Support for women and girls affected by Turner syndrome and their families. Rap sessions, guest speakers, advocacy, literature, newsletter, phone help, buddy system. Meets Sat., 11am-3:30pm (Jan., Apr., July, Oct.), Secaucus Public Library, 1379 Paterson Plank Rd., Secaucus. Pre-registration required. Before attending call 732-217-3021. *Website:* http://www.turnersydromenj.com *E-mail:* tssusnj@turnersyndromenj.com

NATIONAL

Turner Syndrome Society (Canada) *National. 5 chapters. Founded 1981.* Provides support and education to Turner syndrome patients and their families. Tapes, publications, referral to U.S. and Canada groups. Newsletter. Pen pal program, chapter development guidelines and annual conference. Write: Turner Syndrome Society, 323 Chapel St., Ottawa, ON, Canada, K1N 7Z2. Call 1-800-465-6744 or 613-321-2267; Fax: 613-321-2268. *Website:* http://www.turnersyndrome.ca *E-mail:* tssincan@web.net

Turner Syndrome Society of the U.S. *National. 20 chapters. Founded 1987.* Self-help for women, girls and their families affected by Turner syndrome. Increases public awareness about the disorder. Quarterly newsletter, chapter development assistance, advocacy, education and annual conference. Write: Turner Syndrome Society U.S., 10960 Millridge North Dr., Suite 214A,

Houston, TX 77070. Call 1-800-365-9944 or 832-912-6006; Fax: 832-912-6446. *Website:* http://www.turnersyndrome.org *E-mail:* tssus@turnersyndrome.org

Turner Syndrome Support Network *National network. Founded 1989.* Network and exchange of information for parents of children with Turner's syndrome. Information and referrals, phone support, pen pals, conferences, literature, annual convention and newsletter. Membership: US $35yr.; Canada $50/yr.; overseas $60/yr. Write: Turner Syndrome Support Network, c/o MAGIC Foundation, 6645 W. North Ave., Oak Park, IL 60302. Call 1-800-362-4423 or 708-383-0808; Fax: 708-383-0899. *Website:* http://www.magicfoundation.org *E-mail:* mary@magicfoundation.org

TWIN TO TWIN TRANSFUSION SYNDROME

Twin to Twin Transfusion Syndrome Foundation *(MULTILINGUAL) International. 12 national coordinators. Founded 1989.* Dedicated to providing immediate and lifesaving educational, emotional and financial support for families, medical professionals and caregivers before, during and after pregnancy with twin to twin transfusion syndrome. Dedicated to saving the babies, improving their future health and care, furthering medical research, providing neonatal intensive care, special needs and bereavement support. Pen pals, newsletter, literature, phone support, visitation, conferences. Guidelines for professionals on multiple birth loss during pregnancy. Help in starting new chapters. International registry. Website in many languages. Write: TTTS, 411 Longbeach Parkway, Bay Village, OH 44140. Call 1-800-815-9211 or 440-899-8887. *Website:* http://www.tttsfoundation.org *E-mail:* info@tttsfoundation.org

UNDIAGNOSED ILLNESS

NATIONAL

Hearts and Hands *Model. 1 group in NC. Founded 1993.* Emotional, spiritual and educational support for persons with either rare or undiagnosed illnesses and their families. Also has a registry for loin pain hematuria syndrome. Write: Hearts and Hands, c/o Winoka Plummer, 1648 Oliver's Crossing Circle, Winston-Salem, NC 27127. Call 336-785-7612. *Website:* http://www.geocities.com/hotsprings/spa/2464/index.html

In Need Of Diagnosis, Inc. (INOD) *International. Founded 2006.* Provides information and mutual support to those who have an undiagnosed illness. Has an "E-List" to enable persons in need of diagnosis to communicate, exchange information and provide each other with support. Promotes changes in the healthcare system to facilitate the prompt and accurate diagnosis of medical disorders, especially rare disorders. Write: In Need Of Diagnosis, Inc., P.O. Box 536456, Orlando, FL 32853-6456. Call 1-888-894-9190 or 407-405-6363; Fax: 407-898-4234. *Website:* http://www.inod.org *E-mail:* meggenetti@aol.com

Syndromes Without A Name (SWAN) USA *National. Founded 2004.* Mutual support network and information for parents of children with an undiagnosed or unnamed condition. Newsletter and E-list discussion group for parents to share information and provide each other with support. Write: Syndromes Without A Name, 1745 Lorna Lane, Otsego, MI 49078. Call 1-888-880-7926 or 269-694-6061. *Website:* http://www.undiagnosed-usa.org/ *E-mail:* amyclugston@undiagnosed-usa.org

UREA CYCLE DISORDERS

NATIONAL

National Urea Cycle Disorders Foundation *National network. Founded 1989.* Links families, friends and professionals who are dedicated to the identification, treatment and cure of urea cycle disorders, genetic disorders causing an enzyme deficiency in the urea cycle. Networks families together for support, educates professionals, public and supports research. Phone support, literature and newsletter. Dues $35. Write: National Urea Cycle Disorders Foundation, 75 South Grand Ave., Pasadena, CA 91105. Call 1-800-386-8233; Fax: 626-578-0823. *Website:* http://www.nucdf.org *E-mail:* info@nucdf.org

ONLINE

ASA Kids *Online.* Opportunity for parents of children with argininosuccinic aciduria to come together for support and information. Discussion board, stories on affected children and links. *Website:* http://disc.yourwebapps.com/indices/106610.html

TRUE Kids (Transplanted to Resolve Ure-cycle Enzyme-deficiency) *Online.* Mutual support and information for families of transplanted children with urea cycle disorder. *Website:* http://disc.yourwebapps.com/indices/153415.html

Urea Cycle Disorder Discussion Board *Online.* Opportunity for parents caring for a child with a urea cycle disorder to discuss concerns and ideas. Goal is to increase awareness of urea cycle disorders in order to improve diagnosis. *Website:* http://disc.yourwebapps.com/indices/157587.html

VATER / VACTERLS

NATIONAL

TEF/VATER Support Network *International. 6 groups. Founded 1990.* Offers support and encouragement for parents of children with tracheoesophageal fistula, esophageal atresia and VATER. Aims to bring current information to parents and the medical community. Newsletter, information and referrals and phone support. Write: TEF/VATER Support Network, c/o Greg and Terri Burke, 15301 Grey Fox Rd., Upper Marlboro, MD 20772. Call 301-952-6837; Fax: 301-952-9152. *E-mail:* tefvater@ix.netcom.com

VELO-CARDIO-FACIAL SYNDROME / SHPRINTZEN SYNDROME / 22Q11 DELETION SYNDROME

Velo-Cardio-Facial Syndrome Educational Foundation, Inc. *National network. Founded 1996.* Support and resource network for families coping with velo-cardio-facial syndrome (aka Shprintzen syndrome, 22q11 Deletion syndrome). Provides family programs, parent-to-parent networking, educational materials, newsletter and annual conference. Write: Velo-Cardio-Facial Syndrome Educational Foundation, Inc., P.O. Box 874, Milltown, NJ 08850. Call 1-866-823-7335 or 732-238-8803. *Website:* http://www.vcfsef.org *E-mail:* info@vcfsef.org

VENTILATOR USERS

International Ventilator Users Network *International network. Founded 1987.* Information sharing between ventilator users and health care professionals experienced in home mechanical ventilation. Annual directory ($12). Quarterly newsletter (free with membership dues of $30). Write: International Ventilator Users Network, 4207 Lindell Blvd., Suite 110, St. Louis, MO 63108-2030. Call 314-534-0475; Fax: 314-534-5070. *Website:* http://www.post-polio.org/ivun *E-mail:* ventinfo@post-polio.org

*We can also refer callers to over 100 individuals who are seeking others to help start new support groups throughout NJ. For more information call **1-800-367-6274.***

VESTIBULAR DISORDERS / INNER EAR PROBLEMS
(see also deaf, hard-of-hearing)

Vestibular Disorders Association *International. 125 independent groups. Founded 1983.* Information, referrals and support for people affected by disorders caused by inner ear problems. Public education, group development assistance, support group resource kit, quarterly newsletter, library of resources and support network. Distributes several videotapes and publishes 70 documents, including full-length books on Meniere's disease and benign paroxysmal positional vertigo (BPPV). Write: Vestibular Disorders Association, P.O. Box 13305, Portland, OR 97213. Call 1-800-837-8428 or 503-229-7705; Fax: 503-229-8064. *Website:* http://www.vestibular.org *E-mail:* info@vestibular.org

VITILIGO

NATIONAL

American Vitiligo Research Foundation *National. 36+ groups and 4 international groups. Founded 1995.* Raise awareness, educate and support not only the patients but family members also. Networking, literature, newsletter, information and referrals, yearly seminars and conferences. Billboards and public services announcements. Write: American Vitiligo Research Foundation, P.O. Box 7540, Clearwater, Fla. 33758. Call 727-461-3899; Fax: 727-461-4796. *Website:* http://www.avrf.org *E-mail:* vitiligo@avrf.org

ONLINE

Vitiligo Support International, Inc. *Online. Founded 2000.* Provides social support, information and resources to persons affected by vitiligo. Active message boards, chats and international physician referral. Supports research by providing volunteer participants from its membership. Includes "Just for Kids" page. Write: Vitiligo Support International, Inc., P.O. Box 4008, Valley Village, CA 91617. Call 818-752-9002. *Website:* http://www.vitiligosupport.org *E-mail:* info@vitiligosupport.org

VOMITING, CYCLIC

Cyclic Vomiting Syndrome Association *International. 30+ affiliated groups. Founded 1993.* Mutual support and information for families and professionals dealing with cyclic vomiting syndrome, abdominal migraine and related disorders. Networking, phone support, educational materials, research support and newsletter. Write: Cyclic Vomiting Syndrome Association, 2819 West

Highland Blvd., Milwaukee, WI 53208. Call 414-342-7880; Fax: 414-342-8980. *Website:* http://www.cvsaonline.org *E-mail:* cvsa@cvsaonline.org

VON HIPPEL LINDAU

VHL Family Alliance (Von Hippel-Lindau Syndrome) *(MULTILINGUAL) International network. 28 US chapters; 11 foreign affiliates. Founded 1993.* Opportunity for families affected by VHL to share their knowledge and experiences with each other and the medical community. Goal is to improve diagnosis, treatment and quality of life for VHL families. Newsletter, phone support, education, tissue bank and handbook. Literature available in Spanish, German, French, Japanese, Dutch and other languages. Funds research. Assistance in starting local chapters. Write: VHL Family Alliance, 2001 Beacon St., Suite 208, Boston, MA 02135-7787. Call 1-800-767-4845 or 617-277-5667; Fax: 858-712-8712. *Website:* http://www.vhl.org *E-mail:* info@vhl.org

VULVAR DISORDERS

National Vulvodynia Association, Inc. *National. 100 affiliated groups. Founded 1994.* Provides information and support to women with vulvodynia. Educates health care professionals and the public about this condition. Newsletter, literature, phone support, advocacy, information and referrals. Write: National Vvlvodynia Association, P.O. Box 4491, Silver Spring, MD 20914-4491. Call 301-299-0775 or 301-949-5114; Fax: 301-299-3999. *Website:* http://www.nva.org *E-mail:* chris@nva.org

WAGR SYNDROME / ANIRIDIA

International WAGR Syndrome Association *International network. 3 affiliated groups. Founded 2000.* Provides information and support to persons with WAGR Syndrome or aniridia, their families, physicians and teachers. Literature, free bi-annual newsletter, networking, phone support, information and referral. Encourages research. E-mail group. Write: International WAGR Syndrome Association, P.O. Box 392, Allen Park, MI 48101. Call 210-481-9288. *Website:* http://www.wagr.org *E-mail:* reachingout@wagr.org

WALDENSTROM'S MACROGLOBULINEMIA

International Waldenstrom's Macroglobulinemia Foundation *International. 40 affiliated groups. Founded 1994.* Provides support and information to persons with Waldenstrom macroglobulinemia, their families and caregivers. Information and referrals, phone support, conferences, newsletter and literature (some literature available in French and Spanish). Regular support group meetings. Provides assistance in starting new groups. Write: International Waldenstrom's Macroglobulinemia Foundation, 3932D Swift Rd., Sarasota, FL 34231. Call 941-927-4963; Fax: 941-927-4467. *Website:* http://www.iwmf.com *E-mail:* info@iwmf.com

WEGENER'S GRANULOMATOSIS / VASCULITIS

Vasculitis Foundation *National. 35 affiliated groups. Founded 1986.* Emotional support and information for patients with life-threatening uncommon Wegener's granulomatosis and related vasculitis illnesses. Provides information to patients and physicians about this disorder. Educates families, friends and general public about the devastating effects of Vasculitis, it's symptoms and treatment. Dues $25/US; $30/Int'l. (includes bimonthly newsletter). Write: Vasculitis Foundation, P.O. Box 28660, Kansas City, MO 64188-8660. Call 1-800-277-9474 (Mon.-Fri., 8:30am-5pm CST); Fax: 816-436-8211. *Website:* http://www.vasculitisfoundation.org *E-mail:* vf@vasculitisfoundation.org

WILLIAMS SYNDROME

Williams Syndrome Association *National network. 16 chapters. Founded 1982.* Purpose is to encourage research related to Williams syndrome, find and support families with Williams syndrome, and share information among parents and professionals re: educational, medical and behavioral experiences. Newsletter. Write: Williams Syndrome Association, P.O. Box 297, Clawson, MI 48017-0297. Call 1-800-806-1871 or 248-244-2229. *Website:* http://www.williams-syndrome.org *E-mail:* info@williams-syndrome.org

WILSON'S DISEASE

Wilson's Disease Association *International network. Founded 1979.* Provides information and referrals about Wilson's disease, a genetic disorder that causes excessive amounts of copper accumulation in the body, affecting the liver and brain. Provides mutual support and aid for those affected by the disease and their families. Promotes research into treatment and cure. Quarterly newsletter. Provides phone support network. Offers e-mail group. Write: Wilson's Disease Association, 1802 Brookside Dr., Wooster, OH 44691. Call 1-888-264-1450 or 330-264-1450. *Website:* http://www.wilsonsdisease.org *E-mail:* kimberly.symonds@wilsonsdisease.org

Can't find an appropriate group in your area? The Clearinghouse helps people start groups. Give us a call at 1-800-367-6274.

WORSTER-DROUGHT SYNDROME

(see also cerebral palsy)

Worster-Drought Syndrome Support Group *Model.* Provides support and information for families of children with worster-drought, a form of cerebral palsy. Offers phone support in the United Kingdom. Pen pals, networking of families, literature and newsletter. Write: Worster-Drought Syndrome, c/o Contact a Family, 209-211 City Road, London EC1V 1JN, UK. Call 020 7383 3555; Fax: 020 7383 0259. *Website:* http://www.wdssg.org.uk/ *E-mail:* national.contact@wdssg.org.uk

XERODERMA PIGMENTOSUM

Xeroderma Pigmentosum Society *International network. Founded 1995.* Provides sharing of support, information and coping skills for families affected by xeroderma pigmentosum. Quarterly informational newsletter. Promotes research into finding a cure. Information and referrals, phone support, conferences, literature, advocacy in community, education and protection. Free window tinting on homes of patients. Camp Sundown for patients of all ages and their families. Write: XP Society, 437 Snydertown Rd., Craryville, NY 12521. Call 518-851-2612 (voice/fax). *Website:* http://www.xps.org *E-mail:* carn@xps.org

X-LINKED HYOPHOSPHATEMIA / FAMILIAL HYPOPHOSPHATEMIC RICKETS / VITAMIN D RESISTANT RICKETS

ONLINE

XLH Network *Online. Founded 1996.* Volunteer organization offering support and information for individuals and families affected by X-linked hypophosphatemia (aka X-linked hypophosphatemic rickets, familial hypophosphatemic rickets or vitamin D resistant rickets). Also open to those affected by similar disorders including autosomal dominant hypophosphatemic rickets and tumor-induced osteomalacia. Open to interested professionals dedicated to understanding in terms of support, research and developing new treatments. Exchanges and disseminates information. Offers an online brochure and members listserv. Write: The XLH Network, Inc., c/o Joan Reed, 4562 Stoneledge Lane, Manlius, NY 13104. *Website:* http://www.xlhnetwork.org *E-mail:* joan.reed@xlhnetwork.org

MENTAL HEALTH RESOURCES

Offers assistance and advocacy for mental health consumers and families when they are experiencing difficulties with the mental health system. Also provides referrals to mental health providers by county.

MENTAL HEALTH ADMINISTRATORS

ATLANTIC	Sally Williams	609-645-7700 ext. 4307
BERGEN	Susan Boggia	201-634-2753
BURLINGTON	Gary Miller	609-265-5610
CAMDEN	Chuck Steinmetz	856-663-3998
CAPE MAY	Patricia Devaney	609-465-1055
CUMBERLAND	Ethan Aronoff	856-453-7804
ESSEX	Joseph Scarpelli	973-571-2821
GLOUCESTER	Kathleen Spinosi	856-218-4101
HUDSON	Jim Gallagher	201-271-4344
HUNTERDON	Cathy Zahn	908-788-1253
MERCER	Michele Madiou	609-989-6574
MIDDLESEX	Lori Dillon	732-745-4518
MONMOUTH	Charles D. Brown	732-431-7200
MORRIS	Laurie Becker	973-285-6852
OCEAN	Jill Perez	732-506-5374
PASSAIC	Francine Vince	973-881-2834
SALEM	Arnold G. Bradway	856-339-8618
SOMERSET	Pam Mastro	908-704-6302

SUSSEX	Cindy Armstrong 973-948-6000 ext. 225
UNION	Katie Regan 908-527-4846
WARREN	Shannon Brennan 908-475-6081

COMMUNITY HEALTH LAW PROJECT

Promotes protecting the rights of persons with any disability. Community Health Law Project represents low income individuals who are disabled physically, have a mental illness and/or are elderly and unable to afford private attorneys. Offers counseling, referrals, advocacy, training, education, etc. *Website*: http://www.chlp.org

CAMDEN	856-858-9500
ESSEX	973-680-5599; TTY/TTD 973-680-1116
MERCER	609-392-5553
MONMOUTH	732-502-0059
UNION	908-355-8282

FAMILY PROGRAMS

STATEWIDE

Intensive Family Support Services Offers supportive activities to assist families who have a relative diagnosed with mental illness. Families are offered a variety of services based on the individual's need. Services are available to any family and are free of charge. Psychoeducation, single family consultations, family support, respite, advocacy and referrals. Call 1-866-626-4437.

"As a kid I learned that my brother and I could walk forever on a railroad track and never fall off – if we just reached across the track and held each other's hand." -- Steve Potter

MENTAL HEALTH ASSOCIATIONS

STATEWIDE

Mental Health Association in New Jersey Helps mental health consumers and their families explore services available in their community. Also advocates for needed services. Write: MHA in NJ, 88 Pompton Ave., Verona, NJ 07044. Call 973-571-4100; Fax: 973-857-1777. *Website*: http://www.mhanj.org *E-mail*: info@mhanj.org

ATLANTIC	609-272-1700
CAMDEN	856-522-0639
ESSEX	973-509-9777
HUDSON	201-653-4700
MONMOUTH	732-542-6422
MORRIS	973-334-3496
OCEAN	732-905-1132
PASSAIC	973-478-4444

MENTAL HEALTH PACT TEAMS

ATLANTIC	609-404-1974
BERGEN	201-398-9110
BURLINGTON	609-261-6627
CAMDEN	856-428-7632
CAPE MAY	609-463-8990
CUMBERLAND	856-455-8316
ESSEX	973-466-1300
GLOUCESTER	856-251-1414
HUDSON	201-653-3980
HUNTERDON	908-835-8660

MERCER	609-394-5285
MIDDLESEX	732-257-6100
MONMOUTH	732-842-2000 ext. 4301 or 4302
MORRIS	1-888-626-2111 or 973-625-7084
OCEAN	732-349-0515
PASSAIC	973-470-3516
SALEM	856-691-8579
SOMERSET	908-704-8252
SUSSEX	1-888-626-2111 or 973-625-7084
UNION	908-352-0242
WARREN	908-835-8660

*"We must never forget that we may also find meaning in life even
confronted with a hopeless situation, when facing a fate
that cannot be changed. For what then matters is to bear witness
to the uniquely human potential at its best, which is to transform
a personal tragedy into a triumph, to turn one's predicament
into a human achievement..." –Victor Frankl*

LOCAL COMMUNITY HELPLINES

These helplines provide information and referrals to local services and agencies. Many also provide crisis intervention and listening services. Some publish directories of local community services.

ATLANTIC

Intergenerational Services Dial 211 (may not be available from public or cell phones, or from some larger workplace phone systems) or 1-888-426-9243 (24 hr.) Provides information and referral services to local services and agencies.

BERGEN

Community Resource Council 201-343-4900 (Mon.-Fri., 9am-5pm) Information and referral services, crisis intervention. Youth helpline 1-866-FOR-R-YOUTH.

Contact We Care 908-232-2880 (24 hr.) Crisis and suicidal helpline, listening, information and referrals. Covers Bergen, Essex, Middlesex, Morris, Passaic, Somerset and Union counties. *Website:* http://www.contactwecare.org

First Call For Help Dial 211 (may not be available from public or some cell phones and from some larger workplace phone systems) or 1-800-435-7555 (24 hr.). Provides information and referral for local services and agencies. *Website:* http://www.nj211.org *E-mail:* info@nj211.org

BURLINGTON

Contact of Burlington County Call 211 (may not be available from some public, cell phones or from some larger workplace phone systems) 856-234-8888 (crisis intervention, rape care and sexual assault services and reassurance "care calls"); Teen Line: 856-234-0634. All services are free. *Website:* http://www.contactburlco.org *E-mail:* contact333@contactburlco.org

CAMDEN

Contact Community Helplines *(South Jersey only)* 1-877-266-8222 (24 hr. crisis counseling); 856-795-4980 (reassurance calls to elderly and hearing impaired shut-ins (Mon.-Fri., 9am-4:30pm). Provides information, referrals and listening service. Sponsored by United Way. *Website:* http://www.contacthelplines.org *E-mail:* info@contacthelplines.org

First Call For Help *(South Jersey only)* Dial 211 (may not be available from public or cell phones, or from some larger workplace phone systems) 1-800-331-7272 or 856-663-2255 (8am-4:30pm). Will take calls after 4:30pm for emergencies. Information and referrals. Sponsored by UOSS Community Information Systems. *Website:* http://www.infonet.org

CAPE MAY

First Call For Help 609-729-2255 (Mon.-Fri., 8:30am-4:30pm) Information and referrals to local services and agencies. Sponsored by United Way.

CUMBERLAND

Contact Community Helplines *(South Jersey only)* 1-877-266-8222 (24 hr. crisis counseling) Listening, information and referrals. Serves Gloucester, Salem and Cumberland Counties. Sponsored by Contact USA. *Website:* http://www.contacthelplines.org *E-mail:* info@contacthelplines.org

ESSEX

Contact We Care 908-232-2880 (24 hr.) Crisis and suicidal helpline, listening service, information and referrals. Covers Bergen, Essex, Middlesex, Morris, Passaic, Somerset and Union counties. *Website:* http://www.contactwecare.org

First Call for Help Dial 211 (may not be available from public or cell phones and from some larger workplace phone systems) or 1-800-435-7555 (24 hr.) Information and referrals to local services and agencies. *Website:* http://www.nj211.org *E-mail:* info@nj211.org

GLOUCESTER

CONTACT Community Helplines *(South Jersey only)* 1-877-266-8222 (24 hr. crisis counseling); 856-795-4980 (Mon.-Fri., 9am-4:30pm reassurance calls). Provides information, referrals and listening services. Sponsored by United Way. *Website:* http://www.contacthelplines.org *E-mail:* info@contacthelplines.org

First Call For Help-Gloucester County Dial 211 (may not be available from public or cell phones, or from some larger workplace phones) or 1-800-648-0132 (24 hr.). Information, referrals, active listening, crisis counseling and referrals for homeless. Serves Gloucester County. Funded by United Way.

HUDSON

First Call for Help of Essex and West Hudson *(BILINGUAL)* Dial 211 (may not be available from public or cell phones and from some larger workplace phone systems) or 1-800-435-7555 (24 hr.). Information and referrals to local services and agencies. *Website:* http://www.nj211.org *E-mail:* info@nj211.org

HUNTERDON

Hunterdon Helpline 1-800-272-4630, 908-735-4357 or 908-782-4357 (24 hr.); TDD also available. Information and referrals, friendly visits and reassurance calls offered to the elderly, suicide prevention hotline, assistance for the homeless and hungry. Links Transport Service. Professional and volunteer run. Sponsored by United Way. *Website:* http//helplinehc.org

MERCER

Contact of Mercer County 609-896-2120 or 609-585-2244 (24 hr.) Crisis and suicidal helpline, listening, information and referrals. Kids Line: 609-896-4434. *Website:* http://www.contactofmercer.org *E-mail:* contactofmercercounty@verizon.net

Consider passing this Directory on to a student or staff member - browsing through the Directory pages can often provide helpful education as to the wide variety of groups available.

MIDDLESEX

Contact We Care 908-232-2880 (24 hr.) Crisis and suicidal helpline, listening, information and referrals. Covers Bergen, Essex, Middlesex, Morris, Passaic, Somerset and Union counties. *Website:* http://www.contactwecare.org

MONMOUTH

211 of Northern New Jersey Dial 211 (may not be available from public or cell phones, or from some larger workplace phone systems) or 1-800-435-7555 (24 hr.). Provides information and referrals to local services and agencies.

MORRIS

Contact We Care 908-232-2880 (24 hr.) Crisis and suicidal helpline, listening service, information and referrals. Covers Bergen, Essex, Middlesex, Morris, Passaic, Somerset and Union counties. *Website:* http://www.contactwecare.org

First Call For Help Dial 211 (may not be available from public or some cell phones and from some larger workplace phone systems) or 1-800-435-7555 (24 hr.). Provides information and referral for local services and agencies. *Website:* http://www.nj211.org *E-mail:* info@nj211.org

Peer-to-Peer Support Line 1-877-760-4987 (5-10pm) Non-crisis peer counseling for mental health consumers. Provides support, information and resources.

OCEAN

Contact - First Call For Help 732-240-6105 (24 hr.) Provides information and referral for local services and agencies. *Website:* http://www.contactocean.org *E-mail:* contactofoceanco@aol.com

Contact of Ocean County 732-240-6100 (24 hr.) Provides crisis intervention and listening services. Information and referrals on local services and agencies. *Website:* http://www.contactocean.org *E-mail:* contactofoceanco@aol.com

PASSAIC

Contact We Care 908-232-2880 (24 hr.) Crisis and suicidal helpline, listening, information and referrals. Covers Bergen, Essex, Middlesex, Morris, Passaic, Somerset and Union counties. *Website:* http://www.contactwecare.org

First Call For Help Dial 211 (may not be available from public or cell phones and from some larger workplace phone systems) or 1-800-435-7555 (24 hr.). Provides information and referral for local services and agencies. *Website:* http://www.nj211.org *E-mail:* info@nj211.org

SALEM

Contact Community Helplines *(South Jersey only)* 1-877-266-8222 (24 hr. crisis counseling) Provides information, referrals and listening services. *Website:* http://www.contacthelplines.org *E-mail:* info@contacthelplines.org

SOMERSET

211 of Northern New Jersey Dial 211 (may not be available from public or cell phones, from some larger workplace phone systems) or call 1-800-435-1555 (24 hr.). Provides information and referrals to local and regional services and agencies. *Website:* http://www.somersetonline.org

Contact We Care 908-232-2880 (24 hr.) TDD: 908-232-3333 (7am-11pm) Crisis and suicidal helpline, listening, information and referrals. Covers Bergen, Essex, Middlesex, Morris, Passaic, Somerset and Union counties. *Website:* http://www.contactwecare.org

SUSSEX

Sussex County Helpline Dial 211 (may not be available from public or cell phones, or from some larger workplace phone systems) or 1-877-661-4357 (24 hr.). Confidential listening, information and referrals. Also offers assistance in homeless emergencies and protective services. Funded by United Way.

"It is expressly at those times when we feel needy that we will benefit the most from giving."
-- Ruth Ross

UNION

Contact We Care 908-232-2880 (24 hr.) Crisis and suicidal helpline, listening, information and referrals. Covers Bergen, Essex, Middlesex, Morris, Passaic, Somerset and Union counties. *Website:* http://www.contactwecare.org

First Call For Help Dial 211 (may not be available from public or cell phone, also from some larger work place numbers) or 1-800-435-7555 (24 hr.). Provides information and referral to local services and agencies. *Website:* http://www.nj211.org *E-mail:* info@nj211.org

WARREN

NORWESCAP First Call for Help 1-877-661-4357 (Mon.-Fri.; 8am-4:30pm) Information and referrals. Central Holiday Intake (meals on holidays). Information on housing for persons with AIDS. Funded in part by United Way. *Website:* http://www.norwescap.org

Warren County Office for the Disabled 1-877-589-2253 Provides information and referral services to people with all types of disabilities. The office also offers community outreach and disability awareness education programs.

"It's not enough to have lived.

We should be determined to live for something.

May I suggest that it be creating joy for others,
sharing what we have for the betterment of
personkind, bringing hope to the lost and love to the lonely."

-Leo Buscaglia

PSYCHIATRIC EMERGENCY SERVICES

The psychiatric emergency services listed below provide crisis/suicide intervention with trained professionals. Some counties provide mobile crisis services. All are available 24 hours a day. Hotlines should be contacted only in case of real mental health emergencies.

ATLANTIC
Atlantic City Medical Center 609-344-1118

BERGEN
Psychiatric Emergency Screening Program 201-262-4357

BURLINGTON
Screening Crisis Intervention Program 609-835-6180

CAMDEN
Steininger Center 856-428-4357

CAPE MAY
Burdette Tomlin Memorial Hospital 609-465-5999

CUMBERLAND
Cumberland County Guidance Center 856-455-5555

ESSEX
East Orange General Hospital 973-672-9685
Newark Beth Israel Hospital 973-926-7416
University of Medicine and Dentistry of NJ 973-623-2323

GLOUCESTER
Community Mental Health Center of Gloucester County ... 856-845-9100

HUDSON
Bayonne Hospital 201-858-5286
Jersey City Medical Center 201-915-2210

HUNTERDON
Hunterdon Medical Center 908-788-6400

MERCER
Helene Fuld Medical Center   609-394-6086

MIDDLESEX
University of Medicine and Dentistry of NJ   732-235-5700

MONMOUTH
CentraState Medical Center   732-780-6023
Monmouth Medical Center   732-923-6999
Riverview Medical Center   732-219-5325

MORRIS
Chilton Memorial Hospital   973-831-5078
Morristown Memorial Hospital   973-540-0100
Saint Clare's Health Services   973-625-0280

OCEAN
Kimball Medical Center   732-886-4474

PASSAIC
Chilton Memorial Hospital   973-831-5078
St. Mary's Hospital   973-470-3025

SALEM
Salem County Healthcare Commons   856-299-3001

SOMERSET
Somerset County Department of Human Services   908-526-4100

SUSSEX
Newton Memorial Hospital   973-383-0973

UNION
Trinitas Hospital   908-994-7131 or 908-668-2599

WARREN
Family Guidance Center of Warren County   908-454-5141

"I'm glad I understand that while language is a gift, listening is a responsibility."
-- Nikki Giovanni

T O L L – F R E E   H E L P L I N E S

The following toll-free numbers may be a helpful, cost-free resource for persons seeking additional information on a particular subject. These non-profit agencies provide information and referrals, literature and other services. If not indicated as a *(New Jersey)* toll-free number, the helpline is a national resource.

ADOPTION / FOSTER FAMILIES

Foster and Adoptive Family Services *(New Jersey)* 1-800-222-0047 (Mon.-Fri., 9am-6pm) Provides training, offers support services, answers questions on becoming a foster or adoptive parent, scholarships to foster and adoptive youth, holiday toy drive and fostering wishes for children. Sponsored by Division of Youth and Family Services. *Website:* http://www.fafsonline.org. *E-mail*: mawrachow@fafsonline.org.

National Adoption Center 1-800-862-3678 (Mon.-Fri., 9am-5pm) Information on adoption agencies and support groups. Network for matching parents and children with special needs. Fax: 215-735-9410 *Website:* http://www.adopt.org/ *E-mail*: NAC@adopt.org

AGING / SENIOR CITIZENS

Alliance for Aging Research 1-800-639-2421 Citizen advocacy organization that strives to improve the health and independence of older Americans through public and private research. Promotes healthy aging among people of all ages. Provides statistics on the health and well-being of older persons. *Website:* http://www.agingresearch.org

Eldercare Locator 1-800-677-1116 (Mon.-Fri., 9am-8pm EST) Provides information for families and friends of the elderly (ages 60+). Referrals to area agencies on aging for information on insurance, medicaid, taxes and respite care. Information for disabled also provided on these subjects. *Website:* http://www.eldercare.gov *E-mail*: eldercarelocator@infospherix.com

Freedom Eldercare *(New Jersey)* 1-866-737-3336 (24 hr.) Free information and referral service to assist individuals in navigating the complex healthcare system. Specialists represent the fields of nursing, social work and geriatric care management. *Website:* http://www.freedomeldercare.com

National Council on Aging 1-800-424-9046 (Mon.-Fri., 9am-5pm EST) Information to the aged, families and professionals. *Website:* http://www.ncoa.org

National Institute on Aging *(BILINGUAL)* 1-800-222-2225 (voice/TTY); TDD: 1-800-222-4225 (Mon.-Fri., 8:30am-5pm EST) Provides publications on topics of interest to older adults, doctors, nurses, social activities directors, health educators and the public. Sponsored by federal government. *Website:* http://www.nia.nih.gov *E-mail:* niaic@nia.nih.gov

NJ EASE *(New Jersey)* 1-877-222-3737 (Mon.-Fri., 8:30am-5pm) Provides information to seniors, disabled, veterans and their caregivers on available local benefits and programs. Information on housing options, nursing homes, elder abuse issues, assisted living facilities, transportation, nutrition, caregivers, insurance, healthcare, long-term care, social activities, volunteer opportunities and care management. Fax: 973-285-6883.

Senior Citizen Information and Referral *(New Jersey)* 1-800-792-8820 (Mon.-Fri., 8:30am-5pm) Provides information and referrals to services for senior citizens (ages 60+) and their caregivers. Elder abuse issues. Makes referrals to local county offices on aging. Sponsored by NJ Department of Health and Senior Services. *Website:* http://www.state.nj.us/health/senior

AIDS

AIDS Information *(BILINGUAL)* 1-800-448-0440; TTY: 1-888-480-3739 (Mon.-Fri., noon-5pm EST) Resource information on clinical trials for AIDS and HIV+ patients. Information about current treatments and prevention techniques. Provides live online assistance. *Website:* http://aidsinfo.nih.gov *E-mail:* contactus@aidsinfo.nih.gov

American Social Health Association *(BILINGUAL)* 1-800-227-8922 or 919-361-8488 (Mon.-Fri., 9am-6pm EST) Provides information, materials and referrals concerning all types of sexually transmitted infections. Specialists will answer questions via phone or e-mail on transmission, risk reduction, prevention, testing and treatment. *Website:* http://www.ashastd.org or http://www.iwannaknow.org (for teens)

We can also refer callers to over 100 individuals who are seeking others to help start new support groups throughout NJ. Give us a call for more information. **1-800-367-6274**

CDC National Prevention Information Network *(BILINGUAL)* 1-800-458-5231 (Mon.-Fri., 9am-8pm EST); TTY: 1-800-243-7012 or 919-361-4892 Provides information on resources, educational materials, sexually transmitted diseases (including AIDS/HIV), tuberculosis and communities at risk. Many different services and publications offered. *Website:* http://www.cdcnpin.org *E-mail:* info@cdcnpin.org

CDC National STD/AIDS Hotline *(BILINGUAL)* 1-800-232-4636 (24 hr.); TTY: 1-888-232-6342 (24 hr.) Education and research about AIDS, HIV and sexually transmitted diseases. *Website:* http://www.cdc.gov *E-mail:* cdcinfo@cdc.gov

Gay Men's Health Crisis *(BILINGUAL)* 1-800-243-7692 (Mon.-Fri., 10am-9pm; Sat. noon-3pm EST) Provides information and referrals for persons affected by AIDS (including gay men, lesbians, bisexuals, transgenders, straights and immigrants). Write: Gay Men's Health Crisis, 119 West 24th St., New York, NY 10011. *Website:* http://www.gmhc.org *E-mail:* lynns@gmhc.org

New Jersey AIDS/STD Hotline *(New Jersey)* 1-800-624-2377; TTY: 973-926-8008 (24 hr.) Information and referral on AIDS/STD. Counseling and treatment information. Referrals to testing locations. Sponsored by NJ Department of Health.

Project Inform *(BILINGUAL)* 1-800-822-7422 (Mon.-Fri., 10am-4pm PST) Information about experimental drugs, treatment of AIDS, volunteer training programs, quarterly newsletter and journal. *Website:* http://www.projectinform.org *E-mail:* info@projectinform.org

ALCOHOL

Addictions Hotline of NJ *(New Jersey)* 1-800-238-2333 (voice/TDD; 24 hr.) Crisis counseling, information and referrals for all kinds of drug and alcohol related issues (both prescription and illegal drugs). Sponsored by NJ Division of Narcotics and Drug Abuse, Office on Prevention.

Community Recovery *(New Jersey)* 1-800-292-8262 Offers services for veterans who are experiencing problems with drugs or alcohol. The program offers a wide variety of services throughout the state.

"I believe we are all here to be bright torches that light one another's way."
– Bernie S. Siegel

National Association for Children of Alcoholics 1-888-554-2627 (8:30am-5pm EST) Advocates for children and families affected by alcoholism and other drug dependencies. Helps children hurt by parental alcohol and drug abuse. Newsletter, advocacy, policy making, literature, videos and educational materials. *Website:* http://www.nacoa.org *E-mail:* nacoa@nacoa.org

National Clearinghouse for Alcohol and Drug Information *(BILINGUAL)* 1-800-729-6686 or 301-468-2600; Spanish: 1-877-767-8432; TTY: 1-800-487-4889 Information on alcohol, tobacco, drug abuse and prevention. Referrals to treatment centers, research, groups, drugs in the work place, community programs, AIDS and addiction. *Website:* http://www.ncadi-samhsa.gov *E-mail:* ncadi-info@samhsa.hhs.gov

National Council on Alcoholism and Drug Dependence 1-800-622-2255 (24 hr.) Provides information on counseling and treatment services for alcohol or drug abuse. Prevention, education programs and newsletter. *Website:* http://www.ncadd.org *E-mail:* national@mcadd.org

National Organization on Fetal Alcohol Syndrome 1-800-666-6327 Provides information and referrals on fetal alcohol syndrome. Offers free packet of information. Write: National Organization on Fetal Alcohol Syndrome, 900 17th St. NE, Washington, DC 20006. *Website:* http://www.nofas.org

ALOPECIA AREATA

Locks of Love 1-888-896-1588 (recorded information) or 561-963-1677 Provides custom hairpieces to financially disadvantaged children with long-term medical hair loss. Uses donated hair. *Website:* http://www.locksoflove.org/ *E-mail:* info@locksoflove.org

ALZHEIMER'S DISEASE

Alzheimer's Disease Education and Referral Center *(BILINGUAL)* 1-800-438-4380 or 301-495-3311 (Mon.-Fri., 8:30am-5:30pm EST) Provides information and publications on Alzheimer's disease to health and service professionals, patients, their families, caregivers and public. Sponsored by National Institute on Aging. *Website:* http://www.alzheimers.org *E-mail:* adear@alzheimers.org

Alzheimer's Disease Helpline *(New Jersey)* 1-800-424-2494 Information, counseling, referrals and support for Alzheimer's and related disorders. Also offers assistance for caregivers.

American Health Assistance Foundation 1-800-437-2423 (Mon.-Fri., 9am-5pm EST) Provides educational information and funds research for Alzheimer's disease, glaucoma and macular degeneration. *Website:* http://www.ahaf.org

ATTORNEY

Legal Services of New Jersey *(BILINGUAL)* *(New Jersey)* 1-888-576-5529 or 732-572-9100 (Mon.-Fri., 8am-5:30pm) Provides free legal advice over the phone for low income persons for civil cases (housing, landlord, tenant, public assistance and entitlements, family law and domestic violence, consumer law and bankruptcy, employment law, immigration, etc). *Website:* http://www.lsnj.org

National Organization of Social Security Claimant's Reps 1-800-431-2804 (Mon.-Fri., 9am-5:30pm EST) Provides referrals to social security lawyers who assist claimants in getting social security. *Website:* http://www.nosscr.org

BLIND

American Foundation for the Blind 1-800-232-5463; TDD: 212-502-7662 (Mon.-Fri., 8:30am-4:30pm EST) Clearinghouse of information and referrals for the blind. Catalog of publications available. *Website:* http://www.afb.org *E-mail:* afbinfo@afb.net

American Health Assistance Foundation 1-800-437-2423 (Mon.-Fri., 9am-5pm EST) Provides educational information and funds research for Alzheimer's disease, glaucoma and macular degeneration. *Website:* http://www.ahaf.org

Braille Institute 1-800-272-4553 (Mon.-Fri., 8:30am-5pm PST) Provides publications, cassettes and free books for visually impaired children. Free Braille calendar. Referrals to resources. Tapes on vision loss available to companies and organizations. *Website:* http://www.brailleinstitute.org *E-mail:* info@brailleinstitute.org

DB-Link: National Consortion on Deaf-Blindness 1-800-438-9376 (voice); TTY: 1-800-854-7013 Information and referral on education, health, employment, technology, communication and recreation for children who are deaf/blind. Newsletter. *Website:* http://www.nationaldb.org *E-mail:* info@nationaldb.org

Glaucoma Research Foundation 1-800-826-6693 or 415-986-3162 (Mon.-Fri., 8:30am-5pm PST) Non-profit, phone support network for persons with glaucoma. Provides free literature and funds research. *Website:* http://www.glaucoma.org *E-mail:* info@glaucoma.org

Guide Dog Foundation 1-800-548-4337 Provides dogs to the blind free of charge. *Website:* http://www.guidedog.org *E-mail:* info@guidedog.org

Guiding Eyes for the Blind 1-800-942-0149 or 914-245-4024 (Mon.-Fri., 9am-5pm EST) Dedicated to enriching the lives of blind and visually impaired men and women by providing them with guide dogs free of charge. Write: Guiding Eyes for the Blind, 611 Granite Springs Rd., Yorktown Heights, NY 10598. *Website:* http://www.guidingeyes.org *E-mail:* info@guidingeyes.org or student@guidingeyes.org (for students interested in guide dog training).

Hadley School for the Blind 1-800-323-4238 or 847-446-8111; TTY: 847-441-8111 (Mon.-Fri., 8am-4:30pm CST) Provides free distance education to blind and visually impaired persons using Braille materials, large print or audio-cassettes. *Website:* http://www.hadley.edu *E-mail:* info@Hadley.edu

Library of Congress National Library Service for the Blind and Physically Handicapped 1-800-424-8567; TDD: 202-707-0744 (Mon-Fri, 8:00am-4:30pm EST) Refers callers to libraries that have information on books on tapes and in Braille available for qualified blind or handicapped persons who can't read standard print. Fax: 202-707-0712. *Website:* http://www.loc.gov/nls *E-mail:* nls@loc.gov

New Jersey Library for the Blind and Handicapped *(New Jersey)* 1-800-792-8322; TTY: 1-877-882-5593 (Mon.-Fri., 9am-4pm; Sat., 9am-3pm except July/Aug.) Information on provision of recorded materials, large print, Braille and radio reading service. Deaf and hard of hearing awareness program offers over 700 videos, books on hearing loss and deafness. Assistive devices such as: TTYs, baby cry signalers, bed vibrators, closed captioned decoders and assistive listening devices. Sign language interpreting services for library events. Sponsored by Bureau of State Library, Thomas Edison State College. *Website:* http://www.njlbh.org *E-mail:* njlbh@njstatelib.org

NJ Commission for the Blind and Visually Impaired *(New Jersey)* 1-877-685-8878 (Mon.-Fri., 9am-5pm voice mail) Information and referral for persons with a visual impairment regarding educational, social, occupational and vocational services. Sponsored by the NJ Commission for the Blind and Visually Impaired. *Website:* http://www.cbvi.nj.gov

Prevent Blindness America 1-800-331-2020 (Mon.-Fri. 8:30am-5pm CST) Fights vision loss through research, education and direct services. Provides referrals to local services. Offers literature on vision, eye health and safety. *Website:* http://www.preventblindness.org *E-mail:* info@preventblindness.org

Recording For The Blind and Dyslexic 1-866-732-3585 (Mon.-Fri., 8:30am-4:30pm EST); Fax: 609-987-8116 Provides information on recorded textbooks and consumer publications to eligible persons with print and learning disabilities. Information on volunteer programs for recording CDs. Membership $100/1st year; $35/subsequent years. *Website:* http://www.rfbd.org *E-mail:* custserv@rfbd.org

Research to Prevent Blindness 1-800-621-0026 or 212-752-4333 (Mon.-Fri., 9am-5pm EST) Provides publications and information on various eye diseases including macular degeneration, cataracts, glaucoma, diabetic retinopathy, corneal disease, retinitis pigmentosa, amblyopia/strabismus and uveitis. Funds research. *Website:* http://www.rpbusa.org

Retinitis Pigmentosa International 1-800-344-4877 (8am-7pm PST) Provides support and information for persons affected by retinitis pigmentosa and their families. Supports research. *Website:* http://www.rpinternational.org *E-mail:* info@rpinternational.org

BRAIN TUMOR

Pediatric Brain Tumor Foundation 1-800-253-6530 or 828-665-6891 Mission is to find the cause and cure of pediatric brain tumors through the support of research; to aid in the early detection of children's brain tumors; to improve the quality of life of children through better and less invasive treatments and to provide hope, emotional support and information to children and their families. Write: Pediatric Brain Tumor Foundation., 302 Ridgefield Court, Asheville, NC 28806-2210. *Website:* http://www.pbtfus.org or http://www.ride4kids.org *E-mail:* pbtfus@pbtfus.org

BUSINESS

SCORE (Service Corps of Retired Executives) 1-800-634-0245 (Mon.-Fri., 8:30am-5pm EST) Provides counseling for starting or maintaining businesses. Referrals to local chapters. *Website:* http://www.score.org

U.S. Small Business Administration *(BILINGUAL)* 1-800-827-5722; TTY: 704-344-6640 (Mon.-Fri., 9am-5pm EST) Provides information, training and literature on starting and financing small businesses. *Website:* http://www.sba.gov *E-mail*: answerdesk@sba.gov

CANCER

AMC Cancer Information and Counseling Line 1-800-525-3777 (Mon.-Fri., 8:30-5pm MST) Provides current medical information and counseling for cancer issues. *Website:* http://www.amc.org

American Cancer Society *(BILINGUAL) (New Jersey)* 1-800-227-2345 (24 hr.) Provides information on issues related to cancer (services, transportation, encouragement and support). *Website:* http://www.cancer.org

American Cancer Society *(MULTILINGUAL)* 1-800-227-2345 (24 hr.) Information and referral on various issues related to cancer (treatment, services, literature, transportation, equipment, encouragement and support). English, Spanish and Chinese speaking. *Website:* http://www.cancer.org

Anderson Network 1-800-345-6324 (Mon.-Fri., 8am-5pm CST) Matches cancer patients with others with exact diagnosis for support. *Website:* http://www.mdanderson.org

BLOCH Cancer Hotline 1-800-433-0464 Networks persons with cancer and home volunteers with same type of cancer. Free books about cancer. *Website:* http://www.blochcancer.org *E-mail*: hotline@hrblock.com

Cancer Care, Inc. *(BILINGUAL)* 1-800-813-4673 Free counseling for cancer patients and their families. Financial assistance, information and referrals, community and professional education. Teleconference programs. On-going telephone and in-person support groups. *Website:* http://www.cancercare.org *E-mail*: info@cancercare.org

Cancer Hope Network 1-877-467-3638 (9am-5:30pm EST) One-on-one support offered to cancer patients and their families undergoing cancer treatment from trained volunteers who have survived cancer themselves. *Website:* http://www.cancerhopenetwork.org *E-mail*: info@cancerhopenetwork.org

"The life I touch for good or ill will touch another life, and that in turn another, until who knows where the trembling stops or in what far place my touch will be felt."
-- Frederick Buechner

Cancer Information Service *(BILINGUAL)* 1-800-422-6237 Provides information about cancer and cancer-related resources to patients, the public and health professionals. Offers one-on-one smoking cessation counseling and literature. Free publications. Sponsored by National Cancer Institute. *Website:* http://www.cancer.gov

Cancer Research Institute 1-800-992-2623 or 212-688-7515 (Mon.-Fri., 9am-5pm EST) Provides general cancer resource information. Supports leading-edge research aimed at developing immunologic methods of preventing, treating and curing cancer. *Website:* http://www.cancerreseaach.org *E-mail:* info@cancerresearch.org

CureSearch 1-800-458-6223 Active in the search to cure childhood cancer. Involved with research, care, public awareness, fundraising, information and e-newsletter. *Website:* http://www.curesearch.org *E-mail:* info@curesearch.org

Dana Farber Cancer Institute Family Studies Cancer Risk Line 1-800-828-6622 Information regarding familial cancers. *Website:* http://www.partners.org

Gilda Radner Familial Ovarian Cancer Registry 1-800-682-7426 (Mon.-Fri., 9am-5:30pm EST) Information on the warning signs of cancer, diagnostic tests and family history. Sponsored by Roswell Park Cancer Institute. *Website:* http://www.ovariancancer.com

Gynecologic Cancer Foundation 1-800-444-4441 Makes referrals to physicians who specialize in the treatment of gynecological cancer. Brochures, literature and online resources. *Website:* http://www.wcn.org *E-mail:* info@thegcf.org

Hereditary Cancer Institute 1-800-648-8133 (Mon.-Fri., 8am-5pm CST) Studies family-linked cancer. Counseling, information on clinical trials, cancer and hereditary factors.

International Myeloma Foundation 1-800-452-2873 (8am-5pm PST) Information, seminars, grants and newsletter on myeloma. *Website:* http://www.myeloma.org *E-mail:* info@myeloma.org

Locks of Love 1-888-896-1588 (recorded information) or 561-963-1677 (office) Provides custom hairpieces to financially disadvantaged children with long-term medical hair loss. Uses donated hair. *Website:* http://www.locksoflove.org/ *E-mail:* info@locksoflove.org

Look Good...Feel Better 1-800-227-2345 Helps cancer patients improve their appearance during treatment. Free workshops across the country. *Website:* http://www.cancer.org

Lung Cancer Alliance 1-800-298-2436 (9am-5pm, Mon.-Fri. EST) Operates a national "phone buddies" program, comprehensive helpline and many other additional services for persons with lung cancer and their families. *Website:* http://www.lungcanceralliance.org *E-mail:* info@lungcanceralliance.org

Ovarian Cancer Research Fund 1-800-873-9569 Dedicated to advancing and supporting laboratory and clinical research that promotes the development of new therapies and techniques for early detection, screening and treatment of ovarian cancer. Educational outreach, public awareness projects, including videos and resource materials available. *Website:* http://www.ocrf.org

Patient Advocate Foundation 1-800-532-5274 (8am-8pm EST) Provides education and legal counseling to cancer patients (relative to a diagnosis) concerning managed care, discrimination, insurance and financial issues. *Website:* http://www.patientadvocate.org *E-mail:* help@patientadvocate.org

Skin Cancer Foundation 1-800-754-6490 (Mon.-Fri., 9am-5pm EST) Provides educational materials and information on skin cancer and treatment. *Website:* http://www.skincancer.org *E-mail:* info@skincancer.org

Susan G. Komen Breast Cancer Foundation *(BILINGUAL)* 1-800-462-9273 (Mon.-Fri., 8:30am-5:30pm CST) Information on breast cancer and breast health. *Website:* http://www.komen.org/

CAREERS

Career Information Hotline *(New Jersey)* 1-800-222-1309 (Mon.-Fri., 8:30am-4:30pm) Provides descriptions and outlooks on various careers. Has information on New Jersey vocational schools, national colleges, graduate school programs and New Jersey day care centers. Publishes a sample resume and information on job interviews. Not a job search agency. Sponsored by NJ Department of Labor. *Website:* http://www.lwd.state.nj.us/labor

National Job Corps Information Line 1-800-733-5627 *(BILINGUAL)* (24 hr.) Referrals to job corps training for persons ages 16-24. Helps persons to earn high school equivalency diplomas. *Website:* http://www.jobcorps.dol.gov

CHARITY / SERVICE ORGANIZATION

AmVets 1-800-244-6350 Makes referrals to used clothing collection agencies and provides pick-up information.

Goodwill Industries 1-800-741-0186 Provides employment and training services for people with disabilities and other disadvantaging conditions (welfare dependency, illiteracy, criminal history, homeless). Write: Goodwill Industries International, 15810 Indianola Drive, Rockville, MD 20855. *Website:* http://www.goodwill.org

Volunteers of America 1-800-899-0089 (8am-6pm Mon.-Fri. EST) Provides local human service programs and opportunities for individual and community involvement in volunteer programs that deal with social problems. Also has Retiree Volunteer Coalition. *Website:* http://www.volunteersofamerica.org *E-mail:* info@voa.org

CHILD ABUSE

American Humane Association 1-800-227-4645 Mission is to protect children and animals from abuse, neglect and cruelty. Advocates on behalf of children (capital/corporal punishment, child protective services, medical neglect, etc) and animals.

Child Abuse Hotline *(New Jersey)* 1-877-652-2873 or 1-877-NJ ABUSE (24 hr.); TDD: 1-800-835-5510 (24 hr.) Accepts reports of child abuse or neglect. Emergency response for children at risk. Anonymous if callers prefer. Sponsored by Division of Youth and Family Services.

Child Help Inc. *(BILINGUAL)* 1-800-422-4453 (24 hr.) General information on child abuse and related issues. Referrals to local agencies for child abuse reporting. Crisis counseling. *Website:* http://www.childhelp.org

Child Welfare Information Gateway *(BILINGUAL)* 1-800-394-3366 (Mon.-Fri., 8:30am-5:30pm EST) Provides information on all aspects of child maltreatment. *Website:* http://www.childwelfare.gov *E-mail:* info@childwelfare.gov

Prevent Child Abuse New Jersey *(New Jersey)* 1-800-244-5373 Provides information workshops, literature and child abuse prevention information. Aim is to prevent child abuse (not for reports of active abuse situations). *Website:* http://www.preventchildabuse.org

Project Child Find *(New Jersey)* 1-800-322-8174; TDD: 609-984-8432 (Mon.-Fri., 8:15am-4:15pm) Information and referrals for children, from birth to 21 years, with any developmental delay. Sponsored by Department of Education.

U.S. Customs Service *(BILINGUAL)* 1-800-232-5378 Will take reports on child pornography on the internet. Aim is to stop this form of child sexual abuse.

CHILD CARE

Childcare Hotline *(New Jersey)* 1-800-332-9227 (Mon.-Fri., 9am-5pm) Callers can obtain the telephone number of their local childcare resource and referral system to get information about various childcare options and subsidized childcare services. Caregivers can also learn how to become a registered family day care provider. Provides information on how to evaluate the child care environment to make an informed decision on the selection process.

National Association for Family Child Care *(BILINGUAL)* 1-800-359-3817 (Mon.-Fri. 8am-5pm MST) Provides information and training for in-home care providers. Newsletter. *Website:* http://www.nafcc.org

National Child Care Information Center 1-800-616-2242 (Mon.-Fri., 8:30am-5:30pm EST). Provides information to enhance and promote quality child care. *Website:* http://nccic.acf.hhs.gov *E-mail:* info@nccic.org

CHILD SUPPORT

New Jersey Child Support Information *(New Jersey)* 1-800-621-5437 (for existing cases); 1-877-655-4371 (customer service) Provides information on child support issues and problems. *Website:* http://www.njchildsupport.org

CHOLESTEROL

UAB Eat Right 1-800-231-3438 (Mon.-Fri., 9am-5pm EST) Information on nutrition and related topics (weight loss and cholesterol). Sponsored by Nutrition Information Services.

"Beginning today, treat everyone you meet as if they were going to be dead by midnight. Extend to them all the care, kindness and understanding you can muster, and do it with no thought of any reward. Your life will never be the same again." -- Og Mandino

COMPLAINT

Directors Action Line *(New Jersey)* 1-800-331-3937 (Mon.-Fri., 9am-5pm) Responds to concerns and questions about the Division of Youth and Family Service and its services. Also answers questions regarding DYFS and refers callers to other assistance if needed.

Long Term Care Systems *(New Jersey)* 1-800-792-9770 (Mon.-Fri., 8:45am-4:45pm; answering machine other times) Complaint line for hospitals, nursing homes, residential care facilities and assisted living. Sponsored by State Facilities.

CONSUMER

FDA Consumer Affairs 1-888-463-6332 (Mon.-Fri., 10am-4pm) Information on any FDA-regulated product (food and drugs). Has information on rare illnesses, starting businesses, freedom of information act, health and medical issues. Free literature. Referrals to toll-free numbers. Assists in emergency situations. *Website:* http://www.fda.gov

National Do Not Call Registry 1-888-382-1222 An opportunity to limit the telemarketing calls that are received. The registry was created to offer consumers a choice regarding telemarketing calls. *Website:* http://www.donotcall.gov

New Jersey Division of Consumer Affairs *(New Jersey)* 1-800-242-5846 (8:30am-5pm) Takes complaints against businesses, advisory and professional boards, health clubs, home repairs, car dealerships and charities. Information on Lemon Law (automobiles), weights and measures, legalized games of chance, Bureau of Securities, etc. *Website:* http://www.njconsumeraffairs.com *E-mail*: askconsumeraffairs@lps.state.nj.us

Opt Out *(BILINGUAL)* 1-888-567-8688 Organization that removes your name and address from all mailing lists offered by the main consumer credit reporting agencies (Trans Union, Experian, Equifax and Innovis) which advertise and send out new charge card offers. When writing include your first, middle and last name (including Jr., Sr., etc), current address, previous address (if you've moved in the last six months), social security number, date of birth and signature.

Toy Safety Hotline 1-877-486-9723 (8:30am-5pm EST) Provides information on toy safety. Brochures. Information on best selling age-appropriate toys. *Website:* http://www.toyassociation.org

U.S. Consumer Product Safety Commission *(BILINGUAL)* 1-800-638-2772 TTY: 1-800-638-8270 Computer operated recorded information on product safety. Takes reports on unsafe products. Fax: 301-504-0124. *Website:* http://www.cpsc.gov *E-mail:* info@cpsc.gov

CREDIT COUNSELING

Consumer Credit Counseling Services 1-800-388-2227 With touch-tone phone, callers can find out about credit counseling services in their local areas. Sponsored by the National Foundation for Consumer Credit.

CRIME VICTIMS

Consumer Response Center *(BILINGUAL)* 1-877-382-4357 Assistance for people who are victims of fraud. Complaints are shared with law enforcement agencies. Does not resolve individual disputes. Sponsored by Federal Trade Commission. *Website:* http://www.ftc.gov

GAINS Center 1-800-311-4246 (option #2) (Mon.-Fri., 8:30am-5pm EST) Provides information on services for people with co-occurring mental health and substance abuse disorders who come in contact with the justice system. Provides technical assistance, needs assessment and literature to communities. Write: GAINS Center, Policy Research, Inc., 345 Delaware Ave., Delmar, NY 12054. *Website:* http://gainscenter.samhsa.gov *E-mail:* gains@prainc.com

Juvenile Justice Clearinghouse 1-800-851-3420 (Mon.-Fri., 10am-6pm EST) Information and referrals regarding juvenile justice programs and Department of Justice. *Website:* http://www.ncjrs.gov

National Center for Victims of Crime 1-800-394-2255 Provides information, referrals and advocacy to crime victims nationwide. An affiliate to the National Crime Victim Bar Association which provides referrals to file civil suit against perpetrators and other responsible individuals. Also operates Stalking Resource Center which provides training and technical assistance on the issue of stalking. Write: National Center for Victims of Crime, 2000 M St. NW, Suite 480, Washington, DC 20036. *Website:* http://www.ncvc.org *E-mail:* gethelp@ncvc.org

National Criminal Justice Reference Service 1-800-851-3420 (Mon.-Fri., 10am-6:00pm EST) Provides information on all aspects of the criminal justice system and support for victims. *Website:* http://www.ncjrs.gov

National Institute of Corrections 1-800-995-6423 or 202-307-3106 (Mon.-Fri., 8am-5pm EST) Provides information and technical assistance regarding those diagnosed with a mental illness in prison. Write: National Institute of Corrections, 320 First St. NW, Washington, DC 20534. *Website:* http://www.nicic.org

Stalking *(New Jersey)* 1-800-572-7233 (Domestic Violence Hotline; 24 hr.) Support and information for anyone with a restraining order, who is being stalked in New Jersey. Sponsored by the Prevention of Violence Against Women.

Trafficking in Persons and Worker Exploitation Helpline *(MULTILINGUAL)* 1-888-428-7581 (voice/TTY; Mon.-Fri., 9am-5pm EST) Provides opportunity to report trafficking crimes or get help. "Human trafficking" is a form of slavery and involuntary servitude - examples include sexual exploitation, sweatshop workers, exploitation of agricultural workers and individuals working as domestic servants.

Victims of Crime Compensation Agency *(New Jersey)* 1-800-242-0804 Provides counseling, information on compensation and referrals for victims of violent crimes. Can help in emergency situations for qualified persons, otherwise leave message. *Website:* http://www.njvictims.org

We Tip Hotlines *(BILINGUAL)* 1-800-782-7463 (general); 1-800-873-7283 (felony) Takes reports on crimes or felonies.

CYSTIC FIBROSIS

Children's Organ Transplant Association 1-800-366-2682 (Mon.-Fri., 8am-5pm EST) Provides public education on organ transplants. Assists families in fund-raising for transplant and transplant-related expenses. Assistance for all children and adults with cystic fibrosis who are U.S. citizens in need of an organ transplant. *Website:* http://www.cota.org *E-mail:* cota@cota.org

Cystic Fibrosis Foundation 1-800-344-4823 (Mon.-Fri., 8:30am-6:30pm EST); Pharmacy: 1-800-541-4959 Provides information, brochures, insurance information, pharmaceutical services and updates on research. *Website:* http://www.cff.org *E-mail:* info@cff.org

"I am of the opinion that my life belongs to the community, and as long as I live it is my privilege to do for it whatever I can." – George Bernard Shaw

DEAF

ASHA Hearing and Speech Helpline *(BILINGUAL)* 1-800-638-8255 (voice/TDD; Mon.-Fri., 8:30am-5pm EST) Information on speech, hearing and language disabilities. Referrals to ASHA certified clinics. Database of information on listening devices. Sponsored by American Speech Language and Hearing Association. *Website:* http://www.asha.org *E-mail*: actioncenter@asha.org

Better Hearing Institute 1-800-327-9355 or 703-684-3391 Information and literature on any hearing-related issue. *Website:* http://www.betterhearing.org

DB-Link: National Consortion on Deaf/Blindness 1-800-438-9376 (voice); TTY: 1-800-854-7013 Information and referral on education, health, employment, technology, communication, recreation for children who are deaf-blind. Newsletter. All services are free of charge. *Website:* http://nationaldb.org *E-mail*: info@nationaldb.org

Described and Captioned Media Program (DCMP) *(BILINGUAL)* 1-800-237-6213 (voice); TTY: 1-800-237-6819; (Mon-Fri., 8:30am-5pm EST) Provides free loan described and captioned educational media, clearinghouse of information related to educational media access and a gateway to internet resources related to accessibility. Free registration and services. Sponsored by US Dept. of Education and administered by the National Association of the Deaf. *Website:* http://www.cfv.org *E-mail*: info@cvf.org

Dial-A-Hearing Screening Test 1-800-222-3277 (Mon.-Fri., 9am-5pm EST) Offers over the phone hearing screening for persons (aged 14+). Provides hearing information and referral services. *E-mail*: dahst@aol.com

Division of Deaf and Hard of Hearing *(New Jersey)* 1-800-792-8339 (voice/TTY) or 609-984-7281 (Mon.-Fri., 8:30am-4:30pm) Information and referral for the deaf and hard of hearing. Interpreter referral service. Sensitivity training available for the public. *Website:* http://www.state.nj.us/humanservices/ddhh/index.html

HEAR Now 1-800-648-4327 (Mon.-Fri., 8am-5pm CST) Helps financially needy individuals obtain hearing aids. Collects used hearing aids for recycling. Information and referrals. Automated telephone line, leave message and call will be returned within two days. *Website:* http://www.sotheworldmayhear.org *E-mail*: nonprofit@starkey.com

Hearing Aid 1-800-521-5247 (ext. 3) or 734-522-7200 (Mon.-Fri., 8am-5pm EST) Provides general literature on hearing aids and hearing loss. Referrals to hearing instrument specialists. Leave name and address, information will be mailed. Sponsored by International Hearing Society. *Website:* http://www.ihsinfo.org *E-mail*: amarkey@ihsinfo.org

Hearing Aid Assistance to the Aged and Disabled (HAAAD) *(New Jersey)* 1-800-792-9745 (24 hr.) Provides a $100 reimbursement to eligible persons who purchase a hearing aid. Sponsored by NJ State Dept. of Health, Div. of Senior Affairs.

John Tracy Clinic for Preschool Deaf Children *(BILINGUAL)* 1-800-522-4582 (Mon.-Fri., 8am-4pm PST) Information and support for parents and preschool deaf children. Free correspondence course for parents. *Website:* http://www.jtc.org

National Cued Speech Association 1-800-459-3529 (voice/TTY) or 301-915-8009 (voice/TTY) Encourages and supports the use of cued speech for communication, language development and literacy. Networking, literature, advocacy, phone support, conferences, family camps, information and referrals. *Website:* http://www.cuedspeech.org *E-mail*: info@cuedspeech.org

National Institute on Deafness and Other Communication Disorders *(BILINGUAL)* 1-800-241-1044; TTY: 1-800-241-1055 Referrals to national agencies on hearing, speech, language, smell, taste, voice and balance disorders. Publishes fact sheets, brochures, information packets and newsletters. *Website:* http://www.nidcd.nih.gov *E-mail*: nidcdinfo@nidcd.nih.gov

New Jersey Library for the Blind and Handicapped *(New Jersey)* 1-800-792-8322; TTY: 1-877-882-5593 (Mon.-Fri., 9am-4pm; Sat., 9am-3pm except July/Aug.). Information on provision of recorded materials, large print, Braille and radio reading service. Deaf and hard of hearing awareness program offers over 700 videos, books on hearing loss and deafness. Assistive devices such as: TTYs, baby cry signalers, bed vibrators, closed captioned decoders, and assistive listening devices. Sign language interpreting services for library events. Sponsored by Bureau of State Library, Thomas Edison State College. *Website:* http://www.njstatelib.org *E-mail*: njlbh@njstatelib.org

"We don't accomplish anything in this world alone...and whatever happens is the result of the whole tapestry of one's life and all the weavings of individual threads from one to another that creates something." – Sandra Day O'Connor

DENTAL

Dental Care for Handicapped 1-888-471-6334 (Mon.-Fri., 8am-5pm MST) Information on free dental care for qualified elderly, disabled or chronically ill patients. Services include dentures, crowns or other significant dental work. *Website:* http://www.nfdh.org

DEPRESSION

National Institute of Mental Health Information Line *(BILINGUAL)* 1-800-421-4211 Offers free brochures on depression and anxiety. Sponsored by National Institute of Mental Health. *Website:* http://www.nimh.nih.gov

Speak Up When You're Down *(New Jersey)* 1-800-328-3838 (24 hr.) Resources for anyone experiencing postpartum depression, their families and friends. *Website:* http://www.njspeakup.gov

DIABETES

National Diabetes Education Program 1-800-438-5383 or 1-800-860-8747 *(BILINGUAL)* (Mon.-Fri., 8:30am-5pm EST) Provides educational information on diabetes. Publishes "Do Your Level Best" kit and diabetes kit to public and health care professionals. Sponsored by National Institute of Diabetics, Digestive and Kidney Diseases and Center for Diabetes Control and Prevention.

National Institute of Diabetes and Digestive and Kidney Diseases 1-800-891-5390 (kidney); 1-800-860-8747 (diabetes); 1-800-891-5359 (digestive diseases) (Mon.-Fri., 8:30am-5:00pm EST) Provides referrals and literature on a broad range of subjects concerning diabetes, digestive disorders, kidney disease, metabolic and endocrine disorders, hematologic diseases, urologic disorders. *Website:* http://www.niddk.nih.gov *E-mail:* nkudic@info.niddk.nih.gov

DISABILITY

Abledata 1-800-227-0216 (Mon.-Fri., 8:30am-5:30pm EST) Provides information, publications and consumer reviews of all types of assistive technologies for persons with disabilities. Sponsored by National Institute On Disability and Rehabilitation Research and U.S. Deptartment of Education. *Website:* http://www.abledata.com/ *E-mail:* abledata@orcmacro.com

Access Board *(BILINGUAL)* 1-800-872-2253 or 202-272-0080 (voice); 1-800-993-2822 or 202-272-0082 (TTY) Advocates for accessibility. Provides publications and forms to press charges against agencies that are not accessible. *Website:* http://www.access-board.gov *E-mail:* info@access-board.gov

ADA Technical Assistance Line *(BILINGUAL)* 1-800-514-0301; TDD: 1-800-514-0383 (Mon.-Fri. 9am-5:30pm; Thurs. 12:30-5:30pm EST) Provides free publications on the American Disabilities Act. A new publication will be available each month in a limited supply. *Website:* http://www.ada.gov

Assistive Technology Advocacy Center of NJ *(New Jersey)* 1-800-342-5832 (Mon.-Fri., 9am-5pm) Maintains listing of used equipment available for sale.

Canine Companions for Independence 1-866-224-3647 (Mon.-Fri., 8am-5pm PST) Trains dogs to assist people with physical and developmental disabilities. Also has opportunities for people interested in volunteering to raise puppies. *Website:* http://www.cci.org

Childcare Plus 1-800-235-4122 Information and referrals to families of children (birth to 5). Provides training for childcare providers and other early childcare professionals. *Website:* http://www.ccplus.org *E-mail:* ccplus@ruralinstitute.umt.edu

Disability Rights New Jersey (DRNJ) *(New Jersey)* 1-800-922-7233 (NJ only) or 609-292-9742; TTY: 609-633-7106 (Mon.-Fri., 9am-5pm) Provides legal assistance and advocacy services to citizens of New Jersey with any type of disability (both physical and mental). Information and referral services, educational programs, technical assistance and training. *Website:* http://www.njpanda.org *E-mail:* advocate@njpanda.org

Disabled American Veterans 1-877-426-2838 (8:30am-4:30pm EST) Provides free, professional assistance to veterans and their families in obtaining benefits and services earned through military service and provided by the Department of Veterans Affairs and other agencies of the government. Guidelines for developing chapters. *Website:* http://www.dav.org *E-mail:* feedback@davmail.org

"One's life has value so long as one attributes value to the life of others by means of love, friendship and compassion." – Simone De Beauvoir

Disabled and Alone 1-800-995-0066 or 212-532-6740 (Mon.-Fri., 9am-5pm EST) Helps families and caretakers of a loved one with a disability answer the question, "Who will look after my loved one when I am gone?" by creating a "life plan" and carrying out each family's plan for their disabled loved one, as directed and funded by the family. Write: Disabled and Alone/Life Services for the Handicapped, 61 Broadway, Suite 510, New York, NY 10006. *Website:* http://www.disabledandalone.org *E-mail:* info@disabledandalone.org

Division of Disability Services *(New Jersey)* 1-888-285-3036; TDD: 1-877-294-4356 Information and referral services for persons of all ages with disabilities. Serves as the chief link between state government and the county offices on disabilities. Publishes a statewide directory of disability services. *Website:* http://www.state.nj.us/humanservices/dds

Easter Seals National Headquarters Disability Helpline *(BILINGUAL)* 1-800-221-6827 (Mon.-Fri., 8:30am-5pm CST) Provides disability resource packets for children and adults with disabilities. Online directory available. *Website:* http://www.easterseals.com

Family Support Center of New Jersey *(New Jersey)* 1-800-372-6510 (Mon.-Fri., 8am-5pm) Information and referral agency offering services to individuals with a disability or families who live with a family member with special needs. Also works with professionals who service this community. A support network for parents is also available through the center. *Website:* http://www.fscnj.org *E-mail:* jacqui.moskowitz@fscnj.org

Friends' Health Connection *(New Jersey)* 1-800-483-7436 A communication support network that connects patients and caregivers with any disorder, illness or handicap. Members are networked with each other based on health problem, symptoms, lifestyle, interests, occupation, location and other criteria. Communicate via letters, phone and e-mail. It is intended for emotional support, not for romantic purposes. Also provides educational, therapeutic and recreational programs. Membership $9.95. Write: Friends' Health Connection, P.O. Box 114, New Brunswick, NJ 08903. *Website:* http://www.friendshealthconnection.org *E-mail:* info@friendshealthconnection.org

Job Accommodation Network 1-800-526-7234 (voice); 1-877-781-9403 (TTY) (Mon.-Fri., 9am-6pm EST) Information on accommodations for people with disability. Sponsored Office of Disability Employment Policy and Deptartment of the Labor. *Website:* http://www.jan.wvu.edu *E-mail:* jan@jan.wvu.edu

Library of Congress National Library Service for the Blind and Physical Handicapped 1-800-424-8567; TDD: 202-707-0744 (Mon.-Fri., 8:30am-5pm EST) Refers callers to libraries that have information on books on tapes and in Braille available for qualified blind or handicapped persons who can't read standard print. *Website:* http://www.loc.gov/nls *E-mail:* nls@loc.gov

National Accessible Apartment Clearinghouse 1-800-421-1221 Maintains a database of over 80,000 accessible apartments nationwide. Helps people with disabilities find accessible apartments. Owners and managers may also use this service to register their accessible units. Fax: 703-248-9440. *Website:* http://www.accessibleapartments.org *E-mail:* clearinghouse@naahq.org

National Council on Independent Living 1-877-525-3400 or 202-207-0334; TTY: 202-207-0340 Provides information and referrals to independent living centers. *Website:* http://www.ncil.org *E-mail:* ncil@ncil.org

National Dissemination Center for Children with Disabilities *(BILINGUAL)* 1-800-695-0285 (voice/TTY) or 202-884-8200 (voice/TTY) (Mon.-Fri., 9am-5pm EST) Provides information on disabilities with a special focus on children (birth to age 22). Services include information, referrals, technical assistance to parents, educators, caregivers and advocates. Referrals to support groups. Most publications are free. *E-mail:* nichcy@aed.org

National Institute for Rehab Engineering 1-800-736-2216 or 973-853-6585 Provides information, advice and referrals to people with all types of disabilities about assistive technology equipment. Aim is to help people with disabilities to be more independent and self-sufficient. *E-mail:* nire@warwick.net

New Jersey Library for the Blind and Handicapped *(BILINGUAL) (New Jersey)* 1-800-792-8322; TTY: 1-877-882-5593 (Mon.-Fri., 9am-4pm; Sat., 9am-3pm except July/Aug.) Information on provision of recorded materials, large print, Braille and radio reading service. Deaf and hard of hearing awareness program offers over 700 videos, books on hearing loss and deafness. Assistive devices such as: TTYs, baby cry signalers, bed vibrators, closed captioned decoders and assistive listening devices. Sign language interpreting services for library events. Sponsored by Bureau of State Library, Thomas Edison State College. *Website:* http://www.njlbh.org *E-mail:* njlbh@njstatelib.org

NJ WINS (Work Incentive Programs) *(New Jersey)* 1-877-659-4672 Enables social security administration beneficiaries with disabilities to make informed choices about work and assist them in exploring work incentives that are available. *Website:* http://www.njwins.org

Northeast ADA Center *(BILINGUAL)* *(New Jersey)* 1-800-949-4232 (Voice, TTY and Spanish) Provides free technical assistance to employers, individuals with disabilities, state and local government agencies and others in the implementation of the Americans with Disabilities Act. They also provide free training workshops and awareness programs. *Website:* http://www.northeastada.org

Project Child Find 1-800-322-8174; TTY: 609-984-8432 (Mon.-Fri., 8:15am-4:15pm EST) Information and referrals for children, from birth to 21 years, with any developmental delay. Sponsored by Deptartment of Education.

Special Needs Advocate for Parents (SNAP) 1-800-872-5827 Support for parents of special needs children. Referrals to educational advocates, support groups, attorneys and other resources. Medical insurance problem solving. Assistance with estate planning. Newsletter, speakers' bureau and interactive bulletin boards. *E-mail*: info@ucp.org

Technical Assistance Alliance for Parents Centers 1-888-248-0822; TTY: 952-838-0190 (Mon.-Fri., 8am-5:30pm CST) Support and education for families of children with any disability. Advocates for the Individuals with Disabilities Education Act. Literature, training sessions, information and referrals. *Website:* http://www.taalliance.org *E-mail*: alliance@taalliance.org

Through the Looking Glass *(BILINGUAL)* 1-800-644-2666 (Mon.-Fri., 8:30am-5pm PST) or 510-848-1112; TTY: 1-800-804-1616 Phone support, newsletter, information and referrals for disabled parents or parents of disabled children. Write: Through the Looking Glass, 2198 Sixth Street, Suite 100, Berkeley, CA 94710-2204. *Website:* http://www.lookingglass.org *E-mail*: tlg@lookingglass.org

U.S. Equal Employment Opportunity Commission *(MULTILINGUAL)* 1-800-669-4000; TTY: 1-800-669-6820 Information, speakers, technical assistance, training and referrals regarding enforcing ADA and prohibiting discrimination in employment of disabled persons. *Website:* http://www.eeoc.gov

University of Montana Rural Institute 1-800-732-0323 (Mon.-Fri., 8am-5pm MST) Provides support, education, research and service for children and adults with disabilities who live in rural areas. Technological services, early intervention, personnel development, research and assistive technology services are available. *E-mail*: rural@ruralinstitute.umt.edu

DISCRIMINATION

Equal Employment Opportunity *(New Jersey)* 1-800-669-4000 (Mon.-Fri., 8am-8pm); TTY: 1-800-669-6820 Investigates allegations of discrimination due to race, creed, age, religion, gender or disabilities. Sponsored by Federal Government. *Website:* http://www.eeoc.gov

Office for Civil Rights *(BILINGUAL)* 1-800-368-1019 (Mon.-Fri., 8:30am-5:30pm EST) Refers people who feel they have been discriminated against. Sponsored by the Department of Health and Human Services. *Website:* http://www.hhs.gov.ocr/

DOMESTIC VIOLENCE

National Domestic Abuse Helpline for Men and Women 1-888-743-5754 Provides crisis intervention and support services to men and women who are dealing with domestic violence. *Website:* http://www.dahmw.org/

National Domestic Violence Hotline 1-800-799-7233; TTD: 1-800-787-3224 (24 hr.) Information and referrals for victims of domestic violence. *Website:* http://www.ndvh.org

NJ Domestic Violence Hotline *(New Jersey)* 1-800-572-7233 (24 hr.) Information and referrals for victims or perpetrators of domestic violence. *Website:* http://www.womanspace.org

DOWN SYNDROME

National Down Syndrome Society 1-800-221-4602 or 212-460-9330 (Mon.-Fri., 9am-5pm EST) Free packets to new parents, information on education, support groups, medical research, conferences, newsletter, phone support and referrals. Fax: 212-979-2873. *Website:* http://www.ndss.org *E-mail*: info@ndss.org

DRUG ABUSE

Addiction and the Family 1-800-488-3784 Provides general information on drug abuse and treatment. Brochures and referrals to crisis counseling. Publications. Affiliated with Phoenix House.

Addictions Hotline of NJ *(New Jersey)* 1-800-238-2333 (Voice/TDD) (24 hr.) Crisis counseling, information and referrals for all kinds of drug and alcohol related issues (both prescription and illegal drugs). Sponsored by NJ Division of Narcotics and Drug Abuse, Office on Prevention, Trenton.

Community Recovery *(New Jersey)* 1-800-292-8262 Offers services for veterans who are experiencing problems with drugs or alcohol. The program offers a wide variety of services throughout the state.

Drug Policy Information Clearinghouse 1-800-666-3332 (Mon.-Fri., 10am-6pm EST) Sends out information on drug abuse and publications on national drug policies. *Website:* http://www.whitehousedrugpolicy.gov

National Association for Children of Alcoholics 1-888-554-2627 (8:30am-5pm EST) Advocates for children and families affected by alcoholism and other drug dependencies. Helps children hurt by parental alcohol and drug abuse. Newsletter, advocacy, policy making, literature, videos and educational materials. *Website:* http://www.nacoa.org *E-mail:* nacoa@nacoa.org

National Clearinghouse for Alcohol and Drug Information *(BILINGUAL)* 1-800-729-6686 or 301-468-2600; Spanish: 1-877-767-8432; TTY: 1-800-487-4889 Information on alcohol, tobacco and drug abuse. Information on prevention, referrals to treatment centers, research, groups, drugs in the work place, community programs, AIDS, addiction and drug abuse. *Website:* http://www.ncadi-samhsa.gov *E-mail:* ncadi-info@samhsa.hhs.gov

National Council on Alcoholism and Drug Dependence 1-800-622-2255 Provides information on counseling and treatment services for alcohol or drug abuse. Prevention and education programs. Newsletter. *E-mail:* national@ncadd.org *Website:* http://www.ncadd.org

National Inhalant Prevention Center 1-800-269-4237 Provides information and referrals to persons concerned about inhalants. Literature, training, quarterly newsletter, technical assistance, conducts national inhalant and poisons awareness week. *Website:* http://www.inhalants.org *E-mail:* nipc@io.com

National PRIDE Youth Programs 1-800-668-9277 (Mon.-Fri., 8:30am-4pm EST) Trains youth volunteers on how to conduct drug prevention education. *Website:* http://www.prideyouthprograms.org *E-mail:* info@prideyouthprograms.org

DWARFISM

Little People's Research Fund, Inc. 1-800-232-5773 or 410-747-1100 (Mon.-Fri., 9am-5pm EST) Networks parents together. Referrals (primarily research) and literature on dwarfism. *Website:* http://www.lprf.org

DYSLEXIA / LEARNING DISABILITIES

International Dyslexia Association 1-800-222-3123 or 410-296-0232 (Mon.-Fri., 8:30am-4:30pm EST) Provides information and referrals for persons with dyslexia. *Website:* http://www.interdys.org *E-mail:* info@interdys.org

National Center for Learning Disabilities 1-888-575-7373 Provides information and referrals for learning disabled adults and children. *Website:* http://www.ld.org

Recording For The Blind and Dyslexic 1-866-732-3585 (Mon.-Fri., 8am-4:30pm) Information on recorded textbooks and consumer publications to eligible persons with print or learning disabilities. Information on volunteer programs for recording CDs. Membership $100/1st year; $35/yearly thereafter. Fax: 609-987-8116. *Website:* http://www.rfbd.org *E-mail:* custserv@rfbd.org

EATING DISORDERS

National Eating Disorders Association 1-800-931-2237 (8:30am-4:30pm Mon.-Fri. PST) Provides information on local professional services and support groups nationwide for persons with eating disorders. Free literature and training conferences. *Website:* http://www.myneda.org *E-mail:* info@nationaleatingdisorders.org

New Jersey Eating Disorders Helpline *(New Jersey)* 1-800-624-2268 (Mon.-Fri., 10am-5pm) Provides information and referrals for dealing with all types of eating disorders. Feel free to leave a message and your call will be returned. *Website:* http://www.edhelp.com *E-mail:* livctr@aol.com

EDUCATION

Federal Student Aid Information Center 1-800-433-3243 (Mon-Fri, 8am-midnight; Sat. 9am-6pm EST) Information available regarding information on student aid. Sponsored by U.S. Department of Education. *Website:* http://www.federalstudentaid.ed.gov

Goodwill Industries 1-800-741-0186 Provides employment and training services for people with disabilities and other disadvantaging conditions (welfare dependency, illiteracy, criminal history and homeless). Write: Goodwill Industries International, 15810 Indianola Drive, MD 20855. *Website:* http://www.goodwill.org

HESAA Hotline, The *(New Jersey)* 1-800-792-8670; TDD: 609-588-2526 (Mon.-Fri., 9am-5pm) Information on colleges and universities, financial aid, adult evening and Vo-Tech education. *Website:* http://www.hesaa.org

National Job Corps Information Line 1-877-872-5627 (24 hr.) *(BILINGUAL)* Referrals to job corps training for persons ages 16-24. Helps persons earn high school equivalency diplomas. Sponsored by Department of Labor. *Website:* http://www.dol.gov

ENERGY / UTILITIES

Energy Efficiency and Renewable Energy Clearinghouse 1-877-337-3463 (Mon.-Fri., 9am-7pm EST) Free information on energy efficiency and renewable energy. Assists consumers who need information on energy efficiency and renewable energy (transportation, homes). Provides referrals to appropriate organizations. Sponsored by the Department of Energy. *Website:* http://www.eere.energy.gov

Lifeline Utility Assistance Program *(New Jersey)* 1-800-792-9745 (24 hr.) Utility assistance to residents of NJ who are 65+ years old or who are 18 and older and receive Social Security Disability and meet the income eligibility guidelines. Recipients may receive up to $150.

NJ Weatherization and Home Energy Assistance Program *(New Jersey)* 1-800-510-3102 Provides home weatherization and insulation. Heating and cooling assistance to eligible New Jersey residents.

ENVIRONMENTAL

American Public Information on Environment 1-800-320-2743 (Mon.-Fri., 8:30am-5pm CST) Information, education and aid to families with environmental concerns. *Website:* http://www.americanpie.org *E-mail:* info@americanpie.org

Center for Disease Control and Prevention Helpline 1-800-232-4636; TTY: 1-888-232-6348 Provides information on emergency preparedness and response including bioterrorism, chemical emergencies, radiation emergencies, mass casualties, natural disasters, severe weather, recent outbreaks and incidence. *Website:* http://www.cdc.gov

Chemical Information Referral Center *(BILINGUAL)* 1-800-424-9300 Takes calls from emergency personnel (firefighters, police) responding to emergency chemical or other hazardous spills. Companies must call 1-800-262-8200 to register (registration fee is required) and then be eligible to report emergency spills with the referral center. *Website:* http://www.chemtrec.com *E-mail:* customerservice@chemtrec.com

EPA (Environmental Protection Agency) Safe Drinking Water *(BILINGUAL)* 1-800-426-4791 (Mon.-Fri., 10am-4pm EST) Provides information on safe drinking water and policy regulations on a variety of environmental concerns. *Website:* http://www.epa.gov/safewater *E-mail:* sdwa@epa.gov

Indoor Air Quality Information Clearinghouse 1-800-438-4318 (Mon.-Fri., 9am-5pm EST) Provides information and referral on indoor air quality, pollutants and sources, health effects, control methods, commercial building operations and maintenance. Sponsored by the EPA. *Website:* http://www.epa.gov/iaq/ *E-mail:* iaqinfo@aol.com

National Lead Information Center and Clearinghouse *(BILINGUAL)* 1-800-424-5323 (Mon.-Fri., 8am-6pm EST) Provides information on lead-based paint for the home and safe work practices for renovating. Distributes EPA literature. *Website:* http://www.epa.gov/lead *E-mail:* hotline.lead@epamail.epa.gov

EPILEPSY

Epilepsy Information Service 1-800-642-0500 Answers general questions on epilepsy. Free literature, conducts workshops and conferences. *Website:* http://www.WFUBMC.edu

EYE CARE

Eye Care America *(BILINGUAL)* Seniors: 1-800-222-3937; Diabetes Eye Care: 1-800-272-3937; Glaucoma: 1-800-391-3937 Assists financially disadvantaged persons in obtaining medical eye care. Sponsored by American Academy of Ophthalmology Foundation. *Website:* http://www.aao.org

FACIAL DIFFERENCES

Children's Craniofacial Association 1-800-535-3643 (Mon.-Fri., 8:30am-4:30pm CST) Provides information and support for children with craniofacial disfigurement and their families. Makes referrals to doctors and support groups. Disseminates educational booklets. Information on free medical clinics, Cher's Family Retreat and advocacy. *Website:* http://www.ccakids.com

FACES: The National Craniofacial Association. 1-800-332-2373 (Mon.-Fri. 9am-5pm EST) Dedicated to assisting children and adults with craniofacial disorders resulting from disease, accident or birth. Financial assistance, referrals to support groups, newsletter, information and referrals to services and medical professionals. Fax: 423-267-3124; *Website:* http://www.faces-cranio.org *E-mail:* faces@mindspring.com

FOOD HANDLING / FOOD CO-OP

Center for Food Safety and Applied Nutrition 1-888-723-3366 (Mon.-Fri., 10am-4pm EST); TTY: 1-800-877-8339 Provides information on food safety, cosmetics, nutrition, dietary supplements, food additives, food labeling and food biotechnology. Sponsored by FDA. *Website:* http://www.cfsan.fda.gov

Feeding America 1-800-771-2303 Provides hunger relief through a network of over 200 food banks and food-rescue programs. *Website:* http://www.feedingamerica.org

Meat and Poultry Hotline *(BILINGUAL)* 1-800-535-4555 or 1-888-674-6854 (Mon.-Fri., 10am-4pm EST) Answers safe handling questions. Information on food handling. Helps persons understand labels on meat and poultry. Will answer questions about safe handling procedures. Sponsored by US Department of Agriculture. *Website:* http://www.fsis.usda.gov *E-mail:* mphotline.fsis@usda.gov

S.T.O.P. (Safe Tables Our Priority) 1-800-350-7867 Support, education and advocacy for victims and families of victims of foodborne infectious diseases (E.coli, Salmonella Listeria, Shigella, Vibrio and many others). Newsletter, phone and online networking. *Website:* http://www.safetables.org *E-mail:* director@safetables.org

"The influence of each human being on others in this life is a kind of immortality."
— John Quincy Adams

FOOT CARE

Foot Care Information Center 1-800-366-8227 *(BILINGUAL)* Provides literature and referrals on foot care and podiatric medicine. Referrals to podiatrist. Sponsored by American Podiatric Medical Association. *Website:* http://www.apma.org

GAMBLING

Council on Compulsive Gambling of New Jersey *(New Jersey)* 1-800-426-2537 (24 hr.) or 609-588-5515 Information to help compulsive gamblers. Referrals to self-help groups, in-patient treatment programs, counseling services, speakers' bureau and free evaluations for the compulsive gambler. *Website:* http://www.800gambler.org *E-mail*: ccgnj@800gambler.org

National Council on Problem Gambling 1-800-522-4700 Information, referrals to support groups and counseling for compulsive gamblers. *Website:* http://www.ncpgambling.org *E-mail*: ncpg@ncpgambling.org

GASTROINTESTINAL DISORDERS

National Institute of Diabetes and Digestive and Kidney Diseases 1-800-891-5390 (kidney); 1-800-860-8747 (diabetes); 1-800-891-5359 (digestive diseases) (Mon.-Fri., 8:30am-5:00pm EST) Provides referrals and literature on a broad range of subjects concerning diabetes, digestive disorders, kidney disease, metabolic and endocrine disorders, hematologic diseases and urologic disorders. *Website:* http://www.niddk.nih.gov *E-mail*: nkudic@info.niddk.nih.gov

GRANTS / FUNDING

Foundation Center Customer Service 1-800-424-9836 Provides information on grant providers and funders. Grant writing for non-profit projects. Offers course on proposal writing. Free library. *Website:* http://www.foundationcenter.org

HEALTH

Alliance for Informed Choice on Vaccinations *(New Jersey)* 1-800-613-9925. To address the concerns about the safety of vaccines and the right to informed consent. Literature, advocacy and phone help.

American Board of Medical Specialties 1-866-275-2267 or 847-491-9091 Will tell you if your physician is board certified. *Website:* http://www.abms.org

American Dietetic Association *(BILINGUAL)* 1-800-877-1600 Information on diet. Referrals to dietitians. Brochures sometimes available. Sponsored by National Center for Nutrition and Dietetics. *Website:* http://www.eatright.org

American Health Assistance Foundation 1-800-437-2423 (Mon.-Fri., 9am-5pm EST) Provides educational information and funds research for Alzheimer's disease, glaucoma and macular degeneration. *Website:* http://www.ahaf.org

American Running Association 1-800-776-2732 or 301-913-9517 (Mon.-Fri., 9am-5pm) Information on aerobic sports. Referrals to sports medicine clinics, podiatrists and orthopedists. *Website:* http://www.americanrunning.org/ *E-mail:* run@americanrunning.org

CDC Traveler's Health Helpline 1-877-394-8747 Provides information for persons traveling overseas. Includes vaccinations, diseases, safe food and water, traveling with children, persons with special needs, etc. *Website:* http://www.cdc.gov/travel/

Center for Human Genetics 1-800-283-4316 (8am-5pm EST) Provides information on disorders currently under study by the Center for Human Genetics. These include: Alzheimer's, ALS, asthma, autism, Bethlehem myopathy, Chiari malformation, CMT, cardiovascular, facioscapulohumeral muscular dystrophies, focal segmental glomerulosclerosis, spastic paraparesis, glaucoma, benign intraepithelial dyskeratosis, hypophosphatemic rickets, limb-girdle muscular dystrophy, MS, neural tube defects, osteoarthritis, Parkinson's and tuberous sclerosis. See website for complete list. *Website:* http://www.chg.duhs.duke.edu

Centers for Disease Control and Prevention *(BILINGUAL)* 1-800-232-4636 Provides information on health related topics, vaccinations, traveler's health, grants, genetics, hoaxes, rumors and emergency responses. Information is available via the phone or online. *Website:* http://www.cdc.gov *E-mail:* inquiry@cdc.gov

DES Action USA 1-800-337-9288 Information for women who were prescribed DES during pregnancy and their children. Referrals and education for the public and health workers. Quarterly newsletter.

FDA Office on Orphan Product Development 1-800-300-7469 (Mon.-Fri., 8:30am-4:30pm EST) Provides referrals for persons who need a rare orphan drug. *Website:* http://www.fda.gov/orphan

Health Information *(New Jersey)* 1-800-367-6543 (Mon.-Fri., 8:30am-6pm) Assistance by professionals who route callers to the appropriate department for information. Information on VA Hospitals, health certificates, shots required for overseas, senior services, public health issues, complaints about heath care providers, etc. Sponsored by Department of Health and Senior Services. *Website:* http://www.state.nj.us/health/commiss/contact.shtml

March of Dimes 1-888-663-4637 Dedicated to decreasing the incidence of birth defects, infant mortality, low birth weight and lack of prenatal care. Provides information, referrals and literature. Write: March of Dimes Birth Defect Foundation, 1275 Mamaroneck Ave., White Plains, NY 10605. *Website:* http://www.marchofdimes.com

Medicare + Choice Helpline Assistant *(BILINGUAL)* 1-800-633-4227 Provides information on Medicare, Medigap and health plan options. Publications and audiotapes. Sponsored by federal government. *Website:* http://www.medicare.gov

Minority Health Resource Center 1-800-444-6472; TTD: 301-251-1432 (Mon.-Fri., 9am-5pm EST) Federally-funded library service that provides information and referral to sources on health problems for minorities. *Website:* http://www.omhrc.gov

National Center on Complementary and Alternative Medicine 1-888-644-6226 or 301-519-3153; TTY: 1-866-464-3615 (Mon.-Fri., 8:30am-5pm EST) Provides information on clinical trials and current research projects conducted on alternative medicine. *Website:* http://nccam.nih.gov *E-mail*: info@nccam.nih.gov

National Health Information Center 1-800-336-4797 (Mon.-Fri., 9am-5:30pm EST) Helps the public and health professionals locate health information through identification of health, information resources, information and referral systems. Distributes publications and directories on good health and disease prevention topics. Fax: 301-984-4256. *Website:* http://www.health.gov/NHIC *E-mail*: info@nhic.org

National Immunizations Information Hotline *(BILINGUAL)* 1-800-232-4636; TTY: 1-888-232-6348 Information and referrals on immunizations for infants and adults. Referrals to health care professionals. *Website:* http://www.cdc.gov/nip *E-mail:* nipinfo@cdc.gov

National Institute for Occupational Safety and Health *(BILINGUAL)* 1-800-232-4636 or 513-533-8326 Information on all aspects of occupational health and safety. *Website:* http://www.cdc.gov/niosh *E-mail:* eidtechinfo@cdc.gov (for publications)

National Library of Medicine 1-888-346-3656 (Mon.-Fri., 8:30am-8pm; Sat., 9am-5pm) Provides information and referrals to help callers research health questions. *Website:* http://www.nlm.nih.gov *E-mail:* custserv@nlm.nih.gov

National Reference Center for Bioethics Literature 1-800-633-3849 (Mon.-Fri., 9am-5pm EST) Provides information via e-mail, websites or mail on bioethical topics. Will do limited searches on special topics. Write: National Reference Center for Bioethics, Georgetown University, Box 571212, Washington, DC 20057-1212. *Website:* http://bioethic.georgetown.edu *E-mail:* bioethics@georgetown.edu

National Women's Health Information Center *(BILINGUAL)* 1-800-994-9662; TTY: 1-888-220-5446 (Mon.-Fri., 9am-6pm EST) Provides information and referrals for all women's health questions, including questions on breast feeding. *Website:* http://www.womenshealth.gov

National Women's Health Resource Center 1-877-986-9472 (9am-5:30pm EST) Provides information on women's health issues. Dedicated to helping women make informed decisions about their health. Write: National Women's Health Resource Center, 157 Broad St., Suite 315, Red Bank, NJ 07701. *Website:* http://www.healthywomen.org *E-mail:* info@healthywomen.org

NJ Family Healthline *(New Jersey)* 1-800-328-3838 (24 hr.) Provides information and referral to programs on family planning, pre-natal care, child health, pediatric HIV infection and special child health care. Information on WIC program which provide nutritional assistance for qualified women with children up to age of 5 years. Sponsored by United Way.

NORD (National Organization for Rare Disorders) 1-800-999-6673 or 203-744-0100 (in Connecticut); TDD: 203-797-9590 (Mon.-Fri., 9am-5pm EST) Information and networking for persons with rare disorders. Literature. *Website:* http://www.rarediseases.org *E-mail:* orphan@rarediseases.org

"Su Familia" Health Helpline *(BILINGUAL)* 1-866-783-2645 (Mon.-Fri., 9am-6pm EST) Provides confidential health information to Hispanic patients and their families. Provides bilingual fact sheets for a wide variety of health topics. Sponsored by the National Alliance for Hispanic Health. *Website:* http://www.hispanichealth.org *E-mail:* alliance@hispanichealth.org

To Your Health *(New Jersey)* 1-888-838-3180 Provides educational materials and information to residents of New Jersey within the managed care system. Helps the consumer understand their rights under commercial and government sponsored managed care programs. *Website:* http://www.chlp.org

UAB Eat Right 1-800-231-3438 (Mon.-Fri., 9am-5pm EST). Information on nutrition and related topics (weight loss and cholesterol). Sponsored by Nutrition Information Services.

Visiting Nurse Association of America 1-888-866-8773 or 617-737-3200 Referrals to local Visiting Nurse Associations. *Website:* http://www.vnaa.org *E-mail:* vnaa@vnaa.org

HEART

American Health Assistance Foundation 1-800-437-2423 (Mon.-Fri., 9am-5pm EST) Provides educational information and funds research for Alzheimer's disease, glaucoma and macular degeneration. *Website:* http://www.ahaf.org

American Heart Association *(BILINGUAL)* 1-800-242-8721 (24 hr.) Information on heart health and support groups. *Website:* http://www.americanheart.org

Cardiac Arrhythmias Research and Education Foundation, Inc. 1-800-404-9500 (Mon.-Fri., 9am-5pm CST) Support, education and registry for individuals and families affected by long QT syndrome and other genetic arrhythmias. Helps to create community forums for mutual support. *Website:* http://www.longqt.org *E-mail:* care@longqt.org

Texas Heart Institute Heart Information Service 1-800-292-2221 (8am-4pm CST) Answers questions on cardiovascular health via phone, mail or e-mail. Literature on aneurisms, cholesterol, heart transplants, stroke patients, women and heart disease. Information on support groups. *Website:* http://www.texasheartinstitute.org *E-mail:* his@heart.thi.tmc.edu

HOMOSEXUALITY

Gay and Lesbian National Hotline 1-888-843-4564 (Mon.-Fri., 4pm-midnight; Sat., noon-5pm EST) Provides information and referrals for gays, lesbians, transgendered and persons with questions about their sexuality. Information, referrals and peer counseling. *Website:* http://www.glnh.org *E-mail:* info@glbtnationalhelpcenter.org

HOSPICE

Children's Hospice International 1-800-242-4453 (Mon.-Fri., 9am-5pm EST) Refers patients to hospices and specialists in their areas. Bibliography and manuals. *Website:* http://www.chionline.org *E-mail:* info@chionline.org

Hospice Education Institute 1-800-331-1620 (Mon.-Fri., 9am-4:30pm EST) Provides information and referrals regarding hospice care. *Website:* http://www.hospiceworld.org *E-mail:* info@hospiceworld.org

Hospice Foundation of America 1-800-854-3402 (9am-5pm EST) Provides education and information on hospice care. Sponsors research. Offers teleconference series "Living with Grief" for bereaved families. Audiotapes for clergy. Fax: 202-638-5312. *Website:* http://www.hospicefoundation.org *E-mail:* hfaoffice@hospicefoundation.org

National Hospice and Palliative Care Organization 1-800-658-8898; *(SPANISH)* 1-877-658-8896 (Mon.-Fri., 9am-5pm EST) Information for hospice care of terminally ill persons. Referrals to hospice programs nationwide. *Website:* http://www.nhpco.org *E-mail:* caringinfo@nhpco.org

HOSPITAL

Believe In Tomorrow Children's Foundation 1-800-933-5470 (Mon.-Fri., 8:30am-5:00pm EST) Provides retreat housing services to critically ill children and their families. Offers "Hands on Adventures" program for critically ill children. Hospital housing is available for patients at Johns Hopkins Children's Center. *Website:* http://www.believeintomorrow.org

Hill Burton Hotline *(BILINGUAL)* 1-800-638-0742 or 301-443-5656 (Mon.-Fri., 9am-5pm) Using a touchtone phone, caller can get information about free hospital care for eligible persons (low income). Directory of medical centers that are part of Hill Burton program throughout US. *Website:* http://www.hrsa.gov/hillburton/default.htm *E-mail:* dfcrcomm@hrsa.gov

National Association of Hospital Hospitality Houses 1-800-542-9730 (Mon.-Fri., 9am-5pm EST) Makes referrals to hospital hospitality housing programs that provide lodging for families of hospital patients and/or hospital outpatients. *Website:* http://www.nahhh.org

Shriner's Hospital *(BILINGUAL)* 1-800-237-5055 (Mon.-Fri., 8am-5pm EST) Information on free hospital care available to children under the age of 18 needing treatment for burns, spinal cord injury, cleft palate or orthopedic care. If line is busy, leave your phone number including area code.

HOUSING

Community Connections 1-800-998-9999; Federal Relay Service 1-800-483-2209 Provides information about housing and community development, homeless prevention, first-time home buyer programs, veterans, low income housing, HUD, Habitat for Humanity, etc. *Website:* http://www.comcon.org

Hope Now Alliance 1-888-995-4673 *(BILINGUAL)* Provides free housing counseling in order to give struggling homeowners relief from overwhelming mortgage payments. Private partnership organized by the federal government to help homeowners who are struggling to pay the mortgage find the right solution in order to avoid losing their homes.

Housing and Mortgage Finance Agency *(New Jersey)* 1-800-654-6873 (Mon.-Fri., 8am-5pm) Information on mortgages available to first time home buyers and buyers in targeted areas. Offers low down payment and low interest rate mortgages. *Website:* http://www.nj-hmfa.com

National Accessible Apartment Clearinghouse 1-800-421-1221 Maintains a database of over 80,000 accessible apartments nationwide. Helps people with disabilities find accessible apartments. Owners and managers may also use this service to register their accessible units. Fax: 703-248-9440. *Website:* http://www.accessibleapartments.org *E-mail:* clearinghouse@naahq.org

New Jersey Foreclosure Mediation Hotline *(New Jersey)* 1-800-989-5277 (Mon.-Fri., 8am-6pm) Program that provides information to qualified homeowners facing foreclosure with free help from housing counselors, attorneys and a neutral mediator to help resolve their home loan delinquency. Homeowners must meet program criteria for assistance.

New Jersey Tenants Foreclosure Rights *(New Jersey)* 1-888-576-5529 (Legal Services of New Jersey) Helpline for renters affected by the foreclosure of their home. Ensures tenants' rights to stay in their home during a foreclosure and after the resale of the property are protected.

IMMUNE DEFICIENCY

Jeffrey Modell Foundation *(BILINGUAL)* 1-866-463-6474 (24 hr.) Provides information on specific primary immune deficiency diseases. Referrals to major medical centers, psychiatric and social support services. Information on insurance reimbursement.

IMMIGRANT

US Citizenship and Immigration Services *(BILINGUAL)* 1-800-375-5283; TTY: 1-800-767-1833 (Mon.-Fri., 8-10am and 4-6pm) Comprehensive information for immigrants including naturalization processes, adjustment of status for permanent residency and travel documents. Information on international services, employment authorization and immigration medical examinations. *Website:* http://www.uscis.gov/

IMPOTENCE

Impotence Information Center 1-800-843-4315 Provides free information about the causes and treatments of impotence. This includes brochures and a list of local physicians who treat impotence. *Website:* http://www.americanmedicalsystems.com

INCONTINENCE

Incontinence Information Center 1-800-843-4315 Provides free information about the causes and treatments of incontinence. This information consists of brochures and a list of physicians who treat incontinence within the caller's geographic area. *Website:* http://www.americanmedicalsystems.com

INSURANCE

Hurricane Insurance Information Center 1-800-942-4242 (24 hr.) Provides general information on hurricane insurance. *Website:* http://www.disasterinformation.org

Insurance Information Institute 1-800-331-9146 (9am-4:45pm EST) Provides information on home and auto insurance. Also provides hints and literature on preventing theft and accidents. Has information on organizations which have information on Health and Life insurance. *Website:* http://www.iii.org

New Jersey Family Care Hotline *(MULTILINGUAL) (New Jersey)* 1-800-701-0710; TTY: 1-800-701-0720 (Mon. and Thurs. 8am-8pm; Tues., Wed. and Fri., 8am-5pm) Provides information on health insurance to uninsured children and teens up to age 18. *Website:* http://www.njfamilycare.org

KIDNEY DISEASE

American Kidney Fund *(BILINGUAL)* 1-800-638-8299 (Mon.-Thur., 9am-5pm; Fri. 9am-3pm EST) Provides information, referrals and financial assistance to kidney patients. Counselors available to answer questions about kidney disease and transplants. *Website:* http://www.kidneyfund.org

Kidney and Urology Foundation of America *(BILINGUAL)* 1-800-633-6628 (Mon.-Fri., 9am-5pm EST) Dedicated to helping persons afflicted with any debilitating kidney, urologic or related diseases. Offers education, information, health fairs, grants, patient scholarships, physician referrals, fellowship and Pediatric Enrichment program. *Website:* http://www.kidneyurology.org *E-mail*: info@kidneyurology.org

National Institute of Diabetes and Digestive and Kidney Diseases 1-800-891-5390 (kidney); 1-800-860-8747 (diabetes); 1-800-891-5359 (digestive diseases) (Mon.-Fri., 8:30am-5:00pm EST) Provides referrals and literature on a broad range of subjects concerning diabetes, digestive disorders, kidney disease, hematologic diseases, urologic disorders, metabolic and endocrine disorders. *Website:* http://www.niddk.nih.gov/

National Kidney Foundation *(BILINGUAL)* 1-800-622-9010 (Mon.-Fri., 8:30am-5:30pm EST) Provides education and research information on kidney disease. Referrals to local affiliates. *Website:* http://www.kidney.org

LEGISLATION

League of Women Voters *(New Jersey)* 1-800-792-8683 (Mon.-Fri., 8:30am-4:30pm) Provides information regarding voting, New Jersey government and election information. Membership $60/yr. *Website:* www.lwvnj.org

Legislative Information and Bill Room *(New Jersey)* 1-800-792-8630; TDD: 1-800-257-7490 (Mon.-Fri., 8:30am-5pm) Information on the status of bills, calendar and roster. Sponsored by NJ Office of Legislative Services. *Website:* http://www.njleg.state.nj.us *E-mail:* leginfo@njleg.org (legislative matters only).

Project Vote Smart 1-888-868-3762 Non-partisan information about all elected officials and candidates for federal, state and local gubernatorial offices. *Website:* http://www.vote-smart.org

U.S. Government Federal Information Center *(BILINGUAL)* 1-800-688-9889 (voice) Information about federal government programs and agencies including patents, taxes, jobs, social security, passports, visas, department of states, veteran affairs, rules and regulations. *Website:* http://www.usa.gov

LEPROSY

American Leprosy Missions 1-800-543-3135 (Mon.-Fri., 8am-noon EST) Provides information on projects and programs that fight leprosy in 23 countries. *Website:* http://www.leprosy.org *E-mail:* amlep@leprosy.org

LIFE-THREATENING ILLNESS

Caring Connections 1-800-658-8898 (Mon.-Fri., 9am-5pm EST) Provides information and education concerning end-of-life issues. Includes caregiver questions. *Website:* http://www.caringinfo.org *E-mail:* consumers@nhpco.org

Catastrophic Illness in Children Relief Fund *(New Jersey)* 1-800-335-3863 Provides financial assistance to families of children 21 and under who have experienced an illness or condition which is not covered by insurance or any State or Federal program. For medical bills which exceed 10% over the family income.

Friends of Karen, Inc. *(New Jersey)* 1-800-637-2774 (NJ/NY/CT) (Mon.-Fri, 9am-5pm) Dedicated to providing emotional, financial and advocacy support to children with life-threatening illnesses and their families. Provides assistance in the NY metropolitan area, northern New Jersey and Fairfield, Connecticut. Information packets available. *Website:* http://www.friendsofkaren.org

LITERACY

Literacy Volunteers of New Jersey, Inc. *(New Jersey)* 1-800-848-0048 (Mon.-Thurs., 9am-4pm) Refers callers who read below 5th grade level and persons for whom English is a second language to LVA programs statewide. Also has information on other adult education programs. Refers potential volunteers to LVA training programs.

National Literacy Hotline *(BILINGUAL)* 1-800-228-8813 (24 hr.) Information and referrals to local literacy programs. Referrals for both volunteers and people needing literacy services. *Website:* http://www.nifl.gov

LUNG DISEASE

Allergy and Asthma Network - Mothers of Asthmatics *(BILINGUAL)* 1-800-878-4403 Provides emotional support and patient education resources for persons with asthma and allergies. Newsletter. *Website:* http://www.aanma.org *E-mail:* info@aanma.org

National Jewish Lung Line 1-800-222-5864 (Mon.-Fri., 8am-4:30pm MST) Information and referrals. Registered nurses answer questions on all types of lung diseases. Referrals to doctors and free literature. *Website:* http://www.nationaljewish.org *E-mail:* lungline@njc.org

Office on Smoking and Health 1-800-232-4636 (24 hr.) Provides information on the affects of tobacco on health, how to stop smoking, second hand smoke and other current topics relating to tobacco. Sponsored by Federal Government. *Website:* http://www.cdc.gov/tobacco *E-mail:* cdcinfo@cdc.gov

LYME DISEASE

Lyme Disease *(New Jersey)* 1-800-792-8831 (Mon.-Fri., 8am-5pm) Provides NJ residents with information about Lyme disease. Sponsored by the NJ Dept. of Health.

National Lyme Disease Foundation 1-800-886-5963 (need a touch-tone phone) Provides information and referrals for Lyme disease. Education, literature and advocacy.

MARRIAGE

Retrouvaille 1-800-470-2230 (leave message with your town and state, a return call may take several days) National. For couples who have a seriously troubled marriage. Couples spend one weekend together working to save their relationship. Program is volunteer-run by couples whose marriages were saved by their having participated in a Retrouvaille weekend. The program may have a Catholic priest involved as a resource person for some sessions, it is open to couples of any and no faith. The weekend experience is followed by several weekly support group meetings. Suggested donation is $350, but Retrouvaille never turns anyone away.

MARROW TRANSPLANTS

Caitlin Raymond International Bone Marrow Registry 1-800-726-2824 or 508-334-8969 (Mon.-Fri., 8:30am-5pm EST) Comprehensive international resource for patients and physicians conducting a search for unrelated bone marrow or cord blood donor. Write: Caitlin Raymond International Registry, University of Massachusetts Medical Center, 55 Lake Ave. N., Worcestor, MA 01655. *Website:* http://www.crir.org *E-mail:* info@CRIR.org

National BMT LINK 1-800-546-5268 (Mon.-Fri., 8:30am-4:30pm EST) Provides information and referral for bone marrow and stem cell transplants for patients, family and professionals. Referrals to support groups. Peer-support, online phone support groups, information on becoming a donor and educational booklets. *Website:* http://www.nbmtlink.org

National Marrow Donor Program 1-800-627-7692, 1-800-654-1247 or 1-800-526-7809 (Mon.-Fri., 8am-5pm CST) Provides information on bone marrow and stem cell transplants and information on becoming a marrow donor. Maintains computerized data bank of available tissue-typed marrow donors nationwide. Provides patient advocacy to assist patients through the donor search and transplant process. *Website:* http://www.marrow.org

MENTAL HEALTH

Compeer 1-800-836-0475 (Mon.-Fri., 8:30am-5pm) Provides volunteer "friends" for children and adults who receive mental health treatment. *Website:* http://www.compeer.org *E-mail:* info@compeer.org

Family Support Resources *(New Jersey)* 1-866-626-4437 (24 hr.) Automated information line provides local NJ contacts for Intensive Family Support Services and National Alliance on Mental Illness groups. Sponsored by NAMI-NJ.

Girl's and Boy's Town National Hotline *(BILINGUAL)* 1-800-448-3000; TDD: 1-800-448-1833 (24 hr.) Provides crisis intervention, information and referrals for general population. Free and confidential. Short-term crisis intervention. Works with children and families. *Website:* http://www.girlsandboystown.org

Mental Health America 1-800-969-6642; TDD: 1-800-433-5959 (Mon.-Fri., 9am-5pm EST) Provides free information on over 200 mental health topics including bipolar disorder, depression, bereavement, post-traumatic stress disorder and warning signs of mental illness. Referrals to local mental health services. Distributes free national directory of local mental health associations and offers low-cost materials. Advocates to remove stigma of mental illness and for mental health benefits parity. *Website:* http://www.mentalhealthamerica.net

National Alliance for Research on Schizophrenia and Depression 1-800-829-8289 Provides information on schizophrenia, depression and bipolar disorder. Has information on research being conducted on these disorders. Newsletter, literature and brochures. *Website:* http://www.narsad.org

National Institute of Mental Health Information Center 1-866-615-6464 or 301-443-4513 (Mon.-Fri., 8:30am-5pm EST) Provides information and literature on anxiety, phobias, obsessive-compulsive and depression. Leave name and mailing address and they will mail literature to you. *Website:* http://www.nimh.nih.gov

National Mental Health Services Information Center *(BILINGUAL)* 1-800-789-2647 Refers callers to many mental health organizations nationwide. *Website:* http://www.mentalhealth.samhsa.gov

NJ Mental Health Cares Helpline *(New Jersey)* 1-866-202-4357 (Mon.-Fri., 8am-8pm); TTY: 1-877-294-4356 Provides information and referral to all public mental health services in New Jersey. Answers questions regarding mental health and illness. Staffed by mental health professionals.

NJ Psychiatric Association *(New Jersey)* 1-800-345-0143 (Mon.-Thurs., 9am-1pm) Provides referrals to psychiatrists. Lists by language, geographical areas and problems. Information packets available. *Website:* http://wwwpsychnj.org *E-mail:* psychnj@optonline.net

NJ Psychological Association *(New Jersey)* 1-800-281-6572 or 973-243-9800 (Mon.-Fri., 8:30am-4:30pm) Provides referrals to psychologists in your area by specialty and language. *Website:* http://www.psychologynj.org *E-mail*: NJPA@psychologynj.org

State Division of Mental Health Helpline *(New Jersey)* 1-800-382-6717 (Mon.-Fri., 8:30am-5pm) Provides information on state mental health services and takes complaints about them. *Website:* http://www.state.nj.us/humanservices/dmhs *E-mail*: dmhsmail@dhs.state.nj.us

Summit Oaks Hospital *(New Jersey)* (Serves NJ/NY/CT) 1-800-753-5223 (24 hr.) Information for drug or psychiatric problems. Referrals to community mental health centers. Sponsored by Summit Oaks Hospital.

TARA 1-888-482-7227 or 212-966-6514 Education and advocacy organization. Provides information on borderline personality to families, consumers and providers. Referrals to clinicians, treatment programs, self-help groups, BPD Journal, speakers' bureau, professional conferences and advocacy. *Website:* http://www.tara4bpd.org *E-mail:* taraapd@aol.com

Value Options *(New Jersey)* 1-877-652-7624 (24 hr.) TTD: 866-896-6975 Provides comprehensive information on all emotional, behavioral and mental health services for children up to the age of 18 and their families. *Website:* http://www.conewjersey.com

MENTAL RETARDATION

American Association on Intellectual and Development Disabilities 1-800-424-3688 (Mon.-Fri., 9am-5pm EST) General information on mental retardation. *Website:* http://www.aaidd.org *E-mail:* anam@aaidd.org

Clearinghouse on Aging and Developmental Disabilities 1-800-996-8845; TTY: 312-413-0453 Aim is to promote independence, productivity, inclusion and self-determination of older adults with mental retardation. Provides training, technical assistance and materials to patients, families and professionals. Write: Clearinghouse on Aging and Developmental Disabilities, Department of Disability and Human Development (MC626), University of Illinois, 1640 W. Roosevelt Rd., Chicago, IL 60608-6904.

METABOLIC DISORDER

National Institute of Diabetes and Digestive and Kidney Diseases 1-800-891-5390 (kidney); 1-800-860-8747 (diabetes); 1-800-891-5359 (digestive diseases) (Mon.-Fri., 8:30am-5:00pm EST) Provides referrals and literature on a broad range of subjects concerning diabetes, digestive disorders, kidney disease, hematologic diseases, urologic disorders, metabolic and endocrine disorders. *Website:* http://www.niddk.nih.gov *E-mail:* nkudic@info.niddk.nih.gov

NIH Osteoporosis and Related Bone Diseases Resource Center *(MULTILINGUAL)* 1-800-624-2663 or 202-223-0344 (Mon.-Fri., 8:30am-5pm EST); TDD: 202-466-4315 Provides written information to patients, professionals and the public. Resources and information on metabolic bone diseases such as osteoporosis, Paget's disease, osteogenesis imperfecta and primary hyperparathyroidism. Annotated bibliography on current research available to professionals. *Website:* http://www.osteo.org *E-mail:* niamsboneinfo@mail.nih.gov

World Life Foundation 1-800-289-5433 Provides support, research, information and referrals for persons interested in rare metabolic disorders. Provides air transportation for ambulatory patients who need non-emergency treatment.

MILITARY / VETERANS

Army Community Service/Family Support *(New Jersey)* 1-800-877-2380 (Mon.-Fri., 8am-4:30pm) Military affiliated only. Family advocacy, parent education, employment readiness, relocation assistance, support groups and a wide variety of resources.

Army Wounded Soldier and Family Hotline 1-800-984-8523 (Mon.-Fri., 7am-7pm EST) Offers wounded and injured soldiers and family members a way to seek help to resolve medical issues and to provide an information channel of soldier medically related issues directly to senior Army leadership so they can improve how Army serves the medical needs of soldiers and their families.

Community Recovery *(New Jersey)* 1-800-292-8262 Offers services for veterans who are experiencing problems with drugs or alcohol. The program offers a wide variety of services throughout the state.

Department of Veterans Affairs 1-800-827-1000 (Mon.-Fri., 8am-4pm EST) Provides comprehensive information on available programs and services for veterans including pensions, vocational rehab, survivor's benefits, presidential memorial certificates, education programs and home loan programs for dependents. Special programs for disabled, homeless, minority and women veterans. *Website:* http://www.va.gov/ or http://www.va.gov/womenvet

Disabled American Veterans 1-877-426-2838 (8:30am-4:30pm EST) Provides free, professional assistance to veterans and their families in obtaining benefits and services earned through military service and provided by the department of Veteran Affairs and other agencies of the government. Guidelines for developing chapters. *Website:* http://www.dav.org *E-mail:* feedback@davmail.org

Disabled Veterans Job Assistance Line 1-800-378-4559 ext. 2 Provides assistance and referrals for returning disabled service members, recently medically retired service members and spouses of disabled service members.

Supports veterans of Operation Iraqi Freedom, Operation Enduring Freedom, as well as all disabled veterans of other conflicts, campaigns or wars and disabled children.

National Veterans Service Fund, Inc. 1-800-521-0198 (Mon.-Fri., 9am-4pm EST) Provides social services for Vietnam and Persian Gulf War veterans and their families. Focuses on those with disabled children. Provides publications and also offers an online bulletin board. *Website:* http://www.nvsf.org

Paralyzed Vets of America 1-800-424-8200 (Mon.-Fri., 8:30am-5pm EST) TTY/TTD: 202-872-1300 Information, referral and advocacy for disabled and paralyzed vets. *Website:* http://www.pva.org

VA Special Issues Helpline 1-800-749-8387 (8am-4pm CST) Refers Gulf war veterans and veterans affected by Agent Orange with medical problems to local Gulf war and Agent Orange coordinators at local VA medical centers. Other special issues addressed.

Veterans Affairs Suicide Hotline 1-800-273-8255 (when connected, press 1) (24 hr) Suicide prevention help for veterans with emotional crisis. Staffed by mental health professionals working with local VA mental health providers to help callers.

Veterans Counseling Hotline *(New Jersey)* 1-866-838-7654 (24 hr.) Provides peer support, clinical assessment and case management, family resources and referral to a comprehensive mental health network of providers if necessary. Developed by the NJ Department of Military and Veterans Affairs.

Veterans of the Vietnam War, Inc. 1-800-843-8626 (Mon.-Fri., 8am-4pm) or 570-603-9740 (general information) Membership organization open to all veterans and their supporters. Educates public about post-traumatic stress disorder, veteran health issues, Agent Orange and POW/MIA issues. Maintains a Find-a-Vet locator service, publishes newsletter, works with homeless veterans and incarcerated vets. Write: VVNW, 805 South Township Blvd., Pittston, PA 18640. *Website:* http://www.vvnw.org *E-mail*: vvnwnatl@epix.net

MISSING CHILDREN

Child Find of America Hotline 1-800-426-5678 (Mon.-Fri., 9am-5pm EST) Helps parents to locate children. Helps lost children who need assistance. Also offers support services. All services are free. *Website:* http://www.childfindofamerica.org *E-mail*: information@childfindofamerica.org

National Center for Missing and Exploited Children 1-800-843-5678 (24 hr.) Information regarding missing and exploited youth. Helps parents locate missing children. *Website:* http://www.missingkids.com

Vanished Children Alliance 1-800-826-4743 (24 hr.) Provides emotional support and technical assistance to families of missing children. Case management, search assistance, family reunification program, information and referral. Write: Vanished Children's Alliance, 991 W. Hedding St., Suite 101, San Jose, CA 95126. *Website:* http://www.vca.org *E-mail:* info@vca.org

MULTIPLE SCLEROSIS

Multiple Sclerosis Foundation 1-800-441-7055 or 1-888-673-6287 (Mon.-Fri., 9am-7pm EST) Support services for those diagnosed with multiple sclerosis. Grants for research, information and referrals on traditional and alternative treatments. Online doctors forum. Newsletter and phone support. *Website:* http://www.msfocus.org *E-mail:* support@msfocus.org

MUSCULAR DYSTROPHY

Muscular Dystrophy Family Foundation, Inc. 1-800-544-1213 (Mon.- Fri., 8:30am-3:30pm) Provides services, resources, home medical equipment and adaptive devices to help people with muscular dystrophy and their families. Provides comprehensive direct services. *Website:* http://www.mdff.org *E-mail:*mdff@mdff.org

NEPHROGENIC DIABETES INSIPIDUS

Nephrogenic Diabetes Insipidus Foundation 1-888-376-6343 Provides information and support to persons affected by nephrogenic diabetes insipidus. *Website:* http://www.ndif.org *E-mail:* info@ndif.org

NEUROLOGICAL DISORDERS

National Institute of Neurological Disorders 1-800-352-9424 (Mon.-Fri., 8:30am-5pm EST) Provides information on neurological disorders and stroke. Sponsored by National Institute of Health. *Website:* http://www.ninds.nih.gov

NICOTINE

NJ Quitline *(New Jersey)* 1-866-657-8677 (24 hr.); TDD: 1-866-228-4327 Information and counseling for anyone who has a nicotine addiction. Serves all of New Jersey. Sponsored by Dept. of Health and Senior Services. *Website:* http://www.njquitnet.com

Office on Smoking and Health 1-800-232-4636 (24 hr.) Provides information on the affects of tobacco on health, how to stop smoking, second hand smoke and other current topics relating to tobacco. Sponsored by Federal Government. *Website:* http://www.cdc.gov/tobacco *E-mail:* cdcinfo@cdc.gov

ORGAN DONATION

Children's Organ Transplant Association 1-800-366-2682 (Mon.-Fri., 8am-5pm EST) Non-profit organization that provides public education on organ transplants. Assists families in fund-raising for transplant and transplant-related expenses. Assistance for all children and adults with cystic fibrosis who are U.S. citizens in need of an organ transplant. *Website:* http://www.cota.org *E-mail:* cota@cota.org

Living Bank - National Organ and Transplant Registry, The *(BILINGUAL)* 1-800-528-2971 Provides donor cards, educational materials and referrals to medical schools for persons wishing to donate their bodies after death. *Website:* http://www.livingbank.org *E-mail:* info@livingbank.org

National Foundation for Transplants 1-800-489-3863 (Mon.-Fri., 8:30am-4:30pm CST) Provides support services, financial assistance and advocacy to adult and child organ and bone marrow transplant candidates and recipients. Assists in fund-raising activities. *Website:* http://www.transplants.org *E-mail:* info@transplants.org

National Minority Organ Tissue Transplant Education Program 1-800-393-2839 Provides educational information on preventative measures and organ transplants. Referrals to physicians. *Website:* http://www.nationalmottep.org

New Jersey Organ and Tissue Sharing Network *(New Jersey)* 1-800-742-7365, 1-800-541-0075 (24 hr. donor referral line) or 973-379-4535 (Mon.-Fri., 8:30am-5pm) Federally designated, state-certified procurement organization responsible for recovering organs and tissues for NJ residents in need of transplants. Issues donors cards. *Website:* http://www.sharenj.org

OSTEOPOROSIS

NIH Osteoporosis and Related Bone Diseases Resource Center *(MULTILINGUAL)* 1-800-624-2663 or 202-223-0344 (Mon.-Fri., 8:30am-5pm EST); TDD: 202-466-4315 Provides written information to patients, professionals and the public of resources and information on metabolic bone diseases such as osteoporosis, Paget's disease, osteogenesis imperfecta and primary hyperparathyroidism. Annotated bibliography on current research available to professionals. *Website:* http://www.niams.nih.gov/bone *E-mail:* niamsboneinfo@mail.nih.gov

Osteoporosis Helpline 1-888-934-2663 Provides general information and fact sheets on the symptoms, causes and treatment of osteoporosis. Offers referrals to osteoporosis specialists. *E-mail:* toneyourbones@uab.edu

PAGET'S DISEASE

NIH Osteoporosis and Related Bone Diseases Resource Center *(MULTILINGUAL)* 1-800-624-2663 or 202-223-0344 (Mon.-Fri., 8:30am-5pm EST); TDD: 202-466-4315 Provides written information to patients, professionals and the public of resources and information on metabolic bone diseases such as osteoporosis, Paget's disease, osteogenesis imperfecta and primary hyperparathyroidism. Annotated bibliography on current research available to professionals. *Website:* http://www.osteo.org *E-mail:* niamsboneinfo@mail.nih.gov

Paget's Foundation 1-800-237-2438 or 212-509-5335 (Mon.-Fri., 9am-5pm EST) Information, brochures, patient's guide, doctor referrals, professional packets and newsletter on Paget's disease of the bone, as well as primary hyperparathyroidism. *Website:* http://www.paget.org *E-mail:* pagetfdn@aol.com

PARENTING

Healthy Families *(New Jersey)* 1-800-244-5373 For any new parent who feels alone, frightened or overwhelmed. Offers support, education, links to health care and assistance in helping to meet the family needs. Stays with person as child grows. Services are free and will work with person to be the best parent they can be.

Kinship Navigator Program *(New Jersey)* 1-877-816-3211 *(BILINGUAL)* (Mon.-Fri., 9am-5pm) Information and referrals for a wide range of services designed for caregivers of sisters, brothers or grandchildren. Support group referrals, child care resources, respite, educational issues, custody, medical resources and other legal issues.

PARKINSON'S DISEASE

National Parkinson's Foundation 1-800-327-4545 (Mon.-Fri., 9:00am-5pm EST) Professional will answer any question on Parkinson disease. *Website:* http://www.parkinson.org *E-mail:* mailbox@parkinson.org

Parkinson's Disease Foundation, Inc. 1-800-457-6676 International. Founded 1957. A leading national presence in Parkinson's disease research, education and public advocacy. Provides educational materials and support service through toll-free helpline, web service and print/video materials. Write: Parkinson's Disease Foundation, 1359 Broadway, Suite 1509, New York, NY 10018. *Website:* http://www.pdf.org *E-mail:* info@pdf.org

PESTICIDE

National Pesticide Information Center 1-800-858-7378 (7 days, 6:30am-4:30pm PST) Information on most aspects of pesticides. Includes information related to antimicrobials, disinfectants and other chemicals designed to kill micro-organisms. Brochures available by calling or going to website. Sponsored by EPA. *Website:* http://npic.orst.edu *E-mail:* npic@ace.orst.edu

PET LOSS

Pet Loss Support Hotline 1-800-565-1526 (Mon.-Fri., 6:30-9:30pm PST) Offers a non-judgmental outlet for people to express their feelings and concerns when faced with difficult times regarding their pets. Staffed by veterinary students with grief training.

PetFriends *(New Jersey)* 1-800-404-7387 (24 hr.) Compassionate phone support, information and referrals to people who have lost, or anticipate losing, a pet through death or other separation.

POISON

New Jersey Poison Control Centers *(New Jersey)* 1-800-222-1222 (24 hr.) Emergency helpline that provides information on medication errors, drug overdoses, food poisoning, food safety, etc.

"Everyday courage has few witnesses. But yours is no less noble because no drum beats for you, and no crowds shout your name." –Robert Lewis Stevenson

POLICE OFFICERS

Cop-to-Cop *(New Jersey)* 1-866-267-2267 (24 hr.) Serves active and retired policemen and their families. Retired officers and mental health professionals offer callers support. Provides support and referrals for counseling, mental health, substance abuse, partial care and inpatient treatment.

PREGNANCY / CHILDBIRTH

Antiepileptic Drug Pregnancy Registry *(MULTILINGUAL)* 1-888-233-2334 (Mon.-Fri., 9:00am-5:00pm EST) Registry of women who are taking antiepileptic drugs and who are pregnant. Helps to determine which medications are associated with increased risks. Physicians are encouraged to refer women. *Website:* http://www.aedpregnancyregistry.org

Family Helpline, The *(MULTILINGUAL)* *(New Jersey)* 1-800-843-5437 (24 hr.) Confidential and untraceable help for teens to talk about all the options available. Refers caller to local confidential assistance. *Website:* http://www.pa-of-nj.org

National Abortion Federation 1-800-772-9100 (Mon.-Fri., 8am-9pm; Sat., 9am-5pm EST) Information and referrals regarding abortions. Financial aid. *Website:* http://www.prochoice.org

National Hispanic Family Health Helpline *(BILINGUAL)* 1-866-783-2645 (Mon.-Fri., 9am-6pm EST) Provides health information on pregnancy, referral to healthcare centers and doctors. Sponsored by the National Alliance for Hispanic Health. http://www.hispanichealth.org *E-mail*: alliance@hispanichealth.org

National Life Center, Inc. 1-800-848-5683 (24 hr.) Provides counseling and information for pregnant women. Referrals to testing sites, baby clothes and formula. *Website:* http://www.nationallifecenter.com *E-mail*: nlc1stway@snip.net

New Jersey Safe Haven Infant Protection Act *(New Jersey)* 1-877-839-2339 (24 hr.) Offers a safe haven for a person voluntarily relinquishing their infant under 30 days old. Completely confidential. Also answers questions from the public and offers support to those considering giving up or abandoning of their infant.

OTIS (Organization of Teratology Information Services) *(MULTILINGUAL)* 1-866-626-6847 (Mon.-Fri., 8:30am-4pm PST) Provides local referrals to agencies that provide information concerning prenatal drug, medication, chemical and other potentially harmful exposures. *Website:* http://www.otispregnancy.org/ *E-mail*: OTISPregnancy@pharmacy.arizona.edu

Planned Parenthood *(BILINGUAL)* 1-800-230-7526 Referrals to neighborhood planned parenthood clinics nationwide. *Website:* http://www.plannedparenthood.org/

Pregnancy Hotline (National Life Center) *(New Jersey)* 1-800-848-5683 (24 hr.) Free, confidential information for pregnant women regarding pregnancy testing, adoption information, legal assistance, baby clothes, formula, adoption referrals and shelters for women and girls. *Website:* http://www.nationallifecenter.com *E-mail*: nlc1stway@snip.net

Pregnancy Hotline 1-800-238-4269 (24 hr.) Information and counseling to pregnant women. Referrals to free pregnancy test facilities, foster and adoption centers. Sponsored by Bethany Christian Services. *Website:* http://www.bethany.org

Safe Place for Newborns/Newborn Lifeline Network 1-877-440-2229 (24 hr.) Provides referrals to locations where mothers can safely and anonymously take their babies to be placed for adoption. *Website:* http://www.safeplacefornewborns.com

PRESCRIPTIONS, LOW COST

PAAD (Pharmaceutical Assistance) *(New Jersey)* 1-800-792-9745 (8am-5pm). Financial assistance to the aged (65 or older) or disabled to help pay for medications. Hearing aid assistance also offered. Sponsored by NJ State Pharmaceutical Assistance Program.

Partnership for Prescription Assistance 1-888-477-2669 Mails a directory of various pharmaceutical assistance programs for persons who cannot afford prescriptions on their own. *Website:* http://www.pparx.org

Rx4NJ (A Partnership for Prescription Assistance) *(New Jersey)* 1-888-793-6765 Information on specific types of discounted or free prescription medications. A no-cost service of NJ pharmaceutical companies. Call or visit their website to answer questions. *Website:* http://www.rx4nj.org

Senior Gold Prescription Discount Program *(New Jersey)* 1-800-792-9745 (Mon.-Fri., 8:30am-5pm) Pharmaceutical assistance to residents of NJ who are (ages 65+). Also available to those who are age 18+, receive social security disability and meet the income eligibility guidelines.

PROSTATE

Prostatitis Foundation 1-888-891-4200 Provides support and education to men with prostatitis. Encourages research funding. Information and referrals. *Website:* http://www.prostatitis.org

PROSTITUTION / SEX INDUSTRY

HIPS Hotline 1-800-676-4477 (24 hr.) Provides crisis peer counseling and support for persons involved in, or affected by, the sex industry. Counseling and information provided for sex workers and their families in a non-judgmental, supportive atmosphere. *Website:* http://www.hips.org

PSYCHIATRIST / PSYCHOLOGIST

New Jersey Psychiatric Association *(New Jersey)* 1-800-345-0143 (Mon.-Thurs., 9am-1pm) Provides referrals to psychiatrists. Lists by language, geographical areas and problems. Information packets available. *Website:* http://www.psychnj.org *E-mail:* psychnj@optonline.net

New Jersey Psychological Association *(New Jersey)* 1-800-281-6572 or 973-243-9800 (Mon.-Fri., 8:30am-4:30pm) Provides referrals to psychologists in your area by specialty and language. *Website:* http://www.psychologynj.org *E-mail:* NJPA@psychologynj.org

RADIATION

Center for Disease Control and Prevention Helpline 1-800-232-4636; TTY: 1-888-232-6348 Provides information on emergency preparedness and response including bioterrorism, chemical emergencies, radiation emergencies, mass casualties, natural disasters, severe weather, recent outbreaks and incidence. *Website:* http://www.cdc.gov

RAPE / INCEST / SEXUAL ABUSE

National Sexual Violence Resource Center 1-877-739-3895 Provides information and referrals relating to all aspects of sexual violence to persons and agencies. Resources include statistics, research, legal, statutes and prevention. Not for crisis situations. *Website:* http://www.nsvrc.org

National Teen Dating Abuse Helpline 1-866-331-9474 (24 hr.); TTY: 1-866-331-8453 Provides support, crisis intervention, problem-solving techniques and referrals for victims of dating abuse ages 13-18, their families and advocates. Limited information and referrals for batterers is available as well.

New Jersey Coalition Against Sexual Assault *(New Jersey)* 1-800-601-7200 (24 hr.) Information and referrals. Provides information on services for sexual assault victims and their families. Also crisis intervention and accompaniment services to hospital, police, court and short-term counseling. Calls are automatically routed to the caller's local county information services. *Website:* http://www.njcasa.org

RAINN (Rape, Abuse and Incest National Network) 1-800-656-4673 (24 hr.) Provides support and confidential crisis counseling for victims of sexual assault. Callers are automatically routed to the crisis center nearest to them. Write: RAINN, 2000 L St., NW, Ste. 406 Washington, DC 20036. *Website:* http://www.rainn.org *E-mail:* info@rainn.org

REHABILITATION

American Medical Rehabilitation Providers Association 1-800-368-3513 or 1-888-346-4624 Refers callers to rehabilitation hospitals or centers. *Website:* http://www.amrpa.org

Center for Assistive Technologies 1-800-726-9119 (voice/TTY) Provides information on products, technology, resources and services for persons with disabilities. *Website:* http://www.assistivetech.net or http://www.catea.org *E-mail:* catea@coa.gavtech.edu

National Rehabilitation Information Center 1-800-346-2742; TTY: 301-459-5984 (Mon.-Fri., 9am-5pm EST) Library and information center on disability and rehabilitation of all types. Sponsored by U.S. Department of Education. *Website:* http://www.naric.com *E-mail:* naricinfo@heitechservices.com

REYE'S SYNDROME

National Reye's Syndrome 1-800-233-7393 (Mon.-Fri., 9am-5pm EST) Guidance to families affected by Reye's Syndrome. Helps increase public awareness. Fund-raising. *Website:* http://www.reyessyndrome.org *E-mail:* nrsf@reyessyndrome.org

ROSACEA

National Rosacea Society 1-888-662-5874 Information and educational materials on rosacea (a chronic, acne-like condition of the facial skin). *Website:* http://www.rosacea.org *E-mail:* rosacea@aol.com

RUNAWAYS

National Runaway Switchboard 1-800-786-2929 (24 hr.) Provides crisis intervention, information and referrals for runaways regarding shelter, counseling, food pantries and transportation. Suicide and crisis counseling. Greyhound bus tickets available for qualifying kids. Parents are welcome to call for assistance. *Website:* http://www.1800runaway.org *E-mail:* info@1800runaway.org

RURAL ISSUES

Rural Information Center 1-800-633-7701 (Mon.-Fri., 8:30am-4:30pm EST) Information on rural issues. Provides brief database searches for free. *Website:* http://www.ric.nal.usda.gov *E-mail:* ric@nal.usda.gov

SCLERODERMA

Scleroderma Research Foundation 1-800-441-2873 (Mon.-Fri., 9:30am-5:30pm PST) Provides referrals to doctors and clinics nationwide that treat scleroderma. Conducts research into the cause and cure of scleroderma. *Website:* http://www.srfcure.org

SELF-ABUSE

SAFE (Self-Abuse Finally Ends) Alternative Info Line 1-800-366-8288 (Mon.-Fri., 8am-4pm CST) Provides recorded information on dealing with self-abuse and self-mutilation and treatment options. *Website:* http://www.selfinjury.com

SEXUALLY TRANSMITTED DISEASES

American Social Health Association *(BILINGUAL)* 1-800-227-8922 or 919-361-8488 (Mon.-Fri., 9am-6pm EST) Provides information, materials and referrals concerning sexually transmitted infections. Specialists will answer questions via phone or e-mail on transmission, risk reduction, prevention, testing and treatment. *Website:* http://www.ashastd.org or http://www.iwannaknow.org (for teens)

CDC National Prevention Information Network *(BILINGUAL)* 1-800-458-5231 (Mon.-Fri., 9am-8pm EST); TTY: 1-800-243-7012 or 919-361-4892 Provides information on resources, educational materials, sexually transmitted diseases (including AIDS/HIV), tuberculosis and communities at risk via touch tone phone or online. Many different services and publications offered. *Website:* http://www.cdcnpin.org *E-mail:* info@cdcnpin.org

CDC National STD/AIDS Hotline *(BILINGUAL)* 1-800-232-4636 (24 hr.); TTY: 1-888-232-6342 (24 hr.) Education and research about AIDS, HIV and sexually transmitted diseases. *Website:* http://www.cdc.gov *E-mail:* cdcinfo@cdc.gov

SOCIAL SECURITY

National Organization of Social Security Claimant's Reps 1-800-431-2804 (Mon.-Fri., 9am-5:30pm EST) Provides referrals to social security lawyers who assist claimants in getting social security. *Website:* http://www.nosscr.org

NJ WINS (Work Incentive Programs) *(New Jersey)* 1-877-659-4672 Enables social security administration beneficiaries with disabilities to make informed choices about work and assist them in exploring work incentives that are available. *Website:* http://www.njwins.org

Social Security 1-800-772-1213 (Mon.-Fri., 7am-7pm EST); TTY: 1-800-325-0778 (Mon.-Fri., 7am-7pm EST) Provides information on all aspects of social security, supplemental security income and Medicare. Can speak with a person or use touch-tone phone to hear messages. *Website:* http://www.socialsecurity.gov

SPINAL CORD INJURY

Christopher and Dana Reeve Foundation and Paralysis Resource *(MULTILINGUAL)* *(New Jersey)* 1-800-539-7309 Information and referrals. Publishes a free book "Paralysis Resource" for consumers. Book is available in English or Spanish. *Website:* http://www.paralysis.org *E-mail:* info@paralysis.org

Foundation for Spinal Cord Injury Prevention 1-800-342-0330 Dedicated to the prevention, care and cure of spinal cord injuries through public awareness, education and funding research. Free counseling for victims and their families. Networking of patients and families. *Website:* http://www.fscip.org/ *E-mail:* info@fscip.org

National Spinal Cord Injury Hotline *(BILINGUAL)* 1-800-962-9629 (Mon.-Fri., 9am-5pm EST) Information, referral and peer support for spinal cord injured persons and their families. *Website:* http://www.spinalcord.org *E-mail:* info@spinalcord.org

Paralyzed Vets of America 1-800-424-8200; TTY/TTD: 202-872-1300 (Mon.-Fri., 8:30am-5pm EST) Information, referral and advocacy for disabled and paralyzed vets. *Website:* http://www.pva.org

STUTTERING

Stuttering Foundation of America 1-800-992-9392 or 1-800-967-7700 (9am-5pm EST) Information and referrals for stutterers and those who treat stutterers. Phone support and conferences. Maintains a nationwide referral list of speech pathologist that specialize in stuttering. *Website:* http://www.stutteringhelp.org *E-mail:*info@stutteringhelp.org

SUDDEN INFANT DEATH

First Candle/SIDS Alliance *(BILINGUAL)* 1-800-221-7437 (24 hr.) Information on medical research, referrals to local support groups, referrals to community services and education. *Website:* http://www.firstcandle.org *E-mail:* info@firstcandle.org

American SIDS Institute 1-800-232-7437 (24 hr.) Dedicated to the prevention of sudden infant death syndrome. Promotes infant health through research. Education and support for families. *Website:* http://www.sids.org *E-mail:* prevent@sids.org

SUICIDE PREVENTION

Suicide Prevention Helpline *(BILINGUAL)* 1-800-784-2433 or 1-800-273-8255; TTY: 1-800-799-4889 National suicide prevention line that routes callers to a local or regional suicide crisis hotline.

*We can also refer callers to over 100 individuals who are seeking others to help start new support groups throughout NJ. For more information call **1-800-367-6274**.*

SURGERY

American Society of Plastic Surgeons 1-800-635-0635 Referrals to plastic surgeons. Information on particular plastic surgeons as to their particular qualifications. Write: American Society of Plastic Surgeons, 444 E. Algonquin Road, Arlington Heights, IL 60005. *Website:* http://www.plasticsurgery.org

TAXES

NJ Tax Talk *(New Jersey)* 1-800-323-4400 Provides status of refunds and (at certain times of the year) Homestead Rebate applications, order forms and publication or listen to recorded tax topics. To contact customer service call 609-292-6400 (Mon-Fri, 8:30am-4:30pm). *Website:* http://www.state.nj.us/treasury/taxation

IRS Federal Tax Information 1-800-829-1040 (24 hr.) Information regarding federal tax questions, problems and refund information (30 day waiting period for written requests). *Website:* http://www.irs.gov

TRANSPORTATION

ACCESS LINK *(New Jersey)* 1-800-955-2321; TTY: 1-800-955-6765 Provides people with disabilities paratransit service comparable to the local bus service. Specifically for people whose disability prevents them from using existing local bus service.

Air Ambulance Central 1-800-843-8418 (24 hr.) Will fly patients from anywhere for needed medical services. *E-mail:* airmedusa@aol.com

Air Charity Network 1-877-621-7177 Provides referrals to 1200 volunteer pilots who will fly needy patients for medical care. *Website:* http://www.aircharitynetwork.org

American Red Cross 1-800-733-2767 (Mon.-Fri., 8am-5pm EST) Provides disaster relief, emergency, health, safety and community services. *Website:* http://www.redcross.org

Miracle Flights for Kids 1-800-359-1711 (Mon.-Thurs., 7:30am-6pm PST) Arranges airplane travel for children and adults with healthcare problems. Need doctor note and 16 days advance notice. *Website:* http://www.miracleflights.org

National Patient Travel Center 1-800-296-1217 (24 hr.) Information and referral for persons who need cost effective transportation for specialized treatment after an illness or accident. Fax: 757-318-9107. *Website:* http://www.patienttravel.org *E-mail:* info@nationalpatienttravelcenter.org

World Life Foundation 1-800-289-5433 Provides support, research, information and referrals for persons interested in rare metabolic disorders. Provides air transportation for ambulatory patients who need non-emergency treatment.

TRAUMA

American Red Cross 1-866-438-4636 (24 hr.) Provides disaster relief, emergency, health, safety and community services. *Website:* http://www.redcross.org

American Trauma Society 1-800-556-7890 or 301-574-4300 (Mon.-Fri., 8:30am-4:30pm EST) Provides referrals and educational materials on the prevention of physical traumas. *Website:* http://www.amtrauma.org *E-mail:* info@amtrauma.org

Center for Disease Control and Prevention Helpline 1-800-232-4636; TTY: 1-888-232-6348 Provides information on emergency preparedness and response including bioterrorism, chemical emergencies, radiation emergencies, mass casualties, natural disasters, severe weather, recent outbreaks and incidence. *Website:* http://www.cdc.gov

Think First National Injury Prevention Foundation 1-800-844-6556 (Mon.-Fri., 8:30am-5pm CST) Aims to prevent brain, spinal cord and other traumatic injuries through education and training. Information for children and teens. Write: Think First Foundation, 29 W. 120 Butterfield Rd., Suite 105, Warrenville, IL 60555. *Website:* http://www.thinkfirst.org *E-mail:* thinkfirst@thinkfirst.org

UROLOGIC DISEASES

American Urological Association Foundation 1-800-828-7866; 1-866-746-4282 (US only) or 410-689-3700 (Mon.-Fri., 8:30am-5pm EST) Educational information for patients and others interested about urological diseases. *Website:* http://www.auafoundation.org/ *E-mail:* auafoundation@auafoundation.org

Kidney and Urology Foundation of America *(BILINGUAL)* 1-800-633-6628 (Mon.-Fri., 9am-5pm EST) Dedicated to helping persons afflicted with any debilitating kidney, urologic and related diseases. Offers education, information, health fairs, grants, patient scholarships, physician referrals, fellowship and

Pediatric Enrichment program. *Website:* http://www.kidneyurology.org *E-mail:* info@kidneyurology.org

National Institute of Diabetes and Digestive and Kidney Diseases 1-800-891-5390 (kidney); 1-800-860-8747 (diabetes); 1-800-891-5359 (digestive diseases) (Mon.-Fri., 8:30am-5:00pm) Provides referrals and literature on a broad range of subjects concerning diabetes, digestive disorders, kidney disease, hematologic diseases, urologic disorders, metabolic and endocrine disorders. *Website:* http://www.niddk.nih.gov *E-mail:* nkudic@info.niddk.nih.gov

VACCINATIONS

Alliance for Informed Choice on Vaccinations *(New Jersey)* 1-800-613-9925 Addresses the concerns about the safety of vaccines and the right to informed consent. Literature, advocacy and phone help.

Centers for Disease Control and Prevention *(BILINGUAL)* 1-800-232-4636 Provides information on health related topics, vaccinations, traveler's health, grants, genetics, hoaxes, rumors and emergency responses. Information is available via the phone or online. *Website:* http://www.cdc.gov *E-mail:* inquiry@cdc.gov

WELFARE

Division of Family Development *(New Jersey)* 1-800-792-9773 (Mon.-Fri., 8am-4:30pm) Information on welfare and food stamps. Sponsored by Deptartment of Human Services.

Goodwill Industries 1-800-741-0186 Provides employment and training services for people with disabilities and other disadvantaging conditions (welfare dependency, illiteracy, criminal history and homeless). Write: Goodwill Industries International, 9200 Rockville Pike, Bethesda, MD 20814. *Website:* http://www.goodwill.org

WISH GRANTING FOR ILL CHILDREN

A Special Wish Foundation 1-800-486-9474 (Mon.-Fri., 9am-4:30pm EST) Grants wishes to children with terminal illnesses or life threatening disorders. *Website:* http://www.spwish.org *E-mail:* rfickle@spwish.org

Children's Wish Foundation International 1-800-323-9474 (Mon.-Fri., 8:30am-5pm EST) Grants wishes to terminally ill children up to age of 18. *Website:* http://www.childrenswish.org *E-mail:* wish@childrenswish.org

Dream Factory 1-800-456-7556 (Mon.-Fri., 8:00am-4:00pm EST) Grants dreams for children with a life threatening or critical chronic illness. *Website:* http://www.dreamfactoryinc.com *E-mail:* info@dreamfactoryinc.com

Give Kids the World Foundation 1-800-995-5437 or 407-396-1114 (24 hr.) Offers a 51-acre, non-profit resort for use by children with life-threatening illnesses whose one wish is to visit Central Florida's best-loved attractions. *Website:* http://www.gktw.org

Make-A-Wish Foundation 1-800-722-9474 (Mon.-Fri., 7am-4pm MST) Grants wishes to children with serious illnesses or life threatening medical conditions. *Website:* http://www.wish.org

Starlight Children's Foundation 1-800-274-7827 (Mon.-Fri., 9:00am-5:00pm PST) Grants wishes for seriously ill children. Also provides a variety of in-hospital services that focus on distraction entertainment. *Website:* http://www.starlight.org *E-mail:* info@starlight.org

WOMEN

North American Menopause Society 1-800-774-5342 Provides free packets of information on menopause. Referrals to clinicians and discussions groups. *Website:* http://www.menopause.org

Women's Health *(BILINGUAL)* 1-800-994-9662; TTY: 1-888-220-5446 (Mon.-Fri., 9am-6pm EST) Provides information and referrals for all women's health questions and any questions on breast feeding. *Website:* http://www.womenshealth.gov

Women's Health Resource Center *(New Jersey)* 1-877-986-9472 (Mon.-Fri., 9am-5pm) Information and resources about health concerns. By talking with staff, consumers will learn the key questions and issues to discuss with their physicians/health care professionals. *Website:* http://www.healthywomen.org

Women's Referral Central *(New Jersey)* 1-800-322-8092 (24 hr.) Information and referrals on any issues concerning women including education, homelessness, child support, custody, personal growth and domestic violence.

YOUTH

2ND FLOOR Youth Helpline *(New Jersey) (BILINGUAL)* 1-888-222-2228 (24 hr.) Youth helpline for kids (ages 10-24) to call and discuss whatever is on their minds. Message board and resources. *Website:* http://www.2ndfloor.org

Girl's and Boy's Town National Hotline *(BILINGUAL)* 1-800-448-3000; TDD: 1-800-448-1833 (24 hr.) Provides crisis intervention, information and referrals for general population. Free and confidential. Short-term crisis intervention. Works with children and families. *Website:* http://www.boystown.org

Children's Defense Fund 1-800-233-1200 (Mon.-Fri., 9am-5pm CST) Advocacy for children who cannot speak for themselves. Emphasis on low income and disabled children. Develops prevention programs to help children. Training seminars to develop Confident Kids Support Groups. *Website:* http://www.childrensdefense.org *E-mail:* cdfinfo@childrensdefense.org

NineLine 1-800-999-9999 (24 hr.) Nationwide crisis/suicide hotline. Referrals for youth or parents regarding drugs, domestic violence, homelessness, runaways, etc. Message relays and reports of abuse. Helps parents with problems with their kids. If all counselors are busy, stay on line and one will be with you as soon as possible. Sponsored by Nine Line/Covenant House. *Website:* http://www.covenanthouse.org/

Safe Sitter 1-800-255-4089 (Mon.-Fri., 8:00am-4:30pm) Trains adolescents (ages 11-13) on how to be effective baby sitters. *Website:* http://www.safesitter.org *E-mail:* safesitter@safesitter.org

"What's life?

The short answer: a cereal.

The long answer: an opportunity for us all to grow physically, spiritually and emotionally within ourselves and through the interactions with others."
– Ron Culberson

716

SELF-HELP CLEARINGHOUSES

To locate a support group for your concern, review the list below of self-help clearinghouses to see if there is one that serves your community. Our clearinghouse can provide information on other clearinghouse services, both nationally and internationally. Give us a call at 1-800-367-6274 (NJ only) or 973-989-1122. Self-help clearinghouses assist in the finding and forming of local groups. Some clearinghouses also provide training workshops, distribute "how-to" materials, publish directories and offer newsletters.

NATIONAL

American Self-Help Group Clearinghouse Maintains database of national self-help headquarters and model one-of-a-kind groups. Referrals to self-help clearinghouses nationwide. Offers assistance to persons interested in starting new groups. Program Administrator: Ed Madara. Write: American Self-Help Group Clearinghouse, 375 E. McFarlan St., Dover, NJ 07801. Call 973-989-1122; Fax: 973-989-1159. *Website:* http://www.selfhelpgroups.org *E-mail:* ashc@cybernex.net

National Self-Help Clearinghouse Provides information and referrals to self-help groups and regional self-help clearinghouses. Encourages and conducts training of professionals about self-help. Carries out research activities. Publishes manuals and training materials. Write: National Self-Help Clearinghouse, c/o CUNY, Graduate School and University Center, 365 Fifth Ave., Suite 3300, New York, NY 10016. Call 212-817-1822. *Website:* http://www.selfhelpweb.org *E-mail:* info@selfhelpweb.org

CONNECTICUT

Connecticut Self-Help Support Network *Founded 1981.* Information and referrals to support groups. Provides technical assistance in starting and maintaining groups. Group leadership training, educational workshops and conferences. Publishes directory of self-help groups, newsletter and other publications. Write: Connecticut Self-Help Support Network, c/o Elaine Horn, The Consultation Center, 389 Whitney Ave., New Haven, CT 06511. Call 203-624-6982; Fax: 203-562-6355. *Website:* http://www.theconsultationcenter.org *E-mail:* info@theconsultationcenter.org (attention: self-help)

NEW YORK

Institute for Human Services/HELPLINE *(Steuben, Allegany, Schulyer, Yates and Chemung Counties). Founded 1984.* Information and referrals to local services and agencies, as well as local support groups. Provides assistance to new and existing self-help groups. Also acts as a 24-hour crisis and referral line. Newsletter, information and referral. Write: Institute for Human Services/Helpline, 6666 County Rd. ll, Bath, NY 14810. Call 1-800-346-2211 (in NY); Admin: 607-776-9467. *Website:* http://www.ihsnet.org (to find the listing of support groups on the website: on the left side of the home page, under the heading "Programs and Services" click on "2-1-1 helpline", then click on "Helpline Online", next click on the letter "S" or type in the phrase "Support Groups" in the keyword search box) *E-mail:* helpline@ihsnet.org

Mental Health Association of Monroe County Provides information and referrals to local support groups. Assistance in starting new groups, training workshops and how-to materials. Directory of local groups published online. Write: Mental Health Association, 320 North Goodman St., Rochester, NY 14607. Call Cindi Licata 585-325-3145 ext. 113; Fax: 585-325-3188. *Website:* http://www.mharochester.org

New York City Self-Help Center *(Manhattan, Bronx, Staten Island, Queens and Brooklyn).* Information and referrals to support groups in the five boroughs. Receives updated information on support groups and provides assistance to new and developing groups. Write: NYC Self-Help Center, 850 7th Ave., Room 1220, New York, NY 10019. Call 212-586-5770 (Mon.-Thurs. - only open part-time); Admin: 212-399-2685 ext. 209 (Director: Susan Rosenthal); Fax: 212-399-2475. *E-mail:* srosenthal@jbfcs.org

Niagara Self-Help Clearinghouse *(Niagara County). Founded 1985.* Information and referrals to local support groups. Provides technical assistance to new groups. Networks with other community resources. Helps with new group development and holds group leader training. Directory of self-help groups and mental health video/book library. Write: Niagara Self-Help Clearinghouse, c/o MHA in Niagara County, 36 Pine St., Lockport, NY 14094. Call 716-433-3780; Fax: 716-433-3847. *Website:* http://www.mhanc.com

Self-Help Clearinghouse, The *(Rockland County). Founded 1951.* Information and referrals concerning self-help groups. Provides consultation and assistance to new groups that are forming. Publishes newsletter and self-help group directory ($3). Offers assistance starting support groups. Write: Jennifer Conforto, Self-Help Clearinghouse, MHA of Rockland County, Inc., 706 Executive Blvd., Suite F, Valley Cottage, NY 10989. Call 845-267-2172 ext.

422; Fax: 845-267-2169. *Website:* http://www.mharockland.org *E-mail:* hyattm@mharockland.org

Westchester Self-Help Clearinghouse *(Westchester County). Founded 1979.* A central resource for mutual support groups. Provides information and referrals to mutual support groups. Assists in the formation of new groups. Provides community education and publishes a directory of self-help groups every other year. Phone networks for newly separated women and newly widowed men and women. Director: Lenore Rosenbaum, MS. Write: Westchester Self-Help Clearinghouse, 845 N. Broadway, White Plains, NY 10603. Call 914-761-0600 ext. 308; Fax: 914-761-5859. *E-mail:* lrosenbaum@wjcs.com

PENNSYLVANIA

Self-Help Information Network Exchange (SHINE) *(Lackawanna County).* Provides information and referrals to support groups in northeastern Pennsylvania. Sponsors workshops and special events for self-help advocates. Brochure. Community resource library. Write: SHINE, 538 Spruce St., Suite 420, Scranton, PA 18503. Call 570-961-1234 (24 hr.); Admin: 570-347-5616; Fax: 570-341-5816. *Website:* http://www.vacnepa.org *E-mail:* shine@vacnepa.org

"The majority of us lead quiet,
Unheralded lives as we pass through this world.
There will most likely be no ticker-tape parades for us,
No monuments created in our honor.
But that does not lessen our possible impact, for there are
scores of people waiting for someone just like us to come along;
people who will appreciate our compassion, our unique talents.
Someone who will live a happier life merely because we
took the time to share what we had to give.
Too often we underestimate the power of a touch, a smile,
a kind word, a listening ear, an honest compliment, or the
smallest act of caring, all of which have a potential to turn a
life around.
It's overwhelming to consider the continuous opportunities
There are to make our love felt."--Leo Buscaglia

"The journey is not about helping ourselves, but about helping others. We do our best when we use our own skills to make a positive difference in the lives of others. When we do this, we bring enjoyment, hope and fulfillment to others, but we also find that we enjoy the journey more than we ever could have imagined."
– Dave Lieber

INDEX

E

F

G

H

O

S

END NOTE

Our Self-Help Group Clearinghouse publishes this directory of support groups *annually*. Information, phone and e-mail contacts, locations, facilitators, meeting days and times are always changing. New groups are added and disbanded groups removed. Therefore, we advise you not to depend solely upon entries in this directory past one full year of its publication. At, or before that time, please call us to inquire about the availability of the next directory edition. At any time you may also call our helpline, through which we distribute the most up-to-date information on support groups and helplines.

Self-Help Group Clearinghouse Helpline
from anywhere in N.J.
1-800-367-6274